Pro WF

Windows Workflow in .NET 3.0

Bruce Bukovics

Pro WF: Windows Workflow in .NET 3.0

Copyright © 2007 by Bruce Bukovics

ISBN-13 (pbk): 978-1-59059-778-1

ISBN-10 (pbk): 1-59059-778-8

eISBN-13: 978-1-4302-0372-8

Printed and bound in the United States of America 9 8 7 6 5 4 3

Trademarked names may appear in this book. Rather than use a trademark symbol with every occurrence of a trademarked name, we use the names only in an editorial fashion and to the benefit of the trademark owner, with no intention of infringement of the trademark.

Lead Editor: Ewan Buckingham
Technical Reviewer: Sylvain Groulx
Editorial Board: Steve Anglin, Ewan Buckingham, Gary Cornell, Jason Gilmore, Jonathan Gennick, Jonathan Hassell, James Huddleston, Chris Mills, Matthew Moodie, Dominic Shakeshaft, Jim Sumser, Matt Wade
Project Manager: Beth Christmas
Copy Edit Manager: Nicole Flores
Copy Editor: Jennifer Whipple
Assistant Production Director: Kari Brooks-Copony
Production Editor: Katie Stence
Compositor: Susan Glinert
Proofreader: Nancy Riddiough
Indexer: Julie Grady
Artist: April Milne
Cover Designer: Kurt Krames
Manufacturing Director: Tom Debolski

Distributed to the book trade worldwide by Springer-Verlag New York, Inc., 233 Spring Street, 6th Floor, New York, NY 10013. Phone 1-800-SPRINGER, fax 201-348-4505, e-mail orders-ny@springer-sbm.com, or visit http://www.springeronline.com.

For information on translations, please contact Apress directly at 2855 Telegraph Avenue, Suite 600, Berkeley, CA 94705. Phone 510-549-5930, fax 510-549-5939, e-mail info@apress.com, or visit http://www.apress.com.

The information in this book is distributed on an "as is" basis, without warranty. Although every precaution has been taken in the preparation of this work, neither the author(s) nor Apress shall have any liability to any person or entity with respect to any loss or damage caused or alleged to be caused directly or indirectly by the information contained in this work.

The source code for this book is available to readers at http://www.apress.com in the Source Code/ Download section. You will need to answer questions pertaining to this book in order to successfully download the code.

For Teresa

Contents at a Glance

Contents

About the Author

BRUCE BUKOVICS has been a working developer for more than 25 years. During this time, he has designed and developed applications in such widely varying areas as banking, corporate finance, credit card processing, payroll processing, and retail systems.

He has firsthand developer experience with a variety of languages, including C, C++, Delphi, Java, VB, and C#. His design and development experience includes everything from mainframe and client/server to widely distributed n-tier and SOA applications. Most recently, he has been immersed in the .NET 3.0 technology stack, leveraging Windows Presentation Foundation (WPF), Windows Communication Foundation (WCF), and, of course, Windows Workflow Foundation (WF) to help build a new generation of applications.

He considers himself a pragmatic programmer and test driven development evangelist. He doesn't stand on formality and doesn't do things in a particular way just because they have always been done that way. He's willing to look at alternate or unorthodox solutions to a problem if that's what it takes.

He is currently employed at Radiant Systems Inc. in Alpharetta, Georgia, as a lead developer and architect in the central technology group.

About the Technical Reviewer

SYLVAIN GROULX is an independent database software consultant based in Montreal, Quebec. He's been an application developer and DBA over the past 20 years. His current interests include the .NET Framework 3.0 Windows Presentation Foundation, Windows Workflow Foundation, and SQL Server 2005 Services (Broker, Integration, Notification, and Reporting).

As the founder of the Microsoft .NET Architecture User Group in Montreal, he has been an active proponent of .NET technologies and community-based learning initiatives. He is a great enthusiast for C#, which is why he has been actively involved with .NET since the first bits were released in 2000.

He enjoyed many great years as a Microsoft MVP before joining Microsoft Consulting Services. His past roles at Microsoft include project lead and developer consultant. He also spent many years architecting and building custom applications for large enterprise customers.

When not sitting in front of a keyboard, Sylvain is busy playing a round of golf whenever possible.

Acknowledgments

Once again, the folks at Apress have done an outstanding job with this book. It takes a team of very professional people to produce a book like this. You truly made the task of writing this book an enjoyable one. A big thank-you goes out to all of you.

I would like to personally thank Ewan Buckingham who was the editor of this book. Ewan allowed me to write the book that I wanted to write, but he was also there with guidance when I needed it most. Matt Moodie also did some pinch-hitting for Ewan when things got backed up. Jennifer Whipple was the primary copy editor on the book, along with some assistance from Nicole Flores. They both did a great job correcting my prose, refining it without changing my original intent. Katie Stence was the production editor who worked her magic to transform my raw text into the pages that you see before you. And Beth Christmas was the project manager for the book. She was the traffic cop and task master who kept things running smoothly and on schedule.

A good technical book needs a great technical reviewer, and Sylvain Groulx stepped up to the challenge. This was an especially challenging job for Sylvain because I began this book while WF was in a constant state of change, churning with what seemed like monthly CTPs or betas. Yet in spite of this, he was able to keep up with all of the class and namespace changes from one version of WF to the next. Thank you, Sylvain, for making sure that this book is as accurate as possible.

I'd also like to thank all of the folks who contributed to the Microsoft Windows Workflow Foundation forum hosted on MSDN. This active community of developers was an invaluable resource in understanding how some of the undocumented features of WF worked during the early beta and CTP stage.

Most importantly, I must thank my wife, Teresa, and son, Brennen, for their support and patience during this project. When I finished my first book, I honestly thought that it would be a long time before I wrote my second. Little did I know that I was about to embark on this little project without any downtime at all between books. Sorry about that. I love both of you very much, and I'm looking forward to having time to spend with you again. I promise: No more books for a while.

Introduction

I started working with the new Microsoft WinFX technology stack early in the beta and CTP (Community Technology Preview) stage. The foundations in WinFX (Windows Presentation, Windows Communication, and Windows Workflow) have now finally made their way into a shipping Microsoft product: .NET 3.0. I actually started to learn and use all three of these foundations at the same time in my day job. Talk about a massive learning curve.

While I was impressed with the flexibility and capabilities of Windows Presentation Foundation and Windows Communication Foundation, I was somehow inexplicably drawn to Windows Workflow Foundation (WF). WF isn't just a new way to implement a user interface, or a new way to communicate between applications and services. WF represents a completely new way to develop applications. It is declarative, visual, and infinitely flexible. It promotes a model that cleanly separates *what* to do from *when* to do it. This separation allows you to change the workflow model (the *when*) without affecting the *what*. Business logic is implemented as a set of discrete, testable components that are assembled into workflows like building blocks.

Workflow isn't a new concept. But when Microsoft spends years developing a workflow foundation and provides it to us without cost, it is an event worth noting. Other workflow frameworks exist, but WF will soon become the de facto standard workflow framework for Windows applications.

I wrote this book because I'm excited about workflow, and WF in particular. I'm excited about the opportunities that it holds for application developers like us. My hope is that this book will help you to use WF to build an exciting new generation of workflow-enabled applications.

Who Should Read This Book

This book is for all .NET developers who want to learn how to use Windows Workflow Foundation in their own applications. This book is not a primer on .NET or the C# language. To get the most out of the examples that I present in this book, you need a good working knowledge of .NET 1.1 and preferably .NET 2.0. All of the examples are presented in C#, so you should be proficient with C#.

An Overview of This Book

The material in this book is a WF tutorial presented in 17 chapters, with each chapter building upon the ones before it. I've tried to organize the material so that you don't have to jump ahead in order to understand how something works. But since the chapters build upon each other, I do assume that you have read each chapter in order and understand the material that has already been presented.

The short sections that follow provide a brief summary of each chapter.

Chapter 1: A Quick Tour of Windows Workflow Foundation

This chapter provides a brief introduction to WF. In this chapter, you jump right in and develop your first workflow ("Hello Workflow"). You are introduced to some of the fundamental concepts of WF, such as how to pass parameters to a workflow and how to make decisions within a workflow.

Chapter 2: Foundation Overview

The goal of this chapter is to provide a high-level overview of WF in its entirety. This chapter doesn't teach you how to use each individual WF feature, but it does acquaint you with the design time and runtime features that are available with WF. This chapter is a roadmap for the material that is covered in the remainder of the book.

Chapter 3: Activities

Activities are the building blocks of WF and are used to construct complete workflows. This chapter provides a summary of the standard activities that are distributed with WF. This chapter also contrasts two ways to introduce business logic into a workflow: the `CodeActivity` and building your own custom activities.

Chapter 4: Hosting the Workflow Runtime

WF is not a stand-alone application. It is a framework for building your own workflow-enabled applications. This chapter demonstrates how to host the workflow runtime in your own application. Included in this chapter is a set of custom workflow manager classes that assist with hosting of the workflow runtime. These helper classes are used in most of the chapters that follow this one.

Chapter 5: Flow Control

WF includes a rich set of standard activities that support everything from simple branching decisions and while loops to parallel execution and replication. These flow control activities control the execution sequence within a workflow and are covered in this chapter. Most of these activities support `Boolean` conditions that can be specified in code or as declarative rule conditions. These two types of conditions are contrasted in this chapter.

Chapter 6: Local Services

Several core features of WF are implemented as pluggable services. This allows you to choose the implementation of each service that meets your needs. WF also provides for local services that can be implemented by you to serve any purpose. One common use of local services is to facilitate communication between workflow instances and your host application. The focus of this chapter is on implementing and using your own local services.

Chapter 7: Event-Driven Activities

This chapter covers event-driven activities that allow your workflows to wait for the receipt of an external event. Chapter 6 shows you how to implement local services and invoke methods of those services from workflow instances. This chapter demonstrates how to raise events from those local services and handle the events within a workflow.

Chapter 8: Workflow Persistence

Workflow persistence allows you to automatically save the state of running workflow instances and then reload them at a later time. The use of persistence is especially important for long-running workflows where a workflow can be unloaded from memory while it is idle and waiting for an external event.

Chapter 9: State Machine Workflows

WF supports two main types of workflows: sequential and state machine. Up until this point in the book, you have been working with sequential workflows that target system interaction problems. Sequential workflows are best used when the exact sequence of tasks is known at design time. State machine workflows are the focus of this chapter and are designed to easily react to external events. They are especially useful for problems that involve human interaction since the exact sequence of tasks can't be determined at design time.

Chapter 10: Transactions and Compensation

The goal of this chapter is to demonstrate two ways to control the integrity and consistency of work that is performed by a workflow. Transactions allow you to enlist multiple activities into a single logical unit of work. When transactions are used, all of the work is committed or rolled back together without any partial updates. On the other hand, compensation is the process of undoing work that has already completed. Compensation might be necessary if individual activities in a workflow have completed successfully, but later the workflow determines that the work must be undone.

Chapter 11: Workflow Rules

WF includes a general-purpose rules engine that you can also use as an alternate way to declare your business logic. Rules are best thought of as simple statements or assertions about data and not as procedural instructions. Individual rules are grouped into rule sets and are evaluated by the rules engine that is included with WF. Each rule allows you to define the actions to execute when the rule evaluates to `true`, and a separate set of actions when it is `false`.

Chapter 12: Exception and Error Handling

Exception handling is important in any application, and WF provides a way to declaratively handle exceptions. The goal of this chapter is to demonstrate various ways to handle exceptions within the workflow model. This chapter also covers cancellation handlers that are used to execute a set of activities when an executing activity is canceled.

Chapter 13: Dynamic Workflow Updates

Most of the time, you will statically define a workflow and then create instances of it at runtime. WF also provides the ability to dynamically apply updates to an executing workflow, altering the internal structure of the workflow. This chapter demonstrates how to apply dynamic workflow updates from the host application, as well as from within an executing workflow.

Chapter 14: Workflow Tracking

WF provides an instrumentation framework for tracking the execution of each workflow. The tracking framework supports pluggable tracking services that you can implement to meet your needs. The framework is based on tracking profiles that allow you to customize the amount and type of data tracked for each workflow type. The focus of this chapter is using the standard tracking service and also developing your own custom tracking service.

Chapter 15: Web Services and ASP.NET

WF allows you to declaratively access web services from within a workflow. You can also expose a workflow as a web service that can be accessed by any web service client. These topics are covered in this chapter along with the use of WF from an ASP.NET Web Forms application.

Chapter 16: Workflow Serialization and Markup

The goal of this chapter is to demonstrate the use of workflow markup and serialization. Each workflow definition can be declared and expressed in several forms, including markup. Markup declares a workflow in a simple XML form that doesn't require compilation and can be parsed and executed directly by the workflow runtime engine. The advantage of using markup is that it is much easier to modify the workflow definition outside of Visual Studio, since it doesn't require compilation.

Chapter 17: Hosting the Workflow Designers

After workflow serialization and markup is presented in Chapter 16, this chapter shows you how to build your own workflow designer. WF includes the classes that you need to host the workflow designers in your own application. The bulk of this chapter presents a working designer application that enables you to define and modify markup-only workflows.

What You Need to Use This Book

To execute the examples presented in this book, you need a development machine with an OS that supports the .NET 3.0 runtime. Currently, that is Windows XP Service Pack 2, Windows 2003 Server Service Pack 1, or Windows Vista. A fully licensed version of Visual Studio 2005 is also necessary in order to use the visual workflow designers and to work with the example C# code. The workflow designers are not supported on the Express editions of Visual Studio or Visual C#.

The runtime for Windows Workflow Foundation is distributed as part of .NET 3.0. In addition to this, you will need to install the designated version of the Windows SDK that supports workflow development. A separate set of extensions to Visual Studio 2005 must also be downloaded and installed to use the workflow designers, project templates, and workflow debugger.

You should be able to locate download links for all of the necessary files from the Microsoft .NET Framework Development Center (http://msdn2.microsoft.com/en-us/netframework/default.aspx).

Obtaining This Book's Source Code

I have found that the best way to learn and retain a new skill is through hands-on examples. For this reason, this book contains a lot of example source code. I've been frustrated on more than one occasion with technical books that don't print all of the source code in the book. The code may be available for download, but then you need to have a computer handy while you are reading the book. That doesn't work well on the beach. So I've made it a point to present all of the code that is necessary to actually build and execute the examples.

When you are ready to execute the example code, you don't have to enter it yourself. You can download all of the code presented in this book from the Apress site at http://www.apress.com and go to the Source Code/Download section. I've organized all of the downloadable code into separate folders for each chapter with a separate Visual Studio solution for each chapter. The only exception is one shared project that is referenced by projects in most of the chapters of this book. I'd suggest that you also keep your code separate by chapter as you work through the examples in this book.

How to Reach Me

If you have questions or comments about this book or Windows Workflow, I'd love to hear from you. Just send your e-mail to workflow@bukovics.com. To make sure your mail makes it past my spam filters you might want to include the text **ProWF** somewhere in the subject line.

CHAPTER 1

■ ■ ■

A Quick Tour of Windows Workflow Foundation

This chapter presents a brief introduction to Windows Workflow Foundation (WF). Instead of diving deeply into any single workflow topic, it provides you with a sampling of topics that are fully presented in other chapters.

You'll learn why workflows are important and why you might want to develop applications using them. You'll then jump right in and implement your very first functioning workflow. Additional hands-on examples are presented that demonstrate other features of Windows Workflow Foundation.

Why Workflow?

As developers, our job is to solve real business problems. The type and complexity of the problems will vary broadly depending on the nature of the business. But regardless of the complexity of any given problem, we tend to solve problems in the same way: we break the problem down into manageable parts. Those parts are further divided into smaller tasks, and so on.

When we've finally reached a point where each task is the right size to understand and manage, we identify the steps needed to accomplish the task. The steps usually have an order associated with them. They represent a sequence of individual instructions that will only yield the expected behavior when they are executed in the correct order.

In the traditional programming model, you implement a task in code using your language of choice. The code specifies what to do (the execution instructions) along with the sequence of those instructions (the flow of control). You also include code to make decisions (rules) based on the value of variables, the receipt of events, and the current state of the application.

A workflow is simply an ordered series of steps that accomplish some defined purpose according to a set of rules. By that definition, what I just described is a *workflow*.

It might be defined entirely in code, but it is no less a type of workflow. We already use workflows every day we develop software. We might not consider affixing the workflow label to our work, but we do use the concepts even if we are not consciously aware of them.

So why all of this talk about workflows? Why did I write a book about them? Why are you reading it right now?

Workflows Are Different

The workflow definition that I gave previously doesn't tell the whole story, of course. There must be more to it, and there is. To a developer, the word *workflow* typically conjures up images of a highly visual environment where complex business rules and flow of control are declared graphically.

It's an environment that allows you to easily visualize and model the activities (steps) that have been declared to solve a problem. And since you can visualize the activities, it's easier to change, enhance, and customize them.

But there is still more to workflows than just the development environment. Workflows represent a different programming model. It's a model that promotes a clear separation between *what* to do and *when* to do it. This separation allows you to change the *when* without affecting the *what*. Workflows generally use a declarative programming model rather than a procedural one. With this model, business logic can be encapsulated in discrete components. But the rules that govern the flow of control between components are declarative.

General purpose languages such as C# or Visual Basic can obviously be used to solve business problems. But the workflow programming model really enables you to implement your own domain-specific language. With such a language, you can express business rules using terms that are common to a specific problem domain. Experts in that domain are able to view a workflow and easily understand it, since it is declared in terminology that they understand.

For example, if your domain is banking and finance, you might refer to accounts, checks, loans, debits, credits, customers, tellers, branches, and so on. But if the problem domain is pizza delivery, those entities don't make much sense. Instead, you would model your problems using terms such as menus, specials, ingredients, addresses, phone numbers, drivers, tips, and so on. The workflow model allows you to define the problem using terminology that is appropriate for each problem domain.

Workflows allow you to easily model system and human interactions. A *system interaction* is how we as developers would typically approach a problem. You define the steps to execute and write code that controls the sequence of those steps. The code is always in total control.

Human interactions are those that involve real live people. The problem is that people are not always as predictable as your code. For example, you might need to model a mortgage loan application. The process might include steps that must be executed by real people in order to complete the process. How much control do you have over the order of those steps? Does the credit approval always occur first, or is it possible for the appraisal to be done first? What about the property survey? Is it done before or after the appraisal? And what activities must be completed before you can schedule the loan closing? The point is that these types of problems are difficult to express using a purely procedural model because human beings are in control. The exact sequence of steps is not always predictable. The workflow model really shines when it comes to solving human interaction problems.

Why Windows Workflow Foundation?

If workflows are important, then why use Windows Workflow Foundation? Microsoft has provided this foundation in order to simplify and enhance your .NET development. It is not a stand-alone application. It is a software foundation that is designed to enable workflows within your applications. Regardless of the type of application you are developing, there is something in WF that you can leverage.

If you are developing line-of-business applications, you can use WF to orchestrate the business rules. If your application is comprised of a series of human interactions, you can use a WF state machine workflow to implement logic that can react to those interactions. If you need a highly customizable application, you can use the declarative nature of WF workflows to separate the business logic from the execution flow. This allows customization of the flow of control without affecting the underlying business logic. And if you are looking for a better way to encapsulate and independently test your application logic, implement the logic as discrete custom activities that are executed within the WF runtime environment.

There are a number of good reasons to use WF, and here are a few of them:

- It provides a flexible and powerful framework for developing workflows. You can spend your time and energy developing your own framework, visual workflow designer, and runtime environment. Or you can use a foundation that Microsoft provides and spend your valuable time solving real business problems.

- It promotes a consistent way to develop your applications. One workflow looks very similar to the next. This consistency in the programming model and tools improves your productivity when developing new applications and maintaining existing ones.

- It supports *sequential* and *state machine* workflows. Sequential workflows are generally used for system interactions. State machine workflows are well-suited to solving problems that focus on human interaction.

- It supports workflow persistence. The ability to save and later reload the state of a running workflow is especially important when modeling human interactions.

- It supports problem solving using a domain-specific model. Microsoft encourages you to develop your own custom activity components. Each custom component addresses a problem that is specific to your problem domain and uses terminology that is common to the domain.

- It provides a complete workflow ecosystem. In addition to the workflow runtime itself, Microsoft also provides a suite of standard activities, workflow persistence, workflow monitoring and tracking, and a workflow designer that is integrated with Visual Studio which you can also host in your own applications.

- It is free of charge. Because of this and its tight integration with Visual Studio, it will become the de facto standard workflow framework for Windows developers. A growing community of other WF developers is already in place. They are already sharing their ideas, their custom activity components, and other code.

Your Development Environment

In order to develop applications using Windows Workflow Foundation, you'll need to install a minimum set of software components. The minimum requirements are the following:

- Visual Studio 2005 Enterprise, Professional, or Standard

- The .NET 3.0 runtime

- A designated version of the Windows SDK that supports WF

- The Windows Workflow add-in to Visual Studio

Please refer to the Microsoft MSDN site for the latest download and installation instructions.

Hello Workflow

At this point you are ready to create your first workflow. In the world of technology in which we work, it has become customary to begin any new technical encounter with a "Hello World" example.

Not wanting to break with tradition, I present a "Hello Workflow" example in the pages that follow. If you follow along with the steps as I present them, you will have a really simple yet functional workflow application.

In this example, and in the other examples in this chapter, I present important concepts that are the basis for working with all workflows, regardless of their complexity. If you already have experience working with Windows Workflow Foundation, you might feel compelled to skip over this information. If so, go ahead, but you might want to give this chapter a quick read anyway.

To implement the "Hello Workflow" example, you'll create a sequential workflow project, add one of the standard activities to the workflow, and then add code to display "Hello Workflow" on the Console.

Creating the Workflow Project

Workflow projects are created in the same way as other project types in Visual Studio. After starting Visual Studio 2005, you select File ➤ New ➤ Project. A New Project dialog is presented that should look similar to the one shown in Figure 1-1.

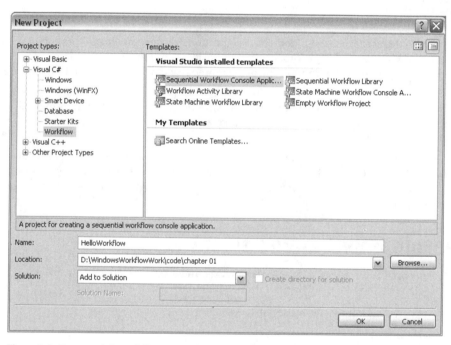

Figure 1-1. *Sequential workflow console application New Project dialog*

After selecting Visual C# as the language, you'll see Workflow as one of the available project template categories. As shown in Figure 1-1, there are several workflow project templates available. For this example, you should choose Sequential Workflow Console Application. This produces a console application that supports the use of Windows Workflow Foundation. A *sequential workflow* is one that executes a series of steps in a defined sequence. That's exactly the type of workflow that we need for this example.

■**Note** Visual Basic developers don't have to worry. The same Workflow project templates are also available for Visual Basic if that's your language of choice.

You should now enter a meaningful name for the project, such as **HelloWorkflow**, select a location, and press OK to create the new project.

Note In the example shown in Figure 1-1, the project will be added to an existing solution named Chapter 01. An existing solution is used in order to neatly organize all of the examples for this book by chapter. This is not a strict requirement and you are free to create individual solutions for each project if you prefer. If you create a new project without first opening or creating a solution, the New Project dialog does not include the Add to Solution option.

After a second or two, the new project is created. The Solution Explorer window shows the source files that are created as part of the project, as shown in Figure 1-2.

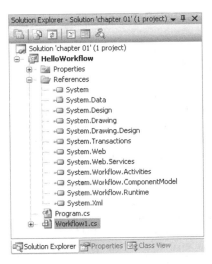

Figure 1-2. *Solution Explorer for the new workflow project*

Notice that I've expanded the References folder in order to show the assembly references for the project. By selecting a workflow project as the template, the assembly references necessary to use WF are added for you. The workflow-related assemblies are the following:

- System.Workflow.Activities
- System.Workflow.ComponentModel
- System.Workflow.Runtime

Within these assemblies, the workflow-related classes are organized into a number of namespaces. In your code, you only need to reference the namespaces that you are actually using.

The project template created a file named Program.cs. Since this is a console application, this file contains the Main method associated with the application. We'll review the generated code for this file shortly.

Introducing the Workflow Designer

Also generated is a file named Workflow1.cs. This file contains the code that defines the workflow and is associated with the visual workflow designer as its editor. When this file is opened, as it is when the project is first created, the initial view of the designer looks like Figure 1-3.

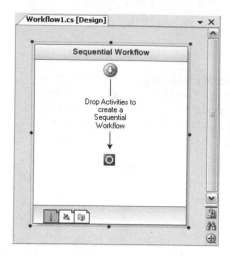

Figure 1-3. *Initial view of the visual workflow designer*

The workflow designer is the primary canvas that you will use to define your workflows. You can also define a workflow entirely in code, in much the same way that you can define an entire Windows form or other user interface elements in code. But one of the best features of WF is the designer, and using it will greatly increase your productivity when defining workflows. The designer supports dragging and dropping of activities onto the workflow canvas from the Visual Studio Toolbox.

Using Workflow Activities

An *activity* represents a step in the workflow and is the fundamental building block of all WF workflows. All activities either directly or indirectly derive from the base System.Workflow. ComponentModel.Activity class. Microsoft supplies a set of standard activities that you can use, but you are encouraged to also develop your own custom activities. Each activity is designed to serve a unique purpose and encapsulates the logic needed to fulfill that purpose.

For a sequential workflow such as this one, the order of the activities in the workflow determines their execution sequence. A sequential workflow has a defined beginning and ending point. As shown in Figure 1-3, previously, these points are represented by the arrow at the top of the workflow and the circle symbol at the bottom. What takes place between these two points is yours to define by dropping activities onto the canvas. Once you've dropped a series of activities onto a workflow, you can modify their execution order by simply dragging them to a new location.

Activities wouldn't be very useful if there wasn't a way to change their default behavior. Therefore, most activities provide a set of properties that can be set at design time. The workflow itself also has properties that can be set at design time.

Figure 1-4 shows just a few of the standard activities that are supplied by Microsoft. I review all of the available activities in Chapter 3.

Figure 1-4. *Partial view of standard activities*

Entering Code

For this simple example, you need to drag and drop the Code activity (CodeActivity) onto the work-flow. The Code activity is a simple way to execute any code that you wish as a step in the workflow. Your workflow should now look like the one shown in Figure 1-5.

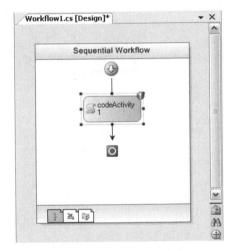

Figure 1-5. *Workflow with single Code activity*

■**Note** As I discuss in Chapter 3, another way to execute your own code is to implement your own custom activity.

The actual class name associated with this activity is CodeActivity. The single instance of this class is given the default name of codeActivity1 when it is dropped onto the workflow. Notice the exclamation point at the top of the activity. This is your indication that there are one or more errors associated with this activity. This is typically the case when the activity has required properties that have not been set.

If you click the exclamation point for the Code activity, you should see an error such as "Property ExecuteCode is not set." To correct this error, you need to set a value for the ExecuteCode property. By selecting codeActivity1 and switching to the Properties window, you'll see the available properties for this activity. The Properties window looks like Figure 1-6.

Figure 1-6. *Property window for codeActivity1*

ExecuteCode is actually a public event of the CodeActivity class. The property requires the name of an event handler for this event. When the Code activity is executed as part of a workflow, the ExecuteCode event is raised and the code you place in the handler is executed.

Enter **codeActivity1_ExecuteCode** in the box and press enter. You could also double click the codeActivity1 in the designer to add a handler for this event. An empty event handler is created for you and the Workflow1.cs file is opened for editing. Listing 1-1 shows the code at this stage.

Listing 1-1. *Workflow1.cs File with Empty ExecuteCode Event Handler*

```
using System;
using System.Workflow.Activities;

namespace HelloWorkflow
{
    public sealed partial class Workflow1 : SequentialWorkflowActivity
    {
        public Workflow1()
        {
            InitializeComponent();
        }

        private void codeActivity1_ExecuteCode(object sender, EventArgs e)
        {

        }
    }
}
```

■**Note** As I mentioned previously, ExecuteCode is actually an event. This implies that somewhere we should see code that assigns the method codeActivity1_ExecuteCode to this event as a handler. That code exists, but is not in this source file. Since this class definition includes the partial keyword, portions of the class definition can be spread across multiple source files.

If you expand the Workflow1.cs file in the Solution Explorer window, you'll see that beneath it there is a source file named Workflow1.designer.cs. The Workflow1.designer.cs file is the other half of this partial class definition and it contains the entries placed there by the Visual Studio Workflow designer. Included with that code is a statement that assigns the codeActivity1_ExecuteCode method as a handler for the ExecuteCode event. Microsoft's design allows for a clean separation of designer-controlled code from our code.

Notice that the Workflow1 class derives from the SequentialWorkflowActivity class. This is the base class that is used for sequential workflows. It is interesting to note that SequentialWorkflowActivity is indirectly derived from the base Activity class. This means that the workflow itself is actually a type of activity. Activities are truly the universal building block of WF.

In order to have this workflow display the obligatory welcome message, you only need to add a call to Console.WriteLine like this:

```
private void codeActivity1_ExecuteCode(object sender, EventArgs e)
{
    Console.WriteLine("Hello Workflow!");
}
```

Hosting the Workflow Runtime

Now that the workflow has been implemented, let's turn our attention to the Program.cs file included in the project. The original code generated for this file is shown in Listing 1-2.

Listing 1-2. *Original Program.cs Generated Code*

```
#region Using directives

using System;
using System.Threading;
using System.Workflow.Runtime;

#endregion

namespace HelloWorkflow
{
    class Program
    {
        static void Main(string[] args)
        {
            WorkflowRuntime workflowRuntime = new WorkflowRuntime();
```

```
AutoResetEvent waitHandle = new AutoResetEvent(false);
workflowRuntime.WorkflowCompleted
    += delegate(object sender, WorkflowCompletedEventArgs e)
    {
        waitHandle.Set();
    };
workflowRuntime.WorkflowTerminated
    += delegate(object sender, WorkflowTerminatedEventArgs e)
    {
        Console.WriteLine(e.Exception.Message);
        waitHandle.Set();
    };

WorkflowInstance instance
    = workflowRuntime.CreateWorkflow(typeof(HelloWorkflow.Workflow1));
instance.Start();

waitHandle.WaitOne();
            }
        }
    }
```

The purpose of this code is to host the workflow runtime and execute the workflow that you just defined. When you create this project from the Sequential Workflow Console Application template, Microsoft is nice enough to generate this boilerplate code. Without making any changes to the code, you can build and run this project and (hopefully) see the correct results.

But before we do that, let's review this code and make one minor addition. The code starts by creating an instance of the WorkflowRuntime class. As the name implies, this is the all-important class that is actually in charge of running the workflow. The class also provides a number of events and methods that permit you to monitor and control the execution of any workflow.

Next, an instance of the AutoResetEvent class is created. This is a thread synchronization class that is used to release a single waiting thread. Thread synchronization you say? Exactly what threads do you need to synchronize? When a workflow executes, it does so in a separate thread that is created and managed by the workflow runtime. This makes sense since the workflow runtime is capable of handling multiple workflows at the same time. In this example, the two threads that must be synchronized are the workflow thread and the main thread of the host console application.

In order for the host console application to know when the workflow has completed, the code subscribes to two events of the WorkflowRuntime class: WorkflowCompleted and WorkflowTerminated. It uses the .NET 2.0 anonymous delegate syntax for this, implementing the event handler code inline rather than referencing a separate method.

When a workflow completes normally, the WorkflowCompleted event is raised and this code is executed:

```
waitHandle.Set();
```

This signals the AutoResetEvent object, which releases the console application from its wait.

If an error occurs, the WorkflowTerminated event is raised and this code is executed:

```
Console.WriteLine(e.Exception.Message);
waitHandle.Set();
```

This displays the error message from the exception and then releases the waiting thread. There are other events that can be used to monitor the status of a workflow, but these are the only two that we need in this example.

Once the workflow runtime has been prepared, an instance of the workflow is created and started with this code:

```
WorkflowInstance instance
    = workflowRuntime.CreateWorkflow(typeof(HelloWorkflow.Workflow1));
instance.Start();
```

The `CreateWorkflow` method has several overloaded versions, but this one simply requires the `Type` of the workflow that you want to create as its only parameter. When a workflow is created, it doesn't begin executing immediately. Instead, a `WorkflowInstance` object is returned from this method and used to start the execution of the workflow.

Finally, the console application suspends execution of the current thread and waits until the `AutoResetEvent` object is signaled with this code:

```
waitHandle.WaitOne();
```

■ **Caution** This workflow is trivial and will execute very quickly. But real-world workflows will require much more time to execute. It is vitally important that the host application waits until the workflow has finished. Otherwise, the host application might terminate before the workflow has had a chance to complete all of its activities.

Running the Application

Before you build and execute this application, add these lines of code to the very end of the `Main` method:

```
Console.WriteLine("Press any key to exit");
Console.ReadLine();
```

This will make it easier to see the results when you execute the project. Without these lines, the console application will execute and then immediately finish, not giving you a chance to see the results.

Now it's time to build and execute the project. You can execute the project by selecting Start Debugging from the Debug menu. Or, if you have the default Visual Studio key mappings still in place, you can simply press F5. If all goes well, you should see these results displayed on the console:

```
Hello Workflow!
Press any key to exit
```

Congratulations! Your first encounter with Windows Workflow Foundation was successful.

Passing Parameters

Workflows would have limited usefulness without the ability to receive parameter input. Passing parameters to a workflow is one of the fundamental mechanisms that permit you to affect the outcome of the workflow.

The preceding example writes a simple string constant to the `Console`. Let's now modify that example so that it uses input parameters to format the string that is written. The parameters will be passed directly from the host console application.

Declaring the Properties

Input parameters can be passed to a workflow as normal .NET CLR (Common Language Runtime) properties. Therefore, the first step in supporting input parameters is to declare the local variables and properties in the workflow class. You can start with the Workflow1.cs file from the previous example and add the following code shown in bold to the Workflow1 class:

```
public sealed partial class Workflow1 : SequentialWorkflowActivity
{
    private String _person = String.Empty;
    private String _message = String.Empty;

    /// <summary>
    /// The target of the greeting
    /// </summary>
    public String Person
    {
        get { return _person; }
        set { _person = value; }
    }

    /// <summary>
    /// The greeting message
    /// </summary>
    public String Message
    {
        get { return _message; }
        set { _message = value; }
    }

    public Workflow1()
    {
        InitializeComponent();
    }

    private void codeActivity1_ExecuteCode(object sender, EventArgs e)
    {
        Console.WriteLine("Hello Workflow!");
    }
}
```

Two local variables and their associated properties define all of the input parameters that are needed for this example.

Next, you can modify the Console.WriteLine statement in the codeActivity1_ExecuteCode method shown previously to use the new variables like this:

```
private void codeActivity1_ExecuteCode(object sender, EventArgs e)
{
    //display the variable greeting
    Console.WriteLine("Hello {0}, {1}", _person, _message);
}
```

Passing Values at Runtime

The Program.cs file requires a few changes in order to pass the new parameters to the workflow. Listing 1-3 shows the revised code for Program.cs in its entirety. The additions and changes from the previous example are highlighted in bold.

Listing 1-3. *Program.cs Code to Pass Runtime Parameters*

```
#region Using directives

using System;
using System.Collections.Generic;
using System.Threading;
using System.Workflow.Runtime;

#endregion

namespace HelloWorkflow
{
    class Program
    {
        static void Main(string[] args)
        {
            WorkflowRuntime workflowRuntime = new WorkflowRuntime();

            AutoResetEvent waitHandle = new AutoResetEvent(false);
            workflowRuntime.WorkflowCompleted
                += delegate(object sender, WorkflowCompletedEventArgs e)
                {
                    waitHandle.Set();
                };
            workflowRuntime.WorkflowTerminated
                += delegate(object sender, WorkflowTerminatedEventArgs e)
                {
                    Console.WriteLine(e.Exception.Message);
                    waitHandle.Set();
                };

            //create a dictionary with input arguments
            Dictionary<String, Object> wfArguments
                = new Dictionary<string, object>();
            wfArguments.Add("Person", "Bruce");
            wfArguments.Add("Message", "did the workflow succeed?");

            WorkflowInstance instance = workflowRuntime.CreateWorkflow(
                typeof(HelloWorkflow.Workflow1),
                    wfArguments);

            instance.Start();

            waitHandle.WaitOne();

            Console.WriteLine("Press any key to exit");
            Console.ReadLine();
        }
    }
}
```

Input parameters are passed to a workflow as a generic Dictionary object. The Dictionary must be keyed by a String and use an Object as the value for each parameter entry. Once the Dictionary object is created, you can use the Add method to specify the value for each parameter that the workflow expects.

Notice that the key to each parameter in the Dictionary is an exact match to one of the workflow public properties. This is not an accident. In order for the parameters to make their way into the workflow, the names must match exactly, including their case. Likewise, the Type of the parameter value must match the expected Type of the property. In this example, both properties are of type String, therefore a string value must be passed in the Dictionary.

Note If you do manage to misspell a parameter name, you'll receive an ArgumentException during execution. For example, if you attempt to pass a parameter named person (all lowercase) instead of Person, you'll receive an ArgumentException with the message "Workflow Services semantic error: The workflow 'Workflow1' has no public writable property named 'person'."

If the parameter name is correct but the value is of the incorrect type, the message will be "Invalid workflow parameter value."

The only other required change is to actually pass the Dictionary object to the workflow. This is accomplished with an overloaded version of the CreateWorkflow method as shown here:

```
WorkflowInstance instance
    = workflowRuntime.CreateWorkflow(typeof(HelloWorkflow.Workflow1),
        wfArguments);
```

When this example application is executed, the results indicate that the parameters are successfully passed to the workflow:

```
Hello Bruce, did the workflow succeed?
Press any key to exit
```

Making Decisions

As you've already seen, workflows use a declarative programming model. Much of your time defining a workflow will be occupied with organizing activities into their proper sequence and setting properties. The real business logic is still there in one form or another. But you can now declare the flow of control between individual activities in the workflow instead of in your code. This separation between your business logic and the rules that control it make workflows a flexible tool for defining complex business problems.

In this next example, you'll see one way to implement simple decisions in a workflow.

Creating a Workflow Library

This example implements a simple calculator using a workflow. The user interface is a Windows Forms application and the workflow is implemented in a separate assembly (a DLL).

Note The purpose of this example isn't to demonstrate the best way to implement a calculator. You could easily develop a self-contained calculator application without a workflow in less code. Instead, this example illustrates the use of a workflow to declare the flow of control and to make simple decisions.

Let's start by creating the workflow project. You can follow the same steps that you used to create the project for the previous examples. However, this time select the Sequential Workflow Library project template. This creates a DLL assembly that supports workflows. Name the project SimpleCalculatorWorkflow. Once the project has been created, you should see the same initial workflow canvas shown in Figure 1-3.

Adding Workflow Properties

This calculator application is extremely simple, but it does support the basic operations of add (+), subtract (-), multiply (x), and divide (/). One of these operations is performed each time the calculator workflow is executed. Each operation works with two integers that are passed in to the workflow. The result of the operation is returned as a Double.

The first step in implementing this workflow is to define these parameters as public properties of the Workflow1 class. The code in Listing 1-4 shows the contents of the Workflow1.cs file after the addition of these variables and properties.

Listing 1-4. *Workflow1.cs File with Calculator Workflow Properties*

```csharp
using System;
using System.Workflow.Activities;

namespace SimpleCalculatorWorkflow
{
    public sealed partial class Workflow1 : SequentialWorkflowActivity
    {
        private String _operation = String.Empty;
        private Int32 _number1;
        private Int32 _number2;
        private Double _result;

        public String Operation
        {
            get { return _operation; }
            set { _operation = value; }
        }

        public Int32 Number1
        {
            get { return _number1; }
            set { _number1 = value; }
        }

        public Int32 Number2
        {
            get { return _number2; }
            set { _number2 = value; }
        }

        public Double Result
        {
            get { return _result; }
            set { _result = value; }
        }
```

```
    public Workflow1()
    {
        InitializeComponent();
    }

}

}
```

The Operation property is used to identify the type of operation and must be one of the valid operation strings (+, -, x, /). As you'll see next, this property is used as the basis for some simple decisions within the workflow. The other properties are the two numbers and the result that are used by each calculation.

Adding IfElse Activities

The workflow must make one very simple decision. It must determine the type of arithmetic operation that is requested and then perform it. To accomplish this, you can use the IfElseActivity.

Open the workflow designer for file Workflow1.cs file and drag the activity labeled IfElse from the Toolbox. After dropping it onto the workflow, the designer should look like Figure 1-7.

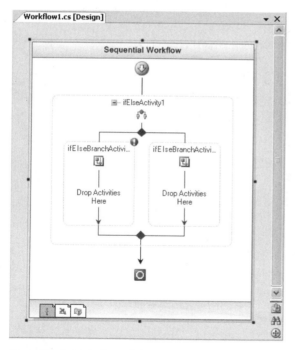

Figure 1-7. *Initial view of IfElseActivity*

The IfElseActivity is actually a container for other activities. It contains a set of two or more IfElseBranchActivity instances. Each one represents a possible branch in a decision tree. The order of the branches is important since the first branch with a true condition is the one that is followed. The evaluation of branches starts with the leftmost branch.

As shown in Figure 1-7, the first two branches are already added for you. As you'll soon see, you're not limited to just those first two branches. You can add as many branches as your workflow requires.

The first branch represents the add operation of the calculator and it will check the `Operation` property for the value +. To enter the first condition, highlight the leftmost `IfElseBranchActivity` class and switch to the Properties window. First, change the `Name` property of the activity to something meaningful such as `ifElseBranchActivityIsAdd`. Although this isn't a strict requirement, a descriptive name makes it easier to identify an activity in the workflow designer.

There are two ways to define a condition. You can use a Code Condition or a Declarative Rule Condition. The code condition is similar to the `CodeActivity` that you've already seen. It works by writing code within an event handler that evaluates to a `Boolean` result. The Declarative Rule Condition must also evaluate to a `Boolean` but it is defined separately from the workflow code. One benefit of rule conditions is that they can be modified at runtime without the need to recompile any code. Since code conditions are just that, code, they require a recompile in order to make any modifications

For this example, select Declarative Rule Condition from the list of available values in the `Condition` property. The full class name that is shown for the rule condition is `System.Workflow. Activities.Rules.RuleConditionReference`.

After selecting the Declarative Rule Condition, expand the `Condition` property to reveal additional properties for the rule. Enter a `ConditionName` of `IsAdd` as a descriptive name for this rule. Each rule must have a unique name. Next, after selecting the `Expression` property, click the ellipsis. This presents the Rule Condition Editor dialog shown in Figure 1-8.

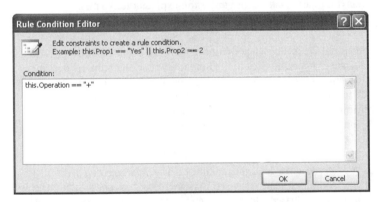

Figure 1-8. *Rule Condition Editor with the first rule*

This dialog is where you enter your `Boolean` expression. As shown in Figure 1-8, enter this code:

```
this.Operation == "+"
```

The Rule Condition Editor has IntelliSense support, therefore you can enter **this** followed by a period, and a list of the available workflow properties will be presented.

This expression will be evaluated when the workflow is executed and a simple `true`/`false` result returned. If the result is `true`, then any additional activities in this branch will be executed. If `false` is returned from the rule, the next `IfElseBranchActivity` is evaluated, and so on. After selecting OK, the dialog is closed and the Properties window should look like Figure 1-9.

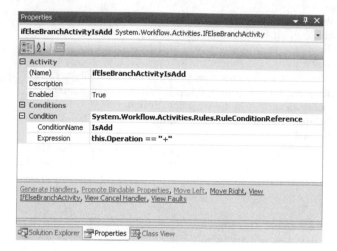

Figure 1-9. *IfElseBranchActivity rule condition properties*

You'll have a total of four rule conditions to add, one for each possible arithmetic operation that the workflow will support. You've just added the IsAdd condition to check for +. Now repeat the process and add a rule condition to the second IfElseBranchActivity to check for the subtraction operation (-). Enter IsSubtract as the ConditionName and enter the expression like this:

```
this.Operation == "-"
```

You need to define two additional IfElseBranch activities in order to check for multiply and divide. To add a new IfElseBranch activity, right-click the ifElseActivity1 object in the designer and select Add Branch. This adds a new branch to the right of any existing branches. Do this three times since you'll need a branch for multiply, divide, and one additional branch. If the rightmost branch doesn't include a conditional expression, it is executed if none of the other branch conditions evaluate to true. As such, it acts as the final else in your decision tree.

Note There are two other ways you can add a new IfElseBranchActivity. After selecting the ifElseActivity1 object, you can select Add Branch from the top-level Workflow menu. If you switch to the Properties window, you can also select Add Branch as one of the available shortcut options at the bottom of the window. If you don't see the commands at the bottom of the Properties window, it is likely that the Commands have been switched off. To enable them, right-click anywhere in the Properties window and make sure Commands is checked.

Once you've added the branches, add the multiply and divide rule conditions. The rule expression for multiply looks like this:

```
this.Operation == "x"
```

The expression for divide looks like this:

```
this.Operation == "/"
```

Adding Calculation Logic

Each IfElseBranchActivity in the workflow represents a separate arithmetic operation. When one of the rule conditions that you just entered is true, any activities within that IfElseBranchActivity are executed. The branches are evaluated one at a time, starting at the left side.

To implement the code for an operation, you can drag and drop a Code activity (CodeActivity) from the Toolbox to the first IfElseBranchActivity container. Drop it in the empty area in the container labeled Drop Activities Here. Now switch to the Properties window for the new CodeActivity and enter a name of AddOperation in the ExecuteCode property. After pressing Enter, an event handler with a name of AddOperation is added to the workflow. Add a line of code to the handler that performs an addition operation on the two numbers. The modified code looks like this:

```
private void AddOperation(object sender, EventArgs e)
{
    _result = _number1 + _number2;
}
```

Repeat these steps for each of the other operations: subtract, multiply, and divide. You also want to throw an exception if an unknown operation is requested. To do this, add a Code activity (CodeActivity) to the final branch and add code that looks like this:

```
private void UnknownOperation(object sender, EventArgs e)
{
    throw new ArgumentException(String.Format(
        "Invalid operation of {0} requested", Operation));
}
```

If you followed all of the steps correctly, the workflow should look like Figure 1-10.

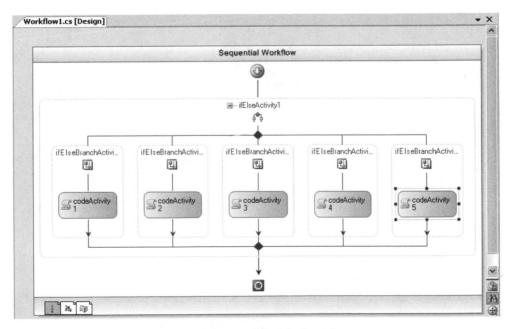

Figure 1-10. *Workflow with multiple IfElseBranchActivity branches*

Listing 1-5 shows the completed code for Workflow1.cs.

Listing 1-5. *Complete Workflow1.cs File*

```csharp
using System;
using System.Workflow.Activities;

namespace SimpleCalculatorWorkflow
{
    public sealed partial class Workflow1 : SequentialWorkflowActivity
    {
        private String _operation = String.Empty;
        private Int32 _number1;
        private Int32 _number2;
        private Double _result;

        public String Operation
        {
            get { return _operation; }
            set { _operation = value; }
        }

        public Int32 Number1
        {
            get { return _number1; }
            set { _number1 = value; }
        }

        public Int32 Number2
        {
            get { return _number2; }
            set { _number2 = value; }
        }

        public Double Result
        {
            get { return _result; }
            set { _result = value; }
        }

        public Workflow1()
        {
            InitializeComponent();
        }

        /// <summary>
        /// Add the numbers
        /// </summary>
        /// <param name="sender"></param>
        /// <param name="e"></param>
        private void AddOperation(object sender, EventArgs e)
        {
            _result = _number1 + _number2;
        }
```

```csharp
/// <summary>
/// Subtract the numbers
/// </summary>
/// <param name="sender"></param>
/// <param name="e"></param>
private void SubtractOperation(object sender, EventArgs e)
{
    _result = _number1 - _number2;
}

/// <summary>
/// Multiply the numbers
/// </summary>
/// <param name="sender"></param>
/// <param name="e"></param>
private void MultiplyOperation(object sender, EventArgs e)
{
    _result = _number1 * _number2;
}

/// <summary>
/// Divide the numbers
/// </summary>
/// <param name="sender"></param>
/// <param name="e"></param>
private void DivideOperation(object sender, EventArgs e)
{
    if (_number2 != 0)
    {
        _result = (Double)_number1 / (Double)_number2;
    }
    else
    {
        _result = 0;
    }
}

/// <summary>
/// Handle invalid operation
/// </summary>
/// <param name="sender"></param>
/// <param name="e"></param>
private void UnknownOperation(object sender, EventArgs e)
{
    throw new ArgumentException(String.Format(
        "Invalid operation of {0} requested", Operation));
}
    }

}
```

Creating the Calculator Client

Now that the workflow is complete, you need a client application that uses it. Create a new project as you've done in the past. This time, instead of a console application, choose Windows Application as the project type. Name the application SimpleCalculator.

Add a project reference to the SimpleCalculatorWorkflow project containing the workflow. Since this Windows application will be hosting the workflow runtime, you'll need to also add these assembly references:

- System.Workflow.Activities
- System.Workflow.ComponentModel
- System.Workflow.Runtime

Note You need to manually add these assembly references since you started with a Windows Application project instead of one of the workflow project templates. The workflow project templates would have added these assembly references for you.

Add a Button object to the form for each number (0 to 9) and each operation (+, -, x, /). Also include a Button for clear (C) and equals (=). You'll also need a TextBox to display the numbers as they are entered and to display the result. The final application should look something like Figure 1-11.

Figure 1-11. *Calculator client application*

Next, you'll need to attach event handlers to the Click event of each button. However, there really are only four different event handlers that you'll need to add:

- NumericButton_Click: Assign this handler to all of the number buttons (0 to 9).
- OperationButton_Click: Assign this handler to all of the operation buttons (+, -, x, /).
- Equals_Click: Assign this handler to the equals button (=).
- Clear_Click: Assign this handler to the clear button (C).

Listing 1-6 shows all of the code that should be added to the Form1.cs file.

Listing 1-6. *Form1.cs Windows Calculator Application*

```csharp
using System;
using System.Collections.Generic;
using System.Threading;
using System.Windows.Forms;
using System.Workflow.Runtime;

namespace SimpleCalculator
{
    public partial class Form1 : Form
    {
        private WorkflowRuntime _workflowRuntime;
        private AutoResetEvent _waitHandle = new AutoResetEvent(false);
        private String _operation = String.Empty;
        private Int32 _number1;
        private Int32 _number2;
        private Double _result;

        public Form1()
        {
            InitializeComponent();

            //start up the workflow runtime. must be done
            //only once per AppDomain
            InitializeWorkflowRuntime();
        }

        /// <summary>
        /// Start the workflow runtime
        /// </summary>
        private void InitializeWorkflowRuntime()
        {
            _workflowRuntime = new WorkflowRuntime();
            _workflowRuntime.WorkflowCompleted
                += delegate(object sender, WorkflowCompletedEventArgs e)
                {
                    _result = (Double)e.OutputParameters["Result"];
                    _waitHandle.Set();
                };
            _workflowRuntime.WorkflowTerminated
                += delegate(object sender, WorkflowTerminatedEventArgs e)
                {
                    MessageBox.Show(String.Format(
                        "Workflow Terminated: {0}", e.Exception.Message),
                        "Error in Workflow");
                    _waitHandle.Set();
                };
        }
```

During construction of the form, the InitializeWorkflowRuntime method is executed. Within this method the workflow runtime is initialized in a similar manner to the previous examples. Only one instance of the WorkflowRuntime can be initialized for each AppDomain. For this reason, initializing the runtime during initial construction of the form makes sense.

One additional requirement for this example is to retrieve the `Result` property when the workflow completes. This property contains the result of the requested calculation. The code to retrieve this value is in the `WorkflowCompleted` event handler for the `WorkflowRuntime` object. When this event is raised by the workflow runtime, the `Result` property is saved in a form member variable. This member variable is later used to update the user interface with the result.

```
private void NumericButton_Click(object sender, EventArgs e)
{
    txtNumber.AppendText(((Button)sender).Text.Trim());
}

private void Clear_Click(object sender, EventArgs e)
{
    Clear();
}

/// <summary>
/// An operation button was pressed
/// </summary>
/// <param name="sender"></param>
/// <param name="e"></param>
private void OperationButton_Click(object sender, EventArgs e)
{
    try
    {
        _number1 = Int32.Parse(txtNumber.Text);
        _operation = ((Button)sender).Text.Trim();
        txtNumber.Clear();
    }
    catch (Exception exception)
    {
        MessageBox.Show(String.Format(
            "Operation_Click error: {0}",
            exception.Message));
    }
}

/// <summary>
/// The equals button was pressed. Invoke the workflow
/// that performs the calculation
/// </summary>
/// <param name="sender"></param>
/// <param name="e"></param>
private void Equals_Click(object sender, EventArgs e)
{
    try
    {
        _number2 = Int32.Parse(txtNumber.Text);

        //create a dictionary with input arguments
        Dictionary<String, Object> wfArguments
            = new Dictionary<string, object>();
        wfArguments.Add("Number1", _number1);
        wfArguments.Add("Number2", _number2);
        wfArguments.Add("Operation", _operation);
```

```
            WorkflowInstance instance
                = _workflowRuntime.CreateWorkflow(
                    typeof(SimpleCalculatorWorkflow.Workflow1),
                        wfArguments);
            instance.Start();

            _waitHandle.WaitOne();

            //display the result
            Clear();
            txtNumber.Text = _result.ToString();
        }
        catch (Exception exception)
        {
            MessageBox.Show(String.Format(
                "Equals error: {0}", exception.Message));
        }
    }
}
```

The `Equals_Click` event handler is where the workflow is created and started. As you saw in Listing 1-3, the input parameters are passed to the workflow as a generic `Dictionary` object. When the object referenced by the `_waitHandle` variable signals that the workflow has completed, the result that is saved in the `WorkflowCompleted` event handler is used to update the user interface.

```
        private void Clear()
        {
            txtNumber.Clear();
            _number1 = 0;
            _number2 = 0;
            _operation = String.Empty;
        }
    }
}
```

■**Note** Remember that in .NET 2.0, Windows applications make use of partial classes to separate your code from the code that is maintained by the forms designer. For this reason, you won't see the code that creates the visual elements for the form (`Button` and `TextBox`). You also won't see the code that adds the event handlers to the `Button.Click` event. All of that code is in the `Form1.Designer.cs` file, not in the `Form1.cs` file shown in Listing 1-6.

Testing and Debugging the Calculator

To test the workflow calculator, you run the `SimpleCalculator` project. All operations work in the expected way. You enter a number, select an operation (+, -, x, /), enter the second number, then press the equals (=) button to see the result. If everything has been implemented correctly, you should see correct results for each type of arithmetic operation.

For example, if you enter 123 + 456 =, you should see the result shown in Figure 1-12.

If you want to step into the code during execution, you can do so in the normal Visual Studio way. You place a breakpoint on a line of code, and the Visual Studio debugger will break execution at that point.

Figure 1-12. *Working workflow calculator*

In addition to the standard way to set a breakpoint in code, you can also set a breakpoint within the workflow designer. To see this, open the designer view of the Workflow1.cs file and make sure the entire workflow is selected. Then press F9 to set a breakpoint for the entire workflow. You can also add a breakpoint from the Debug menu or right-click the workflow and select Breakpoint.

Now when you run the SimpleCalculatorWorkflow project in Debug (F5), the debugger should break when execution of the workflow begins. You can step over workflow activities (F10) or step into (F11) any code in the workflow such as the code activities. Either way, the debugger provides you with a good way to determine which workflow branches are executed.

USING THE WORKFLOW DEBUGGER

The workflow debugger only works if the project that you start is the one containing the workflow. Normally, when testing an application such as this simple calculator, you would start the Windows application, not one of the referenced assemblies. Starting the Windows application doesn't support use of the workflow debugger.

To see the workflow debugger in action, set the SimpleCalculatorWorkflow project as your startup project in Visual Studio. Next, open the project properties and select the Debug tab. The default Start Action is Start Project. Change this to Start External Program and select SimpleCalculator.exe as the startup program. An ellipsis is available that allows you to browse directly to the folder containing this EXE.

Now when you start the SimpleCalculatorWorkflow project in Debug mode, the simple calculator application is launched. The workflow debugger is now enabled and will stop execution on any breakpoints that you've set.

One other interesting feature of the workflow designer is its ability to enable and disable individual activities. For example, right-click the leftmost IfElseBranchActivity in the workflow and select Disable from the context menu. The activity is now shown with a shaded background as a visual cue that it is disabled. This is illustrated in Figure 1-13.

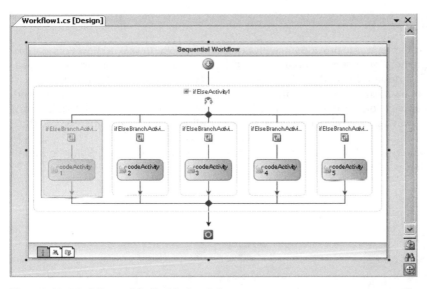

Figure 1-13. *Workflow with disabled activity*

If you run the SimpleCalculator project now, what results should you expect? The activity that you disabled is the one that handled the addition operation (+). Therefore, if you try to add two numbers, you'll receive the error dialog shown in Figure 1-14.

Figure 1-14. *Error dialog when activity is disabled*

Since the branch that checked for the addition operation is now disabled, the only branch that can execute is the rightmost branch that acts as a catchall. The code activity in that branch is responsible for throwing the exception shown in Figure 1-14. If you perform any other operation, the calculator still works correctly because those branches are enabled. If you enable the addition branch again, all operations will be back to normal.

This ability to selectively enable and disable individual activities illustrates some of the flexibility you have with a workflow. You've moved the decision tree for this application out of the code and into a workflow. This technique of disabling activities comes in handy during initial testing and debugging of your workflow applications.

Summary

The purpose of this chapter was to provide you with a quick tour of Windows Workflow Foundation. You started by implementing your first workflow application. This simple example introduced you to the visual workflow designer, workflow activities, the code activity, and the workflow runtime. You then saw how to pass parameters to a workflow in the second example. Finally, you developed a simple calculator application that declares its decision tree, and implements its calculation logic in a workflow. Along the way you were also introduced to rule conditions, output parameters, and the workflow debugger.

In the next chapter, you'll learn about the major components in Windows Workflow Foundation and see how they work together.

CHAPTER 2

■ ■ ■

Foundation Overview

The purpose of this chapter is to provide a grand tour of Windows Workflow Foundation (WF). It is a high-level description of the discrete parts of WF and how they work together. Because of the summary focus of this chapter, it doesn't contain much actual workflow code. As you dig deeper and deeper into WF in later chapters, you'll want to refer back to this chapter to see where individual features fit into the big picture.

The chapter starts with a general discussion of the two major types of workflows, *sequential* and *state machine*. Following that, the major components that are delivered with WF are reviewed. This is a birds-eye view of what you get when you install WF on your development machine. Included is an overview of the WF class libraries, the workflow runtime engine, workflow runtime services, and the workflow design time tools.

The remainder of the chapter is split between runtime and design time features. First, I discuss the workflow runtime environment and review the major WF components that you'll use at runtime. One of your responsibilities when using WF is to provide the host application. The requirements of the host application are summarized along with a discussion of the workflow runtime engine. WF provides the ability to change its default behavior by loading alternate implementations of core services. You can also implement and register local services with the workflow runtime. Both of these types of services are discussed in this chapter. The chapter concludes coverage of the runtime components with a discussion of workflow instances.

The design time environment is covered next. Here I show you the tools that you use to develop workflow applications. In this section, I review workflow authoring modes and project templates followed by a discussion of the workflow designers that are included with WF.

Workflow Types

Workflows come in two varieties: *sequential* and *state machine*. Both workflow types are supported by WF and are described in the sections that follow.

Sequential Workflows

Sequential workflows declare a series of steps that are executed in a prescribed order. Within the workflow, the flow of control is defined with familiar constructs such as if-else branching and while loops.

Sequential workflow behavior can be described with the simple flowchart shown in Figure 2-1.

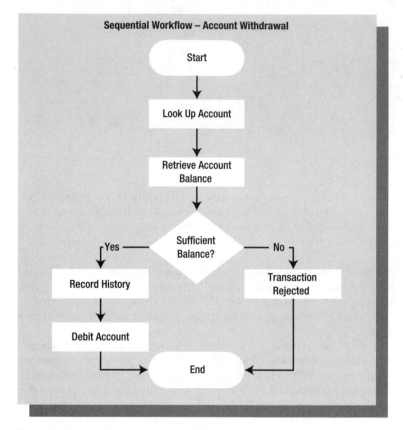

Figure 2-1. *Example sequential workflow*

To illustrate a sequential workflow, Figure 2-1 uses the example of an account withdrawal, such as the kind that would take place at a bank or other financial institution. You'll notice that each step and its sequence within the workflow are clearly defined. Although the workflow does contain a branch, all possible paths through the workflow are explicit. The workflow also has a defined beginning and end. You can't jump in to the middle of the workflow at any point. You must start at the beginning.

State Machine Workflows

State machine workflows don't define a fixed sequence of steps. Instead, they define a set of states, with possible transitions between each state. Each state may contain one or more steps that are executed during state transitions. A simple state machine workflow is illustrated in Figure 2-2.

Figure 2-2 uses the same account withdrawal example used for the sequential workflow. This time the boxes in the figure represent states, not individual steps. Each state can transition to one or more other states. Although they are not shown in the figure, tasks can be executed during the transition to another state.

A state machine workflow is not constrained by a static sequence of steps. Execution does not always have to begin with tasks in the first state. This permits the workflow to be interrupted and resumed if necessary. In WF, the transitions between states are triggered by external events that are raised by the host application. This means that overall control is external to the workflow.

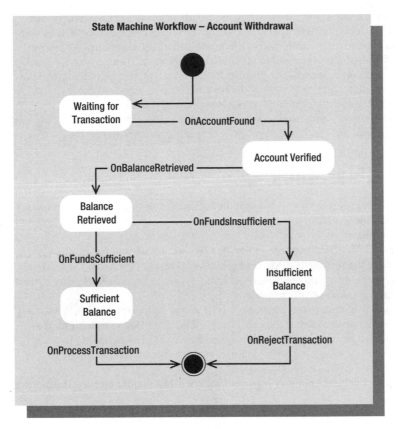

Figure 2-2. *Example state machine workflow*

Choosing a Workflow Type

Both workflow types are suitable for use in a wide variety of applications. You can even use both types within the same application. However, each workflow type targets a different kind of problem. The deciding factor when choosing the workflow type usually comes down to control.

A sequential workflow defines the flow of control within the workflow. Since it specifies the exact sequence of steps within the workflow, it is in control. It works best for system interaction problems where the prescribed steps are known at design time.

State machine workflows don't define a fixed flow of control within the workflow. The exact sequence of state transitions is controlled by external events. For this reason, state machine workflows are well-suited to problems that involve human interaction. Humans don't always do things in a prescribed sequence. Modeling a problem involving human interaction requires flexibility, and a state machine workflow provides this.

In most situations, you can make either type of workflow work. However, choosing the wrong workflow type for the problem may result in a more complicated, inelegant solution. You need to choose the workflow type that feels like a natural fit to the problem.

For the account withdrawal example, which workflow type is best? You could implement a working application using either type. I illustrated the sequential and state machine workflows with the same example problem to show their differences. This doesn't mean that both workflow types are equally suited to solving the problem.

Since the steps needed to complete the transaction are clearly defined and known at design time, the sequential workflow feels like the right choice. Using a state machine model feels forced. This example does involve human interaction since a human is initiating the account withdrawal. But once the transaction is started, that's the end of the human interaction. There is no requirement to enter the workflow at a point other than the beginning. In this situation, the sequential workflow wins. When in doubt, the simplest solution is usually the best.

WF supports both workflow types. Sequential workflows all derive from the `SequentialWorkflowActivity` class. State machine workflows use `StateMachineWorkflowActivity` as their base class. Both classes can be found in the `System.Workflow.Activities` namespace.

Foundation Deliverables

Windows Workflow Foundation provides a number of major components that together provide the infrastructure needed to execute workflows. As the name implies, WF is the foundation on which to build your own workflow applications.

Each component serves a particular purpose in the life of a workflow. But the overall design is very modular, allowing you to use just the features that you need. Some components are used only at design time, while others only enter into the picture at runtime. Others, such as the library of base activities, are leveraged throughout the entire process.

From the design, it's clear that Microsoft has spent a substantial effort architecting WF so that it is very extensible and configurable. Many of the capabilities of WF have been implemented as pluggable components that can be swapped out and replaced by you. If you are not happy with Microsoft's default implementation for a particular feature, you can usually swap it out in favor of one that you develop.

If you were to pigeonhole every one of the components of WF into a major category, the picture would look like Figure 2-3.

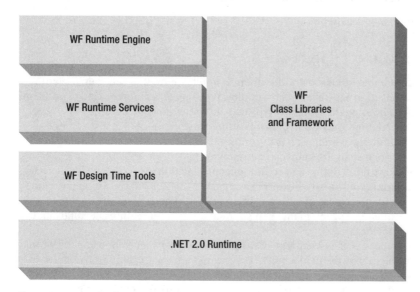

Figure 2-3. *WF component categories*

Each of these major categories is briefly described in the following sections.

Class Libraries and Framework

The class libraries include the base classes and interfaces that you leverage when building workflow applications. They are the building blocks that you use and extend. For example, all activities and workflows derive from the base `Activity` class found in the `System.Workflow.ComponentModel` namespace. Microsoft extended this base class to construct a library of predefined standard activities that are packaged with WF. Your workflows are assembled from a combination of these standard activities and from those that you create yourself.

There are also a number of classes that are included that are used to monitor and control the execution of your workflows. For example, when you create an instance of a workflow, an object of type `WorkflowInstance` (found in the `System.Workflow.Runtime` namespace) is returned. This class enables you to invoke methods on the workflow instance such as `Start`, `Suspend`, and `Terminate`.

As another example, there are classes such as `WorkflowRuntimeService` (found in the `System.Workflow.Runtime.Hosting` namespace) which define the abstract implementation of any services that you develop and register with the runtime. I discuss runtime services in more detail in a following section of the same name.

The term *framework* implies order, structure, and control. It represents much more than just a collection of classes. It provides a defined structure that you use when building applications. It requires that you follow a prescribed set of rules when using portions of the class library. But in return, the framework handles many routine tasks and allows you to concentrate on implementation of your business logic.

The extensive class library included with WF constitutes a workflow framework. The individual classes work together in a specified way to handle the routine tasks associated with a workflow-enabled application.

All workflow-related classes are organized in one of the `System.Workflow` namespaces. Table 2-1 provides an overview of the namespaces included with WF.

Table 2-1. *Workflow Namespaces*

Namespace	Description
`System.Workflow.Activities`	Includes standard activities and related classes that form the building blocks of a workflow
`System.Workflow.Activities.Rules`	Includes conditions and actions that are used to define rules
`System.Workflow.ComponentModel`	Includes core base classes and interfaces that are used by classes in other namespaces
`System.Workflow.ComponentModel.Compiler`	Includes classes that are used to compile workflows
`System.Workflow.ComponentModel.Design`	Includes classes that allow you to extend the design time behavior of activities and workflows
`System.Workflow.ComponentModel.Serialization`	Includes classes that are used during serialization and deserialization of workflows
`System.Workflow.Runtime`	Includes classes used to manage the runtime environment for workflows
`System.Workflow.Runtime.Configuration`	Includes classes used to configure the workflow runtime

Table 2-1. *Workflow Namespaces (Continued)*

Namespace	Description
System.Workflow.Runtime.Hosting	Includes classes related to hosting the workflow runtime such as core services
System.Workflow.Runtime.Tracking	Includes classes that are used by tracking services

Runtime Engine

WF includes a core runtime engine that is represented by the WorkflowRuntime class (found in the System.Workflow.Runtime namespace). The workflow runtime is not a self-contained application. Instead, an instance of this class must be hosted by your application in order to execute and manage workflows. You host the workflow runtime and the runtime hosts the individual workflow instances. The *workflow runtime* is the component that provides an execution environment for the workflow instances.

The WorkflowRuntime class includes methods that permit you to configure and control the workflow runtime. By subscribing to events that are exposed by this class, you can also receive status change notifications. For example, you can receive an event notification when an individual workflow instance starts, terminates, or completes successfully.

Runtime Services

The workflow runtime engine supports the concept of external services. *Services* are class instances that you create and register with the runtime during application startup. Each service fulfills a defined purpose. Services come in two varieties: core and local. The functionality provided by core services is defined by Microsoft. In some cases, the workflow runtime will register its own default implementation of a core service if you don't provide your own. In other cases, the service is optional and a default is not automatically provided for you.

For example, persistence of workflows is important, especially when they are long-running. WF provides the SqlWorkflowPersistenceService class (found in the System.Workflow.Runtime.Hosting namespace) for this purpose. This is a service that handles the persistence duties using a SQL database. When a workflow instance is idled or suspended, its current state can be saved to a database. When the workflow instance is needed again, it is reconstituted within the workflow runtime by retrieving it from the database. By registering this service with the workflow runtime, all of your workflows make use of this functionality. If you prefer another persistence mechanism, you can derive your own persistence service from the abstract WorkflowPersistenceService class and register it with the runtime engine. The persistence service is considered a core workflow service.

Other core services include Commit Work Batch (`DefaultWorkflowCommitWorkBatchService`), runtime thread management (`DefaultWorkflowSchedulerService`), and workflow tracking (`SqlTrackingService`). All of these can be used in their default form or extended and enhanced by you.

On the other hand, local services are developed by you to serve any purpose. One common use of local services is to act as a communications conduit for workflows. The purpose, design, and implementation of this type of service class are completely up to you. You register a local service in a similar way to core services. Once your local service is registered with the runtime, a workflow can invoke methods on the service, or handle events that originate from the service. Local services are an important mechanism used by workflows to communication with other parts of your application.

Design Time Tools

An important benefit of using a workflow model is the ability to visually design and maintain your workflows. WF includes a set of visual tools that allow you to design workflows and custom activities without leaving the Visual Studio environment. The tools are fully integrated with Visual Studio and support the drag-and-drop development experience that you would expect from a Visual Studio add-in. Yes, you can use the WF class libraries to construct workflows without the use of a visual designer. But by doing so, you remove one of the most compelling features of WF.

The design time tools also include a workflow debugger that is integrated with the Visual Studio debugger. By setting breakpoints in the workflow debugger, you can seamlessly step from workflow activities into your code and back again.

In addition to these tools, WF also includes a number of Visual Studio project templates. These templates assist you when creating new workflow projects by setting assembly references and providing boilerplate code.

.NET 2.0 Runtime

WF is part of .NET 3.0 (formerly known as WinFX). The entire WF technology stack is built upon the .NET 2.0 CLR that is also packaged with .NET 3.0. WF doesn't replace the .NET class libraries and managed environment that you use today. Use of WF doesn't prevent you from using any of the native .NET features that your application requires.

Runtime Environment

The previous section describes the major components that are included with WF. This section takes a look at how several key components are used at runtime. Figure 2-4 is a snapshot view of the major workflow components used at runtime. Each runtime component is discussed in more detail in the sections that follow.

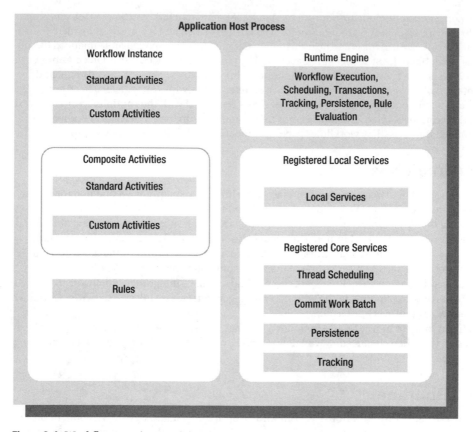

Figure 2-4. *Workflow runtime environment*

Application Host Process

As I mentioned previously, WF is not provided as a complete stand-alone application. It is only a foundation on which to build your applications. You must provide a host application that is responsible for creating an instance of the workflow runtime engine (the WorkflowRuntime class). This design provides the flexibility to host workflows in a wide variety of applications. Some of the possible application types that can act as a workflow host include the following:

- Windows console applications
- Windows service applications
- Windows forms (WinForms) applications
- Windows Presentation Foundation (WPF) applications
- ASP.NET web applications

The startup responsibilities of the host application are shown in Figure 2-5.

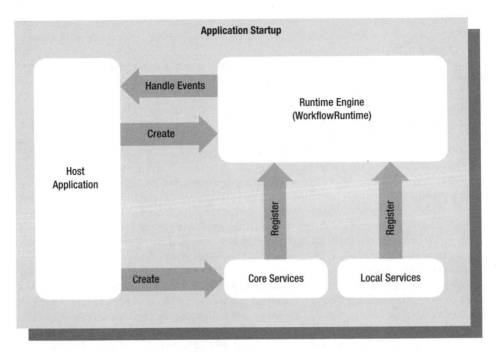

Figure 2-5. *Application startup process*

After initializing an instance of the WorkflowRuntime class, the host application uses it to create and start individual workflow instances. The host can also subscribe to public WorkflowRuntime events that allow it to monitor the progress of each workflow instance.

Caution One restriction on the host application is that it must create only a single instance of the workflow runtime (WorkflowRuntime class) per AppDomain. If you attempt to create a second instance in the same AppDomain, an exception will be thrown. By default, each application has a single AppDomain, so for most applications, this really equates to a single workflow runtime instance per application. You will rarely need more than one instance of the workflow runtime, but if your application creates an additional AppDomain, you can host more than one instance of the workflow runtime.

In addition to initializing the workflow runtime, the host application is also responsible for creating and registering any runtime services that it requires. Runtime services are discussed in more detail in the sections that follow.

Runtime Engine

The workflow runtime engine is represented in your code by the WorkflowRuntime class (found in the System.Workflow.Runtime namespace). You are also permitted to extend this class and use the extended class to initialize the runtime engine. However, only a single instance of the runtime engine can be created for each AppDomain. It is one of the responsibilities of the host application to create the single instance of the workflow runtime engine.

The runtime engine provides an execution environment for your workflows. You don't directly execute workflows within your application. Instead, you ask the runtime engine to create an instance of a workflow which you then instruct to start.

By default, workflows execute asynchronously in a thread that is managed by the runtime engine. This allows you to start multiple workflows from your host application at the same time, with all of them under the control of the runtime engine.

Each workflow can go through multiple execution states throughout its lifetime. For example, all workflows start in the created state and then move into the running state when execution begins. The workflow can also pass into states such as suspended, terminated, or completed. Other events associated with a workflow such as idled, persisted, loaded, or unloaded are possible. It is the runtime engine that manages the life and death of each workflow as it passes through these states.

The runtime engine is also responsible for scheduling and managing execution threads, workflow persistence, workflow transactions (committing of batched work), and workflow tracking. However, while the responsibility for these tasks rests with the runtime engine, it doesn't actually handle these duties by itself. Each of these tasks has been implemented as a runtime service that you create and register with the runtime engine during application startup. This modular design permits you to swap out a default implementation in favor of one that you've developed.

Included in the runtime engine is a flexible rules evaluation engine. This engine is able to evaluate simple rule conditions such as those that you add to an IfElseActivity or WhileActivity. Or it can handle a complex set of rules (called a RuleSet) that you specify within a PolicyActivity. A RuleSet defines multiple rules that are evaluated in sequence and automatically reevaluated based on the actions of rules later in the set.

The workflow runtime engine also exposes several public events that can be handled by the host application. These events allow you to directly monitor the status of each workflow as it passes between execution states. Each event carries with it an instance of the WorkflowInstance class. This class acts as a proxy to the real workflow instance that is managed by the runtime engine. Table 2-2 lists the events exposed by the WorkflowRuntime class that are related to the state of a single workflow instance. This is not an exhaustive list of the events available from the WorkflowRuntime class.

Table 2-2. *WorkflowRuntime Workflow Instance Events*

Event	Description
WorkflowAborted	Raised when a workflow instance has been aborted
WorkflowCompleted	Raised when a workflow instance has completed normally
WorkflowCreated	Raised when a workflow instance is initially created
WorkflowIdled	Raised when a workflow instance has been idled by the runtime engine
WorkflowLoaded	Raised when a workflow instance is loaded into memory by the runtime engine
WorkflowPersisted	Raised when a workflow instance has been persisted
WorkflowResumed	Raised when a workflow instance begins execution once again after it is suspended
WorkflowStarted	Raised when a workflow instance begins execution
WorkflowSuspended	Raised when a workflow instance has been suspended
WorkflowTerminated	Raised when a workflow instance has abnormally terminated
WorkflowUnloaded	Raised when a workflow instance is unloaded from memory by the runtime engine

While it isn't a requirement to subscribe to all of these events, there is a minimum set of events that you do need to handle. You should always subscribe to these events:

- `WorkflowRuntime.WorkflowCompleted`
- `WorkflowRuntime.WorkflowTerminated`

By handling just these events, you'll be able to determine whether a workflow instance has completed successfully or terminated due to some type of problem. Due to the asynchronous way that workflows are executed, your host application will need to use these events to determine when a workflow is no longer executing.

Registered Core Services

As it manages workflow instances, the workflow runtime engine makes use of a set of four core services. These services could have been implemented directly as part of the runtime engine itself. However, the WF team saw fit to implement these services as separate pluggable modules. This allows you to exchange their implementation for your own and provide an implementation that is more appropriate for your application and its execution environment. It's a great extensibility model that enhances the usefulness of WF.

The relationship between the workflow runtime engine and the core services is illustrated in Figure 2-6.

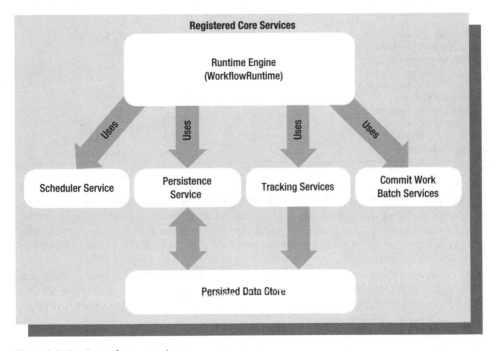

Figure 2-6. *Registered core services*

The core workflow services are listed in Table 2-3.

Table 2-3. *Core Runtime Services*

Type of Service	Description	Optional	Default Implementation	Base Class
Scheduling	Creates and manages the threads used by the runtime engine to execute workflow instances.	No	`DefaultWorkflow➡ SchedulerService`	`WorkflowScheduler➡ Service`
Commit Work Batch	Manages the transactions used by the runtime engine to maintain consistency between the internal workflow state and external data stores.	No	`DefaultWorkflow➡ CommitWorkBatchService`	`WorkflowCommit➡ WorkBatchService`
Persistence	Handles persistence of a workflow instance at the direction of the runtime engine.	Yes	None	`WorkflowPersistence➡ Service`
Tracking	Provides the ability to instrument workflow instances by recording tracking events. Unlike the other core services, you are permitted to register multiple tracking services with the runtime engine.	Yes	None	`TrackingService`

As shown in Table 2-3, WF provides a default implementation for the Scheduling and Commit Work Batch services. These two services are not optional since they provide functionality that the runtime engine relies upon and always expects to exist. If you don't explicitly add your own Scheduling or Commit Work Batch service, the runtime engine will create an instance of the class listed in the "Default Implementation" column.

The Persistence and Tracking services are both optional. If you don't register one of them with the runtime engine, that functionality will not be available to your workflows. For example, if you don't add a Persistence service to the runtime, none of your workflows will be persisted. They will operate as in-memory workflows only.

To register one of these services with the runtime engine, your host application first creates an instance of the appropriate service class. The service is then registered with the runtime by passing the service instance to the `AddService` method of the `WorkflowRuntime` object.

■Note Additional information on how to load and register core services is in Chapter 4.

These core services can only be added to the runtime engine before it is started. Once the StartRuntime method is called on the WorkflowRuntime object, you are no longer allowed to add core services. This restriction only applies to these core services and not to local services, which are covered in the next section.

With the exception of the Tracking service, only one instance of each type of service can be added to the runtime engine. And since these services must be added prior to starting the runtime engine, you are unable to replace a service later. However, you are allowed to create and register multiple instances of the tracking service.

With this design, Microsoft is encouraging you to implement your own services in order to customize and extend the core runtime engine. As a starting point, WF includes multiple implementations of some of the services, each one with a different behavior.

The following tables list the available core service implementations that are included with WF. Table 2-4 lists the available Scheduling services.

Table 2-4. *Available Scheduling Services*

Class Name	Description
DefaultWorkflowSchedulerService	Creates and manages its own threads that are used for workflow execution. This is the default implementation used by the runtime engine.
ManualWorkflowSchedulerService	Permits execution of workflow instances using a thread provided by the host application. Use this service if you need synchronous execution of workflows or if you are hosting the workflow runtime from an ASP.NET application.

Table 2-5 lists the available Commit Work Batch services.

Table 2-5. *Available Commit Work Batch Services*

Class Name	Description
DefaultWorkflowCommitWorkBatchService	The default implementation used by the runtime engine
SharedConnectionWorkflowCommitWorkBatchService	A service implementation that manages database transactions that share a connection across objects

Table 2-6 lists the available Persistence service.

Table 2-6. *Available Persistence Service*

Class Name	Description
SqlWorkflowPersistenceService	A persistence service that uses a SQL database

Table 2-7 lists the available Tracking services.

Table 2-7. *Available Tracking Services*

Class Name	Description
SqlTrackingService	A tracking service implementation that uses a SQL database.
TerminationTrackingService	A tracking service that writes termination events to the system event log. This service is provided as a sample of a custom tracking service.

If you need to implement your own service, you must derive your service class from the base class column shown in Table 2-3 for each service. Alternatively, you can derive your service class from one of the other classes supplied with WF.

Note The Tracking service classes are marked as `sealed` and cannot be used as a base class. If you need to implement a Tracking service, you must derive your class directly from the `TrackingService` class.

Registered Local Services

Local services are optional services that act as a conduit for communication between a workflow instance and your host application. They are also sometimes called *data exchange services*.

A local service provides methods and events that can be used directly by a workflow instance. Using `CallExternalMethodActivity`, a workflow can call a method on a local service. The method is synchronously invoked using the workflow thread. That method can perform any actions that are needed by your application. It could set or query state in your host application, retrieve data from a persisted store such as a database or just about anything else that you need. A method on a local service permits your workflow to reach out beyond the current workflow instance and touch something else.

Events that are exposed by a local service work in the other direction. Using `HandleExternalEventActivity`, a workflow can wait for an event that is raised by a local service. It is up to your application to determine when it should raise the event. While it is waiting for an event, the workflow instance is effectively idled and not consuming an active thread. The capability to wait for events like this is critical to state machine workflows. They typically use external events to trigger additional workflow processing and a change in state.

With a normal C# event, the handling code for the event executes on the same thread used to raise the event. WF events are handled in a different way. When a local service event is raised, the event is added to an internal queue for the workflow instance. Execution of the workflow continues when it picks up the event from the queue. Because of this, local service events are executed on the workflow thread, not the thread used to initially raise them.

The relationship between a workflow instance and local services is illustrated in Figure 2-7.

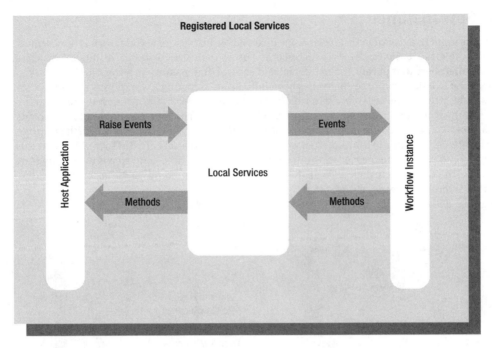

Figure 2-7. *Registered local services*

Developing your own local service is a straightforward task. You first define an ordinary C# `interface` in code. The `interface` should include any methods and events that you want to make available to workflows. Any events that you define should use an event argument class that is derived from `ExternalDataEventArgs`. If you use another `EventArgs` class as your argument base, the event will not be usable by workflows. You must decorate the `interface` with the attribute `ExternalDataExchangeAttribute` in order to identify it as a local service `interface`. This attribute also identifies the `interface` for the workflow designer. Next, you develop a service class that implements the `interface`.

Unlike most of the core services, you are permitted to register more than one local service with the runtime engine. However, only one service is allowed for each `interface` that you define. If you think that you need two or more local services that implement the same `interface`, you'll need to do some refactoring.

Just as with core services, your host application is responsible for creating and registering any local services with the runtime engine. With local services, registration is a two-step process. First you create an instance of the `ExternalDataExchangeService` class (found in the `System.Workflow.Activities` namespace) and add it to the `WorkflowRuntime` instance. Once that is done, you add your local services to the `ExternalDataExchangeService` instance.

The `ExternalDataExchangeService` class can really be thought of as another type of core service. Instead of embedding the code that communicates with your local services directly in the workflow engine, the WF team wisely decided to externalize it. In this way it is pluggable and consistent with the other core services. If you wish, you can derive your own data exchange service from this class and use it to provide your own external communication layer.

Workflow Instance

As the name implies, a *workflow instance* is a single executable instance of a workflow. It is represented in code by the WorkflowInstance class which acts as a proxy to the real workflow instance. This class has public members that permit you to interact and control that instance of a workflow.

Once the workflow runtime engine has been initialized, executing a workflow is a two-step process. First, you use the CreateWorkflow method of the WorkflowRuntime instance to create an instance of the workflow. There are several overloads to this method, but the simplest form accepts a Type object that identifies the workflow you wish to create. When the method is called, the runtime engine creates an instance of the requested workflow and returns a WorkflowInstance object. At this point the workflow is in the Created state but has not yet started. The second step is to actually start execution of the workflow instance. To do this, you call the Start method on the WorkflowInstance object that is returned from CreateWorkflow.

Figure 2-8 illustrates the workflow instance creation process.

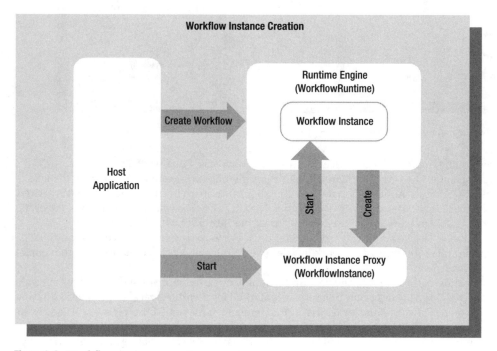

Figure 2-8. *Workflow instance creation*

Identifying a Workflow Instance

Each workflow instance has a unique Guid identifier. The InstanceId property of the WorkflowInstance class returns this ID. This unique ID is important because you can have multiple instances of the same workflow type at the same time. Each instance may be in a different state of execution. The identifier Guid is what you use to uniquely identify a workflow, not its Type. A workflow's Type is only used to create a new instance of a workflow, not to refer to a specific instance.

A workflow's ID can be used in several ways. For example, the WorkflowRuntime class has a GetWorkflow method that retrieves a workflow instance based on its ID. You also use a workflow's ID when raising events that you want handled by a waiting workflow instance. External events that you want to consume in a workflow are required to pass event arguments that are derived from the

ExternalDataEventArgs class. This class has an InstanceId property that must be set to the correct workflow ID. It is this ID that is used to locate the correct instance of the workflow when raising an event.

Workflow Activities

A workflow is composed of one or more activities. Each activity can be categorized in several different ways. First and foremost, there are *standard* and *custom* activities. Standard activities are those that are provided by Microsoft with WF. Activities such as CodeActivity, DelayActivity, IfElseActivity, and SetStateActivity are all standard. They are provided with WF and are available to all developers using WF.

On the other hand, custom activities are not included with WF. They are developed by you, downloaded from a community workflow site, or purchased from a component vendor. They are specialized activities that perform nonstandard tasks. They represent the real power of WF since they extend the original foundation in limitless ways. And they are the key to using workflows as a domain-specific language. Any custom activities that you develop can use terminology that is appropriate for your application's problem domain.

Activities can also be classified as *simple* or *composite*. Simple activities are those that cannot contain other activities. Instead of controlling and managing child activities, they perform a task. Examples of simple activities include CodeActivity, DelayActivity, and SetStateActivity. Composite activities contain other child activities and derive directly or indirectly from the CompositeActivity class. They are responsible for execution of their children. Activities such as IfElseActivity, ListenActivity, ParallelActivity, and StateActivity are all composite activities. In fact, most of the standard activities provided with WF are composite.

Workflow Rules

A workflow can optionally define rules that are evaluated during execution of the workflow instance. Evaluation of the rules is the responsibility of a rules evaluation engine that is part of the workflow runtime.

The rules can be simple Boolean conditions that are defined for activities such as IfElseActivity, WhileActivity, ReplicatorActivity, and ConditionedActivityGroup. All of these activities also support *code conditions*. A code condition specifies a Boolean condition in code and is compiled into the workflow.

The real power of rules is evident when you use the PolicyActivity. This activity encapsulates a set of rules (called a RuleSet) and evaluates them in sequence. However, the sequence isn't necessarily executed statically. After evaluating a rule, the engine may determine that a prior rule requires reevaluation. This might be the case if the current rule modified a value that a prior rule was dependent upon. This type of reevaluation is called *forward chaining*.

As is the case with workflow definition, rules are defined using a declarative model. Rule modeling is seamlessly integrated with workflow modeling. This provides you with a choice where you place your application logic. It can go into code as it always has, into activities of the workflow, or into the rules model.

One advantage that rule conditions have over code conditions is their ability to respond to dynamic updates at runtime. The declared rules are stored separately from the workflow itself. Visual Studio serializes rules to a separate .rules file using the same name as the workflow. Since the rules are declared and evaluated separately from the compiled workflow code, they can be modified at runtime. In contrast, modifications to a code condition would require a recompile of the workflow code.

However, code conditions also have their place in your workflows. Since they are compiled into the workflow, they will generally be faster than rule conditions. They can also support more complex logic in order to determine the final Boolean result. With code conditions, you are free to perform calculations, examine application state, and generally do whatever you need to do in code in order to return a Boolean result.

Design Time Environment

An important part of WF is the design and development time tools that are available for use when developing workflow applications. WF provides a set of class libraries that are used when constructing workflow applications. The visual workflow tools help you to organize the correct elements from the class libraries to define a workflow. Because the workflow class libraries exist, you are not required to use the visual tools to construct your workflows. You can wire together the activities of a workflow entirely in code without the use of a visual designer. However, the visual tools are one of the most compelling features of WF. They bring workflow within reach of the general community of .NET developers.

The visual workflow tools provided with WF are fully integrated with Visual Studio. They provide a seamless design and development environment. The use of these tools is the recommended way to develop WF applications. The design time tools available for WF include these:

- Visual Studio project templates that are used to create new workflow projects.

- An integrated workflow designer that supports sequential and state machine workflows.

- An integrated activity designer that is used to design your own custom activities.

- Integrated rule condition, Rule and RuleSet editors that are used to declare and manage individual rules and groups of rules.

- An integrated workflow debugger that permits debugging of workflows from within the Visual Studio environment.

- A command-line workflow compiler (wfc.exe) that is used to compile workflow markup files (.xoml).

■Note The example workflows and code shown in the remainder of this chapter are not complete workflows. They are a partial set of activities that are used only to demonstrate the Visual Studio workflow design tools. For this reason, this code is not included in the downloadable code for this book.

Workflow Authoring Modes

Before I cover the design time tools, a discussion of workflow authoring modes is in order. WF supports three different ways to author workflows. The authoring modes are the following:

- Code-only

- Code-separation

- No-code

Code-Only

Code-only is the default authoring mode and the one that you'll probably use most often. It is similar to the way Windows Forms applications are authored. When you design a workflow in this mode, the WF designer generates code and places it in the Workflow1.designer.cs file. Any code that you directly add to the workflow goes into file Workflow1.cs. The generated code works directly with the workflow object model, adding activities to the workflow, adding children to the activities, and so on. Since the entire workflow is defined in code, it is compiled as a class in the assembly.

Code-Separation

Code-separation saves a serialized form of the workflow model in a markup file named `Workflow1.xoml` and your code in a separate file named `Workflow1.xoml.cs`. The markup in the `.xoml` file uses a syntax known as XAML to save the serialized form of the workflow. XAML is a general-purpose, XML-based markup language that represents a hierarchy of objects. In this case, the objects represent the activities within the workflow. At compile time, the markup file (`.xoml`) is compiled with the code-beside file (`.xoml.cs`).

You can add a code-separation workflow to a project by selecting Add New Item from the Project menu. Then select either Sequential Workflow (with code separation) or State Machine Workflow (with code separation).

■Note If the `.xoml` file contains XAML, why doesn't it use a `.xaml` extension? XAML is an acronym for eXtensible Application Markup Language. The same XAML syntax is also used extensively by WPF, one of the other foundation pillars of .NET 3.0.

Originally, WF used a different syntax for workflow markup but later changed to the same XAML syntax used by WPF. For historical reasons, the file extensions are still `.xoml`, but internally, they use the XAML syntax. The `.xoml` extension is also used to differentiate workflow XAML from WPF XAML in Visual Studio. Different extensions permit the use of different visual designers when you select a file.

No-Code

No-code workflows are defined entirely in a `.xoml` file. To use the workflow, you can compile it using the command-line workflow compiler (`wfc.exe`) or load it directly into the workflow runtime engine.

No-code workflows allow you to define or modify the structure of the workflow outside of the development environment. For instance, you might use no-code workflows if you host the workflow designer within your own application. After modifying the workflow in the designer, you would serialize it to a `.xoml` file. Later, you could load it into the workflow runtime and start it just like any other workflow. The use of a separate `.xoml` file gives you much more flexibility in managing and distributing your workflows since they are not embedded within an assembly.

The integrated Visual Studio tools for WF don't directly support the no-code authoring of workflows. Don't expect to see a new file type of Sequential Workflow (no-code). If you do want to author no-code workflows, you can start with a code-separation workflow and delete the `Workflow.xoml.cs` file. Or you can simply add an XML file to your project and rename it with a `.xoml` extension. Once you add a root element to the file, you will be able to open it in the workflow designer.

■Note Without a code-beside file such as `Workflow1.xoml.cs`, you cannot add any code to your workflow. This means that any behavior that the workflow requires must already be in the base class that you use for your workflow. Also, if you do drag and drop an activity onto the workflow that does require code-beside (such as a `CodeActivity`), a `Workflow1.xoml.cs` file will be generated and added to the project for you. Once this is done, your no-code workflow is magically transformed into a code-separation workflow.

Project Templates

WF includes a number of project templates that assist you when creating new workflow projects. A project created with one of these templates includes the assembly references that you'll need for a workflow project. Depending on the type of project selected, the appropriate boilerplate code is also included. While the code may not have all of the features that you'll need, it is often a good starting point for your project.

The available workflow project templates are listed in Table 2-8. Each project template is available for C# and VB.

Table 2-8. *Workflow Project Templates*

Template Name	Description
Sequential Workflow Console Application	Creates a console application with a sequential workflow.
Sequential Workflow Library	Creates a library assembly (DLL) with a sequential workflow.
State Machine Workflow Console Application	Creates a console application with a state machine workflow.
State Machine Workflow Library	Creates a library assembly (DLL) with a state machine workflow.
Workflow Activity Library	Creates a library assembly (DLL) with a custom activity.
Empty Workflow Project	Creates a library assembly (DLL) containing the necessary workflow assembly references but without an initial workflow of either type. Use this project as a starting point if you will be using sequential and state machine workflows in your application.

Note All of the workflow projects are capable of supporting both workflow types (sequential or state machine) as well as custom activities. For example, even if you start with the Sequential Workflow Library, you can always add a custom activity or state machine workflow to the project.

Workflow Designer

The visual workflow designer is the real showpiece of the design time tools. Using the designer you can visually design and maintain your workflows instead of coding them by hand. The designer is fully integrated with Visual Studio and supports the type of intuitive drag-and-drop development experience that you would expect.

The workflow designer has several different designer views, with each one tuned to a particular type of workflow or design problem. The individual views are the following:

- Sequential workflow
- State machine workflow
- Fault handlers
- Cancel handler

Sequential Workflow View

Figure 2-9 illustrates the sequential workflow view with a typical sequential workflow.

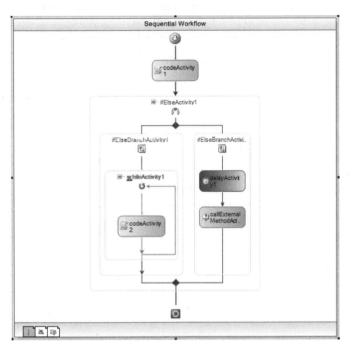

Figure 2-9. *Sequential workflow designer view*

The sequential workflow view is the canvas where your sequential workflows are designed. New activities are added by dragging and dropping them from the Visual Studio Toolbox. If you need to reorder the sequence of activities, you simply drag an activity to its new position within the workflow. Properties of an activity can be set by first selecting the activity, then switching to the Properties window. As an alternative, you can right-click an activity and select Properties. You delete an activity by selecting it and pressing the Delete key, or by right-clicking and selecting Delete.

When the workflow designer is the active window, the Visual Studio Toolbox provides a list of available activities. Figure 2-10 shows a partial view of the Toolbox.

Figure 2-10. *Partial Toolbox view with workflow activities*

Any custom activities and workflows that are in assemblies referenced by the project are also shown at the top of the Toolbox. This means that your custom activities are first-class citizens and they can be dragged and dropped onto a workflow just like standard activities.

A workflow toolbar is also available and is normally active when the workflow designer is the active window. If the workflow toolbar is not visible in your current configuration, you can activate it by right-clicking any Visual Studio toolbar and checking the entry named Workflow. Figure 2-11 shows the default workflow toolbar.

Figure 2-11. *Workflow designer toolbar*

The toolbar allows you to zoom in and out in order to better view all of your workflow design. It also supports enabling and disabling of portions of the workflow and the ability to collapse and expand activities.

Collapsing activities allows you to hide the details behind portions of your workflow. This frees up valuable visual real estate so that you can concentrate on just a portion of the workflow. For example, Figure 2-12 shows the same workflow from Figure 2-9, but this time the IfElseActivity has been collapsed as indicated by the +.

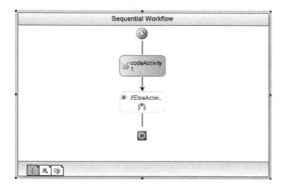

Figure 2-12. *Sequential workflow designer view with IfElseActivity collapsed*

There is also a box in the lower right corner of the workflow designer (not shown here) that provides shortcuts to these same toolbar actions.

State Machine Workflow View

The designer view that is used for state machine workflows is slightly different from the sequential workflow view. Figure 2-13 shows the designer with a sample state machine workflow.

Figure 2-13 shows the top level of the state machine workflow. At this level, states (represented by a StateActivity) are shown instead of individual activities. The lines between states represent transitions between states. You add states by dragging and dropping a StateActivity onto the workflow.

You add activities to a state by dragging and dropping an appropriate activity onto the StateActivity. A StateActivity only accepts a small subset of activities. The list includes EventDrivenActivity, StateInitializationActivity, StateFinalizationActivity, or another StateActivity. One of the most commonly used activities will be an EventDrivenActivity. In Figure 2-13, each of the states has already had an EventDrivenActivity added to it.

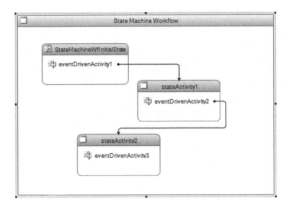

Figure 2-13. *State machine designer view*

To drill down deeper into a state, you double-click the child activity in the state. In the example shown in Figure 2-13, you could double-click the eventDrivenActivity1 in the topmost state. Figure 2-14 shows the contents of this activity.

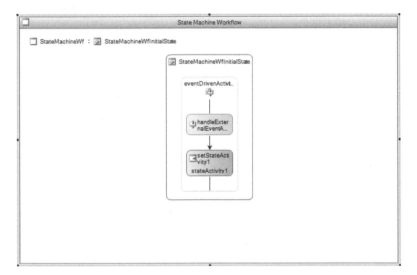

Figure 2-14. *EventDrivenActivity for state machine workflow*

Now the designer reveals the activities that are contained in the EventDrivenActivity. In the example shown in Figure 2-14, the activity contains a HandleExternalEventActivity and a SetStateActivity. The HandleExternalEventActivity waits for receipt of an external event. The SetStateActivity transitions to another state and is what determines the transition lines shown in the top-level state machine view. A more realistic workflow would typically include other activities in addition to SetStateActivity. To return to the level of detail above this one, you click one of the links outside of the EventDrivenActivity. These links return you to a view of the StateActivity or the entire workflow.

Fault Handler View

Exceptions can be thrown at any time during execution of a workflow activity. Within the activity, they can be caught and handled in the normal .NET way using a `try`/`catch` block of code. If they are not handled within the activity that caused the exception, the parent activity is given the opportunity to handle the error. This process continues up the chain of parent activities until it reaches the workflow itself. If it is not handled here, the workflow instance is terminated.

The fault handler view of the workflow designer provides a visual way to define exception handling logic. You use this view to determine which activity should handle the exception and the actions that it should take when a particular type of exception is thrown.

A fault handler can be added to an activity in several ways. You can right-click an activity and select View Faults from the context menu. Or you can select the activity, and then select View Faults from the top-level Workflow menu.

When you select View Faults, you will be presented with a view showing an instance of a `FaultHandlersActivity`. For example, you can add a fault handler to the `EventDrivenActivity` shown in Figure 2-14. To add a handler, right-click the activity and select View Faults Handler. Figure 2-15 shows the fault handler view.

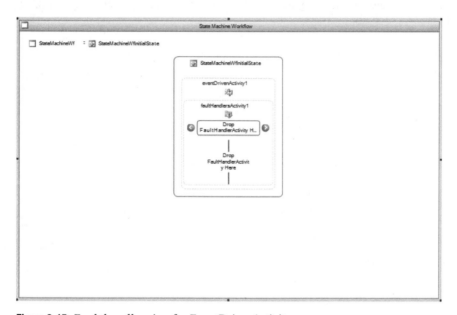

Figure 2-15. *Fault handler view for EventDrivenActivity*

From this view, you can drag and drop any number of `FaultHandlerActivity` objects onto the open `FaultHandlersActivity` (note the difference in the two activity names). Each `FaultHandlerActivity` is associated with a single exception type. The type of exception handled is set in the activity properties. Under each `FaultHandlerActivity`, you add the activities that you want executed when the exception is caught.

Fault handlers can only be added to composite activities. The menu options to add a fault handler are omitted when a simple activity is selected.

To return to the normal view for the composite activity, you right-click and select View <Activity Type>. In this example, the menu option is View Event driven since this is an `EventDrivenActivity`.

Cancel Handler View

The cancel handler view provides a way to define activity cancellation logic. A cancel handler has some similarities to the fault handlers just discussed. Like fault handlers, they are only attached to a composite activity. They are also viewed in a similar way—by right-clicking an activity and selecting View Cancel Handler. Figure 2-16 shows the cancel handler view of the same EventDrivenActivity shown in Figure 2-14.

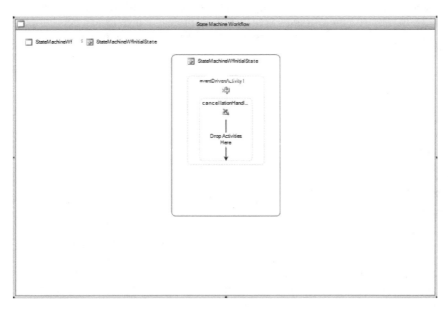

Figure 2-16. *Cancel handler view for EventDrivenActivity*

However, cancel handlers don't catch and handle exceptions. Instead, they specify the cleanup actions that take place when an executing activity is canceled. The need for cancel handlers is best illustrated with an example:

A ListenActivity is a composite activity that allows you to define multiple child activities under it. Assume that each child of the ListenActivity is a HandleExternalEventActivity that listens for a different external event. With this scenario, each HandleExternalEventActivity is executing at the same time waiting for an event. Only one of these children will eventually receive its event and complete execution. The other sibling activities will be canceled by the ListenActivity parent. By entering a cancel handler for the parent ListenActivity, you define the steps to execute when the incomplete children are canceled.

You won't always need a cancel handler. But if your activities require any cleanup when they are canceled, a cancel handler is an appropriate place to define that logic. From the view shown in Figure 2-16, you drag and drop the activities you wish to execute onto the open CancellationHandlerActivity.

Adding Event Handlers

The workflow designer provides other features that assist you when developing workflows. One handy feature is Add Handlers. This option is found in the top-level Workflow menu or in the context menu after right-clicking an activity. If an activity supports one or more events, selecting this option will create empty event handler code for all events. You are still responsible for writing the event handling logic, but this is a quick way to generate the boilerplate code and assign the handlers to the events.

If an activity only supports a single event, you can use the double-click shortcut. When you double-click an activity with a single event, an event handler is created for the event.

Activity Designer

The integrated design tools include an activity designer that is used when you create your own custom activities. If you start with the Workflow Activity Library project or if you add a new item of type Activity to an existing project, you'll see the designer. An example is shown in figure 2-17.

Figure 2-17. *Empty activity designer*

By default, when you add a new Activity item to a project, the new class derives from SequenceActivity. This is a composite activity that supports other child activities. The activity designer permits you to drag and drop other activities onto this custom activity. You then write the code to implement the logic for the custom activity. For example, Figure 2-18 shows the same custom activity after I've added a few child activities.

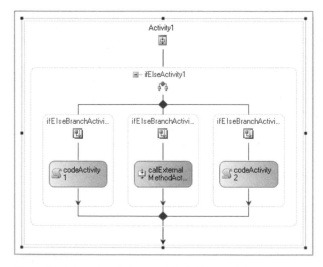

Figure 2-18. *Activity designer with child activities*

Rule Condition Editor

The Rule Condition Editor is where you enter and maintain the rules that are associated with a workflow. Rules are used in two ways. First, they can be used as a simple Boolean condition for an activity that requires a condition. An example of such an activity is IfElseActivity. This activity makes a simple branching decision based on the Boolean result of a rule when it is evaluated.

Secondly, rules can be combined into a RuleSet and used by a PolicyActivity. The individual rules in the RuleSet are evaluated one at a time. However, rules can be reevaluated based on the actions of subsequent rules.

In order to see the Rule Condition Editor, you first need to add an activity that supports a rule condition. To illustrate this, create a new sequential workflow and drop an IfElseActivity onto it. Figure 2-19 shows what your workflow should look like at this point.

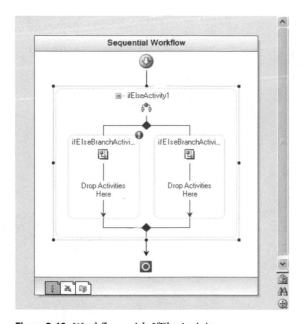

Figure 2-19. *Workflow with IfElseActivity*

Rules act upon fields or properties in the workflow, so the next step is to add a few properties to the workflow. Listing 2-1 shows the Workflow1.cs file with the additions highlighted. Some of these properties are used later in the RuleSet example that follows this one.

Listing 2-1. *Workflow1.cs with Added Fields and Properties*

```
using System;
using System.ComponentModel;
using System.ComponentModel.Design;
using System.Collections;
using System.Drawing;
using System.Workflow.ComponentModel.Compiler;
using System.Workflow.ComponentModel.Serialization;
```

```
using System.Workflow.ComponentModel;
using System.Workflow.ComponentModel.Design;
using System.Workflow.Runtime;
using System.Workflow.Activities;
using System.Workflow.Activities.Rules;

namespace WorkflowProjectScreenShots
{
    public sealed partial class Workflow1 : SequentialWorkflowActivity
    {
        private Double _price;
        private Double _discountAmt;
        private String _discountDesc = String.Empty;

        public String DiscountDesc
        {
            get { return _discountDesc; }
            set { _discountDesc = value; }
        }

        public Double DiscountAmt
        {
            get { return _discountAmt; }
            set { _discountAmt = value; }
        }

        public Double Price
        {
            get { return _price; }
            set { _price = value; }
        }

        public Workflow1()
        {
            InitializeComponent();
        }
    }
}
```

After adding the fields and properties, switch back to the design view shown in Figure 2-19. Right-click the leftmost IfElseBranchActivity and select Properties. For the Condition property, select Declarative Rule Condition and then expand the Condition property. The Property window should now look like Figure 2-20.

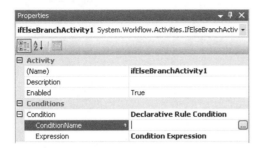

Figure 2-20. *IfElseBranchActivity1 property window*

Each rule condition is required to have a unique name, so enter priceCheck for the ConditionName property. Next, click the ellipsis in the Expression property. This shows the Rule Condition Editor. Since the editor supports IntelliSense, entering **this** followed by a period causes the list of available workflow fields and properties to be displayed. Enter the following condition into the editor: **this.Price >= 100.00.**

Your editor should now look like Figure 2-21.

Figure 2-21. *Rule ConditionEditor with Price condition*

The rule condition you entered is saved when you select OK. Based on this condition, the left-most branch of the IfElseActivity tree is executed when the Price property of the workflow is greater than or equal to 100.00. This same procedure can be followed for any activities that use a simple rule condition such as this.

RuleSet Editor

The RuleSet editor allows you to enter and maintain multiple rules that work together as a group. To demonstrate the RuleSet editor, you can continue where you left off with the last example. Drag and drop a PolicyActivity to the leftmost IfElseBranchActivity. The workflow should now look like Figure 2-22.

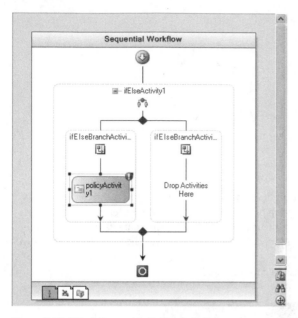

Figure 2-22. *Workflow with PolicyActivity*

Right-click the new `PolicyActivity` and select Properties. In the Properties window, select the ellipsis for the `RuleSetReference` property. The Select RuleSet dialog in Figure 2-23 should now be shown.

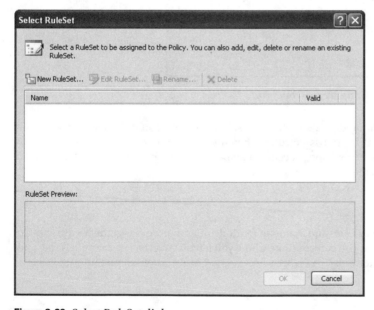

Figure 2-23. *Select RuleSet dialog*

The only available choice from this dialog is New RuleSet, since this is the first RuleSet. After selecting this option, the Rule Set Editor is shown. This is illustrated in Figure 2-24.

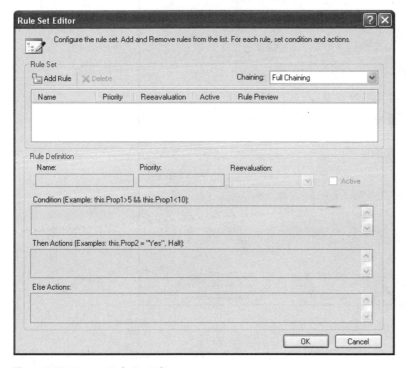

Figure 2-24. *Empty Rule Set Editor*

You can now enter the first rule of the set by selecting Add Rule. Enter **applyDiscount** as the rule name and enter the parameters shown in Table 2-9 into the Condition, Then Actions, and Else Actions boxes of the dialog.

Table 2-9. *applyDiscount Rule Definition*

Rule Element	Code
Condition	`this.Price >= 500.00`
Then Actions	`this.DiscountAmt = 5.0`
Else Actions	`this.DiscountAmt = 2.5`

The finished rule should look like Figure 2-25.

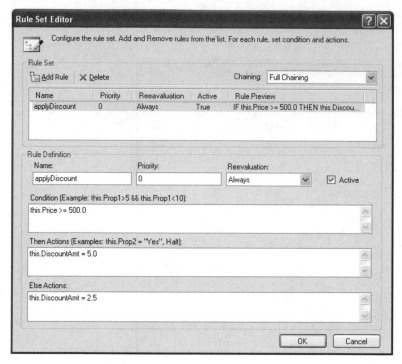

Figure 2-25. *Rule Set Editor with first rule*

You can enter another rule by selecting Add Rule again. This time use `discountDesc` as the rule name and enter the parameters listed in Table 2-10.

Table 2-10. *discountDesc Rule Definition*

Rule Element	Code
Condition	`this.DiscountAmt >= 5.0`
Then Actions	`this.DiscountDesc = "Big Discount"`
Else Actions	`this.DiscountDesc = "Little Discount"`

The second rule should look like Figure 2-26.

During workflow execution, these rules will be evaluated as a set. The `applyDiscount` rule will set the `DiscountAmt` workflow property to 5.0 if the value of the `Price` property is greater than or equal to 500.00. Otherwise, it sets the `DiscountAmt` property to 2.5. Then the `discountDesc` rule sets the `DiscountDesc` property to a descriptive string based on the value of `DiscountAmt`.

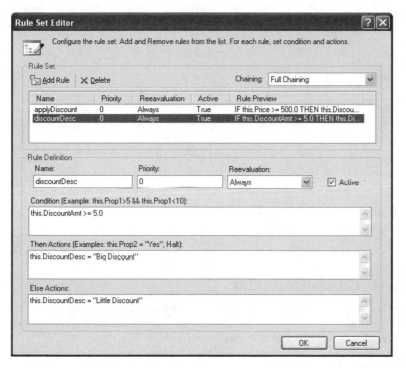

Figure 2-26. *Rule Set Editor with second rule*

Workflow Debugger

The WF design and runtime tools include an integrated workflow debugger. This debugger allows you to add breakpoints to individual activities or the workflow itself from within the workflow designer. To add a breakpoint, you select an activity (or the entire workflow) and press F9. You can also add a breakpoint from the Debug menu, or right-click the activity and select Breakpoint.

Figure 2-27 shows a workflow after a breakpoint has been added to the IfElseBranchActivity on the left. The same breakpoint indicator that Visual Studio uses for code (you will see a red sphere) is used for breakpoints within the workflow designer.

When you execute the workflow project in debug mode (F5), the debugger breaks execution at the location of the workflow breakpoint. Once execution is stopped, you can step over (F10) or step into (F11) individual workflow activities. If you step into an activity that contains code-beside, you'll step directly into the code.

The workflow debugger only works if the project that you start is the one containing the workflow. If your workflow project is an executable (.exe), running the project in debug works fine. If the project containing your workflow is a separate DLL assembly, you'll need to set it as the Start Up project. But since you can't start a DLL directly, you need to change the Start Action for the workflow project. This option is found on the Debug tab of the project properties. The default Start Action is Start Project. Change this to Start External Program and select an .exe as the startup program. Now when you start the workflow project, the .exe is started and your breakpoints are active.

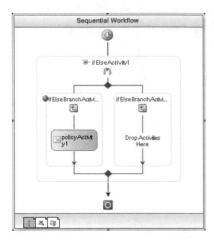

Figure 2-27. *Workflow with breakpoint indicator*

Command-Line Workflow Compiler

WF includes a command-line workflow compiler named `wfc.exe`. This utility is useful when you have defined and saved your workflows as external markup files. The markup files use an extension of `.xoml` and represent a serialized form of the workflow object model.

The `wfc.exe` utility accepts either a single `.xoml` file or a list of files and compiles them to a .NET assembly. If your workflows require code-beside `.cs` or `.vb` files, they can also be included during compilation.

Packaging workflows as separate markup files provides you with additional flexibility. When using code-only workflows (the default authoring style), the entire workflow is defined in code and compiled into an assembly. Once compiled, it is difficult to change the workflow definition. In contrast, workflows that are saved as `.xoml` files are easily modified with any XML or text editor. This provides an opportunity to externally modify the workflow model and then compile them prior to execution. Not all applications require this flexibility, but the command-line compiler is available if you need it.

Summary

The purpose of this chapter was to provide you with a high-level summary of WF. The aim was to show you what WF includes and how the parts fit together rather than how to use any individual part. You learned the differences between sequential and state machine workflows along with some suggestions on when to use each type.

You learned about the workflow runtime environment, including the responsibilities of the host application and the workflow runtime engine. You also learned about core services and local services and how they are used by the runtime engine. Workflow instances were also discussed including a review of activity types and workflow rules.

The Visual Studio workflow designers and tools were reviewed along with project templates, workflow authoring modes, and the workflow debugger.

In the next chapter, you'll learn about activities that are the core building blocks of Windows Workflow Foundation.

CHAPTER 3

■ ■ ■

Activities

The focus of this chapter is the primary building block of all workflows: the activity. This chapter provides a high-level review of the standard activities that are provided with Windows Workflow Foundation (WF). You will become acquainted with the available activities, but you will not learn how to use all of them in detail. This is the one chapter that provides an overview of all of the available activities. Many of the individual activities are difficult to understand unless they are discussed as part of a larger subject area. For this reason, the subsequent chapters in this book each focus on a specific subject area and provide additional detail on the activities that are relevant to that subject.

One area that is covered in detail in this chapter is how to add logic to your workflow. There are two primary ways to accomplish this, using the CodeActivity, and developing your own custom activities. Both mechanisms are explored and compared using a common workflow example. This chapter also provides additional information on enhancing the design time experience when using custom activities.

Understanding Activities

Activities are the primary building blocks of WF. An activity is a discrete, reusable component that is designed to fulfill a defined purpose. WF includes a set of standard activities that you can leverage within your workflows. You are also encouraged to develop your own custom activities to solve your own specialized business problems. For instance, if you are developing a loan application, you might develop custom activities such as AccountSetupActivity, CreditReviewActivity, and LoanFundingActivity. For a point of sale system, you might need custom activities such as ItemLookupActivity, SellItemActivity, and TenderTransactionActivity.

Regardless of the activity's origin (standard or custom), the design time experience working with activities is the same. You start by dragging and dropping an activity onto a workflow or another activity. Then, using the Properties window in Visual Studio, you set properties that are specific to that activity. The properties may control some facet of runtime behavior, or they may be used to wire up the input and output parameters of the activity. It all depends on the needs of the particular activity.

An activity that is capable of hosting other activities is called a *composite activity*. Activities that do not have this capability are called *simple activities*. A composite activity is responsible for the execution of its child activities. A simple activity is only responsible for performing its own work.

Some activities also support events that you can handle with code in the workflow class. In some cases an event handler is optional, while other times one is required. An example is the CodeActivity, which requires you to add an event handler for the ExecuteCode event. If you don't attach a handler for this event, the workflow won't compile. This design time checking is enabled by the presence of validation metadata within the CodeActivity. In this case, the metadata indicates that the ExecuteCode event must be handled, otherwise an error is generated at design time.

A Dual Audience for Activities

The CodeActivity aptly illustrates the dual audience for all activities. First and foremost, activities are designed to solve some defined problem or to perform some defined work. If they don't do anything useful at runtime, they have no real value. While performing their work, they are expected to behave in a particular way in order to cooperate with other workflow activities and the workflow runtime. The workflow runtime and other activities are the runtime audience.

But activities also have a design time audience that is equally important. The design time audience includes the developers that use the activity as a building block for their workflows. An activity's other responsibility is to cooperate with the workflow designer in order to provide an appealing and productive design experience. Using attributes and optional activity components, an activity class exposes metadata to the designer and workflow compiler. An activity that is designed to fully support the design experience is easier to use and helps you to become more productive. By raising an error when the ExecuteCode event handler is omitted, the CodeActivity makes you more productive. It's always preferable to discover your errors at design time rather than run time. An activity that doesn't support the design time experience is only half done.

Class Hierarchy

All activities have a common ancestor, the Activity class (found in the System.Workflow. ComponentModel namespace). This class provides the base contract and functionality that permits an activity to be hosted by WF. Beyond the base Activity class lies a rich set of derived classes, each one providing additional capabilities. Figure 3-1 shows the relationship between some of the most important top-level classes. This is not an exhaustive model of the entire activity class library.

As shown in Figure 3-1, CompositeActivity is derived directly from the Activity class. This is the base class with support for child activities and it serves as the base for all of the other standard activity classes shown in Figure 3-1. If you need to implement a custom composite activity, you can derive directly from CompositeActivity or from one of its descendents. You can also implement a simple custom activity that derives directly from the Activity class. The resulting class would not support child activities.

Moving down to the next layer in the class hierarchy, you see two major branches in the tree. StateActivity represents a state in a state machine workflow. Derived directly from StateActivity is StateMachineWorkflowActivity, which is the base class for a state machine workflow.

■**Note** It is interesting to note that StateMachineWorkflowActivity derives from StateActivity, even though a state machine workflow (represented by StateMachineWorkflowActivity) contains instances of StateActivity (the parent class). The class hierarchy was arranged this way because a state machine workflow itself exhibits the behavior of an individual state. For instance, you can add an EventDrivenActivity to the state machine workflow that provides for global event handling that is applicable to all child states.

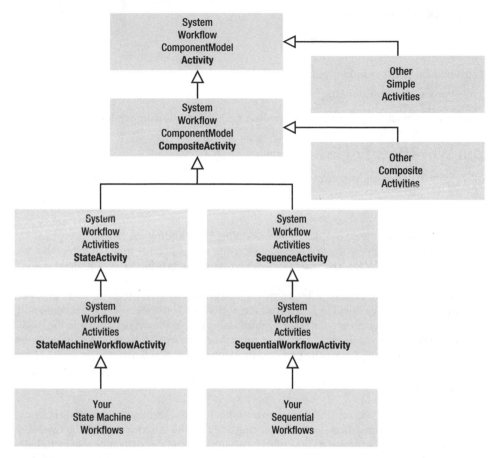

Figure 3-1. *Top level Activity class hierarchy*

Also derived from CompositeActivity is the SequenceActivity class with SequentialWorkflowActivity as its direct child. SequentialWorkflowActivity is the base class for all sequential workflows. The SequenceActivity class supports the execution of an ordered set of child activities.

Exploring Standard Activities

In this section I review the standard activities provided with WF. The goal is to provide a short description of each activity without going into the details on how each activity is used. Detailed coverage of each activity is left to subsequent chapters that target each functional area.

In order to better understand the purpose of each activity and how it relates to the others, I've grouped them into categories. The major activity categories are the following:

- Custom Workflow Logic
- Flow Control
- State Management
- Event Handling

- Local Service Communication
- Rules
- Web Services
- Transactions, Compensation, and Synchronization
- Exceptions and Error Handling

The activities in each of these categories are discussed in the following sections.

Custom Workflow Logic

The single activity in this category permits you to add your own business logic directly to a workflow.

CodeActivity

The CodeActivity is a simple way to add code to a workflow. After adding the CodeActivity to a workflow, you assign a handler to the ExecuteCode event and add your code to the handler. The handler code can perform any work that you need, but it typically acts upon local workflow instance variables.

The CodeActivity can be thought of as a lightweight custom activity. It serves the same purpose to encapsulate and execute business logic. The primary difference is the level of encapsulation and reusability. The CodeActivity encapsulates the business logic within the event handler in the workflow class. It is only reusable within that workflow. A true custom activity encapsulates your business logic as a reusable component that can be executed as a step in any workflow.

Flow Control

The activities in this category control the flow of execution within a workflow. They include many of the familiar programming constructs such as branching and looping. Also included are activities that allow you to execute other activities in parallel or replicate a single activity. I've also included the activities that delay, terminate, and suspend a workflow in this category since they control the flow of execution in their own special way.

IfElseActivity and IfElseBranchActivity

The IfElseActivity permits you to declare multiple conditional branches of execution within a workflow. The IfElseActivity is a composite activity that contains two or more instances of IfElseBranchActivity. At runtime, only one of the defined branches is executed.

Each IfElseBranchActivity contains a condition that is defined by you. The condition can be expressed as a code or rule condition. If the condition evaluates to true, the child activities in the IfElseBranchActivity are executed and the other branches are bypassed. If the condition evaluates to false, the condition in the next IfElseBranchActivity is evaluated, and so on. The final branch is not required to have a condition. If no condition is declared and all prior branch conditions are false, the final branch acts as an else branch and the activities contained within it are executed.

WhileActivity

The WhileActivity repeatedly executes a single child activity as long as its condition is true. The condition can be expressed as a code or rule condition. The condition is checked prior to the start of each iteration, so it is possible that the child activity may never be executed if the condition is initially false.

DelayActivity

The DelayActivity is used to temporarily halt execution of a workflow for a specified amount of time. One popular use of this activity is to set a delay when waiting for an external event. If the external event is never received, the time delay eventually elapses and execution continues.

SequenceActivity

The SequenceActivity is a composite activity that enables you to add multiple child activities that are executed in a defined order. It is especially useful as a child of other activities that only accept a single child. Examples of activities that only accept a single child are the ReplicatorActivity, the WhileActivity, and the ParallelActivity.

ParallelActivity

A ParallelActivity permits you to schedule two or more child branches for execution at the same time. This activity only accepts a SequenceActivity as a child, but within the SequenceActivity you can define other activities that are executed in order. Each SequenceActivity added to the ParallelActivity represents an execution branch.

Contrary to what the activity name implies, the execution branches under a ParallelActivity do not actually execute simultaneously. Each workflow instance executes on a single thread, so true parallel execution of multiple activities isn't possible.

Instead, the ParallelActivity coordinates execution of activities in multiple branches in a round-robin fashion. The first child activity is executed in the first branch. When that activity completes, the first child activity in the second branch executes, and so on. After all branches have had a chance at execution, the next activity in the first branch is executed. If execution of any branch is suspended for any reason (such as a DelayActivity or if the branch is waiting for an external event), execution goes to the next branch. The ParallelActivity doesn't guarantee the sequence in which each branch is executed.

ReplicatorActivity

The ReplicatorActivity creates and executes multiple copies of a single child activity. At runtime, it creates multiple instances of the child activity based on the number of objects in a data collection. Each time a new instance of a child activity is created, it receives the next object in the collection. The data from the collection acts as a parameter that drives the processing within the child activity. If the single child activity is a composite, all of the activities within the composite are executed for each object in the collection.

The ReplicatorActivity enables the development of data-driven workflows, where the exact number of child activity instances can only be determined at runtime. In this sense, it is similar to the C# foreach statement that iterates through the objects in a collection, performing some task with each one.

The ReplicatorActivity supports sequential and parallel execution of the child activity. If you use sequential execution, only one instance of the child activity is created and executed at any one time. Once it completes, the next instance is created, and so on. With parallel execution, all instances of the child activity are initially created and processed in parallel. Just like the ParallelActivity, the ReplicatorActivity doesn't actually execute multiple child activities simultaneously. Instead, it coordinates the execution of the created child activities in a round-robin fashion.

ConditionedActivityGroup

The ConditionedActivityGroup (sometimes referred to as the *CAG*) is used to conditionally execute a series of child activities. Each child activity is associated with its own WhenCondition. The child activity continuously executes as long as its WhenCondition evaluates to true.

The ConditionedActivityGroup also has an optional UntilCondition property that defines a condition used to stop execution. When the UntilCondition is true, the ConditionedActivityGroup cancels all child activities. The WhenCondition and the UntilCondition can be specified as a code or rule condition.

InvokeWorkflowActivity

The InvokeWorkflowActivity is used to start a second workflow. The second workflow executes asynchronously, so this activity will return before the new workflow completes.

You specify the Type of the new workflow by setting the TargetWorkflow property. The activity provides an Invoking event that is raised before the new workflow is initiated. The event handler for this event is a good place to pass parameters and generally set up state for the new workflow.

SuspendActivity

The SuspendActivity stops the execution of the workflow, but doesn't permanently terminate the workflow. It is used in situations where the workflow has an error but the error is recoverable and the workflow can be restarted at the point of failure. Perhaps a parameter is missing or incorrect and it can be easily corrected with some human intervention. To restart a suspended workflow, you call the Resume method on the WorkflowInstance object.

TerminateActivity

The TerminateActivity immediately stops the execution of a workflow instance. This is similar to the SuspendActivity with one very big difference. If you use TerminateActivity, the workflow cannot be resumed and no further processing can take place with that workflow instance. On the other hand, SuspendActivity provides for the resuming of a workflow. You can provide a descriptive error message with the termination by setting the Error property of the TerminateActivity.

State Management

The activities in this category all work with state machine workflows. Included are the activities used to define, initialize, and finalize a state, and transition to a different state.

StateActivity

StateActivity represents a single state and is the primary building block of all state machine workflows. The StateActivity is usually added directly to the top level of a state machine workflow, but it can also be added as a child of another StateActivity.

There is a select group of other activities that are permitted as direct children of a StateActivity. The list includes EventDrivenActivity, StateInitializationActivity, StateFinalizationActivity, and another StateActivity.

SetStateActivity

Where StateActivity defines the state, SetStateActivity is used to transition to a different state. You identify the new state by setting the TargetStateName property of SetStateActivity.

The SetStateActivity is usually declared as a child of an EventDrivenActivity. The EventDrivenActivity is used within a StateActivity to wait for an external event. The event triggers additional processing within that state. After executing other activities to perform some real work, the SetStateActivity is usually included to transition to the next state. When it is used, the SetStateActivity must be declared as the last activity in a series of activities. Placing it somewhere in the middle of a long sequence of activities is not valid.

StateInitializationActivity

The StateInitializationActivity is an optional activity that contains activities to execute when a state is first entered. You can declare a maximum of one StateInitializationActivity in a StateActivity. Each time the workflow transitions to the state, the activities in the StateInitializationActivity are executed before any other activities.

StateFinalizationActivity

StateFinalizationActivity is the reciprocal of StateInitializationActivity. It is a container for activities that you wish to execute just before you transition to another state. It is optional, but if you use it, there can be a maximum of one StateFinalizationActivity for a StateActivity.

Event Handling

The activities in this category are all related to event handling and work with other child activities that receive the event. The activities outlined here don't actually receive the events, but instead, they are containers for other event-driven activities.

ListenActivity and EventDrivenActivity

The ListenActivity is a composite activity that contains two or more instances of EventDrivenActivity. Each EventDrivenActivity defines an execution branch that is waiting for a different event. The EventDrivenActivity is also a composite activity and contains its own set of child activities that are executed when the event is received. Only one EventDrivenActivity branch is ever executed. When one branch receives its event, the other branches are canceled.

The relationship between these two activities is similar to the IfElseActivity and the IfElseBranchActivity discussed previously in the "Flow Control" section. Just like the IfElseActivity, the ListenActivity is the container for multiple branches, only one of which will ever execute. Like the IfElseBranchActivity, the EventDrivenActivity defines a single execution branch.

The ListenActivity cannot be used in a state machine workflow. However, the EventDrivenActivity by itself is often used as a child of the StateActivity. It contains the activities to execute when an event is received and the workflow is in a particular state.

The first child activity of an EventDrivenActivity must be one that implements the IEventActivity interface. This interface is used by the workflow runtime engine to notify an activity that an event has been received. This requirement is necessary since the first activity in an EventDrivenActivity is the one that starts execution of the branch. It must have some way to receive notification of an event, and the IEventActivity is that mechanism. The standard activities that implement this interface are the HandleExternalEventActivity, the WebServiceInputActivity, and the DelayActivity.

EventHandlersActivity and EventHandlingScopeActivity

These activities are used in advanced scenarios where you need to concurrently handle multiple events. Their use is best illustrated by contrasting them with a normal event handling scenario.

In a normal event handling scenario, you define multiple events that can be handled, with each one contained within an `EventDrivenActivity`. These `EventDrivenActivity` branches are added as children to a single `ListenActivity`. In this scenario, when one branch receives its event, the other branches are canceled. Once the first event is received and handled, no further processing of activities takes place within the parent `ListenActivity`.

The `EventHandlersActivity` takes the place of the `ListenActivity`. It is a container for multiple instances of the `EventDrivenActivity`. The big difference between the two is that while the `ListenActivity` cancels the unused branches once an event is received, the `EventHandlersActivity` doesn't. The `EventHandlersActivity` allows concurrent processing of events. When one event is received, the activities within the `EventDrivenActivity` are executed. However, the other event branches are all still alive. They can also receive their events and execute the activities within their branch. The original branch that received its event can even receive it again.

What finally completes the parent activity and causes the event branches to end? That's a job for the `EventHandlingScopeActivity`. The `EventHandlingScopeActivity` can act as the parent of the `EventHandlersActivity` and permits you to also define a set of mainline activities to execute. With all of this in place, you have an activity that is executing a sequence of activities, and also concurrently responding to one or more events. When the mainline sequence of activities completes, all event branches are finally canceled.

Local Service Communication

The activities in this category are used for communication between a workflow and a local service.

CallExternalMethodActivity

The `CallExternalMethodActivity` is used to synchronously invoke a method that you implement in a local workflow service. This is one of the primary mechanisms used by workflows to communicate with the world beyond the current workflow instance.

The method that is invoked must be defined in an `interface`, and that `interface` must be decorated with the `ExternalDataExchangeAttribute`. You identify the method to execute by setting the `InterfaceType` and `MethodName` properties of the `CallExternalMethodActivity`. You don't specify the class that implements the `interface`. Instead, this activity relies on a local service that you register with the runtime engine during startup. Since you can only register a single class instance for each `interface` type, the `InterfaceType` property is sufficient to uniquely identify the local service instance.

If the method requires any input or output parameters, they are defined in the `ParameterBindings` collection of this activity. This collection allows you to bind parameters to properties of the workflow or an activity.

HandleExternalEventActivity

The `HandleExternalEventActivity` is used to receive an event from a local service. Just like the `CallExternalMethodActivity`, the event must be defined in an `interface` decorated with the `ExternalDataExchangeAttribute` and implemented by a registered local service. You identify the event to handle by setting the `InterfaceType` and `EventName` properties of the `HandleExternalEventActivity`. Parameters that are passed with the event populate workflow or activity properties based on the `ParameterBindings` collection of this activity.

Any events that you wish to handle with this activity should derive their `EventArgs` from `ExternalDataEventArgs`. Failure to do this prevents you from passing in parameters with the event.

The HandleExternalEventActivity is never used by itself. It must be contained within an EventDrivenActivity and it must be the first child activity. The EventDrivenActivity defines the execution branch when an event is received. The HandleExternalEventActivity is the activity that actually receives the event and starts execution of the branch.

Rules

The activity in this category is associated with the workflow rules engine.

PolicyActivity

The PolicyActivity enables you to define a set of rules that act upon fields or properties in a workflow. Each rule in the RuleSet is described with if, then, and else syntax by setting the Condition, ThenActions, and ElseActions properties.

Within the ThenActions and ElseActions, you can set a workflow field or property, execute a workflow method, or execute a static method on another class in a referenced assembly.

The rules in a RuleSet are evaluated and executed individually. However, they also work as a group. If an individual Rule modifies a field or property that another Rule depends upon, the dependent Rule may be reevaluated and the actions executed again. This feature is called *forward chaining*.

Many of the standard activities control the flow within the workflow or act as control containers for other activities. In contrast with this, the PolicyActivity is designed to directly change workflow state by allowing you to update field and property values or execute methods.

Web Services

The activities in this category enable your workflow to interact with web services. Using these activities, you can invoke a web service from a workflow or you can expose a workflow to web service clients.

InvokeWebServiceActivity

The InvokeWebServiceActivity is used to invoke a web service from within a workflow. When you drop this activity onto a workflow, the standard Visual Studio Add Web Reference dialog is shown. This allows you to locate the web service and add it as a reference to the current project. In doing so, a proxy class to the web service is generated and included in the project.

It is this proxy that the InvokeWebServiceActivity uses to reference the web service. You identify the proxy class by setting the ProxyClass property. You identify the web service method to invoke by setting the MethodName property and identify the parameter values to pass using the ParameterBindings collection.

WebServiceInputActivity

While the InvokeWebServiceActivity is used to invoke a web service from a workflow, WebServiceInputActivity does the opposite. It exposes the workflow as a web service method. This allows web service clients to call directly into the workflow as if they were invoking any other web service.

The WebServiceInputActivity handles the receipt of the initial web service call. This activity works together with the WebServiceOutputActivity and the WebServiceFaultActivity, which are described next.

The WebServiceInputActivity implements the IEventActivity interface. Because of this, it is also considered an event-driven activity.

WebServiceOutputActivity

The WebServiceOutputActivity is used along with WebServiceInputActivity to expose a workflow to web service clients. The WebServiceOutputActivity is responsible for sending a response to the web service client.

It is only valid to use this activity in a workflow that also includes the WebServiceInputActivity. The two activities act as bookends. You start with the WebServiceInputActivity, followed by any other activities you need to process the web service request. When you are ready to return a response to the web service client, you include the WebServiceOutputActivity.

WebServiceFaultActivity

The WebServiceFaultActivity is used when you need to send a web service fault to a client to indicate an error condition. You can only send one response to a client, using either the WebServiceFaultActivity to indicate a fault, or the WebServiceOutputActivity to send a successful response. You would typically make your response decision in the body of your workflow and then execute only one of these activities.

Transactions, Compensation, and Synchronization

The activities in this category enable you to define a single unit of work that encompasses multiple activities. Also included are activities that enable compensation and synchronized access to variables. *Compensation* is the ability to undo actions that have successfully completed.

TransactionScopeActivity

The TransactionScopeActivity is used to define a logical unit of work that succeeds or fails in its entirety. This is a composite activity that permits you to add other activities to it as children. When the TransactionScopeActivity starts execution, it creates a System.Transactions.Transaction instance to mark the beginning of a new unit of work. All of the child activities within the TransactionScopeActivity use the same transaction during execution.

When all child activities within the TransactionScopeActivity complete normally, the transaction is closed and all pending work is committed. If an unhandled exception is thrown by any child activity, the entire transaction is rolled back and all pending work is returned to its original state.

■Note If your workflow includes the TransactionScopeActivity, you must register a persistence service during workflow runtime initialization.

CompensatableTransactionScopeActivity and CompensatableSequenceActivity

Compensation is the undoing of work that successfully completed but is part of a larger workflow that failed. If activities in a workflow successfully complete, but the workflow later fails due to an error, you need some mechanism to undo the completed work. Compensation is especially useful in long-running workflows where maintaining an active transaction to guarantee the consistency of the data would not be feasible.

The CompensatableTransactionScopeActivity is similar to the TransactionScopeActivity, but it also supports compensation. It provides a transaction for its child activities and commits the transaction when the activity ends. But it also allows you to declare a set of activities to execute if compensation is later necessary.

In like manner, the CompensatableSequenceActivity is a version of the SequenceActivity that supports compensation. Like the SequenceActivity, it allows you to declare an ordered list of child activities. But it also supports the declaration of activities that are executed if the activity requires compensation.

CompensateActivity and CompensationHandlerActivity

The CompensationHandlerActivity is the container for activities that you wish to execute if compensation is necessary. This activity can only be added to an activity that supports the ICompensatableActivity interface. Currently, the only standard activities that support this interface are the CompensatableTransactionScopeActivity and the CompensatableSequenceActivity (discussed in the previous section).

Normally, compensation is triggered when an unhandled exception is thrown within a workflow. If there are any compensatable activities that completed prior to the exception, each one is compensated automatically. The CompensateActivity allows you to manually control the compensation process. Using the CompensateActivity, you can take control over the compensation process and directly execute the compensation logic for an activity.

SynchronizationScopeActivity

The SynchronizationScopeActivity is used to provide controlled access to variables or resources that are shared between parallel branches of execution. It is a composite activity that manages the child activities that you add to it. This activity works in a similar manner to the C# lock statement. If two or more instances of the SynchronizationScopeActivity have the same synchronization handle, their execution is serialized so that the child activities of only one of them are executed at any one time.

This activity is used with composite activities that support multiple parallel execution branches (e.g., ParallelActivity, ConditionedActivityGroup, ReplicatorActivity). If you use a SynchronizationScopeActivity in each of the parallel branches, you can serialize execution of the child activities within each SynchronizationScopeActivity. When the single workflow thread begins execution of a SynchronizationScopeActivity in one execution branch, it will ensure that all of the child activities within the SynchronizationScopeActivity complete before it moves to the next branch of execution. It won't execute scoped child activities within each branch in round-robin (interleaved) fashion as it would without the SynchronizationScopeActivity.

Each SynchronizationScopeActivity has a SynchronizationHandles property. This is a collection of string handles that are used to coordinate the synchronization between instances of the SynchronizationScopeActivity. If two or more SynchronizationScopeActivity instances have the same handle, their children execute in a serialized fashion.

Exceptions and Error Handling

The activities in this category all work with .NET exceptions (classes that are assignable to the base Exception class). One activity is used to throw an exception from within a workflow, while others are used to handle exceptions that have been thrown.

ThrowActivity

The ThrowActivity enables you to throw a .NET exception declaratively as a workflow step. If you encounter error conditions, you are permitted to throw an exception from within any part of your workflow code. This includes code in the workflow itself and any custom activities. This activity allows you to do the same thing as a workflow activity.

You would use the ThrowActivity when you want to throw an exception declaratively in the workflow model rather than from code. The end result is the same as if you used the C# throw statement to throw the exception.

FaultHandlerActivity and FaultHandlersActivity

Two activities are used to catch and handle .NET exceptions within your workflow. The FaultHandlersActivity maintains a collection of FaultHandlerActivity objects and is added as a child of a composite activity. Each FaultHandlerActivity corresponds to a single Exception type and contains the child activities that you wish to execute when handling the exception.

To add a FaultHandlerActivity, you select View Faults from the Workflow menu, or the context menu of a composite activity. When the Fault View is first displayed, it will contain an open FaultHandlersActivity. At this point you can drag and drop a FaultHandlerActivity onto the open FaultHandlersActivity and identify the exception you want to handle. Drag and drop additional FaultHandlerActivity instances to handle other exception types.

CancellationHandlerActivity

The CancellationHandlerActivity is a container for cleanup logic associated with a composite activity. You can add a CancellationHandlerActivity to composite activities to handle cancellation logic for the child activities.

For instance, the ListenActivity is a container for multiple activity branches that are all actively waiting for an event. Once an event is received, the other activities that did not receive their event are canceled. If a CancellationHandlerActivity has been added to the ListenActivity, the set of activities defined within the CancellationHandlerActivity are executed during cancellation.

Standard Activities Summary

Table 3-1 provides a summary of the standard activities that are provided with WF. The activities are presented in alphabetical sequence by activity name. The functional category of each activity is included so that you can refer back to the appropriate section in this chapter that describes the activity.

Table 3-1. *Standard Activity Summary*

Activity Name	Category
CallExternalMethodActivity	Local Service Communication
CancellationHandlerActivity	Exceptions and Error Handling
CodeActivity	Custom Workflow Logic
CompensatableSequenceActivity	Transactions, Composition, and Synchronization
CompensatableTransactionScopeActivity	Transactions, Composition, and Synchronization
CompensateActivity	Transactions, Composition, and Synchronization
CompensationHandlerActivity	Transactions, Composition, and Synchronization
ConditionedActivityGroup	Flow Control
DelayActivity	Flow Control
EventDrivenActivity	Event Handling
EventHandlersActivity	Event Handling
EventHandlingScopeActivity	Event Handling

Table 3-1. *Standard Activity Summary*

Activity Name	Category
FaultHandlerActivity	Exceptions and Error Handling
FaultHandlersActivity	Exceptions and Error Handling
HandleExternalEventActivity	Local Service Communication
IfElseActivity	Flow Control
IfElseBranchActivity	Flow Control
InvokeWebServiceActivity	Web Services
InvokeWorkflowActivity	Flow Control
ListenActivity	Event Handling
ParallelActivity	Flow Control
PolicyActivity	Rules
ReplicatorActivity	Flow Control
SequenceActivity	Flow Control
SetStateActivity	State Management
StateActivity	State Management
StateFinalizationActivity	State Management
StateInitializationActivity	State Management
SuspendActivity	Flow Control
SynchronizationScopeActivity	Transactions, Composition, and Synchronization
TerminateActivity	Flow Control
ThrowActivity	Exceptions and Error Handling
TransactionScopeActivity	Transactions, Composition, and Synchronization
WebServiceFaultActivity	Web Services
WebServiceInputActivity	Web Services
WebServiceOutputActivity	Web Services
WhileActivity	Flow Control

Adding Workflow Logic

In the sections that follow, I review the two ways that you can add custom logic to a workflow. *Custom logic* in this case means adding your own code to a workflow. Without the ability to introduce your own code, you would find it difficult to accomplish most meaningful tasks.

The two primary mechanisms to add code to a workflow are the following:

- Using the CodeActivity
- Developing custom activities

■**Note** You can also define some workflow logic within a RuleSet. Each Rule in the RuleSet can act upon and update workflow variables and also execute methods. Use of the RuleSet for workflow logic is discussed in Chapter 11.

Both of these mechanisms are covered in the remainder of this chapter. To illustrate the differences between implementing code with the CodeActivity and custom activities, I implement the same example workflow with each mechanism. The example that I use is a simple order entry workflow. It consists of these overly simplified steps:

1. Validate the ID of the account that is placing the order and retrieve the available credit for the account.

2. Validate the ID of the product being ordered and retrieve the price of the product.

3. If the account and product are valid, and if the account has sufficient credit to cover the price of the item, proceed with the order.

■**Note** The purpose of the examples that follow is to illustrate how to use the CodeActivity and also create your own custom activities. The examples are not designed to demonstrate how an order entry system should work.

The next section covers the use of the CodeActivity. Following that is a section that covers the steps needed to create and use your own custom activities.

Using the CodeActivity

The CodeActivity is a simple way to add code directly to a workflow. To use it, you drag and drop a CodeActivity onto a workflow or composite activity. You then create a handler for the ExecuteCode event. As a shortcut, you can double-click the CodeActivity to create a handler. Double-clicking adds an empty handler to the workflow using a default name of codeActivty1_ExecuteCode. The actual name of the CodeActivity instance replaces codeActivity1. You can also enter a handler name yourself (or select an existing handler) from the Properties window.

Once you have a handler for the ExecuteCode event, you add code to it. The code in your handler is executed synchronously when the CodeActivity is executed. The other activities in the workflow don't execute until the code in the handler completes. For this reason, you shouldn't perform any blocking tasks, such as waiting for a callback or invoking external services such as a web service.

Using the CodeActivity is a quick and easy way to add your own code to a workflow. But this ease of use does have a price. The code that you add using this activity is implemented in the workflow class itself. This limits the opportunities for reuse to the current workflow only. If you wish to reuse this logic in another workflow, you can't simply drop it on the workflow as you could with a custom activity.

But the CodeActivity does have a place in your workflows. If you simply need to add a few lines of code to a workflow, perhaps needing to set instance variables or call a method or two, then a

`CodeActivity` may be perfect for the job. But when you need to implement workflow logic that may be reused in other workflows, you'll want to implement a custom activity.

Creating the Project

To begin this example, create a new workflow project using the Sequential Workflow Console Application project template. Give the project a meaningful name such as `OrderEntryCode`, which is the one used throughout this example.

■Tip When you create a new project, Visual Studio will also prompt you to save a new solution. You can choose your own name for the solution, but it is generally easier to work with the examples in this chapter if you place all of them in a single Visual Studio solution.

Defining the Workflow Parameters

To process an order, the workflow requires these two parameters:

- `AccountId`: This identifies the account that is placing the order.
- `SalesItemId`: This identifies the product that is being ordered.

In a real application, you might include other parameters such as a quantity for the product being ordered. But since this workflow is only designed as a demonstration of the `CodeActivity`, these parameters should suffice.

Property Types

Parameters can be defined for a workflow (or custom activity) in two ways. You can implement a normal .NET class property, or you can use a dependency property. The property value for a dependency property is stored in a central repository, rather than being implemented as a normal instance variable in your class.

The primary advantage to dependency properties is that they allow binding of property values to instance data at runtime. For example, you can bind the input property of one activity to an output property of another. The actual property values resulting from the binding is determined at runtime. Dependency properties are required when you want to bind properties from one activity to another. However, if you are binding an activity property to a workflow property, the workflow property is not required to be a dependency property. In this case, a normal C# property on the workflow class works fine.

For this example, using dependency properties is not strictly a requirement. This workflow will work correctly without them. However, they are commonly used throughout workflow development, particularly when implementing custom activities. Using dependency properties is a skill that you will need sooner or later. For this reason, it's a good idea to jump right in and start using them now.

Adding Dependency Properties

In order to support dependency properties, a class must derive from the base `DependencyObject` class. The root `System.Workflow.ComponentModel.Activity` class derives from `DependencyObject`, so all workflow and activity classes support dependency properties.

To implement a dependency property, you register the property with the dependency system using the DependencyProperty.Register static method. You then define a .NET property in the normal way with the get and set keywords. However, within the get and set sections of the property definition, you use the GetValue and SetValue methods of the base DependencyObject class to retrieve and set property values.

All of this is best illustrated with a real example. To define the AccountId property for this workflow as a dependency property, you add this code to the Workflow1.cs file:

```
public static DependencyProperty AccountIdProperty
    = System.Workflow.ComponentModel.DependencyProperty.Register(
    "AccountId", typeof(Int32), typeof(Workflow1));


/// <summary>
/// Identifies the account
/// </summary>
[Description("Identifies the account")]
[Category("CodeActivity Example")]
[Browsable(true)]
[DesignerSerializationVisibility(DesignerSerializationVisibility.Visible)]
public Int32 AccountId
{
    get
    {
        return ((Int32)(base.GetValue(Workflow1.AccountIdProperty)));
    }
    set
    {
        base.SetValue(Workflow1.AccountIdProperty, value);
    }
}
```

By convention, the name of the static DependencyProperty returned by the Register method takes the form of MyValueProperty. MyValue is replaced with your property name. Following that convention, the property defined in the previous code for AccountId defines a static DependencyProperty named AccountIdProperty. This static field doesn't contain the value of the property. Instead, it defines the dependency property that is registered with the dependency system.

As shown in the previous code, the get and set sections of the property call the GetValue or SetValue methods to retrieve or update the property value. The property values are stored in a repository that is keyed by the static DependencyProperty field. This is the field that is returned by the Register method. The repository acts like a Dictionary object that holds the current values of each property based on a unique key.

This may seem like a lot of code just to define a property, but it is necessary in order to take advantage of the activity binding features of WF. You'll find that all dependency properties are defined in exactly the same way. Once you've implemented one property, the others are simply a matter of cutting and pasting.

To help with the drudgery of adding a dependency property, WF includes a Visual Studio code snippet for dependency properties. To use this, right-click the location in your source code where you want to add the property and select Insert Snippet. Then select Workflow, then DependencyProperty – Property. A dependency property with the appropriate boilerplate code is added.

■**Caution** Windows Presentation Foundation (WPF) is another one of the foundations included with .NET 3.0. It also uses the concept of dependency properties and dependency objects. However, be aware that even though the class names are the same, they are not the same class. The DependencyObject and DependencyProperty used by WF are found in the System.Workflow.ComponentModel namespace. The WPF classes with the same names are found in the System.Windows namespace. They are not interchangeable. Perhaps sometime in the distant future, Microsoft will see fit to merge these classes into a common technology foundation that is shared by WPF and WF. Until then, be careful if you are developing an application that uses both foundations.

In addition to the AccountId property defined previously, the workflow also requires a dependency property named SalesItemId that is implemented in the same way. It is also an Int32.

The workflow also needs several local instance variables that will be used to store workflow state between activity steps. As activities are added to the workflow, you will see how these variables are used. Since these variables are only used locally within the workflow, they don't need to be exposed as properties. They are defined like this:

```
private Boolean isAccountVerified;
private Boolean isSalesItemVerified;
private Decimal availableCredit;
private Decimal salesItemAmount;
```

After adding the variables and dependency properties, the Workflow1.cs file should look like Listing 3-1.

Listing 3-1. *Workflow1.cs File with Properties and Variables*

```
using System;
using System.ComponentModel;
using System.Workflow.ComponentModel;
using System.Workflow.Activities;

namespace OrderEntryCode
{
    /// <summary>
    /// Order entry workflow using CodeActivity
    /// </summary>
    public sealed partial class Workflow1 : SequentialWorkflowActivity
    {
        private Boolean isAccountVerified;
        private Boolean isSalesItemVerified;
        private Decimal availableCredit;
        private Decimal salesItemAmount;

        public Workflow1()
        {
            InitializeComponent();
        }

        #region Public workflow properties

        public static DependencyProperty AccountIdProperty
            = System.Workflow.ComponentModel.DependencyProperty.Register(
            "AccountId", typeof(Int32), typeof(Workflow1));
```

```csharp
/// <summary>
/// Identifies the account
/// </summary>
[Description("Identifies the account")]
[Category("CodeActivity Example")]
[Browsable(true)]
[DesignerSerializationVisibility(DesignerSerializationVisibility.Visible)]
public Int32 AccountId
{
    get
    {
        return ((Int32)(base.GetValue(Workflow1.AccountIdProperty)));
    }
    set
    {
        base.SetValue(Workflow1.AccountIdProperty, value);
    }
}

public static DependencyProperty SalesItemIdProperty
    = System.Workflow.ComponentModel.DependencyProperty.Register(
    "SalesItemId", typeof(Int32), typeof(Workflow1));

/// <summary>
/// Identifies the item to sell
/// </summary>
[Description("Identifies the item to sell")]
[Category("CodeActivity Example")]
[Browsable(true)]
[DesignerSerializationVisibility(DesignerSerializationVisibility.Visible)]
public Int32 SalesItemId
{
    get
    {
        return ((Int32)(base.GetValue(Workflow1.SalesItemIdProperty)));
    }
    set
    {
        base.SetValue(Workflow1.SalesItemIdProperty, value);
    }
}

#endregion
    }
}
```

Validating the Account

After switching to the workflow designer view, drag and drop a CodeActivity onto the workflow. This code activity is responsible for validating the AccountId property that was passed as an input to the workflow. If the AccountId is valid, the isAccountVerified variable is set to true and the availableCredit variable is set to the credit limit for the account.

Using the Properties window, change the name of the CodeActivity to codeLookupAccount. It is always a good idea to give each activity a meaningful name since this name is what you initially see in the workflow designer view.

Next, double-click the new CodeActivity, and a handler named codeLookupAccount_ExecuteCode is added to the workflow for the ExecuteCode event. In a real-world application, the code in this handler might locate the account using a database query or some other mechanism. But in this simple demonstration application, the code can be much simpler. To simulate a lookup of an account based on the AccountId property, add the following code to the handler:

```
private void codeLookupAccount_ExecuteCode(object sender, EventArgs e)
{
    //simulate an account lookup
    switch (AccountId)
    {
        case 1001:
            isAccountVerified = true;
            availableCredit = 100.00M;
            break;
        case 2002:
            isAccountVerified = true;
            availableCredit = 500.00M;
            break;
        default:
            isAccountVerified = false;
            availableCredit = 0;
            break;
    }
}
```

Now that the code is in place to validate the account, the workflow can make decisions based on the instance variables that were set. After switching to the workflow designer view, drag and drop an IfElseActivity directly under the CodeActivity just added. The code for this activity will determine whether the AccountId property is valid by checking the isAccountVerified variable.

When the IfElseActivity is added, it already contains two instances of the IfElseBranchActivity. The left branch represents the processing that should take place if the account is valid. The right branch is executed if the account is invalid. Rename the left IfElseBranchActivity to ifAccountVerified to reflect its purpose.

From the Properties window, set the Condition property for the ifAccountVerified activity to Declarative Rule Condition. This indicates that the IfElseBranchActivity uses a rule condition rather than a code condition. After expanding the Condition property, set the ConditionName property to a meaningful name such as checkIsAccountVerified. Each rule condition in a workflow must have a unique name.

Now select the ellipsis in the Expression property and enter this condition:

```
this.isAccountVerified == True
```

> **Tip** Remember that the Rule Condition Editor supports IntelliSense. Entering **this** followed by a period causes the list of available workflow fields and properties to be displayed.

After selecting OK in the Rule Condition Editor, the Properties window should now look like Figure 3-2.

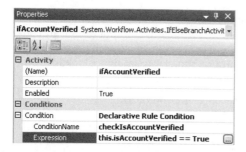

Figure 3-2. *Properties window for ifAccountVerified branch*

Before you add more activities to this main branch on the left, go ahead and finish the right-side branch. This side represents the activities that you want to execute if the account is invalid. Select the IfElseBranchActivity on the right side and change its name to ifAccountInvalid to better describe its purpose. Next, drag and drop a CodeActivity onto the ifAccountInvalid activity, change its name to codeBadAccountId, and double-click the activity to add a code handler. Add this code to the handler to write a message to the Console when the account is invalid:

```
private void codeBadAccountId_ExecuteCode(object sender, EventArgs e)
{
    Console.WriteLine("AccountId {0} is invalid", AccountId);
}
```

Validating the Product

Continuing with the left-side branch, drag and drop another CodeActivity onto the ifAccountVerified activity. The purpose of this CodeActivity is to validate the ID of the product that is being ordered and determine the price of the product. If the SalesItemId property is valid, the isSalesItemVerified variable is set to true and the salesItemAmount is set to the product price.

Change the name of this CodeActivity to codeLookupItem and then double-click the activity to add an event handler. Add this code to the handler:

```
private void codeLookupItem_ExecuteCode(object sender, EventArgs e)
{
    //simulate an item lookup to retrieve the sales amount
    switch (SalesItemId)
    {
        case 501:
            isSalesItemVerified = true;
            salesItemAmount = 59.95M;
            break;
```

```
        case 502:
            isSalesItemVerified = true;
            salesItemAmount = 199.99M;
            break;
        default:
            isSalesItemVerified = false;
            salesItemAmount = 0;
            break;
    }
}
```

Entering the Order

The workflow must make one more decision based on the isSalesItemVerified and salesItemAmount instance variables. If the product is valid (if isSalesItemVerified is true) and the salesItemAmount is less than or equal to the available credit for the account (the availableCredit variable), then the order is accepted. If either of these conditions is false, an error message should be displayed.

To make this last decision, drag and drop an IfElseActivity under the codeLookupItem activity. Change the names for each IfElseBranchActivity under the IfElseActivity. The left-side branch represents the execution path if the order is accepted and should be named ifCreditAvailable. Name the right-side branch ifItemProblems.

Add a Declarative Rule Condition to the ifCreditAvailable branch on the left side. Use checkAvailableCredit as the ConditionName and enter this as the Expression:

```
this.isSalesItemVerified == True &&
this.salesItemAmount <= this.availableCredit
```

Drag and drop a CodeActivity onto the ifCreditAvailable activity and name it codeEnterOrder. Double-click the activity to add an event handler and add this code to the event handler:

```
private void codeEnterOrder_ExecuteCode(object sender, EventArgs e)
{
    //simulate the order
    Console.WriteLine(
        "Order entered for account {0}, Item id {1} for {2}",
        AccountId, SalesItemId, salesItemAmount);
}
```

To handle the condition when the product ID is invalid or the account has insufficient credit, drag and drop another CodeActivity onto the ifItemProblems activity. Name the activity codeInsufficientCredit and double-click to add an event handler. Here is the code for this handler:

```
private void codeInsufficientCredit_ExecuteCode(object sender, EventArgs e)
{
    Console.WriteLine(
        "Item {0} invalid or AccountId {1} credit of {2} insufficient",
        SalesItemId, AccountId, availableCredit);
}
```

The final workflow should look like Figure 3-3.

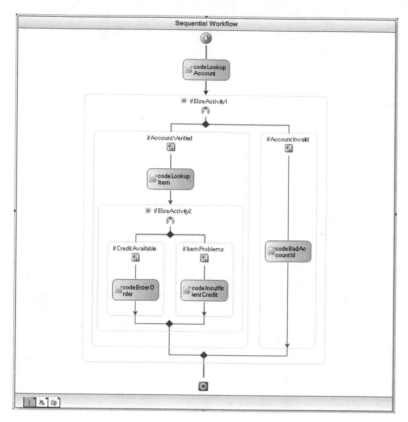

Figure 3-3. *Completed order entry workflow using CodeActivity*

The complete code for the Workflow1.cs file is shown in Listing 3-2.

Listing 3-2. *Complete Workflow1.cs File*

```
using System;
using System.ComponentModel;
using System.Workflow.ComponentModel;
using System.Workflow.Activities;

namespace OrderEntryCode
{
    /// <summary>
    /// Order entry workflow using CodeActivity
    /// </summary>
    public sealed partial class Workflow1 : SequentialWorkflowActivity
    {
        private Boolean isAccountVerified;
        private Boolean isSalesItemVerified;
        private Decimal availableCredit;
        private Decimal salesItemAmount;
```

```
public Workflow1()
{
    InitializeComponent();
}

#region Public workflow properties

public static DependencyProperty AccountIdProperty
    = System.Workflow.ComponentModel.DependencyProperty.Register(
    "AccountId", typeof(Int32), typeof(Workflow1));

/// <summary>
/// Identifies the account
/// </summary>
[Description("Identifies the account")]
[Category("CodeActivity Example")]
[Browsable(true)]
[DesignerSerializationVisibility(DesignerSerializationVisibility.Visible)]
public Int32 AccountId
{
    get
    {
        return ((Int32)(base.GetValue(Workflow1.AccountIdProperty)));
    }
    set
    {
        base.SetValue(Workflow1.AccountIdProperty, value);
    }
}

public static DependencyProperty SalesItemIdProperty
    = System.Workflow.ComponentModel.DependencyProperty.Register(
    "SalesItemId", typeof(Int32), typeof(Workflow1));

/// <summary>
/// Identifies the item to sell
/// </summary>
[Description("Identifies the item to sell")]
[Category("CodeActivity Example")]
[Browsable(true)]
[DesignerSerializationVisibility(DesignerSerializationVisibility.Visible)]
public Int32 SalesItemId
{
    get
    {
        return ((Int32)(base.GetValue(Workflow1.SalesItemIdProperty)));
    }
    set
    {
        base.SetValue(Workflow1.SalesItemIdProperty, value);
    }
}
```

```csharp
#endregion

/// <summary>
/// CodeActivity handler for looking up an account
/// </summary>
/// <param name="sender"></param>
/// <param name="e"></param>
private void codeLookupAccount_ExecuteCode(object sender, EventArgs e)
{
    //simulate an account lookup
    switch (AccountId)
    {
        case 1001:
            isAccountVerified = true;
            availableCredit = 100.00M;
            break;
        case 2002:
            isAccountVerified = true;
            availableCredit = 500.00M;
            break;
        default:
            isAccountVerified = false;
            availableCredit = 0;
            break;
    }
}


/// <summary>
/// Identify the item to order based on the SalesItemId
/// </summary>
/// <param name="sender"></param>
/// <param name="e"></param>
private void codeLookupItem_ExecuteCode(object sender, EventArgs e)
{
    //simulate an item lookup to retrieve the sales amount
    switch (SalesItemId)
    {
        case 501:
            isSalesItemVerified = true;
            salesItemAmount = 59.95M;
            break;
        case 502:
            isSalesItemVerified = true;
            salesItemAmount = 199.99M;
            break;
        default:
            isSalesItemVerified = false;
            salesItemAmount = 0;
            break;
    }
}
```

```csharp
/// <summary>
/// Process a validated order
/// </summary>
/// <param name="sender"></param>
/// <param name="e"></param>
private void codeEnterOrder_ExecuteCode(object sender, EventArgs e)
{
    //simulate the order
    Console.WriteLine(
        "Order entered for account {0}, Item id {1} for {2}",
        AccountId, SalesItemId, salesItemAmount);
}

/// <summary>
/// The AccountId is invalid
/// </summary>
/// <param name="sender"></param>
/// <param name="e"></param>
private void codeBadAccountId_ExecuteCode(object sender, EventArgs e)
{
    Console.WriteLine("AccountId {0} is invalid", AccountId);
}

/// <summary>
/// The Item is invalid or the account has insufficient credit
/// </summary>
/// <param name="sender"></param>
/// <param name="e"></param>
private void codeInsufficientCredit_ExecuteCode(object sender, EventArgs e)
{
    Console.WriteLine(
        "Item {0} invalid or AccountId {1} credit of {2} insufficient",
        SalesItemId, AccountId, availableCredit);
}
    }
}
```

Running the Workflow

Now that the workflow is fully implemented, you can turn your attention to the code that executes it. Since this is a Console application, the project template generates boilerplate code for the Program.cs file to host the workflow runtime and execute the workflow.

However, to test this application, you'll want to execute the workflow multiple times with different input parameters each time. To facilitate this, the standard Program.cs that comes with the project template requires a few adjustments. The revised code is shown in Listing 3-3.

Listing 3-3. *Complete Program.cs File*

```csharp
#region Using directives

using System;
using System.Collections.Generic;
using System.Threading;
using System.Workflow.Runtime;
```

```
#endregion

namespace OrderEntryCode
{
    /// <summary>
    /// Execute OrderEntry workflow with CodeActivity
    /// </summary>
    public class Program : IDisposable
    {
        private WorkflowRuntime _workflowRuntime;
        private AutoResetEvent _waitHandle = new AutoResetEvent(false);

        public Program()
        {
            InitializeWorkflowRuntime();
        }

        #region IDisposable Members

        /// <summary>
        /// Dispose of the workflow runtime
        /// </summary>
        public void Dispose()
        {
            _workflowRuntime.StopRuntime();
            _workflowRuntime.Dispose();
        }
```

The Program class implements IDisposable. This isn't strictly a requirement, but is done in order to allow use of the using syntax in the Main method. Within the Dispose method, StopRuntime and Dispose are called on the WorkflowRuntime instance. This ensures that all resources used by the workflow runtime engine are released and available for garbage collection.

```
        #endregion

        /// <summary>
        /// Start the workflow runtime
        /// </summary>
        private void InitializeWorkflowRuntime()
        {
            _workflowRuntime = new WorkflowRuntime();
            _workflowRuntime.WorkflowCompleted
                += delegate(object sender, WorkflowCompletedEventArgs e)
                {
                    _waitHandle.Set();
                };
            _workflowRuntime.WorkflowTerminated
                += delegate(object sender, WorkflowTerminatedEventArgs e)
                {
                    Console.WriteLine(e.Exception.Message);
                    _waitHandle.Set();
                };
        }
```

During construction of the Program class, an instance of the WorkflowRuntime class is initialized. This class represents the workflow runtime engine. During initialization, the code also adds event handlers for the WorkflowCompleted and WorkflowTerminated events. These events are handled in order to know when each instance of the workflow has completed.

```
/// <summary>
/// Run the workflow
/// </summary>
/// <param name="wfArguments"></param>
public void RunWorkflow(Dictionary<String, Object> wfArguments)
{
    //create the workflow instance and start it
    WorkflowInstance instance = _workflowRuntime.CreateWorkflow(
            typeof(OrderEntryCode.Workflow1), wfArguments);
    instance.Start();

    //wait for the workflow to complete
    _waitHandle.WaitOne();
}
```

A RunWorkflow method is added to make it easier to execute an instance of the workflow. It calls the CreateWorkflow method of the WorkflowRuntime instance to create a workflow. This method returns a WorkflowInstance which is then started using the Start method. The RunWorkflow method then waits for the AutoResetEvent instance (_waitHandle) to be signaled. This is necessary since workflow execution is asynchronous within the runtime engine. The _waitHandle variable is signaled by the WorkflowCompleted and WorkflowTerminated event handlers.

```
static void Main(string[] args)
{
    using (Program instance = new Program())
    {
        //create a dictionary with input arguments
        Dictionary<String, Object> wfArguments
            = new Dictionary<string, object>();
        wfArguments.Add("AccountId", 1001);
        wfArguments.Add("SalesItemId", 501);
        //run the workflow
        instance.RunWorkflow(wfArguments);

        //change the parameters and run the workflow
        //one more time with another account and item
        wfArguments.Clear();
        wfArguments.Add("AccountId", 2002);
        wfArguments.Add("SalesItemId", 502);
        instance.RunWorkflow(wfArguments);

        //try the workflow gain, this time the account
        //should have insufficient funds for the order.
        wfArguments.Clear();
        wfArguments.Add("AccountId", 1001);
        wfArguments.Add("SalesItemId", 502);
        instance.RunWorkflow(wfArguments);
```

```
                    //run the workflow again with an invalid account
                    wfArguments.Clear();
                    wfArguments.Add("AccountId", 9999);
                    wfArguments.Add("SalesItemId", 501);
                    instance.RunWorkflow(wfArguments);

                    Console.WriteLine("Press any key to exit");
                    Console.ReadLine();
                }
            }
        }
    }
```

The static Main method is where everything comes together. Workflow parameters are added to a Dictionary of Object that is keyed by a String. The parameter names exactly match the dependency properties added to the workflow (AccountId and SalesItemId). The workflow is then executed by calling the RunWorkflow method which accepts the Dictionary of parameters.

The workflow is executed a total of four times, each time a different combination of AccountId and SalesItemId are passed. These combinations were chosen to demonstrate the results of each possible execution path within the workflow. When you execute this program, the results look like this:

```
Order entered for account 1001, Item id 501 for 59.95
Order entered for account 2002, Item id 502 for 199.99
Item 502 invalid or AccountId 1001 credit of 100.00 insufficient
AccountId 9999 is invalid
Press any key to exit
```

Evaluating the Approach

The results indicate that the workflow is executing as you would expect and is producing the correct results. The advantage to using the CodeActivity is that it is relatively simple to implement. All of the code is self-contained in the workflow class. For simple workflow tasks, this is a viable approach.

However, the downside of the CodeActivity is that the code is not reusable beyond the current workflow. Since it is fully contained within the workflow class, the code needed to implement an activity is not reusable by other workflows. It is not packaged as a self-contained component that can be easily dragged and dropped onto another workflow. The code is also not independently testable. To test a single CodeActivity, you need to execute the entire workflow.

Creating your own custom activities solves these problems, but does require additional work to implement. The next section of this chapter covers the steps necessary to create your own custom activities.

Developing Custom Activities

Developing custom activities is the second way to add your own code to a workflow. In this section, I show you how to develop and use custom activities. To illustrate this, I implement the same order entry example workflow from the previous CodeActivity section. The difference is that custom activities are implemented instead of placing all of the code in CodeActivity event handlers.

Why Custom Activities?

Just as when you use a CodeActivity, the code in a custom activity can act upon property values and can perform any tasks that you require. CodeActivity works with properties and instance variables of the workflow. On the other hand, a custom activity works with its own set of properties that explicitly define the inputs and outputs of the activity. The individual activities are then wired together in a workflow, with the input properties of one activity bound to the output properties of another (or to properties of the workflow).

Custom activities have several advantages over CodeActivity. They permit you to develop discrete, testable components that can be reused by multiple workflows. Once implemented, the logic contained within them is readily available with a simple drag-and-drop from the Toolbox. Because they are discrete components, they are independently testable. You don't have to wait until a custom activity is used within a workflow to test it. It can be tested and documented independently. On the other hand, reuse of a CodeActivity is limited to the current workflow. It is not a self-contained component that can be reused by other workflows or independently tested.

Custom activities also permit you to develop your own domain-specific language. Each custom activity is given a name that corresponds with its real purpose and is based on the problem domain. This enables you to express business rules using terminology that is common to the problem domain. Experts in that domain are able to view the resulting workflow model and immediately understand it since it is declared in terms that they understand.

However, be aware that custom activities do have one major disadvantage over the CodeActivity: they are more complex and do require additional effort to develop.

Designing for Two Audiences

Custom activities should be developed with two possible audiences in mind. Obviously, they must be functional and solve some real-world problem, otherwise their worth is suspect. In addition, they must be implemented so that they cooperate with other activities within a workflow. I call this the *workflow runtime audience*. It consists of the other activities that live and work alongside the custom activity in a workflow. This audience also includes the workflow runtime engine. Each activity must satisfy a contract with the runtime engine and must exhibit the behavior that is expected by the runtime.

Secondly, custom activities are used by workflow developers at design time. This is the design time audience of developers that want to use your custom activity. Activities that are intuitive and that fully cooperate with the Visual Studio workflow designer are more likely to be used correctly. Custom activities that don't provide property descriptions or don't validate their parameters at design time are not taking full advantage of the available design tools. They don't enhance the design experience for a workflow developer.

Custom activities do require additional effort, especially compared to other mechanisms to add workflow logic such as using a CodeActivity. Much of this additional effort comes not in implementing the actual workflow logic, but in addressing the design time needs of the workflow developer. Tasks such as implementing dependency properties, adding property attributes and implementing design time validation define the metadata for an activity. Those tasks take effort, but they do enhance the design time experience and make the custom activity easier to use. And isn't that one of the reasons you want to develop workflow applications?

Creating the Project

Like the previous example, this one begins by creating a new workflow project. Select the Sequential Workflow Console Application project template for your project. Give the project a meaningful name such as OrderEntryActivities, which is the project name used throughout this example.

When developing a workflow that uses custom activities, it usually makes sense to develop all of the activities first. The activities are the building blocks of the workflow and they must be available in order to build upon them. Once the custom activities are implemented, it's a simple matter to add them to the workflow.

Implementing the Account Validation Activity

The first custom activity to be developed is responsible for validating the ID of the account and determining the amount of credit available for the account.

To add a custom activity, select the `OrderEntryActivities` project, then select Add Activity from the Project menu. You can also add an activity by right-clicking the project and selecting Add Activity from the context menu. Name this activity `ValidateAccountActivity` to help identify its purpose. It is a standard naming convention that all activity names end with the word *Activity*.

Determining the Base Activity

By default, the new activity derives from the base class `SequenceActivity`. This base class is a composite activity that enables you to host other child activities. In this example, you don't need this capability, so you can change the base class to a simple activity that is more suitable. Switch to the code view of the `ValidateAccountActivity.cs` file and change the base class to `Activity` instead of `SequenceActivity`. The `Activity` class can be found in the `System.Workflow.ComponentModel` namespace.

■Note You can develop this custom activity using `SequenceActivity` as its base without any problems. While it doesn't present any problems, it might cause some confusion. When you drag and drop a composite activity such as this onto a workflow, it is shown visually in the designer as an activity that accepts other child activities. Since these custom activities don't support execution of child activities, you wouldn't want to give an incorrect indication that they do.

Defining the Activity Properties

Each custom activity should be designed as a stand-alone component with its own set of input and output parameters. By designing the activity in this way, it is decoupled from all other activities and any host workflows that might use it. The activity isn't aware of any other activities in the workflow. It only knows about the property values that have been passed to it. A fully independent custom activity such as this provides the greatest potential for reuse. It also allows for complete independent testing of the activity apart from other activities and workflows.

In order to support the binding of properties in this activity to other activities, dependency properties are used instead of normal .NET properties. An overview of dependency properties is presented in the previous `CodeActivity` example. The dependency properties required by this activity are the following:

- `AccountId`: An `Int32` that identifies the account to be validated
- `IsAccountVerified`: A `Boolean` that indicates whether the `AccountId` is valid
- `AvailableCredit`: A `Decimal` that contains the amount of available credit for the account

Listing 3-4 shows the `ValidateAccountActivity.cs` file after these property definitions have been added.

Listing 3-4. *ValidateAccountActivity.cs File with Property Definitions*

```
using System;
using System.ComponentModel;
using System.Workflow.ComponentModel;
using System.Workflow.Activities;

namespace OrderEntryActivities
{
    /// <summary>
    /// Validate the account and determine the available credit
    /// </summary>
    public partial class ValidateAccountActivity : Activity
    {
        public ValidateAccountActivity()
        {
            InitializeComponent();
        }

        #region Public workflow properties

        public static DependencyProperty AccountIdProperty
            = System.Workflow.ComponentModel.DependencyProperty.Register(
            "AccountId", typeof(Int32), typeof(ValidateAccountActivity));

        /// <summary>
        /// Identifies the account
        /// </summary>
        [Description("Identifies the account")]
        [Category("Custom Activity Example")]
        [Browsable(true)]
        [DesignerSerializationVisibility(DesignerSerializationVisibility.Visible)]
        public Int32 AccountId
        {
            get
            {
                return ((Int32)(base.GetValue(
                    ValidateAccountActivity.AccountIdProperty)));
            }
            set
            {
                base.SetValue(ValidateAccountActivity.AccountIdProperty, value);
            }
        }

        public static DependencyProperty AvailableCreditProperty
            = System.Workflow.ComponentModel.DependencyProperty.Register(
            "AvailableCredit", typeof(Decimal), typeof(ValidateAccountActivity));

        /// <summary>
        /// The credit amount available for the account
        /// </summary>
        [Description("The credit amount available for the account")]
        [Category("Custom Activity Example")]
```

```
            [Browsable(true)]
            [DesignerSerializationVisibility(DesignerSerializationVisibility.Visible)]
            public Decimal AvailableCredit
            {
                get
                {
                    return ((Decimal)(base.GetValue(
                        ValidateAccountActivity.AvailableCreditProperty)));
                }
                set
                {
                    base.SetValue(
                        ValidateAccountActivity.AvailableCreditProperty, value);
                }
            }

            public static DependencyProperty IsAccountVerifiedProperty
                = System.Workflow.ComponentModel.DependencyProperty.Register(
                "IsAccountVerified", typeof(Boolean), typeof(ValidateAccountActivity));

            /// <summary>
            /// Determines if the account is valid
            /// </summary>
            [Description("Determines if the account is valid")]
            [Category("Custom Activity Example")]
            [Browsable(true)]
            [DesignerSerializationVisibility(DesignerSerializationVisibility.Visible)]
            public Boolean IsAccountVerified
            {
                get
                {
                    return ((Boolean)(base.GetValue(
                        ValidateAccountActivity.IsAccountVerifiedProperty)));
                }
                set
                {
                    base.SetValue(
                        ValidateAccountActivity.IsAccountVerifiedProperty, value);
                }
            }

        #endregion
        }
}
```

Implementing Activity Logic

The actual execution logic in a custom activity is placed in the Execute method. This is a virtual method provided by the base class and should be overridden in your class. This method is called synchronously by the workflow runtime as soon as the activity is executed. The code to simulate the lookup and validation of an account looks like this:

```
/// <summary>
/// Validate the account
/// </summary>
/// <param name="executionContext"></param>
/// <returns></returns>
protected override ActivityExecutionStatus Execute(
    ActivityExecutionContext executionContext)
{
    //simulate an account lookup
    switch (AccountId)
    {
        case 1001:
            IsAccountVerified = true;
            AvailableCredit = 100.00M;
            break;
        case 2002:
            IsAccountVerified = true;
            AvailableCredit = 500.00M;
            break;
        default:
            IsAccountVerified = false;
            AvailableCredit = 0;
            break;
    }

    return base.Execute(executionContext);
}
```

Based on the value of the AccountId property, the code sets the IsAccountVerified and AvailableCredit properties. Once this activity is added to the workflow, these property values will be used by rule conditions and also bound to properties in other activities.

The Execute method must return an ActivityExecutionStatus value as its result. This enumeration defines a set of possible values that indicate the current status of the running activity instance. The default value returned from the base.Execute method is ActivityExecutionStatus.Closed. This indicates that the activity has completed its work and is the value that you want to return.

The Execute method is passed an ActivityExecutionContext instance. This provides information about the execution environment of the activity. It provides methods to retrieve local services, run other child activities, and provide tracking data. You don't need to be concerned with any of these activities for this example activity.

Adding this Execute method code to Listing 3-4 completes the ValidateAccountActivity activity.

Implementing the Product Validation Activity

The purpose of the second custom activity is to validate the product to be sold. Add another new activity to the project and name it ValidateProductActivity. Switch to the code view for the ValidateProductActivity.cs file and change the base class to Activity instead of SequenceActivity.

Listing 3-5 shows the ValidateProductActivity.cs file in its entirety, including the dependency property definitions and the Execute method.

Listing 3-5. *Complete ValidateProductActivity.cs File*

```
using System;
using System.ComponentModel;
using System.Workflow.ComponentModel;
using System.Workflow.Activities;

namespace OrderEntryActivities
{
    /// <summary>
    /// Validate a product ID and retrieve its cost
    /// </summary>
    public partial class ValidateProductActivity : Activity
    {
        public ValidateProductActivity()
        {
            InitializeComponent();
        }

        #region Public workflow properties

        public static DependencyProperty SalesItemIdProperty
            = System.Workflow.ComponentModel.DependencyProperty.Register(
            "SalesItemId", typeof(Int32), typeof(ValidateProductActivity));

        /// <summary>
        /// Identifies the product
        /// </summary>
        [Description("Identifies the product")]
        [Category("Custom Activity Example")]
        [Browsable(true)]
        [DesignerSerializationVisibility(DesignerSerializationVisibility.Visible)]
        public Int32 SalesItemId
        {
            get
            {
                return ((Int32)(base.GetValue(
                    ValidateProductActivity.SalesItemIdProperty)));
            }
            set
            {
                base.SetValue(ValidateProductActivity.SalesItemIdProperty, value);
            }
        }

        public static DependencyProperty SalesItemAmountProperty
            = System.Workflow.ComponentModel.DependencyProperty.Register(
            "SalesItemAmount", typeof(Decimal), typeof(ValidateProductActivity));
```

```csharp
/// <summary>
/// The cost of the product
/// </summary>
[Description("The cost of the product")]
[Category("Custom Activity Example")]
[Browsable(true)]
[DesignerSerializationVisibility(DesignerSerializationVisibility.Visible)]
public Decimal SalesItemAmount
{
    get
    {
        return ((Decimal)(base.GetValue(
            ValidateProductActivity.SalesItemAmountProperty)));
    }
    set
    {
        base.SetValue(
            ValidateProductActivity.SalesItemAmountProperty, value);
    }
}

public static DependencyProperty IsSalesItemVerifiedProperty
    = System.Workflow.ComponentModel.DependencyProperty.Register(
    "IsSalesItemVerified", typeof(Boolean),
    typeof(ValidateProductActivity));

/// <summary>
/// Determines if the SalesItemId valid
/// </summary>
[Description("Determines if the SalesItemId valid")]
[Category("Custom Activity Example")]
[Browsable(true)]
[DesignerSerializationVisibility(DesignerSerializationVisibility.Visible)]
public Boolean IsSalesItemVerified
{
    get
    {
        return ((Boolean)(base.GetValue(
            ValidateProductActivity.IsSalesItemVerifiedProperty)));
    }
    set
    {
        base.SetValue(
            ValidateProductActivity.IsSalesItemVerifiedProperty, value);
    }
}

#endregion
```

The dependency properties required by this activity are the following:

- SalesItemId: An Int32 that identifies the product to be validated
- IsSalesItemVerified: A Boolean that indicates whether the SalesItemId is valid
- SalesItemAmount: A Decimal that contains the cost of the product

```
/// <summary>
/// Validate the product ID and determine the product cost
/// </summary>
/// <param name="executionContext"></param>
/// <returns></returns>
protected override ActivityExecutionStatus Execute(
    ActivityExecutionContext executionContext)
{
    //simulate an item lookup to retrieve the sales amount
    switch (SalesItemId)
    {
        case 501:
            IsSalesItemVerified = true;
            SalesItemAmount = 59.95M;
            break;
        case 502:
            IsSalesItemVerified = true;
            SalesItemAmount = 199.99M;
            break;
        default:
            IsSalesItemVerified = false;
            SalesItemAmount = 0;
            break;
    }

    return base.Execute(executionContext);
}
    }
}
```

The Execute method contains the business logic for this activity. If the SalesItemId value is valid, the IsSalesItemVerified property is set to true and the SalesItemAmount property is set to an example product cost. Otherwise, IsSalesItemVerfied is set to false.

Implementing the Order Entry Activity

The final custom activity simulates entering of the order. It really doesn't need to do much, other than to prove that the workflow reached this critical point with all of the correct property values.

Add another activity to the project, name it EnterOrderActivity and change the base class from SequenceActivity to Activity. Listing 3-6 shows the complete EnterOrderActivity.cs file.

Listing 3-6. *Complete EnterOrderActivity.cs File*

```
using System;
using System.ComponentModel;
using System.Workflow.ComponentModel;
using System.Workflow.Activities;
```

```csharp
namespace OrderEntryActivities
{
    /// <summary>
    /// Enter a validated order
    /// </summary>
    public partial class EnterOrderActivity : Activity
    {
        public EnterOrderActivity()
        {
            InitializeComponent();
        }

        #region Public workflow properties

        public static DependencyProperty AccountIdProperty
            = System.Workflow.ComponentModel.DependencyProperty.Register(
            "AccountId", typeof(Int32), typeof(EnterOrderActivity));

        /// <summary>
        /// Identifies the account
        /// </summary>
        [Description("Identifies the account")]
        [Category("Custom Activity Example")]
        [Browsable(true)]
        [DesignerSerializationVisibility(DesignerSerializationVisibility.Visible)]
        public Int32 AccountId
        {
            get
            {
                return ((Int32)(base.GetValue(
                    EnterOrderActivity.AccountIdProperty)));
            }
            set
            {
                base.SetValue(EnterOrderActivity.AccountIdProperty, value);
            }
        }

        public static DependencyProperty SalesItemIdProperty
            = System.Workflow.ComponentModel.DependencyProperty.Register(
            "SalesItemId", typeof(Int32), typeof(EnterOrderActivity));

        /// <summary>
        /// Identifies the product
        /// </summary>
        [Description("Identifies the product")]
        [Category("Custom Activity Example")]
        [Browsable(true)]
        [DesignerSerializationVisibility(DesignerSerializationVisibility.Visible)]
```

```
public Int32 SalesItemId
{
    get
    {
        return ((Int32)(base.GetValue(
            EnterOrderActivity.SalesItemIdProperty)));
    }
    set
    {
        base.SetValue(EnterOrderActivity.SalesItemIdProperty, value);
    }
}

public static DependencyProperty SalesItemAmountProperty
    = System.Workflow.ComponentModel.DependencyProperty.Register(
    "SalesItemAmount", typeof(Decimal), typeof(EnterOrderActivity));

/// <summary>
/// The cost of the product
/// </summary>
[Description("The cost of the product")]
[Category("Custom Activity Example")]
[Browsable(true)]
[DesignerSerializationVisibility(DesignerSerializationVisibility.Visible)]
public Decimal SalesItemAmount
{
    get
    {
        return ((Decimal)(base.GetValue(
            EnterOrderActivity.SalesItemAmountProperty)));
    }
    set
    {
        base.SetValue(EnterOrderActivity.SalesItemAmountProperty, value);
    }
}

#endregion
```

The dependency properties required by this activity are the following:

- AccountId: An Int32 that identifies the account that is placing the order

- SalesItemId: An Int32 that identifies the product being ordered

- SalesItemAmount: A Decimal that contains the cost of the product

```
/// <summary>
/// Enter a validated order
/// </summary>
/// <param name="executionContext"></param>
/// <returns></returns>
```

```
        protected override ActivityExecutionStatus Execute(
            ActivityExecutionContext executionContext)
        {
            //simulate the order
            Console.WriteLine(
                "Order entered for account {0}, Item id {1} for {2}",
                AccountId, SalesItemId, SalesItemAmount);

            return base.Execute(executionContext);
        }
    }
}
```

Defining the Workflow Parameters

Now that the custom activities are implemented, you can turn your attention to the workflow itself. First, the workflow requires the same two dependency properties that were added to the workflow in the CodeActivity example (shown in Listing 3-1). The dependency properties are the following:

- AccountId: An Int32 that identifies the account that is placing the order
- SalesItemId: An Int32 that identifies the product being ordered

Listing 3-7 shows the Workflow1.cs file after the properties have been added.

Listing 3-7. *Workflow1.cs File with Dependency Properties*

```
using System;
using System.ComponentModel;
using System.Workflow.ComponentModel;
using System.Workflow.Activities;

namespace OrderEntryActivities
{
    /// <summary>
    /// Order entry workflow using custom activities
    /// </summary>
    public sealed partial class Workflow1 : SequentialWorkflowActivity
    {
        public Workflow1()
        {
            InitializeComponent();
        }

        #region Public workflow properties

        public static DependencyProperty AccountIdProperty
            = System.Workflow.ComponentModel.DependencyProperty.Register(
            "AccountId", typeof(Int32), typeof(Workflow1));

        /// <summary>
        /// Identifies the account
        /// </summary>
        [Description("Identifies the account")]
        [Category("CodeActivity Example")]
        [Browsable(true)]
```

```
        [DesignerSerializationVisibility(DesignerSerializationVisibility.Visible)]
        public Int32 AccountId
        {
            get
            {
                return ((Int32)(base.GetValue(Workflow1.AccountIdProperty)));
            }
            set
            {
                base.SetValue(Workflow1.AccountIdProperty, value);
            }
        }

        public static DependencyProperty SalesItemIdProperty
            = System.Workflow.ComponentModel.DependencyProperty.Register(
            "SalesItemId", typeof(Int32), typeof(Workflow1));

        /// <summary>
        /// Identifies the item to sell
        /// </summary>
        [Description("Identifies the item to sell")]
        [Category("CodeActivity Example")]
        [Browsable(true)]
        [DesignerSerializationVisibility(DesignerSerializationVisibility.Visible)]
        public Int32 SalesItemId
        {
            get
            {
                return ((Int32)(base.GetValue(Workflow1.SalesItemIdProperty)));
            }
            set
            {
                base.SetValue(Workflow1.SalesItemIdProperty, value);
            }
        }

        #endregion
    }
}
```

Notice that the private instance variables used in the CodeActivity example have been omitted from this workflow. Those variables are needed in that example since they are used to pass state between each execution of a CodeActivity. In this example, the same data is passed directly between activities using their bound dependency properties. This eliminates the need for the private instance variables.

Defining the Workflow

After building the solution and switching to the design view for the Workflow1.cs file, you're ready to define the workflow.

Once a custom activity is implemented, it is available for use from the Visual Studio Toolbox just like the standard activities provided by Microsoft. Figure 3-4 shows a portion of the Toolbox that includes the custom activities that you just developed. The list of available custom activities is automatically generated by Visual Studio based on the activities that are found in any referenced assemblies.

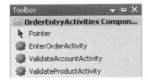

Figure 3-4. *Toolbox with custom activities*

Validating the Account

Start the workflow definition by dragging and dropping an instance of ValidateAccountActivity onto the workflow. The default name of validateAccountActivity1 given to the activity is fine as is.

You now need to wire up the AccountId property of this activity to the AccountId property of the workflow. To do this, switch to the Properties window for the activity. This is shown in Figure 3-5.

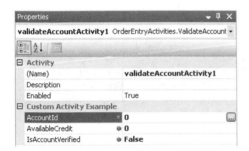

Figure 3-5. *Properties window for validateAccountActivity1*

To assign the AccountId property, select the ellipsis to the right of the property value. This opens the binding dialog shown in Figure 3-6.

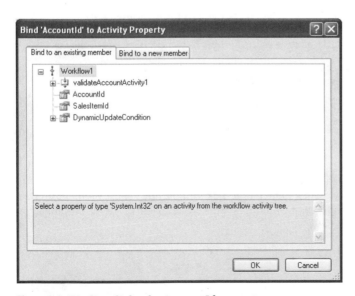

Figure 3-6. *Binding dialog for AccountId property*

This dialog allows you to select a dependency property of the workflow or another activity to bind to this property. *Binding* means that at runtime, the value of this activity property is set to the value obtained from another activity or the workflow. The use of dependency properties is what makes this kind of binding possible.

In this case, you want to bind the AccountId property of this activity to the AccountId of the workflow. At runtime, this property value is passed to the workflow in the Dictionary containing the workflow parameters. Therefore, by binding this activity property to the workflow property, this activity receives the workflow input parameter named AccountId. Select AccountId from the list and select OK to complete the binding.

The other properties shown in Figure 3-5 (AvailableCredit and IsAccountVerified) are outputs of this activity and do not need to be bound to another property at this time. Later, you will use those properties in other activities and rule conditions.

Now drag and drop an IfElseActivity directly under validateAccountActivity1. The purpose of this activity is to branch execution based on the IsAccountVerified property of validateAccountActivity1. The IfElseBranchActivity on the left side represents the processing that should take place if the account is valid. The right branch is executed if the account is invalid. Rename the left IfElseBranchActivity to ifAccountVerified to reflect its purpose, and the right branch to ifAccountInvalid.

From the Properties window, set the Condition property for the ifAccountVerified activity to Declarative Rule Condition. This indicates that the IfElseBranchActivity uses a rule condition rather than a code condition. After expanding the Condition property, set the ConditionName property to a meaningful name such as checkIsAccountVerified. Each rule condition in a workflow must have a unique name.

Now select the ellipsis in the Expression property and enter this condition:

```
this.validateAccountActivity1.IsAccountVerified == True
```

This rule condition definition is slightly different than the one that you entered in the CodeActivity example earlier in this chapter. In this case, you are not evaluating a property or variable of the workflow. Instead, you are referencing the IsAccountVerified dependency property of validateAccountActivity1, the custom activity instance.

Finish out the right-side branch of the IfElseActivity by dragging and dropping a CodeActivity onto the ifAccountInvalid activity. Name it codeBadAccountId and double-click the activity to add a handler for the ExecuteCode event. Add this code to the handler to write a message to the Console when the AccountId is invalid:

```
private void codeBadAccountId_ExecuteCode(object sender, EventArgs e)
{
    Console.WriteLine("AccountId {0} is invalid", AccountId);
}
```

Validating the Product

Drag and drop an instance of ValidateProductActivity onto the ifAccountVerified activity. As you did with the previous custom activity, switch to the Properties window and set the bindings for one of the dependency properties. This time set the binding for the SalesItemId property, binding it to the SalesItemId property of the workflow.

Now drag and drop another `IfElseActivity` under `validateProductActivity1`. The purpose of this activity is to branch execution based on the validity of the product and the account's available credit. Name the left side of the branch `ifCreditAvailable` and the right side `ifItemProblems`.

Add a Declarative Rule Condition to the `ifCreditAvailable` branch on the left side. Use `checkAvailableCredit` as the `ConditionName` and enter this as the `Expression`:

```
this.validateProductActivity1.IsSalesItemVerified == True &&
this.validateProductActivity1.SalesItemAmount <=
this.validateAccountActivity1.AvailableCredit
```

To handle the condition when the product ID is invalid or the account has insufficient credit, drag and drop a `CodeActivity` onto the `ifItemProblems` activity on the right side. Name the activity `codeInsufficientCredit` and double-click to add an event handler. Here is the code for this handler:

```
private void codeInsufficientCredit_ExecuteCode(object sender, EventArgs e)
{
    Console.WriteLine(
        "Item {0} invalid or AccountId {1} credit of {2} insufficient",
        SalesItemId, AccountId,
        this.validateAccountActivity1.AvailableCredit);
}
```

Entering the Order

Drag and drop an instance of the `EnterOrderActivity` onto the `ifCreditAvailable` branch on the left side. Bind the properties of the activity as shown in Table 3-2.

Table 3-2. *Property Bindings for enterOrderActivity1*

Property	Binding
AccountId	Activity=Workflow1, Path=AccountId
SalesItemAmount	Activity=validateProductActivity1, Path=SalesItemAmount
SalesItemId	Activity=Workflow1, Path=SalesItemId

The binding syntax shown in Table 3-2 is also shown within the Properties window. The Activity identifies the activity or workflow that owns the property being bound to. The Path identifies the property that you are binding to.

Figure 3-7 shows the completed workflow using the custom activities.

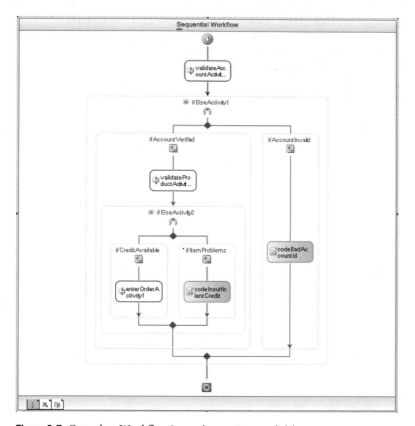

Figure 3-7. *Complete Workflow1.cs using custom activities*

Listing 3-8 shows the code that you need to add to the Workflow1.cs file for the CodeActivity handlers.

Listing 3-8. *CodeActivity Handler Code for the Workflow1.cs File*

```
using System;
using System.ComponentModel;
using System.Workflow.ComponentModel;
using System.Workflow.Activities;

namespace OrderEntryActivities
{
    /// <summary>
    /// Order entry workflow using custom activities
    /// </summary>
    public sealed partial class Workflow1 : SequentialWorkflowActivity
    {

...
```

```csharp
        private void codeBadAccountId_ExecuteCode(object sender, EventArgs e)
        {
            Console.WriteLine("AccountId {0} is invalid", AccountId);
        }

        private void codeInsufficientCredit_ExecuteCode(object sender, EventArgs e)
        {
            Console.WriteLine(
                "Item {0} invalid or AccountId {1} credit of {2} insufficient",
                SalesItemId, AccountId,
                this.validateAccountActivity1.AvailableCredit);
        }
    }
}
```

Running the Workflow

The code to host the workflow runtime and execute the workflow goes into the `Program.cs` file. You can use the same code shown in Listing 3-3 with the few minor changes that are highlighted in Listing 3-9. The only difference is the namespace changes that are highlighted in the listing.

Listing 3-9. *Complete Program.cs File for Custom Activity Workflow*

```csharp
#region Using directives

...

#endregion

namespace OrderEntryActivities
{
    /// <summary>
    /// Execute OrderEntry workflow with custom activities
    /// </summary>
    public class Program : IDisposable
    {

...

        /// <summary>
        /// Run the workflow
        /// </summary>
        /// <param name="wfArguments"></param>
        public void RunWorkflow(Dictionary<String, Object> wfArguments)
        {
            //create the workflow instance and start it
            WorkflowInstance instance = _workflowRuntime.CreateWorkflow(
                    typeof(OrderEntryActivities.Workflow1), wfArguments);
            instance.Start();

            //wait for the workflow to complete
            _waitHandle.WaitOne();
        }
```

...

```
    }
}
```

When executed, you should see these results:

```
Order entered for account 1001, Item id 501 for 59.95
Order entered for account 2002, Item id 502 for 199.99
Item 502 invalid or AccountId 1001 credit of 100.00 insufficient
AccountId 9999 is invalid
Press any key to exit
```

UNIT TESTING CUSTOM ACTIVITIES

One of the advantages of custom activities is that they facilitate unit testing. Since each custom activity is a self-contained component with clearly identified inputs and outputs, it is easy to develop automated unit tests for each activity. You then have some level of assurance that each custom activity functions correctly before you begin to use it within workflows. And the tests can be executed each time you modify the activity to guard against unanticipated changes in behavior.

One popular (and free) unit test framework for .NET is NUnit (http://www.nunit.org). When using NUnit, you develop normal C# classes that test aspects of a custom activity. Each NUnit test class is decorated with an attribute that identifies it as a test fixture. Within the class, methods represent individual test cases. NUnit also supports test and fixture setup and teardown methods.

For example, you can develop a set of NUnit tests for the ValidateAccountActivity just developed. First, download and install NUnit if you haven't already done so. Next, create an Empty Workflow Project and name it ActivitiesUnitTest. Add a normal C# class to the project and name it ValidateAccountActivityTest. By convention, unit test classes generally use the same name as the class they are testing with a Test suffix. Add a reference to the NUnit.Framework assembly to the project, along with a reference to the OrderEntryActivities project developed earlier in this chapter.

Here are the contents of the ValidateAccountActivityTest.cs file:

```
using System;
using System.Threading;
using System.Collections.Generic;
using System.Workflow.Runtime;
using NUnit.Framework;

namespace ActivitiesUnitTest
{
    /// <summary>
    /// NUnit tests for the ValidateAccountActivity
    /// </summary>
    [TestFixture]
    public class ValidateAccountActivityTest
    {
        private WorkflowRuntime _workflowRuntime;
        private AutoResetEvent _waitHandle = new AutoResetEvent(false);
        private WorkflowCompletedEventArgs _completedArgs;
```

```
[TestFixtureSetUp]
public void TestFixtureSetup()
{
    _workflowRuntime = new WorkflowRuntime();
    _workflowRuntime.WorkflowCompleted
        += delegate(object sender, WorkflowCompletedEventArgs e)
        {
            //save the completed event args
            _completedArgs = e;
            _waitHandle.Set();
        };
    _workflowRuntime.WorkflowTerminated
        += delegate(object sender, WorkflowTerminatedEventArgs e)
        {
            Assert.Fail(
                "Workflow terminated: {0}", e.Exception.Message);
            _waitHandle.Set();
        };
}

[TestFixtureTearDown]
public void TestFixtureTearDown()
{
    if (_workflowRuntime != null)
    {
        _workflowRuntime.StopRuntime();
    }
}
```

The methods that have the TestFixtureSetUp and TestFixtureTearDown attributes are executed once per test fixture. A test fixture is the entire class. In these methods, I add code to start the WorkflowRuntime and set up event handlers. In the TestFixtureTearDown method I stop the runtime.

```
/// <summary>
/// Test for a valid account
/// </summary>
[Test]
public void ValidAccountTest()
{
    Dictionary<String, Object> wfArguments
        = new Dictionary<string, object>();
    wfArguments.Add("AccountId", 1001);

    WorkflowInstance instance = _workflowRuntime.CreateWorkflow(
        typeof(OrderEntryActivities.ValidateAccountActivity),
        wfArguments);
    Assert.IsNotNull(instance,
        "Could not create workflow instance");
    instance.Start();

    _waitHandle.WaitOne(5000, false);
```

```
        Assert.IsNotNull(_completedArgs,
            "Completed workflow event args should not be null");

        Decimal credit
            = (Decimal)_completedArgs.OutputParameters["AvailableCredit"];
        Assert.AreEqual((Decimal)100.00, credit,
            "AvailableCredit value is incorrect");

        Boolean accountVerified
            = (Boolean)_completedArgs.OutputParameters["IsAccountVerified"];
        Assert.IsTrue(accountVerified,
            "IsAccountVerified value is incorrect");
    }
```

The ValidAccountTest method has a Test attribute that identifies it as a unit test. This particular method validates the behavior of ValidateAccountActivity when a valid AccountId is passed as input. Since this custom activity is self-contained and doesn't depend on any external resources, it is a simple matter to set up just the parameters that are required by this activity. At this level of testing, you are only concerned with this one activity, not with its use within a workflow.

An instance of the custom activity is created and started just like a workflow. All workflow classes are derived from the base Activity class. Any class that derives from Activity can be executed by the workflow runtime as if it were a complete workflow.

The Assert class is included with NUnit and provides a number of methods that you can use to test for expected results. Several of those methods are demonstrated in this example code. When using the methods of the Assert class, you are declaring the conditions that should be true. If a condition is false, the assertion throws an exception that is caught and displayed by the NUnit GUI or console applications.

```
    /// <summary>
    /// Test for an invalid account
    /// </summary>
    [Test]
    public void InValidAccountTest()
    {
        Dictionary<String, Object> wfArguments
            = new Dictionary<string, object>();
        wfArguments.Add("AccountId", 9999); //invalid

        WorkflowInstance instance = _workflowRuntime.CreateWorkflow(
            typeof(OrderEntryActivities.ValidateAccountActivity),
            wfArguments);
        Assert.IsNotNull(instance,
            "Could not create workflow instance");
        instance.Start();

        _waitHandle.WaitOne(5000, false);

        Assert.IsNotNull(_completedArgs,
            "Completed workflow event args should not be null");
```

```
        Decimal credit
            = (Decimal)_completedArgs.OutputParameters["AvailableCredit"];
        Assert.AreEqual((Decimal)0, credit,
            "AvailableCredit value is incorrect");

        Boolean accountVerified
            = (Boolean)_completedArgs.OutputParameters["IsAccountVerified"];
        Assert.IsFalse(accountVerified,
            "IsAccountVerified value is incorrect");
    }
```

This second method is almost exactly like the first, but It tests the behavior of the activity when an invalid `AccountId` is passed to the activity.

```
    }
}
```

After building this project, you can execute it from the `nunit-gui.exe` or `nunit-console.exe` programs that are provided with NUnit. The NUnit GUI application provides you with a clear visual indication of the success or failure of each test.

Evaluating the Approach

The runtime results from this workflow are the same as the previous example that used the `CodeActivity`. However, the design time results are much different.

The `CodeActivity` example did not result in components that were reusable. All of the code was limited to reuse within the workflow.

This example produced a set of custom activities that can be reused in other workflows. Each activity is a stand-alone component that is decoupled from other activities. Each activity is only aware of the input properties that it receives. It has no knowledge of other activities or any code within the workflow class. Using dependency properties, you are able to bind a property in one activity to another. This approach provides you with the flexibility to wire up the activities in any sequence necessary to solve your business problems.

Use the `CodeActivity` approach for situations that require small amounts of trivial code that you don't anticipate reusing. Use custom activities when you want to develop reusable components that fully encapsulate their logic.

Enhancing the Design Experience

The previous section covered the basics of developing and using your own custom activities. In addition to those implementation tasks, you can optionally add other features to an activity in order to enhance the design time experience. The following design time features are highlighted in this section:

- *Validating the activity*. Adding validation to an activity allows you to catch configuration errors at design time, before you execute the activity within a workflow.

- *Customizing Toolbox behavior*. You can customize the actions of an activity when it is dragged from the Visual Studio Toolbox to the workflow designer.

- *Implementing a custom designer and theme*. You can take complete control over the design experience by developing your own custom designer for the activity. Using a theme, you can change the fonts and colors along with other visual attributes.

The tasks in this section don't help your activity to run any better. Rather, the aim of these tasks is to make developing workflows using custom activities a more pleasant and productive experience.

Validating the Activity

When developing a custom activity, you have the option of providing design time validation. The most common type of validation checks for missing properties, but you can perform any validation logic that you need. For instance, if your activity is a composite, you can verify that a child activity of a specified type has been added.

The goal of validation is to assist the developer at design time by identifying error and warning conditions. A custom activity that provides this type of validation enhances the design experience by providing clues to the proper use of the activity. The developer doesn't have to wait until the workflow is executed to find out that a property was not set. They are notified of missing properties and other errors at design time via visual clues in the designer along with compiler warnings and errors.

Adding validation to a custom activity consists of two steps:

1. Implementing a custom validator class

2. Assigning the validator class to the custom activity class

The custom validator class must derive directly or indirectly from the Validator class (found in the System.Workflow.ComponentModel.Compiler namespace). There are several classes supplied with WF that derive from Validator, but these two are most commonly used as a base class for a custom validator:

- ActivityValidator: A base validator class used for simple activities

- CompositeActivityValidator: A base validator class used for composite activities

Implementing the Sample Activity

To illustrate adding validation to an activity, this example develops a simple custom activity, implements a validation class, and then assigns the validation class to the activity.

To start the example, create a new workflow project using the Empty Workflow Project template. This creates a DLL assembly that can be referenced by other projects. A DLL assembly is more appropriate when you want to add custom activities to the Toolbox. Assign the project the name CustomActivityComponents. Select Add Activity from the Project menu to create a new custom activity, and name the new activity MyCustomActivity.

After changing to the code view for MyCustomActivity.cs, change the base class for the activity from SequenceActivity to Activity. This changes the activity from a composite to a simple activity.

Next, the activity needs properties to validate, so add these dependency properties to the activity:

- MyString: A String property

- MyInt: An Int32 property

Listing 3-10 shows the code for MyCustomActivity.cs after the dependency properties have been added.

Listing 3-10. *MyCustomActivity.cs with Dependency Properties*

```
using System;
using System.ComponentModel;
using System.Workflow.ComponentModel;
using System.Workflow.ComponentModel.Compiler;
using System.Workflow.Activities;
```

```csharp
namespace CustomActivityComponents
{
    /// <summary>
    /// A custom activity that demonstrates activity components
    /// </summary>
    public partial class MyCustomActivity : Activity
    {
        public MyCustomActivity()
        {
            InitializeComponent();
        }

        public static DependencyProperty MyStringProperty
            = System.Workflow.ComponentModel.DependencyProperty.Register(
            "MyString", typeof(string), typeof(MyCustomActivity));

        [Description("A String property")]
        [Category("Custom Activity Components")]
        [Browsable(true)]
        [DesignerSerializationVisibility(DesignerSerializationVisibility.Visible)]
        public string MyString
        {
            get
            {
                return ((string)(base.GetValue(
                    MyCustomActivity.MyStringProperty)));
            }
            set
            {
                base.SetValue(MyCustomActivity.MyStringProperty, value);
            }
        }

        public static DependencyProperty MyIntProperty
            = System.Workflow.ComponentModel.DependencyProperty.Register(
            "MyInt", typeof(Int32), typeof(MyCustomActivity));

        [Description("An Int32 property")]
        [Category("Custom Activity Components")]
        [Browsable(true)]
        [DesignerSerializationVisibility(DesignerSerializationVisibility.Visible)]
        public Int32 MyInt
        {
            get
            {
                return ((Int32)(base.GetValue(MyCustomActivity.MyIntProperty)));
            }
            set
            {
                base.SetValue(MyCustomActivity.MyIntProperty, value);
            }
        }
    }
}
```

Implementing the Validation Class

To implement a custom validation class for this activity, add a new class to the project and name it MyCustomActivityValidator. The standard naming convention for validator classes is the activity name followed by the word *Validator*.

Since the activity that you will be validating is a simple activity, you should use ActivityValidator as your base class. This class is in the System.Workflow.ComponentModel.Compiler namespace so you'll need to add a using statement for this namespace.

Validation can be done in a number of ways, but the most basic is to override the base Validate method and add your validation there. Listing 3-11 shows the complete source for the custom validator class.

Listing 3-11. *Complete MyCustomActivityValidator.cs File*

```
using System;
using System.Workflow.ComponentModel.Compiler;

namespace CustomActivityComponents
{
    /// <summary>
    /// Validator for MyCustomActivity
    /// </summary>
    public class MyCustomActivityValidator : ActivityValidator
    {
        public override ValidationErrorCollection Validate(
            ValidationManager manager, object obj)
        {
            ValidationErrorCollection errors = base.Validate(manager, obj);
            //only validate a single custom activity type
            if (obj is MyCustomActivity)
            {
                MyCustomActivity activity = obj as MyCustomActivity;
                //only do validation when the activity is in a workflow
                if (activity.Parent != null)
                {
                    if (activity.MyInt == 0)
                    {
                        errors.Add(
                            ValidationError.GetNotSetValidationError(
                                "MyInt"));
                    }

                    if (activity.MyString == null ||
                        activity.MyString.Length == 0)
                    {
                        errors.Add(new ValidationError(
                            "MyString Property is incorrect", 501));
                    }
                }
            }
            return errors;
        }
    }
}
```

The first thing that is done in the Validate method is to execute the Validate method of the base class. This is done because the base class may also set error conditions for the activity and you'll want to see those errors. The Validate method returns an instance of ValidationErrorCollection which is a collection of errors and warnings. As you will see in this example, it is possible to return more than one error for an activity.

Next, the code checks the Type of the object passed in to the method. For simplicity, this validation class is designed to only validate a single custom activity, but you can design one that works with an entire family of activities.

After casting the object passed in to the correct activity Type, the Parent property of the activity is checked for null. This code is necessary to avoid errors when compiling the custom activity itself. Without this code, MyCustomActivity won't compile due to the error conditions that are defined here. This is not the desired behavior for a validator. Instead, you only want to perform validation when the activity is actually used within a workflow. Checking the Parent property of the activity for null prevents validation during compilation of the activity.

The validation of both activity properties now takes place. Each property is flagged with an error in a slightly different way. The static ValidationError.GetNotSetValidationError method is a helper used to flag a required property as not set. This static method is used for the MyInt property. As you will see, this produces slightly different visual cues at design time compared to the MyString property. When the MyString property is in error, an instance of the ValidationError object is created without the assistance of a helper method. Regardless of how a ValidationError object is created, it is added to the ValidationErrorCollection object that is the return value for the method.

Assigning the Validator to the Activity

Now that both the activity and the validator have been implemented, you tie them together with the ActivityValidator attribute. This attribute is added to the activity class to identify the class that provides validation logic. Add this attribute to the MyCustomActivity class like this:

```
[ActivityValidator(typeof(MyCustomActivityValidator))]
public partial class MyCustomActivity : Activity
{
    //class details not shown
}
```

Testing the Activity

After building the project, you're ready to test the validation logic of the custom activity. Drag and drop an instance of MyCustomActivity from the Toolbox to Workflow1.cs in workflow design view. Almost immediately, you should see a red indicator (the exclamation point) at the top of the activity informing you of the validation errors. This is illustrated in Figure 3-8.

The Properties window also provides an error indicator for the MyInt property. This property is flagged with an error since the static ValidationError.GetNotSetValidationError method was used to generate the error for that property. In contrast with this, the code manually creates a ValidationError object for the MyString property. This is illustrated in Figure 3-9.

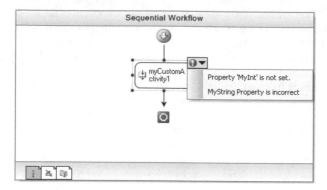

Figure 3-8. *Custom activity with validation errors*

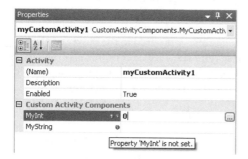

Figure 3-9. *Properties window with validation error*

In addition to the visual error cues, you should receive these compile errors when you build the project:

```
Activity 'myCustomActivity1' validation failed: Property 'MyInt' is not set.
Activity 'myCustomActivity1' validation failed: MyString Property is incorrect
Property 'MyInt' is not set.
MyString Property is incorrect
```

Once you set both of these properties (just choose any integer value and any string), all of the error indicators are removed and the project builds without any errors.

Adding validation to a custom activity does take additional effort. But that effort is rewarded by catching errors during workflow design rather than waiting until runtime. Because it actually helps to catch errors, design time validation improves the design experience more than the other design features that are discussed next.

Customizing Toolbox Behavior

There are a number of ways you can affect the design time behavior of a custom activity. As you might expect, you can determine the image that is used to represent the activity within the workflow designer and the Visual Studio Toolbox. You can also implement code that is executed when an activity is first dragged and dropped onto a workflow. This code can perform initialization tasks such as creating a complete tree of child activities or setting default values for properties. These features are illustrated with the following example.

Implementing the Activity

Start by adding a new custom activity to the same CustomActivityComponents project used in the previous validation example. Name the activity MyCompositeActivity. This time, you'll want to leave the default base class of SequenceActivity alone, since you need a composite activity to complete this example.

This activity does not require any properties in order to demonstrate these design time features. The only remaining tasks for this activity are to add attributes, which will be done after the ActivityToolboxItem class is implemented.

Implementing the ActivityToolboxItem Class

The ActivityToolboxItem class visually represents the activity in the Visual Studio Toolbox. It also contains code that is executed when an activity is dragged from the Toolbox to the design surface of the workflow designer.

To illustrate one possible way to use this class, add a new class to the CustomActivityComponents project and name it MyCompositeActivityToolboxItem. The standard naming convention is to use the activity name followed by *ToolboxItem*.

Use ActivityToolboxItem as the base class. ActivityToolboxItem can be found in the System. Workflow.ComponentModel.Design namespace. The next step is to override the CreateComponentsCore method and add code. This method is executed when the activity is added to the workflow designer. By adding your own code here, you have complete control over the activity creation process within the designer. Listing 3-12 contains the completed code for this class.

Listing 3-12. *Complete MyCompositeActivityToolboxItem.cs File*

```
using System;
using System.ComponentModel;
using System.ComponentModel.Design;
using System.Runtime.Serialization;
using System.Workflow.Activities;
using System.Workflow.ComponentModel.Design;

namespace CustomActivityComponents
{
    /// <summary>
    /// Defines custom activity when a MyCompositeActivity
    /// is dragged from the Toolbox to a workflow
    /// </summary>
    [Serializable]
    public class MyCompositeActivityToolboxItem : ActivityToolboxItem
    {
        /// <summary>
        /// Default constructor
        /// </summary>
        public MyCompositeActivityToolboxItem()
            : base()
        {
        }

        /// <summary>
        /// Serialization constructor
        /// </summary>
        /// <param name="info"></param>
```

```
    /// <param name="context"></param>
    public MyCompositeActivityToolboxItem(
        SerializationInfo info, StreamingContext context)
            : base(info, context)
    {
    }

    protected override IComponent[] CreateComponentsCore(IDesignerHost host)
    {
        //create the primary activity
        MyCompositeActivity activity = new MyCompositeActivity();
        //add an IfElseActivity
        IfElseActivity ifElse = new IfElseActivity("ifElse1");
        //add 3 branches to the IfElseActivity
        ifElse.Activities.Add(new IfElseBranchActivity("ifFirstCondition"));
        ifElse.Activities.Add(new IfElseBranchActivity("ifSecondCondition"));
        ifElse.Activities.Add(new IfElseBranchActivity("elseBranch"));
        activity.Activities.Add(ifElse);

        return new IComponent[] { activity };
    }
  }
}
```

The code in the `CreateComponentsCore` method creates an instance of `MyCompositeActivity`. But it doesn't stop there. It also adds an `IfElseActivity` as a child activity, along with three `IfElseBranchActivity` instances under it. Finally, the root `MyCompositeActivity` is returned to the caller. This kind of code assists developers who use your activity by prebuilding a standard set of child activities. Perhaps these are child activities that users of your activity usually end up adding manually.

Notice that the code also includes explicit constructors, including one that is used for serialization. Failure to include the serialization constructor will prevent activities that use this class from being manually added to the Visual Studio Toolbox.

Adding Attributes to the Activity

The final step in this example is to add an attribute to the activity that instructs it to use the new `MyCompositeActivityToolboxItem` class just implemented. Listing 3-13 shows the completed code for `MyCompositeActivity.cs`.

Listing 3-13. *Completed MyCompositeActivity.cs*

```
using System;
using System.ComponentModel;
using System.Drawing;
using System.Workflow.Activities;

namespace CustomActivityComponents
{
    /// <summary>
    /// A composite activity that demonstrates ToolboxItem and
    /// ToolboxBitmap
    /// </summary>
    [ToolboxBitmap(typeof(MyCompositeActivity), "Resources.graphhs.png")]
```

```
[ToolboxItem(typeof(MyCompositeActivityToolboxItem))]
public partial class MyCompositeActivity : SequenceActivity
{
    public MyCompositeActivity()
    {
        InitializeComponent();
    }
}
}
```

The ToolboxItem attribute assigns the MyCompositeActivityToolboxItem class to the activity. Once this is done, the code that was added to the CreateComponentsCore method is executed whenever an instance of this activity is added to a workflow by dragging it from the Toolbox.

The ToolboxBitmap attribute assigns an image that represents the activity within the workflow designer and the Toolbox. The image shown in this code is one of the stock images that are distributed with Visual Studio. Feel free to substitute your own image, or use one of the images provided with Visual Studio.

Note Visual Studio 2005 includes a collection of images that you can use when creating your own software. By default, the images are distributed as a ZIP file in the \Program Files\Microsoft Visual Studio 8\ Common7\VS2005ImageLibrary folder. The file name is VS2005ImageLibrary.zip. You can unzip this file and directly reference the graphics that you want to include in your application.

The ToolboxBitmap attribute shown in Listing 3-13 assumes that the image has been added to a Resources folder under the project and that the Build Action for the image file is set to Embedded Resource. If this is not done, the activity will not be able to find the image and the default image will be used. This image file (graphhs.png) can be found in the \bitmaps\commands\pngformat folder after you unzip the Visual Studio 2005 image library.

Testing the Activity

After building the project, you are ready to test these new design time features. Open up an existing workflow file in the designer (or add a new Sequential Workflow to the project). Now drag and drop an instance of MyCompositeActivity onto the workflow. Your results should look like Figure 3-10.

As Figure 3-10 shows, you end up with much more than a single activity. The code added to the CreateComponentsCore of the MyCompositeActivityToolboxItem class successfully creates the IfElseActivity and the three branches under it. The top-level image that is shown for myCompositeActivity1 is the one that is specified in the ToolboxBitmap attribute.

Note While the custom image is shown within the workflow designer, it isn't shown by default in the Toolbox. Custom activities can appear in the Toolbox in two ways: they can be manually added by you, or they can appear because a referenced assembly contains a custom activity. A custom image is only shown in the Toolbox when an activity is manually added to the Toolbox. You do this by right-clicking a tab in the Toolbox and selecting the Choose Items option. If a custom activity appears in the Toolbox automatically because it is in a referenced assembly, the default image is shown.

When developing your own custom activities, you won't always need to use these design time features. But they are available to customize the design experience if necessary.

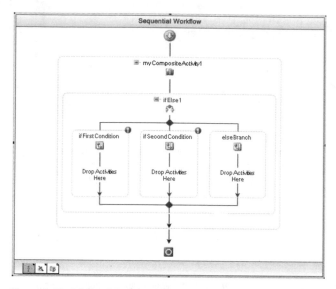

Figure 3-10. *Adding MyCompositeActivity to a workflow*

Customizing the Designer

When you implement a custom activity, you also have the option of customizing the visual designer for that activity. By creating a custom designer class, you can control the design time behavior for the activity as well as change the designer visually. For instance, you can make small adjustments to the designer visually such as changing the background color or the border. A more practical use of a custom designer class is to restrict the type of child activity that can be added to a custom activity.

Every activity type is associated with a default designer. If you don't implement your own designer, you'll get the default. All designers derive from the base ActivityDesigner class (found in the System.Workflow.ComponentModel.Design namespace). Other designers are provided with WF, with each one solving a different type of design problem. For instance, the CompositeActivityDesigner serves as the base class for all composite activity designers. Derived from CompositeActivityDesigner are other designers such as ParallelActivityDesigner and SequentialActivitydesigner that provide a slightly different design experience and serve more the specialized needs of their respective activities.

When implementing your own designer it is important to start with a base designer class that meets most of your needs. This allows you to make slight adjustments to a standard designer instead of implementing everything yourself. For example, you wouldn't use the base ActivityDesigner for a composite activity since that designer doesn't support child activities.

In addition to a designer class, you can implement a designer theme class to apply a style to the designer. The ActivityDesignerTheme class is the base for all designer themes. Derived from this base is a CompositeDesignerTheme that should be used for designers supporting composite activities.

Just like the other design time activity features, the designer and theme are applied declaratively to the activity using attributes. The designer class to use for an activity is assigned with the Designer attribute. The theme to use is assigned by placing the ActivityDesignerTheme attribute on the designer class, not on the activity class.

A simple custom theme and designer are illustrated with the following example.

Implementing a Style

In this example, you will create a new theme and designer for the MyCompositeActivity class used in the prior example. Instead of implementing a new activity for this example, you can add these additional features to the previous example.

Start by adding a new class to the CustomActivityComponents project. Name the class MyCompositeActivityTheme. Listing 3-14 shows the completed code for the new theme.

Listing 3-14. *Completed MyCompositeActivityTheme.cs*

```
using System;
using System.Drawing;
using System.Drawing.Drawing2D;
using System.Workflow.ComponentModel.Design;

namespace CustomActivityComponents
{
    /// <summary>
    /// Custom theme for MyCompositeActivityDesigner
    /// </summary>
    public class MyCompositeActivityTheme : CompositeDesignerTheme
    {
        public MyCompositeActivityTheme(WorkflowTheme theme)
            : base(theme)
        {
            this.BackColorStart = Color.LightSteelBlue;
            this.BackColorEnd = Color.Gainsboro;
            this.BorderStyle = DashStyle.DashDot;
            this.BorderColor = Color.DarkBlue;
            this.BackgroundStyle = LinearGradientMode.Vertical;
            this.ConnectorStartCap = LineAnchor.RectangleAnchor;
            this.ConnectorEndCap = LineAnchor.DiamondAnchor;
            this.ShowDropShadow = true;
        }
    }
}
```

The new theme uses CompositeDesignerTheme as the base class since this theme will be used by a designer that supports composite activities. In the constructor of the theme, the code changes the background color, the border style and color, and so on.

Implementing a Designer

To implement a new designer for the activity, add a new class to the CustomActivityComponents project and name this class MyCompositeActivityDesigner. To illustrate one use of a custom designer, this code restricts the type of child activity that can be added to MyCompositeActivity. The completed code is shown in Listing 3-15.

Listing 3-15. *Completed MyCompositeActivityDesigner.cs*

```
using System;
using System.Collections.Generic;
using System.Collections.ObjectModel;
using System.Workflow.ComponentModel;
using System.Workflow.ComponentModel.Design;
using System.Workflow.Activities;
```

```
namespace CustomActivityComponents
{
    /// <summary>
    /// Custom designer for MyCompositeActivity
    /// </summary>
    [ActivityDesignerTheme(typeof(MyCompositeActivityTheme))]
    public class MyCompositeActivityDesigner : SequentialActivityDesigner
    {
        /// <summary>
        /// Static list of acceptable child activities
        /// </summary>
        private static List<Type> _allowedActivityTypes = new List<Type>();
        static MyCompositeActivityDesigner()
        {
            //initialize list of allowed child types
            _allowedActivityTypes.Add(typeof(IfElseActivity));
            _allowedActivityTypes.Add(typeof(IfElseBranchActivity));
            _allowedActivityTypes.Add(typeof(CodeActivity));
        }

        /// <summary>
        /// Determine if an activity can be added
        /// </summary>
        /// <param name="insertLocation"></param>
        /// <param name="activitiesToInsert"></param>
        /// <returns></returns>
        public override bool CanInsertActivities(HitTestInfo insertLocation,
            ReadOnlyCollection<Activity> activitiesToInsert)
        {
            //allow only selected activity types
            Boolean result = true;
            if (activitiesToInsert != null)
            {
                foreach (Activity activity in activitiesToInsert)
                {
                    result = (_allowedActivityTypes.Contains(activity.GetType()));
                    if (result == false)
                    {
                        break;
                    }
                }
            }
            return result;
        }
    }
}
```

The SequentialActivityDesigner class was chosen as the base because it provides the default behavior that includes support for child activities.

To restrict the type of child activity that is allowed, the code overrides the CanInsertActivities method. This method is executed when a new child activity is dragged over the parent activity. If true is returned, the child is allowed to be added to the parent. Return false to prohibit the addition of that child to the activity.

The logic in CanInsertActivities could have been implemented in a number of ways. This example code uses a static List of activity types that are permitted as children. If the activities being inserted are all in the permitted list, true is returned. If any of the activities to insert are not in the list, false is returned and the child addition is prohibited. The list of permitted activity types is built in a static initializer for the class.

Finally, the ActivityDesignerTheme attribute assigns the new MyCompositeActivityTheme to this designer.

Adding Attributes to the Activity

The final step to use the new designer and theme is to assign them to the activity. To do this, add the Designer attribute to the MyCompositeActivity class. The revised code for this activity is shown in Listing 3-16, with the new attribute highlighted.

Listing 3-16. *Revised MyCompositeActivity.cs File*

```
using System;
using System.ComponentModel;
using System.Drawing;
using System.Workflow.Activities;

namespace CustomActivityComponents
{
    /// <summary>
    /// A composite activity that demonstrates ToolboxItem and
    /// ToolboxBitmap
    /// </summary>
    [ToolboxBitmap(typeof(MyCompositeActivity), "Resources.graphhs.png")]
    [ToolboxItem(typeof(MyCompositeActivityToolboxItem))]
    [Designer(typeof(MyCompositeActivityDesigner))]
    public partial class MyCompositeActivity : SequenceActivity
    {
        public MyCompositeActivity()
        {
            InitializeComponent();
        }
    }
}
```

Testing the Activity

After building the project, you can test the new designer and theme.

■**Tip** Changes such as this that affect the theme for a designer are only seen once you restart Visual Studio. After building the project, you should shut down and restart Visual Studio in order to see the new theme. This only applies to theme changes. If you change the logic within a designer, those changes take effect immediately after building the project.

Open up an existing workflow file in the designer (or add a new Sequential Workflow to the project). Now drag and drop an instance of MyCompositeActivity onto the workflow. Your results should look like Figure 3-11.

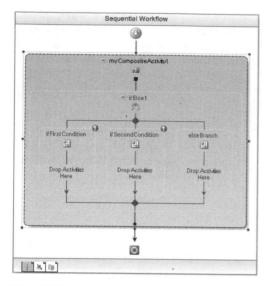

Figure 3-11. *MyCompositeActivity with a custom designer and theme*

Since this book isn't presented in living color, I can't show you the new background colors of the designer. But you should be able to tell from Figure 3-11 that the designer looks different than previous examples. The border also has a dash-dot pattern, and the top and bottom connectors for the activity are different than the standard ones.

■**Note** The IfElse activity and its associated branches are automatically added because of the custom ToolboxItem that is assigned to the activity. This behavior is discussed in the previous example.

To test the new designer behavior, try to drag and drop several activities on to the top portion of the activity (just beneath the myCompositeActivity1 name). First try an activity that is allowed, such as the CodeActivity. If you try to add an activity that is prohibited, such as the DelayActivity, it will not be allowed.

■**Note** While the MyCompositeActivity restricts the type of activity that you can add as a child, the embedded IfElseBranchActivity instances do not have this restriction. Those child activities each have their own designer that does not have the same restrictions as the custom MyCompositeActivity designer. For this reason, you can drag and drop restricted activities within these other child activities.

This example briefly touched on what you can accomplish if you implement your own activity designer. For most activities, you can rely upon the standard designers and themes. But if you are developing a custom activity with a special set of requirements, you do have the flexibility to implement your own designer.

Summary

This chapter provided you with an overview of the standard activities that are provided with WF. Detailed information on how to use each standard activity was not the focus of the chapter. Instead, the purpose of this chapter was to acquaint you with each standard activity and prepare you for more detailed discussions in subsequent chapters.

The major portion of the chapter was used to compare the two primary mechanisms for adding code to a workflow. A common workflow example was used to contrast the use of `CodeActivity` with developing your own custom activities. Additional information was also provided on how to make your custom activities easier to use at design time.

The next chapter provides additional information on hosting the workflow runtime engine within your applications. It explores additional workflow runtime events, shows you how to load workflow services, and introduces a set of helper classes that assist with the hosting duties.

CHAPTER 4

■■■

Hosting the Workflow Runtime

The focus of this chapter is hosting the workflow runtime within your applications. A simple hosting example is used to illustrate the basic requirements for workflow hosting. A set of workflow manager classes are then developed that address some of the problems and limitations of the first example.

The workflow runtime exposes a number of events that can be handled by your host application. These events allow you to monitor the status changes of running workflows. The examples in this chapter demonstrate how you can handle and use these events within your applications.

This chapter also shows you how to add core workflow services to the runtime in code and via the application configuration file. Core workflow services allow you to customize the behavior of the workflow runtime engine by loading an alternate implementation of a service. Examples in this chapter load the persistence service and an alternate implementation of the scheduler service.

When a workflow is created, an instance of the WorkflowInstance class is returned. This class exposes several methods that permit you to take direct actions on a workflow instance. Several of these methods are demonstrated in this chapter.

Finally, workflows normally execute asynchronously within the workflow runtime engine. However, they can also execute synchronously if you load an alternate scheduler service. The use of this alternate service for synchronous workflow execution is demonstrated in this chapter.

Overview of Hosting

Windows Workflow Foundation (WF) was designed to be hosted by your application. It is not a complete stand-alone application that is ready for execution. You must build the application that hosts WF. This was an important design decision for the WF team, and a good one. Use of WF is not confined to a limited set of predefined application types. This design provides you with the flexibility to use WF in the widest variety of your own applications.

When incorporating WF into your application, you need to be aware of your application's responsibilities toward WF. An application that hosts WF has several responsibilities, including these:

- Creating and starting an instance of the workflow runtime engine (represented in code by the WorkflowRuntime class).

- Subscribing and reacting to events published by the workflow runtime engine.

- Optionally creating and registering core workflow services with the runtime engine. These are services that are used for workflow persistence, thread scheduling, transaction management, and workflow tracking.

- Optionally creating and registering local services with the runtime engine. These are services that are primarily used as a communication conduit between the host application and executing workflows.

- Creating and starting workflow instances using the workflow runtime engine.

- Continuing to execute until all running workflows have completed. By default, workflows run asynchronously within the workflow runtime engine once they are started. For this reason, the host application must monitor the status of running workflows in order to determine when it is appropriate to exit.

- Performing an orderly shutdown of the workflow runtime engine prior to exiting.

These host application responsibilities are demonstrated in the examples in this chapter.

Note The use of local services is not covered in this chapter. In-depth coverage of local services is provided in Chapter 6.

Simple Workflow Hosting

This first example illustrates hosting the workflow runtime with a Console application. It is a bare-bones example that is similar to the hosting applications used in the previous chapters. The example code accomplishes its main objective: It hosts a workflow. But it doesn't necessarily do it in the most elegant, reusable way. If you are looking for the bare minimum amount of code that you need to host a workflow, this is it. If you want something more, you can find it in the examples that follow this one.

To implement this example, you will first create a very simple workflow that will serve as the test workflow to execute. It is executed by this first hosting example as well as other examples in this chapter. In order to reuse this workflow, you'll package it as a separate DLL assembly that can be referenced by other projects. You'll then implement a simple Console application that hosts the workflow runtime and starts execution of the sample workflow.

Implementing a Test Workflow

The workflow that you implement here is only used to demonstrate hosting of the workflow runtime engine. The workflow itself doesn't really accomplish any useful work, other than to notify you that it executed by writing a message to the Console. It receives one String parameter as input and updates one output parameter with a different String value. The workflow also includes a small built-in delay that helps it to mimic a longer running workflow. As you will see in the next example, the delay also triggers status changes in the workflow instance.

To begin, create a new workflow project using the Empty Workflow Project template. This creates a DLL assembly project that is capable of containing any type of workflow or custom activity. Name the project SharedWorkflows.

Tip You will also be prompted to save a solution file when you create this new project. It is easier to work with the examples in this chapter if you place all of them in a single Visual Studio solution.

I use the SharedWorkflows project name for most of the remaining chapters in this book. The name itself has no real meaning, other than to signify that it contains workflows (along with activities and related classes) that are used (or shared) by other applications. While other chapters use this same project name, each chapter assumes that you are creating a new SharedWorkflows project and not reusing one from another chapter. You will find it easier to work with the examples in this book if you place the code for each chapter in its own folder.

Add a new sequential workflow to the project. You can do this by first selecting the SharedWorkflows project in the Solution Explorer and then selecting Add Sequential Workflow from the Project menu and accept the default name of Workflow1.

Designing the Workflow

Using the workflow designer view, you now need to drag and drop two activities onto the workflow. First add a CodeActivity to the workflow, followed by a DelayActivity directly under the CodeActivity. You can use the default names that are assigned to these activity instances. Switch to the Properties window for delayActivity1 and set the TimeDuration property to 00:00:05. This sets the delay to five seconds. Before leaving the designer, you also need to assign an event handler to the ExecuteCode event of codeActivity1. The simplest way to do this is to double-click codeActivity1 to add an empty code handler.

The completed workflow is shown in Figure 4-1.

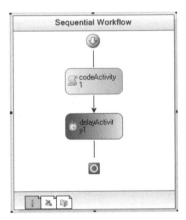

Figure 4-1. *Completed workflow for host application testing*

Implementing Workflow Code

The remainder of the implementation work is done in code instead of the workflow designer. The workflow requires two properties, one that is used as input and one as output. The example code implements these properties using dependency properties instead of standard C# properties. Add these dependency properties to the Workflow1.cs file:

- InputString: This is a String property that is used as a parameter passed from the host application to the workflow.

- Result: This is a String property that the workflow code will update and it will be displayed by the host application when the workflow concludes.

■**Tip** Remember that an easy way to add a dependency property is to use the code snippet that is provided with WF. To do this, right-click the location in your source code where you want to add the property and select Insert Snippet. Then select Workflow, then DependencyProperty – Property. A dependency property with the appropriate boilerplate code is added. You then change the property name and Type to match the properties InputString and Result.

Once the properties have been defined, you need to add code to the codeActivity1 event handler to write a message to the Console and update the Result property. The complete code for Workflow1.cs (including the dependency properties) is shown in Listing 4-1.

Listing 4-1. *Complete Workflow1.cs File*

```
using System;
using System.ComponentModel;
using System.ComponentModel.Design;
using System.Collections;
using System.Drawing;
using System.Workflow.ComponentModel.Compiler;
using System.Workflow.ComponentModel.Serialization;
using System.Workflow.ComponentModel;
using System.Workflow.ComponentModel.Design;
using System.Workflow.Runtime;
using System.Workflow.Activities;
using System.Workflow.Activities.Rules;

namespace SharedWorkflows
{
    public sealed partial class Workflow1 : SequentialWorkflowActivity
    {
        #region Public Dependency Properties

        public static DependencyProperty InputStringProperty
            = System.Workflow.ComponentModel.DependencyProperty.Register(
                "InputString", typeof(string), typeof(Workflow1));

        [Description("The workflow input string parameter")]
        [Category("Hosting the workflow runtime")]
        [Browsable(true)]
        [DesignerSerializationVisibility(DesignerSerializationVisibility.Visible)]
        public string InputString
        {
            get
            {
                return ((string)(base.GetValue(Workflow1.InputStringProperty)));
            }
            set
            {
                base.SetValue(Workflow1.InputStringProperty, value);
            }
        }

        public static DependencyProperty ResultProperty
            = System.Workflow.ComponentModel.DependencyProperty.Register(
                "Result", typeof(string), typeof(Workflow1));

        [Description("The workflow result")]
        [Category("Hosting the workflow runtime")]
        [Browsable(true)]
        [DesignerSerializationVisibility(DesignerSerializationVisibility.Visible)]
        public string Result
```

```
    {
        get
        {
            return ((string)(base.GetValue(Workflow1.ResultProperty)));
        }
        set
        {
            base.SetValue(Workflow1.ResultProperty, value);
        }
    }

    #endregion

    public Workflow1()
    {
        InitializeComponent();
    }

    private void codeActivity1_ExecuteCode(object sender, EventArgs e)
    {
        //provide some indication that the workflow executed
        Console.WriteLine("{0} executing, parameter={1}",
            this.WorkflowInstanceId, InputString);
        //return the InstanceId in the workflow parameter
        Result = String.Format("{0} result property",
            this.WorkflowInstanceId);
    }
  }
}
```

The code in the codeActivity1_ExecuteCode handler references the WorkflowInstanceId property of the workflow. This property is a Guid that uniquely identifies an executable instance of the workflow. When the CodeActivity executes, the identifier is written to the Console along with the input parameter.

Implementing a Simple Host Application

The host application for this example will be a Console application. This application will create an instance of the workflow runtime, subscribe to a few selected events, create and start multiple instances of the test workflow and display the results. To keep this example as simple as possible, no workflow services are used. The next example demonstrates the use of workflow services.

Create a new project and select the Sequential Workflow Console Application template. This creates a Console application that is capable of hosting the workflow runtime. Name the project ConsoleHosting. This project requires a project reference to the SharedWorkflows project implemented in the previous step. This reference is needed since a workflow is created based upon its Type. The workflow Type that this code will execute is found in the SharedWorkflows project.

Note You can delete the Workflow1.cs file from the ConsoleHosting project. This project is used as a workflow host only. It doesn't require a workflow of its own since you will be executing the test workflow from the SharedWorkflows project.

Listing 4-2 shows the complete `Program.cs` code that hosts the workflow runtime and executes the test workflow.

Listing 4-2. *Complete Program.cs File*

```
#region Using directives

using System;
using System.Collections.Generic;
using System.Threading;
using System.Workflow.Runtime;
using System.Workflow.Runtime.Hosting;

#endregion

namespace ConsoleHosting
{
    /// <summary>
    /// Simple workflow hosting
    /// </summary>
    public class Program : IDisposable
    {
        private WorkflowRuntime _workflowRuntime;
        private AutoResetEvent _waitHandle = new AutoResetEvent(false);
        private String _result = String.Empty;

        public Program()
        {
            InitializeWorkflowRuntime();
        }

        public String Result
        {
            get { return _result; }
            set { _result = value; }
        }
```

The code begins by defining several instance variables. The _workflowRuntime variable is an instance of the WorkflowRuntime class. This class is the public proxy to the actual workflow runtime engine and provides a way for the host application to interact with the runtime engine. The _waitHandle variable is an AutoResetEvent instance used to signal the completion of a workflow instance. The _result variable is a String that will be set to the value of the Result workflow property as each instance completes. The _result variable is exposed as a public property of the Program class so that the code in the Main method can access and display the value.

```
        #region IDisposable Members

        /// <summary>
        /// Dispose of the workflow runtime
        /// </summary>
        public void Dispose()
        {
            _workflowRuntime.StopRuntime();
            _workflowRuntime.Dispose();
        }
```

```
    #endregion

    /// <summary>
    /// Start the workflow runtime
    /// </summary>
    private void InitializeWorkflowRuntime()
    {
        _workflowRuntime = new WorkflowRuntime();
        _workflowRuntime.WorkflowCompleted
            += delegate(object sender, WorkflowCompletedEventArgs e)
            {
                //retrieve the output parameter value
                if (e.OutputParameters.ContainsKey("Result"))
                {
                    _result = (String)e.OutputParameters["Result"];
                }
                _waitHandle.Set();
            };
        _workflowRuntime.WorkflowTerminated
            += delegate(object sender, WorkflowTerminatedEventArgs e)
            {
                Console.WriteLine(e.Exception.Message);
                _waitHandle.Set();
            };

        //start execution of the runtime engine
        _workflowRuntime.StartRuntime();
    }
```

The InitializeWorkflowRuntime method is executed from the Program class constructor. This method is responsible for creating a WorkflowRuntime instance and subscribing to selected events of the class. The host application must create only a single instance of the WorkflowRuntime for each AppDomain. Most simple applications are implemented as a single AppDomain, so this restriction really means that a single WorkflowRuntime is created for an entire application.

The WorkflowCompleted event signals that a workflow has completed. In the handler code for the WorkflowCompleted event, the code captures the current value of the workflow's Result property. This event passes WorkflowCompletedEventArgs as the event arguments. The OutputParameters property of WorkflowCompletedEventArgs is a Dictionary of Object keyed by a String that contains the final values of all output workflow properties. Output properties are those that are readable and have a get statement in their property definition. In the test workflow, the InputString and Result properties are both considered output parameters and are found in the OutputParameters collection.

The event handlers for both of the events (WorkflowCompleted and WorkflowTerminated) set the _waitHandle variable to its signaled state. This signal notifies any waiting code that the workflow has completed.

After adding event handlers, the workflow runtime engine is started by calling the StartRuntime method. Calling this method isn't strictly required in this example since the runtime will automatically start when you create your first workflow. This example doesn't add any core workflow services, but if it did, they would be registered with the workflow runtime prior to calling the StartRuntime method.

The Program class also implements the IDisposable interface. Within the Dispose method, an orderly shutdown and disposal of the WorkflowRuntime instance takes place. Implementing IDisposable permits use of the using statement that ensures cleanup in the event of an error condition.

```
/// <summary>
/// Run the workflow
/// </summary>
/// <param name="wfArguments"></param>
public void RunWorkflow(Dictionary<String, Object> wfArguments,
    Type workflowType)
{
    //create the workflow instance and start it
    WorkflowInstance instance = _workflowRuntime.CreateWorkflow(
            workflowType, wfArguments);
    instance.Start();

    //wait for the workflow to complete
    _waitHandle.WaitOne();
}
```

The RunWorkflow method contains the code to create and start an instance of the test workflow. It is passed a Dictionary object containing any workflow parameters and a Type object that identifies the workflow to execute. The CreateWorkflow method of the WorkflowRuntime object is used to create an instance of the requested workflow. CreateWorkflow returns an instance of the WorkflowInstance class which contains properties and methods related to this single workflow instance.

When a workflow is first created, it does not immediately start execution. To begin execution of the workflow, the Start method is called on the instance object returned from the CreateWorkflow method.

After starting the workflow, the RunWorkflow method uses the _waitHandle variable to pause execution of the thread until the workflow has completed. When the Start method is called on the workflow instance, execution of the workflow begins on a separate thread managed by the workflow runtime engine. When the WorkflowCompleted or WorkflowTerminated events are raised, the handler code sets the _waitHandle variable to the signaled state and this code is release from its wait. With this arrangement, the RunWorkflow method simulates synchronous execution of the workflow. The calling code isn't aware that the actual workflow execution is asynchronous on a different thread.

```
static void Main(string[] args)
{
    using (Program instance = new Program())
    {
        //create a dictionary with input arguments
        Dictionary<String, Object> wfArguments
            = new Dictionary<string, object>();
        wfArguments.Add("InputString", "one");
        //run the workflow
        instance.RunWorkflow(wfArguments,
            typeof(SharedWorkflows.Workflow1));
        Console.WriteLine(instance.Result);

        wfArguments.Clear();
        wfArguments.Add("InputString", "two");
        instance.RunWorkflow(wfArguments,
            typeof(SharedWorkflows.Workflow1));
        Console.WriteLine(instance.Result);
```

```
                wfArguments.Clear();
                wfArguments.Add("InputString", "three");
                instance.RunWorkflow(wfArguments,
                    typeof(SharedWorkflows.Workflow1));
                Console.WriteLine(instance.Result);

                Console.WriteLine("Press any key to exit");
                Console.ReadLine();
            }
        }
    }
}
```

The static Main method of the application contains the code to execute the test workflow three times. It first creates an instance of the Program class, wrapping it within a using statement for safety. If any problems occur that interrupt the normal flow of control, the using statement will make sure Dispose is called on the Program object.

A Dictionary of Object keyed by a String is created and populated with the InputString parameter. The parameter name must exactly match the name of a writable workflow property. The RunWorkflow method of the Program class is now executed to create, start, and wait for completion of the workflow. The full Type name of SharedWorkflows.Workflow1 is specified since the code didn't previously add a using statement for the SharedWorkflows namespace. When the workflow completes, the value of the Result property is written to the Console.

When this test application is run, I see these results:

```
5858fb5e-b9f0-417d-8454-79a479c21a19 executing, parameter=one
5858fb5e-b9f0-417d-8454-79a479c21a19 result property
9f926ef4-a708-41f3-bc0f-c8e1083d4b66 executing, parameter=two
9f926ef4-a708-41f3-bc0f-c8e1083d4b66 result property
dbcb49da-5029-44d0-8a8c-576d31af3b99 executing, parameter=three
dbcb49da-5029-44d0-8a8c-576d31af3b99 result property
Press any key to exit
```

Your results will certainly be different since the Guid assigned to each workflow instance is designed to be globally unique. If you do happen to get these *exact* results, you might want to contact Microsoft immediately and tell them that they have a very big problem.

The results show that three separate instances of the workflow were executed. The workflow instances were executed sequentially, one at a time, and each instance received a different input parameter.

Evaluating the Approach

This approach to workflow hosting works, and it actually could be used if you have very limited workflow needs. But the code does have its share of problems and limitations. They include the following:

- The code to manage the workflow runtime and the workflow instances is completely embedded within the Program.cs file. This means it can't be easily reused by any other applications. The code doesn't provide a reusable and consistent way to manage workflows.

- The code is only designed to handle a single workflow at a time. It has the capability to wait for only a single workflow to complete. Because of this limitation, you must wait for one workflow instance to complete before starting another.

- In order to handle multiple workflow instances, you also need to solve the problem of output parameters. A single instance variable is used within the Program class to store the result of all workflows. To run multiple workflow instances, you need a way to keep the output from each workflow instance separate from the others.

- The output parameter to retrieve when a workflow instance completes (Result) is hard-coded in the WorkflowCompleted event handler. This means that only workflows of the same Type can be handled by this code.

- The event handling code only handles two of the workflow runtime events. Other event notifications may become important as your workflows become more sophisticated.

The next example provides a set of reusable classes that address many of these limitations.

Improved Workflow Hosting

The aim of this second example is to solve some of the workflow hosting problems and limitations of the prior example. This example implements a custom workflow manager class and a related workflow instance wrapper class. These classes encapsulate much of the code needed to host and interact with the workflow runtime. After implementing the manager classes, a host Console application is developed that uses them to execute the same test workflow used in the previous example.

Implementing the Workflow Instance Wrapper

The workflow manager classes should be packaged so that they are easily reusable by other projects. To do this, create a DLL assembly project, using the Empty Workflow Project template. In the example code that follows, I've named this project Bukovics.Workflow.Hosting. This assembly name implies a slightly larger scope than the other projects in this chapter. That's appropriate since it contains reusable classes that can be incorporated into other projects in this book, regardless of the chapter.

■**Note** The classes presented in this section are not quite ready for production use but are a good starting point. For instance, the manager class handles most of the workflow runtime events by raising its own event with a formatted message. The host application simply handles this event and writes this message to the Console. You might want to handle some of those events in a different way. However, these classes are a good starting point and represent a big improvement over the previous example.

The first class that you'll implement wraps the WorkflowInstance class provided by WF. The wrapper class is used to encapsulate each workflow instance, isolating its state from other instances. For example, the Program class instance variables used in the previous example (the wait handle and the output parameters) are moved into this wrapper. This is one small step toward supporting the execution of multiple workflows at the same time.

Add a new class to the Bukovics.Workflow.Hosting project and name it WorkflowInstanceWrapper. This is just an ordinary C# class, not a workflow class. The complete code for this class is shown in Listing 4-3 and discussed following the listing.

Listing 4-3. *Complete WorkflowInstanceWrapper.cs File*

```
using System;
using System.Threading;
using System.Collections.Generic;
using System.Workflow.Runtime;
```

```csharp
namespace Bukovics.Workflow.Hosting
{
    /// <summary>
    /// A container for a workflow instance
    /// </summary>
    [Serializable]
    public class WorkflowInstanceWrapper
    {
        private WorkflowInstance _workflowInstance;
        private ManualResetEvent _waitHandle = new ManualResetEvent(false);

        private Dictionary<String, Object> _outputParameters
            = new Dictionary<string, object>();
        private Exception _exception;
        private String _reasonSuspended = String.Empty;

        public WorkflowInstanceWrapper(WorkflowInstance instance)
        {
            _workflowInstance = instance;
        }

        #region Public Properties and Methods

        /// <summary>
        /// Get the workflow instance Id
        /// </summary>
        public Guid Id
        {
            get
            {
                if (_workflowInstance != null)
                {
                    return _workflowInstance.InstanceId;
                }
                else
                {
                    return Guid.Empty;
                }
            }
        }

        /// <summary>
        /// A collection of output parameters
        /// </summary>
        public Dictionary<String, Object> OutputParameters
        {
            get { return _outputParameters; }
            set { _outputParameters = value; }
        }

        /// <summary>
        /// A wait handle that the host application can use
        /// if it wants to halt processing until the
        /// workflow has completed.
        /// </summary>
```

```csharp
        public ManualResetEvent WaitHandle
        {
            get { return _waitHandle; }
            set { _waitHandle = value; }
        }

        /// <summary>
        /// An Exception object if one was thrown from the workflow
        /// </summary>
        public Exception Exception
        {
            get { return _exception; }
            set { _exception = value; }
        }

        /// <summary>
        /// A string that identifies the ReasonSuspended a workflow was
        /// suspended
        /// </summary>
        public String ReasonSuspended
        {
            get { return _reasonSuspended; }
            set { _reasonSuspended = value; }
        }

        /// <summary>
        /// The real workflow instance
        /// </summary>
        public WorkflowInstance WorkflowInstance
        {
            get { return _workflowInstance; }
        }

        /// <summary>
        /// Signal that the workflow has finished and the host
        /// application can stop waiting
        /// </summary>
        public void StopWaiting()
        {
            _waitHandle.Set();
        }

        #endregion
    }
}
```

The class defines several instance variables. The _workflowInstance variable is the
WorkflowInstance that is passed into the constructor. It represents the real workflow instance that
this class is wrapping. A ManualResetEvent is also defined as an instance variable. This wait handle is
used to signal the completion of this workflow instance. This code uses a ManualResetEvent for this
purpose instead of the AutoResetEvent used in the prior example. In that example, AutoResetEvent is
used because the same variable is used to signal the completion of each workflow instance. This

class will wrap only a single workflow instance so the `ManualResetEvent` is appropriate. Once this wait handle is signaled at the completion of a workflow, there is no need to reset it.

Three other instance variables are defined in order to record the workflow result. The `_outputParameters` variable is a `Dictionary` that will contain the value of any output parameters when the workflow completes normally. The `_exception` and `_reasonSuspended` variables will be used if the workflow terminates abnormally or is suspended.

These variables are all exposed as public properties, along with the wait handle, the `WorkflowInstance`, and a property that returns the `Guid` ID of the workflow instance. The `StopWaiting` public method is also provided to set the wait handle to a signaled state.

Implementing the Workflow Manager Class

The next class that you will implement is the workflow manager. Its purpose is to handle the major interactions with the actual `WorkflowRuntime` instance. It doesn't replace the `WorkflowRuntime` class. Instead, it helps you to interact with it in a consistent way by taking over many of the mundane workflow management tasks. Routine tasks such as creating and starting a workflow are handled by this class. As a `WorkflowInstance` object is returned from the `CreateWorkflow` method of `WorkflowRuntime`, it is wrapped in a `WorkflowInstanceWrapper` and added to a `Dictionary` keyed by the workflow instance ID.

This class also contains event handlers for the `WorkflowRuntime` events. When a workflow completes or terminates, the handler code finds the `WorkflowInstanceWrapper` in the collection and sets the output parameters, the exception, or the suspension reason. Doing this saves the results, good or bad, from the workflow, making them available for use by the host application.

To create this class, add another class to the `Bukovics.Workflow.Hosting` project and name it `WorkflowRuntimeManager`. The complete code for this class is shown in Listing 4-4.

Listing 4-4. *Complete WorkflowRuntimeManager.cs File*

```
using System;
using System.Collections.Generic;
using System.Threading;
using System.Workflow.Runtime;

namespace Bukovics.Workflow.Hosting
{
    /// <summary>
    /// A wrapper class to manage workflow creation
    /// and workflow runtime engine events
    /// </summary>
    public class WorkflowRuntimeManager : IDisposable
    {
        private WorkflowRuntime _workflowRuntime;
        private Dictionary<Guid, WorkflowInstanceWrapper> _workflows
            = new Dictionary<Guid, WorkflowInstanceWrapper>();

        /// <summary>
        /// Constructor
        /// </summary>
        /// <param name="instance"></param>
```

```
        public WorkflowRuntimeManager(WorkflowRuntime instance)
        {
            _workflowRuntime = instance;
            if (instance == null)
            {
                throw new NullReferenceException(
                    "A non-null WorkflowRuntime instance is required");
            }

            //subscribe to all workflow runtime events
            SubscribeToEvents(instance);
        }
```

The class defines two instance variables. The _workflowRuntime variable holds a reference
to the WorkflowRuntime instance that is passed in to the constructor. The _workflows variable is a
Dictionary of WorkflowInstanceWrapper objects keyed by the workflow instance Guid. Both of these
variables are also exposed as public properties.

During construction, the SubscribeToEvents method is executed to add handlers for the
WorkflowRuntime events.

```
        /// <summary>
        /// Create and start a workflow
        /// </summary>
        /// <param name="workflowType"></param>
        /// <param name="parameters"></param>
        /// <returns>A wrapped workflow instance</returns>
        public WorkflowInstanceWrapper StartWorkflow(Type workflowType,
            Dictionary<String, Object> parameters)
        {
            WorkflowInstance instance = _workflowRuntime.CreateWorkflow(
                workflowType, parameters);
            WorkflowInstanceWrapper wrapper
                = AddWorkflowInstance(instance);
            instance.Start();
            return wrapper;
        }
```

The StartWorkflow method is used to create and start a workflow. This method expects two
arguments: the Type of the workflow to start and a Dictionary containing any input parameters.
The WorkflowInstance that is returned from the CreateWorkflow method is wrapped in a
WorkflowInstanceWrapper by the AddWorkflowInstance private method. After constructing
a WorkflowInstanceWrapper, the AddWorkflowInstance method adds it to the Dictionary of workflows.

```
        #region Public properties and Events

        /// <summary>
        /// Get the WorkflowRuntime instance
        /// </summary>
        public WorkflowRuntime WorkflowRuntime
        {
            get { return _workflowRuntime; }
        }
```

```
/// <summary>
/// Get a Dictionary of workflow instance wrappers
/// </summary>
public Dictionary<Guid, WorkflowInstanceWrapper> Workflows
{
    get { return _workflows; }
}

/// <summary>
/// Event for logging messages from this class
/// </summary>
public event EventHandler<WorkflowLogEventArgs> MessageEvent;

#endregion
```

A public event named MessageEvent is also defined. This event is raised from the WorkflowRuntime event handlers. It is designed to pass a formatted String message to the host application. The host application can then choose to display the message on the Console or handle the message in some other way.

```
#region Workflow collection management

/// <summary>
/// Remove a single instance from the workflow Dictionary
/// </summary>
/// <param name="workflowId"></param>
public void ClearWorkflow(Guid workflowId)
{
    if (_workflows.ContainsKey(workflowId))
    {
        _workflows.Remove(workflowId);
    }
}

/// <summary>
/// Clear all workflows from the Dictionary
/// </summary>
public void ClearAllWorkflows()
{
    _workflows.Clear();
}

/// <summary>
/// Add a new workflow instance to the Dictionary
/// </summary>
/// <param name="instance"></param>
/// <returns>A wrapped workflow instance</returns>
private WorkflowInstanceWrapper AddWorkflowInstance(
    WorkflowInstance instance)
{
```

```
            WorkflowInstanceWrapper wrapper = null;
            if (!_workflows.ContainsKey(instance.InstanceId))
            {
                wrapper = new WorkflowInstanceWrapper(instance);
                _workflows.Add(wrapper.Id, wrapper);
            }
            return wrapper;
        }

        /// <summary>
        /// Find a workflow instance by Id
        /// </summary>
        /// <param name="workflowId"></param>
        /// <returns></returns>
        public WorkflowInstanceWrapper FindWorkflowInstance(Guid workflowId)
        {
            WorkflowInstanceWrapper result = null;
            if (_workflows.ContainsKey(workflowId))
            {
                result = _workflows[workflowId];
            }
            return result;
        }

        /// <summary>
        /// Wait for all workflow instances to complete
        /// </summary>
        /// <param name="msecondsTimeout"></param>
        public void WaitAll(Int32 msecondsTimeout)
        {
            if (_workflows.Count > 0)
            {
                WaitHandle[] handles = new WaitHandle[_workflows.Count];
                Int32 index = 0;
                foreach (WorkflowInstanceWrapper wrapper
                    in _workflows.Values)
                {
                    handles[index] = wrapper.WaitHandle;
                    index++;
                }
                WaitHandle.WaitAll(handles, msecondsTimeout, false);
            }
        }
    }

        #endregion
```

Also included are methods that maintain and reference the Dictionary of workflows. ClearWorkflow removes a single WorkflowInstanceWrapper from the Dictionary while ClearAllWorkflows removes all entries. The WaitAll method is used to suspend the current thread until all workflows have completed. Each WorkflowInstanceWrapper exposes a WaitHandle property so a host application can choose to wait for a single workflow or all workflows.

```
#region IDisposable Members

/// <summary>
/// Cleanup the workflow runtime
/// </summary>
public void Dispose()
{
    if (_workflowRuntime != null)
    {
        _workflowRuntime.StopRuntime();
        _workflowRuntime.Dispose();
    }
    ClearAllWorkflows();
}

#endregion
```

The class also implements IDisposable and performs an orderly shutdown of the WorkflowRuntime within the Dispose method.

```
#region Workflow Event Handling

/// <summary>
/// Subscribe to all events that we care about
/// </summary>
/// <param name="runtime"></param>
private void SubscribeToEvents(WorkflowRuntime runtime)
{
    runtime.Started
        += new EventHandler<WorkflowRuntimeEventArgs>(
            runtime_Started);
    runtime.Stopped
        += new EventHandler<WorkflowRuntimeEventArgs>(
            runtime_Stopped);
    runtime.WorkflowAborted
        += new EventHandler<WorkflowEventArgs>(
            runtime_WorkflowAborted);
    runtime.WorkflowCompleted
        += new EventHandler<WorkflowCompletedEventArgs>(
            runtime_WorkflowCompleted);
    runtime.WorkflowCreated
        += new EventHandler<WorkflowEventArgs>(
            runtime_WorkflowCreated);
    runtime.WorkflowIdled
        += new EventHandler<WorkflowEventArgs>(
            runtime_WorkflowIdled);
    runtime.WorkflowLoaded
        += new EventHandler<WorkflowEventArgs>(
            runtime_WorkflowLoaded);
    runtime.WorkflowPersisted
        += new EventHandler<WorkflowEventArgs>(
            runtime_WorkflowPersisted);
    runtime.WorkflowResumed
        += new EventHandler<WorkflowEventArgs>(
            runtime_WorkflowResumed);
```

```
    runtime.WorkflowStarted
        += new EventHandler<WorkflowEventArgs>(
            runtime_WorkflowStarted);
    runtime.WorkflowSuspended
        += new EventHandler<WorkflowSuspendedEventArgs>(
            runtime_WorkflowSuspended);
    runtime.WorkflowTerminated
        += new EventHandler<WorkflowTerminatedEventArgs>(
            runtime_WorkflowTerminated);
    runtime.WorkflowUnloaded
        += new EventHandler<WorkflowEventArgs>(
            runtime_WorkflowUnloaded);
}

void runtime_Started(object sender, WorkflowRuntimeEventArgs e)
{
    LogStatus(Guid.Empty, "Started");
}

void runtime_Stopped(object sender, WorkflowRuntimeEventArgs e)
{
    LogStatus(Guid.Empty, "Stopped");
}

void runtime_WorkflowCreated(object sender, WorkflowEventArgs e)
{
    LogStatus(e.WorkflowInstance.InstanceId, "WorkflowCreated");
}

void runtime_WorkflowStarted(object sender, WorkflowEventArgs e)
{
    LogStatus(e.WorkflowInstance.InstanceId, "WorkflowStarted");
}

void runtime_WorkflowIdled(object sender, WorkflowEventArgs e)
{
    LogStatus(e.WorkflowInstance.InstanceId, "WorkflowIdled");
}
```

Most of the WorkflowRuntime event handlers simply raise the MessageEvent so that the host application can display a message on the Console. One aim of this example is to demonstrate when these events are raised during a workflow's lifetime. Writing to the Console is an easy way to accomplish that. If you wish to turn this into real production code, you might perform other processing for some of these event handlers.

```
void runtime_WorkflowCompleted(object sender, WorkflowCompletedEventArgs e)
{
    LogStatus(e.WorkflowInstance.InstanceId, "WorkflowCompleted");
    WorkflowInstanceWrapper wrapper
        = FindWorkflowInstance(e.WorkflowInstance.InstanceId);
    if (wrapper != null)
    {
        wrapper.OutputParameters = e.OutputParameters;
        wrapper.StopWaiting();
    }
}
```

```
void runtime_WorkflowTerminated(object sender,
    WorkflowTerminatedEventArgs e)
{
    LogStatus(e.WorkflowInstance.InstanceId, "WorkflowTerminated");
    WorkflowInstanceWrapper wrapper
        = FindWorkflowInstance(e.WorkflowInstance.InstanceId);
    if (wrapper != null)
    {
        wrapper.Exception = e.Exception;
        wrapper.StopWaiting();
    }
}

void runtime_WorkflowSuspended(object sender, WorkflowSuspendedEventArgs e)
{
    LogStatus(e.WorkflowInstance.InstanceId, "WorkflowSuspended");
    WorkflowInstanceWrapper wrapper
        = FindWorkflowInstance(e.WorkflowInstance.InstanceId);
    if (wrapper != null)
    {
        wrapper.ReasonSuspended = e.Error;
    }
}

void runtime_WorkflowResumed(object sender, WorkflowEventArgs e)
{
    LogStatus(e.WorkflowInstance.InstanceId, "WorkflowResumed");
}

void runtime_WorkflowPersisted(object sender, WorkflowEventArgs e)
{
    LogStatus(e.WorkflowInstance.InstanceId, "WorkflowPersisted");
}

void runtime_WorkflowLoaded(object sender, WorkflowEventArgs e)
{
    LogStatus(e.WorkflowInstance.InstanceId, "WorkflowLoaded");
}

void runtime_WorkflowAborted(object sender, WorkflowEventArgs e)
{
    LogStatus(e.WorkflowInstance.InstanceId, "WorkflowAborted");
    WorkflowInstanceWrapper wrapper
        = FindWorkflowInstance(e.WorkflowInstance.InstanceId);
    if (wrapper != null)
    {
        wrapper.StopWaiting();
    }
}

void runtime_WorkflowUnloaded(object sender, WorkflowEventArgs e)
{
    LogStatus(e.WorkflowInstance.InstanceId, "WorkflowUnloaded");
}
```

Several of the key event handlers perform additional work. The WorkflowCompleted, WorkflowTerminated, and WorkflowAborted event handlers all signal that a workflow has completed by setting the state of the WaitHandle property. The WorkflowSuspended handler does not set the WaitHandle since it is assumed that you will eventually resume a workflow if you suspended it.

Since these same event handlers are executed for all workflow instances, the code must first find the correct WorkflowInstanceWrapper object in the collection of workflows. The WorkflowInstance.InstanceId property of the event arguments contains the Guid that uniquely identifies the workflow instance. Depending on which event handler is executed, a different property of the WorkflowInstanceWrapper is updated. For instance, if the WorkflowCompleted event is raised, the OutputParameters property is set. If WorkflowTerminated is raised, the Exception property is set to the Exception passed with the event.

```
private void LogStatus(Guid instanceId, String msg)
{
    if (MessageEvent != null)
    {
        String formattedMsg;
        if (instanceId == Guid.Empty)
        {
            formattedMsg = String.Format("Runtime - {0}", msg);
        }
        else
        {
            formattedMsg = String.Format("{0} - {1}", instanceId, msg);
        }

        //raise the event
        MessageEvent(this, new WorkflowLogEventArgs(formattedMsg));
    }
}

#endregion
}

/// <summary>
/// An EventArgs for logging a message from
/// the WorkflowRuntimeManager
/// </summary>
public class WorkflowLogEventArgs : EventArgs
{
    private String _msg = String.Empty;
    public WorkflowLogEventArgs(String msg)
    {
        _msg = msg;
    }

    public String Message
    {
        get { return _msg; }
    }
}
}
```

This is obviously much more code than you used in the previous example, and you haven't even implemented a workflow host application yet. What have you accomplished with all of this additional code? You have a workflow manager class that can start a workflow and also react to status changes for that workflow instance. When a workflow completes, the results of the workflow are associated with the correct workflow instance, making them available to the host application. All of this permits a host application to execute and manage multiple workflows at the same time. Best of all, this code is now reusable by multiple host applications. You no longer need to rewrite all of this code each time you need to execute a workflow.

Hosting with the Workflow Manager

To illustrate the use of the workflow manager classes, you can implement another `Console` application that executes the same test workflow as the previous examples. Create a new project, select the Sequential Workflow Console Application template, and name the project `ConsoleHostingManaged`. You'll need to add two additional assembly references to this project. First, you need a reference to the `SharedWorkflows` project that contains the test workflow. Second, add a reference to the `Bukovics.Workflow.Hosting` project that includes the workflow manager classes that you just developed.

■**Note** As in the previous example, you can delete the `Workflow1.cs` that is generated when you create the `ConsoleHostingManaged` project. This project is used as a workflow host only. It doesn't require a workflow of its own since you will be executing the test workflow from the `SharedWorkflows` project.

In addition to demonstrating the use of the workflow manager classes for workflow hosting, this application will also show you how to load one of the core workflow services (the persistence service). There are two different ways to load and register a runtime service that will be demonstrated. To make it easier to run the same workflow tests with slight variations, the code that executes the tests will be placed in its own class, instead of directly in the `Program.cs` file. The `Program.cs` file will only have a small amount of code that initiates the test.

■**Note** This example assumes that your development environment is already set up with the necessary database and persistence schema required by the `SqlWorkflowPersistenceService`. Please refer to the "Setup Steps for Persistence Testing" sidebar in this chapter for information on how to set up a test environment on your machine.

Add a new class (a normal C# class, not a workflow class) to the `ConsoleHostingManaged` project and name it `WorkflowTest`. The entire contents of this class are shown in Listing 4-5 and also available in the book's code download package.

Listing 4-5. *Complete WorkflowTest.cs File*

```
using System;
using System.Collections.Generic;
using System.Text;
using System.Workflow.Runtime;
using System.Workflow.Runtime.Hosting;

using Bukovics.Workflow.Hosting;
```

```
namespace ConsoleHostingManaged
{
    /// <summary>
    /// Workflow hosting using custom wrapper classes
    /// </summary>
    public class WorkflowTest
    {
        public static void Run()
        {
            Console.WriteLine("Running test with persistence service ");

            using (WorkflowRuntimeManager manager
                = new WorkflowRuntimeManager(new WorkflowRuntime()))
            {
                //add event handler to log messages from the manager
                manager.MessageEvent += delegate(
                    Object sender, WorkflowLogEventArgs e)
                {
                    Console.WriteLine(e.Message);
                };
```

The Run method is the method that will be executed from the static Main method of the application to execute the workflow tests. The method starts by creating an instance of the WorkflowRuntimeManager, protecting it with a using statement. When the using block goes out of scope, the Dispose method will be called on the WorkflowRuntimeManager object.

The WorkflowRuntimeManager constructor is passed a new instance of the WorkflowRuntime class. It was a conscious decision in the design of the WorkflowRuntimeManager class to construct the WorkflowRuntime externally like this. This provides additional flexibility since you may need to configure the workflow runtime before you pass it to the WorkflowRuntimeManager constructor.

An event handler is added for WorkflowRuntimeManager.MessageEvent. This event is raised when the manager class handles one of the WorkflowRuntime events. The code in this class simply logs the message to the Console.

```
                //add services to the workflow runtime before it is started
                AddServices(manager.WorkflowRuntime);

                //start the workflow runtime. It will also autostart if
                //we don't do it here.
                manager.WorkflowRuntime.StartRuntime();
```

After creating the WorkflowRuntime and its wrapper, the private AddServices method is executed to add any core workflow services to the runtime.

After adding any core workflow services, the StartRuntime method is called on the WorkflowRuntime. As the code comments indicate, this isn't strictly required since the workflow runtime will automatically start if this method call is omitted. While this method call isn't required, it is important to note that all core services must be added prior to starting the runtime engine. If you attempt to add a core service after calling this method (or automatically starting the runtime), an exception is thrown.

```
                //create a dictionary with input arguments
                Dictionary<String, Object> wfArguments
                    = new Dictionary<string, object>();
                wfArguments.Add("InputString", "one");
                //run the workflow
                manager.StartWorkflow(
                    typeof(SharedWorkflows.Workflow1), wfArguments);
```

Once the core services have been added and the runtime engine is up and running, it's time to run the test workflow. A Dictionary is created to pass input parameters to the workflow. After adding a value for the InputString parameter, the workflow is started using the StartWorkflow method of the WorkflowRuntimeManager class.

```
//run another instance with different parameters
wfArguments.Clear();
wfArguments.Add("InputString", "two");
manager.StartWorkflow(
    typeof(SharedWorkflows.Workflow1), wfArguments);

//run another instance with different parameters
wfArguments.Clear();
wfArguments.Add("InputString", "three");
manager.StartWorkflow(
    typeof(SharedWorkflows.Workflow1), wfArguments);
```

This example executes the workflow three times, just like the previous example. However, there is one major difference. The previous example runs one workflow at a time and waits for it to complete before starting the next workflow. Because this code uses the workflow manager class that you implemented, it can start all of the workflows at once and wait for them all to complete.

```
//wait for all workflow instances to complete
manager.WaitAll(15000);

//display the results from all workflow instances
foreach (WorkflowInstanceWrapper wrapper
    in manager.Workflows.Values)
{
    if (wrapper.OutputParameters.ContainsKey("Result"))
    {
        Console.WriteLine(wrapper.OutputParameters["Result"]);
    }
    else
    {
        //must be a problem - see if there is an exception
        if (wrapper.Exception != null)
        {
            Console.WriteLine("{0} - Exception: {1}",
                wrapper.Id, wrapper.Exception.Message);
        }
    }
}
manager.ClearAllWorkflows();
```

After starting all of the workflows, the WaitAll method of the WorkflowRuntimeManager is called. This suspends the current thread until all started workflow instances have completed (either successfully or not). Once all workflow instances have signaled that they are completed, the WaitAll method returns. The results of each workflow are then written to the Console.

```
    }
}
```

```
/// <summary>
/// Add any services needed by the runtime engine
/// </summary>
/// <param name="instance"></param>
private static void AddServices(WorkflowRuntime instance)
{
    String connStringPersistence = String.Format(
        "Initial Catalog={0};Data Source={1};Integrated Security={2};",
        "WorkflowPersistence", @"localhost\SQLEXPRESS", "SSPI");

    instance.AddService(
        new SqlWorkflowPersistenceService(connStringPersistence, true,
            new TimeSpan(0, 2, 0), new TimeSpan(0, 0, 5)));
}

    }
}
```

The AddServices method is responsible for adding a persistence service to the workflow runtime. The persistence service was chosen as an example because it aptly illustrates the general process used to add any of the core workflow services. If you need other services, you can add them here in a similar manner. Adding a service to the workflow runtime involves these two steps:

1. Create an instance of the service class, configuring it with constructor arguments or setting properties after construction.

2. Use the AddService method of the WorkflowRuntime class to register it.

■**Note** This example does not teach you everything you need to know about workflow persistence. You can refer to Chapter 8 for more information on this subject. The workflow persistence service is used here only to demonstrate how to use a workflow service. The steps outlined here for adding the persistence service apply equally to the other services. All of the core workflow services provided with WF are covered in detail in their respective chapters.

Each service class may have a different set of arguments used to construct an instance of the class. In this case, the SqlWorkflowPersistenceService is passed these parameters:

- ConnectionString: This is a SQL Server connection string that identifies the server and database used to persist and retrieve workflows.

- UnloadOnIdle: This is a Boolean that indicates whether workflows should be unloaded when they become idle.

- InstanceOwnershipDuration: This is a TimeSpan that indicates how long a workflow runtime instance maintains ownership of a workflow instance. It is primarily used in environments where you have a farm of multiple workflow hosts that all work with the same persistence store.

- LoadingInterval: This is a TimeSpan that determines how often the persistence service polls for idled workflows that are ready to be reloaded.

SETUP STEPS FOR PERSISTENCE TESTING

Several examples in this chapter use the `SqlWorkflowPersistenceService` to demonstrate how to add core services to the workflow runtime. The `SqlWorkflowPersistenceService` is a core service provided with WF that persists workflows and uses SQL Server as its data store. The service assumes that SQL Server is available either locally on your development machine or elsewhere on a local network. It further assumes that a database has already been created with an expected schema and a set of expected stored procedures.

Follow the steps outlined here to set up your test environment prior to executing any tests that use the SQL persistence service:

1. If you haven't already done so, install either the full or Express version of SQL Server 2005. The examples in this chapter use a local copy of SQL Server Express. SQL Server Express is distributed with Visual Studio and is also freely downloadable from Microsoft. Optionally, you may also want to download a free copy of SQL Server Management Studio Express from Microsoft. This is a utility that allows you to easily manage databases and objects within a database. It isn't absolutely necessary, but it does make the job of managing SQL Server much easier. The following steps use the `sqlcmd` command-line utility that is distributed with SQL Server. If you have optionally installed SQL Server Management Studio Express, you can use it instead of `sqlcmd` to execute the SQL commands and scripts.

2. Create a local database to use for workflow persistence. You can do this using the `sqlcmd` command-line utility. Open a Windows command prompt and enter this command (don't forget to replace "`localhost\SQLEXPRESS`" with your own server name if necessary):

   `sqlcmd -S `**`localhost\SQLEXPRESS`**` -E -Q "create database WorkflowPersistence"`

   This creates a local database named `WorkflowPersistence` using the default settings for a new database.

3. Now that you have a database, you need to populate it with the tables and stored procedures that the `SqlWorkflowPersistenceService` expects. The SQL scripts to create these objects are distributed with the WF runtime and are located in this directory:
   `[`*`WindowsFolder`*`]\Microsoft.Net\Framework\v3.0\Windows Workflow Foundation\SQL\`
   `[`*`Language`*`]`. `[`*`WindowsFolder`*`]` is the actual folder where Windows is installed and `[`*`Language`*`]` is the language based on the regional settings of your machine. For my machine, it's `EN` for English. Within this folder, you'll see a number of SQL scripts including the two that you need for workflow persistence: `SqlPersistenceService_Schema.sql` and `SqlPersistenceService_Logic.sql`.

4. Using your open command prompt, switch to the directory where the SQL scripts are located. Now using `sqlcmd`, execute the first script like this (all entered on a single line):

   `sqlcmd -S `**`localhost\SQLEXPRESS`**` -E -d WorkflowPersistence`
   `    -i SqlPersistenceService_Schema.sql`

5. Execute `sqlcmd` again to create the stored procedures:

   `sqlcmd -S `**`localhost\SQLEXPRESS`**` -E -d WorkflowPersistence`
   `    -i SqlPersistenceService_Logic.sql`

If all of these steps succeed, a local database named `WorkflowPersistence` should be populated with the tables and stored procedures that are required for workflow persistence. The workflow persistence examples in this chapter assume that this is the database name and that it is available on the local instance of SQL Server Express (`localhost\SQLEXPRESS`). If you change the database or server name, you'll need to adjust the example code (`WorkflowTest.cs`) or `App.Config` file accordingly.

Running the Test

The only remaining task is to add code to the static `Main` method of the `Program.cs` file to execute the `Run` method of the `WorkflowTest` class. Listing 4-6 shows the complete code for `Program.cs`.

Listing 4-6. *Complete Program.cs File*

```
using System;

namespace ConsoleHostingManaged
{
    /// <summary>
    /// Test workflow hosting using custom wrapper classes
    /// </summary>
    public class Program
    {
        static void Main(string[] args)
        {
            WorkflowTest.Run();

            Console.WriteLine("Press any key to exit");
            Console.ReadLine();
        }
    }
}
```

When I run this test on my machine, I see these results:

```
Running test with persistence service
Runtime - Started
0aa6cdd0-7986-4ee9-9912-4916728f9a1d - WorkflowCreated
0aa6cdd0-7986-4ee9-9912-4916728f9a1d - WorkflowStarted
dc3eb854-439c-4c26-b6c3-df37495df52c - WorkflowCreated
dc3eb854-439c-4c26-b6c3-df37495df52c - WorkflowStarted
fe6d398b-2e53-4632-aaa3-4ee77b497157 - WorkflowCreated
fe6d398b-2e53-4632-aaa3-4ee77b497157 - WorkflowStarted
0aa6cdd0-7986-4ee9-9912-4916728f9a1d executing, parameter=one
dc3eb854-439c-4c26-b6c3-df37495df52c executing, parameter=two
0aa6cdd0-7986-4ee9-9912-4916728f9a1d - WorkflowIdled
0aa6cdd0-7986-4ee9-9912-4916728f9a1d - WorkflowPersisted
0aa6cdd0-7986-4ee9-9912-4916728f9a1d - WorkflowUnloaded
dc3eb854-439c-4c26-b6c3-df37495df52c - WorkflowIdled
dc3eb854-439c-4c26-b6c3-df37495df52c - WorkflowPersisted
dc3eb854-439c-4c26-b6c3-df37495df52c - WorkflowUnloaded
fe6d398b-2e53-4632-aaa3-4ee77b497157 executing, parameter=three
fe6d398b-2e53-4632-aaa3-4ee77b497157 - WorkflowIdled
fe6d398b-2e53-4632-aaa3-4ee77b497157 - WorkflowPersisted
fe6d398b-2e53-4632-aaa3-4ee77b497157 - WorkflowUnloaded
9dfa8627-4d60-4f7e-ac28-231808eecfab - WorkflowLoaded
403a0f19-0e58-4f40-83a0-d48eae2a44a2 - WorkflowLoaded
9dfa8627-4d60-4f7e-ac28-231808eecfab - WorkflowPersisted
9dfa8627-4d60-4f7e-ac28-231808eecfab - WorkflowCompleted
403a0f19-0e58-4f40-83a0-d48eae2a44a2 - WorkflowPersisted
403a0f19-0e58-4f40-83a0-d48eae2a44a2 - WorkflowCompleted
0aa6cdd0-7986-4ee9-9912-4916728f9a1d - WorkflowLoaded
0aa6cdd0-7986-4ee9-9912-4916728f9a1d - WorkflowPersisted
```

```
0aa6cdd0-7986-4ee9-9912-4916728f9a1d - WorkflowCompleted
dc3eb854-439c-4c26-b6c3-df37495df52c - WorkflowLoaded
fe6d398b-2e53-4632-aaa3-4ee77b497157 - WorkflowLoaded
dc3eb854-439c-4c26-b6c3-df37495df52c - WorkflowPersisted
dc3eb854-439c-4c26-b6c3-df37495df52c - WorkflowCompleted
fe6d398b-2e53-4632-aaa3-4ee77b497157 - WorkflowPersisted
fe6d398b-2e53-4632-aaa3-4ee77b497157 - WorkflowCompleted
0aa6cdd0-7986-4ee9-9912-4916728f9a1d result property
dc3eb854-439c-4c26-b6c3-df37495df52c result property
fe6d398b-2e53-4632-aaa3-4ee77b497157 result property
Runtime - Stopped
```

As was the case previously, your results will be different since the Guid values are globally unique. Looking at the results, you see that the Runtime Started event is first received. This corresponds to the call to the StartRuntime method.

Following this, the three workflows are created and started in rapid succession. If you follow all of the events for just a single workflow instance, you'll see that the events are raised in this order:

1. *Created*: The workflow instance is created.

2. *Started*: Execution of the workflow instance begins.

3. *Idled*: The workflow is not actively processing. Remember that the test workflow includes the DelayActivity with a short delay. When the delay starts, the workflow is no longer actively consuming the thread and enters this idled state.

4. *Persisted*: Since a persistence service is loaded, the workflow is persisted to the database when it goes into the idled state.

5. *Unloaded*: The UnloadOnIdle argument is set to true in the constructor of the persistence service. This causes the workflow to be unloaded from memory during the time it is idled.

6. *Loaded*: After the DelayActivity completes, the workflow is ready to be loaded back into memory by the persistence service. The next time the persistence service polls for workflows ready to be loaded, this instance is loaded.

7. *Persisted*: This event signals the removal of the workflow from the database.

8. *Completed*: The workflow finally completes.

From these results, it is clear that the three workflows are executing at the same time, with their events interspersed. Once all workflows complete, the Result property for each workflow is displayed. Finally, the Stopped event is raised when the WorkflowRuntimeManager goes out of scope and the Dispose method is called.

Configuring the Runtime with App.Config

The previous example demonstrates how to add core services to the workflow runtime in code. If you prefer, you can also configure workflow services declaratively with entries in the application configuration file (App.Config). The advantage to this approach is that you don't need to rebuild your application if you require a change to the service configuration.

A .NET application configuration file is an XML file that contains multiple configuration sections. Each section must conform to a schema that is defined by the configuration class associated with that section. For executable applications (those with an .exe extension), the application configuration file has the same name as the application with a .config suffix appended. For instance, the application configuration file for MyApp.exe would be MyApp.exe.config. Other hosting environments such as ASP.NET have their own set of configuration files such as Web.Config.

The basic configuration schema for the workflow runtime section looks like this:

```
<WorkflowRuntime Name="ApplicationName" >
  <CommonParameters>
      <!--Add parameters common to all services-->
  </CommonParameters>
  <Services>
      <!--Add core services here-->
  </Services>
</WorkflowRuntime>
```

This example builds upon the code from the previous ConsoleHostingManaged project, making just a few slight changes to the startup code of the host application. The same persistence service will be added to the workflow runtime. The only difference is the mechanism used to add it.

Adding the App.Config

To begin, add an application configuration file to the ConsoleHostingManaged project from the previous example. To do this, select the project in the Solution Explorer, then select Add New Item from the Project menu. Now select Application Configuration File and use the default name of App.Config.

■Note When a project is built, the App.Config file is renamed to correspond to the actual output file name. For example, for a project named MyApp.exe, the App.Config file is renamed to MyApp.exe.config in the output directory.

Listing 4-7 shows the App.Config entries that you need to add.

Listing 4-7. *App.Config for the ConsoleHostingManaged Project*

```
<?xml version="1.0" encoding="utf-8" ?>
<configuration>
  <configSections>
    <section name="WorkflowRuntime"
      type="System.Workflow.Runtime.Configuration.WorkflowRuntimeSection,
        System.Workflow.Runtime, Version=3.0.00000.0, Culture=neutral,
        PublicKeyToken=31bf3856ad364e35" />
  </configSections>
  <WorkflowRuntime Name="ConsoleHostingManaged" >
    <CommonParameters>
      <!--Add parameters common to all services-->
      <add name="ConnectionString"
           value="Initial Catalog=WorkflowPersistence;
             Data Source=localhost\SQLEXPRESS;
             Integrated Security=SSPI;" />
    </CommonParameters>
    <Services>
      <!--Add core services here-->
      <add type="System.Workflow.Runtime.Hosting.SqlWorkflowPersistenceService,
        System.Workflow.Runtime, Version=3.0.00000.0,
        Culture=neutral, PublicKeyToken=31bf3856ad364e35"
        UnloadOnIdle="true" LoadIntervalSeconds="5" />
    </Services>
```

```
    </WorkflowRuntime>
</configuration>
```

You first need to associate the `WorkflowRuntime` section with a class that is capable of processing that section. This is accomplished by adding the section element under `configSections`. The `WorkflowRuntimeSection` class (found in the `System.Workflow.Runtime.Configuration` namespace) is the class provided with WF for this purpose.

Next you add the `WorkflowRuntime` section. The `Name` attribute is set to `ConsoleHostingManaged` to match the project name. The `CommonParameters` element contains parameters that have global scope and are available for use by any core workflow services that you add. In this example, the `ConnectionString` parameter is added with the connection string to use for the persistence service.

Finally, the `Services` element contains a child element that adds the `SqlWorkflowPersistenceService`. Note the two additional attributes, `UnloadOnIdle` and `LoadIntervalSeconds`. These serve the same purpose as the overloaded constructor for this class used in the previous example.

Using the App.Config for Workflow Runtime Configuration

In the previous example, the code needed to configure the workflow runtime and execute a series of tests is all contained in a `WorkflowTest` class. To configure the runtime using an `App.Config` file instead, you need to make a few modifications to this code. Or you can make a copy of this class and modify the copy. In the example code that follows, I've chosen to make a copy of this class, rename it, and modify the copy. This allows me to do A/B comparisons between the two versions (with and without the `App.Config`).

Before you change any code, you need to add an additional assembly reference to the project. To load the configuration from an `App.Config` file, the `System.Configuration` assembly must be referenced by the project.

Copy the `WorkflowTest.cs` file and name the copy `WorkflowAppConfigTest.cs`. Remember to change the class name to match. The revised version of this code is shown in Listing 4-8.

Listing 4-8. *Complete WorkflowAppConfigTest.cs File*

```
using System;
using System.Collections.Generic;
using System.Text;
using System.Workflow.Runtime;
using System.Workflow.Runtime.Hosting;

using Bukovics.Workflow.Hosting;

//System.Configuration must be added as an assembly reference
//in order to load workflow service configuration from
//the App.Config file

namespace ConsoleHostingManaged
{
    /// <summary>
    /// Workflow hosting using custom wrapper classes and
    /// configuring the workflow runtime from the App.Config
    /// </summary>
    public class WorkflowAppConfigTest
    {
```

```
public static void Run()
{
    Console.WriteLine("Running test configured with App.Config");

    using (WorkflowRuntimeManager manager
        = new WorkflowRuntimeManager(
            new WorkflowRuntime("WorkflowRuntime")))
    {
        //add event handler to log messages from the manager
        manager.MessageEvent += delegate(
            Object sender, WorkflowLogEventArgs e)
        {
            Console.WriteLine(e.Message);
        };

        //start the workflow runtime. It will also autostart if
        //we don't do it here.
        manager.WorkflowRuntime.StartRuntime();

        //create a dictionary with input arguments
        Dictionary<String, Object> wfArguments
            = new Dictionary<string, object>();
        wfArguments.Add("InputString", "one");
        //run the workflow
        manager.StartWorkflow(
            typeof(SharedWorkflows.Workflow1), wfArguments);

        //run another instance with different parameters
        wfArguments.Clear();
        wfArguments.Add("InputString", "two");
        manager.StartWorkflow(
            typeof(SharedWorkflows.Workflow1), wfArguments);

        //run another instance with different parameters
        wfArguments.Clear();
        wfArguments.Add("InputString", "three");
        manager.StartWorkflow(
            typeof(SharedWorkflows.Workflow1), wfArguments);

        //wait for all workflow instances to complete
        manager.WaitAll(15000);

        //display the results from all workflow instances
        foreach (WorkflowInstanceWrapper wrapper
            in manager.Workflows.Values)
        {
            if (wrapper.OutputParameters.ContainsKey("Result"))
            {
                Console.WriteLine(wrapper.OutputParameters["Result"]);
            }
```

```
                else
                {
                    //must be a problem - see if there is an exception
                    if (wrapper.Exception != null)
                    {
                        Console.WriteLine("{0} - Exception: {1}",
                            wrapper.Id, wrapper.Exception.Message);
                    }
                }
            }
        }
        manager.ClearAllWorkflows();
    }
  }
 }
}
```

The most important change is highlighted in the code in Listing 4-8. The code now uses an over-loaded constructor for the `WorkflowRuntime` class that accepts the name of a configuration section. The `WorkflowRuntime` string literal corresponds to the name of the section you added to the `App.Config`. In addition to this change, the `AddServices` method (and the reference to it) have been removed since it is no longer needed.

Running the Test

To execute this test, you only have to modify one line in the `Program.cs` file. Just replace the call to `WorkflowTest.Run` with `WorkflowAppConfigTest.Run`. The revised `Program.cs` file is shown in Listing 4-9.

Listing 4-9. *Revised Program.cs File to Execute App.Config Test*

```
using System;

namespace ConsoleHostingManaged
{
    /// <summary>
    /// Test workflow hosting using custom wrapper classes
    /// </summary>
    public class Program
    {
        static void Main(string[] args)
        {
            WorkflowAppConfigTest.Run();

            Console.WriteLine("Press any key to exit");
            Console.ReadLine();
        }
    }
}
```

When I execute this on my machine, I see these results:

```
Running test configured with App.Config
Runtime - Started
bfb9df1c-7c89-4609-a70b-2155870751a9 - WorkflowCreated
bfb9df1c-7c89-4609-a70b-2155870751a9 - WorkflowStarted
bfb9df1c-7c89-4609-a70b-2155870751a9 executing, parameter=one
e662a9b8-0cfc-4ee0-8688-4f721f7109d0 - WorkflowCreated
e662a9b8-0cfc-4ee0-8688-4f721f7109d0 - WorkflowStarted
1060d8cb-764b-4100-81bb-556fe2bd5dd9 - WorkflowCreated
1060d8cb-764b-4100-81bb-556fe2bd5dd9 - WorkflowStarted
e662a9b8-0cfc-4ee0-8688-4f721f7109d0 executing, parameter=two
bfb9df1c-7c89-4609-a70b-2155870751a9 - WorkflowIdled
bfb9df1c-7c89-4609-a70b-2155870751a9 - WorkflowPersisted
bfb9df1c-7c89-4609-a70b-2155870751a9 - WorkflowUnloaded
1060d8cb-764b-4100-81bb-556fe2bd5dd9 executing, parameter=three
e662a9b8-0cfc-4ee0-8688-4f721f7109d0 - WorkflowIdled
e662a9b8-0cfc-4ee0-8688-4f721f7109d0 - WorkflowPersisted
e662a9b8-0cfc-4ee0-8688-4f721f7109d0 - WorkflowUnloaded
1060d8cb-764b-4100-81bb-556fe2bd5dd9 - WorkflowIdled
1060d8cb-764b-4100-81bb-556fe2bd5dd9 - WorkflowPersisted
1060d8cb-764b-4100-81bb-556fe2bd5dd9 - WorkflowUnloaded
bfb9df1c-7c89-4609-a70b-2155870751a9 - WorkflowLoaded
e662a9b8-0cfc-4ee0-8688-4f721f7109d0 - WorkflowLoaded
1060d8cb-764b-4100-81bb-556fe2bd5dd9 - WorkflowLoaded
bfb9df1c-7c89-4609-a70b-2155870751a9 - WorkflowPersisted
bfb9df1c-7c89-4609-a70b-2155870751a9 - WorkflowCompleted
e662a9b8-0cfc-4ee0-8688-4f721f7109d0 - WorkflowPersisted
e662a9b8-0cfc-4ee0-8688-4f721f7109d0 - WorkflowCompleted
1060d8cb-764b-4100-81bb-556fe2bd5dd9 - WorkflowPersisted
1060d8cb-764b-4100-81bb-556fe2bd5dd9 - WorkflowCompleted
bfb9df1c-7c89-4609-a70b-2155870751a9 result property
e662a9b8-0cfc-4ee0-8688-4f721f7109d0 result property
1060d8cb-764b-4100-81bb-556fe2bd5dd9 result property
Runtime - Stopped
Press any key to exit
```

The workflow instance Guid values are different, and the exact sequence of some of the workflow events are different. But overall, this test produces the same results. The persistence service is clearly being loaded and used since the WorkflowPersisted, WorkflowUnloaded, and WorkflowLoaded events are being raised.

Controlling a Workflow Instance

The WorkflowInstance class exposes a number of methods that allow you to manually interact with a workflow instance. For example, you can call the Suspend method to suspend a workflow, the Terminate method to terminate it, and so on. All you need to call these methods is a reference to the WorkflowInstance object for the workflow.

This next example illustrates several of these instance methods. It uses the same test workflow used in the previous examples and the same ConsoleHostingManaged project. To begin, copy the WorkflowAppConfigTest.cs file from the last example and name the copy InstanceMethodsTest.cs. Change the class name to match the new file name. Listing 4-10 shows the revised code for this file with some of the key changes highlighted.

Listing 4-10. *Complete InstanceMethodsTest.cs File*

```
using System;
using System.Collections.Generic;
using System.Text;
using System.Workflow.Runtime;
using System.Workflow.Runtime.Hosting;

using Bukovics.Workflow.Hosting;

namespace ConsoleHostingManaged
{
    /// <summary>
    /// Demonstrate methods of the WorkflowInstance
    /// </summary>
    public class InstanceMethodsTest
    {
        public static void Run()
        {
            Console.WriteLine("Running test of WorkflowInstance methods");

            using (WorkflowRuntimeManager manager
                = new WorkflowRuntimeManager(
                    new WorkflowRuntime("WorkflowRuntime")))
            {
                //add event handler to log messages from the manager
                manager.MessageEvent += delegate(
                    Object sender, WorkflowLogEventArgs e)
                {
                    Console.WriteLine(e.Message);
                };

                //start the workflow runtime. It will also autostart if
                //we don't do it here.
                manager.WorkflowRuntime.StartRuntime();

                //create a dictionary with input arguments
                Dictionary<String, Object> wfArguments
                    = new Dictionary<string, object>();
                wfArguments.Add("InputString", "one");
                //run the workflow
                WorkflowInstanceWrapper instance = manager.StartWorkflow(
                    typeof(SharedWorkflows.Workflow1), wfArguments);

                //manually terminate the workflow instance
                instance.WorkflowInstance.Terminate("Manually terminated");
                //wait for this instance to end
                instance.WaitHandle.WaitOne(10000, false);

                //run another instance with different parameters
                wfArguments.Clear();
                wfArguments.Add("InputString", "two");
```

```
        instance = manager.StartWorkflow(
            typeof(SharedWorkflows.Workflow1), wfArguments);
        //give the workflow time to start execution
        System.Threading.Thread.Sleep(1000);

        //suspend the workflow
        instance.WorkflowInstance.Suspend("Manually suspended");
        //now resume the workflow we just suspended
        instance.WorkflowInstance.Resume();
        //wait for the instance to end
        instance.WaitHandle.WaitOne(10000, false);

        //display the results from all workflow instances
        foreach (WorkflowInstanceWrapper wrapper
            in manager.Workflows.Values)
        {
            if (wrapper.OutputParameters.ContainsKey("Result"))
            {
                Console.WriteLine(wrapper.OutputParameters["Result"]);
            }
            //must be a problem - see if there is an exception
            if (wrapper.Exception != null)
            {
                Console.WriteLine("{0} - Exception: {1}",
                    wrapper.Id, wrapper.Exception.Message);
            }
            //was it suspended?
            if (wrapper.ReasonSuspended.Length > 0)
            {
                Console.WriteLine("{0} - Suspended: {1}",
                    wrapper.Id, wrapper.ReasonSuspended);
            }
        }
        manager.ClearAllWorkflows();
    }
  }
 }
}
```

The code starts and configures the WorkflowRuntime the same way as the prior example, loading the persistence service using the App.Config entries. This time only two workflows are executed. As each workflow is started by the StartWorkflow method, the returned WorkflowInstanceWrapper is saved in a local variable. The wrapper provides a WorkflowInstance property that the code uses to manually control the workflow instance.

Immediately after the first workflow is started, the code calls the Terminate method on it like this:

```
//manually terminate the workflow instance
instance.WorkflowInstance.Terminate("Manually terminated");
```

As the method name implies, this causes the workflow instance to immediately terminate. When a workflow is terminated, the WorkflowTerminated event is raised. This event passes a WorkflowTerminatedException in the Exception property of the WorkflowTerminatedEventArgs. The String passed to the Terminate method is used as the Exception message. The handler for this event in the WorkflowRuntimeManager class saves the Exception in the WorkflowInstanceWrapper. This allows the host application code to interrogate and use this Exception as it sees fit.

The code also illustrates how to wait for a single workflow instance instead of waiting for all instances at the same time. Here is the code that does this:

```
instance.WaitHandle.WaitOne(10000, false);
```

The second workflow is started in the normal way and allowed to begin execution for 1 second (Thread.Sleep blocks the current thread for 1000 milliseconds). The Suspend method is then called, immediately followed by the Resume method. It doesn't really make sense to immediately resume a workflow that you just suspended, but this does illustrate how these methods work. The Suspend method also allows you to pass a String describing the reason the workflow instance was suspended.

The section of code that displays the results of each workflow has been modified slightly. It now includes code that displays the ReasonSuspended property if it has been populated.

To execute this code, modify the Program.cs file in the project so that it executes the InstanceMethodsTest.Run method. The revised Program.cs code is shown in Listing 4-11.

Listing 4-11. *Revised Program.cs File for InstanceMethodsTest*

```
using System;

namespace ConsoleHostingManaged
{
    /// <summary>
    /// Test workflow hosting using custom wrapper classes
    /// </summary>
    public class Program
    {
        static void Main(string[] args)
        {
            InstanceMethodsTest.Run();

            Console.WriteLine("Press any key to exit");
            Console.ReadLine();
        }
    }
}
```

When I execute this code on my machine, I see these results:

```
Running test of WorkflowInstance methods
Runtime - Started
8a2933b3-d1e0-4499-9fab-a4261089957b - WorkflowCreated
8a2933b3-d1e0-4499-9fab-a4261089957b - WorkflowStarted
8a2933b3-d1e0-4499-9fab-a4261089957b - WorkflowPersisted
8a2933b3-d1e0-4499-9fab-a4261089957b - WorkflowTerminated
40919898-251a-4e7f-a228-8919468057db - WorkflowCreated
40919898-251a-4e7f-a228-8919468057db - WorkflowStarted
40919898-251a-4e7f-a228-8919468057db executing, parameter=two
40919898-251a-4e7f-a228-8919468057db - WorkflowIdled
40919898-251a-4e7f-a228-8919468057db - WorkflowPersisted
40919898-251a-4e7f-a228-8919468057db - WorkflowUnloaded
40919898-251a-4e7f-a228-8919468057db - WorkflowLoaded
40919898-251a-4e7f-a228-8919468057db - WorkflowSuspended
40919898-251a-4e7f-a228-8919468057db - WorkflowResumed
```

```
40919898-251a-4e7f-a228-8919468057db - WorkflowPersisted
40919898-251a-4e7f-a228-8919468057db - WorkflowCompleted
8a2933b3-d1e0-4499-9fab-a4261089957b - Exception: Manually terminated
40919898-251a-4e7f-a228-8919468057db result property
40919898-251a-4e7f-a228-8919468057db - Suspended: Manually suspended
Runtime - Stopped
Press any key to exit
```

The test results show that the first workflow instance was terminated as expected. The second workflow instance executed long enough for its CodeActivity to display a message, but was then suspended and immediately resumed. The final results display the Exception message from the terminated workflow and the result from the second workflow that completed. The suspended message is also shown for the second workflow.

You won't always need to directly take control of a workflow instance like this. But if you do need this capability, the WorkflowInstance methods are available.

Synchronous Workflow Execution

One of the core workflow services is the scheduler service. This service is responsible for thread management within the workflow runtime engine. If you don't load your own scheduler service, the DefaultWorkflowSchedulerService class is automatically loaded by the runtime. This default service executes workflows asynchronously using a thread pool.

If you would like to execute your workflows synchronously, you can override this default behavior by adding the ManualWorkflowSchedulerService to the runtime yourself. This is another scheduler service that is provided with WF. The difference is that this service uses the host application's thread for workflow execution.

To demonstrate the use of this service, create a new project, select the Sequential Workflow Console Application template, and name the project ConsoleManualScheduler. For this example, you will execute the same test workflow found in the SharedWorkflows project, so add a reference to that project now. You can delete the Workflow1.cs file generated by the project template since you won't need it.

Listing 4-12 contains the complete code that you will need for the Program.cs file.

Listing 4-12. *Complete Program.cs File*

```csharp
#region Using directives

using System;
using System.Collections.Generic;
using System.Workflow.Runtime;
using System.Workflow.Runtime.Hosting;
using System.Threading;

#endregion

namespace ConsoleManualScheduler
{
    /// <summary>
    /// Use the ManualWorkflowSchedulerService to
    /// synchronously execute a workflow
    /// </summary>
```

```
public class Program
{
    static void Main(string[] args)
    {
        using (WorkflowRuntime workflowRuntime = new WorkflowRuntime())
        {
            String wfResult = String.Empty;
            AutoResetEvent waitHandle = new AutoResetEvent(false);

            workflowRuntime.WorkflowCompleted
                += delegate(object sender, WorkflowCompletedEventArgs e)
                {
                    //retrieve the output parameter value
                    if (e.OutputParameters.ContainsKey("Result"))
                    {
                        wfResult = (String)e.OutputParameters["Result"];
                        waitHandle.Set();
                    }
                };
```

After creating an instance of the WorkflowRuntime, the code adds a handler for the
WorkflowCompleted event. Even though the code will be executing the workflow synchronously,
there is still a need for a WaitHandle (AutoResetEvent or ManualResetEvent) to signal the completion
of a workflow. That's because this particular workflow includes a DelayActivity. The need for
the WaitHandle is explained in more detail later in this section. You also need to handle the
WorkflowCompleted event in order to retrieve the Result property from the workflow when it completes.

```
            //add the manual scheduler service prior to
            //starting the workflow runtime. Use the constructor that
            //allows us to set the useActiveTimers to true.
            ManualWorkflowSchedulerService scheduler =
                new ManualWorkflowSchedulerService(true);
            workflowRuntime.AddService(scheduler);
            //start the workflow runtime
            workflowRuntime.StartRuntime();
```

Next, the alternate scheduler service is added to the workflow runtime. The constructor that is
used for the ManualWorkflowSchedulerService is the one that allows you to set a value for the
useActiveTimers parameter. If true is passed (as it is in this example), the scheduler service will use
one of its own internal timers to automatically reactivate a workflow if it includes a DelayActivity
(as this one does). If you pass false to the constructor instead, the scheduler service won't reactivate
the workflow automatically at the end of the delay. The host application would then be responsible
for resuming the workflow after the delay.

You don't have to explicitly call the StartRuntime method. However, it is called here to emphasize
that the scheduler service must be added prior to starting the workflow runtime.

```
                //create a dictionary with input arguments
                Dictionary<String, Object> wfArguments
                    = new Dictionary<string, object>();
                wfArguments.Add("InputString", "one");
```

```
//create the workflow instance
WorkflowInstance instance = workflowRuntime.CreateWorkflow(
    typeof(SharedWorkflows.Workflow1), wfArguments);
//indicate that it should execute when we provide a thread
instance.Start();
```

After creating a `Dictionary` containing the input parameter, an instance of the workflow is created. The `Start` method is called on the `WorkflowInstance` even though this doesn't actually start execution of the workflow. But it is necessary, otherwise the workflow instance will not be in the correct state and won't execute.

```
//run the workflow instance synchronously on our thread
scheduler.RunWorkflow(instance.InstanceId);


//since the workflow contains a DelayActivity, the RunWorkflow
//method will return immediately at the start of the delay.
//use the waitHandle to signal the actual completion of
//the workflow when the DelayActivity completes.
waitHandle.WaitOne(7000, false);
```

The `RunWorkflow` method is a blocking call since the workflow runtime is using the host application's thread to execute the workflow. When this call returns, the host code then waits for the `waitHandle` to be signaled. This marks the completion of the workflow once the `DelayActivity` has completed its delay. If the workflow did not include the `DelayActivity` (or if it was disabled), this additional wait would not be necessary.

```
//display the workflow result
Console.WriteLine(wfResult);

Console.WriteLine("Press any key to exit");
Console.ReadLine();
        }
    }
  }
}
```

When I execute this test on my machine, I see these results:

```
2a8e7a0c-f9e7-44ad-8ac8-0916a83bad50 executing, parameter=one
2a8e7a0c-f9e7-44ad-8ac8-0916a83bad50 result property
Press any key to exit
```

You can use the `ManualWorkflowSchedulerService` when your host environment is more suited to synchronous execution of workflows. For instance, this service is typically used when you host the workflow runtime within the ASP.NET environment.

Summary

The focus of this chapter was hosting the workflow runtime within your applications. The first example application demonstrated the basic requirements for workflow hosting. Following that, a set of workflow manager classes were developed to address some of the problems and limitations of the first example. These classes provide a reusable and consistent way to host the workflow runtime in your applications. Their design permits execution of multiple workflows at the same time by tracking workflow instances and associating the workflow results with the correct instance.

The examples in this chapter also demonstrated how to use several of the WorkflowRuntime events to track the status of each workflow instance. The WorkflowInstance class exposes several methods that permit you to take direct action with an instance of a workflow, and several of these methods were demonstrated in one of the chapter's examples.

Core workflow services can be added to the workflow runtime engine to modify the default behavior. This chapter included examples that loaded a persistence service in two different ways. First, the service was added in code, followed by an example that loaded the same service via the application configuration file. Another example illustrated the use of an alternate scheduler service. This alternate implementation permits synchronous execution of workflows.

In the next chapter, you'll learn how to control the flow of execution within a workflow using a number of the standard activities.

CHAPTER 5

■■■

Flow Control

One of the great advantages to workflows is that they enable you to declaratively control the flow of execution. No longer are you required to tightly couple the business logic (the *what* and *how*) with the flow control (the *when*). You can develop discrete, independent activities containing your reusable business logic and then knit them together using the flow control activities.

The purpose of this chapter is to present the flow control activities that are included with Windows Workflow Foundation (WF). Many of these activities permit you to define conditions that determine when an activity executes, so the chapter begins with a brief discussion of the two types of conditions: code and rule.

The IfElseActivity allows you to declare simple branching decisions within a workflow. The use of this activity is demonstrated with two example workflows. The first example is implemented with code conditions and the second uses rule conditions.

The WhileActivity provides the ability to repeatedly execute an activity while a condition is true. The ParallelActivity enables the definition of multiple branches of child activities with turn-based execution of each branch. The ReplicatorActivity is similar to the C# foreach statement, creating an instance of a child activity for each element in a collection of input data. This activity is useful when you need a data-driven workflow that can easily adapt and respond to the incoming data. This chapter includes a full discussion of each of these activities along with example workflows that demonstrate their use.

Also included is coverage of the ConditionedActivityGroup, a complex hybrid activity that exhibits some of the behavior of the WhileActivity and the ParallelActivity. The chapter concludes with a discussion of the InvokeWorkflowActivity, TerminateActivity, and SuspendActivity.

Condition Types

Many of the flow control activities can evaluate conditions that you define. Conditions come in two flavors: *code* and *rule*. Code conditions are implemented as a method in the workflow. The method must return a true or false value by setting the Result property of the ConditionalEventArgs that are passed to the method. Since they are implemented as code, the logic that evaluates to true or false is baked into the workflow. You can't modify it without rebuilding the workflow class. A code condition is represented in a workflow by an instance of the CodeCondition class (found in the System. Workflow.Activities namespace).

Rule conditions are declarative and are serialized to a separate .rules file as XML. Each .rules file is associated with an individual workflow. For example, for a code workflow named MyWorkflow, the code for the workflow is implemented in file MyWorkflow.cs and any associated rules are serialized as XML to file MyWorkflow.rules. A separate MyWorkflow.Designer.cs file contains the code that is maintained by the workflow designer.

Rule conditions are represented in a workflow by an instance of the `RuleConditionReference` class (found in the `System.Workflow.Activities.Rules` namespace). This class specifies the name of the `RuleCondition` to evaluate at runtime. Each rule condition must have a name that is unique within the workflow.

The main benefit to using a `RuleCondition` is that it is part of the workflow model, not the workflow implementation (the code). You can dynamically update rules at runtime without rebuilding any code.

■**Note** Declaring a simple `Boolean` condition is just one use of a general-purpose rules evaluation engine. In Chapter 11, you'll learn more about the capabilities of the rules engine that is included with WF. This rules engine can evaluate complex `RuleSet` objects containing multiple `Rule` objects.

How are code and rule conditions used in a workflow? Any activity that uses a condition implements a property of type `ActivityCondition`. Typically, the property name is `Condition`, but this is not a requirement. Examples of activities that implement the `Condition` property are `IfElseBranchActivity` and `WhileActivity`. Other activities, such as the `ReplicatorActivity`, use a different property name. The `CodeCondition` and `RuleConditionReference` classes are both direct descendents of `ActivityCondition`. This means that any activity that accepts a condition can use either a code or a rule condition.

■**Note** Some of the terminology used for rules and rule conditions is similar and confusing. In particular, the `RuleCondition`, `Rule`, and `RuleSet` classes are often confused. The `RuleCondition` is the class that is used in this chapter to define simple rule conditions. The `Rule` class includes a `RuleCondition` as well as other properties such as `ThenActions` and `ElseActions`. Those properties define what to do after evaluating a `RuleCondition`. A `RuleSet` is a collection of `Rule` objects that are evaluated together. Use of the `Rule` and `RuleSet` classes is discussed in Chapter 11.

Using the IfElseActivity

When you need to make simple branching decisions within your workflow, you will usually reach for the `IfElseActivity`. This is a composite activity that permits you to declare multiple conditional branches of execution within a workflow. Each conditional branch is represented by a child `IfElseBranchActivity` that defines a condition and any child activities you want executed when the condition is `true`.

Each `IfElseBranchActivity` is evaluated one at a time, starting with the leftmost branch. If the branch condition evaluates to `true`, the child activities defined within the branch are executed. If the condition is `false`, the next branch in order is evaluated, and so on. Once a branch evaluates to `true`, the activities defined in all other branches are bypassed and are not executed. At runtime, only one branch within an `IfElseActivity` is executed.

When you add an `IfElseActivity` to a workflow, two instances of the `IfElseBranchActivity` are automatically added. If you need additional branches, you can add them by first selecting the `IfElseActivity`, then selecting Add Branch from the Workflow or context-sensitive menu.

Each `IfElseBranchActivity` that defines a condition is similar to a C# `if` statement. The rightmost `IfElseBranchActivity` is not required to have a defined condition. If a final condition is omitted, this branch acts like a C# `else` statement, executing when no other conditions evaluate to `true`.

The workflow example that follows demonstrates how to use the IfElseActivity to make simple branching decisions. For comparison, the same workflow is implemented twice. First, it is implemented using code conditions, followed by the same workflow using rule conditions.

Using an IfElseActivity with Code Conditions

In this example, you will implement a sequential workflow that illustrates the use of the IfElseActivity using code conditions. The conditions will check the value of an input parameter to determine whether it is negative, positive, or exactly equal to zero. Each branch under the IfElseActivity uses a CodeActivity to write a message to the Console. When you execute this workflow, the messages will indicate which IfElseBranchActivity actually executed based on the value of the input parameter.

To implement a workflow, you first need to create a workflow project. Select the Empty Workflow Project template and name the project SharedWorkflows. This creates a DLL assembly that can be referenced by other projects. You will use this same project for all workflows in this chapter.

■**Tip** When you create a new project, Visual Studio will also prompt you to save a new solution. You can choose your own name for the solution, but it is generally easier to work with the examples in this chapter if you place all of them in a single Visual Studio solution.

Adding a Workflow Property

Add a new sequential workflow to the SharedWorkflows project and name it IfElseCodeWorkflow. Before you add any activities to the workflow, switch to code view and add the single property that is used as an input parameter to the workflow. For this example, use a dependency property instead of a normal C# property. The property is named TestNumber and is an Int32. Listing 5-1 shows the code for the IfElseCodeWorkflow.cs file after the property is added.

Listing 5-1. *IfElseCodeWorkflow.cs File with Input Property*

```
using System;
using System.ComponentModel;
using System.ComponentModel.Design;
using System.Collections;
using System.Drawing;
using System.Workflow.ComponentModel.Compiler;
using System.Workflow.ComponentModel.Serialization;
using System.Workflow.ComponentModel;
using System.Workflow.ComponentModel.Design;
using System.Workflow.Runtime;
using System.Workflow.Activities;
using System.Workflow.Activities.Rules;

namespace SharedWorkflows
{
    public sealed partial class IfElseCodeWorkflow : SequentialWorkflowActivity
    {
        public static DependencyProperty TestNumberProperty
            = System.Workflow.ComponentModel.DependencyProperty.Register(
                "TestNumber", typeof(Int32), typeof(IfElseCodeWorkflow));
```

```
[Description("A number to test")]
[Category("Flow Control")]
[Browsable(true)]
[DesignerSerializationVisibility(DesignerSerializationVisibility.Visible)]
public Int32 TestNumber
{
    get
    {
        return ((Int32)(base.GetValue(
            IfElseCodeWorkflow.TestNumberProperty)));
    }
    set
    {
        base.SetValue(IfElseCodeWorkflow.TestNumberProperty, value);
    }
}

public IfElseCodeWorkflow()
{
    InitializeComponent();
}

    }
}
```

Adding an IfElseActivity

After switching to the workflow designer view, drag and drop an IfElseActivity from the Toolbox to the workflow. Notice that two instances of the IfElseBranchActivity have been added for you. This initial view of the workflow is shown in Figure 5-1.

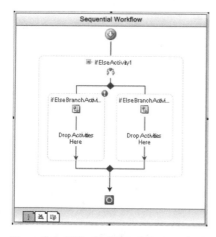

Figure 5-1. *IfElseCodeWorkflow with IfElseActivity*

For this example, you'll need an additional branch so go ahead and add it now. You can do this in several ways. You can select the parent ifElseActivity1, right-click, and select Add Branch from the context-sensitive menu. Or, after selecting ifElseActivity1, you can also select Add Branch from the Workflow menu. Finally, you can switch to the Properties window and select the Add Branch command at the bottom of the Properties window.

■**Tip** If you don't see the commands at the bottom of the Properties window, it is likely that the Commands option has been switched off. To enable this option, right-click anywhere in the Properties window and make sure the Commands option is checked.

Figure 5-2 shows the revised workflow with three `IfElseBranchActivity` branches.

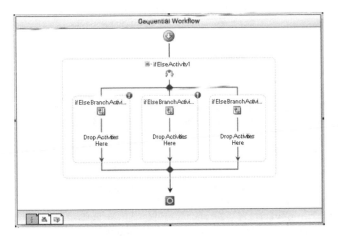

Figure 5-2. *IfElseCodeWorkflow with three branches*

Adding Code Conditions

Next, you will declare a code condition for the leftmost branch. Select `ifElseBranchActivity1` and switch to the Properties window. Under the `Condition` property, select Code Condition. Expand the `Condition` property and enter a name for your code condition handler. This will be the name of the method added to the workflow that implements the condition. This first condition will check the input parameter for a negative value so a `Condition` name of `CheckForNegative` is appropriate. Figure 5-3 shows the property window with the condition name entered.

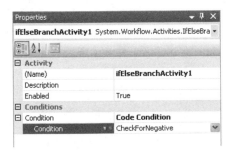

Figure 5-3. *Property window for CheckForNegative code condition*

From the code view, add code to the new CheckForNegative method that checks the input parameter (TestNumber) for a negative value. The code for this method looks like this:

```
private void CheckForNegative(object sender, ConditionalEventArgs e)
{
    e.Result = (TestNumber < 0);
}
```

The Boolean Result property of the ConditionalEventArgs is set to the result of this simple condition. This provides the Boolean result that the workflow runtime engine needs in order to determine whether to execute the child activities under this IfElseBranchActivity.

Add a similar code condition to ifElseBranchActivity2 (the middle branch). This condition will check the TestNumber for a positive value so name the code condition CheckForPositive. The code for this condition handler looks like this:

```
private void CheckForPositive(object sender, ConditionalEventArgs e)
{
    e.Result = (TestNumber > 0);
}
```

The last branch (ifElseBranchActivity3) doesn't need a code condition. It will act as the else condition if the first two branch conditions are false. In this example, if the TestNumber is not negative and is not positive then it must be equal to zero.

Adding Branch Activities

Now that you've defined the simple decisions that the workflow must make, you can add the activities that you wish to execute under each branch. After switching back to the workflow designer view, drag and drop one CodeActivity directly under each IfElseBranchActivity. These activities will execute code that writes a message to the Console to let you know which branch executed.

It's a good idea to rename each of these activities before you add the ExecuteCode handler for each activity. Otherwise, you'll end up with method names that don't describe their real purpose. Moving from left to right, use names of codeActivityIsNegative, codeActivityIsPositive, and codeActivityIsZero for the activities. Now add handlers for the ExecuteCode method of each CodeActivity by double-clicking each activity. Add code to each ExecuteCode handler to write an appropriate message to the Console. Listing 5-2 shows the additional code that you need to add to the IfElseCodeWorkflow.cs file, including the ExecuteCode handlers for each CodeActivity.

Listing 5-2. *Additional Code for the IfElseCodeWorkflow.cs File*

```
using System;
using System.ComponentModel;
using System.Workflow.ComponentModel;
using System.Workflow.Activities;

namespace SharedWorkflows
{
    public sealed partial class IfElseCodeWorkflow : SequentialWorkflowActivity
    {

    ...

        private void CheckForNegative(object sender, ConditionalEventArgs e)
        {
            e.Result = (TestNumber < 0);
        }
```

```csharp
        private void CheckForPositive(object sender, ConditionalEventArgs e)
        {
            e.Result = (TestNumber > 0);
        }

        private void codeActivityIsNegative_ExecuteCode(
            object sender, EventArgs e)
        {
            Console.WriteLine("TestNumber {0} is negative", TestNumber);
        }

        private void codeActivityIsPositive_ExecuteCode(
            object sender, EventArgs e)
        {
            Console.WriteLine("TestNumber {0} is positive", TestNumber);
        }

        private void codeActivityIsZero_ExecuteCode(
            object sender, EventArgs e)
        {
            Console.WriteLine("TestNumber {0} is zero", TestNumber);
        }
    }
}
```

Figure 5-4 shows the designer view of the completed workflow.

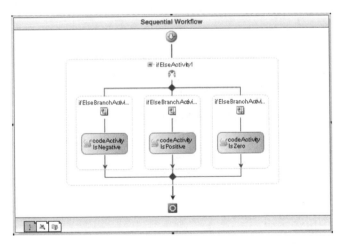

Figure 5-4. *Complete IfElseCodeWorkflow*

Testing the Workflow

To execute the `IfElseCodeWorkflow`, create a new project using the Sequential Workflow Console Application template. Name this project `ConsoleIfElse`. You can delete the `Workflow1.cs` file that is created with the new project since you won't need it. Add a reference to the `SharedWorkflows` project so that you can reference the example workflow.

In order to simplify the task of hosting the workflow runtime, this project will make use of the workflow manager classes developed in Chapter 4. These classes handle some of the mundane tasks associated with hosting the runtime. In that chapter, these classes are implemented in the Bukovics. Workflow.Hosting project. Add that project to this Visual Studio solution and add a reference to that project now.

Add a class named IfElseCodeTest to the ConsoleIfElse project. The code to execute the workflow goes into this class instead of directly into the Program.cs file. Listing 5-3 shows the complete code for the IfElseCodeTest.cs file.

Listing 5-3. *Complete IfElseCodeTest.cs File*

```
#region Using directives

using System;
using System.Collections.Generic;
using System.Text;
using System.Threading;
using System.Workflow.Runtime;
using System.Workflow.Runtime.Hosting;

using Bukovics.Workflow.Hosting;

#endregion

namespace ConsoleIfElse
{
    /// <summary>
    /// Execute IfElse workflow with Code conditions
    /// </summary>
    public class IfElseCodeTest
    {
        public static void Run()
        {
            using (WorkflowRuntimeManager manager
                = new WorkflowRuntimeManager(new WorkflowRuntime()))
            {
                Console.WriteLine("Executing IfElseCodeWorkflow");

                //create a dictionary with input arguments
                Dictionary<String, Object> wfArguments
                    = new Dictionary<string, object>();

                //run the first workflow
                wfArguments.Add("TestNumber", -100);
                manager.StartWorkflow(
                    typeof(SharedWorkflows.IfElseCodeWorkflow), wfArguments);

                //run the second workflow
                wfArguments.Clear();
                wfArguments.Add("TestNumber", +200);
                manager.StartWorkflow(
                    typeof(SharedWorkflows.IfElseCodeWorkflow), wfArguments);
```

```
            //run the third workflow
            wfArguments.Clear();
            wfArguments.Add("TestNumber", 0);
            manager.StartWorkflow(
                typeof(SharedWorkflows.IfElseCodeWorkflow), wfArguments);

            manager.WaitAll(2000);

            Console.WriteLine("Completed IfElseCodeWorkflow\n\r");
        }
    }
}
}
```

After initializing the WorkflowRuntime and creating an instance of the WorkflowRuntimeManager helper class, the code executes the IfElseCodeWorkflow three times. First it passes a negative number, then a positive number, and finally zero.

Note For a full description of the inner workings of the WorkflowRuntimeManager class, refer to Chapter 4.

The code in this test class is executed from the Program.cs file like this:

```
using System;

namespace ConsoleIfElse
{
    public class Program
    {
        static void Main(string[] args)
        {
            //execute the workflow tests
            IfElseCodeTest.Run();

            Console.WriteLine("Press any key to exit");
            Console.ReadLine();
        }
    }
}
```

When this project is built and executed, the results look like this:

```
Executing IfElseCodeWorkflow
TestNumber -100 is negative
TestNumber 200 is positive
TestNumber 0 is zero
Completed IfElseCodeWorkflow

Press any key to exit
```

The results are what you might expect to see from this workflow, proving that the IfElseActivity and the code conditions are executing properly.

Note Be aware that this example is starting all three instances of the workflow at the same time. Since they are executing asynchronously, there is no guarantee that they will complete in the same sequence in which they were started. It is possible that your workflows may complete in a different sequence, giving you slightly different results.

Using an IfElseActivity with Rule Conditions

Now that you have implemented this workflow using code conditions, you can try it again using rule conditions. This will demonstrate the difference between the two mechanisms to declare a condition.

To begin, add another sequential workflow to the SharedWorkflows project. This time name the workflow IfElseRuleWorkflow. Add the same dependency property for TestNumber to the workflow.

Adding Rule Conditions

Using the workflow designer, add the IfElseActivity (with the two initial IfElseActivityBranch instances) and the third IfElseActivityBranch as you did before. Select the ifElseBranchActivity1 (the one on the left side) and switch to the Properties window. This time, select Declarative Rule Condition for the Condition property. Expand the Condition property and enter a ConditionName of checkForNegative. You must provide a unique name for ConditionName since all conditions for a workflow are serialized to the same .rules file. Once a named condition has been added, you can reuse it by selecting it from the list of available conditions.

Select the ellipsis in the Expression property to bring up the Rule Condition Editor dialog. This dialog is where you enter the Rule condition. This first condition checks the TestNumber property for a negative value like this:

```
this.TestNumber < 0
```

Since the editor supports IntelliSense, entering **this** followed by a period causes the list of available workflow fields and properties to be displayed. You can then select the property that you wish to test (TestNumber) from the list.

Figure 5-5 shows the Rule Condition Editor with this condition already entered.

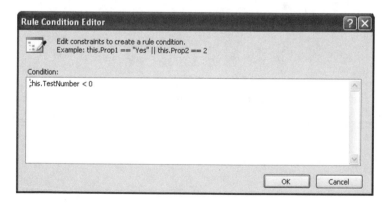

Figure 5-5. *Rule Condition Editor for ifElseActivityBranch1*

After selecting OK, the Property window should look like Figure 5-6.

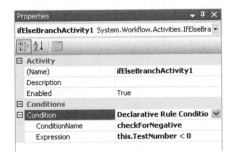

Figure 5-6. *Property window for ifElseActivityBranch1*

This condition is very simple, but you can build complex conditions using the standard set of relational, arithmetic, and logical operators. The supported operators are summarized in Table 5-1.

Table 5-1. *Supported Rule Condition Operators*

Operator	Supported Symbols
Equality	==, =
Greater than	>
Greater than or equal	>=
Less than	<
Less than or equal	<=
Logical and	&&, AND
Logical or	‖, OR
Logical not	!, NOT
Bitwise and	&
Bitwise or		
Addition	+
Subtraction	-
Multiplication	*
Division	/
Modulus	MOD
Operator precedence	(,)
Indexer	[,]

The indexer symbols ([,]) are used to reference variables that support an index such as a simple array or collection, for example

```
this.Field1Array[1] > 0
```

or

```
this.Field1Array[this.Field2] > 0
```

Tip You don't need to enter `If` in front of a condition. The `If` is implied and is flagged as an error by the Rule Condition Editor if you enter it.

Repeat these steps to enter a condition for the second branch (`ifElseBranchActivity2`). Name this condition `checkForPositive`. This condition checks the `TestNumber` property for a positive value like this:

```
this.TestNumber > 0
```

Adding Branch Activities

Finish the workflow by adding the three instances of `CodeActivity` to the workflow, adding `ExecuteCode` handlers, and adding the same code that writes messages to the `Console`.

The completed code for this workflow is shown in Listing 5-4.

Listing 5-4. *Complete IfElseRuleWorkflow.cs File*

```
using System;
using System.ComponentModel;
using System.Workflow.ComponentModel;
using System.Workflow.Activities;

namespace SharedWorkflows
{
    public sealed partial class IfElseRuleWorkflow : SequentialWorkflowActivity
    {
        public static DependencyProperty TestNumberProperty
            = System.Workflow.ComponentModel.DependencyProperty.Register(
                "TestNumber", typeof(Int32), typeof(IfElseRuleWorkflow));

        [Description("A number to test")]
        [Category("Flow Control")]
        [Browsable(true)]
        [DesignerSerializationVisibility(DesignerSerializationVisibility.Visible)]
        public Int32 TestNumber
        {
            get
            {
                return ((Int32)(base.GetValue(
                    IfElseRuleWorkflow.TestNumberProperty)));
            }
```

```
        set
        {
            base.SetValue(IfElseRuleWorkflow.TestNumberProperty, value);
        }
    }

    public IfElseRuleWorkflow()
    {
        InitializeComponent();
    }

    private void codeActivityIsNegative_ExecuteCode(
        object sender, EventArgs e)
    {
        Console.WriteLine("TestNumber {0} is negative", TestNumber);
    }

    private void codeActivityIsPositive_ExecuteCode(
        object sender, EventArgs e)
    {
        Console.WriteLine("TestNumber {0} is positive", TestNumber);
    }

    private void codeActivityIsZero_ExecuteCode(
        object sender, EventArgs e)
    {
        Console.WriteLine("TestNumber {0} is zero", TestNumber);
    }
  }
}
```

Testing the Workflow

You can test the rule condition version of the workflow using the code that you implemented in the last example. All that is required is one small change. Open the IfElseCodeTest.cs file in the ConsoleIfElse project and change all IfElseCodeWorkflow references to IfElseRuleWorkflow.

After building the solution, you should be able to execute the ConsoleIfElse project and see these results:

```
Executing IfElseRuleWorkflow
TestNumber -100 is negative
TestNumber 200 is positive
TestNumber 0 is zero
Completed IfElseRuleWorkflow

Press any key to exit
```

Using the WhileActivity

You use the WhileActivity when you want to repeatedly execute a child activity while a condition is true. It is very similar to the C# while statement. Just like the IfElseActivity, the condition can be specified using either a code or a rule condition.

The condition is evaluated prior to execution of the child activity. Therefore, it is possible to execute the child activity zero times if the condition is initially false. This is the same behavior as the C# while statement.

The WhileActivity only accepts a single child activity. On the surface, this appears to be a severe limitation. However, that single child activity may be a composite activity that contains children of its own. One activity that is typically used as a child of the WhileActivity is the SequenceActivity. The SequenceActivity is simply a container for child activities that are executed in order.

In the example that follows, you will create a simple workflow that demonstrates the use of the WhileActivity. This example also demonstrates the use of the SequenceActivity as a container for other child activities.

Implementing the Workflow

Add a new sequential workflow to the same SharedWorkflows project used in the previous examples in this chapter. Name the workflow WhileWorkflow. This workflow requires a single Int32 property named TestNumber, implemented as a dependency property. Listing 5-5 shows the WhileWorkflow.cs file after the property has been added.

Listing 5-5. *WhileWorkflow.cs File with Property Added*

```
using System;
using System.ComponentModel;
using System.Workflow.ComponentModel;
using System.Workflow.Activities;

namespace SharedWorkflows
{
    public sealed partial class WhileWorkflow : SequentialWorkflowActivity
    {
        public static DependencyProperty TestNumberProperty
            = System.Workflow.ComponentModel.DependencyProperty.Register(
                "TestNumber", typeof(Int32), typeof(WhileWorkflow));

        [Description("A number to test")]
        [Category("Flow Control")]
        [Browsable(true)]
        [DesignerSerializationVisibility(DesignerSerializationVisibility.Visible)]
        public Int32 TestNumber
        {
            get
            {
                return ((Int32)(base.GetValue(
                    WhileWorkflow.TestNumberProperty)));
            }
```

```
        set
        {
            base.SetValue(WhileWorkflow.TestNumberProperty, value);
        }
    }

    public WhileWorkflow()
    {
        InitializeComponent();
    }
  }
}
```

Adding the WhileActivity

After switching to the workflow designer view, drag and drop a WhileActivity on to the workflow. Figure 5-7 shows the workflow with the empty WhileActivity.

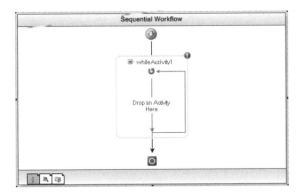

Figure 5-7. *WhileWorkflow with WhileActivity*

This WhileActivity will use a rule condition that checks the TestNumber property for a value greater than zero. This means that any activity that you add as a child of the WhileActivity will be repeatedly executed until the TestNumber property is less than or equal to zero. Add the rule condition by selecting whileActivity1, switching to the Properties window, and entering a condition with the properties shown in Table 5-2.

Table 5-2. *Condition for whileActivity1*

Property	Value
Condition	Declarative Rule Condition
ConditionName	checkIterationNumber
Expression	this.TestNumber > 0

Figure 5-8 shows the Properties window after the condition has been entered.

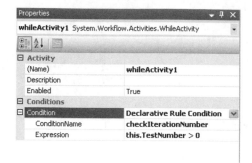

Figure 5-8. *Properties window for whileActivity1*

Adding Children with a SequenceActivity

The WhileActivity only accepts a single activity as a child. If you want to repeatedly execute more than one activity, you need to add a single activity that can contain other children. One such container is SequenceActivity. Drag and drop a SequenceActivity as a child of whileActivity1.

Now drag and drop two CodeActivity instances as children of the SequenceActivity. The first CodeActivity will write a message to the Console showing the current value of the TestNumber property. Name this activity codeWriteNumber. The second CodeActivity will decrement the TestNumber so that the WhileActivity condition is eventually false. Name this activity codeProcessIteration.

Add code handlers for each CodeActivity. The completed code for the WhileWorkflow.cs file is shown in Listing 5-6 with the latest changes highlighted.

Listing 5-6. *Complete WhileWorkflow.cs File*

```
using System;
using System.ComponentModel;
using System.Workflow.ComponentModel;
using System.Workflow.Activities;

namespace SharedWorkflows
{
    public sealed partial class WhileWorkflow : SequentialWorkflowActivity
    {
        public static DependencyProperty TestNumberProperty
            = System.Workflow.ComponentModel.DependencyProperty.Register(
                "TestNumber", typeof(Int32), typeof(WhileWorkflow));

        [Description("A number to test")]
        [Category("Flow Control")]
        [Browsable(true)]
        [DesignerSerializationVisibility(DesignerSerializationVisibility.Visible)]
        public Int32 TestNumber
        {
            get
            {
                return ((Int32)(base.GetValue(
                    WhileWorkflow.TestNumberProperty)));
            }
```

```
        set
        {
            base.SetValue(WhileWorkflow.TestNumberProperty, value);
        }
    }

    public WhileWorkflow()
    {
        InitializeComponent();
    }

    private void codeWriteNumber_ExecuteCode(
        object sender, EventArgs e)
    {
        Console.WriteLine("TestNumber is {0}", TestNumber);
    }

    private void codeProcessIteration_ExecuteCode(
        object sender, EventArgs e)
    {
        TestNumber--;  //decrement iteration count
    }
  }
}
```

Figure 5-9 shows the completed workflow in the designer view.

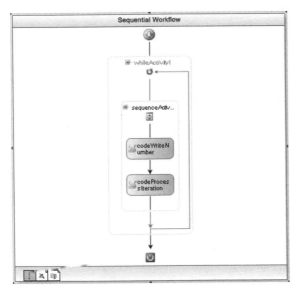

Figure 5-9. *Complete WhileWorkflow*

Testing the Workflow

Create a new project using the Sequential Workflow Console Application template and name the project ConsoleWhile. Add a reference to the SharedWorkflows and the Bukovics.Workflow.Hosting projects. Delete the Workflow1.cs file since it isn't required.

Add a new C# class to the ConsoleWhile project and name it WhileTest. The complete code for this class is shown in Listing 5-7.

Listing 5-7. *Complete WhileTest.cs File*

```csharp
#region Using directives

using System;
using System.Collections.Generic;
using System.Text;
using System.Threading;
using System.Workflow.Runtime;
using System.Workflow.Runtime.Hosting;

using Bukovics.Workflow.Hosting;

#endregion

namespace ConsoleWhile
{
    /// <summary>
    /// Execute workflow with WhileActivity
    /// </summary>
    public class WhileTest
    {
        public static void Run()
        {
            using (WorkflowRuntimeManager manager
                = new WorkflowRuntimeManager(new WorkflowRuntime()))
            {
                //create a dictionary with input arguments
                Dictionary<String, Object> wfArguments
                    = new Dictionary<string, object>();

                //run the first workflow
                Console.WriteLine("Executing WhileWorkflow Test 1");
                wfArguments.Add("TestNumber", 5);
                manager.StartWorkflow(
                    typeof(SharedWorkflows.WhileWorkflow), wfArguments);
                manager.WaitAll(2000);
                Console.WriteLine("Completed WhileWorkflow Test 1\n\r");

                //run the second workflow
                Console.WriteLine("Executing WhileWorkflow Test 2");
                wfArguments.Clear();
                wfArguments.Add("TestNumber", 0);
```

```
            manager.StartWorkflow(
                typeof(SharedWorkflows.WhileWorkflow), wfArguments);
            manager.WaitAll(2000);
            Console.WriteLine("Completed WhileWorkflow Test 2\n\r");
        }
    }
  }
}
```

This code uses the same pattern that should be familiar to you by now. After creating the WorkflowRuntime and the WorkflowRuntimeManager, it executes the WhileWorkflow twice. The first time it passes the number 5 as the TestNumber parameter. This should result in the child activities of the workflow executing five times. During each iteration, the handler for the CodeActivity will write the current value of the TestNumber property on the Console for you to see. The second workflow is passed a value of zero. This should result in the WhileActivity condition being initially false and the child activities not executed at all.

All that is left is to execute the static WhileTest.Run method from the Program.cs file like this:

```
using System;

namespace ConsoleWhile
{
    public class Program
    {
        static void Main(string[] args)
        {
            //execute the workflow tests
            WhileTest.Run();

            Console.WriteLine("Press any key to exit");
            Console.ReadLine();
        }
    }
}
```

When executed, the results look like this:

```
Executing WhileWorkflow Test 1
TestNumber is 5
TestNumber is 4
TestNumber is 3
TestNumber is 2
TestNumber is 1
Completed WhileWorkflow Test 1

Executing WhileWorkflow Test 2
Completed WhileWorkflow Test 2

Press any key to exit
```

As expected, the first workflow executes five times. Each time, the TestNumber property is decremented. The second workflow never executes the child activities since the rule condition for the WhileActivity is initially false.

Using the ParallelActivity

A ParallelActivity permits you to schedule two or more child branches for execution at the same time. Each branch of execution is represented by a child SequenceActivity. The SequenceActivity is the only activity allowed as a direct child of the ParallelActivity. The SequenceActivity is the container for any number and type of child activities that you wish to execute.

The ParallelActivity doesn't really execute multiple branches simultaneously. Each workflow instance executes on a single thread, so true parallel execution of multiple activities isn't possible. Instead of true parallel execution, the ParallelActivity coordinates execution of activities in each branch, giving each SequenceActivity a turn at execution. Once an activity in a branch executes, the next branch takes its turn. When that branch executes an activity, execution moves to the next branch, and so on. Once all branches have had a chance to execute, the process starts again with the first (leftmost) branch, executing the next activity in that branch (if there is one).

Each branch gets a turn at execution, but this doesn't mean that each branch always executes an activity. A branch may contain an activity that causes the execution of that branch to be delayed. For instance, a branch may be waiting on receipt of an external event, or may contain a DelayActivity. In this case, execution of the branch is bypassed and the next branch receives its turn. When execution returns to the waiting branch, the situation is evaluated once again. If the branch is no longer waiting, it takes its turn at execution. If it is still in a wait state, the branch loses its turn at execution and the next branch executes.

The actual execution sequence within a ParallelActivity is not guaranteed. Because an execution branch may be required to wait for an external event or a DelayActivity, the actual execution sequence is unpredictable.

■**Tip** When using a ParallelActivity, avoid designing workflows that rely on a particular order of execution for the child activities.

In the example that follows, you will create a workflow that demonstrates the use of the ParallelActivity. In a second example, you will modify the workflow by adding a DelayActivity. This illustrates the difference in execution order when a delay is introduced to one of the SequenceActivity branches within the ParallelActivity.

Implementing the Workflow

This example uses some standard activities that have already been discussed. It uses a WhileActivity in order to execute the ParallelActivity more than once. Executing the ParallelActivity more than once illustrates the behavior as activities in one branch complete prior to those in another branch. Like other examples, the CodeActivity is used to write messages to the Console.

You begin this example by adding a new sequential workflow to the SharedWorkflows project. This is the same project used throughout this chapter to house the workflows. Name the new workflow ParallelWorkflow. This workflow uses the now familiar TestNumber property (Int32) to control the number of iterations in a WhileActivity. Listing 5-8 shows the ParallelWorkflow.cs file after the TestNumber property is defined.

Listing 5-8. *ParallelWorkflow.cs File with Property Added*

```
using System;
using System.ComponentModel;
using System.Workflow.ComponentModel;
using System.Workflow.Activities;
```

```
namespace SharedWorkflows
{
    public sealed partial class ParallelWorkflow : SequentialWorkflowActivity
    {
        public static DependencyProperty TestNumberProperty
            = System.Workflow.ComponentModel.DependencyProperty.Register(
                "TestNumber", typeof(Int32), typeof(ParallelWorkflow));

        [Description("A number to test")]
        [Category("Flow Control")]
        [Browsable(true)]
        [DesignerSerializationVisibility(DesignerSerializationVisibility.Visible)]
        public Int32 TestNumber
        {
            get
            {
                return ((Int32)(base.GetValue(
                    ParallelWorkflow.TestNumberProperty)));
            }
            set
            {
                base.SetValue(ParallelWorkflow.TestNumberProperty, value);
            }
        }

        public ParallelWorkflow()
        {
            InitializeComponent();
        }

    }
}
```

Since this workflow includes a larger number of activities than previous examples, I'll show you what the completed workflow should look like first. This provides you with a visual guide to building the workflow. Figure 5-10 shows the completed ParallelWorkflow.

Using Figure 5-10 as a guide, drag and drop a WhileActivity onto the workflow. Set the condition for the WhileActivity using the properties shown in Table 5-3.

Table 5-3. *Condition for ParallelWorkflow whileActivity1*

Property	Value
Condition	Declarative Rule Condition
ConditionName	checkIterationCount
Expression	this.TestNumber > 0

Next, drag and drop a ParallelActivity as a child of the WhileActivity. The WhileActivity only accepts a single child activity and the ParallelActivity qualifies in that regard. When you add the ParallelActivity, the two SequenceActivity instances are already created for you. Each one represents a separate branch of execution. If you need additional branches, you can add them by selecting the ParallelActivity and then choosing Add Branch from the Workflow or context menu.

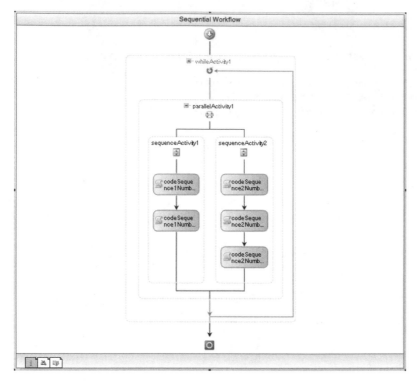

Figure 5-10. *Completed ParallelWorkflow*

Next, add the five CodeActivity instances shown in Figure 5-10. Add two instances to the left-side branch and three to the right side. Before you add any code handlers for the activities, rename them according to this list:

- codeSequence1Number1
- codeSequence1Number2
- codeSequence2Number1
- codeSequence2Number2
- codeSequence2Number3

The first two names apply to the CodeActivity instances under the left branch (sequence 1). The last three go on the right (sequence 2). As you will soon see, the activity names are important since you will write the names to the Console to observe their order of execution.

Four of these CodeActivity instances will share the same event handler for the ExecuteCode event. To add the common handler, select the first CodeActivity (codeSequence1Number1), switch to the Properties window, and enter commonCode_ExecuteCode as the handler name for the ExecuteCode property. Assign this same handler to three of the other CodeActivity instances by selecting it from the list of available handler methods.

One of the activities (it really doesn't matter which one) requires slightly different code in its handler. In the example code, I've chosen codeSequence1Number2 to receive its own ExecuteCode handler. You can create a handler for it by double-clicking the activity.

The code in both of the handler methods writes the activity name to the Console. When the workflow executes, you'll be able to determine the actual execution sequence based on these Console messages. In addition to writing the Console message, the code in the codeSequence1Number2 handler also decrements the TestNumber property. The WhileActivity condition checks this property prior to execution of the ParallelActivity. In this example, it doesn't matter which child activity decrements this property. As long as the property is decremented prior to the next iteration of the WhileActivity, the workflow should execute correctly.

The completed code for ParallelWorkflow.cs, including the ExecuteCode handlers, is shown in Listing 5-9.

Listing 5-9. *Complete ParallelWorkflow.cs File*

```
using System;
using System.ComponentModel;
using System.Workflow.ComponentModel;
using System.Workflow.Activities;

namespace SharedWorkflows
{
    public sealed partial class ParallelWorkflow : SequentialWorkflowActivity
    {
        public static DependencyProperty TestNumberProperty
            = System.Workflow.ComponentModel.DependencyProperty.Register(
                "TestNumber", typeof(Int32), typeof(ParallelWorkflow));

        [Description("A number to test")]
        [Category("Flow Control")]
        [Browsable(true)]
        [DesignerSerializationVisibility(DesignerSerializationVisibility.Visible)]
        public Int32 TestNumber
        {
            get
            {
                return ((Int32)(base.GetValue(
                    ParallelWorkflow.TestNumberProperty)));
            }
            set
            {
                base.SetValue(ParallelWorkflow.TestNumberProperty, value);
            }
        }

        public ParallelWorkflow()
        {
            InitializeComponent();
        }

        private void commonCode_ExecuteCode(object sender, EventArgs e)
        {
            Console.WriteLine(((Activity)sender).Name);
        }
```

```
        private void codeSequence1Number2_ExecuteCode(
            object sender, EventArgs e)
        {
            Console.WriteLine(((Activity)sender).Name);
            TestNumber--;
        }
    }
}
```

Testing the Workflow

You can use a Console application to execute the ParallelWorkflow. To implement this application, create a new project using the Sequential Workflow Console Application template. Name the project ConsoleParallel. Add the usual references to the SharedWorkflows and Bukovics.Workflow.Hosting projects. Delete the Workflow1.cs file since it isn't needed.

Add a new class to the project and name it ParallelTest. Listing 5-10 shows the complete listing for the ParallelTest.cs file.

Listing 5-10. *Complete ParallelTest.cs File*

```
#region Using directives

using System;
using System.Collections.Generic;
using System.Workflow.Runtime;

using Bukovics.Workflow.Hosting;

#endregion

namespace ConsoleParallel
{
    /// <summary>
    /// Execute workflow with ParallelActivity
    /// </summary>
    public class ParallelTest
    {
        public static void Run()
        {
            using (WorkflowRuntimeManager manager
                = new WorkflowRuntimeManager(new WorkflowRuntime()))
            {
                //create a dictionary with input arguments
                Dictionary<String, Object> wfArguments
                    = new Dictionary<string, object>();
```

```
                //run the first workflow
                Console.WriteLine("Executing ParallelWorkfow");
                wfArguments.Add("TestNumber", 2);
                manager.StartWorkflow(
                    typeof(SharedWorkflows.ParallelWorkflow), wfArguments);
                manager.WaitAll(2000);
                Console.WriteLine("Completed ParallelWorkfow \n\r");
            }
        }
    }
}
```

This code executes the ParallelWorkflow passing it a value of 2 for the TestNumber parameter. This means the ParallelActivity and all of its child activities should execute twice.

To run this test, you need to execute the ParallelTest.Run static method from the Program.cs file like this:

```
using System;

namespace ConsoleParallel
{
    public class Program
    {
        static void Main(string[] args)
        {
            //execute the workflow tests
            ParallelTest.Run();

            Console.WriteLine("Press any key to exit");
            Console.ReadLine();
        }
    }
}
```

When executed, the results look like this:

```
Executing ParallelWorkfow
codeSequence1Number1
codeSequence2Number1
codeSequence1Number2
codeSequence2Number2
codeSequence2Number3
codeSequence1Number1
codeSequence2Number1
codeSequence1Number2
codeSequence2Number2
codeSequence2Number3
Completed ParallelWorkfow

Press any key to exit
```

The results clearly demonstrate the turn-based behavior of the ParallelActivity. The execution order is illustrated in Figure 5-11.

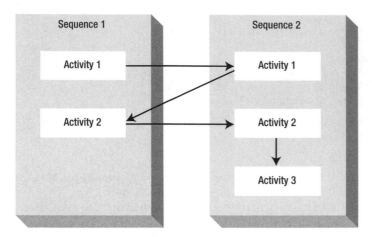

Figure 5-11. *ParallelWorkflow execution sequence*

The first activity in the first sequence is executed, followed by the first activity in the second sequence. Execution then returns to the first sequence with the second activity. The second activity in the second sequence then receives its turn. Finally, since the first sequence only has two activities, the third and final activity in the second sequence is executed.

All of those activities are executed during the first iteration of the WhileActivity. Since we passed a 2 as the TestNumber parameter, the WhileActivity processes the ParallelActivity one more time. The second iteration looks exactly like the first.

These results illustrate an important point. All branches of a ParallelActivity must reach completion before the activity is considered complete. In this example, the first sequence has only two child activities. Once that sequence finishes its work, it has to wait until the second sequence completes its final activity before starting again. Even though the ParallelActivity contains multiple branches of parallel execution, it is still viewed as a single activity by its parent activity.

Adding a DelayActivity

In this next example, you will make one small modification to the ParallelWorkflow just completed. You need to add a DelayActivity under the left-side SequenceActivity, between the two CodeActivity instances.

As its name indicates, the DelayActivity permits you to introduce an arbitrary time delay to a workflow. During a delay, the workflow (or in this case, one of the SequenceActivity branches) enters an idled state. The modified workflow is shown in Figure 5-12.

The purpose of the delay is to demonstrate its effect on the order of execution controlled by the ParallelActivity. Switch to the Properties window for the DelayActivity and set the TimeoutDuration property to **00:00:00.2** (two-tenths of a second). This should provide just enough of a delay to cause a slightly different order of execution.

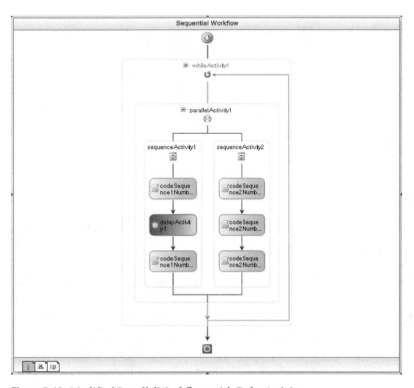

Figure 5-12. *Modified ParallelWorkflow with DelayActivity*

When you rebuild the solution and execute the workflow again, you should see these results:

```
Executing ParallelWorkflow
codeSequence1Number1
codeSequence2Number1
codeSequence2Number2
codeSequence2Number3
codeSequence1Number2
codeSequence1Number1
codeSequence2Number1
codeSequence2Number2
codeSequence2Number3
codeSequence1Number2
Completed ParallelWorkflow

Press any key to exit
```

The execution order for the modified workflow is illustrated in Figure 5-13.

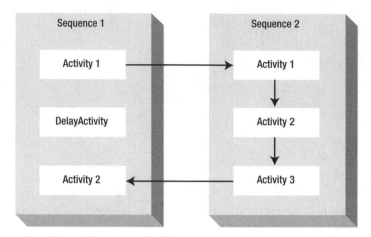

Figure 5-13. *ParallelWorkflow execution sequence with DelayActivity*

The order of execution starts just like the workflow version without the DelayActivity, executing the first activity for each sequence. At this point in the original workflow, the second activity for the first sequence is executed. However, in this version, the DelayActivity now executes. That delay causes execution to move to the next activity in the second sequence. The first sequence gave up its turn at execution since it was processing a delay. When the first sequence has another turn at execution, it is still in the middle of the delay. So once again, execution moves back to the second sequence, executing the third and final activity in that sequence. Finally, when the first sequence has a turn again, the last activity in that sequence executes.

Using the ReplicatorActivity

One of the most useful C# keywords is foreach. With its simple syntax, this little keyword enables you to easily iterate through the elements in an array or collection. Within the scope of the foreach statement, you define the code you wish to execute for each instance.

Windows Workflow Foundation provides a feature that is similar to foreach with the ReplicatorActivity. This activity creates and executes multiple copies of a single child activity. The child activity that you define is considered a template for each child instance that is created. The ReplicatorActivity is passed a collection of seed data to process in its InitialChildData property. The InitialChildData property is an IList, so any array or collection that implements IList can be the input of the ReplicatorActivity.

When the ReplicatorActivity executes, an instance of the template activity is cloned and executed for each element in the InitialChildData collection. There are several ways that a child activity can access the collection element that is associated with it. The examples that follow demonstrate two different ways to accomplish this. Figure 5-14 illustrates the behavior of the ReplicatorActivity.

The ReplicatorActivity supports two different modes of operation that you set with the ExecutionType property. An ExecutionType of Sequence means only one instance of a child activity is created and executed at any one time. Once that activity completes, the next instance is created, and so on. An ExecutionType of Sequence is the default if you don't set this property. If you set the ExecutionType to Parallel, the ReplicatorActivity creates all of the child instances at the same time and executes them in parallel. *Parallel* in this context means the same kind of execution you saw with the ParallelActivity, where activities each take their turn at execution. They don't actually execute at the same time on multiple threads.

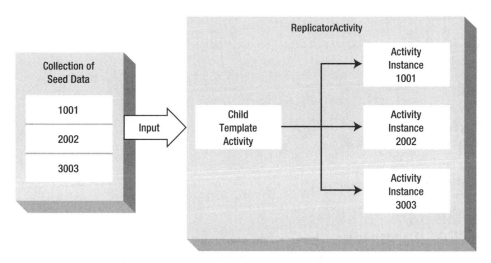

Figure 5-14. *Behavior of the ReplicatorActivity*

In the following examples, you will implement two workflows that use the ReplicatorActivity. The first example uses an ExecutionType of Sequence and demonstrates one way for a child activity to retrieve its data. The second example uses an ExecutionType of Parallel and demonstrates an alternate mechanism to access instance data using a custom activity.

Implementing the Sequence Workflow

This first example workflow uses a ReplicatorActivity with an ExecutionType of Sequence. To keep this workflow as simple as possible, a CodeActivity is used as the child of the ReplicatorActivity. A collection of strings is passed to the workflow as the seed data to be processed. Each instance of the CodeActivity that is created by the ReplicatorActivity processes one of the strings in the collection, writing the string to the Console.

■**Caution** The code presented in this example only works with an ExecutionType of Sequence. The reason for this is discussed in more detail in the comments following Listing 5-12.

Start the example by adding a new sequential workflow to the SharedWorkflows project. Name the new workflow ReplicatorWorkflow. Add a dependency property named InputList to the workflow. This property has a type of List<String> that is a generic List of type String. Listing 5-11 shows the ReplicatorWorkflow.cs file after the dependency property has been added.

Listing 5-11. *ReplicatorWorkflow.cs File with Dependency Property*

```
using System;
using System.ComponentModel;
using System.Workflow.ComponentModel;
using System.Workflow.Activities;
using System.Collections.Generic;
```

```
namespace SharedWorkflows
{
    public sealed partial class ReplicatorWorkflow : SequentialWorkflowActivity
    {
        public static DependencyProperty InputListProperty
            = System.Workflow.ComponentModel.DependencyProperty.Register(
                "InputList", typeof(List<String>), typeof(ReplicatorWorkflow));

        [Description("A list of strings to process")]
        [Category("Flow Control")]
        [Browsable(true)]
        [DesignerSerializationVisibility(DesignerSerializationVisibility.Visible)]
        public List<String> InputList
        {
            get
            {
                return ((List<String>)(base.GetValue(
                    ReplicatorWorkflow.InputListProperty)));
            }
            set
            {
                base.SetValue(ReplicatorWorkflow.InputListProperty, value);
            }
        }

        public ReplicatorWorkflow()
        {
            InitializeComponent();
        }

    }
}
```

Next, drag and drop a `ReplicatorActivity` onto the workflow. Switch to the Properties window and verify that the `ExecutionType` property is set to `Sequence`. This is the default. From the Properties window, bind the `InitialChildData` property to the `InputList` property of the workflow. You show the Bind Property dialog by double-clicking the Bind Property icon within the property. You can also select the ellipsis on the right side of the property. Once the dialog is shown, you select the workflow's `InputList` property as the binding target.

A `ReplicatorActivity` only accepts a single child activity. The child activity is a template for the activities that are cloned at runtime. An instance of this template activity is executed for each element in the `InitialChildData` collection. Drag and drop a `CodeActivity` as the only child of the `ReplicatorActivity`.

Double-click the `CodeActivity` to add a handler for the `ExecuteCode` event. The code that you will add to this handler should write one of the input strings to the `Console`. However, you must first identify which element in the collection is associated with the current instance of the `CodeActivity`.

This example demonstrates the first way that an activity can retrieve its input parameter from the collection. Listing 5-12 shows the completed `ReplicatorWorkflow.cs` with the additional code highlighted.

Listing 5-12. *Complete ReplicatorWorkflow.cs File*

```
using System;
using System.ComponentModel;
using System.Workflow.ComponentModel;
using System.Workflow.Activities;
using System.Collections.Generic;

namespace SharedWorkflows
{
    public sealed partial class ReplicatorWorkflow : SequentialWorkflowActivity
    {
        public static DependencyProperty InputListProperty
            = System.Workflow.ComponentModel.DependencyProperty.Register(
                "InputList", typeof(List<String>), typeof(ReplicatorWorkflow));

        [Description("A list of strings to process")]
        [Category("Flow Control")]
        [Browsable(true)]
        [DesignerSerializationVisibility(DesignerSerializationVisibility.Visible)]
        public List<String> InputList
        {
            get
            {
                return ((List<String>)(base.GetValue(
                    ReplicatorWorkflow.InputListProperty)));
            }
            set
            {
                base.SetValue(ReplicatorWorkflow.InputListProperty, value);
            }
        }

        public ReplicatorWorkflow()
        {
            InitializeComponent();
        }

        /// <summary>
        /// Handler for the CodeActivity that is replicated
        /// </summary>
        /// <param name="sender"></param>
        /// <param name="e"></param>
        private void codeActivity1_ExecuteCode(object sender, EventArgs e)
        {
            Object data = String.Empty;
            if (sender is Activity)
            {
```

```
        //retrieve the instance data from the parent activity
        if (((Activity)sender).Parent is ReplicatorActivity)
        {
            ReplicatorActivity rep
                = ((Activity)sender).Parent as ReplicatorActivity;
            data = rep.InitialChildData[rep.CurrentIndex];
        }
    }
    Console.WriteLine("CodeActivity instance data: {0}", data);
}
    }
}
```

When the codeActivity1_ExecuteCode executes for each instance of the CodeActivity, it retrieves its input data from the parent ReplicatorActivity. To do this it must execute several steps. First, notice that it uses the sender argument for this purpose instead of directly referencing the replicatorActivity1 from the workflow. In general, this is the pattern that you should use when referencing other activities, particularly when accessing child activities. For a complete explanation, refer to the sidebar "Accessing Activities in a Context-Safe Way" later in this chapter.

The sender in this case is the current instance of the CodeActivity. The code casts this as a generic Activity in order to reference its parent property as a ReplicatorActivity. The CurrentIndex property of the ReplicatorActivity is the index into the InitialChildData property. The index identifies the element in the collection that is associated with this instance of the CodeActivity.

This example works because the ExecutionType property of the ReplicatorActivity is set to Sequence. If you set it to Parallel instead, the workflow will not execute correctly. The reason for this is in the way child activities are created for the two ExecutionType values. When Sequence is used, child activities are created and executed one at a time. The CurrentIndex property is incremented as each child activity is created. Since the value of the CurrentIndex is always coordinated with the instance of the child activity, everything works correctly. On the other hand, when Parallel is used, all instances of the child activity are created immediately. By the time the first activity begins execution, the CurrentIndex has already been incremented to the last element in the InitialChildData collection. This would cause the CodeActivity handler to always reference the last element in the collection.

Figure 5-15 shows the complete ReplicatorWorkflow.

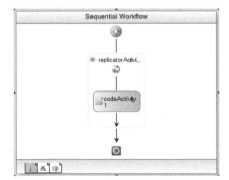

Figure 5-15. *Complete ReplicatorWorkflow*

Testing the Sequence Workflow

To test the workflow, create a new project using the Sequential Workflow Console Application template and name the project ConsoleReplicator. Add a reference to the SharedWorkflows and Bukovics.Workflow.Hosting projects and delete the Workflow1.cs file.

Add a new class to the project and name it ReplicatorTest. Listing 5-13 shows the complete listing for the ReplicatorTest.cs file.

Listing 5-13. *Complete ReplicatorTest.cs File*

```csharp
#region Using directives

using System;
using System.Collections.Generic;
using System.Workflow.Runtime;

using Bukovics.Workflow.Hosting;

#endregion

namespace ConsoleReplicator
{
    /// <summary>
    /// Execute workflow with ReplicatorActivity
    /// </summary>
    public class ReplicatorTest
    {
        public static void Run()
        {
            using (WorkflowRuntimeManager manager
                = new WorkflowRuntimeManager(new WorkflowRuntime()))
            {
                //create a dictionary with input arguments
                Dictionary<String, Object> wfArguments
                    = new Dictionary<string, object>();

                //create and populate a list of strings to process
                List<String> inputList = new List<string>();
                inputList.Add("one");
                inputList.Add("two");
                inputList.Add("three");
                wfArguments.Add("InputList", inputList);

                Console.WriteLine("Executing ReplicatorWorkflow");
                manager.StartWorkflow(
                    typeof(SharedWorkflows.ReplicatorWorkflow), wfArguments);
                manager.WaitAll(2000);
                Console.WriteLine("Completed ReplicatorWorkflow\n\r");
            }
        }
    }
}
```

The InputList parameter is defined as a List<String> that corresponds to the definition of the workflow property. Three strings are passed in this collection as test data. When the workflow is executed, three instances of the CodeActivity should be created and executed, with each one writing one of the strings to the Console.

To run this test, you need to execute the ReplicatorTest.Run static method from the Program.cs file like this:

```
using System;

namespace ConsoleReplicator
{
    public class Program
    {
        static void Main(string[] args)
        {
            //execute the workflow tests
            ReplicatorTest.Run();

            Console.WriteLine("Press any key to exit");
            Console.ReadLine();
        }
    }
}
```

When this test is executed, you should see these results:

```
Executing ReplicatorWorkflow
CodeActivity instance data:  one
CodeActivity instance data:  two
CodeActivity instance data:  three
Completed ReplicatorWorkflow

Press any key to exit
```

Implementing the Parallel Workflow

This second ReplicatorActivity example demonstrates using an ExecutionType of Parallel. When Parallel is used, all instances of the child activity are created immediately. As I already mentioned, the approach used in the previous example won't work when ExecutionType is set to Parallel. The problem is that you can no longer rely upon the CurrentIndex property to point to the correct element in the collection of input data.

This example demonstrates another way to provide the input parameter to each child activity instance. Instead of allowing each child instance to retrieve its own data, the code will pass the correct data element to the child as it is created. To accomplish this, the child activity must have a property that can accept the data to process. For this reason, this example uses a custom activity as the child of the ReplicatorActivity instead of a CodeActivity.

Implementing a Custom Activity

To begin this example, add a new activity to the SharedWorkflows project and name it ConsoleMessageActivity. This is the custom activity that writes a message to the Console. Change the base class from SequenceActivity to Activity since this example doesn't require a composite activity.

This activity requires one property named Message that is of type String. This property will be set to the correct value as the activity is created by the ReplicatorActivity. You also need to override the Execute method and add code to write the Message property to the Console. The complete code for the ConsoleMessageActivity.cs file is shown in Listing 5-14.

Listing 5-14. *Complete ConsoleMessageActivity.cs File*

```csharp
using System;
using System.ComponentModel;
using System.Workflow.ComponentModel;

namespace SharedWorkflows
{
    public partial class ConsoleMessageActivity : Activity
    {
        public static DependencyProperty MessageProperty
            = System.Workflow.ComponentModel.DependencyProperty.Register(
            "Message", typeof(string), typeof(ConsoleMessageActivity));

        [Description("A String message to write to the Console")]
        [Category("Flow Control")]
        [Browsable(true)]
        [DesignerSerializationVisibility(DesignerSerializationVisibility.Visible)]
        public string Message
        {
            get
            {
                return ((string)(base.GetValue(
                    ConsoleMessageActivity.MessageProperty)));
            }
            set
            {
                base.SetValue(ConsoleMessageActivity.MessageProperty, value);
            }
        }

        public ConsoleMessageActivity()
        {
            InitializeComponent();
        }

        protected override ActivityExecutionStatus Execute(
            ActivityExecutionContext executionContext)
        {
            //write the message
            if (Message != null)
            {
                Console.WriteLine(Message);
            }
            return base.Execute(executionContext);
        }

    }
}
```

■Tip It's a good idea to build the SharedWorkflows project at this point. Doing so will make sure that the custom activity builds correctly and that it is added to the Visual Studio Toolbox before you need to use it in a workflow.

Implementing the Workflow

Next, add a new sequential workflow to the SharedWorkflows project and name it ReplicatorParallelWorkflow. This workflow requires the same InputList property (List<String>) that you added to the last workflow (ReplicatorWorkflow).

Drag and drop a ReplicatorActivity onto the workflow. Bind the InitialChildData property to the InputList property of the workflow as you did in the previous example. For this example, you need to set the ExecutionType property of the ReplicatorActivity to Parallel.

The ReplicatorActivity exposes several events that are raised during execution. One event that this example uses is ChildInitialized. This event is raised during the creation of a child activity instance. This is your opportunity to pass the correct input data element to the child activity. Add a handler named replicatorActivity1_ChildInitialized to this event.

To make this example more interesting, drag and drop a SequenceActivity as the child of the ReplicatorActivity. Then add an instance of the custom ConsoleMessageActivity as the child of the SequenceActivity. There are no properties or event handlers you need to set for either of these activities. With the SequenceActivity in place, you could add any number of other child activities and all of them would be executed for each element in the input collection.

You could have successfully implemented the workflow with the ConsoleMessageActivity as the direct child of the ReplicatorActivity. The SequenceActivity is not really required and has been added for demonstration purposes only. Adding it complicates things just enough to make the code more interesting and realistic. Now, the child activity that is cloned is the SequenceActivity, not the custom ConsoleMessageActivity. This will have a direct effect on the code that follows.

The key to this workflow is the code that you need to add to the replicatorActivity1_ChildInitialized handler. This code, along with the complete ReplicatorParallelWorkflow.cs file, is shown in Listing 5-15.

Listing 5-15. *Complete ReplicatorParallelWorkflow.cs File*

```
using System;
using System.ComponentModel;
using System.Workflow.ComponentModel;
using System.Workflow.Activities;
using System.Collections.Generic;

namespace SharedWorkflows
{
    public sealed partial class ReplicatorParallelWorkflow :
        SequentialWorkflowActivity
    {
        public static DependencyProperty InputListProperty
            = System.Workflow.ComponentModel.DependencyProperty.Register(
                "InputList", typeof(List<String>),
                typeof(ReplicatorParallelWorkflow));
```

```csharp
        [Description("A list of strings to process")]
        [Category("Flow Control")]
        [Browsable(true)]
        [DesignerSerializationVisibility(DesignerSerializationVisibility.Visible)]
        public List<String> InputList
        {
            get
            {
                return ((List<String>)(base.GetValue(
                    ReplicatorParallelWorkflow.InputListProperty)));
            }
            set
            {
                base.SetValue(
                    ReplicatorParallelWorkflow.InputListProperty, value);
            }
        }

        public ReplicatorParallelWorkflow()
        {
            InitializeComponent();
        }

        /// <summary>
        /// Executed as each child activity instance is initialized
        /// </summary>
        /// <param name="sender"></param>
        /// <param name="e"></param>
        private void replicatorActivity1_ChildInitialized(
            object sender, ReplicatorChildEventArgs e)
        {
            //find the activity that needs the input string
            ConsoleMessageActivity cma = e.Activity.GetActivityByName(
                "consoleMessageActivity1", true) as ConsoleMessageActivity;
            //pass the input parameter to the child activity
            if (cma != null)
            {
                cma.Message = e.InstanceData as String;
            }
        }
    }
}
```

The ChildInitialized handler is executed as each instance of the child activity is created. The purpose of this code is to set the Message property of the custom ConsoleMessageActivity activity to the correct element of the input data collection. For our convenience, the InstanceData property of the ReplicatorChildEventArgs passes the data that should be associated with this instance.

The most interesting part of the code is the way it finds and references the ConsoleMessageActivity. First, it accesses the Activity property of the ReplicatorChildEventArgs. This property represents the root activity that has been cloned from the template. In this workflow, that is the SequenceActivity, not the ConsoleMessageActivity. The GetActivityByName method of the Activity is called to retrieve the ConsoleMessageActivity instance by its name (consoleMessageActivity1). The second parameter of this method is passed true to limit the search of activities to the current activity. Passing false would search for the activity globally within the entire scope of the workflow.

You might think that you could simply access the consoleMessageActivity1 workflow variable instead of all of these steps. After all, it represents the ConsoleMessageActivity that you want to execute, right? It is, but it is only a template for the real child activities that are cloned from this template. Setting a property on this template activity will only affect the next instance that is created from the template, not the current one. The proper way to reference the current child activity in this event handler is to go through the Activity property of the ReplicatorChildEventArgs. This references the activity in a context-safe way. For more information on execution contexts and their importance, refer to the sidebar "Accessing Activities in a Context-Safe Way" in the next section.

The completed ReplicatorParallelWorkflow is shown in Figure 5-16.

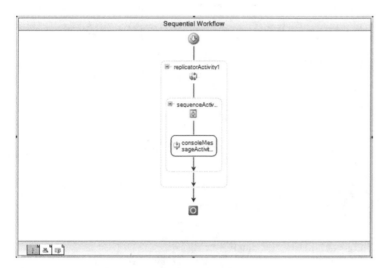

Figure 5-16. *Complete ReplicatorParallelWorkflow*

Testing the Parallel Workflow

To test the ReplicatorParallelWorkflow, you can modify the existing ReplicatorTest.cs file in the ConsoleReplicator project. Just change all ReplicatorWorkflow references to ReplicatorParallelWorkflow and rebuild the project. When you execute the ConsoleReplicator application, the results should look like this:

```
Executing ReplicatorParallelWorkflow
one
two
three
Completed ReplicatorParallelWorkflow

Press any key to exit
```

ACCESSING ACTIVITIES IN A CONTEXT-SAFE WAY

WF includes several looping activities that process child activities multiple times. These include the ReplicatorActivity, the WhileActivity, and the ConditionedActivityGroup. These activities appear to execute the same child activity over and over again, but the truth is they don't. Instead, they create a clone of the original child activity and execute the clone.

Every activity runs within an execution context. The context is simply an execution environment that contains one or more activities. The context determines the set of parent and child activities that you can safely reference. The execution context is represented in code by the ActivityExecutionContext class. An instance of this class is passed to many of the Activity methods such as Execute.

Understanding that there is an execution context becomes important when using one of these looping activities. In particular, you need to be aware of the execution context when writing event handler code within the workflow class itself. Why? This is a problem because code in the workflow class has access to the variables that represent the child activities. This isn't the case when writing code in a custom activity class. When you are writing code in the workflow class, you might be tempted to directly reference these local variables. You need to resist that temptation.

To illustrate this, consider the ReplicatorParallelWorkflow example in this chapter. The workflow class includes a variable named consoleMessageActivity1, which refers to the ConsoleMessageActivity added to the workflow. This activity isn't a direct child of the workflow, but instead, the tree of activities looks like this:

```
replicatorParallelWorkflow
    replicatorActivity1
        sequenceActivity1
            consoleMessageActivity1
```

This workflow has event handler code for the ChildInitialized event that references the current instance of the ConsoleMessageActivity. The potential problem arises in this handler code. If you reference the consoleMessageActivity1 variable, you are referencing the activity that is part of this original tree of activities. Because the workflow is using the ReplicatorActivity, the consoleMessageActivity1 is simply a template activity. Modifying it will only change future instances of the activity as they are cloned. If it is your intent to modify the template, feel free to do so. But if your intent is to reference the current instance of the activity, this workflow variable won't help you at all.

To determine what the code should do within the ChildInitialized handler, you need to understand that the tree of activities now looks like this:

```
replicatorParallelWorkflow
    replicatorActivity1
        sequenceActivity1 (template A)
            consoleMessageActivity1 (template B)
        sequenceActivity1 (cloned instance A1)
            consoleMessageActivity1 (cloned instance B1)
```

Prior to calling the handler for the ChildInitialized event, the ReplicatorActivity clones its only direct child (sequenceActivity1). Since this is a deep clone, all children are also cloned (consoleMessageActivity1). The result is a brand-new instance of the SequenceActivity and ConsoleMessageActivity that I've labeled cloned instance A1 and B1. This cloned set of activities lives within a new execution context.

Now the real fun begins. How do you reference the B1 instance (the ConsoleMessageActivity) in order to set its Message property? The ChildInitialized event passes an instance of ReplicatorChildEventArgs that has an Activity property. This activity represents the root of the execution context. In this case, that's the cloned A1 instance of the SequenceActivity. You can now find the B1 instance that you really need in two different ways. The example code calls e.Activity.GetActivityByName, passing in the name of the activity like this:

```
ConsoleMessageActivity cma = e.Activity.GetActivityByName(
    "consoleMessageActivity1", true) as ConsoleMessageActivity;
```

The second parameter value of `true` is also passed to the method to indicate that the activity search should only look within children of the current activity. You could also accomplish the same thing using this code:

```
ConsoleMessageActivity cma
    = ((SequenceActivity)e.Activity).Activities[0]
        as ConsoleMessageActivity;
```

If you replaced `e.Activity` with `this` in this code, you would incorrectly reference the original template activity (template A) instead of the newly cloned instance (A1).

Be aware that when the `SequenceActivity` is cloned, its `Parent` property doesn't change. The parent of the cloned activity (A1) is still `replicatorActivity1`. This allows you to use the `Parent` property as you normally would without any changes in behavior.

This discussion focuses on the `ReplicatorActivity` example and the `ChildInitialized` event handler. But you will see this same behavior in the other looping activities. Any time you are using one of these activities, you should be mindful of the execution context.

Using ReplicatorActivity Events

The `ReplicatorActivity` exposes several useful events that you may want to handle, depending on your needs. The most useful events are summarized in Table 5-4.

Table 5-4. *ReplicatorActivity Events*

Event	Description
Initialized	This event is raised as the `ReplicatorActivity` begins execution. This is a good place to perform any one-time initialization of the `ReplicatorActivity` or to set additional properties on the template child activity. Setting additional properties here will affect any instances of the child activity that are created later.
ChildInitialized	This event is raised immediately after a child activity is cloned and before it begins execution. This is your opportunity to pass data to an individual instance of the child activity.
ChildCompleted	This event is raised immediately after an instance of the child activity completes execution.
Completed	This event is raised when the `ReplicatorActivity` has completed execution.

Interrupting Execution

The `ReplicatorActivity` normally processes all elements in the `InitialChildData` collection, creating an instance of the child activity for each one. However, you can optionally define a condition that is capable of interrupting the normal execution of the child activities.

The `ReplicatorActivity` includes an `UntilCondition` property that you can define using a code or rule condition. This condition is checked when the `ReplicatorActivity` first begins execution, prior to the creation of any child activities. It is also checked again after each child activity completes.

If this condition evaluates to true, no further processing of activities takes place. No new child activities are created and any that might be executing are canceled. Think of this as a C# break statement that interrupts the normal operation of the foreach.

Because it is possible that not all child instances completed, the ReplicatorActivity provides the AllChildrenComplete property. A value of true for this property indicates that all child instances completed.

Using the ConditionedActivityGroup

The ConditionedActivityGroup (sometimes called the *CAG*) is a composite activity that enables the construction of fairly complex workflows. It is really a hybrid activity, exhibiting some of the behavior of a ParallelActivity and a WhileActivity.

You use the ConditionedActivityGroup by adding one or more child activities that you wish to execute. Like the ParallelActivity, child activities are executed from left to right and each child activity is given a turn at execution. If the child is a composite, only one of its children is executed during any given turn.

Each child activity can optionally declare a WhenCondition. This can be a code or rule condition that determines whether the child activity should execute. If a condition is defined and it evaluates to true, the child is executed once during its next turn. The child activity will continue to execute once during its turn until the WhenCondition evaluates to false. If no WhenCondition is defined, the child activity is executed only once.

The WhenCondition is evaluated when the CAG first begins execution, and also each time one of its direct child activities completes. Because the conditions are evaluated over and over again, it is possible for the actions of one child to have an impact on the condition for another child. For example, the condition for the first child may initially evaluate to false. But a subsequent child may modify a workflow variable or property that is used in the first child's condition. When the conditions are evaluated again, the change in variable or property value may cause the first child to execute.

The ConditionedActivityGroup also supports an optional UntilCondition. Like the other condition properties, this can be a code or a rule condition. If defined, this property specifies a condition that causes the CAG to end execution early. If the UntilCondition is not defined, the CAG completes when all of its children have completed and no WhenCondition evaluates to true. With the UntilCondition defined, the CAG will end when the UntilCondition is true, or when all child activities have completed normally.

Implementing the Workflow

To demonstrate the use of the ConditionedActivityGroup, the example that follows implements an overly simplified fast food ordering workflow. A collection of items that have been ordered is passed in as a workflow parameter. Each element in the collection represents an item that has been ordered. The assumption is that each kind of item (sandwich, fries, drink, combo) requires different processing that will be handled by a different child activity.

The workflow doesn't know the quantity of each item that has been ordered, so that's where the looping behavior of the CAG comes into play. The WhenCondition for each child activity looks for a particular kind of food item (sandwich, fries, drink, combo). The individual child activities may be executed more than once, depending on their conditions. As each item is processed, it is removed from the collection of items. The CAG completes when there are no more items in the collection that require processing.

The combo item is unique since it actually represents the combination of a sandwich, fries, and a drink. The activity code for this kind of item actually adds a sandwich, fries, and a drink to the collection of items. This processes the combo item by exploding it into its individual line items. This nicely illustrates the behavior of the CAG, since adding these new items to the collection causes the conditions of the other child activities to evaluate to true, resulting in new items for them to process.

To start this example, add a new sequential workflow to the SharedWorkflows project and name the new workflow CAGWorkflow. Add a property named LineItems to the workflow. This property has a type of List<String>, which is a generic List of type String.

■**Note** Unlike other examples in this chapter, this workflow defines LineItems as a standard C# property instead of a dependency property. The reason is simply to emphasize that you can use either type of property in a workflow. There are additional capabilities that are available to you if you use a dependency property, but this example doesn't require them. See Chapter 3 for a discussion of workflow properties.

Listing 5-16 shows the CAGWorkflow.cs file after the property is added.

Listing 5-16. *CAGWorkflow.cs File with LineItems Property*

```
using System;
using System.ComponentModel;
using System.Collections.Generic;
using System.Workflow.Activities;

namespace SharedWorkflows
{
    public sealed partial class CAGWorkflow : SequentialWorkflowActivity
    {
        private List<String> _lineItems;

        public List<String> LineItems
        {
            get { return _lineItems; }
            set { _lineItems = value; }
        }

        public CAGWorkflow()
        {
            InitializeComponent();
        }

    }
}
```

After switching to the workflow designer view, drag and drop a ConditionedActivityGroup to the workflow. Figure 5-17 shows the workflow with the empty CAG.

As you can see in Figure 5-17, the CAG is composed of two distinct sections. The top section is like a filmstrip that contains the list of child activities that have been added. This is where you drag and drop new activities, or select an existing activity for modification.

The bottom section of the CAG is a preview or edit area for the currently selected activity. By clicking the small button to the left of Previewing, you can switch back and forth between Previewing and Editing. If the child activity that you add is itself a composite activity, you will need to switch to Editing mode in order to add children to it. Once the composite activity is in Editing mode, you drag and drop new child activities onto the bottom section of the CAG to add them to the composite activity.

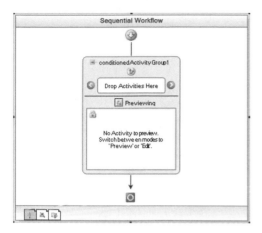

Figure 5-17. *Workflow with empty CAG*

Drag and drop four instances of the CodeActivity onto the top filmstrip area of the CAG. Each one of these activities corresponds to a kind of item to process (sandwich, fries, drink, combo). To keep the purpose of each activity clear, change the names of these activities to codeSandwich, codeFries, codeDrink, and codeCombo.

Each CodeActivity requires a different WhenCondition. When the condition is true, the activity is executed. All conditions should be set as a Declarative Rule Condition. The ConditionName and Expression properties for each condition are shown in Table 5-5.

Table 5-5. *CodeActivity Conditions*

Activity Name	ConditionName	Expression
codeSandwich	checkForSandwich	this.LineItems.Contains("sandwich")
codeFries	checkForFries	this.LineItems.Contains("fries")
codeDrink	checkForDrink	this.LineItems.Contains("drink")
codeCombo	checkForCombo	this.LineItems.Contains("combo")

Double-click each CodeActivity to add a handler for the ExecuteCode event. The complete code for the CAGWorkflow.cs file is shown and discussed in Listing 5-17.

Listing 5-17. *Complete CAGWorkflow.cs File*

```
using System;
using System.ComponentModel;
using System.Collections.Generic;
using System.Workflow.Activities;

namespace SharedWorkflows
{
    public sealed partial class CAGWorkflow : SequentialWorkflowActivity
    {
        private List<String> _lineItems;
```

```
public List<String> LineItems
{
    get { return _lineItems; }
    set { _lineItems = value; }
}

public CAGWorkflow()
{
    InitializeComponent();
}

private void codeSandwich_ExecuteCode(object sender, EventArgs e)
{
    Console.WriteLine("Process sandwich");
    ProcessLineItem("sandwich");
}

private void codeFries_ExecuteCode(object sender, EventArgs e)
{
    Console.WriteLine("Process fries");
    ProcessLineItem("fries");
}

private void codeDrink_ExecuteCode(object sender, EventArgs e)
{
    Console.WriteLine("Process drink");
    ProcessLineItem("drink");
}
```

Each of the ExecuteCode handlers writes a message to the Console, and then calls the private ProcessLineItem method. In a real application, ProcessLineItem would perform some real work, but in this demonstration, it simply removes an item with the correct string value from the LineItems collection.

```
private void codeCombo_ExecuteCode(object sender, EventArgs e)
{
    //a combo is composed of a sandwich, fries and drink.
    //add these individual items to the LineItems collection
    //and remove the combo item.
    Console.WriteLine("Process combo - adding new items");
    ProcessLineItem("combo");
    LineItems.Add("sandwich");
    LineItems.Add("fries");
    LineItems.Add("drink");
}
```

The codeCombo_ExecuteCode method handles the combo item. For a combo, it adds individual sandwich, fries, and drink line items to the LineItems collection. This causes those new items to be processed the next time the child activities receive their turn at execution.

```
/// <summary>
/// Indicate an item has been processed by removing it
/// from the collection
/// </summary>
/// <param name="item"></param>
```

```
        private void ProcessLineItem(String item)
        {
            Int32 itemIndex = LineItems.IndexOf(item);
            if (itemIndex >= 0)
            {
                LineItems.RemoveAt(itemIndex);
            }
        }
    }
}
```

Figure 5-18 shows the completed CAG with the first CodeActivity highlighted.

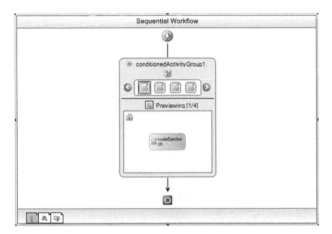

Figure 5-18. *Completed CAGWorkflow*

Testing the Workflow

To test the CAGWorkflow, create a new Sequential Workflow Console Application and name it ConsoleCAG. Add a reference to the SharedWorkflows and Bukovics.Workflow.Hosting projects and delete the Workflow1.cs file since it isn't needed.

Add a new class to the project and name it CAGTest. Listing 5-18 shows the complete listing for the CAGTest.cs file.

Listing 5-18. *Complete CAGTest.cs File*

```
#region Using directives

using System;
using System.Collections.Generic;
using System.Workflow.Runtime;

using Bukovics.Workflow.Hosting;

#endregion
```

```
namespace ConsoleCAG
{
    /// <summary>
    /// Execute workflow with ConditionedActivityGroup
    /// </summary>
    public class CAGTest
    {
        public static void Run()
        {
            using (WorkflowRuntimeManager manager
                = new WorkflowRuntimeManager(new WorkflowRuntime()))
            {
                Dictionary<String, Object> wfArguments
                    = new Dictionary<string, object>();
                List<String> items = new List<string>();
                items.Add("sandwich");
                items.Add("drink");
                items.Add("fries");
                items.Add("drink");
                items.Add("combo");
                wfArguments.Add("LineItems", items);

                Console.WriteLine("Executing CAGWorkflow");
                manager.StartWorkflow(
                        typeof(SharedWorkflows.CAGWorkflow), wfArguments);
                manager.WaitAll(3000);
                Console.WriteLine("Completed CAGWorkflow\n\r");
            }
        }
    }
}
```

The code creates a generic List<String> containing the items to order. Included in the list is a combo. The combo should cause additional items to be created and processed by the activities within the ConditionedActivityGroup.

The final step is to add code to the Program.cs file to execute this static Run method like this:

```
using System;

namespace ConsoleCAG
{
    public class Program
    {
        static void Main(string[] args)
        {
            //execute the workflow tests
            CAGTest.Run();

            Console.WriteLine("Press any key to exit");
            Console.ReadLine();
        }
    }
}
```

When I execute this test application, I see these results:

```
Executing CAGWorkflow
Process sandwich
Process fries
Process drink
Process combo - adding new items
Process sandwich
Process fries
Process drink
Process drink
Completed CAGWorkflow

Press any key to exit
```

By reviewing these results, you can determine the execution order of the child activities. The sandwich, fries, and the drink are processed in that order. This order corresponds to the sequence of child activities within the CAG, not the sequence of elements in the input collection.

When the combo is processed, it adds another entry of a sandwich, fries, and a drink. After processing the combo, execution moves back to the leftmost CodeActivity, which processes the newly added sandwich entry. The fries from the combo are next, followed by the last remaining original item, a drink. The final drink processed is added by the combo.

The ConditionedActivityGroup is a slightly complicated yet powerful activity. Use it in those situations where you need parallel execution of a set of child activities, each with its own looping condition.

Using the InvokeWorkflowActivity

The InvokeWorkflowActivity (found in the System.Workflow.Activities namespace) enables you to execute a new workflow as a step in the current workflow. This provides another level of code reuse similar to custom activities, but on a larger scale.

The steps necessary to use this activity are fairly simple:

1. Drag and drop the InvokeWorkflowActivity to the desired location in your workflow.

2. Set the TargetWorkflow property to the Type of the workflow you wish to execute.

3. Set values for any parameters required by the TargetWorkflow.

When setting the TargetWorkflow property, a dialog is provide that allows you to navigate to the correct Type from a list of all referenced Activity types. Only classes that derive from the Activity class are shown in the list. In order to reference the new workflow Type, you must first add a reference to the project or assembly containing the workflow.

Once you set the TargetWorkflow property, the Parameters property is updated with any properties that are defined in the TargetWorkflow. This allows you to set values for any required properties from within the Properties window. You can set static values for these properties or bind each property to a property in the current workflow or another activity.

The InvokeWorkflowActivity provides an Invoking event that you can handle in code. This event is raised just prior to the creation of the new workflow and is your opportunity to perform any setup tasks that might be required prior to starting the new workflow.

One important aspect of the InvokeWorkflowActivity is that it completes as soon as it starts the new workflow. It doesn't wait for the new workflow to complete. The new workflow executes asynchronously on another thread and doesn't have any direct connection to the InvokeWorkflowActivity once it is started. This means that InvokeWorkflowActivity is a good way to launch other workflows, but the other workflows are expected to be autonomous. Once the new workflow is launched, there are no guarantees concerning the order of execution for the two workflows.

Since the new workflow instance executes on its own thread, there is no way to retrieve output parameters from the instance. There is no built-in mechanism that allows the invoking workflow to retrieve output parameters from the invoked workflow. However, the invoked workflow can use local services to return any output data to the host application.

Note WF doesn't support recursive execution of workflows. This means that an invoked workflow is not allowed to directly or indirectly invoke the original workflow.

Using the TerminateActivity

The TerminateActivity is used to declaratively end the current workflow. Normally, a sequential workflow will follow a flow of execution that has a defined beginning and end. It may take a few twists and turns along the way, but it eventually reaches the end. A state machine workflow normally transitions from state to state and isn't required to have defined beginning and end points. The TerminateActivity allows you to short-circuit the normal flow of execution by terminating the workflow before it reaches a normal end.

To use the TerminateActivity, you drag and drop it onto the desired location in your workflow. You can specify a String error message using the Error property.

When you terminate a workflow, the WorkflowTerminated event of the WorkflowRuntime class is raised, passing an instance of WorkflowTerminatedEventArgs. The Exception property of WorkflowTerminatedEventArgs contains a WorkflowTerminatedException with the message you set with the Error property.

Using the SuspendActivity

The SuspendActivity is similar to the TerminateActivity. They both end execution of the current workflow and they allow you to do this declaratively in the workflow definition. The difference is that SuspendActivity permits you to resume the suspended workflow; TerminateActivity ends the workflow without the ability to start it again.

To use the SuspendActivity, drag and drop it onto the desired location in your workflow. Just like the TerminateActivity, SuspendActivity provides an Error property that you can use to provide a String message. The message might be used to describe the reason for suspending the workflow. You typically suspend a workflow when it has a recoverable error. This might be a problem with an input parameter or something else that can be corrected with human intervention and then resumed.

When you suspend a workflow, the WorkflowSuspended event of the WorkflowRuntime class is raised, passing an instance of WorkflowSuspendedEventArgs. The Error property of WorkflowSuspendedEventArgs contains the message that you passed to the Error property of the SuspendActivity.

Also included in the WorkflowSuspendedEventArgs is the WorkflowInstance property. This permits you to identify and control the workflow instance just suspended. The reason for suspending a workflow rather than terminating it is so you can resume it later. When you need to resume the workflow, you can call the Resume method on this WorkflowInstance object. The Resume method causes the workflow to resume execution immediately following the SuspendActivity.

Caution When you suspend a workflow, you indicate that you are not done with the workflow. You must either resume or cancel the workflow to indicate its final resolution. Failure to do this will result in workflows being persisted indefinitely (if a persistence service is used) or using precious memory within the workflow runtime.

Summary

The focus of this chapter was the standard flow control activities that are included with Windows Workflow Foundation (WF). These are the activities that permit you to control the sequence of execution within your workflows.

In this chapter you learned about code and rule conditions and saw each type of condition demonstrated using the IfElseActivity. The IfElseActivity permits simple branching decisions within a workflow. This chapter also demonstrated the use of the WhileActivity, the ParallelActivity, the ReplicatorActivity, and the ConditionedActivityGroup. Finally, the chapter ends with a discussion of the InvokeWorkflowActivity, the TerminateActivity, and the SuspendActivity.

In the next chapter, you will learn how to develop and use local workflow services.

CHAPTER 6

■ ■ ■

Local Services

Windows Workflow Foundation (WF) provides the ability to optionally register services with the workflow runtime engine. This ability provides an extensible way to modify the behavior of the workflow runtime. WF defines a set of core workflow services that handle thread scheduling, workflow persistence, transactions, and workflow tracking. The designers of WF could have embedded the implementation of these services in the runtime engine itself, but they wisely chose to externalize them, placing their implementations in pluggable services. This places you in control. You decide which services to use (some are optional) and which implementation to use for each service.

WF also supports another kind of service known as a *local* service (sometimes called a *data exchange service*). This is a service that you design and implement yourself. A local service can serve just about any purpose, but one general use is to facilitate communications between workflow instances and the host application. In contrast with this, *core* workflow services each have a purpose (e.g., persistence, tracking) that has been defined by Microsoft. You can develop alternate implementations for each core service, but that doesn't change their defined purpose.

The goal of this chapter is to discuss the implementation and use of local services. An example local service is first implemented and then added to the workflow runtime engine, making it available to workflow instances. A local service can be created via code or from entries in an application configuration file. Both mechanisms are demonstrated in this chapter.

Once a local service is loaded, it can be referenced and used from a workflow instance. Three different ways to use a local service are demonstrated. First, the example local service is used directly from code in the workflow class. Then a custom activity is developed that uses the same local service. Finally, the standard `CallExternalMethodActivity` is demonstrated. This activity allows you to declaratively invoke a method on a local service without any code.

Understanding Local Services

The primary purpose of local services is to serve the needs of your workflows. Only you really know what those needs are. You might need to query or set application state, retrieve or update data in a persistent store such as a database, or communicate with nonworkflow objects and other components in the application. By implementing functionality as a local service, you make it centrally available to multiple workflow instances.

Workflows interact with local services in these two ways:

- Calling a method on a local service
- Waiting for an event to be raised by a local service

When a workflow interacts with a local service, it may indirectly interact with other parts of the application. For instance, a workflow may invoke a method on a local service, but that method may invoke a method on another object or raise an event that is handled elsewhere within the application.

Conversely, a workflow may wait for and handle a local service event, but another component else-where in the application must be responsible for raising the event.

This relationship between the host application, local services, and workflow instances is illus-trated in Figure 6-1 from Chapter 2.

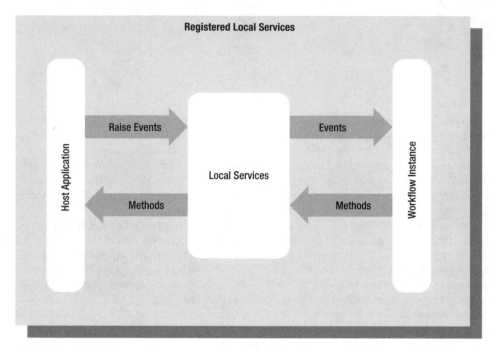

Figure 6-1. *Local service interaction*

■**Note** This chapter demonstrates how to implement a local service and call methods on it from a workflow. It doesn't cover event handling. That subject is discussed in Chapter 7.

Calling a method on a local service is done synchronously using the thread from the current workflow instance. This means that the method shouldn't perform long-running tasks that will block the workflow thread for a long period of time.

Regardless of their defined purpose, all local services are designed, implemented, and used in a similar way. The next few sections of this chapter provide a high-level overview of the steps necessary to implement and use a local service. After this brief overview, the remainder of the chapter demon-strates these steps with example code.

Implementing a Local Service

To implement a local service and make it available to workflow instances, follow these steps:

1. Define the service contract using a normal C# interface. This defines the methods and events that you wish to make available to workflow instances.

2. Decorate the interface with the ExternalDataExchangeAttribute (found in the System. Workflow.Activities namespace). This identifies the interface as a local service interface.

3. Develop a normal C# class that implements the interface you just defined.

4. Create an instance of the class and add it to the workflow runtime engine. This is done just once during initialization of the workflow runtime.

All local services are uniquely identified by their interface type. This means that only one instance of a service is allowed for each service interface. However, you are permitted to register more than one local service, as long as each service implements a different interface. As you will soon see, services are always referenced by their interface type, not the service class name.

Because there is only a single instance of each service, multiple workflow instances may be calling methods on the same service object at the same time. Make sure you keep this in mind when designing the methods of your service. You'll need to make sure that they access data in a thread-safe way.

Using a Local Service

Now that the local service is registered with the workflow runtime it is available for use by any workflow instance. There are two ways for you to call a method on the local service:

- Use the GetService method to obtain a reference to the service and call one of the methods defined by the service interface. This is how you use a local service directly from workflow or activity code. There are several workflow-related classes that implement the GetService method. Two of these are illustrated in the examples that follow.

- Use the CallExternalMethodActivity. This activity permits you to declaratively call a local service method as a step in a workflow. No workflow or activity code is needed when using this activity.

Implementing and Using a Local Service

In this first example, you will implement a local service and then use it from a workflow. To illustrate a somewhat realistic use of a local service, this simple service mimics a financial adjustment to an account. The workflow will call a method on the service, passing in an account ID and the adjustment amount. The service locates the account, updates the account balance, and returns a reference to the updated account object.

This first example demonstrates how to reference and call this service from a CodeActivity. Subsequent examples demonstrate different ways to reference a local service using a custom activity and the CallExternalMethodActivity.

Implementing the Account Class

To begin, create a new project using the Empty Workflow Project template and name the project SharedWorkflows. This creates a DLL assembly that can be referenced by other projects.

■**Tip** It is easier to work with the examples in this chapter if you place all of the projects in a single Visual Studio solution.

Now add a new C# class to the SharedWorkflows project and name it Account. This is a normal C# class, not a workflow class. The purpose of this class is to define a test object that can be modified by the local service. You will see how this class is used as test data by the service implementation in Listing 6-3. Listing 6-1 shows the complete code for the Account.cs file.

Listing 6-1. *Complete Account.cs File*

```csharp
using System;

namespace SharedWorkflows
{
    /// <summary>
    /// Defines an account
    /// </summary>
    [Serializable]
    public class Account
    {
        private Int32 _id;
        private String _name = String.Empty;
        private Double _balance;

        public Int32 Id
        {
            get { return _id; }
            set { _id = value; }
        }

        public String Name
        {
            get { return _name; }
            set { _name = value; }
        }

        public Double Balance
        {
            get { return _balance; }
            set { _balance = value; }
        }
    }
}
```

Declaring the Service Contract

Next, you need to declare a contract that the service class will implement. This takes the form of a normal C# interface that defines all the methods and events that you wish to make available to workflows. Add a new interface to the SharedWorkflows project and name it IAccountServices. Listing 6-2 shows the complete code you need for the IAccountServices.cs file.

Listing 6-2. *Complete IAccountServices.cs File*

```csharp
using System;
using System.Workflow.Activities;

namespace SharedWorkflows
{
    /// <summary>
    /// Defines account services that are available to workflows
    /// </summary>
    [ExternalDataExchange]
```

```
public interface IAccountServices
{
    /// <summary>
    /// Adjust the balance of an account
    /// </summary>
    /// <param name="id"></param>
    /// <param name="adjustment"></param>
    /// <returns>Account</returns>
    Account AdjustBalance(Int32 id, Double adjustment);
}
}
```

To keep this example simple, only a single method is defined. The `AdjustBalance` method accepts an account ID and the amount of the adjustment that should be applied to the account.

Notice that the `interface` is decorated with the `ExternalDataExchangeAttribute`. This is required in order to add a local service to the workflow runtime. This attribute identifies the `interface` as a local service contract and the class that implements it as a local service. If you attempt to add an object to the workflow runtime that doesn't include this attribute on its `interface`, an exception is thrown.

Implementing the Local Service Class

The next step is to develop a class that implements the `interface` that you just defined (`IAccountServices`). To do this, add another C# class to the `SharedWorkflows` project and name it `AccountService`. The complete code for this class is shown in Listing 6-3 and discussed afterward.

Listing 6-3. *Complete AccountService.cs File*

```
using System;
using System.Collections.Generic;

namespace SharedWorkflows
{
    /// <summary>
    /// Provides account services to workflows
    /// </summary>
    public class AccountService : IAccountServices
    {
        private Dictionary<Int32, Account> _accounts
            = new Dictionary<int, Account>();

        public AccountService()
        {
            PopulateTestData();
        }

        #region IAccountServices Members

        /// <summary>
        /// Adjust the balance for an account
        /// </summary>
        /// <param name="id"></param>
        /// <param name="adjustment"></param>
        /// <returns>Account</returns>
```

```
public Account AdjustBalance(Int32 id, Double adjustment)
{
    Account account = null;
    if (_accounts.ContainsKey(id))
    {
        account = _accounts[id];
        account.Balance += adjustment;
    }
    return account;
}

#endregion

#region Generate Test Data

private void PopulateTestData()
{
    Account account = new Account();
    account.Id = 101;
    account.Name = "Neil Armstrong";
    account.Balance = 100.00;
    _accounts.Add(account.Id, account);

    account = new Account();
    account.Id = 102;
    account.Name = "Michael Collins";
    account.Balance = 99.95;
    _accounts.Add(account.Id, account);

    account = new Account();
    account.Id = 103;
    account.Name = "Buzz Aldrin";
    account.Balance = 0;
    _accounts.Add(account.Id, account);
}

#endregion
    }
}
```

Most importantly, this class implements the IAccountServices interface. This identifies it as a local service since that interface contains the ExternalDataExchangeAttribute. In order to mimic an adjustment to an account, the class contains a Dictionary of Account objects that are populated with test data upon construction. The AdjustBalance method locates an account from the Dictionary, updates the balance, and returns the modified account object. This is far from a real-world example, but it is enough to illustrate the use of this local service.

While this service only implements the AdjustBalance method, it is permitted to implement other public methods as necessary. For instance, you might need other methods that are used by the host application to interact with the local service. If these additional methods are not part of the IAccountServices interface (the contract with the workflows), they are not visible to workflow instances.

Implementing the Workflow

To test this local service, add a new sequential workflow to the SharedWorkflows project and name it BalanceAdjustmentWorkflow. The workflow requires two input properties (Id and Adjustment) and one property used as output (Account). These properties are shown in Listing 6-4.

Listing 6-4. *BalanceAdjustmentWorkflow.cs File with Properties Added*

```csharp
using System;
using System.Workflow.Activities;

namespace SharedWorkflows
{
    public sealed partial class BalanceAdjustmentWorkflow
        : SequentialWorkflowActivity
    {
        private Int32 _id;
        private Double _adjustment;
        private Account _account;

        public Int32 Id
        {
            get { return _id; }
            set { _id = value; }
        }

        public Double Adjustment
        {
            get { return _adjustment; }
            set { _adjustment = value; }
        }

        public Account Account
        {
            get { return _account; }
            set { _account = value; }
        }

        public BalanceAdjustmentWorkflow()
        {
            InitializeComponent();
        }
    }
}
```

After switching to the workflow designer view, drag and drop a CodeActivity onto the workflow. Change the name of the CodeActivity to codeAdjustAccount and then double-click it to add a handler for the ExecuteCode event. You will fully implement the code for this handler in just a few steps. The workflow now looks like Figure 6-2.

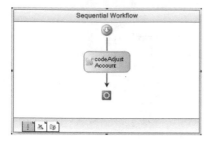

Figure 6-2. *Complete BalanceAdjustmentWorkflow*

This workflow will illustrate the first way to access the local service and invoke the AdjustBalance method. The base Activity class defines a method named OnActivityExecutionContextLoad that will be used to obtain a reference to the service. This virtual method is executed when the activity execution context is loaded. This occurs when the workflow begins execution or whenever it is reloaded from a persistence store.

Passed with the OnActivityExecutionContextLoad method is an object that implements the IServiceProvider interface. This interface includes the GetService method that permits you to retrieve a reference to a service.

Override this method in the BalanceAdjustmentWorkflow and enter this code:

```
protected override void OnActivityExecutionContextLoad(
    IServiceProvider provider)
{
    base.OnActivityExecutionContextLoad(provider);

    //retrieve the account service from the workflow runtime
    _accountServices = provider.GetService(typeof(IAccountServices))
        as IAccountServices;
    if (_accountServices == null)
    {
        //we have a big problem
        throw new InvalidOperationException(
            "Unable to retrieve IAccountServices from runtime");
    }
}
```

The GetService method is passed the Type of the service you are requesting. The Type is always an interface since local services are uniquely identified by their interface. To make the local service available to other code in the workflow class, the reference to it is stored in an instance variable named _accountService that you need to define. Define the variable like this:

```
private IAccountServices _accountServices;
```

The final bit of workflow code that you need is in the ExecuteCode handler for the CodeActivity. This code calls the AdjustBalance method of the IAccountServices object just retrieved and passes the Id and Adjustment properties as arguments. The Account property is set to the result of the method. The code for this event handler looks like this:

```
private void codeAdjustAccount_ExecuteCode(object sender, EventArgs e)
{
    //apply the adjustment to the account
    Account = _accountServices.AdjustBalance(Id, Adjustment);
}
```

The completed code for the BalanceAdjustmentWorkflow.cs file is shown in Listing 6-5.

Listing 6-5. *Complete BalanceAdjustmentWorkflow.cs File*

```
using System;
using System.Workflow.Activities;

namespace SharedWorkflows
{
    public sealed partial class BalanceAdjustmentWorkflow
        : SequentialWorkflowActivity
    {
        private Int32 _id;
        private Double _adjustment;
        private Account _account;
        private IAccountServices _accountServices;

        public Int32 Id
        {
            get { return _id; }
            set { _id = value; }
        }

        public Double Adjustment
        {
            get { return _adjustment; }
            set { _adjustment = value; }
        }

        public Account Account
        {
            get { return _account; }
            set { _account = value; }
        }

        public BalanceAdjustmentWorkflow()
        {
            InitializeComponent();
        }

        protected override void OnActivityExecutionContextLoad(
            IServiceProvider provider)
        {
            base.OnActivityExecutionContextLoad(provider);

            //retrieve the account service from the workflow runtime
            _accountServices = provider.GetService(typeof(IAccountServices))
                as IAccountServices;
            if (_accountServices == null)
            {
                //we have a big problem
                throw new InvalidOperationException(
                    "Unable to retrieve IAccountServices from runtime");
            }
        }
```

```
        private void codeAdjustAccount_ExecuteCode(object sender, EventArgs e)
        {
            //apply the adjustment to the account
            Account = _accountServices.AdjustBalance(Id, Adjustment);
        }
    }
}
```

Testing the Workflow

To test the workflow, create a new project using the Sequential Workflow Console Application template. Name this project ConsoleLocalServices. You can delete the Workflow1.cs file that is created with the new project since you won't need it. Add a reference to the SharedWorkflows project in order to reference the workflow.

This project makes use of the workflow manager classes developed in Chapter 4. These classes simplify workflow runtime hosting by handling some of the mundane tasks. In that chapter, these classes are implemented in the Bukovics.Workflow.Hosting project. Add that project to this Visual Studio solution and add a reference to that project now.

Add a class named LocalServiceTest to the ConsoleLocalServices project. The code to execute the workflow goes into this class instead of directly into the Program.cs file. Listing 6-6 shows the complete code for the LocalServiceTest.cs file.

Listing 6-6. *Complete LocalServiceTest.cs File*

```
using System;
using System.Collections.Generic;
using System.Workflow.Runtime;
using System.Workflow.Activities;

using Bukovics.Workflow.Hosting;
using SharedWorkflows;

namespace ConsoleLocalServices
{
    public class LocalServiceTest
    {
        public static void Run()
        {
            using (WorkflowRuntimeManager manager
                = new WorkflowRuntimeManager(new WorkflowRuntime()))
            {
                //add services to the workflow runtime
                AddServices(manager.WorkflowRuntime);
                manager.WorkflowRuntime.StartRuntime();

                //create a dictionary with input arguments
                Dictionary<String, Object> wfArguments
                    = new Dictionary<string, object>();
```

```
            //run the first workflow
            Console.WriteLine("Executing BalanceAdjustmentWorkflow");
            wfArguments.Add("Id", 101);
            wfArguments.Add("Adjustment", -25.00);
            WorkflowInstanceWrapper instance = manager.StartWorkflow(
                typeof(SharedWorkflows.BalanceAdjustmentWorkflow),
                wfArguments);
            manager.WaitAll(2000);

            Account account
                = instance.OutputParameters["Account"] as Account;
            if (account != null)
            {
                Console.WriteLine(
                    "Revised Account: {0}, Name={1}, Bal={2:C}",
                    account.Id, account.Name, account.Balance);
            }
            else
            {
                Console.WriteLine("Invalid Account Id\n\r");
            }

            Console.WriteLine("Completed BalanceAdjustmentWorkflow\n\r");
        }
    }

    /// <summary>
    /// Add any services needed by the runtime engine
    /// </summary>
    /// <param name="instance"></param>
    private static void AddServices(WorkflowRuntime instance)
    {
        //add the external data exchange service to the runtime
        ExternalDataExchangeService exchangeService
            = new ExternalDataExchangeService();
        instance.AddService(exchangeService);

        //add our custom local service
        //to the external data exchange service
        exchangeService.AddService(new AccountService());
    }
  }
}
```

After creating an instance of the WorkflowRuntime and WorkflowRuntimeManager classes, the AddServices method is invoked to add the local service. This method first creates an instance of the ExternalDataExchangeService and adds it to the WorkflowRuntime instance. The AccountService is then created and added to the ExternalDataExchangeService. That's really all there is to adding a local service to the workflow runtime.

The remainder of the code creates a `Dictionary` containing the `Id` and `Adjustment` parameters, starts an instance of the `BalanceAdjustmentWorkflow`, and then writes the results to the `Console`.

The final bit of required code goes into the `Program.cs` file to execute the static `Run` method of the `LocalServiceTest` class. The `Program.cs` code looks like this:

```
using System;

namespace ConsoleLocalServices
{
    public class Program
    {
        static void Main(string[] args)
        {
            LocalServiceTest.Run();

            Console.WriteLine("Press any key to exit");
            Console.ReadLine();
        }
    }
}
```

When executed on my machine, the results look like this:

```
Executing BalanceAdjustmentWorkflow
Revised Account: 101, Name=Neil Armstrong, Bal=$75.00
Completed BalanceAdjustmentWorkflow

Press any key to exit
```

Since I am formatting the balance as currency, your results may look different if your computer uses a different regional setting. This account started with a balance of 100.00 and the test applied an adjustment of –25.00. Therefore, the result of 75.00 is correct and the workflow succeeded.

Use this approach when you need to reference a service directly from code in the workflow class. This would be the case if you use activities such as `CodeActivity` that add event handlers to the workflow class.

Loading from App.config

In Chapter 4, you saw that core workflow services could be loaded and configured using an application configuration file (`App.config`). You can also load local services in a similar manner. Declaring them in an application configuration file enables you to externally configure your workflow application. If you need to change the set of local services that are loaded, you can accomplish that without rebuilding the application.

To load local services in this manner, you need to add the appropriate entries to the application configuration file and then use a different constructor for the `ExternalDataExchangeService` class in the workflow runtime startup code.

Listing 6-7 shows an `App.config` file that loads the same local service used in the previous example.

Listing 6-7. *App.config That Loads Local Services*

```xml
<?xml version="1.0" encoding="utf-8" ?>
<configuration>
  <configSections>
    <section name="WorkflowRuntime"
      type="System.Workflow.Runtime.Configuration.WorkflowRuntimeSection,
        System.Workflow.Runtime, Version=3.0.00000.0, Culture=neutral,
        PublicKeyToken=31bf3856ad364e35" />
    <section name="LocalServices"
      type="System.Workflow.Activities.ExternalDataExchangeServiceSection,
        System.Workflow.Activities, Version=3.0.0.0, Culture=neutral,
        PublicKeyToken=31bf3856ad364e35"/>
  </configSections>
  <WorkflowRuntime Name="ConsoleLocalServices" >
    <CommonParameters>
      <!--Add parameters common to all services-->
    </CommonParameters>
    <Services>
      <!--Add core services here-->
    </Services>
  </WorkflowRuntime>

  <LocalServices>
    <Services>
      <!--Add local services here-->
      <add type="SharedWorkflows.AccountService,
        SharedWorkflows,Version=1.0.0.0,
        Culture=neutral, PublicKeyToken=null" />
    </Services>
  </LocalServices>

</configuration>
```

■**Note** Chapter 4 discusses the `WorkflowRuntime` section of this configuration file in detail. Refer to that chapter for more information.

First, an entry has been added to the `configSections` that identifies the `LocalServices` section. This associates the `LocalServices` section with the `ExternalDataExchangeServiceSection` class that processes it. Next, the individual local services that you wish to load are added to the `LocalServices` section.

To actually use these entries, you need to modify the code that initializes the workflow runtime engine so that it uses these configuration file sections. Listing 6-8 shows a revised version of the `LocalServiceTest.cs` file used in the previous example (in the `ConsoleLocalServices` project).

Listing 6-8. *LocalServiceTest.cs Using App.config Entries*

```csharp
using System;
using System.Collections.Generic;
using System.Workflow.Runtime;
using System.Workflow.Activities;
```

```
using Bukovics.Workflow.Hosting;
using SharedWorkflows;

namespace ConsoleLocalServices
{
    public class LocalServiceTest
    {
        public static void Run()
        {
            using (WorkflowRuntimeManager manager
                = new WorkflowRuntimeManager(
                    new WorkflowRuntime("WorkflowRuntime")))
            {
                //add services to the workflow runtime
                AddServices(manager.WorkflowRuntime);
                manager.WorkflowRuntime.StartRuntime();

                //create a dictionary with input arguments
                Dictionary<String, Object> wfArguments
                    = new Dictionary<string, object>();

                //run the first workflow
                Console.WriteLine("Executing BalanceAdjustmentWorkflow");
                wfArguments.Add("Id", 101);
                wfArguments.Add("Adjustment", -25.00);
                WorkflowInstanceWrapper instance = manager.StartWorkflow(
                    typeof(SharedWorkflows.BalanceAdjustmentWorkflow),
                    wfArguments);
                manager.WaitAll(2000);

                Account account
                    = instance.OutputParameters["Account"] as Account;
                if (account != null)
                {
                    Console.WriteLine(
                        "Revised Account: {0}, Name={1}, Bal={2:C}",
                        account.Id, account.Name, account.Balance);
                }
                else
                {
                    Console.WriteLine("Invalid Account Id\n\r");
                }

                Console.WriteLine("Completed BalanceAdjustmentWorkflow\n\r");
            }
        }
```

```
        /// <summary>
        /// Add any services needed by the runtime engine
        /// </summary>
        /// <param name="instance"></param>
        private static void AddServices(WorkflowRuntime instance)
        {
            //add the external data exchange service to the runtime
            ExternalDataExchangeService exchangeService
                = new ExternalDataExchangeService("LocalServices");
            instance.AddService(exchangeService);
        }
    }
}
```

> **Note** When loading configuration entries from a file, the project requires a reference to the System. Configuration assembly.

The highlighted code has been changed from the previous example. First, the constructor for the WorkflowRuntime class is passed the name of the configuration file section that contains the entries it needs. In this example, the name of that section is WorkflowRuntime. To load local services, the constructor for ExternalDataExchangeService is also passed the name of a configuration file section. In this case, the name LocalServices is passed since this is the section that contains the local service entries.

After making these changes and rebuilding, you should be able to execute the ConsoleLocalServices project and see exactly the same results as before.

Using a Custom Activity

The previous example demonstrates how to reference and use a local service directly from code in the workflow class. That example makes the service method call from the ExecuteCode event handler of a CodeActivity. In this example, you will see how to reference a local service from a custom activity. The general mechanism used to reference a local service is the same, but the actual implementation is slightly different.

> **Tip** For this example, you can choose to implement a new workflow or modify the one used in the previous example. All of the workflow input and output parameters are the same as the previous example, so modifying the existing workflow requires the least amount of work. The instructions that follow assume that you are modifying the existing workflow.

Implementing a Custom Activity

To begin, add a new activity to the SharedWorkflows project that was used in the previous example and name the activity AdjustAccountActivity. Change the base class from SequenceActivity to Activity since a composite activity is not needed.

The complete code that you need for the AdjustAccountActivity.cs file is shown in Listing 6-9 and discussed within the listing and afterward.

Listing 6-9. *Complete AdjustAccountActivity.cs File*

```
using System;
using System.ComponentModel;
using System.Workflow.ComponentModel;
using System.Workflow.Activities;

namespace SharedWorkflows
{
    public partial class AdjustAccountActivity : Activity
    {
        public static DependencyProperty IdProperty
            = System.Workflow.ComponentModel.DependencyProperty.Register(
            "Id", typeof(Int32), typeof(AdjustAccountActivity));

        [Description("Identifies the account")]
        [Category("Local Services")]
        [Browsable(true)]
        [DesignerSerializationVisibility(DesignerSerializationVisibility.Visible)]
        public Int32 Id
        {
            get
            {
                return ((Int32)(base.GetValue(AdjustAccountActivity.IdProperty)));
            }
            set
            {
                base.SetValue(AdjustAccountActivity.IdProperty, value);
            }
        }

        public static DependencyProperty AdjustmentProperty
            = System.Workflow.ComponentModel.DependencyProperty.Register(
            "Adjustment", typeof(Double), typeof(AdjustAccountActivity));

        [Description("The adjustment amount")]
        [Category("Local Services")]
        [Browsable(true)]
        [DesignerSerializationVisibility(DesignerSerializationVisibility.Visible)]
        public Double Adjustment
        {
            get
            {
                return ((Double)(base.GetValue(
                    AdjustAccountActivity.AdjustmentProperty)));
            }
            set
            {
                base.SetValue(AdjustAccountActivity.AdjustmentProperty, value);
            }
        }
```

```
public static DependencyProperty AccountProperty
    = System.Workflow.ComponentModel.DependencyProperty.Register(
    "Account", typeof(Account), typeof(AdjustAccountActivity));

[Description("The revised Account object")]
[Category("Local Services")]
[Browsable(true)]
[DesignerSerializationVisibility(DesignerSerializationVisibility.Visible)]
public Account Account
{
    get
    {
        return ((Account)(base.GetValue(
            AdjustAccountActivity.AccountProperty)));
    }
    set
    {
        base.SetValue(AdjustAccountActivity.AccountProperty, value);
    }
}
```

The activity requires the same three properties that are defined in the workflow class (Id, Adjustment, and Account). However, the properties of this activity will be bound to those of the workflow. Therefore, they must be dependency properties instead of C# properties.

```
public AdjustAccountActivity()
{
    InitializeComponent();
}

protected override ActivityExecutionStatus Execute(
    ActivityExecutionContext executionContext)
{
    IAccountServices accountServices =
        executionContext.GetService<IAccountServices>();
    if (accountServices == null)
    {
        //we have a big problem
        throw new InvalidOperationException(
            "Unable to retrieve IAccountServices from runtime");
    }

    //apply the adjustment to the account
    Account = accountServices.AdjustBalance(Id, Adjustment);

    return base.Execute(executionContext);
}
```

The highlighted code in the Execute method shows how to reference and use the local service. In the previous example, you used the OnActivityExecutionContextLoad method of the workflow to retrieve the local service. This method is invoked when the activity execution context is loaded. Here, the ActivityExecutionContext is passed as an argument to the Execute method, slightly simplifying the process of retrieving a service.

The ActivityExecutionContext supports two overloaded versions of the GetService method. The one used in this code is a generic method that is passed IAccountServices to identify the local service to retrieve. Using the generic method saves you the trouble of casting the result to the correct type.

Once the reference to the local service is retrieved, the call to the AdjustBalance method is straightforward and is similar to the previous example.

■Tip It's a good idea to build the SharedWorkflows project at this point. Doing so will ensure that the custom activity builds correctly and is available in the Toolbox prior to the next step.

Modifying the Workflow

To complete this example, modify the BalanceAdjustmentWorkflow that you developed earlier in the chapter.

After opening the BalanceAdjustmentWorkflow in the workflow designer view, delete the CodeActivity and replace it with the new AdjustAccountActivity that you just implemented. Figure 6-3 shows the revised workflow.

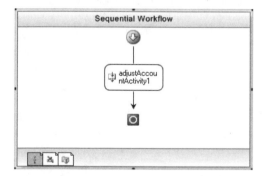

Figure 6-3. *BalanceAdjustmentWorkflow with AdjustAccountActivity*

Before leaving the designer view, you need to bind the three activity properties to the workflow properties of the same name. Doing this causes the input parameters for the workflow to be passed to the custom activity when it is executed. Likewise, the output property of the activity (the Account property) is bound to the Account property of the workflow. This permits the host application to retrieve this output parameter and show the results. Table 6-1 shows the property bindings for adjustAccountActivity1.

Table 6-1. *Property Bindings for adjustAccountActivity1*

Property	Binding
Account	Activity=BalanceAdjustmentWorkflow, Path=Account
Adjustment	Activity=BalanceAdjustmentWorkflow, Path=Adjustment
Id	Activity=BalanceAdjustmentWorkflow, Path=Id

Listing 6-10 shows the revised listing for the `BalanceAdjustmentWorkflow.cs` file.

Listing 6-10. *Revised BalanceAdjustmentWorkflow.cs File*

```
using System;
using System.Workflow.Activities;

namespace SharedWorkflows
{
    public sealed partial class BalanceAdjustmentWorkflow
        : SequentialWorkflowActivity
    {
        private Int32 _id;
        private Double _adjustment;
        private Account _account;

        public Int32 Id
        {
            get { return _id; }
            set { _id = value; }
        }

        public Double Adjustment
        {
            get { return _adjustment; }
            set { _adjustment = value; }
        }

        public Account Account
        {
            get { return _account; }
            set { _account = value; }
        }

        public BalanceAdjustmentWorkflow()
        {
            InitializeComponent();
        }
    }
}
```

The original version of this file can be seen in Listing 6-5. If you compare the two versions, you'll see that you don't need to add anything to the workflow class. However, gone are the `_accountServices` variable, the code for the `OnActivityExecutionContextLoad` method, and the `codeAdjustAccount_ExecuteCode` method.

Testing the Workflow

You can execute this revised version of the workflow using the same `ConsoleLocalServices` application used in the previous example. The application doesn't require any changes.

> ■**Note** You can execute the version of ConsoleLocalServices that loaded the local service via code or from the App.config file. Both versions should provide the same results.

When I execute this on my machine, I see these results, which are the same as the previous example:

```
Executing BalanceAdjustmentWorkflow
Revised Account: 101, Name=Neil Armstrong, Bal=$75.00
Completed BalanceAdjustmentWorkflow

Press any key to exit
```

Accessing a local service from a custom activity is more straightforward than the approach shown for a CodeActivity. A custom activity also permits you to use a local service declaratively as part of the workflow model rather than in workflow code. The downside is that you end up defining the properties twice (once in the workflow and again in the custom activity). But the big benefit of a custom activity is that it is self-contained and reusable in other workflows. And the workflow code that retrieved and saved the reference to the local service is now gone, greatly simplifying the code in the workflow class.

The next example explores one more way to invoke a method on a local service.

Using the CallExternalMethodActivity

Microsoft provides the standard CallExternalMethodActivity that you can use to invoke a method on a local service. The big advantage to using this activity is that it doesn't require any code (other than the local service itself). Like a custom activity, the call to the local service is declared as part of the workflow model rather than in workflow code.

To use the CallExternalMethodActivity, you first select the service you wish to call by choosing an interface from the list of referenced assemblies. Once an interface is selected, you choose the method you wish to call. Finally, you bind or set any parameters that are required by the method.

> ■**Note** This example builds upon the prior example, modifying the BalanceAdjustmentWorkflow instead of starting from scratch.

Implementing the Workflow

To demonstrate the use of the CallExternalMethodActivity, open the BalanceAdjustmentWorkflow that you developed in the previous example (in the SharedWorkflows project). In design view, delete the custom activity (adjustAccountActivity1) and replace it with an instance of CallExternalMethodActivity.

Switch to the Properties window for this activity and select the ellipsis for the InterfaceType property. Figure 6-4 shows the type selection dialog that you should now see.

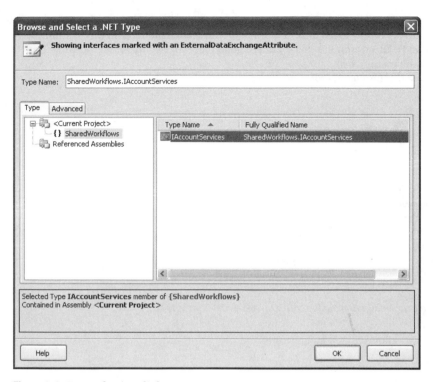

Figure 6-4. *Type selection dialog*

The purpose of this dialog is to select the interface that identifies the local service you wish to use. Only interfaces that are decorated with the ExternalDataExchangeAttribute are shown in this dialog. The list of available interfaces is built from the referenced assemblies as well as the current project. If the interface you want is missing from the list, then either you're missing an assembly reference, or the interface is missing the ExternalDataExchangeAttribute.

As shown in Figure 6-4, I've selected the IAccountServices interface from the SharedWorkflows project (the current project). After pressing OK, you are returned to the Properties window.

The next step is to select the MethodName property. In this example, the interface only supports a single method so the choice of the AdjustBalance method is a simple one. Once you select a method, any input arguments are shown in the Parameters section of the Properties window. Since the AdjustBalance method returns a result, it is also shown in the Parameters section.

The final step is to set or bind the parameters for the method call. In this example, you need to bind all of the parameters to workflow properties. This allows the input parameters (Id and Adjustment) to be passed from the workflow to the method, and the result (an Account object) to be passed back to the workflow Account property. Table 6-2 shows the bindings that you need.

Table 6-2. *Parameter Bindings for callExternalMethodActivity1*

Property	Binding
(ReturnValue)	Activity=BalanceAdjustmentWorkflow, Path=Account
adjustment	Activity=BalanceAdjustmentWorkflow, Path=Adjustment
id	Activity=BalanceAdjustmentWorkflow, Path=Id

The `CallExternalMethodActivity` provides a `MethodInvoking` event that you can optionally handle in code. This event is raised just prior to the call on the service method. In this example you don't need to handle this event. But this event is a good place to execute any setup code that is necessary prior to the method call.

Figure 6-5 shows the completed Properties window.

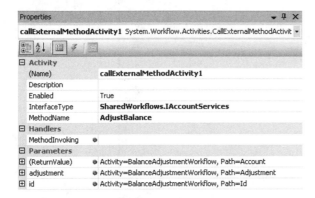

Figure 6-5. *Complete Properties window for callExternalMethodActivity1*

The completed workflow looks like Figure 6-6.

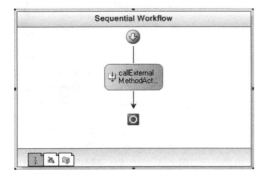

Figure 6-6. *BalanceAdjustmentWorkflow with CallExternalMethodActivity*

If you started with the version of the `BalanceAdjustmentWorkflow` that you developed in the previous example, there are no additional coding changes. The `BalanceAdjustmentWorkflow.cs` file should look like Listing 6-10 without any additional changes.

Testing the Workflow

To test the revised version of the workflow, simply execute the `ConsoleLocalServices` application that you used for the previous examples. No changes to the application code are necessary.

When I execute this on my machine, I see the same consistent results:

```
Executing BalanceAdjustmentWorkflow
Revised Account: 101, Name=Neil Armstrong, Bal=$75.00
Completed BalanceAdjustmentWorkflow

Press any key to exit
```

Using the CallExternalMethodActivity is the simplest way to call a local service method. It allows you to easily bind the method parameters to workflow properties or those of another activity. And it accomplishes this with zero code.

Use CallExternalMethodActivity when the method call is isolated and not part of a larger sequence of calls. A custom activity might make more sense if you have a series of related methods to call on the same service and wish to encapsulate them all into a single activity.

Summary

In this chapter, you saw how to implement and use local services. Unlike core services, local services can serve any purpose that you define. An example local service was implemented and then used by workflow instances. A local service must be loaded into the workflow runtime in order to use it. Loading of local services can be accomplished via code or from entries in an application configuration file. Both ways to load services were demonstrated in this chapter.

Three different ways were demonstrated to access and use local services from a workflow. First, a local service was used directly from code in the workflow class. Then a custom activity was developed that used the same local service. Finally, the standard CallExternalMethodActivity that is provided with WF was used to invoke a method on the same local service.

The next chapter discusses the second half of the local service story: events.

CHAPTER 7

■■■

Event-Driven Activities

Event-driven activities suspend execution of a workflow until an event is received. The event is commonly raised externally by a local service, but it can also be raised internally from within a workflow. These types of activities are vital to state machine workflows, since they are typically used to trigger state transitions. But they are also a valuable tool for sequential workflows.

The previous chapter began the discussion of local services. It covered the steps needed to implement a local service and then call a method on the service from a workflow. This chapter completes the local services story. It shows you how to implement and raise events in a local service and then handle them within a workflow. Demonstrated in this chapter are the typical patterns used to call an external method and then wait for a response from the host application in the form of one or more events.

The chapter begins with a general discussion of event-driven activities, followed by an example that uses HandleExternalEventActivity to process local service events. This example implements a local service that provides bidirectional communication between a workflow and the host application.

Windows Workflow Foundation (WF) provides an alternative to using CallExternalMethodActivity and HandleExternalEventActivity to communicate with a local service. Using a command-line utility (wca.exe), you can generate strongly typed custom activities that derive from these standard activities. The second example in this chapter demonstrates how to use this utility to generate the custom activities and then use them in a workflow.

The normal correlation logic routes local service events back to the correct workflow based on the workflow instance ID. However, in some situations, this type of correlation isn't sufficient. You may need a workflow that waits for multiple instances of the same event. WF provides a set of correlation attributes that enable you to control which activity within a workflow receives the event. These correlation attributes are demonstrated in the third example of the chapter.

The chapter concludes with a discussion and an example that demonstrates the use of EventHandlingScopeActivity and EventHandlersActivity. Unlike the more common form of event handling, these activities enable you to concurrently handle multiple events while executing a main line set of activities.

Using Event-Driven Activities

WF includes a group of activities that work together to provide event handling within a workflow. Some of these activities wait for an external event (e.g., HandleExternalEventActivity), while others trigger and handle an event internally (e.g., DelayActivity). In both cases, the activities implement the IEventActivity interface, which is a requirement for any activity that handles an event.

Other activities are composites that act as containers for these event handler activities. EventDrivenActivity is similar to SequenceActivity in that it contains a set of child activities that are executed in sequence. However, EventDrivenActivity requires that the first child activity implement

IEventActivity. When this first child executes, it immediately begins waiting for its event. Execution of the entire EventDrivenActivity is suspended until the event is received or the activity is canceled. When the event is received, the other child activities within the EventDrivenActivity are executed.

Other activities, such as ListenActivity, act as containers for multiple instances of EventDrivenActivity. Each EventDrivenActivity represents a branch of execution that is triggered by a different event. The EventDrivenActivity is the only child activity permitted by the ListenActivity. Figure 7-1 illustrates the relationship between these activities.

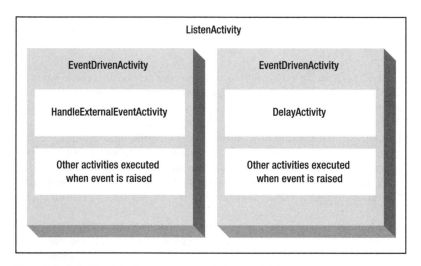

Figure 7-1. *Relationship between event-driven activities*

Figure 7-1 shows two instances of the EventDrivenActivity, one with a HandleExternalEventActivity child activity and the other with a DelayActivity. When one of these activities receives its event, the activities defined under it are executed. Any other EventDrivenActivity branches are canceled by the parent ListenActivity.

Additional EventDrivenActivity instances could have been added, but a minimum of two is required. For instance, in a loan processing workflow, you might need to handle both an approve and a reject event. To implement this, you place each event in its own EventDrivenActivity.

The DelayActivity is useful since it enables you to declare the activities to execute when an expected event is never received. It is for this reason that the ListenActivity requires a minimum of two EventDrivenActivity branches. The assumption is that one of them handles an event that you expect you will receive, and the other handles the condition that occurs when the event is never received.

■**Note** This part of the chapter covers the most frequently used activities. Other, more specialized activities such as the EventHandlingScopeActivity are covered later in this chapter. The WebServiceInputActivity is also an event-driven activity that implements IEventActivity. It is discussed in Chapter 15.

In the next section, I discuss and demonstrate the steps necessary to use the HandleExternalEventActivity to handle an event from a local service.

Using the HandleExternalEventActivity

The HandleExternalEventActivity is one of the most frequently used event handling activities. You often use it in combination with the CallExternalMethodActivity to enable two-way communication between a workflow instance and a local service. You use the CallExternalMethodActivity to invoke a local service method, and then you use the HandleExternalEventActivity to wait for the response in the form of an event.

■**Note** The CallExternalMethodActivity was first discussed in Chapter 6. Additional information on this activity can be found in that chapter.

Generally, the steps necessary to use the HandleExternalEventActivity in a workflow are as follows:

1. Implement the class that will be used as the event arguments. In order to handle the event with HandleExternalEventActivity, the event arguments must derive from ExternalDataEventArgs.

2. Define the event in a local service interface. A local service interface is one that has been decorated with the ExternalDataExchangeAttribute and implemented by a local service class.

3. Implement the event in a local service class.

4. Provide some mechanism in the local service class to raise the event. This might take the form of a public method that the host application can invoke to raise the event. Or the local service may raise the event itself based on its own internal logic.

5. Add an instance of the ListenActivity to a workflow. This creates an initial set of two EventDrivenActivity instances as children of the ListenActivity. Each EventDrivenActivity represents a separate execution branch that must be started by an activity implementing IEventActivity.

6. Add the HandleExternalEventActivity to one of the EventDrivenActivity branches. The HandleExternalEventActivity has a number of properties that must be set at design time. You first select the interface that identifies the local service. After selecting an interface, you select the event that you wish to handle from the list of available events.

7. Complete the second EventDrivenActivity instance by adding an activity that implements IEventActivity. If you don't have another external event that you wish to handle, you can use a DelayActivity.

You must also decide how you want to handle the event arguments when the event is received. Presumably, the event arguments carry data that the workflow requires in order to continue processing. One option is to define a parameter binding that sets a workflow property to the value of the event arguments when they are received. You can then use the event arguments elsewhere in your workflow by referencing the workflow property. Another option is to add a code handler to the Invoked event of the HandleExternalEventActivity. This enables you to work with the event arguments directly in this handler as they are received.

The workflow instance ID (a Guid) plays a critical role in workflow event processing. When a local service raises an event, the workflow instance ID must be passed to the constructor of the base event arguments class (ExternalDataEventArgs). This ID determines the workflow instance that will receive the event.

In the example that follows, you will walk through each of these steps to implement a simple guess-the-number game. The workflow will randomly choose a number and allow you to make guesses until you finally choose the correct number. Each time you make an incorrect guess, the workflow sends you a `string` message with a hint. The host application for this example is a Windows Forms application.

A local service enables two-way communication between the workflow and the host application. The local service provides a method that is called by the workflow to pass the hint message. The workflow uses the `CallExternalMethodActivity` to invoke this method. The local service also provides an event that the workflow handles with a `HandleExternalEventActivity`. This event is raised by the host application to pass the latest guess to the workflow.

The local service also includes public members that are used only by the host application. A method is included that enables the host application to raise the event to the workflow. Another event is included that is raised by the local service to pass the hint message to the host application.

Creating the Project

To begin this example, create a new project using the Empty Workflow Project template, and name the project `SharedWorkflows`. This creates a DLL assembly that can be referenced by the Windows Forms application that will host the workflow runtime.

Implementing the Event Arguments Class

Before you can define an event in the local service `interface`, you need to define the event arguments class that the event will pass. Add a new C# class to the `SharedWorkflows` project and name it `GuessReceivedEventArgs`. An instance of this class is passed with the event as it is raised and contains the latest guess. The class is derived from `ExternalDataEventArgs` since this is a requirement in order to handle the event with `HandleExternalEventActivity`. This base class provides the `InstanceId` property, which identifies the workflow instance that should receive the event.

The complete code for the `GuessReceivedEventArgs.cs` file is shown in Listing 7-1.

Listing 7-1. *Complete GuessReceivedEventArgs.cs File*

```
using System;
using System.Workflow.Activities;

namespace SharedWorkflows
{
    /// <summary>
    /// Passes a guess from the local service to a workflow
    /// </summary>
    [Serializable]
    public class GuessReceivedEventArgs : ExternalDataEventArgs
    {
        private Int32 _nextGuess;

        public GuessReceivedEventArgs(Guid instanceId, Int32 nextGuess)
            : base(instanceId)
        {
            _nextGuess = nextGuess;
        }
```

```
        public Int32 NextGuess
        {
            get { return _nextGuess; }
            set { _nextGuess = value; }
        }
    }
}
```

The constructor passes the `instanceId` parameter to the base class. Without this ID, the workflow runtime would have no way to identify the correct workflow instance to receive the event.

Defining the Service Interface

Now you are ready to define the `interface` for the local service. Add a C# interface to the `SharedWorkflows` project and name it `IGuessingGame`. This `interface` defines the public members that will be used by the workflow. First, it defines the `GuessReceived` event that passes the latest guess to the workflow and allows it to continue processing. It also defines the `SendMessage` method that the workflow invokes to pass hint messages to the local service.

Listing 7-2 shows the complete code for `IGuessingGame.cs`.

Listing 7-2. *Complete IGuessingGame.cs File*

```
using System;
using System.Workflow.Activities;

namespace SharedWorkflows
{
    /// <summary>
    /// Defines the methods and events that
    /// are exposed to workflows for the
    /// number guessing game.
    /// </summary>
    [ExternalDataExchange]
    public interface IGuessingGame
    {
        /// <summary>
        /// Send a message from the workflow to the local service
        /// </summary>
        /// <param name="message"></param>
        void SendMessage(String message);

        /// <summary>
        /// Notify the workflow that a new guess has been received
        /// </summary>
        event EventHandler<GuessReceivedEventArgs> GuessReceived;
    }
}
```

Notice that the `interface` is decorated with the `ExternalDataExchangeAttribute`. This is required to identify this as a local service `interface` and make it available to workflows. The `GuessReceived` event uses the `GuessReceivedEventArgs` that you implemented in the previous step.

Implementing the Local Service

The local service class implements the IGuessingGame interface to provide communication with workflow instances. This service must also communicate with the host application. When a string message is received from a workflow, it must be forwarded to the host application so it can be shown to the user. And when the user makes a guess, the new guess must be passed to the workflow by raising the GuessReceived event.

To forward a message to the host application, the service provides a MessageReceived event. This event is not part of the IGuessingGame interface and is not used by workflow instances. Instead, the event is handled by the host application and raised by the SendMessage method as it is called by a workflow. To implement the event arguments class for this event, add a C# class to the SharedWorkflows project and name it MessageReceivedEventArgs. Listing 7-3 shows the complete code for the MessageReceivedEventArgs.cs file.

Listing 7-3. *Complete MessageReceivedEventArgs.cs File*

```
using System;
using System.Workflow.Activities;

namespace SharedWorkflows
{
    /// <summary>
    /// Passes a message from the workflow to the local service
    /// </summary>
    [Serializable]
    public class MessageReceivedEventArgs : ExternalDataEventArgs
    {
        private String _message;

        public MessageReceivedEventArgs(Guid instanceId, String message)
            : base(instanceId)
        {
            _message = message;
        }

        public String Message
        {
            get { return _message; }
            set { _message = value; }
        }
    }
}
```

■**Note** The MessageReceivedEventArgs class derives from ExternalDataEventArgs, even though it is not used by workflows. The use of this base class is not a requirement in this case, since it is not used by workflows. However, this event does need to pass the workflow instance ID to the host application, and this base class provides the InstanceId property that serves that purpose. Therefore, ExternalDataEventArgs is used here as a convenience instead of implementing an InstanceId property directly in this class.

Now you are ready to implement the local service class itself. Add another C# class to the SharedWorkflows project and name it GuessingGameService.

Listing 7-4 shows the complete code for the GuessingGameService.cs file.

Listing 7-4. *Complete GuessingGameService.cs File*

```
using System;
using System.Workflow.Runtime;

namespace SharedWorkflows
{
    public class GuessingGameService : IGuessingGame
    {
        #region IGuessingGame Members

        /// <summary>
        /// Called by a workflow to send a message to the host
        /// </summary>
        /// <param name="message"></param>
        public void SendMessage(string message)
        {
            if (MessageReceived != null)
            {
                MessageReceivedEventArgs args
                    = new MessageReceivedEventArgs(
                        WorkflowEnvironment.WorkflowInstanceId,
                        message);
                MessageReceived(this, args);
            }
        }

        /// <summary>
        /// Handled by a HandleExternalEventActivity in a workflow
        /// </summary>
        public event EventHandler<GuessReceivedEventArgs> GuessReceived;

        #endregion

        #region Public Members (not part of the service contract)

        /// <summary>
        /// Handled by the host application to receive messages
        /// </summary>
        public event EventHandler<MessageReceivedEventArgs> MessageReceived;

        /// <summary>
        /// Called by the host application to raise the
        /// GuessReceived event
        /// </summary>
        /// <param name="args"></param>
        public void OnGuessReceived(GuessReceivedEventArgs args)
        {
```

```
        if (GuessReceived != null)
        {
            //must pass null as the sender otherwise
            //the correct workflow won't receive the event.
            GuessReceived(null, args);
        }
    }

    #endregion
}
}
```

The `GuessingGameService` implements the `IGuessingGame` interface and has a total of four members. Two are defined by `IGuessingGame` and used by workflow instances, and two are used to interact with the host application. Table 7-1 recaps how each member is used.

Table 7-1. *GuessingGameService Members*

Member	Used By	Description
SendMessage	Workflow	A method that is invoked by a workflow instance to send a message to the host application. This method raises the `MessageReceived` event.
GuessReceived	Workflow	An event that is handled by a workflow instance to receive the next guessed number. This event is raised when the host application calls the `OnGuessReceived` method.
MessageReceived	Host	An event that is handled by the host application to receive a hint message from a workflow instance. This event is raised by the `SendMessage` method.
OnGuessReceived	Host	A method that is invoked by the host application to send a new guess to a workflow instance. This method raises the `GuessReceived` event that is handled by the workflow instance.

Notice that the `SendMessage` method uses the static `WorkflowEnvironment.WorkflowInstanceId` method to retrieve the workflow instance ID. This is a convenient way to obtain the workflow instance ID associated with the current thread. This works because this method is invoked by a workflow that is executing on its own workflow thread. By passing the instance ID with the `MessageReceived` event, it is available to the host application when it raises the `GuessReceived` event.

Implementing the Workflow

The responsibilities of the workflow include randomly choosing a number to guess, passing hint messages to the host application, and processing each guess as it is received. The workflow should continue to execute until a correct guess is received.

To begin development of the workflow, add a new sequential workflow to the `SharedWorkflows` project and name it `GuessingGameWorkflow`. The first order of business is to randomly select the target number to guess. This is initialization work that should be executed just once as the workflow begins. An appropriate place to execute this code is in the `Initialized` event for the workflow. This event is raised just prior to execution of the first activity. Switch to the Properties window for the workflow and add a handler named `OnInitialized` to the `Initialized` event.

The workflow also requires a few instance variables and properties. Listing 7-5 shows the code for the GuessingGameWorkflow at this point, including the OnInitialized code that you need to add.

Listing 7-5. *GuessingGameWorkflow.cs File with Initialization Code*

```
using System;
using System.Workflow.Activities;

namespace SharedWorkflows
{
    /// <summary>
    /// The guessing game workflow
    /// </summary>
    public sealed partial class GuessingGameWorkflow
        : SequentialWorkflowActivity
    {
        #region Variables and Properties

        private Int32 _theNumber;
        private Boolean _isComplete = false;
        private String _message = String.Empty;

        public String Message
        {
            get { return _message; }
            set { _message = value; }
        }

        public Boolean IsComplete
        {
            get { return _isComplete; }
            set { _isComplete = value; }
        }

        #endregion

        public GuessingGameWorkflow()
        {
            InitializeComponent();
        }

        /// <summary>
        /// Initialize variables as the workflow is started
        /// </summary>
        /// <param name="sender"></param>
        /// <param name="e"></param>
        private void OnInitialized(object sender, EventArgs e)
        {
            Random random = new Random();
            _theNumber = random.Next(1, 10);
            Message = "Please guess a number between 1 and 10.";
        }

    }
}
```

The Message property is the hint message that will be passed back to the host application (via the local service method call). The IsComplete property will be used by a WhileActivity to determine when the workflow is complete. The OnInitialized event handler randomly generates a number and saves it in a variable named _theNumber. It also sets an initial value for the Message property.

■**Tip** This workflow contains a number of activities, and it is easy to get lost in the detailed instructions. As a guide, you can look ahead to Figure 7-6 and see what the completed workflow should look like.

After switching to the workflow designer view, drag and drop a CallExternalMethodActivity onto the empty workflow. The purpose of this activity is to call the SendMessage method of the local service to pass the initial welcome message to the user. From the Properties window for this activity, select the ellipsis for the InterfaceType property. The type selector dialog shown in Figure 7-2 appears.

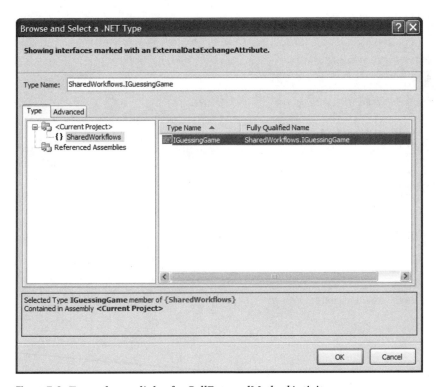

Figure 7-2. *Type selector dialog for CallExternalMethodActivity*

This is your opportunity to select the local service interface containing the method you wish to call. As shown in Figure 7-2, you should select IGuessingGame and then click OK.

Once you select the `interface`, you can choose the method to call using the `MethodName` property. For this example, select `SendMessage` as the `MethodName`. Once the method is chosen, the Parameters section of the Properties window is updated with the list of parameters required by the `SendMessage` method. Bind the `message` parameter to the `Message` property of the workflow. This means that as the `SendMessage` method is invoked, the current value of the `Message` workflow property will be passed as the `message` parameter. The Properties window for this activity should now look like Figure 7-3.

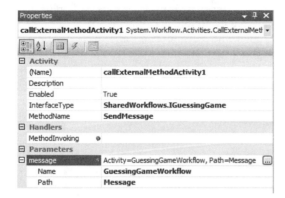

Figure 7-3. *Properties for callExternalMethodActivity1*

After this initial message is sent to the user, the remainder of the workflow should repeat until the user correctly guesses the number. To accomplish this, drag and drop a `WhileActivity` just below `callExternalMethodActivity1`. Add a declarative rule condition named `checkIsComplete` that contains the following expression:

`!this.IsComplete`

This condition will cause the child of the `WhileActivity` to repeat as long as the `IsComplete` workflow property is `false`. Figure 7-4 shows the completed Properties window for the `WhileActivity`.

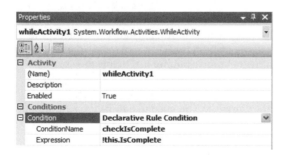

Figure 7-4. *Properties window for WhileActivity*

The WhileActivity requires a single child activity, so drag and drop a ListenActivity onto it. The ListenActivity creates two initial EventDrivenActivity instances as children. All of the remaining activities that you add will be children of one of these EventDrivenActivity instances. The EventDrivenActivity on the left will wait for the GuessReceived event, while the one on the right takes care of things if the event is never received.

To handle the GuessReceived event, drag and drop a HandleExternalEventActivity as a child of the EventDrivenActivity on the left side. Just as you did with the CallExternalMethodActivity, select the IGuessingGame as the InterfaceType. Select GuessReceived as the EventName. To handle the GuessReceived event, add a handler for the Invoked event by double-clicking the HandleExternalEventActivity. This adds a code handler with a default name of handleExternalEventActivity1_Invoked. You will add code to this handler after you add a few more activities to the workflow. The Properties window for the HandleExternalEventActivity should look like Figure 7-5.

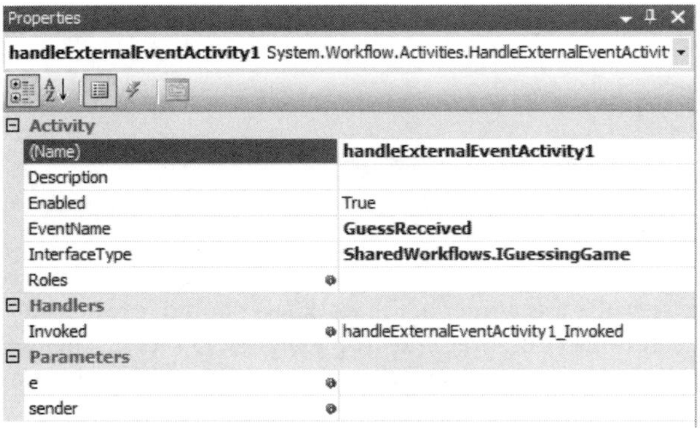

Figure 7-5. *Properties window for HandleExternalEventActivity*

The code handler for the GuessReceived event will determine if the user correctly guessed the number or if the user should guess something higher or lower. In any case, a message will be passed back to the user. Therefore, the next step is to once again use CallExternalMethodActivity to invoke the SendMessage method. All of the property values of this CallExternalMethodActivity instance are exactly the same as the previous instance. The easiest way to add another instance is to select the previous instance (callExternalMethodActivity1), select Copy from the Edit menu (or the right-click context menu), and then select Paste after positioning the mouse pointer just below the HandleExternalEventActivity. This should create a new activity named callExternalMethodActivity2 with all of the same property values of the original activity.

To complete the visually designed portion of the workflow, you need to handle the situation that occurs when the GuessReceived event is never received. To accomplish this, drag and drop a DelayActivity onto the EventDrivenActivity on the right side. Set the TimeoutDuration to one minute (00:01:00). Next, drag and drop a TerminateActivity directly beneath the DelayActivity. This will terminate the workflow if a guess has not been received within one minute.

Figure 7-6 shows the completed workflow.

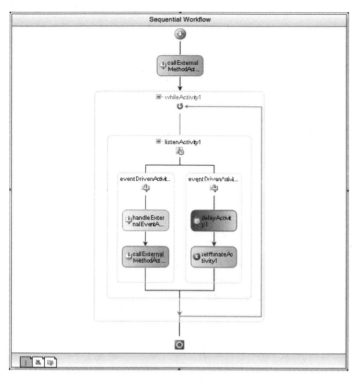

Figure 7-6. *Completed GuessingGameWorkflow*

Listing 7-6 shows the completed code for GuessingGameWorkflow.cs, including the code that you need to add to the handleExternalEventActivity1_Invoked method.

Listing 7-6. *Complete GuessingGameWorkflow.cs File*

```
using System;
using System.Workflow.Activities;

namespace SharedWorkflows
{
    /// <summary>
    /// The guessing game workflow
    /// </summary>
    public sealed partial class GuessingGameWorkflow
        : SequentialWorkflowActivity
    {
        #region Variables and Properties

        private Int32 _theNumber;
        private Boolean _isComplete = false;
        private String _message = String.Empty;
```

```csharp
public String Message
{
    get { return _message; }
    set { _message = value; }
}

public Boolean IsComplete
{
    get { return _isComplete; }
    set { _isComplete = value; }
}

#endregion

public GuessingGameWorkflow()
{
    InitializeComponent();
}

/// <summary>
/// Initialize variables as the workflow is started
/// </summary>
/// <param name="sender"></param>
/// <param name="e"></param>
private void OnInitialized(object sender, EventArgs e)
{
    Random random = new Random();
    _theNumber = random.Next(1, 10);
    Message = "Please guess a number between 1 and 10.";
}

/// <summary>
/// The event was received
/// </summary>
/// <param name="sender"></param>
/// <param name="e"></param>
private void handleExternalEventActivity1_Invoked(
    object sender, ExternalDataEventArgs e)
{
    GuessReceivedEventArgs eventArgs
        = e as GuessReceivedEventArgs;
    if (eventArgs != null)
    {
        if (eventArgs.NextGuess < _theNumber)
        {
            Message = "Try a higher number.";
        }
        else if (eventArgs.NextGuess > _theNumber)
        {
            Message = "Try a lower number.";
        }
```

```
            else
            {
                Message = String.Format(
                    "Congratulations! You correctly guessed {0}.", _theNumber);
                IsComplete = true;
            }
        }
    }
}
```

The handleExternalEventActivity1_Invoked method is executed when the GuessReceived event is raised. The code first casts the event arguments to the correct type (GuessReceivedEventArgs) and then decides which message to send to the user. If the user correctly guessed the number, then the IsComplete property is also set to true. Doing this stops further processing of the WhileActivity.

Implementing the Host Application

The host application for this example is a Windows Forms application instead of a simple Console application. This makes sense since the user must be able to easily interact with the running workflow.

The host application will be responsible for hosting the workflow runtime engine, adding the GuessingGameService to the runtime, responding to messages from the workflow, and passing guesses to the workflow.

Add a new project to the solution using the Windows Application project template and name the project GuessingGame. Since this isn't a workflow project template, it doesn't automatically include the workflow assembly references that you need. Add these references to the project now:

- System.Workflow.Activities
- System.Workflow.ComponentModel
- System.Workflow.Runtime
- SharedWorkflows
- Bukovics.Workflow.Hosting

The SharedWorkflows and Bukovics.Workflow.Hosting references are project references. The Bukovics.Workflow.Hosting project was originally developed in Chapter 4 and contains a set of workflow manager classes that assist with hosting duties.

Visually, the application is fairly simple and should look something like Figure 7-7.

Figure 7-7. *Visual design of the GuessingGame application*

The aim of this chapter (and book) isn't to teach you how to write Windows Forms applications. So feel free to improve on this visual design if you have the urge. The basic requirements are a Label to display messages from the workflow, a TextBox used to enter a new guess, a Button to start a new workflow, and another Button to send a guess to the workflow.

Before entering any code for this form, make sure you add Click event handlers for both buttons. Listing 7-7 shows the complete code for this form, which is discussed with comments within the listing.

Listing 7-7. *Complete Form1.cs for the GuessingGame Project*

```
using System;
using System.Windows.Forms;

using System.Workflow.Activities;
using System.Workflow.Runtime;

using Bukovics.Workflow.Hosting;
using SharedWorkflows;

namespace GuessingGame
{
    /// <summary>
    /// The WinForm for the number guessing game
    /// </summary>
    public partial class Form1 : Form
    {
        private WorkflowRuntimeManager _workflowManager;
        private GuessingGameService _gameService;
        private Guid _instanceId = Guid.Empty;
```

The Form1 class defines several instance variables. One holds a reference to the WorkflowRuntimeManager, another holds a reference to the GuessingGameService, and another is used to store the workflow instance ID.

```
        public Form1()
        {
            InitializeComponent();
        }

        protected override void OnLoad(EventArgs e)
        {
            base.OnLoad(e);

            //create workflow runtime and manager
            _workflowManager = new WorkflowRuntimeManager(
                new WorkflowRuntime());

            //add the external data exchange service to the runtime
            ExternalDataExchangeService exchangeService
                = new ExternalDataExchangeService();
            _workflowManager.WorkflowRuntime.AddService(exchangeService);

            //add our local service
            _gameService = new GuessingGameService();
            exchangeService.AddService(_gameService);
```

```
    //subscribe to the service event that sends us messages
    _gameService.MessageReceived
        += new EventHandler<MessageReceivedEventArgs>(
            gameService_MessageReceived);

    //handle the terminated event
    _workflowManager.WorkflowRuntime.WorkflowTerminated
        += new EventHandler<WorkflowTerminatedEventArgs>(
            WorkflowRuntime_WorkflowTerminated);
}
```

The OnLoad event of the form is used to initialize the workflow runtime engine. During initialization, an instance of the GuessingGameService is created and added to the engine. The code subscribes to the MessageReceived event of this service. Within the handler for this event, the workflow hint message is processed and shown to the user. The WorkflowTerminated event of the WorkflowRuntime is also handled in order to display a message when the workflow has been terminated. This occurs when a guess hasn't been received before the DelayActivity fires in one minute.

```
protected override void OnFormClosed(FormClosedEventArgs e)
{
    base.OnFormClosed(e);
    //clean up the workflow runtime
    if (_workflowManager != null)
    {
        _workflowManager.Dispose();
    }
}

private void btnStart_Click(object sender, EventArgs e)
{
    //start the workflow without any parameters
    _workflowManager.StartWorkflow(
        typeof(GuessingGameWorkflow), null);

    btnGuess.Enabled = true;
}
```

The Click event handler for the Start button (btnStart_Click) is where a new instance of the GuessingGameWorkflow is started. The workflow doesn't require any input parameters.

```
private void btnGuess_Click(object sender, EventArgs e)
{
    //pass the guess to the running workflow
    try
    {
        Int32 nextGuess = Int32.Parse(txtNextNumber.Text);
        //raise the GuessReceived event in the game service
        _gameService.OnGuessReceived(
            new GuessReceivedEventArgs(_instanceId, nextGuess));
    }
    catch (FormatException)
    {
        MessageBox.Show("Could not parse the number");
    }
```

```
        catch (OverflowException)
        {
            MessageBox.Show("The number exceeded the allowed limits");
        }
        catch (EventDeliveryFailedException)
        {
            MessageBox.Show(
                "Your guess was not delivered.\n\rStart a new game.",
                "Game Ended", MessageBoxButtons.OK, MessageBoxIcon.Asterisk);
        }
        catch (Exception exception)
        {
            MessageBox.Show(exception.Message);
        }
    }
```

The Click event handler for the Guess button (btnGuess_Click) parses the input string and, if it is a valid number, passes it to the workflow by calling the OnGuessReceived method of the GuessingGameService. The GuessReceivedEventArgs require a workflow instance ID as one of its parameters. The instance ID that is used here was saved in the handler for the MessageReceived event.

```
        private delegate void UpdateDelegate();

        private void gameService_MessageReceived(object sender,
            MessageReceivedEventArgs e)
        {
            UpdateDelegate theDelegate = delegate()
            {
                //update the UI with the message
                lblMessage.Text = e.Message;
                txtNextNumber.SelectAll();
                txtNextNumber.Focus();
            };

            //save the workflow instance ID. we will need it
            //when we make the return trip with a guess.
            _instanceId = e.InstanceId;

            //execute the anonymous delegate on the UI thread
            this.Invoke(theDelegate);
        }
```

The handler for the MessageReceived event (gameService_MessageReceived) is responsible for saving the workflow instance ID and also updating the user with the latest hint message. Unfortunately, updating the user isn't quite as simple as setting the Text property of the Label to the new message. Windows Forms controls have *thread affinity*, which means they can be updated only by the thread that created them. The thread that is raising the MessageReceived event is actually the workflow thread. In order to update the Label control, the code uses the Invoke method of the form, which executes the code on the primary user interface thread. The Invoke method requires a delegate that references the code to execute and an anonymous delegate is used to keep all of the code in one place.

```
        void WorkflowRuntime_WorkflowTerminated(object sender,
            WorkflowTerminatedEventArgs e)
        {
            MessageBox.Show(
                "Sorry, but the time expired since your last guess.",
                "Start a New Game", MessageBoxButtons.OK,
                MessageBoxIcon.Information);
        }
    }
}
```

■**Caution** Always be careful when updating a user interface with workflow data. If the method or event handler was invoked by a workflow, it is executing on a workflow thread, and you can't directly update user interface controls on that thread.

Testing the Workflow

After building the GuessingGame project, you should be ready to take it out for a test drive. Figure 7-8 shows the application after you click the Start button. Clicking the Start button begins the workflow.

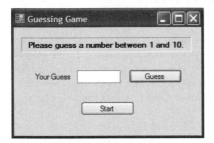

Figure 7-8. *Starting the Guessing Game*

As you can see from Figure 7-8, as the workflow begins, you see the original welcome message asking you to guess the number. Figure 7-9 shows the result after I guessed an incorrect number.

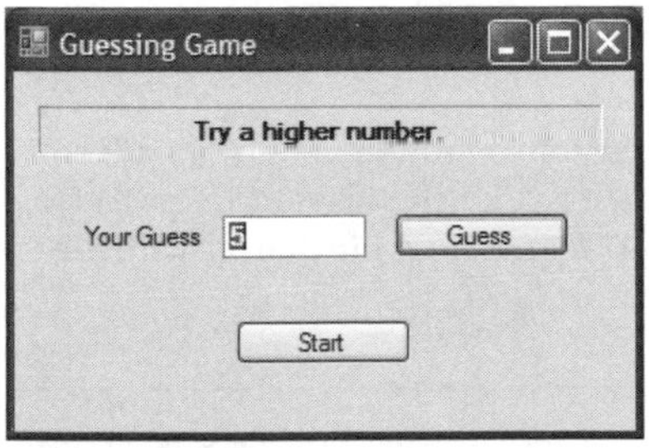

Figure 7-9. *Guessing Game with an incorrect guess*

A similar message would be presented if I need to guess a lower number. Once I correctly guess the number, the message shown in Figure 7-10 is presented.

Figure 7-10. *Guessing Game with a correct guess*

Once you correctly guess a number, the workflow completes and is no longer available to accept guesses. If you click the Start button again, another workflow instance is started. This application works correctly because it is able to send the workflow instance ID back with the GuessReceivedEventArgs. The workflow runtime uses this ID to locate the correct workflow instance that should receive the event. If this host application supported it, you could have multiple workflow instances running at the same time, all waiting for a guess. The instance ID passed with the GuessReceived event would be used to route the event to the correct workflow instance.

Generating Communication Activities

Using CallExternalMethodActivity and HandleExternalEventActivity, a workflow can communicate with a local service. In order for these activities to work, you must first select the InterfaceType and then choose either a MethodName or EventName (depending on which activity is used). WF offers an alternative way to communicate with a local service. Using the wca.exe utility, you can generate a set of strongly typed custom activities. Each generated activity corresponds to one of the local service methods or events. If you use these custom activities, you no longer need to select the interface type and the member name.

This command-line utility is the Workflow Communication Activity Generator, wca.exe. You pass it the name of a compiled assembly containing one or more local service interfaces (those decorated with ExternalDataExchangeAttribute). The output from the utility is one or more source files containing the generated activities. One file is generated for any methods and another for any events. The naming convention of the files uses the interface name followed by .Invokes.cs or .Sinks.cs. Once the source files are generated, you simply add them to the project and build it. The custom activities are then available from the Visual Studio Toolbox just like any other activity.

Generating the Activities

To demonstrate the use of the wca.exe utility, you can generate custom communication activities for the IGuessingGame interface used in the last example. You can then modify the GuessingGameWorkflow to replace the CallExternalMethodActivity and HandleExternalEventActivity instances with the new custom-generated activities.

■**Note** The wca.exe utility is executed from a command prompt. It is included with the Windows SDK, not with Visual Studio. You can execute the utility directly from the \bin directory where the Windows SDK was installed. Or, you can execute the setenv.cmd found in the Windows SDK \bin directory to set the environment variables that allow you to execute wca.exe from any directory.

From a command prompt, switch to the SharedWorkflows project directory from the last example. To generate communication activities for this project, enter this command:

```
wca /collapseArgs bin\debug\SharedWorkflows.dll
```

This assumes that you've already built the debug version of this project and that the assembly is in the default location under the project directory. I'm using the optional /collapseArgs parameter, which generates one property named E for the event arguments. Without this option, the utility generates a property for each public field and property of the event arguments.

■**Note** The wca.exe utility supports other command-line options. Please consult MSDN for the current documentation, or enter wca.exe without any parameters for a short description of the available options.

When I execute this command, these two files are generated:

- IGuessingGame.Invokes.cs
- IGuessingGame.Sinks.cs

The first file contains a custom activity named SendMessage that corresponds to the IGuessingGame method with the same name. This class uses the standard CallExternalMethodActivity class as its base. The second file has an activity named GuessReceived that derives from the standard HandleExternalEventActivity class. Both activities are generated using the same namespace as the interface (SharedWorkflows).

After adding these two source files to the SharedWorkflows project and rebuilding, you should see the two new activities in the Visual Studio Toolbox, as shown in Figure 7-11.

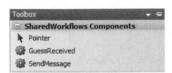

Figure 7-11. *Toolbox with generated communication activities*

■**Note** If you are developing your own custom activities, you should normally follow the naming convention of adding the Activity suffix to the class name. Unfortunately, Microsoft didn't follow its naming convention with these generated activities. Instead of generating a name of SendMessage, it really should be SendMessageActivity.

Modifying the Workflow

To use the generated activities, you simply need to replace the current CallExternalMethodActivity and HandleExternalEventActivity instances with the custom activities. Open the GuessingGameWorkflow from the last example (in the SharedWorkflows project). Delete callExternalMethodActivity1 and callExternalMethodActivity2, and replace them with instances of the new SendMessage activity. Bind the message parameter for the activity to the Message workflow property.

Then replace handleExternalEventActivity1 with a GuessReceived activity. For this activity, you can set the Invoked event to use the same handleExternalEventActivity1_Invoked handler as the original version.

The revised workflow is shown in Figure 7-12.

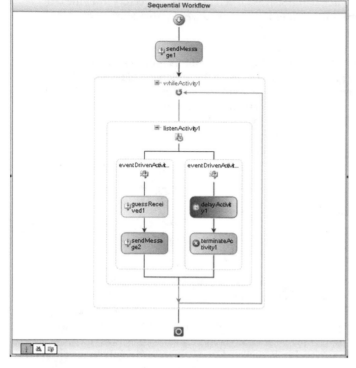

Figure 7-12. *Revised GuessingGameWorkflow with custom activities*

After building the project, you should be able to start the GuessingGame application and begin guessing numbers. The results that you see should be exactly the same as the example that used the standard activities.

Using generated communication activities slightly simplifies your workflow design experience. You no longer have to select the InterfaceType and the method or event since this information is baked into the custom activity. If you use the same methods and events a number of times in multiple workflows, this slight improvement can really add up.

Manually Controlling Correlation

In the previous examples, you've seen that as local service events are raised, they are routed to the correct workflow instance. The magic that accomplishes this is the workflow instance ID that is passed with the ExternalDataEventArgs. The InstanceId property of ExternalDataEventArgs identifies the workflow instance that should receive the event.

It is common for a workflow to wait for multiple events, using a different HandleExternalEventActivity instance to wait for each event. The standard event routing also handles this situation, passing the event to the correct HandleExternalEventActivity instance in the workflow. When one event is received, all other EventDrivenActivity branches are canceled.

This type of event routing is sufficient for most situations. However, what happens if a workflow must handle multiple instances of the same event? This might be the case if the workflow includes an activity such as a ParallelActivity that permits multiple branches of execution. Each execution branch may be waiting for the same type of event. The standard event routing will identify the correct workflow instance, but how do you determine which activity should receive the event? This situation is illustrated in Figure 7-13.

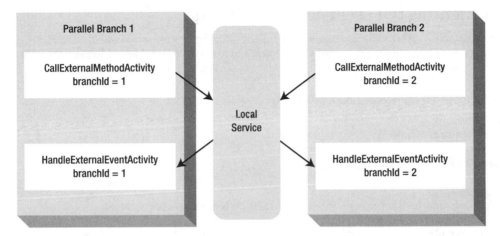

Figure 7-13. *A workflow that requires correlation*

Figure 7-13 shows two parallel branches of execution. Each branch executes the same set of activities, first using CallExternalMethodActivity to invoke a local service method, and then waiting for an event with HandleExternalEventActivity. The problem arises when both of the HandleExternalEventActivity instances are waiting for the same type of event. When designing a workflow such as this one, you need to logically associate the activities within a single branch with each other. When a branch uses CallExternalMethodActivity to invoke a method, you want any events that result from that method to be returned to an activity in the original branch. To put it another way, when one branch passes a branchId of 1 to a method, an event that passes back a branchId of 1 should be handled by an activity in the same branch.

The solution to this problem is to manually control the event routing using a set of *correlation attributes*. These are attributes that you apply to the local service interface. They identify a parameter that is used to correlate an event back to the correct activity within a workflow.

There are three correlation attributes:

- CorrelationParameterAttribute: You place this attribute on the interface itself to identify the name of the correlation parameter. Once the parameter is identified, the correlation logic will look for this parameter name in all methods and events. If it finds the parameter name, the correlation logic will use the parameter value to route an event back to the correct activity.

- CorrelationAliasAttribute: You place this attribute on a member to provide an alias name for the correlation parameter. You use this attribute when the parameter names in the method or event are not consistent with the parameter name specified in the CorrelationParameterAttribute.

- CorrelationInitializerAttribute: This member-level attribute identifies the member in the interface that initializes the correlation parameter. It tells the runtime that the parameter named by the CorrelationParameterAttribute is being initialized by this method or event.

The following example demonstrates the use of these correlation attributes. In this example, you will implement a simple local service with a single method and single event. The workflow that uses the local service has a ParallelActivity that creates two separate branches of execution. Each branch of execution contains the same set of activities, first invoking the local service method and then waiting for the event. Since each branch of execution is waiting for the same type of event, this example illustrates the problem that the correlation attributes solve.

Implementing the Event Arguments Class

To begin this example, you will define the event arguments class that will be passed with the local service event. Add a new C# class to the SharedWorkflows project and name it CorrelationExampleEventArgs. The complete code for the CorrelationExampleEventArgs.cs file is shown in Listing 7-8.

Listing 7-8. *Complete CorrelationExampleEventArgs.cs File*

```
using System;
using System.Workflow.Activities;

namespace SharedWorkflows
{
    /// <summary>
    /// EventArgs to demonstrate the use of correlation attributes
    /// </summary>
    [Serializable]
    public class CorrelationExampleEventArgs : ExternalDataEventArgs
    {
        private Int32 _branchId;
        private Int32 _eventData;

        public CorrelationExampleEventArgs(Guid instanceId,
            Int32 branchId, Int32 eventData)
            : base(instanceId)
        {
            _branchId = branchId;
            _eventData = eventData;
        }

        public Int32 BranchId
        {
            get { return _branchId; }
            set { _branchId = value; }
        }

        public Int32 EventData
        {
            get { return _eventData; }
            set { _eventData = value; }
        }
    }
}
```

This class is derived from ExternalDataEventArgs, which is a requirement for any local service event arguments. The BranchId property will be the correlation parameter that identifies the correct activity to receive the event. The EventData property allows the local service to pass additional data with the event. The value of this property will be written to the Console to help verify that the correct activity received the event.

Defining the Service Interface

Next, add a new C# interface to the SharedWorkflows project and name it ICorrelationExample. This interface defines the local service members that are made available to workflows. Listing 7-9 shows the complete ICorrelationExample.cs file.

Listing 7-9. *Complete ICorrelationExample.cs File*

```
using System;
using System.Workflow.Activities;

namespace SharedWorkflows
{
    /// <summary>
    /// Defines methods and events to demonstrate the
    /// use of correlation attributes.
    /// </summary>
    [ExternalDataExchange]
    [CorrelationParameter("branchId")]
    public interface ICorrelationExample
    {
        /// <summary>
        /// Called by the workflow to start the
        /// correlation example
        /// </summary>
        /// <param name="branchId"></param>
        [CorrelationInitializer]
        void StartDemonstration(Int32 branchId);

        /// <summary>
        /// An event that is handled by the workflow
        /// </summary>
        [CorrelationAlias("branchId", "e.BranchId")]
        event EventHandler<CorrelationExampleEventArgs> EventReceived;
    }
}
```

Like all local service interfaces, this one is decorated with the ExternalDataExchange attribute. The three correlation attributes have also been applied to the interface. The CorrelationParameterAttribute is used to identify the parameter named branchId as the correlation parameter. This means that the value of that parameter is used to coordinate the routing of the event back to the correct activity. The CorrelationInitializerAttribute identifies the StartDemonstration method as the member that initializes the correlation parameter. When the StartDemonstration method is invoked by a workflow, it marks the beginning of a new series of local service calls that should be correlated. The workflow runtime takes note of the value of the branchId at this point. The CorrelationAliasAttribute provides an alias name of e.BranchId for the branchId correlation parameter. This is needed for the event since the event arguments are always passed with a name of e. The BranchId property of the event arguments must be associated with the correlation parameter.

Implementing the Local Service

To implement the local service, add a new C# class to the SharedWorkflows project and name it CorrelationExampleService. The complete code for this service is shown in Listing 7-10.

Listing 7-10. *Complete CorrelationExampleService.cs File*

```
using System;
using System.Workflow.Runtime;

namespace SharedWorkflows
{
    /// <summary>
    /// Local service used to demonstrate correlation
    /// </summary>
    public class CorrelationExampleService : ICorrelationExample
    {
        #region ICorrelationExample Members

        public void StartDemonstration(int branchId)
        {
            if (EventReceived != null)
            {
                EventReceived(null, new CorrelationExampleEventArgs(
                    WorkflowEnvironment.WorkflowInstanceId,
                    branchId, branchId));
            }
        }

        public event EventHandler<CorrelationExampleEventArgs> EventReceived;

        #endregion
    }
}
```

This service class implements both of the members defined by the ICorrelationExample interface. To keep this example as simple as possible, the StartDemonstration method raises the EventReceived event, allowing the workflow to immediately handle the event. The original branchId that is passed as a method argument is returned as the EventData.

Implementing the Workflow

To define the workflow, add a new sequential workflow to the SharedWorkflows project and name it CorrelationExampleWorkflow. The complete workflow that you will define is shown in Figure 7-14 and described in detail after the figure.

As you can see from Figure 7-14, the workflow has a single ParallelActivity that contains two SequenceActivity instances. The easiest way to define this workflow is to concentrate on the left-side SequenceActivity first. Once it is complete, you can copy and paste it to the right side, and then make just a few minor changes.

Starting with the left-side SequenceActivity, drag and drop a CallExternalMethodActivity as the first child. Set the InterfaceType property to SharedWorkflows.ICorrelationExample and select StartDemonstration as the MethodName. Once you select the MethodName, the Parameters section of the Properties window will be updated to include a branchId parameter. You can set the branchId parameter to a literal 1.

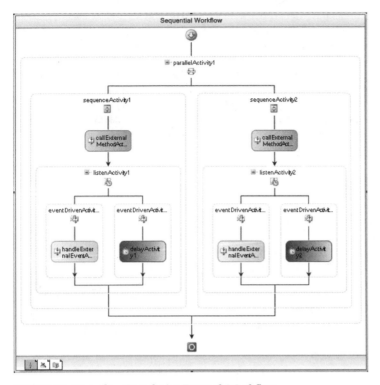

Figure 7-14. *Complete CorrelationExampleWorkflow*

Since the interface includes correlation attributes, the Properties window will also include a CorrelationToken property along with a child property of OwnerActivityName. These properties provide a unique name to this correlation. You can enter the literal branch1 for the CorrelationToken and choose the workflow (CorrelationExampleWorkflow) as the OwnerActivityName. This means that the CorrelationToken of branch1 must be unique within the entire workflow. The Properties window for callExternalMethodActivity1 should look like Figure 7-15.

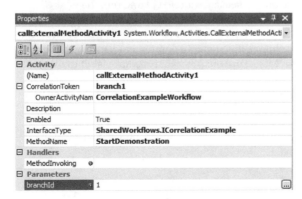

Figure 7-15. *Properties window for callExternalMethodActivity1*

Next, add a ListenActivity under the CallExternalMethodActivity. Add a HandleExternalEventActivity under the left-side EventDrivenActivity. Select SharedWorkflows. ICorrelationExample as the InterfaceType, and then select EventReceived as the EventName. Enter the same values for the CorrelationToken and OwnerActivityName as you did in the CallExternalMethodActivity (branch1). This associates this HandleExternalEventActivity with the previous CallExternalMethodActivity. It tells the workflow runtime that the branchId that was passed to the CallExternalMethodActivity should be used to route the event back to this activity.

To add a code handler for the Invoked event, double-click the handleExternalEventActivity1. You will add the code for this handler after you have completed the visual portion of the workflow design. Figure 7-16 shows the Properties window for handleExternalEventActivity1.

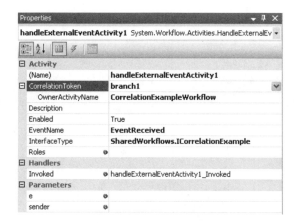

Figure 7-16. *Properties window for handleExternalEventActivity1*

To complete the ListenActivity, you should add a DelayActivity to the right-side EventDrivenActivity. You can set the TimeoutDuration to ten seconds (00:00:10).

To create a duplicate set of activities for the right-side execution branch, you can copy and paste the left-side branch. To do this, select sequenceActivity1 (on the left side), right-click it, and select Copy. Then right-click and select Paste while the mouse pointer is positioned under parallelActivity1. This should create a sequenceActivity3 along with all of the child activities that you just added. You can then delete the original empty sequenceActivity2 and rename sequenceActivity3 to sequenceActivity2.

You now need to make a few minor adjustments to the new copy of the execution branch on the right. Select callExternalMethodActivity2 and change the branchId parameter to 2. Also change the CorrelationToken to branch2 instead of branch1. Make sure the OwnerActivityName is set to the workflow name (CorrelationExampleWorkflow).

Make similar changes to handleExternalEventActivity2, changing the CorrelationToken to branch2. Also change the name of the Invoked event handler to handleExternalEventActivity2_Invoked.

Now you can add code to the two Invoked event handlers. Listing 7-11 shows the complete listing for the CorrelationExampleWorkflow.cs file.

Listing 7-11. *Complete CorrelationExampleWorkflow.cs File*

```csharp
using System;
using System.Workflow.Activities;

namespace SharedWorkflows
{
    /// <summary>
    /// Workflow that demonstrates correlation
    /// </summary>
    public sealed partial class CorrelationExampleWorkflow :
        SequentialWorkflowActivity
    {
        public CorrelationExampleWorkflow()
        {
            InitializeComponent();
        }

        private void handleExternalEventActivity1_Invoked(
            object sender, ExternalDataEventArgs e)
        {
            if (e is CorrelationExampleEventArgs)
            {
                Console.WriteLine("Received data for branch 1: {0}",
                    ((CorrelationExampleEventArgs)e).EventData);
            }
        }

        private void handleExternalEventActivity2_Invoked(
            object sender, ExternalDataEventArgs e)
        {
            if (e is CorrelationExampleEventArgs)
            {
                Console.WriteLine("Received data for branch 2: {0}",
                    ((CorrelationExampleEventArgs)e).EventData);
            }
        }
    }
}
```

Each event code handler writes a message to the Console. The EventData property of the event arguments is written to verify that the correct event is received by each handler.

Testing the Workflow

To test this correlation example, you will use a simple Console application. Create a new project using the Sequential Workflow Console Application project template and name the project ConsoleCorrelation. You can remove the Workflow1 that the project template generates since it won't be needed. Add project references to the SharedWorkflows project and Bukovics.Workflow.Hosting.

Add a new C# class to the project and name it CorrelationTest. This class will contain the code to initialize the workflow runtime, add the CorrelationExampleService, and start the CorrelationExampleWorkflow. The complete code for CorrelationTest.cs is in Listing 7-12.

Listing 7-12. *Complete CorrelationTest.cs File*

```csharp
using System;
using System.Collections.Generic;
using System.Workflow.Runtime;
using System.Workflow.Activities;

using Bukovics.Workflow.Hosting;
using SharedWorkflows;

namespace ConsoleCorrelation
{
    public class CorrelationTest
    {
        public static void Run()
        {
            using (WorkflowRuntimeManager manager
                = new WorkflowRuntimeManager(new WorkflowRuntime()))
            {
                //add services to the workflow runtime
                AddServices(manager.WorkflowRuntime);
                manager.WorkflowRuntime.StartRuntime();

                //run the first workflow
                Console.WriteLine("Executing CorrelationExampleWorkflow");
                manager.StartWorkflow(
                    typeof(SharedWorkflows.CorrelationExampleWorkflow), null);
                manager.WaitAll(10000);

                Console.WriteLine("Completed CorrelationExampleWorkflow\n\r");
            }
        }

        /// <summary>
        /// Add any services needed by the runtime engine
        /// </summary>
        /// <param name="instance"></param>
        private static void AddServices(WorkflowRuntime instance)
        {
            //add the external data exchange service to the runtime
            ExternalDataExchangeService exchangeService
                = new ExternalDataExchangeService();
            instance.AddService(exchangeService);

            //add our custom local service
            //to the external data exchange service
            exchangeService.AddService(new CorrelationExampleService());
        }
    }
}
```

This rather unremarkable code is similar to the hosting code that you've seen for other examples. After creating the WorkflowRuntime and the WorkflowRuntimeManager classes, it adds an instance of the CorrelationExampleService. Once this runtime environment is initialized, the CorrelationExampleWorkflow is started.

The code to execute this test goes into the `Program.cs` file and looks like this:

```
using System;

namespace ConsoleCorrelation
{
    public class Program
    {
        static void Main(string[] args)
        {
            //execute the workflow tests
            CorrelationTest.Run();

            Console.WriteLine("Press any key to exit");
            Console.ReadLine();
        }
    }
}
```

When I execute the `ConsoleCorrelation` program, I see these results:

```
Executing CorrelationExampleWorkflow
Received data for branch 1: 1
Received data for branch 2: 2
Completed CorrelationExampleWorkflow

Press any key to exit
```

This shows that the event containing a `branchId` of 1 was processed by the `branch1` event handler. Likewise, the event containing a `branchId` of 2 was handled by the `branch2` handler.

You won't always need to use the correlation attributes to manually control correlation. But if multiple portions of your workflow are waiting to receive the same type of event, they will likely be necessary.

Using the EventHandlingScopeActivity

In the most common event handling scenario, you define multiple events that can be handled, with each one contained within an `EventDrivenActivity`. These `EventDrivenActivity` branches are added as children to a single `ListenActivity`. In this scenario, when one branch receives its event, the other branches are canceled. Once the first event is received and handled, no further processing of activities takes place within the parent `ListenActivity`. This is the type of event handling that you've seen so far in this chapter.

The `EventHandlingScopeActivity` is a dramatically different type of event handling activity. It has two discrete sections: a main line child activity and a set of event handling activities. The single main line child activity executes in a normal manner. Although `EventHandlingScopeActivity` accepts only a single child, the child can be a composite activity such as a `SequenceActivity` that enables you to add any number of child activities. When the main line activity (and all of its children) completes, the entire `EventHandlingScopeActivity` comes to an end.

In addition to the main line child activity, event handling activities are contained within a single `EventHandlersActivity` that is a child of `EventHandlingScopeActivity`. The `EventHandlersActivity` is the parent for one or more `EventDrivenActivity` instances, with each one acting as a separate branch of execution. Each `EventDrivenActivity` contains one or more child activities, but the first child must implement IEventActivity (e.g., HandleExternalEventActivity) in order to start execution of the branch.

When an event is received, the activities within the EventDrivenActivity are executed. However, unlike the more common event handling of ListenActivity, the other event branches are all still alive. They can also receive their events and execute the activities within their execution branch. The original branch that received its event can even receive it again.

These activities are used in advanced scenarios where you need to concurrently handle multiple events and execute a main line set of activities at the same time. In the example that follows, you will implement a workflow using the EventHandlingScopeActivity. It contains a main line set of activities that execute while a condition is true. It also handles three external events, one of which is being used to set the condition for the main line activities.

Defining the Service Interface

To begin this example, you will define the interface for the local service. Add a new C# interface to the SharedWorkflows project and name it IScopeExample. Listing 7-13 shows the complete code for the IScopeExample.cs file.

Listing 7-13. *Complete IScopeExample.cs File*

```
using System;
using System.Workflow.Activities;

namespace SharedWorkflows
{
    /// <summary>
    /// Defines the methods and events that
    /// demonstrate the use of EventHandlingScopeActivity
    /// and EventHandlersActivity.
    /// </summary>
    [ExternalDataExchange]
    public interface IScopeExample
    {
        /// <summary>
        /// Notify the host that the example workflow started
        /// </summary>
        void Started();

        event EventHandler<ExternalDataEventArgs> EventOne;

        event EventHandler<ExternalDataEventArgs> EventTwo;

        event EventHandler<ExternalDataEventArgs> EventStop;
    }
}
```

The Started method will be invoked by the workflow when it first begins execution. The three events will be handled by the workflow using HandleExternalEventActivity instances.

Implementing the Local Service

To implement the local service, add a new C# class to the SharedWorkflows project and name it ScopeExampleService. Listing 7-14 contains the complete code for ScopeExampleService.cs.

Listing 7-14. *Complete ScopeExampleService.cs File*

```csharp
using System;

using System.Workflow.Activities;
using System.Workflow.Runtime;

namespace SharedWorkflows
{
    /// <summary>
    /// Local service used with the
    /// EventHandlingScopeActivity example.
    /// </summary>
    public class ScopeExampleService : IScopeExample
    {
        private Guid _instanceId;

        #region IScopeExample Members

        public void Started()
        {
            //save the workflow instance ID
            _instanceId = WorkflowEnvironment.WorkflowInstanceId;
        }

        public event EventHandler<ExternalDataEventArgs> EventOne;

        public event EventHandler<ExternalDataEventArgs> EventTwo;

        public event EventHandler<ExternalDataEventArgs> EventStop;

        #endregion

        #region Methods to raise events from the host

        public void OnEventOne()
        {
            if (EventOne != null)
            {
                EventOne(null, new ExternalDataEventArgs(_instanceId));
            }
        }

        public void OnEventTwo()
        {
            if (EventTwo != null)
            {
                EventTwo(null, new ExternalDataEventArgs(_instanceId));
            }
        }
```

```
        public void OnEventStop()
        {
            if (EventStop != null)
            {
                EventStop(null, new ExternalDataEventArgs(_instanceId));
            }
        }

        #endregion
    }
}
```

In addition to the three events, this service includes three methods that are invoked by the host application to raise the events. The `Started` method saves the workflow instance ID as a variable. This ID is later used when raising the individual events.

■**Caution** Since this local service saves the workflow instance ID as a local variable, it doesn't support more than one workflow instance at a time. This approach is fine for this simple example, but it is not suitable as production code. Please refer to the prior examples in this chapter for implementations that pass the workflow instance ID back to the host application.

Implementing the Workflow

Add a new sequential workflow to the `SharedWorkflows` project and name it `ScopeExampleWorkflow`. The workflow requires one property that will be used in a declarative rule condition. The `ScopeExampleWorkflow.cs` file with the `IsComplete` property is shown in Listing 7-15.

Listing 7-15. *Partial ScopeExampleWorkflow.cs File*

```
using System;
using System.Workflow.Activities;

namespace SharedWorkflows
{
    /// <summary>
    /// Workflow that demonstrates EventHandlingScopeActivity
    /// </summary>
    public sealed partial class ScopeExampleWorkflow
        : SequentialWorkflowActivity
    {
        private Boolean _isComplete = false;
```

```
        public Boolean IsComplete
        {
            get { return _isComplete; }
            set { _isComplete = value; }
        }

        public ScopeExampleWorkflow()
        {
            InitializeComponent();
        }
    }
}
```

Defining the Main Line

After switching to the workflow designer view, you will define the main line of execution. Start by dragging and dropping an EventHandlingScopeActivity to the empty workflow. This activity supports a single activity as its only child, so drop a SequenceActivity onto the EventHandlingScopeActivity.

The first thing this workflow main line should do is call the Started method of the local service. To accomplish this, add a CallExternalMethodActivity as the first child of the SequenceActivity. Wire up the properties for this activity by setting the InterfaceType to SharedWorkflows. IScopeExample, and then select Started as the MethodName. This method doesn't request any parameters.

After calling the Started method, the workflow should continuously execute a set of activities. To implement this, add a WhileActivity just below the CallExternalMethodActivity. Set a declarative rule condition with an expression that checks the IsComplete workflow property. Name the condition checkIsComplete and enter the expression like this:

```
!this.IsComplete
```

This will execute all child activities of the WhileActivity until the IsComplete property is set to true.

WhileActivity accepts only a single child, so add a SequenceActivity to it now. Under the SequenceActivity, add a CodeActivity and rename it codeMainlineMessage. This workflow will have a number of CodeActivity instances, and giving each of them a meaningful name will make it easier to identify the purpose of each CodeActivity event handler. After renaming the CodeActivity, double-click it to add a handler for the ExecuteCode event. You will add the code to this handler after you've completed the visual portion of the workflow design.

Finally, add a DelayActivity under the CodeActivity. Set the TimeoutDuration to one second (00:00:01). This slight delay is added between iterations of the WhileActivity to produce a more readable set of messages that will be written to the Console. Figure 7-17 shows the completed main line of the workflow.

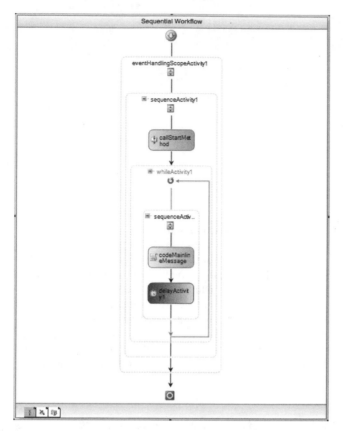

Figure 7-17. *Main line of ScopeExampleWorkflow*

Defining the Event Handlers

The next step is to add the event handlers to the EventHandlingScopeActivity. There will be a total of three different events that you will handle. To add event handlers to the EventHandlingScopeActivity, you need to change to an alternate design view for this activity. Select the EventHandlingScopeActivity, right-click it, and then select View Event Handlers. Alternatively, you can select the activity and then select View Event Handlers from the main Workflow menu. Once you change the view, you should see an empty EventHandlersActivity instance as shown in Figure 7-18.

To add a handler for the first event, drag and drop an EventDrivenActivity to the filmstrip area of the EventHandlersActivity. The workflow should now look like Figure 7-19.

The EventHandlersActivity contains two distinct areas. The top filmstrip area is where you will drag and drop instances of EventDrivenActivity. It allows you to scroll left and right if the activity contains more events than will fit in a single view. To define the activities for a given EventDrivenActivity, select the activity, and then drag and drop the child activities onto the lower area.

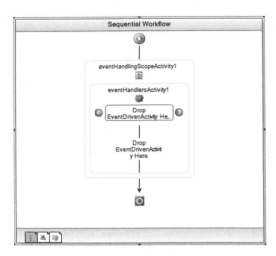

Figure 7-18. *Viewing event handlers*

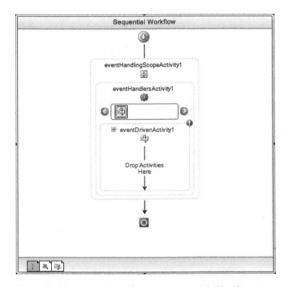

Figure 7-19. *EventHandlersActivity with the first EventDrivenActivity*

Now you can define one or more child activities by dragging and dropping them onto the lower area. The first child event of an `EventDrivenActivity` must be the one that waits for the event and implements `IEventActivity`. Add a `HandleExternalEventActivity` to the lower area now. The workflow should now look like Figure 7-20.

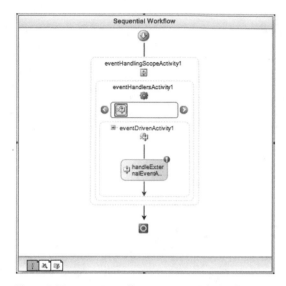

Figure 7-20. *EventHandlersActivity with the first HandleExternalEventActivity*

This activity will wait for EventOne from the local service, so rename it to handleEventOne to help describe its purpose. After switching to the Properties window, set the InterfaceType to SharedWorkflows.IScopeExample and select EventOne as the EventName. Double-click the activity to add a handler for the Invoked event. You will add code to all of these event handlers after just a few additional steps. Figure 7-21 shows the completed Properties window for this activity.

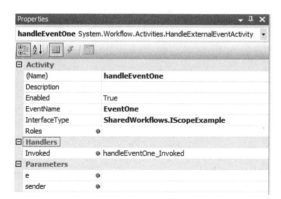

Figure 7-21. *Properties window for the handleEventOne activity*

You can now repeat the process for the other two local service events. For each one, add an EventDrivenActivity to the filmstrip area, and then add a HandleExternalEventActivity to the lower area. The second event to handle is EventTwo and the third event is EventStop. Figure 7-22 shows the completed set of event handlers with the last event still selected.

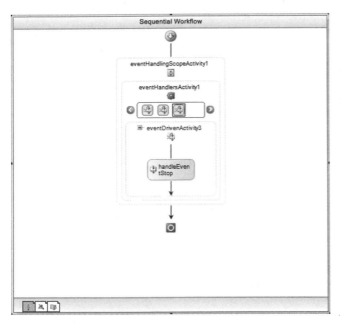

Figure 7-22. *Completed event handlers*

You can now add code to the workflow that writes messages to the Console for each event. Listing 7-16 shows the complete code for the ScopeExampleWorkflow.cs file, including all event handling code.

Listing 7-16. *Complete ScopeExampleWorkflow.cs File*

```
using System;
using System.Workflow.Activities;

namespace SharedWorkflows
{
    /// <summary>
    /// Workflow that demonstrates EventHandlingScopeActivity
    /// </summary>
    public sealed partial class ScopeExampleWorkflow
        : SequentialWorkflowActivity
    {
        private Boolean _isComplete = false;

        public Boolean IsComplete
        {
            get { return _isComplete; }
            set { _isComplete = value; }
        }

        public ScopeExampleWorkflow()
        {
            InitializeComponent();
        }
```

```
        private void codeMainlineMessage_ExecuteCode(
            object sender, EventArgs e)
        {
            Console.WriteLine("Executing the workflow main line");
        }

        private void handleEventOne_Invoked(
            object sender, ExternalDataEventArgs e)
        {
            Console.WriteLine("Got EventOne");
        }

        private void handleEventTwo_Invoked(
            object sender, ExternalDataEventArgs e)
        {
            Console.WriteLine("Got EventTwo");
        }

        private void handleEventStop_Invoked(
            object sender, ExternalDataEventArgs e)
        {
            Console.WriteLine("Got EventStop");

            //set the variable that will tell the WhileActivity to stop
            _isComplete = true;
        }
    }
}
```

In addition to writing a message to the Console, the code for the EventStop event also sets _isComplete to true. This will cause the condition for the WhileActivity to return false and the main line set of activities (and the workflow) will complete.

Testing the Workflow

To test this workflow, create a new project using the Sequential Workflow Console Application project template and name the project ConsoleScope. You can remove the Workflow1 that the project template generates since it won't be needed. Add project references to the SharedWorkflows project and Bukovics.Workflow.Hosting.

Add a new C# class to the project and name it ScopeTest. This class will contain the code to initialize the workflow runtime, add the ScopeExampleService, and start the ScopeExampleWorkflow. Once the workflow is up and running, public methods of the local service are invoked to raise events that will be handled by the workflow. The complete code for ScopeTest.cs is in Listing 7-17.

Listing 7-17. *Complete ScopeTest.cs File*

```
using System;
using System.Threading;
using System.Workflow.Runtime;
using System.Workflow.Activities;

using Bukovics.Workflow.Hosting;
using SharedWorkflows;
```

```csharp
namespace ConsoleScope
{
    /// <summary>
    /// Test the ScopeExampleWorkflow
    /// </summary>
    public class ScopeTest
    {
        private static ScopeExampleService _scopeService;

        public static void Run()
        {
            using (WorkflowRuntimeManager manager
                = new WorkflowRuntimeManager(new WorkflowRuntime()))
            {
                //add services to the workflow runtime
                AddServices(manager.WorkflowRuntime);
                manager.WorkflowRuntime.StartRuntime();

                //start the workflow
                Console.WriteLine("Executing ScopeExampleWorkflow");
                manager.StartWorkflow(
                    typeof(SharedWorkflows.ScopeExampleWorkflow), null);

                //allow the main line of the workflow to execute
                Thread.Sleep(3000);
                //fire some events
                _scopeService.OnEventOne();
                Thread.Sleep(100);
                _scopeService.OnEventOne();
                Thread.Sleep(100);
                _scopeService.OnEventOne();
                Thread.Sleep(100);
                _scopeService.OnEventTwo();
                Thread.Sleep(100);
                _scopeService.OnEventOne();
                //let the main line execute by itself again
                Thread.Sleep(3000);
                //signal that the workflow should stop
                _scopeService.OnEventStop();

                manager.WaitAll(10000);

                Console.WriteLine("Completed ScopeExampleWorkflow\n\r");
            }
        }

        /// <summary>
        /// Add any services needed by the runtime engine
        /// </summary>
        /// <param name="instance"></param>
        private static void AddServices(WorkflowRuntime instance)
        {
            //add the external data exchange service to the runtime
            ExternalDataExchangeService exchangeService
```

```
                    = new ExternalDataExchangeService();
                instance.AddService(exchangeService);

                //add our custom local service
                //to the external data exchange service
                _scopeService = new ScopeExampleService();
                exchangeService.AddService(_scopeService);
            }
        }
    }
```

A small amount of delay was added between each event to make the output a bit cleaner. The delays also provide the main line activities with time to execute once per second.

The final bit of code to execute the Run method of this test class goes into the Program.cs file and looks like this:

```
using System;

namespace ConsoleScope
{
    public class Program
    {
        static void Main(string[] args)
        {
            //execute the workflow tests
            ScopeTest.Run();

            Console.WriteLine("Press any key to exit");
            Console.ReadLine();
        }
    }
}
```

When I execute the ConsoleScope application, I see these results:

```
Executing ScopeExampleWorkflow
Executing the workflow main line
Executing the workflow main line
Executing the workflow main line
Got EventOne
Got EventOne
Got EventOne
Got EventTwo
Executing the workflow main line
Got EventOne
Executing the workflow main line
Executing the workflow main line
Got EventStop
Completed ScopeExampleWorkflow

Press any key to exit
```

Due to differences in machine speed and configuration, it is possible that the sequence of events may be slightly different when you execute this on your machine. But the basic set of events should look very similar to my results.

Looking at the results, you can clearly see that the main line of activities is executing at a rate of once per second. After a short delay, the host application begins raising events, including multiple firings of the same event (EventOne). Finally, when the EventStop event is raised, the main line activities and the workflow complete.

The EventHandlingScopeActivity is a powerful, yet complex activity. Use it in situations where you want to execute a main line set of activities in a normal way, but also concurrently respond to one or more events.

Summary

The focus of this chapter was event-driven activities, which temporarily suspend execution of the workflow to wait until an event is received. This chapter demonstrated using these activities with a sequential workflow, but they are also an important key to implementing state machine workflows.

The first example in this chapter implemented a workflow that used CallExternalMethodActivity and HandleExternalEventActivity to provide two-way communication with a local service. The local service also interacted with the host application, acting as a communication conduit.

The second example showed you how to use the wca.exe utility to generate a set of custom activities. The generated activities are strongly typed to a particular local service interface. They provide an alternative to the more generalized CallExternalMethodActivity and HandleExternalEventActivity.

The use of optional correlation attributes was demonstrated in the third example. These attributes are used in situations where a workflow is required to wait for multiple instances of the same event. They help to route the event to the correct activity within the workflow.

This chapter concluded with an example that demonstrated the use of EventHandlingScopeActivity and EventHandlersActivity. These activities are more powerful and complex than the more common event handling activities. They are used in situations where you need to execute a main line set of activities and also concurrently respond to multiple events.

In the next chapter, you will learn about workflow persistence, which permits long-running workflows.

■■■

CHAPTER 8

Workflow Persistence

An important capability of workflows is that they can be *persisted* (saved and reloaded at a later time). Workflow persistence is especially important when developing applications that coordinate human interactions, since those interactions could take a long period of time. But persistence is also applicable to other types of applications. Without persistence, the lifetime of your workflows is limited. When the host application is shut down, any workflow instances simply cease to exist.

Workflow persistence is implemented as one of the optional core workflow services. You need to load a persistence service only if your application requires it.

After taking a brief look at reasons to use persistence, this chapter examines how persistence works in the Windows Workflow Foundation (WF) world. WF includes a standard persistence service that works with SQL Server. This chapter includes an example that demonstrates how to use this persistence service.

The WF persistence logic was implemented as external services in order to permit you to provide your own persistence implementation. The second half of this chapter demonstrates how to implement your own custom persistence service and use it in an application.

Understanding Persistence

Before jumping into a live example of workflow persistence, this section of the chapter provides an overview of how persistence works in WF. This overview provides background information that will make the examples that follow it easier to understand.

This section begins with a review of several reasons to use workflow persistence.

Why Persist Workflows?

Up to this point, you have seen workflows that perform only short-lived tasks. You have seen that multiple instances of a workflow can be started by an application, but each workflow exists only in memory, within the workflow runtime engine. While these in-memory workflows are very useful and can be used to accomplish many tasks, they are limited. When the host application or the workflow runtime is stopped, the workflow instances cease to exist. Their lifetime is tightly bound to a single host application. Workflows that only exist in memory are limited in several ways.

Workflow persistence means to save the complete state of a workflow to a durable store such as a SQL database or file. Once persisted, the workflow can be removed from memory and reloaded at a later time. Here are some of the reasons to use persistence with your workflows:

- *Human interaction tasks*: Workflows that are designed to interact with humans are typically long running. They may take minutes, hours, days, or weeks to complete. It isn't practical to keep such a workflow alive in memory for that length of time. Persistence of the workflow provides a way to unload it while it is waiting for the next human event, and then reload it when the event is received.

- *State machine workflows*: These workflows are designed around a set of defined states, with interactions that cause a transition to a different state. The kinds of tasks that are modeled with a state machine workflow usually require persistence of the workflow while waiting for the next transition.

- *Scalability*: In-memory workflows are limited to execution within a single application host. To provide scalability, some applications may require multiple workflow runtime hosts, perhaps running on multiple servers. A persisted workflow can be loaded and executed on a different server than the one that started it.

- *Resource consumption*: Without a persistence mechanism, workflows must stay in memory. They have nowhere else to go. If a workflow is waiting for an external input, such as an event, it is actually idle. With a persistence mechanism in place, the idled workflow can be persisted and unloaded from memory. Once the external event is received, the workflow is loaded back into memory and processing can continue. Swapping workflows in and out of memory like this frees resources (memory and workflow threads), making them available for workflows that are actively executing.

- *Application flexibility*: An in-memory workflow can be executed only by the application that started it. Perhaps you have a web-based application that starts a workflow, but you also want to use more traditional applications (e.g., Windows Forms) to work with the workflow. Persisting the workflow allows it to be reloaded by an entirely different class of application.

Not every application requires persistence. If you require only short-lived workflows that execute within a single application, you can probably do without persistence. On the other hand, if your workflows model long-running tasks that are designed around human interactions, or if you need the flexibility to tune the performance of your application, then you likely need persistence.

Persistence Overview

WF implements persistence as one of the optional core workflow services. Instead of providing a static persistence mechanism that is implemented internally by the workflow runtime engine, the WF designers decided to make the implementation externally pluggable. This provides you with total control when it comes to persistence. If you don't need it, you don't have to load the persistence service. If you do need persistence, you load the persistence service that provides the implementation that meets your needs.

WF provides a standard persistence implementation that works with a SQL Server database (SqlWorkflowPersistenceService in the System.Workflow.Runtime.Hosting namespace). You create your own SQL Server database for persistence, but WF provides the scripts to create the necessary tables and stored procedures that this service expects.

If you don't want to use the standard SQL Server persistence service, you can provide your own implementation. WF includes a base class (WorkflowPersistenceService in the System.Workflow. Runtime.Hosting namespace) that you must derive from when implementing your own persistence service. You are permitted to implement the persistence service using any type of durable store that you want. You can persist workflows to binary files, to XML, or to a relational database with your own schema. But you can load only a single persistence service at a time for an instance of the workflow runtime.

You load a persistence service just once, when you are first initializing the workflow runtime engine. Once the service is loaded, the workflow runtime engine uses it at designated times in the life of a workflow to save or load the state of a workflow instance. Persisting a workflow instance doesn't require any manual intervention from you; it is something that is controlled by the workflow runtime engine and occurs automatically.

This is one of the real benefits of using persistence with WF. It eliminates the need to implement your own persistence mechanism to save the state of your application. If your application state is made up of one or more workflow instances, the state is saved for you. Because you are utilizing WF, you get persistence for free.

If a persistence service is loaded, the *state* of the workflow is persisted in these situations:

- When a workflow becomes idle. An example is when a workflow is waiting for an external event or executes a `DelayActivity`.

- When a workflow completes or terminates.

- When a `TransactionScopeActivity` completes. A `TransactionScopeActivity` identifies a logical unit of work that is ended when the activity completes.

- When a `CompensatableSequenceActivity` completes. A `CompensatableSequenceActivity` identifies a set of child activities that are compensatable. *Compensation* is the ability to undo the actions of a completed activity.

- When a custom activity that is decorated with the `PersistOnCloseAttribute` completes.

- When you manually invoke one of the methods on a `WorkflowInstance` that cause a persistence operation. Examples are `Unload` and `TryUnload`. The `Load` method results in a previously unloaded and persisted workflow being retrieved and loaded back into memory.

Note It is important to make a distinction between saving a workflow and saving the *state* of a workflow. Not all persistence operations result in a new serialized copy of a workflow being saved. For instance, when a workflow completes or terminates, the standard SQL Server persistence service (`SqlWorkflowPersistenceService`) actually removes the persisted copy of the workflow. It persisted the workflow in the sense that it updated the durable store with the state of the workflow. If you implement your own persistence service, you may choose to do something else when a workflow completes.

When any of these situations occur, the workflow runtime engine invokes the appropriate methods of the persistence service to save the workflow state. The workflow runtime doesn't know (or care) how the persistence method was implemented. It only knows that a persistence operation was invoked on the service. Obviously, if no persistence service has been loaded, these methods are not invoked and no persistence takes place.

When a workflow must be reloaded into memory, other methods on the persistence service are invoked. These methods retrieve the workflow state from a durable store and deserialize it back into an `Activity` object that the workflow engine can use. This occurs most often when a workflow that was previously idle is now ready for execution. Perhaps the workflow received an external event that it was waiting to receive, or the time span for a `DelayActivity` expired.

To handle a `DelayActivity`, a persistence service must also save the time when the `DelayActivity` is expected to expire. The service will then periodically poll the persisted workflows to see if any have a timer that has expired. If so, the workflow is ready to be reloaded and execution resumes. The `SqlWorkflowPersistenceService` has a `LoadingInterval` property that permits you to control the frequency of this polling interval.

In most scenarios, you will want to unload a workflow from memory when it becomes idle and after it has been persisted. A workflow might become idle if it is waiting to receive an external event.

Unloading an idle workflow makes sense since it frees valuable resources (memory and workflow threads), making them available to workflows that are actively executing. And since you don't know exactly how long the workflow will be idle, it's usually more efficient to unload it.

However, unloading workflows when they become idle is a persistence service option. You can choose to persist idle workflows but continue to keep them in memory. You might do this in an application where workflows are frequently waiting for external events, but the events are received very quickly. In this case, the overhead of unloading and then immediately reloading a workflow might be greater than simply keeping the workflow in memory.

Note Persistence and unloading of idle workflows are related but separate options. You can choose to persist workflows and unload them from memory when they become idle. Or you can persist them and choose to keep them in memory. You cannot choose to unload an idle workflow unless you also persist it; that is not an option.

In the next section, you will learn how to use the standard persistence service for SQL Server (SqlWorkflowPersistenceService).

Using the SqlWorkflowPersistenceService

WF includes the SqlWorkflowPersistenceService class. This class contains the implementation for a persistence service that uses SQL Server as its durable store. Using this service is, by far, the easiest way to introduce persistence to your workflows. The primary requirement is that you must have a version of SQL Server installed (SQL Server 2000 or greater). Since SQL Server Express is now available for free, it is very easy to meet this requirement.

To use SqlWorkflowPersistenceService, you follow these steps:

1. If you haven't already done so, install a version of SQL Server (SQL Server 2000 or greater). This includes the full purchased versions of SQL Server 2000 or SQL Server 2005, or the free versions of SQL Server Express or Microsoft SQL Server Desktop Engine (MSDE).

2. Create a database to use for workflow persistence. This can be a new database that will contain only the persistence tables, or an existing database that is already used by your application.

3. Create the database tables, stored procedures, and other objects that SqlWorkflowPersistenceService expects. WF includes the SQL scripts that create these objects. You simply need to execute them once against your target database.

4. In your host application, create an instance of SqlWorkflowPersistenceService and add it to the workflow runtime engine as a core service. This is done just once during initialization of the workflow runtime. The constructor for SqlWorkflowPersistenceService is where you provide the database connection string, along with other parameters that control the service. You can also load this service using entries in your App.Config file.

That's it. Once you've completed these steps, workflows will be persisted automatically according to the workflow runtime rules outlined in the previous section.

In the sections that follow, you will walk through the development of an application that demonstrates workflow persistence. The application is a Windows Forms application that allows you to start multiple workflow instances and monitor their current status (e.g., idle, persisted, unloaded, complete). The demonstration workflow is extremely simple. It contains a WhileActivity that executes until a workflow property is set to true. Within the WhileActivity, a set of two external events is handled. The first event doesn't really do anything useful. But when that event is raised, it allows the workflow to execute the next iteration of the WhileActivity. That causes the workflow to cycle through the states again (idle, persisted, unloaded) as you watch from the host application. The second event sets the workflow property so that the WhileActivity and the workflow end.

Since the workflows are persisted, you can also stop and restart the application without losing any workflows. When the application starts, it obtains a list of all workflows that are persisted. You can then reload and execute one of the available workflows by raising one of the external events.

Preparing a Database for Persistence

Before you begin development of the demonstration application, you should prepare a database that will be used for workflow persistence.

If you haven't already done so, install a version of Microsoft SQL Server. If you don't have a full retail version available, you can use SQL Server Express, which is distributed with Visual Studio 2005.

Once you have SQL Server installed, you can create a database and populate it with the objects required by SqlWorkflowPersistenceService by following the steps outlined in Chapter 4. Within that chapter, the sidebar titled "Setup Steps for Persistence Testing" outlines the steps necessary to prepare a persistence database.

After you've performed all of these steps, a local database named WorkflowPersistence should now be populated with the tables and stored procedures that are required for workflow persistence. The demonstration application assumes that this is the database name and that it is available on the local instance of SQL Server Express (localhost\SQLEXPRESS). If you change the database or server name, you'll need to adjust the example code accordingly.

Implementing the Local Service

This application requires the ability to raise two different events that are handled by the workflow. To raise these events, you need to implement a local service. Start by creating a new project using the Empty Workflow Project template and name the project SharedWorkflows. This creates a DLL assembly that can be referenced by the Windows Forms demonstration application.

You'll need to first define an interface for the local service. Add a new C# interface to the SharedWorkflows project and name it IPersistenceDemo. Listing 8-1 shows the complete contents of the IPersistenceDemo.cs file.

Listing 8-1. *Complete IPersistenceDemo.cs File*

```csharp
using System;
using System.Workflow.Activities;

namespace SharedWorkflows
{
    /// <summary>
    /// Events exposed by the PersistenceDemoService
    /// </summary>
    [ExternalDataExchange]
    public interface IPersistenceDemo
    {
        event EventHandler<ExternalDataEventArgs> ContinueReceived;

        event EventHandler<ExternalDataEventArgs> StopReceived;
    }
}
```

The interface is decorated with the ExternalDataExchangeAttribute to identify it as the local service interface. The two events that are defined both use ExternalDataEventArgs as their event arguments. This is a requirement in order to handle these events in a workflow.

Next, add a new C# class to the SharedWorkflows project and name it PersistenceDemoService. This is the local service that implements the IPersistenceDemo interface. It is almost as simple as the interface. Listing 8-2 shows the complete PersistenceDemoService.cs file.

Listing 8-2. *Complete PersistenceDemoService.cs File*

```csharp
using System;
using System.Workflow.Activities;

namespace SharedWorkflows
{
    /// <summary>
    /// Implements events that are handled by workflow instances
    /// </summary>
    public class PersistenceDemoService : IPersistenceDemo
    {
        #region IPersistenceDemo Members

        public event EventHandler<ExternalDataEventArgs> ContinueReceived;

        public event EventHandler<ExternalDataEventArgs> StopReceived;

        #endregion

        #region Members used by the host application

        /// <summary>
        /// Raise the ContinueReceived event
        /// </summary>
        /// <param name="args"></param>
        public void OnContinueReceived(ExternalDataEventArgs args)
        {
            if (ContinueReceived != null)
            {
                ContinueReceived(null, args);
            }
        }

        /// <summary>
        /// Raise the StopReceived event
        /// </summary>
        /// <param name="args"></param>
        public void OnStopReceived(ExternalDataEventArgs args)
        {
            if (StopReceived != null)
            {
                StopReceived(null, args);
            }
        }

        #endregion
    }
}
```

In addition to implementing the two `IPersistenceDemo` events, the service includes two methods to raise the events. These methods will be invoked by the host application and are not available to workflows since they are not part of the `interface`.

Implementing the Workflow

To implement the example workflow, add a new sequential workflow to the `SharedWorkflows` project and name it `PersistenceDemoWorkflow`. The workflow requires one property that will be referenced by a condition of the `WhileActivity`, so it's best to add the property before you begin the visual design of the workflow. Listing 8-3 shows the `PersistenceDemoWorkflow.cs` file after the property has been added.

Listing 8-3. *PersistenceDemoWorkflow.cs After Adding a Property*

```
using System;
using System.Workflow.Activities;

namespace SharedWorkflows
{
    /// <summary>
    /// A workflow that demonstrates the behavior of
    /// persistence services
    /// </summary>
    public sealed partial class PersistenceDemoWorkflow :
        SequentialWorkflowActivity
    {
        private Boolean _isComplete = false;

        public Boolean IsComplete
        {
            get { return _isComplete; }
            set { _isComplete = value; }
        }

        public PersistenceDemoWorkflow()
        {
            InitializeComponent();
        }

    }
}
```

The visual design of the workflow is fairly simple. Here's the big picture: The workflow will start with a `WhileActivity`, with a `CompensatableSequenceActivity` as its child. Under the `CompensatableSequenceActivity`, there will be a `ListenActivity` with two `EventDrivenActivity` branches. Each `EventDrivenActivity` will contain a single `HandleExternalEventActivity` that listens for an event from the local service.

To implement the workflow, first switch to the visual workflow designer view, and then drag and drop a `WhileActivity` onto the empty workflow. Add a declarative rule condition to the `WhileActivity` and give it a `ConditionName` of `checkIsComplete`. Enter an `Expression` that checks the value of the `IsComplete` workflow property like this:

```
!this.IsComplete
```

This condition causes the WhileActivity to repeat its child activity until the IsComplete property is set to true.

Next, add a CompensatableSequenceActivity as the direct child of the WhileActivity.

■**Note** We don't actually need the CompensatableSequenceActivity for this workflow to operate correctly. However, adding it here causes additional persistence service methods to be invoked each time the CompensatableSequenceActivity completes. You will see these persistence service methods in action later in this chapter when you develop your own persistence service. That example uses this same workflow to demonstrate a custom persistence service. Adding the CompensatableSequenceActivity now is easier than adding it later.

You can now add a ListenActivity to the CompensatableSequenceActivity, and add a HandleExternalEventActivity under each EventDrivenActivity. Set the InterfaceType for both of the HandleExternalEventActivity instances to SharedWorkflows.IPersistenceDemo.

Rename the HandleExternalEventActivity instance on the left to handleContinueReceived and set the EventName property to ContinueReceived. You don't need to add any code to handle this event. The act of raising the event is enough to demonstrate the behavior of the persistence service when an event is received.

Rename the HandleExternalEventActivity instance on the right to handleStopReceived and set the EventName to StopReceived. When this event is received, you need to set the IsComplete workflow property to true. To do this, double-click the activity to add a handler for the Invoked event named handleStopReceived_Invoked. You will add code to this handler in the next step. This completes the visual design of the workflow. Figure 8-1 shows the completed workflow.

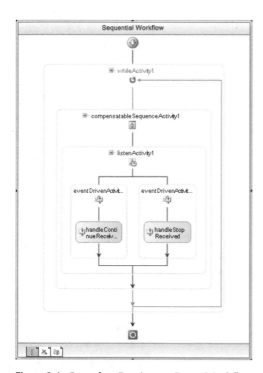

Figure 8-1. *Complete PersistenceDemoWorkflow*

Listing 8-4 shows the completed `PersistenceDemoWorkflow.cs` file, including the event handling code you need to add to the `handleStopReceived_Invoked` method.

Listing 8-4. *Complete PersistenceDemoWorkflow.cs File*

```
using System;
using System.Workflow.Activities;

namespace SharedWorkflows
{
    /// <summary>
    /// A workflow that demonstrates the behavior of
    /// persistence services
    /// </summary>
    public sealed partial class PersistenceDemoWorkflow :
        SequentialWorkflowActivity
    {
        private Boolean _isComplete = false;

        public Boolean IsComplete
        {
            get { return _isComplete; }
            set { _isComplete = value; }
        }

        public PersistenceDemoWorkflow()
        {
            InitializeComponent();
        }

        private void handleStopReceived_Invoked(
            object sender, ExternalDataEventArgs e)
        {
            //tell the WhileActivity to stop
            _isComplete = true;
        }
    }
}
```

Implementing the Host Application

The host application is a Windows Forms application that will allow you to start and then interact with multiple workflow instances. The form will have a `DataGridView` that lists available workflow instances along with a status message for each instance. The `DataGridView` is bound to a collection of objects that contain the workflow instance ID and the status message. The user interface includes buttons that permit you to start a new workflow instance, or interact with an existing workflow instance by raising the `ContinueReceived` or `StopReceived` events.

To begin the host application, add a new Windows Application project to the current solution and name the project `PersistenceDemo`. Since this project isn't created from a workflow project template, you'll need to add references to these assemblies yourself:

- `System.Workflow.Activities`
- `System.Workflow.ComponentModel`

- System.Workflow.Runtime

- SharedWorkflows

- Bukovics.Workflow.Hosting

The SharedWorkflows and Bukovics.Workflow.Hosting references are project references. The Bukovics.Workflow.Hosting project was originally developed in Chapter 4 and contains a set of workflow manager classes that assist with hosting duties.

Implementing a Class for Displaying Workflow Status

Before you begin the visual design of the host application, there is one nonvisual class that you need to add. The application will use a DataGridView to display status information for the available workflows. You need to implement a class that contains the information to display. Instances of this class will be created and placed in a collection that is databound to the DataGridView.

Add a new C# class to the PersistenceDemo project and name it Workflow. Listing 8-5 shows the completed code for this class.

Listing 8-5. *Complete Workflow.cs File*

```csharp
using System;

namespace PersistenceDemo
{
    /// <summary>
    /// Used for display of workflow status in a DataGridView
    /// </summary>
    public class Workflow
    {
        private Guid _instanceId = Guid.Empty;
        private String _statusMessage = String.Empty;
        private Boolean _isCompleted;

        public Guid InstanceId
        {
            get { return _instanceId; }
            set { _instanceId = value; }
        }

        public String StatusMessage
        {
            get { return _statusMessage; }
            set { _statusMessage = value; }
        }

        public Boolean IsCompleted
        {
            get { return _isCompleted; }
            set { _isCompleted = value; }
        }
    }
}
```

Designing the User Interface

The visual design of Form1 in the PersistenceDemo project looks like Figure 8-2.

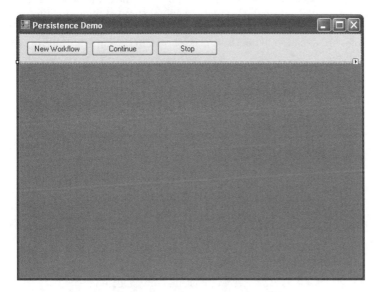

Figure 8-2. *Windows Forms designer for PersistenceDemo Form1*

Table 8-1 lists the set of visual controls that you'll need to add to the form.

Table 8-1. *Form1 Controls*

Control Type	Name	Events to Handle	Description
DataGridView	dataGridView1	SelectionChanged	Bound to a collection of objects that displays the list of available workflow instances along with their status. The DataGridView is the large gray area shown in the lower portion of the form.
Button	btnNewWorkflow	Click	Starts a new workflow instance.
Button	btnContinue	Click	Raises the ContinueReceived event.
Button	btnStop	Click	Raises the StopReceived event.

After adding and naming the visual controls, add event handles for the events listed in Table 8-1. If you use the suggested control names, the names for the event handlers should match the example code shown in Listing 8-6.

Adding Code to the Form

Unlike many of the other examples in this book, this host application contains a fair amount of code. To make it clearer how all of the pieces of code work together, Listing 8-6 shows the completed code for the Form1.cs file with comments embedded within the listing to highlight some of the more interesting sections of code.

A number of instance variables are declared in the Form1 class shown in Listing 8-6. Table 8-2 identifies the variables and their usage.

Table 8-2. *Form1 Instance Variables*

Variable	Description
_workflowManager	Holds a reference to the WorkflowManager object that wraps the WorkflowRuntime.
_persistence	Holds a reference to the persistence service.
_persistenceDemoService	Holds a reference to the local service that implements the events.
_workflows	A dictionary of Workflow objects that are keyed by the workflow instance ID. This collection is bound to the DataGridView for display.
_selectedWorkflow	The Workflow object that is currently selected in the DataGridView.

Listing 8-6. *Complete Form1.cs File*

```csharp
using System;
using System.Data;
using System.Collections.Generic;
using System.Windows.Forms;

using System.Workflow.Activities;
using System.Workflow.Runtime;
using System.Workflow.Runtime.Hosting;

using Bukovics.Workflow.Hosting;
using SharedWorkflows;

namespace PersistenceDemo
{
    /// <summary>
    /// The persistence demo application
    /// </summary>
    public partial class Form1 : Form
    {
        private WorkflowRuntimeManager _workflowManager;
        private WorkflowPersistenceService _persistence;
        private PersistenceDemoService _persistenceDemoService;
        private Dictionary<Guid, Workflow> _workflows
            = new Dictionary<Guid, Workflow>();
        private Workflow _selectedWorkflow;
```

```csharp
public Form1()
{
    InitializeComponent();
}

#region Initialization and shutdown

/// <summary>
/// Initialize the workflow runtime during startup
/// </summary>
/// <param name="e"></param>
protected override void OnLoad(EventArgs e)
{
    base.OnLoad(e);
    //create workflow runtime and manager
    _workflowManager = new WorkflowRuntimeManager(
        new WorkflowRuntime());

    //add services to the workflow runtime
    AddServices(_workflowManager.WorkflowRuntime);

    _workflowManager.WorkflowRuntime.WorkflowCreated
        += new EventHandler<WorkflowEventArgs>(
            WorkflowRuntime_WorkflowCreated);
    _workflowManager.WorkflowRuntime.WorkflowCompleted
        += new EventHandler<WorkflowCompletedEventArgs>(
            WorkflowRuntime_WorkflowCompleted);
    _workflowManager.WorkflowRuntime.WorkflowPersisted
        += new EventHandler<WorkflowEventArgs>(
            WorkflowRuntime_WorkflowPersisted);
    _workflowManager.WorkflowRuntime.WorkflowUnloaded
        += new EventHandler<WorkflowEventArgs>(
            WorkflowRuntime_WorkflowUnloaded);
    _workflowManager.WorkflowRuntime.WorkflowLoaded
        += new EventHandler<WorkflowEventArgs>(
            WorkflowRuntime_WorkflowLoaded);
    _workflowManager.WorkflowRuntime.WorkflowIdled
        += new EventHandler<WorkflowEventArgs>(
            WorkflowRuntime_WorkflowIdled);

    //initially disable these buttons until a workflow
    //is selected in the data grid view
    btnContinue.Enabled = false;
    btnStop.Enabled = false;

    //start the runtime prior to checking for any
    //existing workflows that have been persisted
    _workflowManager.WorkflowRuntime.StartRuntime();

    //load information about any workflows that
    //have been persisted
    RetrieveExistingWorkflows();
}
```

The initialization of the workflow runtime is done in the overridden OnLoad method. This method is invoked when the form is first loaded. The code in this method creates an instance of the WorkflowRuntime and wraps it in a WorkflowRuntimeManager. WorkflowRuntimeManager was developed in Chapter 4 and assists with some of the routine hosting tasks.

The code in the OnLoad method also adds handlers for a number of the WorkflowRuntime events. Events such as WorkflowCreated, WorkflowPersisted, and WorkflowUnloaded are handled in order to update the display when the status of a workflow instance changes.

During startup the OnLoad method executes the AddServices method. This is where an instance of the SqlWorkflowPersistenceService class is created and added to the workflow runtime.

```
/// <summary>
/// Add any services needed by the runtime engine
/// </summary>
/// <param name="instance"></param>
private void AddServices(WorkflowRuntime instance)
{
    //use the standard SQL Server persistence service
    String connStringPersistence = String.Format(
        "Initial Catalog={0};Data Source={1};Integrated Security={2};",
        "WorkflowPersistence", @"localhost\SQLEXPRESS", "SSPI");
    _persistence =
        new SqlWorkflowPersistenceService(connStringPersistence, true,
            new TimeSpan(0, 2, 0), new TimeSpan(0, 0, 5));
    instance.AddService(_persistence);

    //add the external data exchange service to the runtime
    ExternalDataExchangeService exchangeService
        = new ExternalDataExchangeService();
    instance.AddService(exchangeService);

    //add our local service
    _persistenceDemoService = new PersistenceDemoService();
    exchangeService.AddService(_persistenceDemoService);
}
```

The AddServices method first constructs a SQL Server connection string. This code assumes that the name of the database is WorkflowPersistence and that it is managed by a local copy of SQL Server Express. It also assumes that integrated security is used, eliminating the need to specify a SQL Server login and password.

Several overloaded constructors are available for the SqlWorkflowPersistenceService class. The one used here expects a connection string followed by a Boolean value and two TimeSpan values. The Boolean value is the unloadOnIdle parameter. A value of true instructs the persistence service to unload any idle workflows from memory after they have been persisted.

The first TimeSpan value indicates the amount of time that an instance of SqlWorkflowPersistenceService should maintain a lock on a workflow. This is primarily used in situations where you have multiple workflow hosts that are all processing workflows from a common persistence database. For this demonstration application, the value entered here doesn't really matter.

The second TimeSpan value sets the loadingInterval property and determines how often the persistence service polls for workflows that have an expired DelayActivity. The code sets this to five seconds, which is a fairly aggressive value; every five seconds, the persistence service will examine the persisted workflows that have been unloaded due to a DelayActivity. If the delay has expired, they are candidates to be loaded back into memory and execution will resume.

After loading the persistence service, an instance of the PersistenceDemoService class is also created and added to the workflow runtime engine. This is the local service providing the external events that are handled by the workflow.

```
/// <summary>
/// Perform cleanup during application shutdown
/// </summary>
/// <param name="e"></param>
protected override void OnFormClosed(FormClosedEventArgs e)
{
    base.OnFormClosed(e);
    //cleanup the workflow runtime
    if (_workflowManager != null)
    {
        _workflowManager.Dispose();
    }
}

#endregion

#region Workflow event handling

void WorkflowRuntime_WorkflowCreated(object sender,
    WorkflowEventArgs e)
{
    UpdateDisplay(e.WorkflowInstance.InstanceId, "Created");
}

void WorkflowRuntime_WorkflowIdled(object sender,
    WorkflowEventArgs e)
{
    UpdateDisplay(e.WorkflowInstance.InstanceId, "Idled");
}

void WorkflowRuntime_WorkflowLoaded(object sender,
    WorkflowEventArgs e)
{
    UpdateDisplay(e.WorkflowInstance.InstanceId, "Loaded");
}

void WorkflowRuntime_WorkflowUnloaded(object sender,
    WorkflowEventArgs e)
{
    UpdateDisplay(e.WorkflowInstance.InstanceId, "Unloaded");
}
```

```
void WorkflowRuntime_WorkflowPersisted(object sender,
    WorkflowEventArgs e)
{
    UpdateDisplay(e.WorkflowInstance.InstanceId, "Persisted");
}

void WorkflowRuntime_WorkflowCompleted(object sender,
    WorkflowCompletedEventArgs e)
{
    UpdateCompletedWorkflow(e.WorkflowInstance.InstanceId);
    UpdateDisplay(e.WorkflowInstance.InstanceId, "Completed");
}

private delegate void UpdateDelegate();

/// <summary>
/// Update the status message for a workflow
/// </summary>
/// <param name="instanceId"></param>
/// <param name="statusMessage"></param>
private void UpdateDisplay(Guid instanceId, String statusMessage)
{
    UpdateDelegate theDelegate = delegate()
    {
        Workflow workflow = GetWorkflow(instanceId);
        workflow.StatusMessage = statusMessage;
        RefreshData();
        //slow things down so you can see the status changes
        System.Threading.Thread.Sleep(1000);
    };

    //execute the anonymous delegate on the UI thread
    this.Invoke(theDelegate);
}

/// <summary>
/// Updating the bindings for the DataGridView
/// </summary>
private void RefreshData()
{
    //setup binding for DataGridView
    BindingSource source = new BindingSource();
    dataGridView1.DataSource = source;
    source.DataSource = _workflows.Values;

    dataGridView1.Columns[0].MinimumWidth = 250;
    dataGridView1.Columns[1].MinimumWidth = 140;
    dataGridView1.Columns[2].MinimumWidth = 40;

    dataGridView1.Refresh();
}
```

The UpdateDisplay and UpdateCompletedWorkflow methods both refresh the display by updating the bound collection of Workflow objects. The UpdateDisplay method is invoked by all of the handlers for the workflow runtime event (e.g., WorkflowCreated, WorkflowPersisted, WorkflowCompleted). It locates the workflow instance in the internal collection (if it exists) using the private GetWorkflow method. It then updates the status message for the Workflow object.

Notice that the code to update the data bound collection is executed on the UI thread. This is important since you can update a UI control only from the thread that created it. The actual code to execute is wrapped in an anonymous delegate in order to keep the code all in one place.

The call to Thread.Sleep(1000) is used to slow down the display so that you can actually see the status changes. Each workflow will typically cycle through a number of status changes very quickly and you would not see those changes without this short delay.

Caution Be careful when updating the user interface from workflow runtime event handling code. The workflow events are raised from a workflow thread, not the user interface thread.

```
/// <summary>
/// Mark a workflow as completed
/// </summary>
/// <param name="instanceId"></param>
private void UpdateCompletedWorkflow(Guid instanceId)
{
    UpdateDelegate theDelegate = delegate()
    {
        Workflow workflow = GetWorkflow(instanceId);
        workflow.IsCompleted = true;
    };

    //execute the anonymous delegate on the UI thread
    this.Invoke(theDelegate);
}
```

The UpdateCompletedWorkflow method is only invoked by the handler for the WorkflowCompleted event. It updates the IsCompleted property of the Workflow object to indicate that the workflow has completed. This prevents the application from raising additional events for the workflow.

Both of these methods call the RefreshData method, which binds the collection of Workflow objects to the DataGridView.

```
#endregion

#region UI event handlers and management

/// <summary>
/// Start a new workflow
/// </summary>
/// <param name="sender"></param>
/// <param name="e"></param>
private void btnNewWorkflow_Click(object sender, EventArgs e)
{
    //start a new workflow instance
    _workflowManager.StartWorkflow(
        typeof(PersistenceDemoWorkflow), null);
}
```

The Click event handlers for the three buttons are used to start new instances of PersistenceDemoWorkflow or raise one of the local service events. The btnNewWorkflow_Click method is responsible for starting a new workflow instance.

```
/// <summary>
/// Raise the Continue event through the local service
/// </summary>
/// <param name="sender"></param>
/// <param name="e"></param>
private void btnContinue_Click(object sender, EventArgs e)
{
    if (_selectedWorkflow != null)
    {
        _persistenceDemoService.OnContinueReceived(
            new ExternalDataEventArgs(_selectedWorkflow.InstanceId));
    }
}
```

The btnContinue_Click method raises the local service ContinueReceived event.

```
/// <summary>
/// Raise the Stop event through the local service
/// </summary>
/// <param name="sender"></param>
/// <param name="e"></param>
private void btnStop_Click(object sender, EventArgs e)
{
    if (_selectedWorkflow != null)
    {
        _persistenceDemoService.OnStopReceived(
            new ExternalDataEventArgs(_selectedWorkflow.InstanceId));
    }
}
```

The btnStop_Click looks very similar to the code for btnContinue_click. The only difference is the name of the local service method that it executes. Both of these methods reference the _selectedWorkflow variable. This variable contains the Workflow object that was selected in the DataGridView and saved by the dataGridView1_SelectionChanged method.

```
/// <summary>
/// The selected workflow has changed
/// </summary>
/// <param name="sender"></param>
/// <param name="e"></param>
private void dataGridView1_SelectionChanged(
    object sender, EventArgs e)
{
    //save the selected workflow instance
    if (dataGridView1.SelectedRows.Count > 0)
    {
        DataGridViewRow selectedRow = dataGridView1.SelectedRows[0];
        _selectedWorkflow = selectedRow.DataBoundItem as Workflow;
        SetButtonState();
    }
}
```

Before you can raise the ContinueReceived or StopReceived events, you must first identify the workflow instance that should receive the event. This is accomplished by selecting one of the available workflow instances shown in the DataGridView control. The code that saves the selected workflow instance is in the SelectionChanged event handler for the DataGridView (method dataGridView1_SelectionChanged).

```
/// <summary>
/// Enable / Disable buttons
/// </summary>
private void SetButtonState()
{
    if (_selectedWorkflow != null)
    {
        btnContinue.Enabled = !(_selectedWorkflow.IsCompleted);
        btnStop.Enabled = !(_selectedWorkflow.IsCompleted);
    }
    else
    {
        btnContinue.Enabled = false;
        btnStop.Enabled = false;
    }
}

#endregion

#region Collection Management

/// <summary>
/// Retrieve a workflow from our local collection
/// </summary>
/// <param name="instanceId"></param>
/// <returns></returns>
private Workflow GetWorkflow(Guid instanceId)
{
    Workflow result = null;
    if (_workflows.ContainsKey(instanceId))
    {
        result = _workflows[instanceId];
    }
    else
    {
        //create a new instance
        result = new Workflow();
        result.InstanceId = instanceId;
        _workflows.Add(result.InstanceId, result);
    }
    return result;
}

/// <summary>
/// Identify all persisted workflows
/// </summary>
```

```
    private void RetrieveExistingWorkflows()
    {
        _workflows.Clear();
        //retrieve a list of workflows that have been persisted

        foreach (SqlPersistenceWorkflowInstanceDescription workflowDesc
            in ((SqlWorkflowPersistenceService)_persistence).GetAllWorkflows())
        {
            Workflow workflow = new Workflow();
            workflow.InstanceId = workflowDesc.WorkflowInstanceId;
            workflow.StatusMessage = "Unloaded";
            _workflows.Add(workflow.InstanceId, workflow);
        }

        if (_workflows.Count > 0)
        {
            RefreshData();
        }
    }
```

The RetrieveExistingWorkflows method is executed from the OnLoad method. The purpose of this method is to retrieve a list of all workflow instances that are currently persisted. This is done in order to present a list of available workflows when the application first starts.

The SqlWorkflowPersistenceService contains a method named GetAllWorkflows that returns a collection of SqlPersistenceWorkflowInstanceDescription objects. Each one of these objects represents a persisted workflow. This information is used to build a collection of Workflow objects that are bound to the DataGridView and displayed.

```
    #endregion

    }
}
```

Testing the Application

Once all of these individual application pieces are in place, you should be able to start the PersistenceDemo application. Initially, there are no workflows shown, so begin the demonstration by clicking the New Workflow button. This starts a workflow and updates the display to show the workflow instance ID and status message. The application looks like Figure 8-3 after I start a new workflow.

■**Note** Since the workflow instance ID is a Guid and should be globally unique, you should always see different instance IDs than the ones shown here.

Although the StatusMessage column in Figure 8-3 shows a status of Unloaded, the workflow actually cycled through several status messages before it was unloaded. If you watch very closely as you start a new workflow, you will see that the workflow status quickly cycles through Created, Idled, Persisted, and finally Unloaded. These status messages displayed as WorkflowRuntime events are received for the instance.

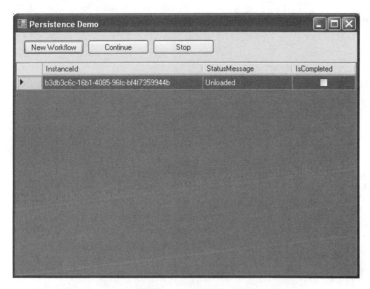

Figure 8-3. *PersistenceDemo application with one workflow*

If you remember the design of the workflow, this series of events makes sense. After the workflow is created, it executes the ListenActivity, which contains activities to handle two different external events. As the workflow is waiting for these events, it is considered idle. This accounts for the immediate move from Created to Idled. Since a persistence service has been loaded, idled workflows are automatically persisted, so the workflow then displays the Persisted status message. Finally, because the persistence service is constructed with a value that instructed it to unload idled workflows, the final status message is Unloaded.

Now that you have a workflow, you can raise the ContinueReceived event by clicking the Continue button. When you do so, watch the StatusMesssage again. You should see the workflow quickly cycle between Loaded, Idled, Persisted, and Unloaded. What would account for this series of events?

Remember that the workflow contains a WhileActivity that continues to execute until the IsComplete property is set to true. That property is set in the workflow when the StopReceived event is raised. When you raised the ContinueReceived event, the persistence service loaded the workflow back into memory in order to process the event. After handling the event, the workflow was again considered idle and was persisted and unloaded once again. This same processing will continue each time you click the Continue button.

To complete the workflow, click the Stop button. This time, the workflow cycles through status messages of Loaded, Persisted, and finally Completed. The application should now look like Figure 8-4.

The really interesting resultsoccur when you start multiple workflows and then close the application without stopping them with the Stop button. Click the New Workflow button three times, waiting for each instance to reach the Unloaded state before starting the next workflow. The application should now look like Figure 8-5.

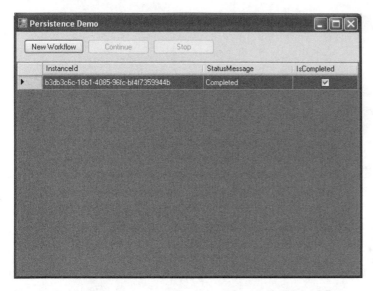

Figure 8-4. *PersistenceDemo application with completed workflow*

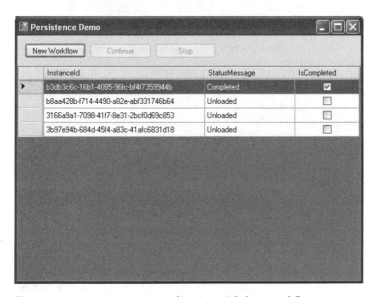

Figure 8-5. *PersistenceDemo application with four workflows*

Now shut down the application and immediately restart it. The application should look like Figure 8-6, showing the three incomplete workflows.

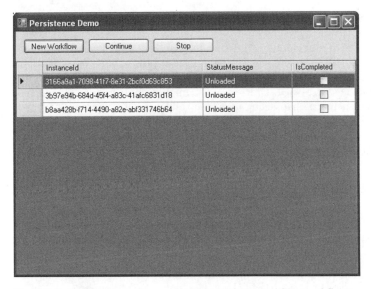

Figure 8-6. *PersistenceDemo application with incomplete workflows*

This list of workflows was retrieved during startup by calling the GetAllWorkflows method of the persistence service.

■**Note** The GetAllWorkflows method doesn't load all of the workflows back into memory. It simply identifies the workflows that are persisted. Each one of these workflows can then be loaded back into memory by raising one of the local service events.

You can now raise events for these three workflows in the same way you did for the first workflow. Just select a workflow, and then click the Continue or Stop button. If you click Continue, the selected workflow will cycle through the same set of status messages you saw previously. If you click the Stop button, the selected workflow will receive the StopReceived event and will complete.

This simple application illustrates several things about the behavior of the SQL Server persistence service.

- Once the persistence service is loaded, workflows are automatically persisted according to a set of internal WF rules.

- A workflow is removed by the persistence service when it is complete. The workflow that you previously completed by clicking the Stop button is now gone when you restart the application.

- Persisted workflows are not dependent on a particular instance of an application. They now live in the durable store that is managed by the persistence service and can be reloaded into memory for execution by any workflow application.

- Workflows that are waiting to receive an event are considered idle. As far as the persistence service and the workflow runtime are concerned, it doesn't matter how long these workflows are idle. It could take minutes, days, weeks, or even longer for you to raise one of the local service events. While they are waiting, they are safely persisted.

Implementing a Custom Persistence Service

The easiest way to add persistence to your workflows is to use the standard SQL Server persistence service that was just demonstrated. However, this service might not always meet your needs. Perhaps you can't or don't want to use SQL Server. You might already be developing your application around another relational database engine (e.g., MySQL, Oracle). Or you might want to use SQL Server, but need to use a different database schema, perhaps using application tables that you've already defined. Or you might need persistence, but don't want the overhead of a relational database at all; your application might work just fine persisting workflows as binary or XML files in a local directory.

The solution is to develop your own persistence service. There are really just a few steps that you need to follow in order to implement and use your own persistence service.

1. Derive your custom persistence class from `WorkflowPersistenceService` (in the `System.Workflow.Runtime.Hosting` namespace).

2. Provide implementations for all of the abstract methods in the base class. Each of these methods is called at various times during the life of a workflow to save or retrieve the state of an entire workflow or part of it.

3. Load the custom persistence service into the workflow runtime in the same manner as the standard service.

Understanding the Abstract Methods

The largest task you face is providing implementations for all of the abstract methods defined by the `WorkflowPersistenceService` class. For this reason, each of the abstract methods is briefly described in the sections that follow.

SaveWorkflowInstanceState

This method is called by the workflow runtime engine to persist the state of the entire workflow. The root `Activity` of the workflow is one of the arguments passed to this method. To save the state of the workflow, you must call the `Save` method on this root `Activity`. This returns a `Stream`, which you can then persist using any type of durable store that you like.

Calling the `Save` method is an important step, because it guarantees that the workflow will be persisted in a form that you can later pass to the static `Load` method of the `Activity` class. This takes place in the `LoadWorkflowInstanceState` method.

When you persist the entire workflow, you will need a primary key to use when referencing the workflow in your durable store. The obvious choice for this key is the workflow instance ID. This `Guid` uniquely identifies the workflow, and using it will avoid any potential problems associated with some other identification scheme. The workflow instance ID is also passed back to you when the workflow runtime requests that you reload a workflow instance.

This method is also called when a workflow is completed or terminates. This final call is your last chance to perform additional processing with the persisted copy of the workflow. If you follow the same approach as the standard persistence service for SQL Server, you will remove the workflow from the durable store when it is completed or terminated. But if your application requires the retention of completed workflows, you can move the workflow to a different set of database tables or archive it in some other way. You can determine the workflow status by calling the static `GetWorkflowStatus` method of the base `WorkflowPersistenceService` class.

The `SaveWorkflowInstanceState` method is also passed a `Boolean` argument named `unlock`. This parameter indicates whether you should unlock the workflow instance after it is persisted. It is your choice to implement workflow locking or not. If implemented, a locking mechanism would record the fact that a workflow instance has been loaded by a particular instance of the workflow runtime and is actively executing. A lock that you record for the workflow instance would prevent other instances of the workflow runtime from working with that workflow instance.

Whenever you are working with a durable store such as a database or a set of files, you should be careful to perform updates in a way that will guarantee the consistency of the data. For databases, this usually means applying individual updates as part of a larger batch of work (a transaction) and then committing all of the changes at once.

Note WF includes a framework for managing and committing batches of work. It works by adding work items to `WorkflowEnvironment.WorkBatch` and then later committing them. Using this mechanism guarantees that updates to your durable store are coordinated with the internal state of the workflow. Use of this WF framework is discussed in Chapter 10. In order to keep the focus of the discussion on workflow persistence, the custom persistence service in this chapter does not use this batching mechanism.

If you are unable to persist the state of a workflow, you should throw an exception of type `PersistenceException`.

LoadWorkflowInstanceState

This method is called to load the previously saved state of a workflow instance. You are passed the instance ID of the workflow to load. Once you retrieve the workflow state from your durable store, you must use the static `Load` method of the `Activity` class to recreate the workflow instance. The return value of this method is the workflow (with a return type of `Activity`) that was loaded.

SaveCompletedContextActivity

The `SaveWorkflowInstanceState` method described previously is called to persist the state of an entire workflow. In contrast, this method saves just a portion of the workflow. Its purpose is to save the activity execution context for completed activities that support compensation.

Every activity runs within an execution context. The context is simply an execution environment that contains one or more activities. The context determines the set of parent and child activities that you can safely reference. Activities that have looping or repeating behavior generate new execution contexts for each of their iterations. For example, the `WhileActivity` loops continuously as long as a specified condition is `true`. But a new activity execution context is created with each iteration. The purpose of this method is to save the state of each of those activity contexts as they complete. Think of each of these contexts as an additional checkpoint in the life of a workflow.

However, individual activity contexts are saved only if the activity supports compensation. *Compensation* is the process of rolling back changes from activities that have successfully completed. This might be needed if the individual activities successfully complete, but later in the workflow the decision is made to undo all of the updates from the individual activities. In order to roll back changes that have already completed, you need the checkpoints that have been saved by this method.

As an example, your workflow might contain a `WhileActivity` that has a `SequenceActivity` as its child (a `WhileActivity` only supports a single child). Assume for this example that the `SequenceActivity` contains several `CodeActivity` instances. As the `WhileActivity` iterates, new activity contexts are created. However, this method will not be called for each context since none of these activities support compensation. If you replace the `SequenceActivity` with a `CompensatableSequenceActivity`, the situation changes. As the name implies, `CompensatableSequenceActivity` supports compensation. Now at the end of each iteration, this method is called, providing you with the opportunity to save a context checkpoint.

If the workflow requires compensation (the actual undoing of the updates), the LoadCompletedContextActivity method is called to reload each activity context that was saved by this method.

Each activity context has its own unique context ID (a Guid) that is different from the workflow instance ID. When saving a completed context with this method, you should provide a mechanism to associate each context ID with the workflow instance ID. This is needed when it is time to reload a persisted context and also to remove all persisted data for a workflow when it is completed.

Just as you do in the SaveWorkflowInstanceState method, you must call the Save method of the activity to serialize the activity to a format that can be reloaded.

LoadCompletedContextActivity

This method is the reciprocal of SaveCompletedContextActivity. It loads completed activity contexts that have been previously saved. It is invoked if and when a workflow requires compensation (undoing) of completed changes.

This method is passed an outerActivity parameter that is the parent Activity of the context to be loaded. You must use the static Load method of the Activity class to load the activity. However, you need to pass this outerActivity to the method in order to properly associate the loaded context with the correct parent activity.

UnlockWorkflowInstanceState

This method is called to unlock a workflow instance outside of the normal load and save methods. For instance, if a workflow is aborted, this method would be called to clean up any locks that you have for the workflow instance.

Since this is an abstract method, you must provide an implementation for it in your derived class. However, you only need to provide actual unlocking logic if you choose to implement a locking mechanism.

UnloadOnIdle

This method returns a Boolean value that indicates whether the workflow that is passed in as an argument should be unloaded when it becomes idle. You can choose to always return true or false, or make your decision based on each individual workflow.

Implementing the Service

In this section, you will develop a custom persistence service. This service is extremely simple, serializing the workflow state to a set of files in the current directory. Although it is simple, this example service does demonstrate the basic steps necessary to implement your own service.

Your custom persistence service might need to be much more elaborate than this one. In particular, this service does not implement workflow instance locking, so it doesn't support multiple workflow hosts that work with the same set of persisted workflows. If you are using a database as your durable store, you should also add support for transactions and batching of work to maintain the consistency of your data.

■**Note** Please refer to Chapter 10 for more information on transactions and batching of work.

To implement the service, add a new C# class to the SharedWorkflows project and name it FileWorkflowPersistenceService. Derive the class from WorkflowPersistenceService and provide implementations for all of the abstract methods discussed previously. Listing 8-7 presents the completed code for the `FileWorkflowPersistenceService.cs` file. Selected portions of the code are discussed within the listing.

Listing 8-7. *Complete FileWorkflowPersistenceService.cs File*

```csharp
using System;
using System.IO;
using System.Collections.Generic;
using System.Workflow.Runtime;
using System.Workflow.Runtime.Hosting;
using System.Workflow.ComponentModel;

namespace SharedWorkflows
{
    /// <summary>
    /// A file-based workflow persistence service
    /// </summary>
    public class FileWorkflowPersistenceService
        : WorkflowPersistenceService
    {
        private String _path = Environment.CurrentDirectory;

        #region Abstract method implementations

        /// <summary>
        /// Persist the current state of the entire workflow
        /// </summary>
        /// <param name="rootActivity"></param>
        /// <param name="unlock"></param>
        protected override void SaveWorkflowInstanceState(
            Activity rootActivity, bool unlock)
        {
            //get the workflow instance ID
            Guid instanceId = WorkflowEnvironment.WorkflowInstanceId;

            //determine the status of the workflow
            WorkflowStatus status =
                WorkflowPersistenceService.GetWorkflowStatus(rootActivity);
            switch (status)
            {
                case WorkflowStatus.Completed:
                case WorkflowStatus.Terminated:
                    //delete the persisted workflow
                    DeleteWorkflow(instanceId);
                    break;
                default:
                    //save the workflow
                    Serialize(instanceId, Guid.Empty, rootActivity);
                    break;
            }
        }
```

The SaveWorkflowInstanceState method contains the code needed to persist the state of the entire workflow. This method calls the static WorkflowEnvironment.WorkflowInstanceId method to retrieve the instance ID for the current workflow. You will see later in the code that this ID is used as part of the file name when persisting the workflow.

This method also determines if it should save the workflow state or delete it based on the workflow status. The status is retrieve by calling the static GetWorkflowStatus method of the base WorkflowPersistenceService class. If the workflow status is Completed or Terminated, any files that have been persisted for this workflow are deleted. A private Serialize method is called to handle the actual persistence of the workflow state.

```
/// <summary>
/// Load an entire workflow
/// </summary>
/// <param name="instanceId"></param>
/// <returns></returns>
protected override Activity LoadWorkflowInstanceState(
    Guid instanceId)
{
    Activity activity = Deserialize(instanceId, Guid.Empty, null);
    if (activity == null)
    {
        ThrowException(instanceId,
            "Unable to deserialize workflow", null);
    }
    return activity;
}
```

The LoadWorkflowInstanceState method loads the requested workflow instance by calling the private Deserialize method.

```
/// <summary>
/// Persist a completed activity context
/// </summary>
/// <remarks>
/// This persists completed activities that were part
/// of an execution scope. Example:  Activities
/// within a CompensatableSequenceActivity.
/// </remarks>
/// <param name="activity"></param>
protected override void SaveCompletedContextActivity(
    Activity activity)
{
    //get the workflow instance ID
    Guid instanceId = WorkflowEnvironment.WorkflowInstanceId;

    //get the context ID, which identifies the activity scope
    //within the workflow instance
    Guid contextId = (Guid)activity.GetValue(
        Activity.ActivityContextGuidProperty);

    //persist the activity for this workflow
    Serialize(instanceId, contextId, activity);
}
```

The SaveCompletedContextActivity method is responsible for saving a completed activity execution context if the activity supports compensation. This method requires two different identifiers to save the context. It retrieves the workflow instance ID and also a separate activity context ID. Both IDs are passed to the private Serialize method that saves the context.

```
/// <summary>
/// Load an activity context
/// </summary>
/// <param name="scopeId"></param>
/// <param name="outerActivity"></param>
/// <returns></returns>
protected override Activity LoadCompletedContextActivity(
    Guid scopeId, Activity outerActivity)
{
    //get the workflow instance ID
    Guid instanceId = WorkflowEnvironment.WorkflowInstanceId;

    Activity activity = Deserialize(instanceId, scopeId, outerActivity);
    if (activity == null)
    {
        ThrowException(instanceId,
            "Unable to deserialize activity", null);
    }
    return activity;
}
```

The LoadCompletedContextActivity retrieves a completed activity context and loads it as a child of the outerActivity parameter that was passed to the method.

```
protected override void UnlockWorkflowInstanceState(
    Activity rootActivity)
{
    //locking not implemented
}

protected override bool UnloadOnIdle(Activity activity)
{
    //always unload on idle
    return true;
}
```

This service always returns true from the UnloadOnIdle method. This means that any workflows that are idled will be removed from memory after they are persisted.

```
#endregion

#region Persistence and File Management

/// <summary>
/// Serialize the workflow or an activity context
/// </summary>
/// <param name="instanceId"></param>
/// <param name="contextId"></param>
/// <param name="activity"></param>
```

```
private void Serialize(
    Guid instanceId, Guid contextId, Activity activity)
{
    try
    {
        String fileName = GetFilePath(instanceId, contextId);
        using (FileStream stream = new FileStream(
            fileName, FileMode.Create))
        {
            activity.Save(stream);
        }
    }
    catch (ArgumentException e)
    {
        ThrowException(instanceId,
            "Serialize: Path has invalid argument", e);
    }
    catch (DirectoryNotFoundException e)
    {
        ThrowException(instanceId,
            "Serialize: Directory not found", e);
    }
    catch (Exception e)
    {
        ThrowException(instanceId,
            "Serialize: Unknown exception", e);
    }
}
```

The Serialize method is responsible for actually saving the workflow state or a completed activity context to a file. This method retrieves the file name using a private GetFilePath method. The file name always uses the workflow instance ID as the high-order part of the file name. If the entire workflow state is being saved, the complete file name is the instance ID and a .wf extension. If the method is saving a completed activity context, the file name contains the workflow instance ID and the context ID with a .wfc extension. This naming convention logically associates all of the saved context files with the parent workflow. This makes it easier to delete all files for a workflow when the workflow is completed.

```
/// <summary>
/// Deserialize a workflow or an activity context
/// </summary>
/// <param name="instanceId"></param>
/// <param name="contextId"></param>
/// <param name="rootActivity"></param>
/// <returns></returns>
private Activity Deserialize(
    Guid instanceId, Guid contextId, Activity rootActivity)
{
    Activity activity = null;
    try
    {
        String fileName = GetFilePath(instanceId, contextId);
        using (FileStream stream = new FileStream(
            fileName, FileMode.Open))
        {
```

```
            activity = Activity.Load(stream, rootActivity);
        }
    }
    catch (ArgumentException e)
    {
        ThrowException(instanceId,
            "Deserialize: Path has invalid argument", e);
    }
    catch (FileNotFoundException e)
    {
        ThrowException(instanceId,
            "Deserialize: File not found", e);
    }
    catch (DirectoryNotFoundException e)
    {
        ThrowException(instanceId,
            "Deserialize: Directory not found", e);
    }
    catch (Exception e)
    {
        ThrowException(instanceId,
            "Deserialize: Unknown exception", e);
    }
    return activity;
}
```

The Deserialize method reverses the process and retrieves the requested file. It uses the static Load method of the Activity class to reload the previously saved file.

```
/// <summary>
/// Delete a workflow and any related activity context files
/// </summary>
/// <param name="instanceId"></param>
private void DeleteWorkflow(Guid instanceId)
{
    try
    {
        String[] files = Directory.GetFiles(
            _path, instanceId.ToString() + "*");

        foreach (String file in files)
        {
            if (File.Exists(file))
            {
                File.Delete(file);
            }
        }
    }
    catch (ArgumentException e)
    {
        ThrowException(instanceId,
            "Delete: Path has invalid argument", e);
    }
```

```
            catch (DirectoryNotFoundException e)
            {
                ThrowException(instanceId,
                    "Delete: Directory not found", e);
            }
            catch (Exception e)
            {
                ThrowException(instanceId,
                    "Delete: Unknown exception", e);
            }
        }

        /// <summary>
        /// Determine the full file path
        /// </summary>
        /// <param name="instanceId"></param>
        /// <param name="contextId"></param>
        /// <returns></returns>
        private String GetFilePath(Guid instanceId, Guid contextId)
        {
            String fullPath = String.Empty;
            if (contextId == Guid.Empty)
            {
                //create a path for the entire workflow.
                //Naming convention is [instanceId].wf
                fullPath = Path.Combine(_path, String.Format("{0}.{1}",
                    instanceId, "wf"));
            }
            else
            {
                //create a path for a single activity context
                //within the workflow.
                //naming convention is [instanceId].[contextId].wfc
                fullPath = Path.Combine(_path, String.Format("{0}.{1}.{2}",
                    instanceId, contextId, "wfc"));
            }
            return fullPath;
        }

        #endregion

        #region Existing Workflow Management

        /// <summary>
        /// Return a list of all workflow IDs that are persisted
        /// </summary>
        /// <returns></returns>
        public List<Guid> GetAllWorkflows()
        {
            List<Guid> workflows = new List<Guid>();
            String[] files = Directory.GetFiles(_path, "*.wf");
```

```
    foreach (String file in files)
    {
        //turn the file name into a Guid
        Guid instanceId = new Guid(
            Path.GetFileNameWithoutExtension(file));
        workflows.Add(instanceId);
    }

    return workflows;
}
```

The GetAllWorkflows was added to the class in order to return a list of workflow instance IDs that are persisted. The host application can call this method to retrieve a list of available workflows.

```
    #endregion

    #region Common Error handling

    /// <summary>
    /// Throw an exception due to an error
    /// </summary>
    /// <param name="instanceId"></param>
    /// <param name="message"></param>
    /// <param name="inner"></param>
    private void ThrowException(Guid instanceId, String message,
        Exception inner)
    {
        if (inner == null)
        {
            throw new PersistenceException(
                String.Format("Workflow: {0} Error: {1}",
                    instanceId, message));
        }
        else
        {
            throw new PersistenceException(
                String.Format("Workflow: {0} Error: {1}: Inner: {2}",
                    instanceId, message, inner.Message), inner);
        }
    }

    #endregion
    }
}
```

Testing the Custom Service

You can test this new persistence service using the same PersistenceDemo application that was used with the SQL Server persistence service earlier in the chapter. A few minor changes are needed to the code and are outlined in this section.

Open the Form1.cs file of the PersistenceDemo project and locate the AddService method. Remove the references to the SqlWorkflowPersistenceService class and the SQL Server connection string since they are no longer needed. In their place, add code to create an instance of the

FileWorkflowPersistenceService class and add it to the workflow runtime. The revised code for the AddService method is shown here:

```
private void AddServices(WorkflowRuntime instance)
{
    //use the custom file-based persistence service
    _persistence = new FileWorkflowPersistenceService();
    instance.AddService(_persistence);

    //add the external data exchange service to the runtime
    ExternalDataExchangeService exchangeService
        = new ExternalDataExchangeService();
    instance.AddService(exchangeService);

    //add our local service
    _persistenceDemoService = new PersistenceDemoService();
    exchangeService.AddService(_persistenceDemoService);
}
```

The other necessary change is to the RetrieveExistingWorkflows method. This method retrieves the list of available workflows that have been persisted. The custom persistence service implements a GetAllWorkflows method, but the return value is different from the SQL Server persistence service. The custom service returns a collection of Guid values. The revised code for the RetrieveExistingWorkflows is shown here:

```
private void RetrieveExistingWorkflows()
{
    _workflows.Clear();
    //retrieve a list of workflows that have been persisted

    foreach (Guid instanceId
        in ((FileWorkflowPersistenceService)_persistence).GetAllWorkflows())
    {
        Workflow workflow = new Workflow();
        workflow.InstanceId = instanceId;
        workflow.StatusMessage = "Unloaded";
        _workflows.Add(workflow.InstanceId, workflow);
    }

    if (_workflows.Count > 0)
    {
        RefreshData();
    }
}
```

That's it. After rebuilding the PersistenceDemo project, you should be able to run it and see the same type of behavior as the previous example that used the SQL Server persistence service.

As you start and interact with workflows, you should see the files used for persistence in the same directory as the executable. For example, when I start a new workflow, I see this file appear in the directory:

e9cdb9d0-ec23-4d05-86a4-9b30b977f259.wf

If I raise the `ContinueReceived` event by clicking the Continue button, I see an additional file created:

```
e9cdb9d0-ec23-4d05-86a4-9b30b977f259.wf
e9cdb9d0-ec23-4d05-86a4-9b30b977f259.c6893b50-9e89-48c0-ae9d-1887615fe384.wfc
```

The second file represents the completed activity context for the `CompensatableSequenceActivity` that is included in the workflow. Additional files are created each time I click the Continue button. When I click the Stop button for the workflow, all of the files for the workflow instance are deleted.

Note Remember that since these are `Guid` values, the file names will be different on your machine.

I can also create multiple workflow instances and then stop and restart the application. Just like the example that used SQL Server, the application presents a list of workflows that have been persisted. I can then interact with them individually by raising events.

Using the standard SQL Server persistence service provides you with easy, out-of-the-box support for persistence. But implementing your own custom persistence service provides you with ultimate flexibility; you are able to implement the service to meet the exact needs of your particular application.

Summary

This chapter focused on workflow persistence. Workflow persistence in WF is implemented as one of the optional core services. This architecture allows you to use the standard SQL Server persistence service that is provided with WF, or implement your own custom persistence service.

Several good reasons to use persistence were covered in the overview section of this chapter. Following the overview of how persistence works in WF, an example application was developed that demonstrated the behavior of the standard SQL Server persistence service.

After the SQL Server persistence example, a custom persistence service was developed and used by the same application. This custom service used simple files as its durable store instead of a relational database such as SQL Server. To illustrate the ability to plug in different implementations of core services, the demo application was modified to use the custom service with minimal effort.

In the next chapter, you will learn about state machine workflows that allow you to more naturally model processes that involve human interaction.

CHAPTER 9

■ ■ ■

State Machine Workflows

The focus of this chapter is state machine workflows. *State machine workflows* are different from sequential workflows in a number of ways. Most importantly, they don't define a hardwired sequence of steps within the workflow. Instead, they define a set of application states with possible transitions between states. Each state can handle multiple external events that trigger execution of child activities including a possible transition to another state.

Because their flow of control is not hardwired into the design of the workflow, they are excellent in situations that require human interaction.

This chapter begins with a brief overview of state machine workflows. This overview includes a discussion of their benefits, as well as a summary of the WF classes that you use when developing state machine workflows.

Following the overview, you will implement an application that uses a state machine workflow to model the basic operations of a car. The example provides step-by-step instructions on how to design and implement the workflow along with a local service that supports the necessary external events. The Windows Forms application enables you to interact with the workflow, raising events that cause the workflow to transition to another state.

Three additional examples in this chapter build upon this first example by making slight improvements to the design. One of these additional examples demonstrates how to eliminate duplicate activities using recursive composition of states. The final two examples show you how to interrogate the workflow runtime to retrieve additional information about a running state machine workflow.

Understanding State Machine Workflows

State machine workflows are different from the sequential workflows that you have used so far. As you are already well aware by now, sequential workflows allow you to define a fixed sequence of execution steps. Each sequential workflow also has a clearly defined starting and ending point.

State machine workflows don't define a fixed sequence of steps. Instead, they define a set of states, with possible transitions between each state. Each state may contain one or more activities that are executed prior to a transition to another state. The execution of these activities is triggered by the receipt of an event. A simple state machine workflow is illustrated in Figure 9-1, seen previously in Chapter 2.

Figure 9-1 illustrates a simple state machine workflow using an account withdrawal example. The boxes in the figure represent *states*, not individual steps. Each state can transition to one or more other states. The state transitions are triggered by the receipt of an event such as OnAccountFound or OnBalanceReceived. Although they are not shown in the figure, a series of activities could be executed for each event prior to the transition to another state.

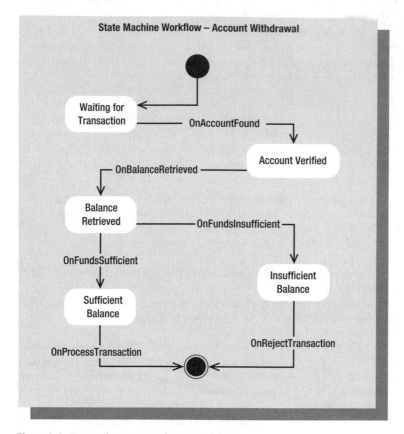

Figure 9-1. *Example state machine workflow*

Why a State Machine Workflow?

You have already seen that you can accomplish quite a bit using sequential workflows. Why do you need state machine workflows?

Each workflow type targets a different kind of problem. The deciding factor when choosing the workflow type usually comes down to control. A sequential workflow defines the flow of control within the workflow. Since it specifies the exact sequence of steps within the workflow, it is in control. It works best for system interaction problems where the prescribed steps are known at design time.

State machine workflows don't define a fixed flow of control within the workflow. The exact sequence of state transitions is controlled by external events. For this reason, state machine workflows are well-suited to problems that involve human interaction. Human interactions are those that involve real live people. The problem is that people are not always predictable and it is difficult to model interactions with them using a series of fixed procedural steps.

For example, you might need to model a mortgage loan application. The process might include steps that must be executed by real people in order to complete the process. How much control do you have over the order of those steps? Does the credit approval always occur first, or is it possible for the appraisal to be done first. What about the property survey? Is it done before or after the appraisal? And what activities must be completed before you can schedule the loan closing?

Humans don't always do things in a prescribed sequence. Modeling a problem involving human interaction requires flexibility and a state machine workflow provides this.

In most situations, you can make either type of workflow work. However, this doesn't mean that both workflow types are equally suited to solving all problems. Choosing the wrong workflow type for the problem may result in a more complicated, inelegant solution. You need to choose the workflow type that feels like a natural fit to the problem.

State Machine Workflow Overview

When you are defining a state machine workflow, you attack the problem differently than when you use a sequential workflow. With a sequential workflow, you generally start by defining the steps needed to accomplish some task. Each step is made up of one or more activities that you add to the workflow and arrange in the proper sequence.

In contrast with this, when defining a state machine workflow, you generally start by identifying the states. Each state in the workflow can directly correspond to a state in the business process that you are modeling. For instance, if you are modeling a loan application process, your states might include application started, account setup, reviewing credit report, verifying employment, underwriting, loan rejected, and loan closed.

Once you have defined the states, you then identify the events that can occur while you are in each state. Continuing with the loan application example for a moment, if you are in the reviewing credit report state, it might make sense to receive events such as credit sufficient and credit insufficient. Each event carries with it logic (in the form of activities) that you wish to execute when the event is received. Events that are defined within a state can only be received while you are in that particular state.

Each event can also trigger a transition to another state as the last step in the logic for that event. If you are in the reviewing credit report state and you receive the credit sufficient event, you might want to transition to the verifying employment state or perhaps the underwriting state. On the other hand, if you receive the credit insufficient event, you would likely want to transition directly to the loan rejected state.

You may also need to handle selected events at any time, regardless of what state you're in. For instance, in the loan application example, the customer may decide that they don't want the loan after all. You need to handle a loan canceled event at any time. These out of band events are accommodated in WF by placing the event handler at a higher level, outside of the current state. States in WF can contain other states. This is called *recursive composition of states*. Any events defined by the outer state are available while the workflow is currently in any of the inner states. Events can also be handled by the workflow itself.

State Machine Classes

To define a state machine workflow, you start with the StateMachineWorkflowActivity class (found in the System.Workflow.Activities namespace). This is the base class for your workflow when you select State Machine Workflow as the Add Item template or when you select one of the State Machine Workflow Project templates. You can add a state machine workflow to any project that supports workflows. This means you can mix and match sequential and state machine workflows in the same project.

Individual states are defined in the workflow using the StateActivity (also in the System. Workflow.Activities namespace). Each event that you wish to handle is represented by an EventDrivenActivity. This is a composite activity that triggers execution when an event is received. The first child of an EventDrivenActivity must support the IEventActivity interface in order to trigger execution of the other child activities when the event is received. When used in a state machine workflow, this typically means that the first event is a HandleExternalEventActivity. Following the HandleExternalEventActivity, you include the other activities that you wish to execute when the event is received.

The only direct child activities that are allowed for the StateMachineWorkflowActivity are the StateActivity and the EventDrivenActivity. This makes sense based on what you already know about state machine workflows. They contain states and can also directly handle events.

Each StateActivity has a select list of direct child activities that it supports. As I already mentioned, it accepts multiple instances of EventDrivenActivity, with each instance associated with one, and only one, event. A StateActivity also accepts a single StateInitializationActivity and a single StateFinalizationActivity. Both of these activities are composites and are optional.

If you include a StateInitializationActivity, the activities that it contains are executed as soon as the StateActivity begins execution. This is done before it begins listening for any events that you have defined. If you include a StateFinalizationActivity, it is executed immediately prior to transitioning to another state.

To transition to another state, you use the SetStateActivity. You include the SetStateActivity as the last child of an EventDrivenActivity instance. Since this activity causes a transition to another state, it doesn't make sense to include other activities following it.

The relationship between these activities is illustrated in Figure 9-2.

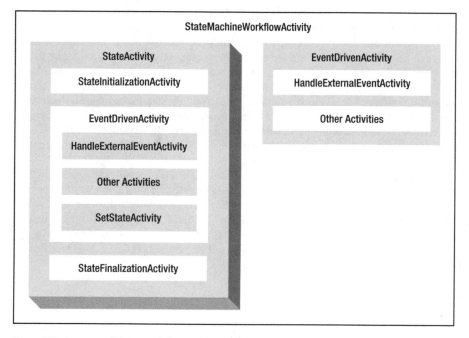

Figure 9-2. *State machine workflow activities*

As shown in Figure 9-2, a state machine workflow (StateMachineWorkflowActivity) contains one or more instances of StateActivity. Each StateActivity contains one or more EventDrivenActivity instances. Each EventDrivenActivity begins with an activity that is capable of receiving an event (HandleExternalEventActivity). Following this activity, you include other activities that you wish to execute when the event is received. Finally, the last child activity of the EventDrivenActivity can be a SetStateActivity which transitions to another state. A similar stack of EventDrivenActivity instances can also be added directly as children of the state machine workflow. These activities enable handling of events regardless of the current state. The StateInitializationActivity and StateFinalizationActivity are optional activities that are children of the StateActivity.

■**Note** You may notice that the `StateMachineWorkflowActivity` class derives from `StateActivity`. This is what enables `StateMachineWorkflowActivity` to exhibit the behavior of a state, such as handling events and acting as the parent for other states.

Initial and Completed States

Since a state machine workflow is composed of multiple states, you may be wondering which state the workflow is in when it first begins execution. The `StateMachineWorkflowActivity` class includes an `InitialStateName` property. This property identifies the initial state and must be set by you when implementing the workflow. Failure to set this property results in an error when you build the project containing the workflow.

The `StateMachineWorkflowActivity` class also includes another important property named `CompletedStateName`. This property identifies the state that causes the completion of the workflow. When you transition to this completion state, this marks the end of the workflow and it stops execution and completes. A completion state is an ordinary `StateActivity`, but if you select it in the `CompletedStateName` property, it takes on this special meaning. One notable restriction is that a completion state cannot contain any children. As soon as you transition to this state, the workflow completes so there is no need to define any children. If any children were defined, they wouldn't be executed.

The `CompletedStateName` property is optional. At first, you might think this is a mistake, since without it the workflow will never complete. This is not a mistake and that is exactly the behavior you will see if you don't include a completion state. The workflow will never complete. Instead, it will continue to transition from state to state and handle the events defined for those states. For some applications, this is exactly the type of behavior that you want. Obviously, for such long-running (never ending) workflows, you would want to make sure that you use a persistence service. Otherwise, the workflow would end prematurely if the host process was ever shut down.

Recursive Composition of States

The `StateActivity` can also include other instances of `StateActivity`. This is called *recursive composition of states*. The primary use of this technique is to allow handling of selected events from more than one state. For example, assume that you have two states: state A and state B. You may have an event that you wish to handle while you are in either state. You have two ways to handle this. Your first option is to define the event within each state, duplicating the stack of activities you've defined to handle the event. This approach is shown in Figure 9-3.

Your second option is to enclose both of these states in a new parent state and handle the event in the parent state. Using this second approach, you could create a new state C, and move states A and B into it as children. You can then add the `EventDrivenActivity` to state C to handle the event. This approach is illustrated in Figure 9-4.

Since it is defined in a common parent state, the event can now be handled when the workflow is currently in state A or B. Although not shown in Figure 9-4, each of the child states (A and B) can still contain their own set of events that they alone handle. You will see an example of this type of state composition in one of the upcoming example workflows.

When you transition to another state using `SetStateActivity`, you can only transition to leaf states. *Leaf states* are those that do not contain other states. Using the previous example, you could transition to state A or B but not to the parent state C since it contains other states. The parent state (C in this example) is also not a valid candidate state for the `InitialStateName` and `CompletedStateName` properties of the state machine workflow. Since you can't transition to a composite parent state, you are not allowed to designate it as the initial or completed state.

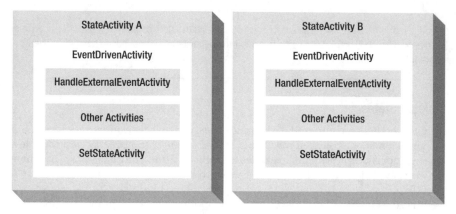

Figure 9-3. *Multiple states with duplicate event handlers*

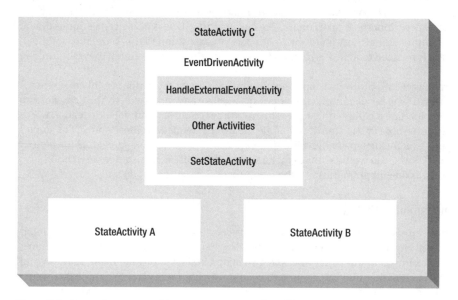

Figure 9-4. *Recursive states with a common event handler*

Implementing a State Machine Workflow

In the example that follows, you will implement an application that uses a state machine workflow. For this example, I chose a familiar subject to model: operating a car. While you wouldn't normally model something like this in a real application, it does illustrate the basic concepts of states, events, and transitions that are important in a state machine workflow. And the subject area is something that most of us can easily relate to.

Designing the Car State Machine

If you think about operating a car, you will immediately think of several states that could be modeled in a workflow. Here are the states that I've chosen for this example:

- *Not Running*: In this state, you are in the car but the engine is not running.

- *Running*: You've now started the engine, but you're not moving.

- *Moving Forward*: The car is moving forward.

- *Moving in Reverse*: The car is moving in reverse.

- *Done with the Car*: You are finished with the car.

There are many other states that you could model, but this list is enough to provide a substantial example. The next step is to identify the events that can occur while you are in each state. Table 9-1 lists the events that are allowed for each state, along with the planned state transitions as each event is handled.

Table 9-1. *State Machine Events by State*

State	Event	State Transition
Not Running	Start the Engine	Running
Not Running	Leave the Car	Done with the Car
Running	Go Forward	Moving Forward
Running	Go in Reverse	Moving in Reverse
Running	Stop Engine	Not Running
Moving Forward	Stop Moving	Running
Moving in Reverse	Stop Moving	Running
All states	Beep Horn	None

If you look at the events outlined in Table 9-1, you will see that they very naturally fall into place once you've identified the states. For instance, if the car is in the Not Running state, you can either Start the Engine or Leave the Car. You can't Go Forward or Go in Reverse because you haven't started the engine yet. Likewise, if you are in the Moving Forward state, the only thing you can do is Stop Moving. You can't Stop Engine or Leave the Car while it is moving. Of course this example could be enhanced to allow other events that control the speed or direction of movement.

Notice that the Beep Horn event is available regardless of the current workflow state. This means that the Beep Horn event will have to be defined at the workflow level instead of within one of the states.

The workflow that you will implement for this state machine will handle all of these events using instances of `HandleExternalEventActivity`. The events will be defined as local service events and raised by the host application. As the workflow receives an event, it will call a local service method to send a simple `String` message back to the host. The messages will provide feedback to the driver of the vehicle about the current state of the workflow. After sending a message to the host, the workflow will transition to the appropriate state.

The host application will be a simple Windows Forms application. It will include a number of buttons that enable you to raise the local service events.

Defining the Local Service Interface

To begin coding the example, create a new project using the Empty Workflow Project template and name the project SharedWorkflows. This creates a DLL assembly that can be referenced by the Windows Forms demonstration application developed later in the "Implementing the Host Application" section.

Now add a new C# interface to this project and name it ICarServices. This interface defines the events and methods that you want to expose to the workflow via a local service. Listing 9-1 shows the complete code that you need for the ICarServices.cs file.

Listing 9-1. *Complete ICarServices.cs File*

```csharp
using System;
using System.Workflow.Activities;

namespace SharedWorkflows
{
    /// <summary>
    /// Define the contract for operating a vehicle
    /// </summary>
    [ExternalDataExchange]
    public interface ICarServices
    {
        /// <summary>
        /// Start the engine
        /// </summary>
        event EventHandler<ExternalDataEventArgs> StartEngine;

        /// <summary>
        /// Stop the engine
        /// </summary>
        event EventHandler<ExternalDataEventArgs> StopEngine;

        /// <summary>
        /// Stop movement of the vehicle
        /// </summary>
        event EventHandler<ExternalDataEventArgs> StopMovement;

        /// <summary>
        /// Move the vehicle forward
        /// </summary>
        event EventHandler<ExternalDataEventArgs> GoForward;

        /// <summary>
        /// Move the vehicle in reverse
        /// </summary>
        event EventHandler<ExternalDataEventArgs> GoReverse;

        /// <summary>
        /// Done with the car
        /// </summary>
        event EventHandler<ExternalDataEventArgs> LeaveCar;
```

```
/// <summary>
/// Beep the horn
/// </summary>
event EventHandler<ExternalDataEventArgs> BeepHorn;

/// <summary>
/// Send a message to the host application
/// </summary>
/// <param name="message"></param>
void OnSendMessage(String message);
    }
}
```

The `interface` is decorated with the `ExternalDataExchange` attribute that identifies it as a local service `interface`, making it available to workflows. All of the events pass an instance of `ExternalDataEventArgs` as their event arguments. None of these events need to pass any additional data with the event, so this base argument class is sufficient.

The `interface` also defines the `OnSendMessage` method. This method will be invoked by the workflow using the `CallExternalMethodActivity` to pass a message back to the host.

Implementing the Local Service

Next, add a new C# class to the `SharedWorkflows` project and name it `CarService`. This is the local service that implements the `ICarServices` interface. Listing 9-2 shows the complete code for the `CarService.cs` file.

Listing 9-2. *Complete CarService.cs File*

```
using System;
using System.Workflow.Activities;
using System.Workflow.Runtime;

namespace SharedWorkflows
{
    /// <summary>
    /// A local service that provides events used to control
    /// a vehicle
    /// </summary>
    public class CarService : ICarServices
    {
        #region ICarServices Members

        public event EventHandler<ExternalDataEventArgs> StartEngine;

        public event EventHandler<ExternalDataEventArgs> StopEngine;

        public event EventHandler<ExternalDataEventArgs> StopMovement;

        public event EventHandler<ExternalDataEventArgs> GoForward;

        public event EventHandler<ExternalDataEventArgs> GoReverse;

        public event EventHandler<ExternalDataEventArgs> BeepHorn;
```

```csharp
        public event EventHandler<ExternalDataEventArgs> LeaveCar;

        /// <summary>
        /// Send a message from a workflow to the host application
        /// </summary>
        /// <param name="message"></param>
        public void OnSendMessage(String message)
        {
            if (MessageReceived != null)
            {
                MessageReceivedEventArgs args
                    = new MessageReceivedEventArgs(
                        WorkflowEnvironment.WorkflowInstanceId,
                        message);
                MessageReceived(this, args);
            }
        }

        #endregion

        #region Members used by the host application

        public event EventHandler<MessageReceivedEventArgs> MessageReceived;

        public void OnStartEngine(ExternalDataEventArgs args)
        {
            if (StartEngine != null)
            {
                StartEngine(null, args);
            }
        }

        public void OnStopEngine(ExternalDataEventArgs args)
        {
            if (StopEngine != null)
            {
                StopEngine(null, args);
            }
        }

        public void OnStopMovement(ExternalDataEventArgs args)
        {
            if (StopMovement != null)
            {
                StopMovement(null, args);
            }
        }

        public void OnGoForward(ExternalDataEventArgs args)
        {
            if (GoForward != null)
            {
                GoForward(null, args);
            }
        }
```

```csharp
        public void OnGoReverse(ExternalDataEventArgs args)
        {
            if (GoReverse != null)
            {
                GoReverse(null, args);
            }
        }

        public void OnBeepHorn(ExternalDataEventArgs args)
        {
            if (BeepHorn != null)
            {
                BeepHorn(null, args);
            }
        }

        public void OnLeaveCar(ExternalDataEventArgs args)
        {
            if (LeaveCar != null)
            {
                LeaveCar(null, args);
            }
        }

        #endregion
    }
}
```

In addition to implementing the ICarServices interface, the service also includes a series of methods that raise the events. These methods are invoked by the host application, not the workflow.

The implementation for the OnSendMessage method takes the String message passed from the workflow and passes it to the host application via a MessageReceived event. This event is used only by the host application and uses an event arguments class named MessageReceivedEventArgs. To implement this class, add a new C# class named MessageReceivedEventArgs to the SharedWorkflows project. Listing 9-3 shows the complete code for the MessageReceivedEventArgs.cs file.

Listing 9-3. *Complete MessageReceivedEventArgs.cs File*

```csharp
using System;
using System.Workflow.Activities;

namespace SharedWorkflows
{
    /// <summary>
    /// Passes a message from the workflow to the local service
    /// </summary>
    [Serializable]
    public class MessageReceivedEventArgs : ExternalDataEventArgs
    {
        private String _message;
```

```
        public MessageReceivedEventArgs(Guid instanceId, String message)
            : base(instanceId)
        {
            _message = message;
        }

        public String Message
        {
            get { return _message; }
            set { _message = value; }
        }
    }
}
```

Implementing the Workflow

To begin defining the workflow, add a new state machine workflow to the SharedWorkflows project and name it CarWorkflow. Normally, I like to define any workflow variables and properties before moving to the visual design of the workflow. However, this workflow doesn't require a single instance variable or property. In fact, you won't add a single line of code to this workflow. Everything will be done in the visual workflow designer. Listing 9-4 is the complete code listing for the CarWorkflow.cs file.

Listing 9-4. *Complete CarWorkflow.cs File*

```
using System;
using System.Workflow.Activities;

namespace SharedWorkflows
{
    /// <summary>
    /// Car state machine workflow
    /// </summary>
    public sealed partial class CarWorkflow
        : StateMachineWorkflowActivity
    {
        public CarWorkflow()
        {
            InitializeComponent();
        }
    }
}
```

After switching back to the visual workflow designer, you should see an empty state machine workflow that looks like Figure 9-5.

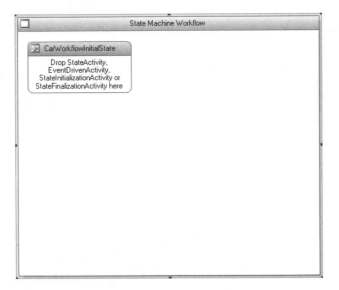

Figure 9-5. *Empty CarWorkflow*

Defining the States

The first order of business is to add all of the states defined in the previous design discussion. The first state is already created for you by the new workflow template. You only need to rename it from the default name of CarWorkflowInitialState to NotRunningState. To add the other states, drag and drop a StateActivity from the Toolbox to an empty area of the workflow. Name each state according to the following list:

- RunningState
- MovingForwardState
- MovingInReverseState
- DoneWithCarState

The workflow should now look like Figure 9-6.

■**Tip** You can arrange the states in a state machine workflow into any position that you like. If the workflow becomes cluttered, you can simply drag the states to new positions.

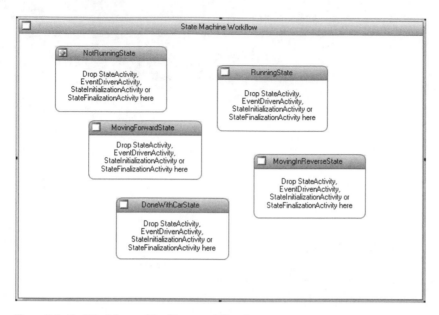

Figure 9-6. *CarWorkflow with all states defined*

Now that the states are defined, this is a good time to identify the initial and completed states. Switch to the Properties window for the workflow and set the InitialStateName property to NotRunningState and the CompletedStateName property to DoneWithCarState. The InitialStateName property identifies the initial state that the workflow will be in when it first begins execution. The CompletedStateName property identifies the state that causes the workflow to complete. The completed Properties window should look like Figure 9-7.

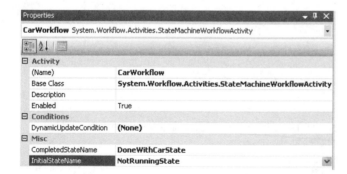

Figure 9-7. *Properties window with Initial and Completed states defined*

Defining the First Event

You can now define the first event for the NotRunningState. Drag and drop an EventDrivenActivity onto the NotRunningState. The workflow should now look like Figure 9-8.

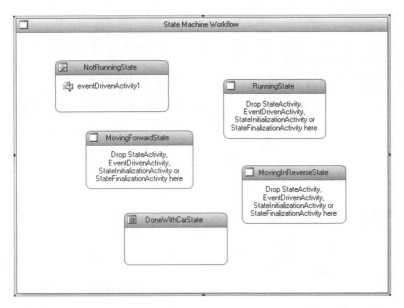

Figure 9-8. *CarWorkflow with first EventDrivenActivity added*

By double-clicking the eventDrivenActivity1 that you just added, the designer view changes to a detailed view of the activity (eventDrivenActivity1). This is shown in Figure 9-9.

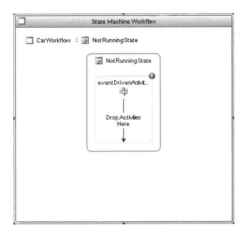

Figure 9-9. *EventDrivenActivity for NotRunningState*

The icons at the top of the view indicate your current designer scope (you are editing the NotRunningState of the CarWorkfow). When you are finished with this view, you can single-click either of these icons to return to the full workflow design view.

It's a good idea to always give the EventDrivenActivity instances a meaningful name since they are shown in the top-level view of the workflow. This EventDrivenActivity will be used to handle the StartEngine event so rename it to eventStartEngine.

To handle the StartEngine event, you'll need to add a set of three activities as children of this eventStartEngine activity. First, add a HandleExternalEventActivity, followed by a CallExternalMethodActivity and a SetStateActivity. Most of the events that you will handle in this workflow will follow this same pattern of three activities.

Set the InterfaceType property of the HandleExternalEventActivity to SharedWorkflows. ICarServices to identify the local service interface that defines the event. Set the EventName to StartEngine. None of the events that you will handle require any code, so there is no need to add an event handler.

Set the same value for the InterfaceType property of the CallExternalMethodActivity, but set the MethodName to OnSendMessage. Enter the String literal **Started Engine** in the message parameter. You can do this directly in the Parameters section of the Properties window. Figure 9-10 shows the completed properties for this activity.

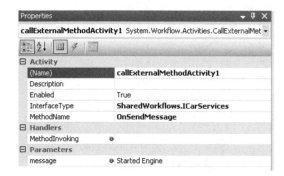

Figure 9-10. *Properties window for callExternalMethodActivity1*

The SetStateActivity includes a TargetStateName property that identifies the state that you will transition to. For this event, set this property to RunningState. Figure 9-11 shows the complete EventDrivenActivity that handles the StartEngine event.

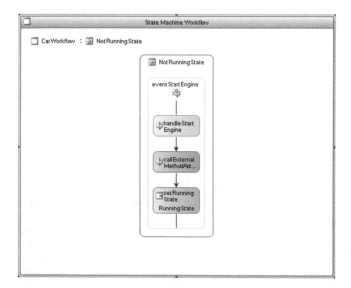

Figure 9-11. *Complete EventDrivenActivity for the StartEngine event*

You can now return to the top-level workflow view by single-clicking the CarWorkflow or NotRunningState icons. Before you add handlers for any additional events, drag and drop a StateInitializationActivity to the NotRunningState. You can also right-click the NotRunningState and select Add StateInitialization to add this activity.

Once added, double-click the new activity to go to the detailed view. This activity is executed as soon as the state is entered and before it begins to wait for any events. When this particular state is first entered, you need to send an initial message to the host application. To do this, drag and drop a CallExternalMethodActivity onto the StateInitializationActivity. Set the InterfaceType property to the same value as before (SharedWorkflows.ICarServices) and set the MethodName to OnSendMessage. Enter **The car is parked and not running** as the message parameter. This will be the initial message that the host application receives when the workflow is first started. The StateInitializationActivity should now look like Figure 9-12.

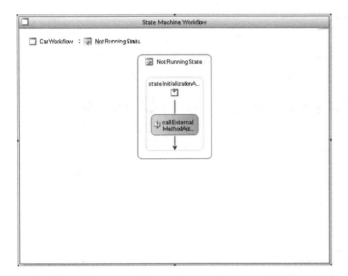

Figure 9-12. *Complete StateInitializationActivity for NotRunningState*

When you return to the top-level workflow view, your workflow should look like Figure 9-13.

Notice that the designer now shows an arrow that indicates the state transition to RunningState. This line is drawn for you based on the TargetStateName property value of the SetStateActivity.

■**Tip** If you need to change the state transition to a different state, you can go back into the detail view and change the value of the TargetStateName property. However, an easier way is to simply drag the line to a new state. This changes the value of the property for you.

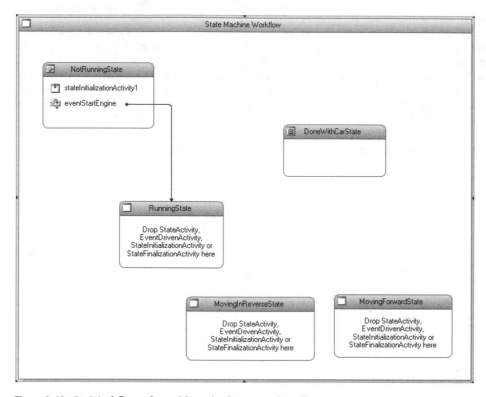

Figure 9-13. *CarWorkflow after adding the first event handler*

Defining the Remaining Events

All of the other events require the same set of three child activities: HandleExternalEventActivity, CallExternalMethodActivity, and SetStateActivity. To define handlers for the remaining events, follow the steps outlined previously for the StartEngine event. Table 9-2 is a summary of all of the events that you need to add. The StartEngine event has already been implemented in the previous section but is included in the table for completeness.

Table 9-2. *CarWorkflow State Event Handling*

State	Event	OnSendMessage message Parameter	State Transition
NotRunningState	StartEngine	Started engine	RunningState
NotRunningState	LeaveCar	Leaving the car	DoneWithCarState
RunningState	StopEngine	Stopping the engine	NotRunningState
RunningState	GoForward	Moving forward	MovingForwardState
RunningState	GoReverse	Moving in reverse	MovingInReverseState
MovingForwardState	StopMovement	Stopping movement	RunningState
MovingInReverseState	StopMovement	Stopping movement	RunningState

Once all of these activities have been added, your workflow should look like Figure 9-14.

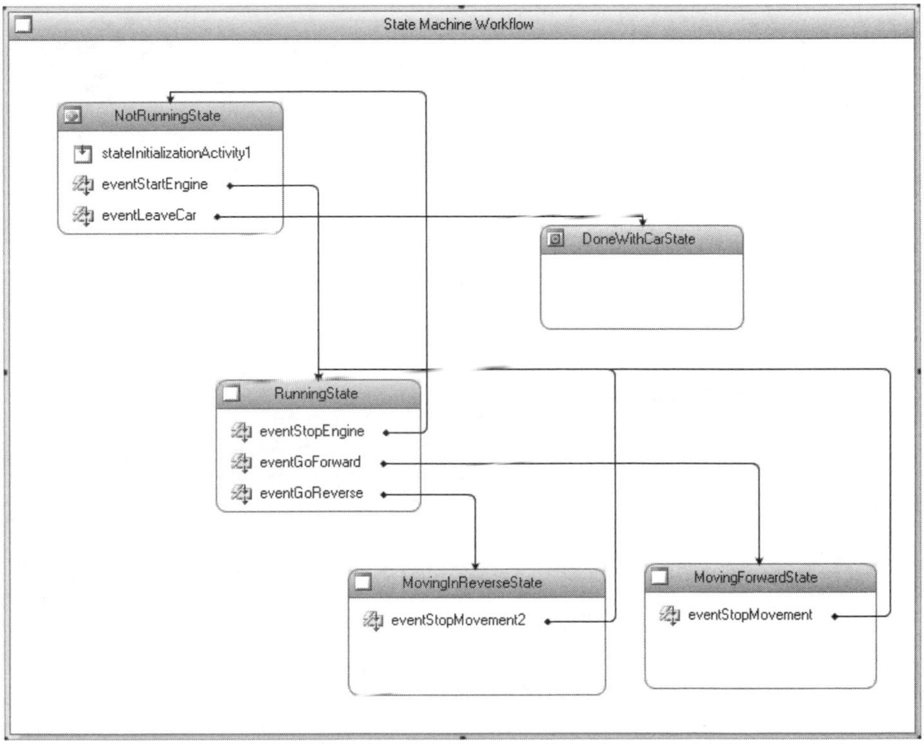

Figure 9-14. *CarWorkflow with completed states*

The only remaining event to handle is BeepHorn. This event is different because you should be able to raise this event regardless of what state the workflow is in. What you really want is to handle this event at the workflow level. Since StateMachineWorkflowActivity is derived directly from StateActivity, it exhibits the behavior of a state. Because of this, you can drag and drop an EventDrivenActivity directly onto the workflow. Once added, you can double-click the EventDrivenActivity and add the event handling activities from the detail designer view as you previously did for the other events.

For the BeepHorn event, enter a string message of **Beep!** for the message parameter of the CallExternalMethodActivity. The BeepHorn is also different in that it doesn't cause a transition to a state. Remember, it isn't even defined in a state. Figure 9-15 shows the complete EventDrivenActivity for the BeepHorn event.

Once the BeepHorn handler is in place, the workflow is complete. Figure 9-16 shows the completed CarWorkflow. Note the EventDrivenActivity at the top of the workflow for the BeepHorn event.

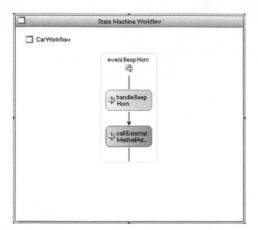

Figure 9-15. *BeepHorn EventDrivenActivity*

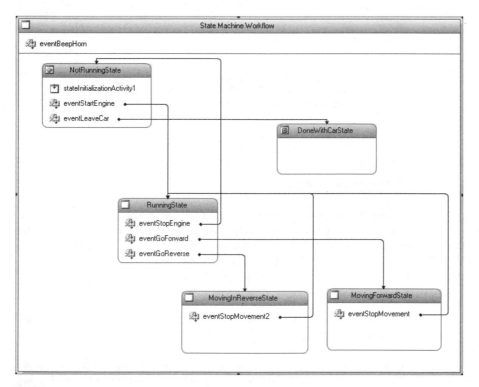

Figure 9-16. *Completed CarWorkflow*

Implementing the Host Application

The host application is a relatively simple Windows Forms application. It displays the status message that the workflow passes to the host by calling the OnSendMessage method. It also includes several buttons that raise the local service events.

To implement the host application, add a new Windows Application project to the current solution. Name the project CarStateMachine. Since this project isn't created from a workflow project template, you'll need to add references to these assemblies yourself:

- System.Workflow.Activities
- System.Workflow.ComponentModel
- System.Workflow.Runtime
- SharedWorkflows
- Bukovics.Workflow.Hosting

The SharedWorkflows and Bukovics.Workflow.Hosting references are project references. The Bukovics.Workflow.Hosting project was originally developed in Chapter 4 and contains a set of workflow manager classes that assist with hosting duties.

Designing the User Interface

The user interface for the CarStateMachine application looks like Figure 9-17.

Figure 9-17. *User interface for CarStateMachine application*

The area above the buttons is actually a Label that is used to display the message from the workflow. Table 9-3 lists all of the controls that you need to add to Form1 of the application.

Table 9-3. *CarStateMachine Controls*

Control	Name	Text Property
Label	lblMessage	Empty string
Button	btnNewCar	New Car
Button	btnStartEngine	Start Engine
Button	btnStopEngine	Stop Engine
Button	btnForward	Forward
Button	btnStop	Stop Moving
Button	btnReverse	Reverse
Button	btnBeepHorn	Beep Horn
Button	btnLeaveCar	Leave Car

After adding all of the Button controls, add Click event handlers for each button. The sample code that follows in Listing 9-5 uses the default name for each event handler.

Adding Code

Listing 9-5 contains the complete code for Form1.cs. Some of the more interesting sections are discussed in the inline comments.

Listing 9-5. *Complete Form1.cs File*

```csharp
using System;
using System.Collections.Generic;

using System.Windows.Forms;
using System.Workflow.Activities;
using System.Workflow.Runtime;

using Bukovics.Workflow.Hosting;
using SharedWorkflows;


namespace CarStateMachine
{
    /// <summary>
    /// Application to test the CarWorkflow
    /// </summary>
    public partial class Form1 : Form
    {
        private WorkflowRuntimeManager _workflowManager;
        private CarService _carService;
        private Guid _instanceId = Guid.Empty;
        private WorkflowInstanceWrapper _instanceWrapper;

        public Form1()
        {
            InitializeComponent();
            EnableEventButtons(false);
        }

        #region Initialization and shutdown

        /// <summary>
        /// Initialize the workflow runtime during startup
        /// </summary>
        /// <param name="e"></param>
        protected override void OnLoad(EventArgs e)
        {
            base.OnLoad(e);
            //create workflow runtime and manager
            _workflowManager = new WorkflowRuntimeManager(
                new WorkflowRuntime());

            //add services to the workflow runtime
            AddServices(_workflowManager.WorkflowRuntime);
        }
```

The initialization of the workflow runtime is similar to other examples that you've seen. The OnLoad method creates the workflow runtime and wraps it in an instance of the custom workflow manager class.

```
/// <summary>
/// Add any services needed by the runtime engine
/// </summary>
/// <param name="instance"></param>
private void AddServices(WorkflowRuntime instance)
{
    //add the external data exchange service to the runtime
    ExternalDataExchangeService exchangeService
        = new ExternalDataExchangeService();
    instance.AddService(exchangeService);

    //add our local service
    _carService = new CarService();
    _carService.MessageReceived
        += new EventHandler<MessageReceivedEventArgs>(
            carService_MessageReceived);
    exchangeService.AddService(_carService);
}
```

The AddServices method is then executed to add the local service (CarService) to the workflow runtime. The code also adds a handler for the MessageReceived event of the CarService. This is how the host application receives messages from the running workflow.

```
/// <summary>
/// Perform cleanup during application shutdown
/// </summary>
/// <param name="e"></param>
protected override void OnFormClosed(FormClosedEventArgs e)
{
    base.OnFormClosed(e);
    //cleanup the workflow runtime
    if (_workflowManager != null)
    {
        _workflowManager.Dispose();
    }
}

#endregion

#region Workflow originated events

private delegate void UpdateDelegate();

void carService_MessageReceived(
    object sender, MessageReceivedEventArgs e)
{
    //save the workflow instance Id
    _instanceId = e.InstanceId;
```

```
        UpdateDelegate theDelegate = delegate()
        {
            //update the message shown in the UI
            lblMessage.Text = e.Message;
        };

        //execute the anonymous delegate on the UI thread
        this.Invoke(theDelegate);
    }
```

In the carService_MessageReceived handler method, the code is careful to update the user interface on the UI thread.

```
    #endregion

    #region UI event handlers

    private void btnNewCar_Click(object sender, EventArgs e)
    {
        _instanceWrapper
            = _workflowManager.StartWorkflow(
                typeof(CarWorkflow), null);

        _instanceId = _instanceWrapper.WorkflowInstance.InstanceId;

        //enable the buttons
        EnableEventButtons(true);
        btnNewCar.Enabled = false;
    }
```

The btnNewCar_Click method is the Click event handler for the New Car button. This method contains the code to start a new workflow. The Click event handlers for the other Button controls simply raise one of the events using a method in the local CarService.

```
    private void btnStartEngine_Click(object sender, EventArgs e)
    {
        try
        {
            _carService.OnStartEngine(GetEventArgs());
        }
        catch (Exception exception)
        {
            HandleException(exception);
        }
    }

    private void btnStopEngine_Click(object sender, EventArgs e)
    {
        try
        {
            _carService.OnStopEngine(GetEventArgs());
        }
        catch (Exception exception)
        {
            HandleException(exception);
        }
    }
```

```csharp
private void btnLeaveCar_Click(object sender, EventArgs e)
{
    try
    {
        _carService.OnLeaveCar(GetEventArgs());
        //disable the buttons
        EnableEventButtons(false);
        btnNewCar.Enabled = true;
    }
    catch (Exception exception)
    {
        HandleException(exception);
    }
}

private void btnForward_Click(object sender, EventArgs e)
{
    try
    {
        _carService.OnGoForward(GetEventArgs());
    }
    catch (Exception exception)
    {
        HandleException(exception);
    }
}

private void btnStop_Click(object sender, EventArgs e)
{
    try
    {
        _carService.OnStopMovement(GetEventArgs());
    }
    catch (Exception exception)
    {
        HandleException(exception);
    }
}

private void btnReverse_Click(object sender, EventArgs e)
{
    try
    {
        _carService.OnGoReverse(GetEventArgs());
    }
    catch (Exception exception)
    {
        HandleException(exception);
    }
}
```

```csharp
        private void btnBeepHorn_Click(object sender, EventArgs e)
        {
            try
            {
                _carService.OnBeepHorn(GetEventArgs());
            }
            catch (Exception exception)
            {
                HandleException(exception);
            }
        }

        private ExternalDataEventArgs GetEventArgs()
        {
            ExternalDataEventArgs args
                = new ExternalDataEventArgs(_instanceId);
            args.WaitForIdle = true;
            return args;
        }
```

When raising external events that are handled by a state machine workflow, it is important to only raise events after the workflow has transitioned to a new state. If you were to raise an event while the workflow is in the middle of transitioning to its new state, the workflow would not be able to handle the event and an EventDeliveryFailedException would be thrown. To prevent this from occurring, you can set the optional WaitForIdle property of the ExternalDataEventArgs class to true. This causes the workflow runtime to wait until the workflow has completed the state transition and is idled before attempting to deliver the event. This property is set in the private GetEventArgs method.

```csharp
        private void HandleException(Exception e)
        {
            if (e is EventDeliveryFailedException)
            {
                MessageBox.Show("Action not allowed", "Not Allowed",
                    MessageBoxButtons.OK, MessageBoxIcon.Warning);
            }
            else
            {
                MessageBox.Show(e.Message, "Unhandled Exception",
                    MessageBoxButtons.OK, MessageBoxIcon.Error);
            }
        }

        #endregion

        #region Internal Helper methods

        private void EnableEventButtons(Boolean enabled)
        {
            btnStartEngine.Enabled = enabled;
            btnStopEngine.Enabled = enabled;
            btnForward.Enabled = enabled;
            btnReverse.Enabled = enabled;
            btnStop.Enabled = enabled;
            btnBeepHorn.Enabled = enabled;
            btnLeaveCar.Enabled = enabled;
        }
```

```
        #endregion

    }
}
```

■**Tip** This example does not use a persistence service. It doesn't make sense to persist the state of the CarWorkflow and then permit you to stop and restart the application. However, real-world applications that are built around state machine workflows do typically require persistence. Make sure you review the requirements of your application to determine whether a persistence service is necessary. Use of a persistence server is covered in Chapter 8.

Testing the Application

All of the necessary parts of this application are now in place. If you build the solution and run the CarStateMachine application, you should see something similar to Figure 9-18.

Figure 9-18. *CarStateMachine application initial display*

■**Note** Your exact placement and sizing of the controls on the form may be different. But hopefully, your application looks similar to what is shown here.

If you press the New Car button, the code handler will start a new instance of the CarWorkflow. When that happens, the initial state (NotRunningState) will be entered and the StateInitializationActivity that you defined for that state will execute. The result is that the application receives the initial message sent by the StateInitializationActivity and should now look like Figure 9-19.

Figure 9-19. *CarStateMachine application with started workflow*

If you are now in the car, the first thing you would logically want to do is to start the car. You can do this by pressing the Start Engine button. The workflow will now send another message to the host application and will transition to the RunningState. The application should now look like Figure 9-20.

Figure 9-20. *CarStateMachine application with running engine*

So far, the application and workflow are working as you would expect. Now that you are in the RunningState, you have three valid choices. You can stop the engine, you can move forward, or you can move in reverse. You know that those are your options because you implemented the workflow. But one very big deficiency in this application is that it doesn't provide any visual feedback. You have no way to visually determine which options are allowed at any point in time.

■**Note** The other examples in this chapter revise this application to correct this and other design deficiencies. One of the later examples shows you how to determine which events are valid in the current workflow state.

If you make an invalid selection, for example, by pressing the Stop Moving button, you should receive the error dialog shown in Figure 9-21.

You are receiving this error because the StopMovement event that you raised was undeliverable. The host application caught the EventDeliveryFailedException that was thrown by the workflow runtime when it was unable to deliver the event. Why was the event undeliverable? The runtime could not deliver the event because you were in a state that did not define a handler for that event.

However, the BeepHorn event is active, regardless of the current state of the workflow. A handler for this event was defined by the workflow directly rather than as a child of a particular state. If you press the Beep Horn button now, the application should look like Figure 9-22.

Figure 9-21. *CarStateMachine application with error dialog*

Figure 9-22. *CarStateMachine application after BeepHorn event*

With this first example, you've seen how to design and implement a simple state machine work-flow along with an application that uses it. In the next example, you will make a minor modification to this workflow that demonstrates the ability to recursively compose states within other states.

Eliminating Duplicate Event Handlers

The workflow in the previous example functions and produces the correct results. However, it isn't the most elegant design in one particular area. The workflow contains a duplicate set of handler activities for the StopMovement event. If you review the design of the CarWorkflow, you will see that this event is handled within MovingForwardState and MovingInReverseState. Both handler imple-mentations are exactly the same.

Generally, when you have a duplicate implementation such as this, it is a good candidate for refactoring. But how can you refactor this to eliminate the duplicate event handler? After all, both of these states need to react to the StopMovement event.

The solution is to use a technique called recursive composition of states. This means you define a parent state that includes other states as its children. If the parent state contains an EventDrivenActivity to handle an event, that event is shared by all of the child states. You still transition to one of the child states, not the parent. But regardless of which child state you are currently in, the shared event is available and can be handled.

Refactoring the CarWorkflow

Using this technique, you can refactor the CarWorkflow to eliminate the duplicate implementation for the StopMovement event. To accomplish this, you will add a new state named MovingState to the workflow. This will be the new parent state for MovingForwardState and MovingInReverseState. You will then move one of the existing EventDrivenActivity instances that handle the StopMovement event to the new MovingState and delete the duplicate implementation.

You can begin these changes by opening the CarWorkflow from the last example (found in the SharedWorkflows project) with the visual workflow designer. Drag and drop a new StateActivity onto the workflow and name it MovingState. Now, drag MovingForwardState and MovingInReverseState into the MovingState, making them children of the new state.

Now that these two states have a common parent state, you can drag the eventStopMovement activity (an EventDrivenActivity) from the MovingForwardState to the parent MovingState. The eventDrivenActivity2 that is in the MovingInReverseState can be deleted since it is no longer needed.

The revised CarWorkflow should now look like Figure 9-23.

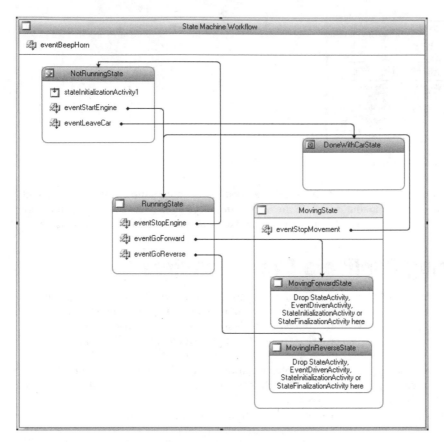

Figure 9-23. *Revised CarWorkflow with recursive states*

Notice that the child states (MovingForwardState and MovingInReverseState) no longer have any child activities of their own. This may be a signal that you really don't need these separate states in this very simple example. However, it is easy to see where an enhanced version of this workflow might require these separate states. For instance, if you want to add the concept of shifting gears, you would permit multiple gears when you are going forward but only a single gear when moving in reverse.

The state transitions from the RunningState continue to point to the child activities, not the new MovingState parent. This is an important point to remember when you compose states that contain other states. You can only transition to a leaf state (one that does not contain other states). Transitioning to a parent state such as MovingState is not permitted.

Testing the Revised Workflow

After you build the SharedWorkflows project, you should be able to run the CarStateMachine application and observe the same behavior as before. In particular, test the Stop Moving button to verify that it works correctly from both of the states within the new MovingState.

As you develop more state machine workflows, you will discover that it is a common requirement to handle the same event in multiple states. This technique of recursive composition of states provides an elegant way to accomplish this without duplicating the event handling activities.

Identifying Available Events

The CarStateMachine application developed in the previous examples has one very big design deficiency: it doesn't provide any feedback to the user to identify the events that are available. Depending on the current state of the CarWorkflow, only a small set of events should be permitted.

In this follow-up example, you will modify the CarStateMachine application to correct this problem. This example uses the GetWorkflowQueueData method of the WorkflowInstance object to identify the events that can be handled by the workflow in its current state. Based on the return value from this method, the application will enable or disable the individual buttons that raise the events. The goal is to prevent the user from raising events that the workflow is incapable of handling.

Interrogating the Workflow Queues

An instance of WorkflowInstance is returned from the WorkflowRuntime when a workflow is started. It contains methods that permit you to interact with the running instance of the workflow.

One of those methods is GetWorkflowQueueData. This method returns a collection of WorkflowQueueInfo objects. A workflow actually receives and processes events via a set of internal queues. Each WorkflowQueueInfo object in the returned collection is associated with one of the queues. Each queue is uniquely named for the external event that it handles. Therefore, you can use these WorkflowQueueInfo objects to identify the events that the workflow is waiting to receive in its current state.

Modifying the CarStateMachine Application

All of the necessary modifications should be made to the Form1.cs file of the CarStateMachine project. First, add an additional using statement to the beginning of this file. The System.Collections.ObjectModel namespace is needed to reference the ReadOnlyCollection that is returned from the GetWorkflowQueueData method. The revised set of using statements looks like this:

```
using System;
using System.Collections.Generic;
using System.Collections.ObjectModel;

using System.Windows.Forms;
using System.Workflow.Activities;
using System.Workflow.Runtime;

using Bukovics.Workflow.Hosting;
using SharedWorkflows;
```

Next, modify the form constructor to set the Tag property of each button. The value used for this property identifies the event that is associated with each button. The Tag property is used later in the code to easily identify the buttons that should be enabled or disabled. The revised constructor looks like this:

```
public Form1()
{
    InitializeComponent();

    //associate each button with the event that it raises
    btnStartEngine.Tag = "StartEngine";
    btnStopEngine.Tag = "StopEngine";
    btnForward.Tag = "GoForward";
    btnReverse.Tag = "GoReverse";
    btnStop.Tag = "StopMovement";
    btnBeepHorn.Tag = "BeepHorn";
    btnLeaveCar.Tag = "LeaveCar";

    EnableEventButtons(false);
}
```

The application will enable or disable the buttons each time the workflow becomes idle. This occurs each time the workflow transitions to a new state and begins waiting for events. To accomplish this, the code needs to handle the WorkflowIdled event of the WorkflowRuntime. A handler is assigned to this event in the revised OnLoad method shown here:

```
protected override void OnLoad(EventArgs e)
{
    base.OnLoad(e);
    //create workflow runtime and manager
    _workflowManager = new WorkflowRuntimeManager(
        new WorkflowRuntime());

    _workflowManager.WorkflowRuntime.WorkflowIdled
        += new EventHandler<WorkflowEventArgs>(
            WorkflowRuntime_WorkflowIdled);

    //add services to the workflow runtime
    AddServices(_workflowManager.WorkflowRuntime);
}
```

The handler method for the WorkflowIdled event looks like this:

```
/// <summary>
/// Handle the WorkflowIdled event
/// </summary>
/// <param name="sender"></param>
/// <param name="e"></param>
private void WorkflowRuntime_WorkflowIdled(
    object sender, WorkflowEventArgs e)
{
    UpdateDelegate theDelegate = delegate()
    {
        //first disable all buttons
        EnableEventButtons(false);

        //determine which events are allowed.
        //Note:  ReadOnlyCollection is in the
        //System.Collections.ObjectModel namespace.
        ReadOnlyCollection<WorkflowQueueInfo> queueInfoData
            = _instanceWrapper.WorkflowInstance.GetWorkflowQueueData();
```

```
            if (queueInfoData != null)
            {
                foreach (WorkflowQueueInfo info in queueInfoData)
                {
                    EventQueueName eventQueue = info.QueueName
                        as EventQueueName;
                    if (eventQueue == null)
                    {
                        break;
                    }

                    //enable the button that is associated
                    //with this event
                    EnableButtonForEvent(eventQueue.MethodName);
                }
            }
        };

        //execute the anonymous delegate on the UI thread
        this.Invoke(theDelegate);
}
```

This handler is executed each time the workflow becomes idled. It begins by calling the GetWorkflowQueueData method of the WorkflowInstance object. This returns a collection of WorkflowQueueInfo objects. Each one of these objects represents one of the internal queues currently in use by the workflow. Each queue is associated with one of the external events.

To identify the events that the workflow can currently handle, you simply inspect the collection of WorkflowQueueInfo objects. The remainder of this handler code iterates through this collection of objects. Each WorkflowQueueInfo object contains a QueueName property which is an instance of an EventQueueName object. The EventQueueName object has a MethodName property that identifies the external event handled by the queue. This name is passed to a private method named EnableButtonForEvent to enable or disable any buttons associated with the event. Note that all of this new code is within the anonymous delegate that is executed on the UI thread. This is important since updates to UI controls must be done on the original thread that created them.

The EnableButtonForEvent method is responsible for enabling or disabling the buttons based on the event name that is passed in. The code for this method looks like this:

```
private void EnableButtonForEvent(String eventName)
{
    //if a control has a Tag property equal
    //to the event name, then enable it
    foreach (Control control in this.Controls)
    {
        if (control is Button &&
            control.Tag != null)
        {
            if (control.Tag.ToString() == eventName)
            {
                control.Enabled = true;
            }
        }
    }
}
```

Testing the Application

After rebuilding the CarStateMachine application, you should be ready to run it. When you do, you should see that the buttons are now enabled and disabled according to the current state of the workflow. For instance, after pressing New Car, the application looks like Figure 9-24.

Figure 9-24. *Revised CarStateMachine after New Car*

If you compare Figure 9-24 with the original version shown in Figure 9-19, you will clearly see the difference. After these enhancements to the application, buttons are only enabled if the event they raise is supported by the current workflow state.

If you press Start Engine, the application looks like Figure 9-25.

Figure 9-25. *Revised CarStateMachine after Start Engine*

The application is now greatly improved since it provides valuable feedback to the user. By selectively enabling and disabling the buttons, the user is prevented from raising an event that is not supported by the current workflow state.

You can use this technique when your application is required to know the possible events that can be raised in the current workflow state.

Accessing Runtime Information

WF also includes the StateMachineWorkflowInstance class (found in the System.Workflow. Activities namespace). This class provides additional runtime information for an instance of a state machine workflow.

You create an instance of this class by passing the constructor a reference to the workflow runtime and the instance ID Guid associated with the state machine workflow. Once created, you can then reference the properties and methods of the StateMachineWorkflowInstance object to interact with the running workflow.

For instance, you can use the CurrentStateName property to retrieve the name of the current state. The CurrentState property returns a reference to the current StateActivity object rather than just the name. Several of the more interesting properties are listed in Table 9-4. This is not a complete list of all properties for this class.

Table 9-4. *Selected StateMachineWorkflowInstance Properties*

Property	Description
CurrentState	Returns a StateActivity representing the current state
CurrentStateName	Returns the String name of the current state
PossibleStateTransitions	Returns a collection of strings that identify the possible states that you can transition to from the current state
States	Returns a collection of StateActivity objects representing all of the leaf states in the workflow

The StateMachineWorkflowInstance class also provides a SetState method. Using this method, you can take direct control of the workflow and direct it to transition to the state that you specify.

Modifying the CarStateMachine Application

To provide a small example of how to use the StateMachineWorkflowInstance class, you can modify the CarStateMachine application once again. This time, you will modify the WorkflowRuntime_ WorkflowIdled method (added in the last example) to display the current state name in the title of the application form. Listing 9-6 is the revised source for this method with the additional code highlighted.

Listing 9-6. *Revised WorkflowRuntime_WorkflowIdled Method*

```
/// <summary>
/// Handle the WorkflowIdled event
/// </summary>
/// <param name="sender"></param>
/// <param name="e"></param>
private void WorkflowRuntime_WorkflowIdled(
    object sender, WorkflowEventArgs e)
{
    UpdateDelegate theDelegate = delegate()
    {
        //first disable all buttons
        EnableEventButtons(false);

        //determine which events are allowed.
        //Note:  ReadOnlyCollection is in the
        //System.Collections.ObjectModel namespace.
        ReadOnlyCollection<WorkflowQueueInfo> queueInfoData
            = _instanceWrapper.WorkflowInstance.GetWorkflowQueueData();
```

```
        if (queueInfoData != null)
        {
            foreach (WorkflowQueueInfo info in queueInfoData)
            {
                EventQueueName eventQueue = info.QueueName
                    as EventQueueName;
                if (eventQueue == null)
                {
                    break;
                }

                //enable the button that is associated
                //with this event
                EnableButtonForEvent(eventQueue.MethodName);
            }
        }

        StateMachineWorkflowInstance stateMachine
            = new StateMachineWorkflowInstance(
                _workflowManager.WorkflowRuntime,
                _instanceWrapper.WorkflowInstance.InstanceId);

        //set the form title to the current state name
        this.Text = String.Format(
            "State: {0}", stateMachine.CurrentStateName);

    };

    //execute the anonymous delegate on the UI thread
    this.Invoke(theDelegate);
}
```

An instance of the StateMachineWorkflowInstance class is constructed by passing the
WorkflowRuntime and the InstanceId of the workflow. Once it is constructed, the code sets the Text
property of the Form to the value of the CurrentStateName property.

Testing the Application

When you run the application, you should see the current state name shown in the title bar of the
application. For instance, after pressing the New Car button, NotRunningState should be displayed
in the title as shown in Figure 9-26.

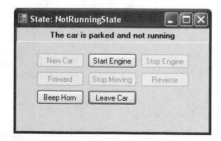

Figure 9-26. *CarStateMachine with NotRunningState shown*

If you press the Start Engine button, you should see that the workflow is in the RunningState. This is shown in Figure 9-27.

Figure 9-27. *CarStateMachine with RunningState shown*

You won't always need to use the StateMachineWorkflowInstance class. But if you need access to runtime information that is related to state machine workflows, keep this class in mind.

Summary

The focus of this chapter was state machine workflows. In the overview section of this chapter, you learned how these workflows are different from the sequential workflows that you have used up to this point. The WF classes and activities that you use when developing state machine workflows were also summarized.

Because of their flexibility, state machine workflows are well-suited to solving problems that involve human interaction. The benefits of using state machine workflows to solve these types of problems were highlighted in the overview.

A major part of this chapter was an application that models the basic operation of a car. This Windows Forms application used a state machine workflow to model several states of a car and then associate a set of events with each state. The host application permitted you to raise the external events that caused the workflow to transition to a new state.

Three additional examples made revisions to the workflow and the host application to simplify the design and add enhancements. Recursive composition of states was used to remove duplicate event handling logic. And the application was further enhanced by retrieving runtime information about the workflow to provide additional feedback to the user.

The next chapter discusses the WF support for transactions and batching of work.

CHAPTER 10

■■■

Transactions and Compensation

Integrity and consistency are important qualities to have when performing work in any application. You generally don't want to perform work in an inconsistent manner, or in a way that might leave the integrity of the data in doubt. These are important qualities for workflow applications as well as traditional applications.

WF supports several mechanisms that are designed to ensure the integrity and consistency of work that you perform. One mechanism supported by WF is *transactions*. Transactions allow you to create logical groups of work that use a resource manager such as a relational database. When work is enlisted in a transaction, it is committed or rolled back together. Either all of the work succeeds, or all of it fails. It is designed to always leave the underlying resource (such as a database) in a consistent state.

WF provides support for transactions with the `TransactionScopeActivity`. After a general discussion of transactions, the first example in this chapter demonstrates the use of this activity to enlist multiple database updates in a single batch of work.

WF also supports *compensation*. Compensation is a standardized way to undo work that is already completed. You can use compensation in those situations where a long-running transaction is not feasible. The second example in this chapter demonstrates the use of the `CompensatableTransactionScopeActivity` and the `CompensatableSequenceActivity`.

WF also provides you with the flexibility to commit other kinds of work under the control of a transaction. By adding work items to a batch of work, you can coordinate the actual committing of the work with an active transaction. The third example in this chapter demonstrates how to use the `IPendingWork` interface to accomplish this.

Understanding Transactions

A transaction is a logical boundary that defines work to be applied atomically. The concept of a transaction to set the logical boundary for some work is not new. Relational databases have supported transactions for decades.

When working with a relational database, you use a transaction when you have several updates that you wish to perform, and you want to ensure that all of the updates either succeed or fail as a complete set. To accomplish this, you begin a transaction, and then perform the first set of updates, then the second, and so on. Finally, after all of the updates have been applied, you signal the end of the transaction by committing the work. If any errors occur along the way, you can instead roll back the work. Rolling back work puts the resource (the relational database) back to its original state prior to your updates. In this way, all of the work within the transaction succeeds or fails as one atomic unit of work.

The Way of Transactions

Over the years, Microsoft has provided a number of ways to use and manage transactions. Today, .NET supports several mechanisms that provide access to transactions. And as you will soon see, WF adds its own mechanism to tap into the power of transactions.

In .NET, transactions can be managed explicitly for a single durable resource such as a relational database. For instance, when working with SQL Server, you can explicitly manage transactions using methods of the SqlConnection and SqlTransaction classes. The BeginTransaction method of the SqlConnection class returns a SqlTransaction. The SqlTransaction object includes the Commit and Rollback methods that you use to complete the transaction.

.NET also permits you to implicitly manage transactions using Enterprise Services. For instance, you can add attributes such as TransactionAttribute and AutoCompleteAttribute to an Enterprise Services component (a class that derives from the ServicedComponent class and is registered with Enterprise Services). These attributes cause the component to automatically create and use a transaction as methods are invoked. Using this approach, you no longer have to explicitly begin and end transactions. Enterprise Services takes care of that for you.

The big advantage to implicitly managed transactions is that you are no longer limited to using a single resource such as a relational database. If you perform work that uses another durable resource manager, that work is automatically enlisted in the current transaction, becoming part of the same unit of work. The most common resource managers are still database servers, but .NET does permit you to write your own resource manager that serves your own special needs.

.NET 2.0 introduced a new transaction framework defined in the System.Transactions namespace. This namespace includes classes such as Transaction and TransactionScope. This framework uses a lightweight transaction that is more efficient and optimized for local use. This is in contrast with a fully distributed transaction that requires the overhead of the Microsoft Distributed Transaction Coordinator (MSDTC) to coordinate the transaction across multiple resources or servers. The new transaction framework still supports fully distributed transactions, but it defers the decision to create one until it is absolutely necessary. When necessary, it promotes a lightweight local transaction to a fully distributed transaction automatically.

The TransactionScope class provides the ultimate in flexibility when working with transactions. Using this class, you can demarcate any code as a transactional code block. Any work done within that code block (work that uses a resource manager) is part of a single atomic transaction. The work performed in the code block is committed by calling the Complete method of the TransactionScope object. If an unhandled exception is thrown anywhere in the code block, or if Complete is not called, the transaction is rolled back.

WF Support for Transactions

WF provides the TransactionScopeActivity that is similar in concept to the TransactionScope class. Like the TransactionScope class, this activity demarcates a block of transactional code. In this case, the block of code is a set of child activities that you add to this composite activity. A new transaction (System.Transactions.Transaction) is created when the TransactionScopeActivity begins execution. Any child activities that are capable of using a transaction use the one provided by the TransactionScopeActivity. When all child activities complete and the TransactionScopeActivity ends, the transaction is committed. If an unhandled exception is thrown during execution of the child activities, the transaction is rolled back and all work is restored to its original state.

The TransactionScopeActivity includes a property named TransactionOptions. This object (an instance of the WorkflowTransactionOptions class) exposes its own set of properties that control the behavior of the transaction. One of the exposed properties is IsolationLevel. By changing the value of the IsolationLevel property, you determine the access to uncommitted or dirty data by the child activities of the TransactionScopeActivity.

The possible values for the IsolationLevel property are defined by the IsolationLevel enum found in the System.Transactions namespace. This is the same enum used to define the isolation level for the `Transaction` class. The default value is `Serializable`, which provides the highest possible level of protection. Other possible values are summarized in the following list:

`Serializable`: This is the highest possible isolation level and the default if a value isn't specified. With this level, data that is read by the current transaction cannot be changed by another transaction. It is named "serializable" since it allows the current transaction to reread the original data prior to any changes and obtain the same results. To enforce this, inserts to the data by another transaction are also prohibited, which makes this level the most restrictive and potentially a source of performance issues. It typically can result in excessive locking within the database as well as time-outs while one transaction has to wait for another to complete. Even though this is the most restrictive isolation level, it is still appropriate for many applications. When an application is correctly designed with short-lived transactions updating a limited amount of data, `Serializable` provides a good balance between integrity and performance.

`RepeatableRead`: Like `Serializable`, this isolation level prevents changes to the same data by another transaction. However, inserts to the data are allowed by other transactions. The transaction is no longer serializable in the sense that a reread of data may result in additional rows. However, this option can improve performance by reducing locking and time-outs.

`ReadCommitted`: This level prevents a transaction from reading data being updated by another uncommitted transaction. Once the second transaction commits the changes, the data can be read.

`ReadUncommitted`: This level allows reading of uncommitted data, otherwise known as *dirty reads*. It provides the greatest possible concurrency and performance; however, this comes at a very big cost. A transaction may be working with data that is in an intermediate state, making business decisions based on data that have not been committed.

The `TransactionOptions` property (a `WorkflowTransactionOptions` instance) also exposes the `TimeoutDuration` property. Setting this property changes the maximum amount of time that the transaction will exist before it times out and rolls back any changes.

When executing a workflow that contains a `TransactionScopeActivity`, a persistence service is required. This is necessary because the workflow runtime automatically persists the workflow when a `TransactionScopeActivity` ends. If you attempt to execute one of these workflows without first loading a persistence service, an `InvalidOperationException` will be thrown.

In addition to the persistence service, the workflow runtime also requires a `WorkflowCommitWorkBatchService` in order to process activities that use transactions. However, unlike persistence, which requires you to explicitly load a persistence service, a default implementation of a `WorkflowCommitWorkBatchService` is loaded for you if you don't explicitly load one. The default version is `DefaultWorkflowCommitWorkBatchService` (found in the `System.Workflow.Runtime.Hosting` namespace). This default service is sufficient for most applications.

■Note WF also includes the `SharedConnectionWorkflowCommitWorkBatchService` class (also found in the `System.Workflow.Runtime.Hosting` namespace). This is a highly specialized version of the service that should be used when you are using the `SqlWorkflowPersistenceService` for persistence and the `SqlTrackingService` for workflow tracking at the same time. In this scenario, both of these services should use the same physical SQL Server database and the same connection string.

The `SharedConnectionWorkflowCommitWorkBatchService` class is optimized to avoid potential performance problems when both the persistence and tracking services are used. The problem arises when the tracking service performs transactional updates to the database. If the persistence and tracking service use different database connections, the transaction is promoted to a distributed transaction using MSDTC. This causes a performance hit that is avoided by this specialized version of the service.

Using the TransactionScopeActivity

The example that follows demonstrates the use of the TransactionScopeActivity to group child activities into a single atomic unit of work. For this example, I've chosen a simple transfer of funds from one account to another. The transfer involves two steps: a debit from one account and a credit to another. Both steps must succeed; otherwise the transfer cannot take place. If either step fails, the entire transfer must be rolled back.

To properly illustrate the transfer, the example uses a table in a SQL Server database to maintain the balance for the two accounts. A custom activity is developed that handles either a debit or a credit to a single account. The test workflow then includes two instances of this activity, one to process the debit and a second instance to handle the credit. Both of these instances are placed in a TransactionScopeActivity to ensure that they perform their work under the control of the same transaction.

Before you implement this example, you will need to create the SQL Server database and the test table that are referenced by the example code. Please refer to the "Preparing the ProWorkflow Database" sidebar for the steps needed to accomplish this. The examples in this chapter also require a workflow persistence service. To set up a SQL Server database to be used for persistence, you can refer to the instructions in Chapter 4.

PREPARING THE PROWORKFLOW DATABASE

The examples in this chapter assume that you have a copy of SQL Server Express installed on your development machine. SQL Server Express is distributed with Visual Studio 2005 and is also available as a free download directly from Microsoft. A fully licensed version of SQL Server 2005 can also be used. However, the database connection strings shown in the example code assume that SQL Server Express is being used. Please make the appropriate adjustments to the connection strings if you are not using SQL Server Express.

A database named ProWorkflow is used for all of the examples in this chapter. To create this database and also execute the SQL scripts needed to create and populate the test tables, you can use the sqlcmd command-line tool provided with SQL Server. Optionally, you can download a free copy of SQL Server Management Studio Express from Microsoft. This is a utility that allows you to graphically manage databases and objects within a database.

First, save the following SQL script to a file named ProWorkflowCreate.sql. This script contains the statements that create the database and the tables needed by all of the examples in this chapter:

```
USE [master]
GO
IF  EXISTS (SELECT name FROM sys.databases
    WHERE name = N'ProWorkflow')
DROP DATABASE [ProWorkflow]
GO
CREATE DATABASE [ProWorkflow]
GO
USE ProWorkflow
GO
SET ANSI_NULLS ON
GO
SET QUOTED_IDENTIFIER ON
GO
IF NOT EXISTS (SELECT * FROM sys.objects
WHERE object_id = OBJECT_ID(N'[dbo].[account]') AND type in (N'U'))
```

```
BEGIN
CREATE TABLE [dbo].[account](
    [accountId] [int] NOT NULL,
    [description] [nvarchar](50) NULL,
    [balance] [money] NULL
) ON [PRIMARY]
END
GO
SET ANSI_NULLS ON
GO
SET QUOTED_IDENTIFIER ON
GO
IF NOT EXISTS (SELECT * FROM sys.objects
WHERE object_id = OBJECT_ID(N'[dbo].[itemInventory]') AND type in (N'U'))
BEGIN
CREATE TABLE [dbo].[itemInventory](
    [itemId] [int] NOT NULL,
    [description] [nvarchar](50) NULL,
    [qtyOnHand] [int] NULL
) ON [PRIMARY]
END
GO
SET ANSI_NULLS ON
GO
SET QUOTED_IDENTIFIER ON
GO
IF NOT EXISTS (SELECT * FROM sys.objects
WHERE object_id = OBJECT_ID(N'[dbo].[orderDetail]') AND type in (N'U'))
BEGIN
CREATE TABLE [dbo].[orderDetail](
    [orderId] [int] NOT NULL,
    [accountId] [int] NOT NULL,
    [itemId] [int] NOT NULL,
    [quantity] [int] NOT NULL
) ON [PRIMARY]
END
```

After creating the database and the objects in it, you need to populate some of the tables with test data. To do this, you can save the following script to a file named `PopulateTestTables.sql`:

```
USE [ProWorkflow]
GO
/*
reset account table
*/
DELETE FROM [account]
GO
INSERT INTO [account]
([accountId],[description],[balance])
VALUES(1001, 'account 1', 100.00)
GO
```

```
INSERT INTO [account]
([accountId],[description],[balance])
VALUES(2002, 'account 2', 100.00)
GO
INSERT INTO [account]
([accountId],[description],[balance])
VALUES(9000, 'company account', 1000.00)
GO
/*
reset itemInventory table
*/
DELETE FROM [itemInventory]
GO
INSERT INTO [itemInventory]
([itemId],[description],[qtyOnHand])
VALUES(51,'hammer', 10)
GO
INSERT INTO [itemInventory]
([itemId],[description],[qtyOnHand])
VALUES(52,'shop vac', 2)
GO
INSERT INTO [itemInventory]
([itemId],[description],[qtyOnHand])
VALUES(53,'extension ladder', 5)
GO
/*
reset orderDetail table
*/
DELETE FROM [orderDetail]
GO
```

Now that you have saved these scripts to files, you can execute them with the sqlcmd utility. Save the following lines to a file named PrepareProWorkflowDatabase.cmd. This allows you to easily execute these commands again in order to reset the test database back to its original state:

```
sqlcmd -S localhost\SQLEXPRESS –E -m-1 -r1 -d master -i ProWorkflowCreate.sql
sqlcmd -S localhost\SQLEXPRESS –E -m-1 -r1
    -d ProWorkflow -i PopulateTestTables.sql
Pause
```

■ **Note** Each sqlcmd is entered on a single line. The second sqlcmd shown is broken into two separate lines to fit the format of this book.

Now open a Windows command prompt and execute the PrepareProWorkflowDatabase.cmd file you just saved. If all goes well, you should have a new ProWorkflow database that contains the tables and test data used by the examples in this chapter.

Implementing the AccountAdjustmentActivity

To begin this example, create a new project using the Empty Workflow Project template and name the project SharedWorkflows. This creates a DLL assembly that will contain the custom activity and the workflow. The custom activity that you will develop reads data from the application configuration file (App.Config). To access the configuration classes in code, you need to add an assembly reference to System.Configuration.

Add a new Activity to the project and name it AccountAdjustmentActivity. This is the custom activity that will process either a debit or a credit to an account. By default, the base class for a new activity is SequenceActivity, which means this is a composite activity. Since this activity doesn't need to support children, you can change the base class from SequenceActivity to Activity.

■ **Note** You can add a new activity to the project in several ways. First, you can right-click the SharedWorkflows project in the Solution Explorer and select Add, then Activity. You can also select the project and then select Add Activity from the main Project menu. You can also right-click the project in the Solution Explorer and select Add New Item, then select Activity.

The AccountAdjustmentActivity requires these three properties:

- Amount: A Decimal that will contain the amount of funds to debit or credit
- AccountId: An Int32 that identifies the account to debit or credit
- IsCredit: A Boolean that is set to true if this is a credit, and false for a debit

All of these properties should be implemented as dependency properties. This is necessary since you will be binding the values for these properties to similar properties of the workflow. Only dependency properties provide support for binding activity properties.

Listing 10-1 shows the complete AccountAdjustmentActivity.cs file that you will need, including the dependency properties and the code that processes the account balance adjustment.

Listing 10-1. *Complete AccountAdjustmentActivity.cs File*

```
using System;
using System.Data;
using System.Data.SqlClient;
using System.Configuration;  //needs assembly reference
using System.ComponentModel;
using System.Workflow.ComponentModel;

namespace SharedWorkflows
{
    /// <summary>
    /// Custom activity that adjusts the balance of an account
    /// </summary>
    public partial class AccountAdjustmentActivity : Activity
    {
        /// <summary>
        /// Amount Dependency Property
        /// </summary>
```

```
public static DependencyProperty AmountProperty
    = System.Workflow.ComponentModel.DependencyProperty.Register(
        "Amount", typeof(Decimal), typeof(AccountAdjustmentActivity));
[Description("The amount of the balance adjustment")]
[Category("ProWorkflow")]
[Browsable(true)]
[DesignerSerializationVisibility(DesignerSerializationVisibility.Visible)]
public Decimal Amount
{
    get
    {
        return ((Decimal)(base.GetValue(
            AccountAdjustmentActivity.AmountProperty)));
    }
    set
    {
        base.SetValue(AccountAdjustmentActivity.AmountProperty, value);
    }
}

/// <summary>
/// AccountId Dependency Property
/// </summary>
public static DependencyProperty AccountIdProperty
    = System.Workflow.ComponentModel.DependencyProperty.Register(
        "AccountId", typeof(Int32), typeof(AccountAdjustmentActivity));
[Description("Identifies the account")]
[Category("ProWorkflow")]
[Browsable(true)]
[DesignerSerializationVisibility(DesignerSerializationVisibility.Visible)]
public Int32 AccountId
{
    get
    {
        return ((Int32)(base.GetValue(
            AccountAdjustmentActivity.AccountIdProperty)));
    }
    set
    {
        base.SetValue(AccountAdjustmentActivity.AccountIdProperty, value);
    }
}

/// <summary>
/// IsCredit Dependency Property
/// </summary>
public static DependencyProperty IsCreditProperty
    = System.Workflow.ComponentModel.DependencyProperty.Register(
        "IsCredit", typeof(Boolean), typeof(AccountAdjustmentActivity));
[Description("True if this is a credit, false for a debit")]
[Category("ProWorkflow")]
[Browsable(true)]
[DesignerSerializationVisibility(DesignerSerializationVisibility.Visible)]
public Boolean IsCredit
```

```
{
    get
    {
        return ((Boolean)(base.GetValue(
            AccountAdjustmentActivity.IsCreditProperty)));
    }
    set
    {
        base.SetValue(AccountAdjustmentActivity.IsCreditProperty, value);
    }
}

public AccountAdjustmentActivity()
{
    InitializeComponent();
}
```

Following the dependency properties, the code contains an overridden Execute method. This is the method that is called by the workflow runtime when the activity is executed. The bulk of the code in this activity is straightforward SQL logic using the ADO.NET classes that work with SQL Server.

```
/// <summary>
/// Perform the adjustment against the account
/// </summary>
/// <param name="executionContext"></param>
/// <returns></returns>
protected override ActivityExecutionStatus Execute(
    ActivityExecutionContext executionContext)
{
    using (SqlConnection connection = new SqlConnection(
        ConfigurationManager.ConnectionStrings
            ["ProWorkflow"].ConnectionString))
    {
        connection.Open();

        if (!IsCredit)
        {
            //if this is a debit, see if the account
            //has a sufficient balance
            Decimal currentBal = GetCurrentBalance(
                connection, AccountId);
            if (currentBal < Amount)
            {
                throw new ArgumentException(
                    "Insufficient balance to process debit");
            }
        }

        //update the account balance
        UpdateBalance(connection, AccountId, Amount, IsCredit);

        connection.Close();
    }

    return base.Execute(executionContext);
}
```

The code in the Execute method first creates an instance of a SqlConnection object. The connection string is retrieved from the application configuration file (App.Config) of the host application. You will see the contents of that file later when you implement the host application. It's always good practice to avoid hard-coded connection strings within your code. The SqlConnection object is wrapped in a using code block. This ensures that the Dispose method of the connection object is called when the code leaves this scope. Calling Dispose also closes the database connection if it is open.

Within the scope of the SqlConnection object, the private GetCurrentBalance method is called if the activity is processing a debit (the IsCredit property is false). The purpose of this method is to retrieve the current balance for the account. If the amount of the debit exceeds the current balance, an exception is thrown.

If no exception is thrown, the code then calls the private UpdateBalance method (shown next). This method updates the balance for the account positively or negatively by the Amount property. If the IsCredit property is true, the balance is increased, otherwise it is reduced.

```
/// <summary>
/// Retrieve the current balance for an account
/// </summary>
/// <param name="accountId"></param>
/// <returns></returns>
private Decimal GetCurrentBalance(
    SqlConnection connection, Int32 accountId)
{
    Decimal balance = 0;
    String sql =
        @"select balance from account where accountId = @AccountId";

    //setup Sql command object
    SqlCommand command = new SqlCommand(sql);
    //setup parameters
    SqlParameter p = new SqlParameter("@AccountId", accountId);
    command.Parameters.Add(p);
    command.Connection = connection;

    Object result = command.ExecuteScalar();
    if (result != null)
    {
        balance = (Decimal)result;
    }

    return balance;
}

/// <summary>
/// Update the account balance
/// </summary>
/// <param name="adjAmount"></param>
/// <returns></returns>
private void UpdateBalance(SqlConnection connection,
    Int32 accountId, Decimal adjAmount, Boolean isCredit)
{
    String sql;
    if (isCredit)
    {
```

```
                sql =
                    @"update account set balance = balance + @AdjAmount
                  where accountId = @AccountId";
            }
            else
            {
                sql =
                    @"update account set balance = balance - @AdjAmount
                  where accountId = @AccountId";
            }
            //setup Sql command object
            SqlCommand command = new SqlCommand(sql);
            //setup parameters
            SqlParameter p = new SqlParameter("@AccountId", accountId);
            command.Parameters.Add(p);
            p = new SqlParameter("@AdjAmount", adjAmount);
            command.Parameters.Add(p);
            command.Connection = connection;

            command.ExecuteNonQuery();
        }
    }
}
```

Implementing the AccountTransferWorkflow

The next step is to implement a workflow that uses the AccountAdjustmentActivity. Add a new sequential workflow to the SharedWorkflows project and name it AccountTransferWorkflow. This workflow requires a set of three dependency properties that will provide input values to the workflow. The required properties are the following:

- Amount: A Decimal that will contain the amount of the transfer
- FromAccountId: An Int32 that identifies the account to debit
- ToAccountId: An Int32 that identifies the account to credit

Listing 10-2 shows the complete listing for the AccountTransferWorkflow.cs after these properties have been defined.

Listing 10-2. *Complete AccountTransferWorkflow.cs File*

```
using System;
using System.ComponentModel;
using System.Workflow.ComponentModel;
using System.Workflow.Activities;

namespace SharedWorkflows
{
    /// <summary>
    /// Workflow that processes a transfer of funds
    /// between two accounts
    /// </summary>
    public sealed partial class AccountTransferWorkflow
        : SequentialWorkflowActivity
```

```
    {
        /// <summary>
        /// Amount Dependency Property
        /// </summary>
        public static DependencyProperty AmountProperty
            = System.Workflow.ComponentModel.DependencyProperty.Register(
                "Amount", typeof(Decimal), typeof(AccountTransferWorkflow));
        [Description("The amount of the balance adjustment")]
        [Category("ProWorkflow")]
        [Browsable(true)]
        [DesignerSerializationVisibility(DesignerSerializationVisibility.Visible)]
        public Decimal Amount
        {
            get
            {
                return ((Decimal)(base.GetValue(
                    AccountTransferWorkflow.AmountProperty)));
            }
            set
            {
                base.SetValue(AccountTransferWorkflow.AmountProperty, value);
            }
        }

        /// <summary>
        /// FromAccountId Dependency Property
        /// </summary>
        public static DependencyProperty FromAccountIdProperty
            = System.Workflow.ComponentModel.DependencyProperty.Register(
                "FromAccountId", typeof(Int32), typeof(AccountTransferWorkflow));
        [Description("Identifies the account")]
        [Category("ProWorkflow")]
        [Browsable(true)]
        [DesignerSerializationVisibility(DesignerSerializationVisibility.Visible)]
        public Int32 FromAccountId
        {
            get
            {
                return ((Int32)(base.GetValue(
                    AccountTransferWorkflow.FromAccountIdProperty)));
            }
            set
            {
                base.SetValue(AccountTransferWorkflow.FromAccountIdProperty, value);
            }
        }

        /// <summary>
        /// ToAccountId Dependency Property
        /// </summary>
        public static DependencyProperty ToAccountIdProperty
            = System.Workflow.ComponentModel.DependencyProperty.Register(
                "ToAccountId", typeof(Int32), typeof(AccountTransferWorkflow));
        [Description("Identifies the account")]
        [Category("ProWorkflow")]
```

```
        [Browsable(true)]
        [DesignerSerializationVisibility(DesignerSerializationVisibility.Visible)]
        public Int32 ToAccountId
        {
            get
            {
                return ((Int32)(base.GetValue(
                    AccountTransferWorkflow.ToAccountIdProperty)));
            }
            set
            {
                base.SetValue(AccountTransferWorkflow.ToAccountIdProperty, value);
            }
        }

        public AccountTransferWorkflow()
        {
            InitializeComponent();
        }
    }
}
```

After switching to the visual workflow designer for the AccountTransferWorkflow you can drag and drop a TransactionScopeActivity onto the empty workflow. For this example, you can use all of the default settings for this activity.

Next, after building the solution, add two instances of the custom AccountAdjustmentActivity as children of the TransactionScopeActivity. Change the name of the first AccountAdjustmentActivity to creditActivity and the second to debitActivity. Tables 10-1 and 10-2 list the property bindings that you should now set for these activities.

Table 10-1. *Property Bindings for creditActivity*

Property	Binding
AccountId	Activity=AccountTransferWorkflow, Path=ToAccountId
Amount	Activity=AccountTransferWorkflow, Path=Amount
IsCredit	true

Table 10-2. *Property Bindings for debitActivity*

Property	Binding
AccountId	Activity=AccountTransferWorkflow, Path=FromAccountId
Amount	Activity=AccountTransferWorkflow, Path=Amount
IsCredit	false

Figure 10-1 shows the completed workflow.

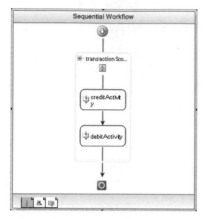

Figure 10-1. *Complete AccountTransferWorkflow*

You may be wondering why I execute the credit activity first, followed by the debit activity. Logically, you would want to first execute the debit, thus ensuring that the account has a sufficient balance to support the transfer. If the debit fails and throws an exception, the credit would never be executed and there would be nothing to roll back.

While a design that executes the debit first makes more sense, it doesn't really demonstrate the TransactionScopeActivity, and that is the real purpose of this workflow. By executing the credit first, this contrived example shows you what happens when the exception is thrown (by the debit activity) after updates have already been applied by the credit activity.

Testing the Workflow

You can test this workflow using a simple Console application. Add a new Sequential Workflow Console Application to the solution and name it ConsoleAccountTransfer. You can delete Workflow1 that was added to this project by the template since it is not needed. Add the following additional references to this project:

- SharedWorkflows
- Bukovics.Workflow.Hosting
- System.Configuration

The SharedWorkflows and Bukovics.Workflow.Hosting references are project references. The Bukovics.Workflow.Hosting project was originally developed in Chapter 4 and contains a set of workflow manager classes that assist with hosting duties. A reference to System.Configuration is needed in order to retrieve values from the application configuration file.

Add a new C# class to the ConsoleAccountTransfer project and name it AccountTransferTest. This class will contain the code to host the workflow runtime and start the workflow. The complete code for this class is shown and discussed in Listing 10-3.

Listing 10-3. *Complete AccountTransferTest.cs File*

```
using System;
using System.Configuration;   //need assembly reference
using System.Collections.Generic;
using System.Data.SqlClient;
using System.Workflow.Runtime;
```

```
using System.Workflow.Activities;
using System.Workflow.Runtime.Hosting;

using Bukovics.Workflow.Hosting;
using SharedWorkflows;

namespace ConsoleAccountTransfer
{
    /// <summary>
    /// Test the AccountTransferWorkflow
    /// </summary>
    public class AccountTransferTest
    {
        public static void Run()
        {
            using (WorkflowRuntimeManager manager
                = new WorkflowRuntimeManager(new WorkflowRuntime()))
            {
                //configure services for the workflow runtime
                AddServices(manager.WorkflowRuntime);
                manager.WorkflowRuntime.StartRuntime();

                //run the workflow using a transfer value that should work

                Console.WriteLine("Executing 1st AccountTransferWorkflow");
                DisplayTestData(1001, 2002, "before");

                //create a dictionary with input arguments
                Dictionary<String, Object> wfArguments
                    = new Dictionary<string, object>();
                wfArguments.Add("FromAccountId", 1001);
                wfArguments.Add("ToAccountId", 2002);
                wfArguments.Add("Amount", (Decimal)25.00);
                //start the workflow
                WorkflowInstanceWrapper instance = manager.StartWorkflow(
                    typeof(SharedWorkflows.AccountTransferWorkflow), wfArguments);
                manager.WaitAll(5000);
                if (instance.Exception != null)
                {
                    Console.WriteLine("EXCEPTION: {0}",
                        instance.Exception.Message);
                }
                DisplayTestData(1001, 2002, "after");
                Console.WriteLine("Completed 1st AccountTransferWorkflow\n\r");

                //run the workflow again using an amount that should fail

                Console.WriteLine("Executing 2nd AccountTransferWorkflow");
                DisplayTestData(1001, 2002, "before");

                wfArguments = new Dictionary<string, object>();
                wfArguments.Add("FromAccountId", 1001);
                wfArguments.Add("ToAccountId", 2002);
                //this transfer amount should exceed the available balance
```

```
            wfArguments.Add("Amount", (Decimal)200.00);
            instance = manager.StartWorkflow(
                typeof(SharedWorkflows.AccountTransferWorkflow), wfArguments);
            manager.WaitAll(5000);
            if (instance.Exception != null)
            {
                Console.WriteLine("EXCEPTION: {0}",
                    instance.Exception.Message);
            }
            DisplayTestData(1001, 2002, "after");
            Console.WriteLine("Completed 2nd AccountTransferWorkflow\n\r");
        }
    }

    /// <summary>
    /// Add any services needed by the runtime engine
    /// </summary>
    /// <param name="instance"></param>
    private static void AddServices(WorkflowRuntime instance)
    {
        //use the standard SQL Server persistence service
        SqlWorkflowPersistenceService persistence =
            new SqlWorkflowPersistenceService(
                ConfigurationManager.ConnectionStrings
                    ["WorkflowPersistence"].ConnectionString,
                true, new TimeSpan(0, 2, 0), new TimeSpan(0, 0, 5));
        instance.AddService(persistence);
    }
```

This class contains the usual code to create an instance of the WorkflowRuntime and wrap it in a WorkflowRuntimeManager instance. The AddServices method is called during startup to add a persistence service to the runtime. The database connection string used when constructing the SqlWorkflowPersistenceService is retrieved from the application configuration file.

```
    #region Display Test Data

    /// <summary>
    /// Display the balances for the test accounts
    /// </summary>
    /// <param name="acctId1"></param>
    /// <param name="acctId2"></param>
    /// <param name="desc"></param>
    private static void DisplayTestData(
        Int32 acctId1, Int32 acctId2, String desc)
    {
        using (SqlConnection connection = new SqlConnection(
            ConfigurationManager.ConnectionStrings
                ["ProWorkflow"].ConnectionString))
        {
            connection.Open();
            Decimal balance = GetCurrentBalance(connection, acctId1);
            Console.WriteLine("Balance {0} test for AccountId {1}: {2}",
                desc, acctId1, balance);
            balance = GetCurrentBalance(connection, acctId2);
```

```
        Console.WriteLine("Balance {0} test for AccountId {1}: {2}",
            desc, acctId2, balance);
        connection.Close();
    }
}
```

The code includes a `DisplayTestData` method that is called before and after the execution of the workflow. This method executes a SQL query against the database to retrieve the current balance. By showing the account balances before and after the workflow, you will be able to compare the expected results to the actual values in the database.

```
/// <summary>
/// Get the balance for an account
/// </summary>
/// <param name="connection"></param>
/// <param name="accountId"></param>
/// <returns></returns>
private static Decimal GetCurrentBalance(
    SqlConnection connection, Int32 accountId)
{
    Decimal balance = 0;
    String sql =
        @"select balance from account where accountId = @AccountId";

    //setup Sql command object
    SqlCommand command = new SqlCommand(sql);
    //setup parameters
    SqlParameter p = new SqlParameter("@AccountId", accountId);
    command.Parameters.Add(p);
    command.Connection = connection;

    Object result = command.ExecuteScalar();
    if (result != null)
    {
        balance = (Decimal)result;
    }

    return balance;
}

#endregion
    }
}
```

The `AccountTransferWorkflow` is executed twice. The first time, it transfers 25.00 between two accounts. The test data for these accounts initially sets their balance to 100.00, so this first workflow execution should succeed. This assumes that this is the first time you've run this test.

The second time the workflow executes, it attempts a transfer of 200.00 between the same accounts. Since this exceeds the balance in the account, the debit should fail and throw an exception. In this case, the beginning and ending balances for the accounts should be the same since any updates that might have been applied for the credit portion of the transfer were rolled back.

You will also need to add an application configuration file to the `ConsoleAccountTransfer` project. You can use the default name of `App.Config` for this file. The contents of this file are shown in Listing 10-4.

Listing 10-4. *App.Config for ConsoleAccountTransfer Project*

```xml
<?xml version="1.0" encoding="utf-8" ?>
<configuration>
  <connectionStrings>
    <!--connection string for workflow persistence database-->
    <add name="WorkflowPersistence" connectionString=
      "Integrated Security=SSPI;Initial Catalog=WorkflowPersistence;
      Data Source=localhost\SQLEXPRESS;Integrated Security=SSPI" />
    <!--connection string for the testing database-->
    <add name="ProWorkflow" connectionString=
      "Integrated Security=SSPI;Initial Catalog=ProWorkflow;
      Data Source=localhost\SQLEXPRESS;Integrated Security=SSPI" />
  </connectionStrings>
</configuration>
```

The App.Config file contains the two database connection strings that the host and workflow require. These connection strings assume that the databases are hosted by a local copy of SQL Server Express. You will need to modify these connection strings if you are using the full version of SQL Server, or if the database names are different than the ones defined here.

Finally, you need to add code to the Program.cs file to execute the static Run method of the test class. That code looks like this:

```csharp
using System;

namespace ConsoleAccountTransfer
{
    public class Program
    {
        static void Main(string[] args)
        {
            //execute the workflow tests
            AccountTransferTest.Run();

            Console.WriteLine("Press any key to exit");
            Console.ReadLine();
        }
    }
}
```

After building, you should be able to execute the ConsoleAccountTransfer project. When I execute this, I see these results:

```
Executing 1st AccountTransferWorkflow
Balance before test for AccountId 1001: 100.0000
Balance before test for AccountId 2002: 100.0000
Balance after test for AccountId 1001: 75.0000
Balance after test for AccountId 2002: 125.0000
Completed 1st AccountTransferWorkflow

Executing 2nd AccountTransferWorkflow
Balance before test for AccountId 1001: 75.0000
Balance before test for AccountId 2002: 125.0000
EXCEPTION: Insufficient balance to process debit
```

```
Balance after test for AccountId 1001: 75.0000
Balance after test for AccountId 2002: 125.0000
Completed 2nd AccountTransferWorkflow

Press any key to exit
```

As expected, the first transfer of 25.00 succeeded. However, the second one (attempting to transfer 200.00) failed and threw an exception. As you can see from the before and after balances, any updates to the database by the credit activity were rolled back due to the exception.

Note The previous results assume that this is the first time you've executed this test. If you run this test a number of times, the numbers for the first workflow execution will be different since 25.00 is transferred with each execution. If you run the test enough times, you will reach the point where the first workflow execution also fails due to an insufficient balance.

You can execute the `PrepareProWorkflowDatabase.cmd` that you saved earlier to drop and recreate the database. This will put the database back to its original state.

The `TransactionScopeActivity` is a simple way to enlist child activities into a transaction. This guarantees that any work the activities perform that uses a resource manager (such as a relational database) will be applied atomically. If an unhandled exception is thrown by any child activity, the entire batch of work will be rolled back.

Understanding Compensation

Like transactions, *compensation* is a mechanism for guaranteeing the integrity and consistency of work that is performed by a workflow. However, each mechanism accomplishes its goal in a different way and is suitable for solving a different set of problems.

Transactions guarantee consistency by grouping work into a single batch and then committing all of the work at once. Either all of the work succeeds or fails. When work is performed under the control of a transaction, you don't have a problem with partial updates. Consistency is guaranteed.

Transactions are typically used to guarantee consistency when applying updates to a relational database or a similar durable store. They work best when their lifetime is kept as short as possible. Long-running transactions are possible, but they quickly result in locking and concurrency problems in a database application. They are best used for a relatively fast sequence of updates that must be applied together to maintain consistency.

Compensation is a general mechanism for undoing work that previously succeeded. In a workflow, you might have a number of activities that successfully complete their work, perhaps even using a `TransactionScopeActivity` to guarantee consistency. But later in the workflow, a critical error is discovered and an exception is thrown. How do you undo the work that already succeeded earlier in the workflow? The `TransactionScopeActivity` is no help to you since the transaction already ended, serving its purpose to maintain consistency.

In this scenario, compensation can be used to undo the previously completed work. You can logically group activities together and specify a compensation handler for the group. Within the compensation handler, you declare the set of activities to execute if compensation is needed. Compensation processing can be triggered automatically by an unhandled exception in the workflow, or explicitly executed using the `CompensateActivity`.

Compensation is well-suited to long-running workflows. Workflows are capable of spanning hours, days, weeks, or even longer. Holding a traditional transaction open for that length of time would be impractical if not impossible. But the workflow may require the ability to undo work that it has already completed. Compensation is the solution when you must undo work in a long-running workflow.

Transactions work automatically with the underlying resource manager (e.g., relational database) to roll back the pending work. Compensation doesn't automatically roll back the work for you. Instead, it provides a standardized place where you can declare the steps necessary to undo the work.

Since you must declare the steps for compensation (declared as a set of activities), you are not limited to working with resource managers (e.g., relational databases). If an action can be undone, you can implement logic to compensate it. For instance, a workflow might invoke a web service to initiate some action with an external application. How might you compensate that action? If the application provides a way to undo the previous action, it would likely take the form of another web service call. Within a compensation handler, you can invoke the web service to undo the previous action.

In a workflow, activities that can be compensated must implement the ICompensatableActivity interface. WF provides two standard activities that implement this interface and are compensatable:

- CompensatableTransactionScopeActivity (in the System.Workflow.ComponentModel namespace)

- CompensatableSequenceActivity (in the System.Workflow.Activities namespace)

Both of these activities are composites that allow you to declare a set of child activities. The CompensatableTransactionScopeActivity supports transactions and compensation. It works exactly like the TransactionScopeActivity discussed in the previous section. However, it also supports compensation, permitting you to undo the work applied by this activity after it has completed.

The CompensatableSequenceActivity works just like a SequenceActivity, permitting you to declare a set of child activities to execute in the specified order. But it also supports compensation, allowing you to declare the set of activities to execute if compensation is needed.

The CompensationHandlerActivity (found in the System.Workflow.ComponentModel namespace) is a container for the activities that you wish to execute during compensation. This composite activity is added to the CompensatableSequenceActivity and the CompensatableTransactionScopeActivity when you define your compensation logic.

As I mentioned previously, the compensation logic is automatically triggered when an unhandled exception is raised within a workflow. If the exception isn't handled, any compensatable activities (CompensatableTransactionScopeActivity or CompensatableSequenceActivity) that have completed are compensated in the reverse order of their original execution. This means the most recently completed activity is compensated first, then the prior activity, and so on. They are compensated by executing the child activities specified within their CompensationHandlerActivity.

You can also explicitly execute the compensation logic using the CompensateActivity. Use this activity when you need finer control over the compensation process. This activity permits you to specify the activity you wish to compensate by setting the TargetActivityName property. This property must be set to a compensatable activity, or it can be set to compensate the entire workflow. The CompensateActivity can only be added to a CompensationHandlerActivity, a FaultHandlerActivity, or a CancellationHandlerActivity.

■**Note** Use of the CompensateActivity is not demonstrated in this chapter. However, it is presented in Chapter 12.

Using Compensatable Activities

The example that follows demonstrates the use of the `CompensatableTransactionScopeActivity` and the `CompensatableSequenceActivity`. The example uses an order entry workflow to illustrate compensation of activities that previously completed.

■Note This example uses the same database and tables that were prepared for the previous example. If you haven't already done so, you'll need to prepare the database, tables, and test data using the instructions found in the "Preparing the ProWorkflow Database" sidebar.

The workflow first reduces inventory for the item that is being ordered (the `itemInventory` table), and then inserts the item into the order table (`orderDetail`). This work is accomplished by two new custom activities that are added as children of a `CompensatableTransactionScopeActivity`. Following this, the `AccountAdjustmentActivity` in the previous example is used to debit and credit accounts for the amount of the order. A `CompensatableSequenceActivity` containing a `CodeActivity` is also included in the workflow to demonstrate its use. The workflow will trigger compensation when an attempt is made to debit funds from an account that has an insufficient balance.

Implementing the InventoryUpdateActivity

This order entry example uses a custom activity that reduces the inventory for the item being ordered. To implement this activity, add a new Activity to the `SharedWorkflows` project used in the previous example. Name this new activity `InventoryUpdateActivity`. You can change the base class from the default of `SequenceActivity` to `Activity` since you don't need a composite activity for this example.

This activity requires these properties that are all implemented as dependency properties:

- `ItemId`: An `Int32` that identifies the item that is being adjusted
- `Quantity`: An `Int32` that contains the amount of the inventory adjustment
- `IsReduction`: A `Boolean` that is set to `true` if this is an inventory reduction, otherwise `false` to increase inventory

Listing 10-5 shows the complete code for the `InventoryUpdateActivity.cs` file, including the dependency properties and the database update logic.

Listing 10-5. *Complete InventoryUpdateActivity.cs File*

```
using System;
using System.Data;
using System.Data.SqlClient;
using System.Configuration;  //needs assembly reference
using System.ComponentModel;
using System.Workflow.ComponentModel;

namespace SharedWorkflows
{
    public partial class InventoryUpdateActivity : Activity
    {
        /// <summary>
        /// ItemId Dependency Property
        /// </summary>
```

```csharp
public static DependencyProperty ItemIdProperty
    = System.Workflow.ComponentModel.DependencyProperty.Register(
        "ItemId", typeof(Int32), typeof(InventoryUpdateActivity));
[Description("Identifies the item to update")]
[Category("ProWorkflow")]
[Browsable(true)]
[DesignerSerializationVisibility(DesignerSerializationVisibility.Visible)]
public Int32 ItemId
{
    get
    {
        return ((Int32)(base.GetValue(
            InventoryUpdateActivity.ItemIdProperty)));
    }
    set
    {
        base.SetValue(InventoryUpdateActivity.ItemIdProperty, value);
    }
}

/// <summary>
/// Quantity Dependency Property
/// </summary>
public static DependencyProperty QuantityProperty
    = System.Workflow.ComponentModel.DependencyProperty.Register(
        "Quantity", typeof(Int32), typeof(InventoryUpdateActivity));
[Description("The quantity of the item to remove from inventory")]
[Category("ProWorkflow")]
[Browsable(true)]
[DesignerSerializationVisibility(DesignerSerializationVisibility.Visible)]
public Int32 Quantity
{
    get
    {
        return ((Int32)(base.GetValue(
            InventoryUpdateActivity.QuantityProperty)));
    }
    set
    {
        base.SetValue(InventoryUpdateActivity.QuantityProperty, value);
    }
}

/// <summary>
/// IsReduction Dependency Property
/// </summary>
public static DependencyProperty IsReductionProperty
    = System.Workflow.ComponentModel.DependencyProperty.Register(
        "IsReduction", typeof(Boolean), typeof(InventoryUpdateActivity));
[Description("True to reduce inventory, false to increase it")]
[Category("ProWorkflow")]
[Browsable(true)]
[DesignerSerializationVisibility(DesignerSerializationVisibility.Visible)]
```

```
public Boolean IsReduction
{
    get
    {
        return ((Boolean)(base.GetValue(
            InventoryUpdateActivity.IsReductionProperty)));
    }
    set
    {
        base.SetValue(InventoryUpdateActivity.IsReductionProperty, value);
    }
}

public InventoryUpdateActivity()
{
    InitializeComponent();
}
```

The overall design and organization of this activity is very similar to the AccountAdjustmentActivity developed in the previous example. It begins by defining the dependency properties that will be referenced during execution.

```
/// <summary>
/// Control updates to inventory
/// </summary>
/// <param name="executionContext"></param>
/// <returns></returns>
protected override ActivityExecutionStatus Execute(
    ActivityExecutionContext executionContext)
{
    using (SqlConnection connection = new SqlConnection(
        ConfigurationManager.ConnectionStrings
            ["ProWorkflow"].ConnectionString))
    {
        connection.Open();
        if (IsReduction)
        {
            //make sure we have sufficient inventory
            Int32 qtyOnHand = GetCurrentInventory(connection, ItemId);
            if (qtyOnHand < Quantity)
            {
                throw new ArgumentException(
                    "Insufficient inventory for item");
            }
        }

        //update the inventory
        UpdateInventory(connection, ItemId, Quantity, IsReduction);

        connection.Close();
    }
    return base.Execute(executionContext);
}
```

This activity is designed to either reduce or increase the inventory for the selected item, depending on the value of the IsReduction property. By supporting an inventory adjustment in both directions, this activity serves a dual purpose. It will be used in the main line of the workflow to reduce inventory, but will also be used to compensate itself within a compensation handler. Within the compensation handler, the IsReduction property will be set to false to indicate that inventory should be increased instead of reduced.

```
/// <summary>
/// Retrieve the current inventory for an item
/// </summary>
/// <param name="connection"></param>
/// <param name="itemId"></param>
/// <returns></returns>
private Int32 GetCurrentInventory(
    SqlConnection connection, Int32 itemId)
{
    Int32 inventory = 0;
    String sql =
        @"select qtyOnHand from itemInventory where itemId = @ItemId";

    //setup Sql command object
    SqlCommand command = new SqlCommand(sql);
    //setup parameters
    SqlParameter p = new SqlParameter("@ItemId", itemId);
    command.Parameters.Add(p);
    command.Connection = connection;

    Object result = command.ExecuteScalar();
    if (result != null)
    {
        inventory = (Int32)result;
    }

    return inventory;
}

/// <summary>
/// Update the inventory
/// </summary>
/// <param name="connection"></param>
/// <param name="itemId"></param>
/// <param name="quantity"></param>
/// <param name="isReduction"></param>
private void UpdateInventory(SqlConnection connection,
    Int32 itemId, Int32 quantity, Boolean isReduction)
{
    String sql;
    if (IsReduction)
    {
        sql =
        @"update itemInventory
          set qtyOnHand = qtyOnHand - @Quantity
          where itemId = @ItemId";
        Console.WriteLine(
            "InventoryUpdateActivity: Reducing inventory");
    }
```

```
            else
            {
                sql =
                @"update itemInventory
                  set qtyOnHand = qtyOnHand + @Quantity
                  where itemId = @ItemId";
                Console.WriteLine(
                    "InventoryUpdateActivity: Compensating inventory");
            }
            //setup Sql command object
            SqlCommand command = new SqlCommand(sql);
            //setup parameters
            SqlParameter p = new SqlParameter("@ItemId", itemId);
            command.Parameters.Add(p);
            p = new SqlParameter("@Quantity", quantity);
            command.Parameters.Add(p);
            command.Connection = connection;

            command.ExecuteNonQuery();
        }
    }
}
```

Implementing the OrderDetailActivity

Another custom activity is needed to insert a row into the orderDetail table to process the order. To implement this activity, add a new Activity to the SharedWorkflow project and name it OrderDetailActivity. Change the base class from SequenceActivity to Activity.

This activity uses a number of dependency properties:

- OrderId: An Int32 that uniquely identifies the order.

- AccountId: An Int32 that identifies the account placing the order.

- ItemId: An Int32 that identifies the item being ordered.

- Quantity: An Int32 containing the quantity of the item being ordered.

- IsAddOrder: A Boolean that is set to true if the item is being added to the order. This property is set to false if the previously ordered item should be removed from the order.

Listing 10-6 shows the complete code for the OrderDetailActivity.cs file.

Listing 10-6. *Complete OrderDetailActivity.cs File*

```
using System;
using System.Data;
using System.Data.SqlClient;
using System.Configuration;  //needs assembly reference
using System.ComponentModel;
using System.Workflow.ComponentModel;

namespace SharedWorkflows
{
```

```csharp
public partial class OrderDetailActivity : Activity
{
    /// <summary>
    /// OrderId Dependency Property
    /// </summary>
    public static DependencyProperty OrderIdProperty
        = System.Workflow.ComponentModel.DependencyProperty.Register(
            "OrderId", typeof(Int32), typeof(OrderDetailActivity));
    [Description("Identifies the order")]
    [Category("ProWorkflow")]
    [Browsable(true)]
    [DesignerSerializationVisibility(DesignerSerializationVisibility.Visible)]
    public Int32 OrderId
    {
        get
        {
            return ((Int32)(base.GetValue(
                OrderDetailActivity.OrderIdProperty)));
        }
        set
        {
            base.SetValue(OrderDetailActivity.OrderIdProperty, value);
        }
    }

    /// <summary>
    /// AccountId Dependency Property
    /// </summary>
    public static DependencyProperty AccountIdProperty
        = System.Workflow.ComponentModel.DependencyProperty.Register(
            "AccountId", typeof(Int32), typeof(OrderDetailActivity));
    [Description("Identifies the account")]
    [Category("ProWorkflow")]
    [Browsable(true)]
    [DesignerSerializationVisibility(DesignerSerializationVisibility.Visible)]
    public Int32 AccountId
    {
        get
        {
            return ((Int32)(base.GetValue(
                OrderDetailActivity.AccountIdProperty)));
        }
        set
        {
            base.SetValue(OrderDetailActivity.AccountIdProperty, value);
        }
    }

    /// <summary>
    /// ItemId Dependency Property
    /// </summary>
```

```csharp
public static DependencyProperty ItemIdProperty
    = System.Workflow.ComponentModel.DependencyProperty.Register(
        "ItemId", typeof(Int32), typeof(OrderDetailActivity));
[Description("Identifies the item being ordered")]
[Category("ProWorkflow")]
[Browsable(true)]
[DesignerSerializationVisibility(DesignerSerializationVisibility.Visible)]
public Int32 ItemId
{
    get
    {
        return ((Int32)(base.GetValue(
            OrderDetailActivity.ItemIdProperty)));
    }
    set
    {
        base.SetValue(OrderDetailActivity.ItemIdProperty, value);
    }
}

/// <summary>
/// Quantity Dependency Property
/// </summary>
public static DependencyProperty QuantityProperty
    = System.Workflow.ComponentModel.DependencyProperty.Register(
        "Quantity", typeof(Int32), typeof(OrderDetailActivity));
[Description("The quantity of the item to order")]
[Category("ProWorkflow")]
[Browsable(true)]
[DesignerSerializationVisibility(DesignerSerializationVisibility.Visible)]
public Int32 Quantity
{
    get
    {
        return ((Int32)(base.GetValue(
            OrderDetailActivity.QuantityProperty)));
    }
    set
    {
        base.SetValue(OrderDetailActivity.QuantityProperty, value);
    }
}

/// <summary>
/// IsAddOrder Dependency Property
/// </summary>
public static DependencyProperty IsAddOrderProperty
    = System.Workflow.ComponentModel.DependencyProperty.Register(
        "IsAddOrder", typeof(Boolean), typeof(OrderDetailActivity));
[Description("True to add the item to the order, false to remove it")]
[Category("ProWorkflow")]
[Browsable(true)]
[DesignerSerializationVisibility(DesignerSerializationVisibility.Visible)]
```

```
public Boolean IsAddOrder
{
    get
    {
        return ((Boolean)(base.GetValue(
            OrderDetailActivity.IsAddOrderProperty)));
    }
    set
    {
        base.SetValue(OrderDetailActivity.IsAddOrderProperty, value);
    }
}

public OrderDetailActivity()
{
    InitializeComponent();
}
```

This activity requires a larger number of dependency properties. As usual, they are defined first in the listing.

```
protected override ActivityExecutionStatus Execute(
    ActivityExecutionContext executionContext)
{
    using (SqlConnection connection = new SqlConnection(
        ConfigurationManager.ConnectionStrings
            ["ProWorkflow"].ConnectionString))
    {
        connection.Open();
        if (IsAddOrder)
        {
            InsertOrderDetail(connection, OrderId,
                AccountId, ItemId, Quantity);
            Console.WriteLine(
                "OrderDetailActivity: Inserting orderDetail row");
        }
        else
        {
            DeleteOrderDetail(connection, OrderId,
                AccountId, ItemId);
            Console.WriteLine(
                "OrderDetailActivity: Compensating orderDetail row");
        }
        connection.Close();
    }
    return base.Execute(executionContext);
}
```

Just like the InventoryUpdateActivity, this activity is designed to operate in two modes. If the IsAddOrder property is set to true, a row is inserted into the database to represent the order for the selected item. This is the desired behavior for the main line of the workflow. If IsAddOrder is set to false, the previously inserted row is deleted. This behavior will be used when this activity is used within a compensation handler.

```csharp
/// <summary>
/// Insert a new order detail row
/// </summary>
/// <param name="connection"></param>
/// <param name="orderId"></param>
/// <param name="accountId"></param>
/// <param name="itemId"></param>
/// <param name="quantity"></param>
private void InsertOrderDetail(SqlConnection connection,
    Int32 orderId, Int32 accountId, Int32 itemId, Int32 quantity)
{
    String sql =
        @"insert into orderDetail
          (orderId, accountId, itemId, quantity)
          values(@OrderId, @AccountId, @ItemId, @Quantity)";

    //setup Sql command object
    SqlCommand command = new SqlCommand(sql);
    //setup parameters
    SqlParameter p = new SqlParameter("@OrderId", orderId);
    command.Parameters.Add(p);
    p = new SqlParameter("@AccountId", accountId);
    command.Parameters.Add(p);
    p = new SqlParameter("@ItemId", itemId);
    command.Parameters.Add(p);
    p = new SqlParameter("@Quantity", quantity);
    command.Parameters.Add(p);
    command.Connection = connection;

    command.ExecuteNonQuery();
}


/// <summary>
/// Delete an order detail row
/// </summary>
/// <param name="connection"></param>
/// <param name="orderId"></param>
/// <param name="accountId"></param>
/// <param name="itemId"></param>
private void DeleteOrderDetail(SqlConnection connection,
    Int32 orderId, Int32 accountId, Int32 itemId)
{
    String sql =
        @"delete from orderDetail
          where orderId = @OrderId
           and  accountId = @AccountId
           and  itemId = @ItemId ";
    //setup Sql command object
    SqlCommand command = new SqlCommand(sql);
    //setup parameters
    SqlParameter p = new SqlParameter("@OrderId", orderId);
    command.Parameters.Add(p);
    p = new SqlParameter("@AccountId", accountId);
    command.Parameters.Add(p);
```

```
                    p = new SqlParameter("@ItemId", itemId);
                    command.Parameters.Add(p);
                    command.Connection = connection;

                    command.ExecuteNonQuery();
                }
            }
        }
```

It isn't necessary to develop activities that are capable of compensating themselves like this. However, you do need to implement the compensation logic somewhere. With a small amount of additional effort, the original activities can be implemented so that they satisfy their original purpose as well as compensation.

Implementing the OrderEntryWorkflow

To implement a workflow that uses these activities, add a new sequential workflow to the SharedWorkflows project. Name it OrderEntryWorkflow.

The OrderEntryWorkflow uses a number of dependency properties:

- OrderId: An Int32 that uniquely identifies the order

- ItemId: An Int32 that identifies the item being ordered

- Quantity: An Int32 containing the quantity of the item being ordered

- Amount: A Decimal containing the amount of funds to transfer from one account to another to pay for the order

- OrderAccountId: An Int32 that identifies the account placing the order

- ToAccountId: An Int32 that identifies the account that should receive the funds resulting from the order

Listing 10-7 shows the OrderEntryWorkflow.cs file after the dependency properties have been defined.

Listing 10-7. *OrderEntryWorkflow.cs File After Adding Dependency Properties*

```
using System;
using System.ComponentModel;
using System.Workflow.ComponentModel;
using System.Workflow.Activities;

namespace SharedWorkflows
{
    public sealed partial class OrderEntryWorkflow
        : SequentialWorkflowActivity
    {
        /// <summary>
        /// OrderId Dependency Property
        /// </summary>
        public static DependencyProperty OrderIdProperty
            = System.Workflow.ComponentModel.DependencyProperty.Register(
                "OrderId", typeof(Int32), typeof(OrderEntryWorkflow));
        [Description("Identifies the order")]
        [Category("ProWorkflow")]
```

```csharp
[Browsable(true)]
[DesignerSerializationVisibility(DesignerSerializationVisibility.Visible)]
public Int32 OrderId
{
    get
    {
        return ((Int32)(base.GetValue(
            OrderEntryWorkflow.OrderIdProperty)));
    }
    set
    {
        base.SetValue(OrderEntryWorkflow.OrderIdProperty, value);
    }
}
/// <summary>
/// ItemId Dependency Property
/// </summary>
public static DependencyProperty ItemIdProperty
    = System.Workflow.ComponentModel.DependencyProperty.Register(
        "ItemId", typeof(Int32), typeof(OrderEntryWorkflow));
[Description("Identifies the item being ordered")]
[Category("ProWorkflow")]
[Browsable(true)]
[DesignerSerializationVisibility(DesignerSerializationVisibility.Visible)]
public Int32 ItemId
{
    get
    {
        return ((Int32)(base.GetValue(
            OrderEntryWorkflow.ItemIdProperty)));
    }
    set
    {
        base.SetValue(OrderEntryWorkflow.ItemIdProperty, value);
    }
}


/// <summary>
/// Quantity Dependency Property
/// </summary>
public static DependencyProperty QuantityProperty
    = System.Workflow.ComponentModel.DependencyProperty.Register(
        "Quantity", typeof(Int32), typeof(OrderEntryWorkflow));
[Description("The quantity of the item to order")]
[Category("ProWorkflow")]
[Browsable(true)]
[DesignerSerializationVisibility(DesignerSerializationVisibility.Visible)]
public Int32 Quantity
{
    get
    {
        return ((Int32)(base.GetValue(
            OrderEntryWorkflow.QuantityProperty)));
    }
```

```csharp
        set
        {
            base.SetValue(OrderEntryWorkflow.QuantityProperty, value);
        }
    }


    /// <summary>
    /// Amount Dependency Property
    /// </summary>
    public static DependencyProperty AmountProperty
        = System.Workflow.ComponentModel.DependencyProperty.Register(
            "Amount", typeof(Decimal), typeof(OrderEntryWorkflow));
    [Description("The amount of the balance adjustment")]
    [Category("ProWorkflow")]
    [Browsable(true)]
    [DesignerSerializationVisibility(DesignerSerializationVisibility.Visible)]
    public Decimal Amount
    {
        get
        {
            return ((Decimal)(base.GetValue(
                OrderEntryWorkflow.AmountProperty)));
        }
        set
        {
            base.SetValue(OrderEntryWorkflow.AmountProperty, value);
        }
    }

    /// <summary>
    /// OrderAccountId Dependency Property
    /// </summary>
    public static DependencyProperty OrderAccountIdProperty
        = System.Workflow.ComponentModel.DependencyProperty.Register(
            "OrderAccountId", typeof(Int32), typeof(OrderEntryWorkflow));
    [Description("Identifies the account placing the order")]
    [Category("ProWorkflow")]
    [Browsable(true)]
    [DesignerSerializationVisibility(DesignerSerializationVisibility.Visible)]
    public Int32 OrderAccountId
    {
        get
        {
            return ((Int32)(base.GetValue(
                OrderEntryWorkflow.OrderAccountIdProperty)));
        }
        sel
        {
            base.SetValue(OrderEntryWorkflow.OrderAccountIdProperty, valuc);
        }
    }
```

```
/// <summary>
/// ToAccountId Dependency Property
/// </summary>
public static DependencyProperty ToAccountIdProperty
    = System.Workflow.ComponentModel.DependencyProperty.Register(
        "ToAccountId", typeof(Int32), typeof(OrderEntryWorkflow));
[Description("Identifies the account to receive funds from the order")]
[Category("ProWorkflow")]
[Browsable(true)]
[DesignerSerializationVisibility(DesignerSerializationVisibility.Visible)]
public Int32 ToAccountId
{
    get
    {
        return ((Int32)(base.GetValue(
            OrderEntryWorkflow.ToAccountIdProperty)));
    }
    set
    {
        base.SetValue(OrderEntryWorkflow.ToAccountIdProperty, value);
    }
}

public OrderEntryWorkflow()
{
    InitializeComponent();
}

    }
}
```

Using the CompensatableTransactionScopeActivity

Before beginning the visual design of the workflow, you will need to build the solution. This is necessary in order to populate the Toolbox with the custom activities.

To begin the visual design of the OrderEntryWorkflow, switch to the workflow designer view and drag a CompensatableTransactionScopeActivity onto the empty workflow. Name this activity orderEntryScope. Now add an instance of InventoryAdjustmentActivity (named inventoryUpdateActivity1) and OrderDetailActivity (orderDetailActivity1) as children of orderEntryScope. Next, you need to set up the property bindings for both of these child activities. Table 10-3 and 10-4 list the property bindings that you need to set.

Table 10-3. *Property Bindings for inventoryUpdateActivity1*

Property	Binding
IsReduction	true
ItemId	Activity=OrderEntryWorkflow, Path=ItemId
Quantity	Activity=OrderEntryWorkflow, Path=Quantity

Table 10-4. *Property Bindings for orderDetailActivity1*

Property	Binding
AccountId	Activity=OrderEntryWorkflow, Path=OrderAccountId
IsAddOrder	true
ItemId	Activity=OrderEntryWorkflow, Path=ItemId
OrderId	Activity=OrderEntryWorkflow, Path=OrderId
Quantity	Activity=OrderEntryWorkflow, Path=Quantity

Figure 10-2 shows the workflow after adding these activities.

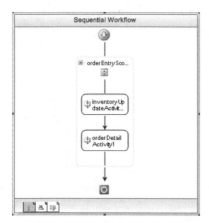

Figure 10-2. *OrderEntryWorkflow with orderEntryScope added*

Remember that the CompensatableTransactionScopeActivity used here as a container also supports transactions just like the TransactionScopeActivity (demonstrated in the previous example). This means that the inventory adjustment and the adding of an order detail row will be done under the control of a transaction. Both operations will succeed, or any partial updates will be rolled back.

Since the orderEntryScope activity is compensatable (an instance of CompensatableTransactionScopeActivity), it supports the declaration of compensation logic. Before moving on to another activity, this is a good time to define that compensation logic. To do this, right-click the orderEntryScope activity and select View Compensation Handler from the context menu. You could also select the activity and then select View Compensation Handler from the top-level Workflow menu. This view presents an empty CompensationHandlerActivity where you can add your own set of compensation handling activities.

You will use the same set of activities as compensation handlers as you used in the main line of the workflow. Add an InventoryAdjustmentActivity and an OrderDetailActivity as children of the CompensationHandlerActivity. Name the activities compensateInventoryActivity and compensateOrderEntry. You can now set the parameter bindings for these activities using the same values shown in Table 10-3 and 10-4. The only exceptions are the following:

- IsReduction should be set to false to indicate that you are increasing inventory instead of reducing it.

- IsAddOrder should be set to false to indicate that you are removing an item from the order instead of adding one.

Figure 10-3 shows the compensation handler for the orderEntryScope activity.

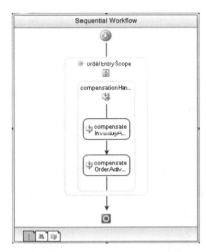

Figure 10-3. *Compensation handler for orderEntryScope*

You can now return to the main designer view by right-clicking the orderEntryScope activity and selecting View CompensatableTransactionScope.

Using the CompensatableSequenceActivity

The next order of business is to drag and drop a CompensatableSequenceActivity directly below the orderEntryScope activity. This is simply a SequenceActivity that also happens to support compensation. It is included here to illustrate how multiple compensatable activities are executed during compensation.

Add a CodeActivity as a child of the CompensatableSequenceActivity and double-click it to add a code handler for the ExecuteCode event. Switch to the compensation handler view by right-clicking the CompensatableSequenceActivity and selecting View Compensation Handler. Once there, add another CodeActivity that will handle the compensation logic. After renaming this activity to compensateCodeActivity, double-click it to add a code handler. Once the compensation CodeActivity has been added, you can return to the main view by selecting View CompensatableSequence.

The code handlers for the two CodeActivity instances should be added to the OrderEntryWorkflow.cs file. Add the following code to these two handlers:

```
private void codeActivity1_ExecuteCode(object sender, EventArgs e)
{
    Console.WriteLine("CodeActivity: Executing code");
}

private void compensateCodeActivity_ExecuteCode(object sender, EventArgs e)
{
    Console.WriteLine("CodeActivity: Executing compensation code");
}
```

Adding the TransactionScopeActivity

The final set of activities in this workflow lives in a TransactionScopeActivity. Add a TransactionScopeActivity instance directly under the CompensatableSequenceActivity. Add two instances of the AccountAdjustmentActivity to the TransactionScopeActivity. Name the first one creditActivity and the second debitActivity.

■**Note** The AccountAdjustmentActivity was developed for the first example in this chapter and should be in the SharedWorkflows project.

These two activities will serve the same purpose they did in the first example of this chapter. The first activity will credit an account the amount of the order, and the second activity will debit another account. It is this debit of the second account that will act as the trigger for compensation of the workflow. When a debit is attempted for an account with an insufficient balance, an exception will be thrown. Since it is an unhandled exception, any compensatable activities that have completed will be compensated.

Tables 10-5 and 10-6 show the property bindings for these debit and credit activities.

Table 10-5. *Property Bindings for creditActivity*

Property	Binding
AccountId	Activity=OrderEntryWorkflow, Path=ToAccountId
Amount	Activity=OrderEntryWorkflow, Path=Amount
IsCredit	true

Table 10-6. *Property Bindings for debitActivity*

Property	Binding
AccountId	Activity=OrderEntryWorkflow, Path=OrderAccountId
Amount	Activity=OrderEntryWorkflow, Path=Amount
IsCredit	false

The finished workflow should look like Figure 10-4.

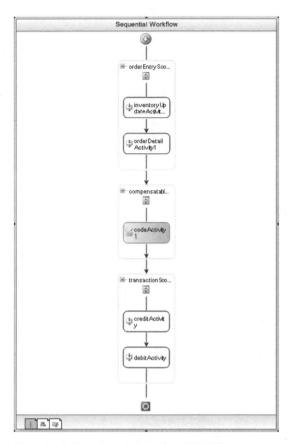

Figure 10-4. *Completed OrderEntryWorkflow*

Testing the Workflow

To test this workflow, add a new Sequential Workflow Console Application to the solution and name it ConsoleOrderEntry. You can delete Workflow1 that was added to this project by the template since it is not needed. Add the following additional references to this project:

- SharedWorkflows
- Bukovics.Workflow.Hosting
- System.Configuration

   Like the previous example, a reference to System.Configuration is needed in order to retrieve values from the application configuration file.

   Add a new C# class to the ConsoleOrderEntry project and name it OrderEntryTest. This class will contain the code to host the workflow runtime and start the workflow. The complete code for this class is shown in Listing 10-8.

Listing 10-8. *Complete OrderEntryTest.cs File*

```
using System;
using System.Configuration;  //need assembly reference
using System.Collections.Generic;
using System.Data.SqlClient;
using System.Workflow.Runtime;
using System.Workflow.Activities;
using System.Workflow.Runtime.Hosting;

using Bukovics.Workflow.Hosting;
using SharedWorkflows;

namespace ConsoleOrderEntry
{
    /// <summary>
    /// Test the OrderEntryWorkflow
    /// </summary>
    public class OrderEntryTest
    {
        public static void Run()
        {
            using (WorkflowRuntimeManager manager
                = new WorkflowRuntimeManager(new WorkflowRuntime()))
            {
                //configure services for the workflow runtime
                AddServices(manager.WorkflowRuntime);
                manager.WorkflowRuntime.StartRuntime();

                Console.WriteLine("Executing OrderEntryWorkflow");
                //create a dictionary with input arguments
                Dictionary<String, Object> wfArguments
                    = new Dictionary<string, object>();
                wfArguments.Add("OrderId", 1234);
                wfArguments.Add("OrderAccountId", 1001);
                wfArguments.Add("ToAccountId", 9000);
                wfArguments.Add("ItemId", 52);
                wfArguments.Add("Quantity", 2);
                wfArguments.Add("Amount", (Decimal)225.00);
                //start the workflow
                WorkflowInstanceWrapper instance = manager.StartWorkflow(
                    typeof(SharedWorkflows.OrderEntryWorkflow), wfArguments);
                manager.WaitAll(20000);
                if (instance.Exception != null)
                {
                    Console.WriteLine("EXCEPTION: {0}",
                        instance.Exception.Message);
                }
                Console.WriteLine("Completed OrderEntryWorkflow\n\r");
            }
        }

        /// <summary>
        /// Add any services needed by the runtime engine
```

```
/// </summary>
/// <param name="instance"></param>
private static void AddServices(WorkflowRuntime instance)
{
    //use the standard SQL Server persistence service
    SqlWorkflowPersistenceService persistence =
        new SqlWorkflowPersistenceService(
            ConfigurationManager.ConnectionStrings
                ["WorkflowPersistence"].ConnectionString,
            true, new TimeSpan(0, 2, 0), new TimeSpan(0, 0, 5));
    instance.AddService(persistence);
}
}
}
```

The workflow runtime hosting logic is similar to other code that you've already seen. The code in bold shows that the transfer amount is 225.00. This exceeds the balance for the debit account (100.00) and will cause the debitActivity of the workflow to throw an exception. This should cause the compensation logic to be executed.

The ConsoleOrderEntry project also requires an application configuration file that defines the database connection strings. Add one to the project now and use the default name of App.Config. The contents look exactly like the one used in the previous example:

```
<?xml version="1.0" encoding="utf-8" ?>
<configuration>
  <connectionStrings>
    <!--connection string for workflow persistence database-->
    <add name="WorkflowPersistence" connectionString=
      "Integrated Security=SSPI;Initial Catalog=WorkflowPersistence;
      Data Source=localhost\SQLEXPRESS;Integrated Security=SSPI" />
    <!--connection string for the testing database-->
    <add name="ProWorkflow" connectionString=
      "Integrated Security=SSPI;Initial Catalog=ProWorkflow;
      Data Source=localhost\SQLEXPRESS;Integrated Security=SSPI" />
  </connectionStrings>
</configuration>
```

The Program.cs file for the ConsoleOrderEntry project requires this code to execute the workflow test:

```
using System;

namespace ConsoleOrderEntry
{
    public class Program
    {
        static void Main(string[] args)
        {
            //execute the workflow tests
            OrderEntryTest.Run();

            Console.WriteLine("Press any key to exit");
            Console.ReadLine();
        }
    }
}
```

■Tip Before executing this test, you should execute the `PrepareProWorkflowDatabase.cmd` that you saved earlier to drop and recreate the database. This will put the database back to its original state.

You can now build and execute the `ConsoleOrderEntry` project. I see these results when I run this test:

```
Executing OrderEntryWorkflow
InventoryUpdateActivity: Reducing inventory
OrderDetailActivity: Inserting orderDetail row
CodeActivity: Executing code
CodeActivity: Executing compensation code
InventoryUpdateActivity: Compensating inventory
OrderDetailActivity: Compensating orderDetail row
EXCEPTION: Insufficient balance to process debit
Completed OrderEntryWorkflow

Press any key to exit
```

Based on these results, you can see that the inventory was first reduced and an `orderDetail` row was inserted. Those activities successfully completed and the transaction they were using was committed. Following that, the `CodeActivity` that is a child of the `CompensatableSequenceActivity` was executed.

At that point, the `creditActivity` and the `debitActivity` were executed. Since the `debitActivity` threw an exception, compensation handlers for any completed activities were executed. Notice that compensation takes place in the reverse order from the original activities. First the compensation for the `CompensatableSequenceActivity` was executed (the `CodeActivity`), followed by the `CompensatableTransactionScopeActivity` (the `InventoryUpdateActivity` and `OrderDetailActivity`). Finally, the hosting code displayed information about the exception that was thrown.

Compensation allows you to handle scenarios that require you to undo previously successful work. This is especially important with long-running workflows where it would be impractical to maintain an open transaction.

Participating in a Batch of Work

You've seen how you can perform work under the control of a transaction with the `TransactionScopeActivity`. Traditionally, that work must involve a resource manager such as a relational database. WF also provides a way for you to enlist work in a transaction without the requirement of a resource manager.

By implementing the `IPendingWork interface`, a local service (or the host application) can perform work that is controlled by a transaction. The work that you perform is completely open-ended and defined by you. This means that you are not limited to work performed on a relational database or other resource manager.

The `IPendingWork interface` defines three members that you must implement. These members are summarized in Table 10-7.

A workflow adds work to a batch using the static `WorkflowEnvironment.BatchWork` property. This property supports an `Add` method that you use to add an object representing some work. The work object should be committed when the transaction completes. What that work is and how it is represented is completely up to you to define. It could be as simple as a `String` or a complex custom object. The only requirement is that the local service understands how to process and commit the work.

Table 10-7. *IPendingWork Members*

Member	Description
MustCommit	Returns a Boolean to indicate whether the current batch of work should be committed immediately or if it can wait until the next commit point
Commit	Called to commit the batch of work
Complete	Called at the end of the transaction to notify you of the success or failure of the transaction

The Add method requires you to also identify the object that will commit the work. In the example that follows, this is the local service that implements IPendingWork. By passing in the object with the Add method, you are able to enlist several different local services in the same transaction. Each service must implement IPendingWork. When the IPendingWork methods are called by the workflow runtime, each service is passed a collection of work items that were added to the batch for that service.

Using the IPendingWork Interface

In this example application, you will develop a local service class that implements the IPendingWork interface. The example workflow will add work items to the collection of pending work using a local service method. The workflow will use a TransactionScopeActivity to enlist the calls to the service method in a transaction. When the transaction completes, the methods of the IPendingWork interface are called on the local service object to commit the pending batch of work.

Implementing the Local Service

To begin this example, you need to define the local service interface. This defines the single method that is exposed to the workflow and is used to add a pending work item. Add a new interface to the SharedWorkflows project and name it IBatchedServices. Listing 10-9 is the complete contents of the IBatchedServices.cs file.

Listing 10-9. *Complete IBatchedServices.cs File*

```
using System;
using System.Workflow.Activities;

namespace SharedWorkflows
{
    /// <summary>
    /// Defines a service that uses IPendingWork
    /// </summary>
    [ExternalDataExchange]
    public interface IBatchedServices
    {
        void DoSomeWork(String message);
    }
}
```

The DoSomeWork method will be invoked by the workflow. In this demonstration, the actual work is a simple String message. In a live application, this object could be any type of object of your own design.

Next, add a new C# class to the SharedWorkflows project and name it BatchedService. This is the local service class that implements IBatchedServices. Listing 10-10 shows the complete contents of the BatchedService.cs. Selected sections of the code are discussed following the listing.

Listing 10-10. *Complete BatchedService.cs File*

```csharp
using System;
using System.Collections;
using System.Workflow.Runtime;
using System.Transactions;

namespace SharedWorkflows
{
    /// <summary>
    /// A local service that demonstrates IPendingWork
    /// </summary>
    public class BatchedService : IBatchedServices, IPendingWork
    {
        #region IBatchedServices Members

        /// <summary>
        /// Method invoked by the workflow to perform work
        /// </summary>
        /// <param name="message"></param>
        public void DoSomeWork(string message)
        {
            //add the requested work to current batch of work
            //for the current workfow
            WorkflowEnvironment.WorkBatch.Add(this, message);
        }

        #endregion

        #region IPendingWork Members

        /// <summary>
        /// Commit the collection of work items
        /// </summary>
        /// <param name="transaction"></param>
        /// <param name="items"></param>
        public void Commit(Transaction transaction, ICollection items)
        {
            foreach (Object item in items)
            {
                Console.WriteLine("Commiting: {0}", item.ToString());
            }
        }

        /// <summary>
        /// Called at the end of the Transaction to notify us
        /// of success or failure of the transaction.
        /// </summary>
        /// <param name="succeeded"></param>
        /// <param name="items"></param>
```

```csharp
        public void Complete(bool succeeded, ICollection items)
        {
            if (succeeded)
            {
                Console.WriteLine("Complete: Transaction succeeded");
            }
            else
            {
                Console.WriteLine(
                    "Complete: Transaction aborted. Need to rollback");
                foreach (Object item in items)
                {
                    Console.WriteLine("Rolling Back: {0}", item.ToString());
                }
            }
        }


        /// <summary>
        /// Tells the workflow runtime that the collection of work
        /// items should be committed now at the current commit point.
        /// </summary>
        /// <param name="items"></param>
        /// <returns></returns>
        public bool MustCommit(ICollection items)
        {
            Console.WriteLine("Returning true for MustCommit");
            return true;
        }

        #endregion
    }
}
```

Notice that this service class implements the IBatchedServices interface as well as IPendingWork. Both interfaces are necessary since the service is exposed to workflows and also acts as an object that is capable of committing pending work. The implementation of the DoSomeWork method adds a work item to the collection of pending work items with this code:

```csharp
WorkflowEnvironment.WorkBatch.Add(this, message);
```

In this case, the actual work is simply the String message that is passed from the workflow when it calls this method. The local service passes a reference to itself (this) as the first argument of the Add method. This identifies itself as the object that will handle committing of this work item.

The Commit method is called by the workflow runtime when the transaction is ready to commit all pending work. In the workflow, this is triggered when the TransactionScopeActivity has completed. The Commit method is passed the current transaction, along with a collection of work items to commit. In this example, the code commits the work items by simply writing them to the Console.

The Complete method is called after all services and resource managers have committed their work. Passed with this method is a Boolean value indicating the success or failure of the transaction. It is possible that another service or resource manager that is participating in the same transaction has an error during the commit processing. In this case, the succeeded argument would be false and the code would use this final opportunity to back out any pending work.

The MustCommit method is called prior to the Commit or Complete methods. This is the opportunity for the local service to indicate whether the work items should be committed immediately or if they can be deferred until a later commit point. The example code returns true which forces the workflow runtime to commit the work items by calling the Commit method.

Implementing the BatchedWorkWorkflow

A simple sequential workflow will be used to demonstrate the use of the custom service. Add a new sequential workflow to the SharedWorkflows project and name it BatchedWorkWorkflow. The workflow will call the DoSomeWork method of the local service several times. Each time, it will pass a different String message to the service method. These calls will be made using instances of the CallExternalMethodActivity. All of these calls will be wrapped in a single TransactionScopeActivity. The workflow does not require any input or output properties or any code that you need to add.

Using the visual workflow designer, drag and drop a TransactionScopeActivity onto the empty workflow. Now add a CallExternalMethodActivity as a child of the TransactionScopeActivity. Set the InterfaceType property to SharedWorkflows.IBatchedServices and select DoSomeWork as the MethodName. Set the message parameter to **work item one**.

You need to add two additional instances of the CallExternalMethodActivity to the TransactionScopeActivity. All of these instances will use the same basic set of properties, so the easiest way to add the new instances is to copy the first one that you just added. To do this, right-click the CallExternalMethodActivity you just added and select Copy. Then right-click an empty area of the TransactionScopeActivity and select Paste. Paste two additional instances of this activity for a total of three CallExternalMethodActivity instances.

Now change the message parameter for the additional instances so that they all send a unique message. The suggested messages for the additional instances are the following:

- work item two
- work item three

The completed workflow should look like Figure 10-5.

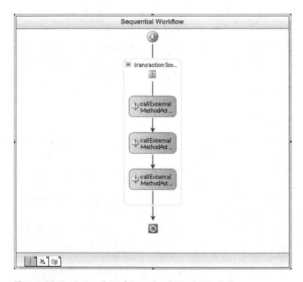

Figure 10-5. *Completed BatchedWorkWorkflow*

Testing the Workflow

Next, create a Console application that will execute this workflow. Add a new Sequential Workflow Console Application to the solution and name it ConsoleBatchedWork. You can delete Workflow1 that was added to this project by the template since it is not needed. Add the following additional references to this project:

- SharedWorkflows
- Bukovics.Workflow.Hosting
- System.Configuration

A reference to System.Configuration is needed in order to retrieve the persistence connection string from the application configuration file.

■**Note** This application doesn't directly reference a database, but it does use the TransactionScopeActivity. Any time you execute a workflow that includes this activity, you must also use a persistence service.

Add a new C# class to the ConsoleBatchedWork project and name it BatchedWorkTest. This class will contain the code to host the workflow runtime and start the workflow. The complete code for this class is shown in Listing 10-11.

Listing 10-11. *Complete BatchedWorkTest.cs File*

```
using System;
using System.Configuration;  //need assembly reference
using System.Workflow.Runtime;
using System.Workflow.Activities;
using System.Workflow.Runtime.Hosting;

using Bukovics.Workflow.Hosting;
using SharedWorkflows;

namespace ConsoleBatchedWork
{
    /// <summary>
    /// Test the BatchedWorkWorkflow
    /// </summary>
    public class BatchedWorkTest
    {
        public static void Run()
        {
            using (WorkflowRuntimeManager manager
                = new WorkflowRuntimeManager(new WorkflowRuntime()))
            {
                //configure services for the workflow runtime
                AddServices(manager.WorkflowRuntime);
                manager.WorkflowRuntime.StartRuntime();
```

```
                Console.WriteLine("Executing BatchedWorkWorkflow");
                //start the workflow
                manager.StartWorkflow(
                    typeof(SharedWorkflows.BatchedWorkWorkflow), null);
                manager.WaitAll(5000);
                Console.WriteLine("Completed BatchedWorkWorkflow\n\r");
            }
        }

        /// <summary>
        /// Add any services needed by the runtime engine
        /// </summary>
        /// <param name="instance"></param>
        private static void AddServices(WorkflowRuntime instance)
        {
            //use the standard SQL Server persistence service
            SqlWorkflowPersistenceService persistence =
                new SqlWorkflowPersistenceService(
                    ConfigurationManager.ConnectionStrings
                        ["WorkflowPersistence"].ConnectionString,
                    true, new TimeSpan(0, 2, 0), new TimeSpan(0, 0, 5));
            instance.AddService(persistence);

            //add the external data exchange service to the runtime
            ExternalDataExchangeService exchangeService
                = new ExternalDataExchangeService();
            instance.AddService(exchangeService);

            //add our local service
            exchangeService.AddService(new BatchedService());
        }
    }
}
```

Notice that in addition to loading the persistence service, the AddServices method also creates an instance of the BatchedService that you implemented in the previous steps.

You also need to add an application configuration file (App.Config) to the ConsoleBatchedWork project. The contents of this file are shown here:

```xml
<?xml version="1.0" encoding="utf-8" ?>
<configuration>
  <connectionStrings>
    <!--connection string for workflow persistence database-->
    <add name="WorkflowPersistence" connectionString=
      "Integrated Security=SSPI;Initial Catalog=WorkflowPersistence;
      Data Source=localhost\SQLEXPRESS;Integrated Security=SSPI" />
  </connectionStrings>
</configuration>
```

Finally, you need to add code to the Program.cs file of the project to actually execute the test. The code for Program.cs is shown here:

```
using System;

namespace ConsoleBatchedWork
{
    public class Program
    {
        static void Main(string[] args)
        {
            //execute the workflow tests
            BatchedWorkTest.Run();

            Console.WriteLine("Press any key to exit");
            Console.ReadLine();
        }
    }
}
```

After building the ConsoleBatchWork project, you should be able to execute it. Here are the results that I see when I execute this:

```
Executing BatchedWorkWorkflow
Returning true for MustCommit
Commiting: work item one
Commiting: work item two
Commiting: work item three
Complete: Transaction succeeded
Completed BatchedWorkWorkflow

Press any key to exit
```

The results show that the MustCommit method was first called, followed by the Commit and Complete methods. The code in the local service committed the pending work by writing it to the Console.

You can use this technique to place work under the control of a transaction. By adding the work to the WorkflowEnvironment.WorkBatch property, you defer the final processing of the work until the transaction is ready to commit. While not shown in this example, the committing of this pending work can be coordinated with other work that uses a resource manager such as a relational database. This enables you to coordinate the database commits with other nondatabase work.

Summary

The focus of this chapter was transactions and compensation. These are the two primary mechanisms supported by WF that help to ensure the integrity and consistency of work that you perform in a workflow application.

In the first example in this chapter, the use of the TransactionScopeActivity was demonstrated. This activity permits you to enlist multiple operations in a single transaction. All of the work in the transaction is committed or rolled back as a single unit.

The second example demonstrated how to implement compensation in a workflow using the `CompensatableTransactionScopeActivity` and the `CompensatableSequenceActivity`. Compensation is used to undo work that previously succeeded in a workflow. You use this mechanism for long-running workflows where enlisting the work in a single transaction would not be feasible.

Finally, the chapter concluded with an example that used the `IPendingWork` interface. By implementing this `interface`, you can defer the actual committing of work within a workflow. The work can then be coordinated with an active transaction and committed along with pending work for resource managers such as a relational database.

In the next chapter, you will learn about the workflow rules engine and how to use it in your applications.

CHAPTER 11

■ ■ ■

Workflow Rules

WF provides a flexible rules evaluation engine that you can use when developing applications. Rules are an alternate way to implement business requirements and they complement the other mechanisms that are provided with WF. A *rule* is simply a declarative statement about your data. Within a rule, you declare a condition that you wish to evaluate at runtime. If the condition evaluates to true, one or more actions that you define are executed. A rule also permits you to define actions to execute when the condition evaluates to false. The rules support in WF includes a rules editor that allows you to declare individual rules and group them together into rule sets.

After a summary of the rules support in WF, a series of examples are presented that demonstrate the features of workflow rules.

The first example walks you through the process of declaring a set of rules and then executing them within a workflow using the PolicyActivity. Rules tracing is also enabled and the *trace log* is reviewed. The trace log provides insights into just how the rules engine evaluates each of the rules.

The chapter then builds on this first example workflow with a series of shorter examples that explore other features of rules. For instance, one example shows you how to adjust the execution sequence for individual rules. Following that example, the rules are modified to reference workflow methods instead of properties. A set of rule attributes are applied to the methods to provide dependency information to the rules engine.

You can also execute rules in code instead of using the PolicyActivity. Two short examples demonstrate ways to execute rules entirely in code. The first example demonstrates code to deserialize and execute a rule set that was previously saved while the second example creates a rule entirely in code.

Understanding Workflow Rules

As you have already seen, WF provides several places where you can place the business logic (business rules) for a workflow-based application. You can implement the business logic in the workflow class itself using event handlers and overridden methods. Or you can implement custom activities that encapsulate the business logic for a task. You can also implement local services that provide functionality that is available to workflows and the host application. And the execution of all of this business logic is declaratively controlled by the workflow model.

In addition to these mechanisms, WF also provides a general-purpose rules engine that is a suitable alternative for some of your business logic. To use the rules engine in an application, you first organize business requirements into individual rules (represented by instances of the Rule class). Rules are then organized into logical groupings known as *rule sets* (the RuleSet class).

Rules and rule sets are not procedural code. The goal when defining rules is not to explicitly define the procedural steps to execute as you would with a conventional language such as C#. Instead, you define simple rules that the rules engine executes for you. Rules are best thought of as individual statements of fact or assertions that you declare about your data. The actual execution and evaluation of the rules is based on the data and the interaction with other rules.

Parts of a Rule

Each rule is composed of three separate parts:

- A *condition* that evaluates to a Boolean result
- A *then* action that is executed if the condition is true
- An *else* action (optional) that is executed if the condition is false

Collectively, these parts form an if-then-else construct that works in a similar way to the C# if-else statement. A rule is executed by evaluating its *condition* and then executing one of the actions (*then* or *else*) depending on the result from the condition. Each action can contain multiple statements that are executed in sequence.

The rule condition is the same one that you've already seen in previous chapters (used in activities such as the IfElseBranchActivity, the WhileActivity, and so on). It can be a simple or compound Boolean expression that references workflow fields, properties, or methods. It can also reference members of objects within the workflow class.

Within an action (*then* or *else*), you can set a workflow field or property (or objects within a workflow) to a new value. You can also execute methods within the workflow or an object within the workflow. Static methods of types in referenced assemblies can also be executed within an action. Rule actions also support specialized statements such as Halt and Update.

Once a rule set has been defined, it can be executed within a workflow in two ways. You can execute a rule set by adding a PolicyActivity to the workflow, or you can execute a rule set directly from code.

During execution of a rule set, each rule is evaluated and the appropriate actions performed. There are several ways that you can control the sequence in which the rules in a rule set are evaluated. By default, rules are executed in alphabetical sequence based on the rule name. You can optionally modify the evaluation sequence by changing the priority of the individual rules. Rules with a higher priority (a larger number) will be evaluated first. Within rules with the same priority, the alphabetical sequence is used.

However, although you *can* affect the evaluation sequence for rules, you generally don't *need* to do so. This is because an important feature of the workflow rules engine is its ability to reevaluate rules. This reevaluation is called *forward chaining*. It works by discovering and monitoring dependencies between rules. If a rule modifies a variable that is referenced in a condition of a previously evaluated rule, forward chaining causes the prior rule to be evaluated again. As you will see later in this chapter, there are several ways to help the rules engine discover dependencies between rules. You can also explicitly control rule dependencies yourself, or turn off forward chaining entirely.

When rules are added to a workflow, they are serialized to a separate .rules file that is built as an embedded resource of the project. The .rules resource is then deserialized during execution. As an alternative, you can also save the .rules file external to the project and deserialize and execute the rules from code. This isolation and separation is one of the major benefits of declaring some of your business logic as rules. Since the rules are encapsulated in their own file, they are much easier to change and dynamically update without modifying other parts of the application.

Why Use Rules?

Rule-based business logic has several advantages when compared to the alternatives. The conventional alternative is to codify and embed the business logic in your application using a procedural language. Here are some of the advantages of a rule-based application:

- Rules provide a clear separation of the business rules (what you want to accomplish) from the procedural code (the process used to enforce the rules). This clear separation eases maintenance of the application and minimizes the chances of unintentionally changing the business rules.

- Rules are a greatly simplified way to declare business requirements and relationships between data. Rules are simple declarative statements and assertions about the data rather than a complicated sequence of steps that merge the real business rules with process and infrastructure code. In a rule-based application, the focus becomes the relationships that are found within the data, not the procedural code.

- Rules enable an easier translation of business requirements into a working application. Rules are expressed in a form that is much closer to the original requirements (they are statements of fact about the data). Therefore, the requirements require less of a transformation than would be required to codify the rules using a procedural language.

- A rule-based application provides greater visibility into the real business rules. By not embedding business rules in procedural code, they are in a form that is more easily visible and understood by business analysts and nondevelopers.

- A rule-based application is more extensible and adaptable. The business requirements are likely to change more often than other aspects of the application (such as the application framework or infrastructure). Declaring the requirements as rules enables you to more quickly and confidently modify them as the requirements change. If rules are persisted externally from the compiled code, they can be modified without the need to rebuild the application.

Using Rules in WF

WF provides a number of classes that support the use of rules within your application. All of the classes related to rules can be found in the `System.Workflow.Activities.Rules` namespace. In the following sections I provide a tour of the primary classes that you will use when building rule-enabled applications.

Defining Rules

The `Rule` class is used to declare a single business rule. The class is the container for a single rule condition and up to two rule actions. One action is executed if the condition evaluates to `true`, and the other action (if one is specified) is executed when the condition is `false`.

The `Condition` property of the `Rule` class references a `RuleCondition` object that defines the condition to be evaluated. `RuleCondition` is actually the base class for the `RuleExpressionCondition` class. When you declare rules using the Rule Set editor that is provided as a Visual Studio designer, you create instances of `RuleExpressionCondition`, not the base `RuleCondition`.

Instances of `RuleExpressionCondition` are also declared and referenced when you use a rule condition in activities such as the `IfElseBranchActivity`, the `WhileActivity`, and the `ConditionedActivityGroup`. You should already be familiar with the entry of rule conditions from working with these other activities. The process of declaring a condition to be used in a `Rule` instance is very similar.

The `Rule` class exposes two properties that define the possible actions that will be executed. The `ThenActions` property defines the actions that will be executed if the expression defined in the `Condition` property evaluates to `true`. The actions defined in the `ElseActions` property are executed when the `Condition` evaluates to `false`. The `ThenActions` is required but the `ElseActions` property is optional. Each one of these properties is a collection that supports multiple actions.

The Rule class also has a Name property that should be used to provide a descriptive name for the Rule. As I already mentioned, the default evaluation sequence for rules within a RuleSet is alphabetical by name. In general, this shouldn't affect the way you name rules. First and foremost, you should provide a good descriptive name for your rules. Don't try to use the rule name as a mechanism to control the evaluation sequence. There are other mechanisms (such as the Priority property) that can be used for that purpose.

The Priority property of the Rule class is used to control the initial evaluation sequence of rules within a RuleSet. By default, new rules are created with a Priority of zero. If there are some rules that you wish to execute before others, you can set their Priority to a larger number. Rules with a larger Priority value are executed prior to those with a smaller Priority. However, remember that forward chaining of rules will ultimately control the evaluation order of rules (unless you disable forward chaining).

■**Tip** Remember that when defining rules, you are declaring simple facts about the data. Your goal is not to implement procedural logic using rule syntax. Don't become overly concerned with the sequence in which your rules will be evaluated. Leave that problem to the rules engine.

Declaring the Rule Condition

When defining a rule condition, your job is to declare a statement that evaluates to a Boolean true or false value. Within a rule condition, you can reference fields, properties, and methods of the workflow. You can also reference members of objects defined within the workflow. Table 11-1 provides a summary of the operators that are supported by a rule condition.

Table 11-1. *Supported Rule Condition Operators*

Operator	Supported Symbols
Equality	==, =
Greater Than	>
Greater Than or Equal	>=
Less Than	<
Less Than or Equal	<=
Logical And	&&, AND
Logical Or	‖, OR
Logical Not	!, NOT
Bitwise And	&
Bitwise Or		
Addition	+
Subtraction	–
Multiplication	*
Division	/

Table 11-1. *Supported Rule Condition Operators*

Operator	Supported Symbols
Modulus	MOD
Operator Precedence	(,)
Indexer	[,]

The indexer symbols ([,]) are used to reference variables that support an index such as a simple array or collection. For example

```
this.Field1Array[1] > 0
```

or

```
this.Field1Array[this.Field2] > 0
```

Declaring the Rule Actions

Both of the action properties of the Rule class (ThenActions and ElseActions) are defined as a collection of RuleAction objects (IList<RuleAction>). The RuleAction class is an abstract class that is the base for several other action classes. The derived RuleStatementAction class is used when you need to modify a field or property or to execute a method. This is the action that you will use most often. Other possible derived actions are RuleHaltAction and RuleUpdateAction.

A RuleStatementAction is constructed when you set a field or property to a new value or when you execute a method. You can reference members (fields, properties, and methods) of the workflow itself (this.Field1), or of an object that is defined within the workflow (this.Field1.PropertyA). You can also execute static methods of a type that is in a referenced assembly.

The RuleStatementAction supports simple static assignments (fieldA = 10, fieldB = true) or more complex calculations (fieldA = fieldC * 3.14). You can also use the operator precedence symbols, "(" and ")" to clarify the sequence to use when calculating a new value.

■ **Note** The statements that you enter in a RuleStatementAction are serialized as CodeDom objects. CodeDom classes are used to represent the internal structure of source code that can be dynamically generated and compiled. If you use the Rule Set editor to work with rules, you won't need to fully understand the details of CodeDom objects. However, if you want to dynamically build rules in code, you will need to get up to speed on the basics of constructing statements using the CodeDom objects. Refer to the CodeDOM Quick Reference in MSDN for a good introduction to the CodeDom classes.

The RuleHaltAction halts the execution of a RuleSet. A RuleHaltAction is generated when you enter the literal halt (or Halt) as one of the actions. When this action is executed, no further execution of the other rules in the RuleSet takes place. However, the current collection of RuleAction objects does complete their execution.

The RuleUpdateAction is used when you want to explicitly identify the dependencies between rules. You generate a RuleUpdateAction when you enter an Update statement as one of the actions. The Update statement identifies the field or property that this action has modified.

Defining RuleSets

Individual Rule objects are associated with a RuleSet. When you use the Rule Set editor in Visual Studio, you first define a RuleSet. Make sure you provide a descriptive name for the RuleSet so that you will be able to easily identify its purpose. Once the RuleSet is created, you add individual Rule instances to it. The collection of Rule objects in a RuleSet is exposed by the Rules property (ICollection<Rule>).

Controlling Forward Chaining Behavior

The RuleSet class includes a ChainingBehavior property that determines how the rules engine will perform forward chaining (if at all). The value for this property is an enum named RuleChainingBehavior. Unfortunately, the Rule Set editor doesn't display the exact enum names, but instead uses slightly different terminology. Table 11-2 summarizes the possible values for ChainingBehavior, which is simply labeled Chaining in the Rule Set editor.

Table 11-2. *RuleChainingBehavior Options*

Enum Value	Rule Set Editor Display	Description
Full	Full Chaining	Automatic forward chaining is enabled. The rules engine automatically detects dependencies between rules. This is the default for a new RuleSet.
UpdateOnly	Explicit Update Only	Automatic detection of forward chaining is disabled. Dependencies between rules must be explicitly identified by including a RuleUpdateAction in the rule actions.
None	Sequential	No forward chaining is performed. Each rule is executed exactly one time.

To illustrate the forward chaining behavior using each of these options, I've defined three simple rules in Table 11-3. For the purpose of this illustration, it really doesn't matter what these rules are attempting to accomplish, what the variables mean, or what problem domain they belong to.

Table 11-3. *Example RuleSet*

Rule	Condition	ThenAction	ElseAction
Rule1	A > 10	B = 60	B = 40
Rule2	B > 50	C = "preferred"	C = "normal"
Rule3	D < 100	B = B * 0.80	

After you review the rules in Table 11-3, you can see that the real inputs that matter are variables A and D. The B and C variables are set internally within the RuleSet, but A and D are referenced by conditions.

If the Full Chaining option is used, the rules engine will automatically determine the dependencies between rules and reevaluate a prior rule if necessary. For this example, assume that A is 12 and D is 99. The rules will be evaluated like this:

1. Rule1 evaluates to true since A has a value of 12, which is greater than 10. This causes B to be set to a value of 60.

2. Rule2 evaluates to true since B has been set to 60 (by Rule1), which is greater than 50. Variable C is now set to "preferred."

3. Rule3 evaluates to true since D is equal to 99, which is less than 100. This causes variable B to be set to 48 (60 * 0.80). Variable B has been changed and one of the prior rules (Rule2) references B in its condition. This causes the reevaluation of Rule2.

4. Rule2 is evaluated again, this time evaluating to false since B is now 48, which is not greater than 50. This causes C to be set to "normal."

5. Rule3 is not evaluated again since it doesn't depend on any variables that were modified since the first time it was evaluated.

The final result is that variable B is set to 48 and C is set to "normal." The input variables A and D are unchanged.

At the opposite end of the spectrum, you can completely disable forward chaining by setting the Chaining property to Sequential (None). If you now execute the same RuleSet using the same variable values, the final outcome would be that variable B is set to 48 and C is set to "preferred." The results are different because only the first three steps in the previous list are executed. After Rule3 is executed, the RuleSet is complete since forward chaining of rules is disabled.

Most of the time you will want to let the rules engine handle the dependency detection for forward chaining. However, you can also use the Explicit Update Only option. This option enables forward chaining, but it places you in control of the dependency discovery. When this option is used, you must explicitly use an Update statement within your actions to identify the variables that have been modified. The rules engine then uses this information to determine when reevaluation of a prior rule is necessary.

To illustrate how this works, a revised version of the example RuleSet is needed. Table 11-4 shows the revised RuleSet that includes the Update statements.

Table 11-4. *Revised Example RuleSet with Update Statements*

Rule	Condition	ThenAction	ElseAction
Rule1	A > 10	B = 60, Update(B)	B = 40, Update(B)
Rule2	B > 50	C = "preferred", Update(C)	C = "normal", Update(C)
Rule3	D < 100	B = B * 0.80, Update(B)	

The Update statements generate a RuleUpdateAction when the rule is serialized to the .rules file. Each Update statement identifies the field or property that has been modified by the other actions in the collection. When this RuleSet is evaluated, it would exhibit the same behavior as the first example, producing a final result of variable B set to 48 and C set to "normal."

You won't generally need to explicitly use Update statements like this. The approach recommended by Microsoft is to use the automatic forward chaining instead. This explicit approach is available if you want to take over total control of the forward chaining.

Suppressing Rule Reevaluation

Another option that affects the behavior of rules evaluation is the ReevaluationBehavior property of the Rule class. This option is simply labeled Reevaluation in the Rule Set editor. The values for this property are defined in an enum named `RuleReevaluationBehavior`. When this option is set to Always (the default), the `Rule` is capable of being reevaluated. If you instead set it to Never, the `Rule` is executed only a single time (although it may be evaluated multiple times until it does execute an action). Even if the rule condition references members that have been modified, it won't be reevaluated if this property is set to Never.

Identifying Dependencies with Attributes

When a rule condition or action references a field or a property, the rules engine can easily identify the dependencies that it uses to control forward chaining of rules. If a field or property is modified by an action, it identifies other rules that reference that same field or property in a condition.

However, when a condition or action executes a method instead, the rules engine is not able to determine the dependencies without your help. For instance, a rule condition might execute a method named `GetAccountStatus` and use the result in an expression. Based on the method name, you and I might make an educated guess that the method returns a value that represents the account status. But the rules engine is incapable of making that same assumption. If another rule executes a method named `ChangeAccountStatus`, we might guess that it modifies the same value that is returned by the first method. But again, the rules engine can't make that connection without our assistance.

WF provides a set of attributes that you can apply to methods (or properties) to solve this problem. Table 11-5 identifies the available attributes.

Table 11-5. *Rule Attributes*

Name	Description
`RuleReadAttribute`	Identifies a field or property that is read by the attributed method or property
`RuleWriteAttribute`	Identifies a field or property that is modified by the attributed method or property
`RuleInvokeAttribute`	Identifies another method or property that is invoked by the attributed method or property

You place one or more of these attributes on a method or property to identify the referenced variables (fields or properties). For instance, you might place the `RuleReadAttribute` on the `GetAccountStatus` method mentioned previously to identify the underlying field that is being retrieved. The code would look like this:

```
[RuleRead("accountStatus")]
public int GetAccountStatus()
{
    return this.accountStatus;
}
```

Now, when the `GetAccountStatus` method is referenced in a `Rule`, the dependency on the `accountStatus` field is clearly identified. If the field or property being referenced is on another object (instead of being defined directly in the workflow class), you modify the path provided to the attribute like this:

```
[RuleRead("Account/AccountStatus")]
public int GetAccountStatus()
{
    return this.Account.AccountStatus;
}
```

In like manner, the `RuleWriteAttribute` can be applied to methods (or properties) to identify the field or property that is being modified. For instance, the made up `ChangeAccountStatus` method might look like this after the `RuleWriteAttribute` has been added:

```
[RuleWrite("Account/AccountStatus")]
public void ChangeAccountStatus(int newStatus)
{
    //code to validate and update Account.AccountStatus
}
```

The `RuleReadAttribute` and the `RuleWriteAttribute` can be used to identify a single field or property that is referenced, or you can specify wild cards. For example, this attribute indicates that all fields and properties of the Account object are modified:

```
[RuleWrite("Account/*")]
```

Note When applying attributes, you can also specify the full name of the attribute. For example, `RuleRead` and `RuleReadAttribute` are synonymous.

Sometimes, the method that is invoked by the `Rule` is not the one that actually references the field or property. Many times, the invoked method simply calls another method that has the direct reference to the field or property. In this case, you can use the `RuleInvokeAttribute` to indicate that one method or property invokes another.

For instance, the `ChangeAccountStatus` method just shown might not actually be the method that updates the `AccountStatus` property. It may defer that to another private method. If that were the case, these two methods would look like this:

```
[RuleWrite("Account/AccountStatus")]
private void ValiateAndUpdateAccountStatus(int newStatus)
{
    //code to validate and update Account.AccountStatus
}

[RuleInvoke("ValiateAndUpdateAccountStatus")]
public void ChangeAccountStatus(int newStatus)
{
    //call other methods and perform other work
    ValiateAndUpdateAccountStatus(newStatus);
    //call other methods and perform other work
}
```

The rules engine can now indirectly determine that invoking the `ChangeAccountStatus` method updates the `AccountStatus` property.

Defining Rules with a PolicyActivity

Now that you have the background on the rules support within WF, it's time to develop a workflow that uses rules. In this example, you will implement a simple workflow that contains a single instance of the PolicyActivity. The PolicyActivity executes a RuleSet that calculates totals for a sales order. It determines the total amount of the order based on the item price and the quantity of the item being ordered. It also determines the amount to charge for shipping of the order. The properties of the order are encapsulated within a SalesItem object that is passed into the workflow by the host application.

Implementing the SalesItem Class

To begin development of this example, create a new project using the Empty Workflow Project template and name the project SharedWorkflows. When creating a new project, you will also be prompted to save the solution file. You can use the same solution for all of the projects in this chapter.

The first order of business is to implement a class that defines the item to be sold. It is an instance of this class that will be passed into the workflow and modified by a RuleSet. Add a normal C# class (not a workflow class) to the SharedWorkflows project and name it SalesItem. Listing 11-1 shows the complete code for the SalesItem.cs file.

Listing 11-1. *Complete SalesItem.cs File*

```csharp
using System;

namespace SharedWorkflows
{
    /// <summary>
    /// A class that defines an item to sell
    /// </summary>
    [Serializable]
    public class SalesItem
    {
        private Int32 _quantity;
        private Double _itemPrice;
        private Double _orderTotal;
        private Double _shipping;
        private Boolean _isNewCustomer;

        public Int32 Quantity
        {
            get { return _quantity; }
            set { _quantity = value; }
        }

        public Double ItemPrice
        {
            get { return _itemPrice; }
            set { _itemPrice = value; }
        }
```

```
        public Double OrderTotal
        {
            get { return _orderTotal; }
            set { _orderTotal = value; }
        }

        public Double Shipping
        {
            get { return _shipping; }
            set { _shipping = value; }
        }

        public Boolean IsNewCustomer
        {
            get { return _isNewCustomer; }
            set { _isNewCustomer = value; }
        }
    }
}
```

The Quantity and ItemPrice properties will be used to determine the final order total. The OrderTotal and Shipping properties are both calculated by execution of the RuleSet. The IsNewCustomer property will also be referenced by the RuleSet to determine if the order qualifies for a special discount.

Declaring the Rules

Now add a new sequential workflow to the SharedWorkflows project and name it SellItemWorkflow. Before you move to the visual design of the workflow, you need to add a property that allows the host application to pass in a SalesItem object. The code for the SellItemWorkflow.cs file is shown in Listing 11-2.

Listing 11-2. *Complete SellItemWorkflow.cs File*

```
using System;
using System.Workflow.Activities;

namespace SharedWorkflows
{
    /// <summary>
    /// Processes a sales item using a RuleSet
    /// </summary>
    public sealed partial class SellItemWorkflow
        : SequentialWorkflowActivity
    {
        private SalesItem _salesItem;

        public SalesItem SalesItem
        {
            get { return _salesItem; }
            set { _salesItem = value; }
        }
```

```
        public SellItemWorkflow()
        {
            InitializeComponent();
        }
    }
}
```

After switching to the workflow designer view, drag and drop a PolicyActivity onto the empty workflow. The job of the PolicyActivity is to execute the RuleSet that is named in the RuleSetReference property. Since you haven't defined a RuleSet yet, the Properties window for the PolicyActivity looks like Figure 11-1.

Figure 11-1. *Unassigned RuleSetReference*

Once you have one or more rule sets defined for this workflow, you will be able to choose a RuleSet from the list and assign it to this property. By clicking the ellipsis on the right side of the RuleSetReference property, you can define a new RuleSet using the Rule Set editor. You are first presented with the rule set selector dialog shown in Figure 11-2.

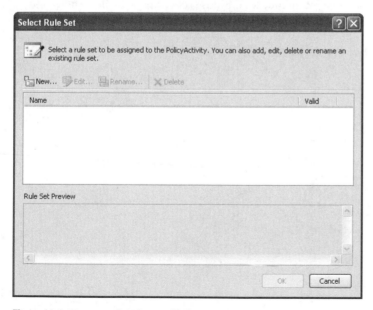

Figure 11-2. *Empty rule selector dialog*

From here, your only available option is to select the New button to create a new RuleSet. This brings up an empty Rule Set editor as shown in Figure 11-3.

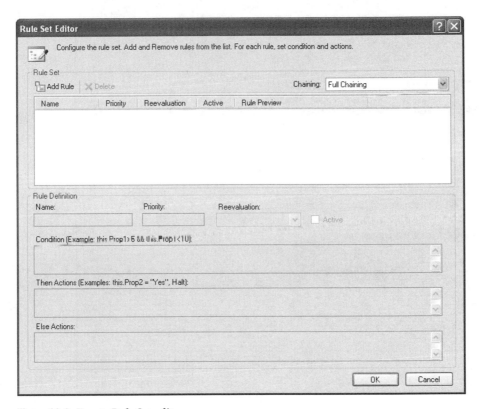

Figure 11-3. *Empty Rule Set editor*

You will be adding a total of three rules to this RuleSet. To add the first rule, select Add Rule, which adds an empty rule to the list, ready for you to define. This is shown in Figure 11-4.

The first rule will determine the total amount of the order (OrderTotal property) based on the Quantity and ItemPrice properties. If the Quantity is greater than 10, a discount of 5% off of the ItemPrice is applied. Otherwise, the total is simply the Quantity multiplied by the ItemPrice. The values that you should enter for this first rule are listed in Table 11-6.

Table 11-6. *CalcTotal Rule Definition*

Property	Value
Name	CalcTotal
Priority	0 (the default)
Reevaluation	Always (the default)
Condition	this.SalesItem.Quantity > 10
Then Actions	this.SalesItem.OrderTotal = this.SalesItem.Quantity * (this.SalesItem.ItemPrice * 0.95)
Else Actions	this.SalesItem.OrderTotal = this.SalesItem.Quantity * this.SalesItem.ItemPrice

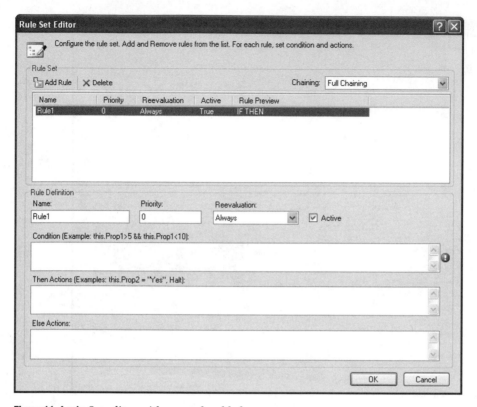

Figure 11-4 rule *Set editor with new rule added*

As you enter the condition and actions, remember that the Rule Set editor supports IntelliSense. You can enter **this** followed by a period to show a list of available members of the workflow class. From there, you can navigate to the SalesItem property, and then enter another period to see the list of SalesItem object members. This rule only requires a single *then* and *else* action. But you are by no means limited to a single action. After entering the first action, you can press the Enter key to begin entry of an expression for another action.

After entering this first rule, the Rule Set editor should look like Figure 11-5.

You can now press the Add Rule button again to begin definition of the second rule. This rule calculates a value for the Shipping property of the SalesItem object. If the total amount of the order (OrderTotal property) is greater than 100, Shipping is free (zero). Otherwise, Shipping is 0.95 for each item. Table 11-7 lists the property values that you need for this rule.

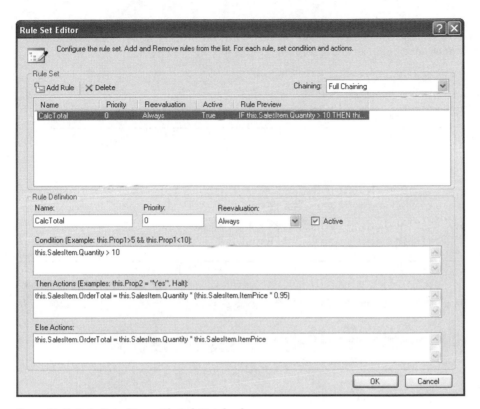

Figure 11-5. *Rule Set editor with CalcTotal rule*

Table 11-7. *CalcShipping Rule Definition*

Property	Value
Name	CalcShipping
Priority	0 (the default)
Reevaluation	Always (the default)
Condition	this.SalesItem.OrderTotal > 100.0
Then Actions	this.SalesItem.Shipping = 0
Else Actions	this.SalesItem.Shipping = this.SalesItem.Quantity * 0.95

In like manner, you can add the third and final rule. This one applies a special discount to the order total of 10.00 if this is a new customer. Table 11-8 lists the property values for this rule. Note that this rule does not contain an *else* action.

Table 11-8. *NewCustomer Rule Definition*

Property	Value
Name	NewCustomer
Priority	0 (the default)
Reevaluation	Always (the default)
Condition	this.SalesItem.IsNewCustomer
Then Actions	this.SalesItem.OrderTotal = this.SalesItem.OrderTotal - 10.0
Else Actions	

Your completed rule set should now look like Figure 11-6.

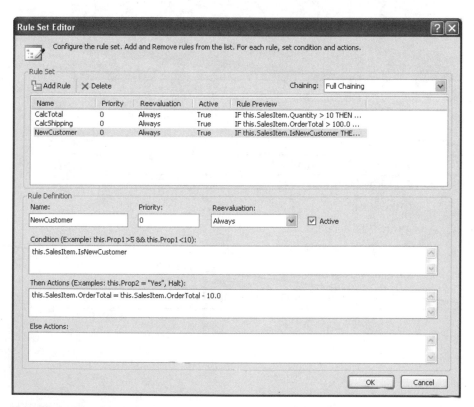

Figure 11-6. *Completed RuleSet*

When you press the OK button, the RuleSet will be saved with a default name of RuleSet1. You can then press the Rename button to give the RuleSet a more appropriate name of CalculateItemTotals. The rename dialog is shown in Figure 11-7.

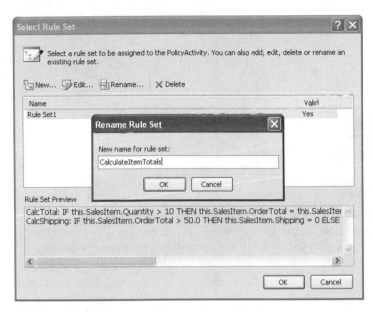

Figure 11-7. *RuleSet rename dialog*

The Properties window for the PolicyActivity now lists CalculateItemTotal as the selected RuleSetReference. This is shown in Figure 11-8.

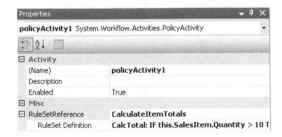

Figure 11-8. *PolicyActivity properties with assigned RuleSetReference*

This completes the definition of the RuleSet for this example. You don't need to add any other activities to the workflow, therefore the completed SellItemWorkflow should look like Figure 11-9.

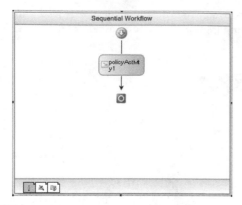

Figure 11-9. *Complete SellItemWorkflow*

Testing the Workflow

The host application to test this workflow will be a `Console` application. Add a new Sequential Workflow Console Application to the solution and name it `ConsoleSellItem`. You can delete `Workflow1` that was added to this project by the template since it is not needed. You will also need to add the following additional references to this project:

- `SharedWorkflows`
- `Bukovics.Workflow.Hosting`

The `SharedWorkflows` and `Bukovics.Workflow.Hosting` references are project references. The `Bukovics.Workflow.Hosting` project was originally developed in Chapter 4. You should add it as an existing project to your current solution in order to reference it.

Add a new C# class to the `ConsoleSellItem` project and name it `SellItemTest`. This class will contain all of the code needed to host the workflow runtime and execute the `SellItemWorkflow`. Listing 11-3 is the complete code for the `SellItemTest.cs` file.

Listing 11-3. *Complete SellItemTest.cs File*

```
using System;
using System.Collections.Generic;
using System.Workflow.Runtime;

using Bukovics.Workflow.Hosting;
using SharedWorkflows;

namespace ConsoleSellItem
{
    /// <summary>
    /// Test the SellItemWorkflow
    /// </summary>
    public class SellItemTest
    {
```

```
public static void Run()
{
    using (WorkflowRuntimeManager manager
        = new WorkflowRuntimeManager(new WorkflowRuntime()))
    {
        manager.WorkflowRuntime.StartRuntime();

        //execute the workflow with parameters that will
        //result in a normal priced item and shipping
        Console.WriteLine("Executing SellItemWorkflow");
        SalesItem item = new SalesItem();
        item.ItemPrice = 10.00;
        item.Quantity = 4;
        item.IsNewCustomer = false;
        ExecuteWorkflow(manager, item);
        Console.WriteLine("Completed SellItemWorkflow\n\r");

        //execute the workflow again with parameters that
        //will cause a discounted price and shipping
        Console.WriteLine("Executing SellItemWorkflow (Discounts)");
        item = new SalesItem();
        item.ItemPrice = 10.00;
        item.Quantity = 11;
        item.IsNewCustomer = false;
        ExecuteWorkflow(manager, item);
        Console.WriteLine("Completed SellItemWorkflow (Discounts)\n\r");

        //execute the workflow once more, this time with the
        //IsNewCustomer property set to true
        Console.WriteLine("Executing SellItemWorkflow (New Customer)");
        item = new SalesItem();
        item.ItemPrice = 10.00;
        item.Quantity = 11;
        item.IsNewCustomer = true;
        ExecuteWorkflow(manager, item);
        Console.WriteLine("Completed SellItemWorkflow (New Customer)\n\r");
    }
}
```

After initializing the workflow runtime, the code executes the SellItemWorkflow three times, each time with a slightly different set of parameters. The results from each execution of the workflow will demonstrate that the RuleSet is being evaluated correctly.

The first workflow execution should result in normal pricing for the item, without any discounts. The second workflow execution should result in a discounted item price and free shipping. The final execution sets the IsNewCustomer parameter to true which should result in an additional discount being applied to the order.

```
/// <summary>
/// Execute the SellItemWorkflow
/// </summary>
/// <param name="item"></param>
private static void ExecuteWorkflow(
    WorkflowRuntimeManager manager, SalesItem item)
{
    DisplaySalesItem(item, "Before");
```

```
            //create a dictionary with input arguments
            Dictionary<String, Object> wfArguments
                = new Dictionary<string, object>();
            wfArguments.Add("SalesItem", item);

            //execute the workflow
            WorkflowInstanceWrapper instance = manager.StartWorkflow(
                typeof(SharedWorkflows.SellItemWorkflow), wfArguments);
            manager.WaitAll(5000);

            if (instance.Exception != null)
            {
                Console.WriteLine("EXCEPTION: {0}",
                    instance.Exception.Message);
            }
            else
            {
                DisplaySalesItem(item, "After");
            }
        }

        /// <summary>
        /// Display the contents of the SalesItem
        /// </summary>
        /// <param name="item"></param>
        /// <param name="message"></param>
        private static void DisplaySalesItem(SalesItem item, String message)
        {
            Console.WriteLine("{0}:", message);
            Console.WriteLine("  ItemPrice    = {0:C}", item.ItemPrice);
            Console.WriteLine("  Quantity     = {0}", item.Quantity);
            Console.WriteLine("  OrderTotal   = {0:C}", item.OrderTotal);
            Console.WriteLine("  Shipping     = {0:C}", item.Shipping);
            Console.WriteLine("  IsNewCustomer = {0}", item.IsNewCustomer);
        }
```

The ExecuteWorkflow is simply a convenience method that executes the workflow with the parameters that have been passed in. Prior to executing the workflow, the DisplaySalesItem method is called to display the current property values for the SalesItem object. The method waits for the workflow to complete and then calls DisplaySalesItem again to display the resulting values.

```
        }
    }
```

You will also need to add code to the Program.cs file to execute the static Run method of this SellItemTest class. The code for the Program.cs file looks like this:

```
using System;

namespace ConsoleSellItem
{
    public class Program
    {
        static void Main(string[] args)
        {
            //execute the workflow tests
            SellItemTest.Run();

            Console.WriteLine("Press any key to exit");
            Console.ReadLine();
        }
    }
}
```

When I execute this test, I see these results:

```
Executing SellItemWorkflow
Before:
  ItemPrice     = $10.00
  Quantity      = 4
  OrderTotal    = $0.00
  Shipping      = $0.00
  IsNewCustomer = False
After:
  ItemPrice     = $10.00
  Quantity      = 4
  OrderTotal    = $40.00
  Shipping      = $3.80
  IsNewCustomer = False
Completed SellItemWorkflow
```

The first workflow execution resulted in a correct OrderTotal of 40.00 (Quantity of 4 * ItemPrice of 10.00). The Shipping was 3.80 (Quantity of 4 * 0.95).

```
Executing SellItemWorkflow (Discounts)
Before:
  ItemPrice     = $10.00
  Quantity      = 11
  OrderTotal    = $0.00
  Shipping      = $0.00
  IsNewCustomer = False
After:
  ItemPrice     = $10.00
  Quantity      = 11
  OrderTotal    = $104.50
  Shipping      = $0.00
  IsNewCustomer = False
Completed SellItemWorkflow (Discounts)
```

The second workflow calculated an OrderTotal of 104.50. Because the Quantity is greater than 10, the 5% discount was applied to the ItemPrice (Quantity of 11 * ItemPrice of 9.50). Because the OrderTotal was greater than 100.00, the Shipping is zero.

```
Executing SellItemWorkflow (New Customer)
Before:
  ItemPrice     = $10.00
  Quantity      = 11
  OrderTotal    = $0.00
  Shipping      = $0.00
  IsNewCustomer = True
After:
  ItemPrice     = $10.00
  Quantity      = 11
  OrderTotal    = $94.50
  Shipping      = $10.45
  IsNewCustomer = True
Completed SellItemWorkflow (New Customer)

Press any key to exit
```

The final workflow execution is the most interesting. It is the one example that set the IsNewCustomer property to true, which should result in an additional 10.00 discount. It calculated a final OrderTotal of 94.50 and Shipping of 10.45. To understand how the RuleSet evaluated the data, a review of each Rule is in order:

- Since the Quantity is greater than 10, the first rule calculated an OrderTotal of 104.50 just like the previous execution (Quantity of 11 * ItemPrice of 9.50).

- The OrderTotal was greater than 100, therefore the second rule calculated shipping of zero.

- The IsNewCustomer property is true, so an additional 10.00 discount was subtracted from the OrderTotal property resulting in a new value of 94.50 (104.50 – 10.00).

- Because the NewCustomer rule modified the OrderTotal, and the CalcShipping rule has a dependency on OrderTotal (it references OrderTotal in its condition), the CalcShipping rule was reevaluated (forward chaining). This time, when the CalcShipping rule was evaluated, the OrderTotal was not greater than 100, therefore the Shipping was calculated as 10.45 (Quantity of 11 * 0.95 per item).

■**Note** This is the conceptual sequence of the rule evaluation that explains how the test results were generated. However, as you will see when you review the trace logs in the next section, the actual sequence of the rule evaluation is slightly different.

Tracing Rules

Since rules are not procedural code, you can't step through each Rule as it is evaluated in the Visual Studio debugger. However, when defining and debugging your rule-based workflows, you can enable tracing for the rules engine. This is often helpful in determining the problem with a Rule when you don't get the results that you expect.

Note The workflow tracking mechanism also allows you to monitor rules evaluation. Please refer to Chapter 14.

Tracing for rules is enabled via entries in the application configuration file (App.config). For instance, Listing 11-4 is an App.config file that will enable tracing of all possible messages for the rules engine.

Listing 11-4. *App.config with Rule Tracing Enabled*

```
<?xml version="1.0" encoding="utf-8" ?>
<configuration>
  <system.diagnostics>
    <switches>
      <add name="System.Workflow.Activities.Rules" value="All" />
      <add name="System.Workflow LogToFile" value="1" />
    </switches>
  </system.diagnostics>
</configuration>
```

The TraceLevel value of All indicates that all possible log messages will be recorded. You can also specify a level of Information or Verbose if you want to filter the level of messages that are logged. The second trace switch enables logging to a file with a fixed name of WorkflowTrace.log. This file will be created in the same directory as the host executable.

To see the rule tracing in action, you can add the App.config file shown in Listing 11-4 to the ConsoleSellItem host application developed in the previous example.

Tip Remember that when you add an application configuration file to a project, it is added with a default name of App.config. But when you build the project, it is renamed to match the output name of the project.

This time, when you execute the application, a WorkflowTrace.log file is created. Portions of the log are shown in the following results. I've truncated the log in order to fit the format of this book:

```
Rule "CalcShipping" Condition dependency: "this/SalesItem/OrderTotal/"
Rule "CalcShipping" THEN side-effect: "this/SalesItem/Shipping/"
Rule "CalcShipping" ELSE side-effect: "this/SalesItem/Shipping/"
Rule "CalcTotal" Condition dependency: "this/SalesItem/Quantity/"
Rule "CalcTotal" THEN side-effect: "this/SalesItem/OrderTotal/"
Rule "CalcTotal" ELSE side-effect: "this/SalesItem/OrderTotal/"
Rule "NewCustomer" Condition dependency: "this/SalesItem/IsNewCustomer/"
Rule "NewCustomer" THEN side-effect: "this/SalesItem/OrderTotal/"
Rule "CalcTotal" THEN actions trigger rule "CalcShipping"
Rule "CalcTotal" ELSE actions trigger rule "CalcShipping"
Rule "NewCustomer" THEN actions trigger rule "CalcShipping"
```

This first part of the log shows you the dependencies between the individual rules that the rules engine was able to identify. Each rule is inspected to determine the fields or properties that the rule is dependent upon, or that the rule modifies. The final lines of this section of the trace show that the actions of the CalcTotal and NewCustomer rules trigger evaluation of the CalcShipping rule.

Following this initial inspection of the rules, the trace shows the actual execution for the first workflow instance:

```
Evaluating condition on rule "CalcShipping".
Rule "CalcShipping" condition evaluated to False.
Evaluating ELSE actions for rule "CalcShipping".
Evaluating condition on rule "CalcTotal".
Rule "CalcTotal" condition evaluated to False.
Evaluating ELSE actions for rule "CalcTotal".
Rule "CalcTotal" side effects enable rule "CalcShipping" reevaluation.
Evaluating condition on rule "CalcShipping".
Rule "CalcShipping" condition evaluated to False.
Evaluating ELSE actions for rule "CalcShipping".
Evaluating condition on rule "NewCustomer".
Rule "NewCustomer" condition evaluated to False.
```

■**Note** The actual trace also includes the workflow instance ID (Guid) with each line of the trace. This allows you to identify the workflow instance that is generating the trace results. The results shown here are for just one of the workflow instances. The complete trace file includes a trace for all of the workflow instances.

This detailed trace shows you the sequence and results for each rule that is evaluated. Notice that the rules are not evaluated in the same sequence in which they are defined. In the Rule Set editor, you defined the rules in CalcTotal, CalcShipping, NewCustomer sequence. But during execution, they are evaluated in CalcShipping, CalcTotal, NewCustomer sequence. This is the default alphabetical sequence for rules that all have the same priority (as these do).

As shown in this trace, there is more forward chaining going on here than was originally thought. The CalcShipping rule is evaluated first, not second as you might expect. The CalcTotal rule is then executed (second, not first). Since the CalcShipping rule is dependent upon the OrderTotal property, which was just modified, the CalcShipping rule is reevaluated, resulting in a recalculation of the Shipping property.

Here is the trace for the third workflow instance (the second instance is very similar to the first and is not shown):

```
Evaluating condition on rule "CalcShipping".
Rule "CalcShipping" condition evaluated to False.
Evaluating ELSE actions for rule "CalcShipping".
Evaluating condition on rule "CalcTotal".
Rule "CalcTotal" condition evaluated to True.
Evaluating THEN actions for rule "CalcTotal".
Rule "CalcTotal" side effects enable rule "CalcShipping" reevaluation.
Evaluating condition on rule "CalcShipping".
Rule "CalcShipping" condition evaluated to True.
Evaluating THEN actions for rule "CalcShipping".
Evaluating condition on rule "NewCustomer".
Rule "NewCustomer" condition evaluated to True.
Evaluating THEN actions for rule "NewCustomer".
Rule "NewCustomer" side effects enable rule "CalcShipping" reevaluation.
Evaluating condition on rule "CalcShipping".
Rule "CalcShipping" condition evaluated to False.
Evaluating ELSE actions for rule "CalcShipping".
```

Based on the data used for this final workflow instance, it was expected that this instance would require forward chaining. From the last few lines of the trace, you can see that forward chaining did cause the CalcShipping rule to be reevaluated after the NewCustomer rule evaluated to true.

Because of the automatic forward chaining of this RuleSet, the correct results are produced regardless of the actual execution sequence of each Rule. Generally, you shouldn't be concerned with manually adjusting the rule priorities to execute the rules in a specific sequence. You should let the rules engine handle those duties (as demonstrated here). However, if you don't like the idea of reevaluating rules, because of possible performance concerns, you can adjust the rule priorities. This is demonstrated in the next section.

Adjusting Rule Sequence

As you saw from the rules evaluation trace listing, rules are executed in alphabetical sequence based on the rule name. But prior to sorting by rule name, the rules are first organized by priority. The rules with the highest priority number are executed first, followed by the rules with the next highest priority, and so on. If multiple rules have the same priority, they are executed in alphabetical sequence within a priority.

The purpose of this example is to demonstrate the effect that the rule priority has on the rules evaluation sequence. This example builds upon the SellItemWorkflow and RuleSet that you developed for the previous example. You will modify the priority of two of the rules and also suppress reevaluation of one of the rules.

Setting the Rule Priority

To begin, open the SellItemWorkflow that you developed in the previous example in the workflow designer. Select the PolicyActivity and open the Rule Set editor from the Properties window for the activity. Using the Rule Set editor, make the following changes to the RuleSet:

1. Change the priority of the CalcTotal rule to 20. This will force this rule to be evaluated first.

2. Change the priority of the CalcShipping rule to 10, causing this rule to be evaluated second.

3. Change the Reevaluation property of the CalcShipping rule from Always to Never. This will suppress reevaluation of this rule, causing the rule to be executed only once.

The RuleSet should look like Figure 11-10 after these changes.

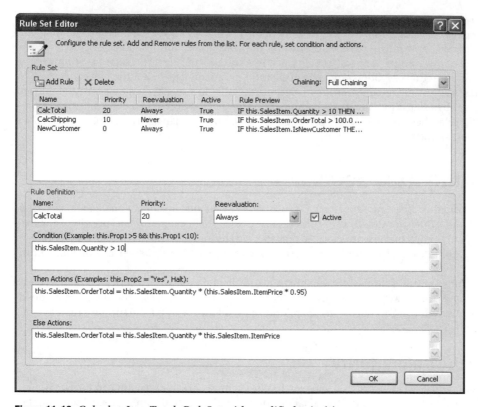

Figure 11-10. *CalculateItemTotals RuleSet with modified priorities*

Testing the Workflow

After saving the changes to the RuleSet by pressing OK and building the SharedWorkflows project, you should be ready to test your changes. When I execute the ConsoleSellItem application, I see these results:

```
Executing SellItemWorkflow
Before:
  ItemPrice     = $10.00
  Quantity      = 4
  OrderTotal    = $0.00
  Shipping      = $0.00
  IsNewCustomer = False
After:
  ItemPrice     = $10.00
  Quantity      = 4
  OrderTotal    = $40.00
  Shipping      = $3.80
  IsNewCustomer = False
Completed SellItemWorkflow
```

```
Executing SellItemWorkflow (Discounts)
Before:
  ItemPrice     = $10.00
  Quantity      = 11
  OrderTotal    = $0.00
  Shipping      = $0.00
  IsNewCustomer = False
After:
  ItemPrice     = $10.00
  Quantity      = 11
  OrderTotal    = $104.50
  Shipping      = $0.00
  IsNewCustomer = False
Completed SellItemWorkflow (Discounts)

Executing SellItemWorkflow (New Customer)
Before:
  ItemPrice     = $10.00
  Quantity      = 11
  OrderTotal    = $0.00
  Shipping      = $0.00
  IsNewCustomer = True
After:
  ItemPrice     = $10.00
  Quantity      = 11
  OrderTotal    = $94.50
  Shipping      = $0.00
  IsNewCustomer = True
Completed SellItemWorkflow (New Customer)

Press any key to exit
```

If you compare these results to the original test (without the rule priority changes), you should notice a change to the final workflow execution (in bold). In the original version of the RuleSet, the Shipping was calculated as 10.45, whereas this time it is calculated as 0.00.

The reason for this difference can be seen in the trace log from this workflow execution. A partial listing of the WorkflowTrace.log file is shown here:

```
Evaluating condition on rule "CalcTotal".
Rule "CalcTotal" condition evaluated to True.
Evaluating THEN actions for rule "CalcTotal".
Evaluating condition on rule "CalcShipping".
Rule "CalcShipping" condition evaluated to True.
Evaluating THEN actions for rule "CalcShipping".
Evaluating condition on rule "NewCustomer".
Rule "NewCustomer" condition evaluated to True.
Evaluating THEN actions for rule "NewCustomer".
```

Because of the rule priority changes that you made, the rules are executed in the same sequence as they are shown in the Rule Set editor. Also, because you disabled reevaluation for the CalcShipping rule, it was only executed once. In the previous version of this workflow, the execution of the NewCustomer rule triggered the CalcShipping rule to be reevaluated, resulting in a different Shipping amount.

You can adjust rule priority like this if necessary. For instance, you may have some rules that must be evaluated only once, or must be evaluated in a particular sequence in order to work properly. Or you may be concerned with the performance hit associated with reevaluation of rules. If those are your business requirements or concerns, then manually adjusting the rule priority is a good way to control the rule sequence.

Using Methods Within Rules

All of the previous example rules reference properties of an object in the rule condition and actions. As an alternative, you can also execute a method within a rule condition or action. This example demonstrates the use of methods by modifying the SellItemWorkflow developed in the previous examples. Instead of referencing the OrderTotal property directly as done in the previous examples, new workflow methods are defined that retrieve or set the OrderTotal. The rule conditions and actions are then modified to invoke the new methods instead of referencing the property directly. The new methods are decorated with one of the rule attributes to identify the underlying field or property that is referenced.

Adding the Access Methods

To begin this example, open the SellItemWorkflow.cs file in the code editor. You need to add two new methods that reference the OrderTotal property of the SellItem object. The revised code for the SellItemWorkflow.cs file is shown in Listing 11-5.

Listing 11-5. *Revised SellItemWorkflow.cs File with Access Methods*

```
using System;
using System.Workflow.Activities;
using System.Workflow.Activities.Rules; //needed for rule attributes

namespace SharedWorkflows
{
    /// <summary>
    /// Processes a sales item using a RuleSet
    /// </summary>
    public sealed partial class SellItemWorkflow
        : SequentialWorkflowActivity
    {
        private SalesItem _salesItem;

        public SalesItem SalesItem
        {
            get { return _salesItem; }
            set { _salesItem = value; }
        }

        public SellItemWorkflow()
        {
            InitializeComponent();
        }
```

```
    [RuleRead("SalesItem/OrderTotal")]
    public Double GetOrderTotal()
    {
        return SalesItem.OrderTotal;
    }

    [RuleWrite("SalesItem/OrderTotal")]
    public void SetOrderTotal(Double newTotal)
    {
        SalesItem.OrderTotal = newTotal;
    }
  }
}
```

The two new methods (GetOrderTotal and SetOrderTotal) are simple access methods that retrieve or update the OrderTotal property. Most importantly, the methods contain the rule attributes that identify the property that is referenced by the method. If a method references more than one property, you can include multiple instances of these attributes on each method.

The GetOrderTotal has the RuleReadAttribute to indicate that the OrderTotal property of the SalesItem object is read by the method. Likewise, the SetOrderTotal method has the RuleWriteAttribute to indicate that the same property is modified by the method. These attributes are used by the rules engine to determine the dependencies when these methods are referenced by a rule.

The path to the variable that you specify in the rule attributes is important. The path is always relative to the target object that the RuleSet is executed against. Since the workflow is using a PolicyActivity to execute the RuleSet, the target object for the RuleSet is the workflow itself. That's why the path includes the workflow property name (SalesItem) followed by the property of this object (OrderTotal).

Using the Methods in the RuleSet

You can now switch to the workflow designer for the SellItemWorkflow, select the PolicyActivity, and open the Rule Set editor from the Properties window. Modify the CalcTotal rule to use the values shown in Table 11-9.

Table 11-9. *CalcTotal Rule Definition Using Methods*

Property	Value
Name	CalcTotal
Priority	0 (the default)
Reevaluation	Always (the default)
Condition	this.SalesItem.Quantity > 10
Then Actions	this.SetOrderTotal(this.SalesItem.Quantity * (this.SalesItem.ItemPrice * 0.95))
Else Actions	this.SetOrderTotal(this.SalesItem.Quantity * this.SalesItem.ItemPrice)

Notice that the actions now use the SetOrderTotal method to update the OrderTotal property. For this example, the Priority and Reevaluation properties are also reset to their original default values.

Tables 11-10 and 11-11 show you the revised values that you'll need to define the `CalcShipping` and `NewCustomer` rules.

Table 11-10. *CalcShipping Rule Definition Using Methods*

Property	Value
Name	`CalcShipping`
Priority	0 (the default)
Reevaluation	Always (the default)
Condition	`this.GetOrderTotal() > 100.0`
Then Actions	`this.SalesItem.Shipping = 0`
Else Actions	`this.SalesItem.Shipping = this.SalesItem.Quantity * 0.95`

Table 11-11. *NewCustomer Rule Definition Using Methods*

Property	Value
Name	`NewCustomer`
Priority	0 (the default)
Reevaluation	Always (the default)
Condition	`this.SalesItem.IsNewCustomer`
Then Actions	`this.SetOrderTotal(this.GetOrderTotal() - 10.0)`
Else Actions	

After saving the `RuleSet` changes by pressing OK and rebuilding the `SharedWorkflows` project, you should be able to test these changes. If you run the same `ConsoleSellItem` application, you should see the same results as the original version of the workflow that referenced the `OrderTotal` directly (the very first example in this chapter).

Identifying Indirect Relationships

It is also possible that the method you invoke from a rule is not the one that directly uses or modifies a field or a property. The method you invoke from a rule may call another method that does the real work. In this case, you can place the `RuleInvokeAttribute` on a method, using it to identify another method that the attributed method calls. The called method would have the `RuleReadAttribute` or the `RuleWriteAttribute` depending on the work done by the method.

For example, you can rewrite the `SetOrderTotal` method introduced in the last example so that it calls another method to update the `OrderTotal` property. The revised code might look like this:

```
[RuleInvoke("PrivateOrderTotalMethod")]
public void SetOrderTotal(Double newTotal)
{
    PrivateOrderTotalMethod(newTotal);
}

[RuleWrite("SalesItem/OrderTotal")]
private void PrivateOrderTotalMethod(Double newTotal)
{
    SalesItem.OrderTotal = newTotal;
}
```

The SetOrderTotal method no longer has a direct dependency on the OrderTotal property. But it now calls the PrivateOrderTotalMethod which does modify this property. The SetOrderTotal method includes the RuleInvokeAttribute, identifying the private method that updates the property. The private method includes the RuleWriteAttribute to indicate that it modifies the OrderTotal property. Because the code identifies this indirect relationship with the rule attributes, the rules engine is able to correctly identify the dependencies.

If you were to make these changes, rebuild the SharedWorkflows project, and execute the ConsoleSellItem application, you would see that the results are the same as the last example.

Executing a RuleSet in Code

In the previous examples, a PolicyActivity was used to execute a RuleSet within a workflow. Using the PolicyActivity is the easiest way to access the rules engine, but as an alternative, you can also execute a RuleSet directly in code.

■**Note** Related information on workflow and rules serialization can be found in Chapter 16.

In this example, you will execute the CalculateItemTotals RuleSet in code rather than from a PolicyActivity. This example assumes that this RuleSet is where you last left it from the prior example. This means that the RuleSet that references the SetOrderTotal and GetOrderTotal access methods is assumed to be the current version.

To execute a RuleSet in code, you will create a new workflow that contains a single CodeActivity instead of a PolicyActivity. The ExecuteCode event handler for the CodeActivity will contain all of the code necessary to deserialize and execute the CalculateItemTotals RuleSet.

■**Note** This example assumes that the SellItemWorkflow that you developed in the previous examples still exists. You need the existing SellItemWorkflow since you will be executing the serialized version of the RuleSet from this workflow. For this reason, you will create a new workflow for this example instead of modifying the existing one.

Implementing the SellItemSerializedWorkflow

To begin this example, add a new sequential workflow to the current solution and name it SellItemSerializedWorkflow. Drag and drop a CodeActivity onto the empty workflow, name it codeExecuteRuleSet, and then double-click the activity to add a handler for the ExecuteCode event. Listing 11-6 shows the complete code that you'll need for the SellItemSerializedWorkflow.cs file.

Listing 11-6. *Complete SellItemSerializedWorkflow.cs File*

```csharp
using System;
using System.IO;
using System.Xml;
using System.Reflection;
using System.Workflow.Activities;
using System.Workflow.Activities.Rules;
using System.Workflow.ComponentModel.Compiler;
using System.Workflow.ComponentModel.Serialization;

namespace SharedWorkflows
{
    /// <summary>
    /// Processes a sales item using a RuleSet definition
    /// that is deserialized from an embedded .rules resource
    /// </summary>
    public sealed partial class SellItemSerializedWorkflow
        : SequentialWorkflowActivity
    {
        private SalesItem _salesItem;

        public SalesItem SalesItem
        {
            get { return _salesItem; }
            set { _salesItem = value; }
        }

        public SellItemSerializedWorkflow()
        {
            InitializeComponent();
        }

        [RuleRead("SalesItem/OrderTotal")]
        public Double GetOrderTotal()
        {
            return SalesItem.OrderTotal;
        }

        [RuleInvoke("PrivateOrderTotalMethod")]
        public void SetOrderTotal(Double newTotal)
        {
            PrivateOrderTotalMethod(newTotal);
        }

        [RuleWrite("SalesItem/OrderTotal")]
        private void PrivateOrderTotalMethod(Double newTotal)
        {
            SalesItem.OrderTotal = newTotal;
        }
```

The SalesItem property and the access methods (GetOrderTotal, SetOrderTotal, and PrivateOrderTotalMethod) can all be copied from the SellItemWorkflow without any changes. They are needed because the current version of the CalculateItemTotals RuleSet references these methods.

```
/// <summary>
/// Execute a RuleSet definition read from
/// a file
/// </summary>
/// <param name="sender"></param>
/// <param name="e"></param>
private void codeExecuteRuleSet_ExecuteCode(
    object sender, EventArgs e)
{
    //get a stream from the embedded .rules resource
    Assembly assembly = Assembly.GetAssembly(typeof(SellItemWorkflow));
    Stream stream = assembly.GetManifestResourceStream(
        "SharedWorkflows.SellItemWorkflow.rules");
```

The ExecuteCode method begins by reading the serialized definition of the rules for the SellItemWorkflow. These rules are saved as an embedded resource in the SharedWorkflows project and are referenced and retrieved as a Stream. This example retrieves the rules from the embedded resource as a convenience since they are readily available in this form. As an alternative, you could just as easily retrieve the rules from an externally saved .rules file. The only requirement is that you create a Stream that can be used by the code that follows.

```
using (XmlReader xmlReader = XmlReader.Create(
    new StreamReader(stream)))
{
    WorkflowMarkupSerializer markupSerializer
        = new WorkflowMarkupSerializer();
    //deserialize the rule definitions
    RuleDefinitions ruleDefinitions
        = markupSerializer.Deserialize(xmlReader) as RuleDefinitions;
```

A special WorkflowMarkupSerializer class is used to deserialize the rules. The result is an instance of the RuleDefinitions class. This class is a container that represents the contents of an entire .rules file. Within it are the definitions for one or more RuleSet instances.

```
if (ruleDefinitions != null)
{
    if (ruleDefinitions.RuleSets.Contains("CalculateItemTotals"))
    {
        RuleSet rs
            = ruleDefinitions.RuleSets["CalculateItemTotals"];
        //validate and execute the RuleSet against this
        //workflow instance
        RuleValidation validation = new RuleValidation(
            typeof(SellItemSerializedWorkflow), null);
```

After deserializing the .rules file (the embedded resource in this case) into a RuleDefinitions object, the CalculateItemTotals RuleSet is retrieved. A RuleValidation object is created next. The RuleValidation object is used to verify whether the rules defined within a RuleSet are valid for a specified type of object. In this case a RuleValidation object is created for a Type of SellItemSerializedWorkflow since the code is about to execute the RuleSet against this workflow.

```
                        if (rs.Validate(validation))
                        {
                            RuleExecution execution
                                = new RuleExecution(validation, this);
                            rs.Execute(execution);
                        }
                        else
                        {
                            foreach (ValidationError error in validation.Errors)
                            {
                                Console.WriteLine(error.ErrorText);
                            }
                        }
```

After validating the RuleSet using the RuleValidation object, a RuleExecution object is created. RuleExecution is an execution wrapper that brings together the RuleValidation object and the target that the RuleSet will be executed against. In this example, the code executes the RuleSet against the workflow instance (this). The Execute method of the RuleSet is then used to execute the RuleSet against the target workflow instance.

If the RuleSet fails validation, the RuleValidation object provides a collection of validation errors that are displayed on the Console.

```
                    }
                }
            }
        }
    }
}
```

Testing the Workflow

To execute this code from the ConsoleSellItem application, you need to make one minor change to the SellItemTest.cs file. Change the name of the workflow that the code starts from SellItemWorkflow to SellItemSerializedWorkflow. The code to change is in the ExecuteWorkflow method and is shown here:

```
private static void ExecuteWorkflow(
    WorkflowRuntimeManager manager, SalesItem item)
{
    DisplaySalesItem(item, "Before");

    //create a dictionary with input arguments
    Dictionary<String, Object> wfArguments
        = new Dictionary<string, object>();
    wfArguments.Add("SalesItem", item);

    //execute the workflow
    WorkflowInstanceWrapper instance = manager.StartWorkflow(
        typeof(SharedWorkflows.SellItemSerializedWorkflow), wfArguments);

    manager.WaitAll(5000);
```

```
    if (instance.Exception != null)
    {
        Console.WriteLine("EXCEPTION: {0}",
            instance.Exception.Message);
    }
    else
    {
        DisplaySalesItem(item, "After");
    }
}
```

After building the solution, you should be able to execute the ConsoleSellItem application. The results for this example should be consistent with the previous results.

Using the PolicyActivity is obviously much easier than this example since it eliminates the need for all of this code. However, part of the appeal of using declarative rules is the ability to load and execute rules that have been persisted separately from other parts of the application. Deserializing and executing rules from a Stream like this provides a great deal of flexibility that your application may require.

Constructing a RuleSet in Code

The previous example deserializes and executes a RuleSet that had been saved as an embedded resource of the project (a .rules file). The RuleSet was originally created by the Rule Set editor. One final alternative that is available when working with rules is to construct the RuleSet completely in code.

■**Note** This is by far the most difficult way to use rules and is not recommended for most applications.

You may have the need to construct a RuleSet in code like this for specialized situations. Perhaps your rule-based application has the need to build rules dynamically based on data obtained at runtime from the end users. In this case, building a RuleSet in code may be the appropriate solution.

Implementing the SellItemInCodeWorkflow

Like the last example, this workflow will include a single CodeActivity. The ExecuteCode handler for this activity will contain the code that builds a RuleSet from scratch and then executes it.

Add a new sequential workflow to the current solution and name it SellItemInCodeWorkflow. Drag and drop a CodeActivity onto the workflow and name it codeExecuteRuleSet. Double-click the activity to add a handler for the ExecuteCode event.

■**Note** The example code shown here only implements the first rule from the previous examples (CalcTotal). The other rules would be constructed in a similar way as this first rule and don't introduce any new concepts that require review here.

Listing 11-7 is the complete code for the SellItemInCodeWorkflow.cs file.

Listing 11-7. *Complete SellItemInCodeWorkflow.cs File*

```
using System;
using System.Workflow.Activities;
using System.Workflow.Activities.Rules;
using System.Workflow.ComponentModel.Compiler;
using System.CodeDom;

namespace SharedWorkflows
{
    /// <summary>
    /// Processes a sales item using a RuleSet composed
    /// and executed in code
    /// </summary>
    public sealed partial class SellItemInCodeWorkflow
        : SequentialWorkflowActivity
    {
        private SalesItem _salesItem;

        public SalesItem SalesItem
        {
            get { return _salesItem; }
            set { _salesItem = value; }
        }

        public SellItemInCodeWorkflow()
        {
            InitializeComponent();
        }
```

This workflow will create a `RuleSet` that works with the same `SalesItem` object used in the previous examples. Therefore, you'll need a `SalesItem` property that allows the host application to pass in a test object.

```
        /// <summary>
        /// Execute a RuleSet in code
        /// </summary>
        /// <param name="sender"></param>
        /// <param name="e"></param>
        private void codeExecuteRuleSet_ExecuteCode(
            object sender, EventArgs e)
        {
            //create references to properties
            CodeThisReferenceExpression codeThis
                = new CodeThisReferenceExpression();
            CodePropertyReferenceExpression quantityRef
                = new CodePropertyReferenceExpression(codeThis, "Quantity");
            CodePropertyReferenceExpression itemPriceRef
                = new CodePropertyReferenceExpression(codeThis, "ItemPrice");
            CodePropertyReferenceExpression orderTotalRef
                = new CodePropertyReferenceExpression(codeThis, "OrderTotal");
```

The `ExecuteCode` event handler begins by creating `CodeDom` reference expression objects. Each of these objects provides a reference for one of the properties of the `SellItem` object.

```
//create the ruleset
RuleSet rs = new RuleSet("CalculateItemTotals");

//
//define the CalcTotal rule
//
Rule rule = new Rule("CalcTotal");

//IF this.SalesItem.Quantity > 10
CodeBinaryOperatorExpression condition
    = new CodeBinaryOperatorExpression(
        quantityRef, CodeBinaryOperatorType.GreaterThan,
        new CodePrimitiveExpression(10));
rule.Condition = new RuleExpressionCondition(condition);
```

Next, a RuleSet and a Rule are created and named. The RuleExpressionCondition is constructed using a CodeBinaryOperatorExpression (another CodeDom object). The condition references the Quantity property and compares it to a value of 10.

```
//THEN this.SalesItem.OrderTotal = this.SalesItem.Quantity *
//  (this.SalesItem.ItemPrice * 0.95)
CodeAssignStatement assignWithDiscount
    = new CodeAssignStatement(orderTotalRef,
        new CodeBinaryOperatorExpression(
            quantityRef, CodeBinaryOperatorType.Multiply,
                new CodeBinaryOperatorExpression(itemPriceRef,
                    CodeBinaryOperatorType.Multiply,
                    new CodePrimitiveExpression(0.95))));
rule.ThenActions.Add(new RuleStatementAction(assignWithDiscount));

//ELSE this.SalesItem.OrderTotal = this.SalesItem.Quantity *
//   this.SalesItem.ItemPrice
CodeAssignStatement assignWithoutDiscount
    = new CodeAssignStatement(orderTotalRef,
        new CodeBinaryOperatorExpression(
            quantityRef, CodeBinaryOperatorType.Multiply,
            itemPriceRef));
rule.ElseActions.Add(new RuleStatementAction(assignWithoutDiscount));
```

The two rule actions (*then* and *else*) are now constructed and added to the Rule object. The code shown in this section is a good example of why you won't want to build a Rule in code as a normal practice. The CodeDom code to construct just this single action is dense and not intuitive at all.

```
//add rule to ruleset
rs.Rules.Add(rule);

//validate and execute the RuleSet against the
//SalesItem property
RuleValidation validation
    = new RuleValidation(typeof(SalesItem), null);
if (rs.Validate(validation))
{
    RuleExecution execution = new RuleExecution(validation, SalesItem);
    rs.Execute(execution);
}
```

```
        else
        {
            foreach (ValidationError error in validation.Errors)
            {
                Console.WriteLine(error.ErrorText);
            }
        }
    }
```

After constructing the Rule and the RuleSet, the code to validate and execute the RuleSet is similar to the previous example. One difference is that this code validates and executes the RuleSet against the SalesItem property of the workflow, not the workflow itself. This was done to illustrate the point that you can execute a RuleSet against any type of object, not just an activity or workflow.

```
        }
    }
}
```

Testing the Workflow

The same ConsoleSellItem application can be used to execute this workflow. You only need to change the name of the workflow to execute as you did in the last example. This time, change the workflow Type to execute to SellItemInCodeWorkflow. When you execute this application, you should see these results:

```
Executing SellItemWorkflow
Before:
  ItemPrice      = $10.00
  Quantity       = 4
  OrderTotal     = $0.00
  Shipping       = $0.00
  IsNewCustomer = False
After:
  ItemPrice      = $10.00
  Quantity       = 4
  OrderTotal     = $40.00
  Shipping       = $0.00
  IsNewCustomer = False
Completed SellItemWorkflow

Executing SellItemWorkflow (Discounts)
Before:
  ItemPrice      = $10.00
  Quantity       = 11
  OrderTotal     = $0.00
  Shipping       = $0.00
  IsNewCustomer = False
After:
  ItemPrice      = $10.00
  Quantity       = 11
  OrderTotal     = $104.50
  Shipping       = $0.00
  IsNewCustomer = False
Completed SellItemWorkflow (Discounts)
```

```
Executing SellItemWorkflow (New Customer)
Before:
  ItemPrice     = $10.00
  Quantity      = 11
  OrderTotal    = $0.00
  Shipping      = $0.00
  IsNewCustomer = True
After:
  ItemPrice     = $10.00
  Quantity      = 11
  OrderTotal    = $104.50
  Shipping      = $0.00
  IsNewCustomer = True
Completed SellItemWorkflow (New Customer)

Press any key to exit
```

The results from this workflow are different from all previous examples because only the first rule is constructed in code. But that single rule is producing the expected results by calculating the OrderTotal.

Constructing a RuleSet directly in code is clearly not the easiest way to incorporate rules into your application. On the contrary, it is the most difficult way to accomplish this. However, if your application has specialized needs and requires that you construct rules from scratch, you have the ability to do so using the classes provided with WF.

Summary

The focus of this chapter was the WF support for rules. In this chapter, you learned that WF provides a rich and flexible rules evaluation engine. Rules provide another way to implement your business logic that complements workflow code, custom activities, and local services.

The chapter began with an overview of the classes used to support rules in WF along with some of the benefits of using rules. Following the overview, an example was presented that walked you through the steps necessary to implement and execute a RuleSet. A PolicyActivity was used by the workflow to execute the RuleSet. This chapter also showed you how to enable rules tracing and how to make use of the trace logs that are produced.

Additional examples in this chapter demonstrated how to control the execution sequence for individual rules and how to control forward chaining and reevaluation of rules. The chapter also showed you how to add rule attributes to methods in order to use them within a rules expression.

In addition to using the PolicyActivity to execute a RuleSet, this chapter also demonstrated how to execute a RuleSet in code. One example showed you how to deserialize a previously saved set of rules and another constructed a RuleSet entirely in code.

In the next chapter, you'll learn about the WF features that assist with workflow exception and error handling.

CHAPTER 12

Exception and Error Handling

The focus of this chapter is exception and error handling. WF provides a way to declaratively handle exceptions within the workflow model. While this doesn't completely eliminate the need to handle exceptions within your code, it does allow you to declare some cleanup logic within the workflow model, enabling easier changes to the logic as it becomes necessary.

This chapter begins with an overview of workflow exception handling. It then presents a series of short examples that demonstrate how to use the FaultHandlerActivity to declaratively define exception logic within a workflow.

Exception handling is used to clean up work for incomplete activities while compensation (covered in Chapter 10) is the undoing of work that has completed. The two mechanisms are designed to address a different set of problems. This chapter includes an example that shows you how to use both mechanisms within the same workflow.

Finally, WF also provides a way to declare activities to execute when a composite activity is canceled. The use of the CancellationHandlerActivity is demonstrated in the final section of the chapter.

Understanding Workflow Exception Handling

In general, the exception handling rules that apply when you develop traditional .NET applications also apply to workflow development. In traditional .NET development, if an exception is thrown directly by you (or as a byproduct of something that you did), you have the option of catching that exception and handling it. This is accomplished in C# with a try/catch block of code. If the exception is caught somewhere in code, the application continues to run. If the exception is not caught anywhere in your code, the application terminates. The exception may be caught directly in the method that caused the exception, or it may be caught farther up the call stack by another method.

Exception handling in workflow applications is similar, but there are some differences. If an exception occurs within workflow or activity code (for instance within an event handler in the workflow class or a method of a custom activity), you have the same opportunity to catch and handle that exception. If you handle the exception, the workflow continues to run. If you don't handle the exception, the workflow is terminated.

But there are differences in the way exceptions are handled in a workflow application compared to a traditional .NET application. The most important differences are summarized here and then discussed:

- An unhandled exception in a workflow terminates the workflow, not the entire application.
- Workflow exception handling is asynchronous.
- Workflow exceptions can be handled in code, or handled declaratively within the workflow model.

An unhandled exception in a workflow won't terminate the entire application. Instead, an unhandled exception will terminate the workflow instance that threw the exception. When this occurs, the workflow runtime notifies the host application of the termination by raising the WorkflowTerminated event of the WorkflowRuntime class.

The workflow runtime is able to defer handling of the exception like this because workflow exception handling is asynchronous. When an unhandled exception is thrown (one that isn't caught directly in code with a try/catch block), it is caught by the workflow runtime and placed in an internal queue for handling (similar to the way external events are handled).

Because an unhandled exception is queued by the workflow runtime, you have additional opportunities to handle it within the workflow. WF provides the FaultHandlerActivity, which allows you to declaratively handle an exception within the workflow model. Just like a C# catch statement, each FaultHandlerActivity is associated with only a single Type of Exception that it handles (catches). The FaultHandlerActivity is a composite activity that allows you to declare child activities to execute in order to handle the exception. Handling the exception usually means cleaning up any partially completed work.

One or more instances of FaultHandlerActivity can be added to a container activity named FaultHandlersActivity (note the plural form of the activity name). A single FaultHandlersActivity can be added to any composite activity. This means that you can declare fault handling logic for composite activities such as the SequenceActivity and the ParallelActivity that are commonly used as a container for other activities. Since the SequentialWorkflowActivity is derived from the SequenceActivity, you can also declare fault handlers globally for an entire sequential workflow. State machine workflows and the StateActivity don't directly support fault handlers. However, the StateInitializationActivity, the StateFinalizationActivity, and the EventDrivenActivity that are commonly used in state machine workflows do support fault handlers.

The activity that throws an exception (or causes it to be thrown) always has the first opportunity to handle the exception. If the exception isn't handled, it is passed to its parent (a composite activity or the workflow). If the parent composite activity has a FaultHandlerActivity that matches the Type of the thrown Exception, the activities within the FaultHandlerActivity are executed. If no matching FaultHandlerActivity is found, the exception is passed up the activity stack to the next parent, and so on. The final opportunity to handle the exception is at the workflow itself (in the case of a sequential workflow). If the workflow doesn't have a FaultHandlerActivity that matches the Type of the thrown Exception, the workflow is terminated.

Where you place the FaultHandlerActivity to handle an exception affects the final outcome of a workflow. For instance, if you place your fault handling activities at the workflow level, an unhandled exception may result in the premature termination of the workflow. The fault handling activities will execute, but no other main line activities of the workflow will execute. This scenario is illustrated in Figure 12-1.

In this scenario, if one of the child activities within SequenceActivityOne throws an unhandled exception, the fault handlers that have been declared at the workflow level will have an opportunity to handle the exception. No other child activities of SequenceActivityOne will execute, nor will any of the child activities of SequenceActivityTwo. As soon as the fault handler activities for the exception are complete, the workflow will terminate.

On the other hand, you can choose to also declare fault handlers for the SequenceActivity instances. This scenario is illustrated in Figure 12-2.

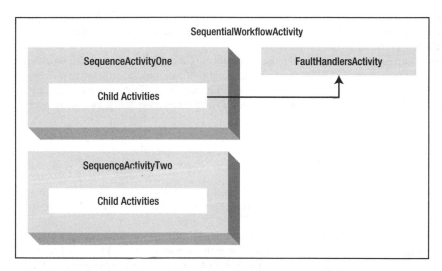

Figure 12-1. *Fault handling at the workflow*

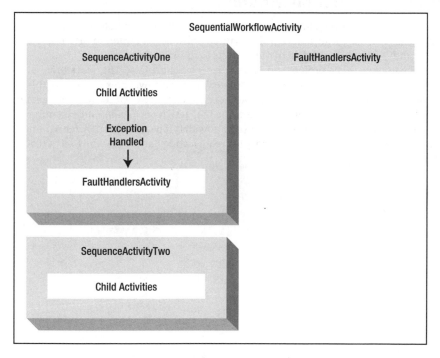

Figure 12-2. *Fault handling by a composite activity*

When the same child activity throws an exception, this time the local fault handlers that have been declared for SequenceActivityOne receive the first opportunity to handle the exception. If the exception can be handled there, there is no need to pass the exception to the workflow for handling. Just like the previous example, no other child activities of SequenceActivityOne will execute. However, the activities within SequenceActivityTwo do execute. They were not affected by the exception that was thrown, caught, and handled entirely within the bounds of SequenceActivityOne. When used this way, you can liken each SequenceActivity instance to a try/catch block in C#. The fault handlers declared within one SequenceActivity were able to catch and handle the exception before it had an adverse affect on other portions of the workflow.

Workflow exception handling doesn't take the place of try/catch blocks within your workflow and activity code. If an exception is thrown (and not caught directly in code), the activity is terminated. Workflow exception handling doesn't prevent that. But using workflow exception handling does provide you with a declarative way to perform cleanup and recovery activities when an exception does occur.

Reviewing Default Behavior

When an unhandled exception is thrown within a workflow instance, the default behavior is to terminate the workflow. The WorkflowTerminated event of the WorkflowRuntime class is then raised to notify the host application of the problem.

Before delving into the options for fault handling within a workflow, this first example demonstrates the default behavior when an unhandled exception is thrown within a workflow. Subsequent examples will build upon this code to explore the fault handling options that are provided by WF.

Implementing the ExceptionWorkflow

The first step is to create a new project using the Empty Workflow Project template and name the project SharedWorkflows. When creating a new project, you will also be prompted to save the solution file. You can use the same solution for all of the projects in this chapter.

Add a sequential workflow to the project and name it ExceptionWorkflow. This workflow requires two CodeActivity instances that you can add to the workflow now. Later versions of this workflow will add other activities. Name the first CodeActivity codeCauseException and the second codeOtherActivity. As the name implies, the purpose of the first activity is to cause an exception. The second will write a message on the Console to let you know that it has executed. After naming each CodeActivity, you can double-click each activity to create a code handler for the ExecuteCode event. The workflow should look like Figure 12-3.

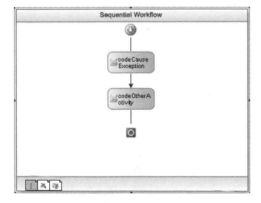

Figure 12-3. *Complete ExceptionWorkflow*

Listing 12-1 is the complete code that you'll need for the ExceptionWorkflow.cs file.

Listing 12-1. *Complete ExceptionWorkflow.cs File*

```
using System;
using System.Workflow.Activities;

namespace SharedWorkflows
{
    /// <summary>
    /// Throw an exception and observe how it is handled
    /// </summary>
    public sealed partial class ExceptionWorkflow
        : SequentialWorkflowActivity
    {
        private Int32 _testNumber;

        public Int32 TestNumber
        {
            get { return _testNumber; }
            set { _testNumber = value; }
        }

        public ExceptionWorkflow()
        {
            InitializeComponent();
        }

        /// <summary>
        /// Throw an exception
        /// </summary>
        /// <param name="sender"></param>
        /// <param name="e"></param>
        private void codeCauseException_ExecuteCode(
            object sender, EventArgs e)
        {
            switch (TestNumber)
            {
                case 1:
                    throw new DivideByZeroException("Error 1");
                case 2:
                    throw new ArithmeticException("Error 2");
                default:
                    break;
            }
        }
    }
```

The `ExecuteCode` handler for the `codeCauseException` activity throws an exception based on the value of the `TestNumber` property. The value for this property is passed in as a workflow parameter from the host application. The ability to throw these two related exception types will be used in subsequent examples to demonstrate how to declare separate handlers for each type of exception.

```
        /// <summary>
        /// Write a message to the Console
        /// </summary>
        /// <param name="sender"></param>
        /// <param name="e"></param>
```

```
            private void codeOtherActivity_ExecuteCode(
                object sender, EventArgs e)
            {
                Console.WriteLine("Executing the other CodeActivity");
            }
        }
    }
}
```

Testing the Workflow

To test the `ExceptionWorkflow`, you can create a `Console` application. Add a new Sequential Workflow Console Application to the solution and name it `ConsoleException`. Delete `Workflow1` that was added to this project by the template since it will not be used. Add these additional references to this project:

- `SharedWorkflows`
- `Bukovics.Workflow.Hosting`

The `SharedWorkflows` and `Bukovics.Workflow.Hosting` references are project references. The `Bukovics.Workflow.Hosting` project was originally developed in Chapter 4. You should add it as an existing project to your current solution in order to reference it.

Add a new C# class to the `ConsoleException` project and name it `ExceptionTest`. This class will have all of the code needed to host the workflow runtime and execute the `ExceptionWorkflow`. Listing 12-2 is the complete code for the `ExceptionTest.cs` file.

Listing 12-2. *Complete ExceptionTest.cs File*

```
using System;
using System.Collections.Generic;
using System.Workflow.Runtime;

using Bukovics.Workflow.Hosting;
using SharedWorkflows;

namespace ConsoleException
{
    /// <summary>
    /// Test the ExceptionWorkflow
    /// </summary>
    public class ExceptionTest
    {
        public static void Run()
        {
            using (WorkflowRuntimeManager manager
                = new WorkflowRuntimeManager(new WorkflowRuntime()))
            {
                manager.WorkflowRuntime.StartRuntime();

                Console.WriteLine("Executing ExceptionWorkflow Value 1");
                ExecuteWorkflow(manager, 1);
                Console.WriteLine("Completed ExceptionWorkflow Value 1\n\r");
```

```
                Console.WriteLine("Executing ExceptionWorkflow Value 2");
                ExecuteWorkflow(manager, 2);
                Console.WriteLine("Completed ExceptionWorkflow Value 2\n\r");
            }
        }

        /// <summary>
        /// Execute the workflow
        /// </summary>
        /// <param name="item"></param>
        private static void ExecuteWorkflow(
            WorkflowRuntimeManager manager, Int32 testNumber)
        {
            //create a dictionary with input arguments
            Dictionary<String, Object> wfArguments
                = new Dictionary<string, object>();
            wfArguments.Add("TestNumber", testNumber);

            //execute the workflow
            WorkflowInstanceWrapper instance = manager.StartWorkflow(
                typeof(SharedWorkflows.ExceptionWorkflow), wfArguments);
            manager.WaitAll(5000);

            if (instance.Exception != null)
            {
                Console.WriteLine("EXCEPTION: {0}: {1}",
                    instance.Exception.GetType().Name,
                    instance.Exception.Message);
            }
        }
    }
}
```

This code executes the ExceptionWorkflow twice, first passing a value of 1 and then with a value of 2. This should cause a DivideByZeroException to be thrown for the first workflow instance and an ArithmeticException for the second.

The WorkflowRuntimeManager and WorkflowInstanceWrapper classes were developed in Chapter 4. If you refer back to the code in that chapter, you'll see that WorkflowRuntimeManager handles the WorkflowTerminated event of the WorkflowRuntime object. When this event is handled, it saves the thrown exception in the Exception property of the WorkflowInstanceWrapper instance. This allows the highlighted code in Listing 12-2 to reference the exception that was thrown by the workflow.

To execute this test, you also need to add the code shown here to the Program.cs file:

```
using System;

namespace ConsoleException
{
    public class Program
    {
        static void Main(string[] args)
        {
            ExceptionTest.Run();
```

```
            Console.WriteLine("Press any key to exit");
            Console.ReadLine();
        }
    }
}
```

When you build and execute the ConsoleException application, you should see these results:

```
Executing ExceptionWorkflow Value 1
EXCEPTION: DivideByZeroException: Error 1
Completed ExceptionWorkflow Value 1

Executing ExceptionWorkflow Value 2
EXCEPTION: ArithmeticException: Error 2
Completed ExceptionWorkflow Value 2

Press any key to exit
```

As expected, the test results show that the workflow exceptions were passed back to the host application via the WorkflowTerminated event. Notice also that there is no sign of the message from the second CodeActivity. This means that as soon as the first CodeActivity raises an unhandled exception, the workflow is terminated without any further processing of activities.

■**Tip** If you execute the test application in debug mode directly from within Visual Studio (F5), you may hit a breakpoint as each exception is thrown. This is the normal behavior when the Visual Studio debug assistants are enabled. If you don't want this behavior, you can execute the application using the Start Without Debugging option (CTRL-F5 if you have the default key mappings). Or you can disable the debug assistants from the Debug, Exceptions main menu.

Using FaultHandlerActivity

The previous example demonstrates the default behavior when a workflow instance raises an unhandled exception. In this example, you will modify the same ExceptionWorkflow from the previous example to handle exceptions within the workflow. You will first add a single FaultHandlerActivity to the workflow that will handle both of the exceptions that are raised. After viewing the results with a single FaultHandlerActivity, you will add a second FaultHandlerActivity to handle the more specific DivideByZeroException.

Handling ArithmeticException

Start by opening the ExceptionWorkflow in the workflow designer. Fault handlers are added from an alternative designer view that is accessible from the main Workflow menu in Visual Studio, or from the context menu of the designer. For instance, if you right-click the ExceptionWorkflow, you should see a context menu that looks like Figure 12-4.

The FaultHandlersActivity designer contains two parts. The top part is a filmstrip viewer that allows you to work with multiple FaultHandlerActivity instances. Each FaultHandlerActivity handles a single Type of Exception. The lower portion of the designer is where you add child activities to the selected FaultHandlerActivity.

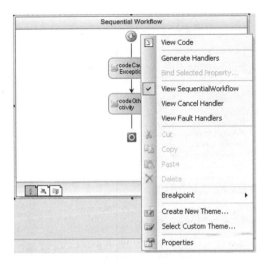

Figure 12-4. *Workflow context menu*

When you select the View Fault Handlers option, the view will change to the empty `FaultHandlersActivity` shown in Figure 12-5. When you are ready to return to the main view, you select View SequentialWorkflow from the context menu.

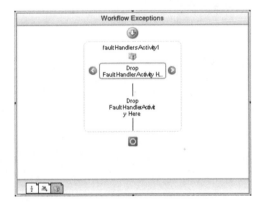

Figure 12-5. *Empty FaultHandlersActivity for ExceptionWorkflow*

You declare activities to handle an exception by first dragging and dropping a `FaultHandlerActivity` onto the top portion (the filmstrip) of the designer. You then add the exception handling child activities to the bottom of the designer. If you have multiple `FaultHandlerActivity` instances, you select one at a time in the top portion of the designer to see their respective child activities in the bottom portion.

For this example, you need to add a `FaultHandlerActivity` to handle `System.ArithmeticException`. Drag and drop a `FaultHandlerActivity` onto the top part of the `FaultHandlersActivity` and name it `faultHandlerArithmetic`. Next, click the ellipsis for the `FaultType` property of the activity to view the Type Selector dialog. This is a common workflow dialog that allows you to select a `Type` from a referenced assembly. In this case, the dialog filters the types so that only those that derive from `System.Exception` are shown. Figure 12-6 shows the Type Selector dialog with the correct `Exception` selected.

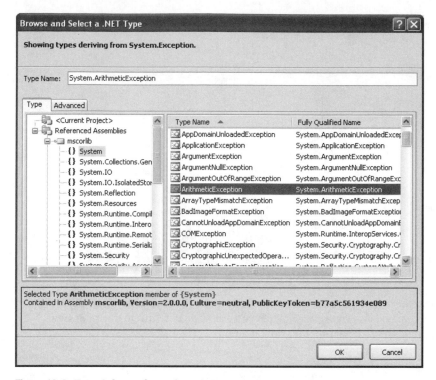

Figure 12-6. *Type Selector for ArthmeticException*

To handle this exception, you will simply write a message to the Console. To do this, drag and drop a CodeActivity onto the bottom pane of the FaultHandlersActivity and name it codeHandleArithmetic. Double-click the new CodeActivity to add a handler for the ExecuteCode event. The Fault Handlers view should now look like Figure 12-7.

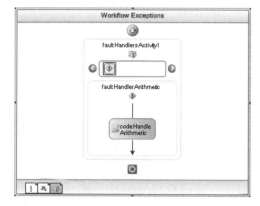

Figure 12-7. *Fault handlers for ExceptionWorkflow*

You're done with the Fault Handlers view for this example, so you can switch back to the main designer view by selecting View SequentialWorkflow from the context or main Workflow menu.

The only remaining task is to add code to the ExecuteCode handler of the new codeHandleArithmetic activity that you added. Switch to the code view and add the code shown in Listing 12-3 to the existing ExceptionWorkflow.cs file.

Listing 12-3. *Revised ExceptionWorkflow.cs File*

```
using System;
using System.Workflow.ComponentModel;
using System.Workflow.Activities;

namespace SharedWorkflows
{
    /// <summary>
    /// Throw an exception and observe how it is handled
    /// </summary>
    public sealed partial class ExceptionWorkflow
        : SequentialWorkflowActivity
    {

...

        /// <summary>
        /// Handle an ArithmeticException
        /// </summary>
        /// <param name="sender"></param>
        /// <param name="e"></param>
        private void codeHandleArithmetic_ExecuteCode(
            object sender, EventArgs e)
        {
            //get the parent fault handler activity in order
            //to retrieve the Exception message
            FaultHandlerActivity faultActivity
                = ((Activity)sender).Parent as FaultHandlerActivity;
            String message = String.Empty;
            if (faultActivity != null)
            {
                message = faultActivity.Fault.Message;
            }
            Console.WriteLine("Handle ArithmeticException: {0}",
                message);
        }
    }
}
```

The goal of this code is to handle the exception by writing the Exception.Message property to the Console. To obtain the message, the code must first navigate to the FaultHandlerActivity that caught the exception. It does this using the Parent property of the sender parameter. The sender in this case is the CodeActivity, therefore the Parent is the FaultHandlerActivity. The FaultHandlerActivity has a Fault property which contains a reference to the Exception that was raised. Once you have a reference to this activity, the message is written to the Console.

This time when you execute the ConsoleException application, the results look like this:

```
Executing ExceptionWorkflow Value 1
Handle ArithmeticException: Error 1
Completed ExceptionWorkflow Value 1

Executing ExceptionWorkflow Value 2
Handle ArithmeticException: Error 2
Completed ExceptionWorkflow Value 2

Press any key to exit
```

The highlighted lines were written by the codeHandleArithmetic activity. Since the exceptions were handled within the workflow, the host application was not notified of the exception. And the additional CodeActivity (codeOtherActivity) within the main line of the workflow still didn't execute. Since the first CodeActivity threw an exception, the flow of control immediately went to the FaultHandlerActivity that handled the exception.

Even though there were two different types of exceptions thrown, the single FaultHandlerActivity that you added was able to handle both of them. This works because both of the exceptions derive from the same parent exception class of System.ArithmeticException.

Handling DivideByZeroException

The ExceptionWorkflow now handles both of the possible exceptions with a single FaultHandlerActivity for System.ArithmeticException. In this short example, you will add a second FaultHandlerActivity to explicitly handle DivideByZeroException.

Open the ExceptionWorkflow in the workflow designer again and switch to the Fault Handler view for the workflow. Drag and drop a second FaultHandlerActivity onto the filmstrip area of the FaultHandlersActivity and name it faultHandlerDivide. Set the FaultType property of this new activity to System.DivideByZeroException. Add a child CodeActivity to faultHandlerDivide and name it codeHandleDivide. Once the CodeActivity is named, you can double-click it to add a code handler for the ExecuteCode event.

If you build the project now, it might build, but then again, it might not. You see, I neglected to say exactly where you should place the new FaultHandlerActivity. Where you place the new FaultHandlerActivity (faultHandlerDivide) in relation to the original one (faultHandlerArithmetic) makes all the difference. FaultHandlerActivity instances must be placed from left to right, starting with the most specific Type of Exception and moving to more general types to the right.

If you place the new activity faultHandlerDivide to the right of faultHandlerArithmetic, your project won't build. You should receive these errors:

```
Error 1 Activity 'faultHandlersActivity1' validation failed:
A FaultHandlerActivity for exception type 'DivideByZeroException'
must be added before the handler for exception type 'ArithmeticException'.
Error 2 A FaultHandlerActivity for exception type 'DivideByZeroException'
must be added before the handler for exception type 'ArithmeticException'.
```

To solve this little problem, you can drag the faultHandlerDivide activity to the left of faultHandlerArithmetic. You can also select one of the activities and right-click to bring up the context menu. Depending on which activity you've selected, you should see a Move Left or Move Right option that changes the activity sequence.

If you got the activities in the proper sequence, congratulations! You were either very lucky or you instinctively understood that the sequence of FaultHandlerActivity instances works the same way as the C# catch statements. You must place the most specific exception handler first, followed by handlers for more general exceptions.

To complete the workflow, you need to add code to the codeHandleDivide ExecuteCode handler. The code is almost exactly the same as the code handler for the other exception. The code that you need to add to the ExceptionWorkflow.cs file is shown in Listing 12-4.

Listing 12-4. *Revised ExceptionWorkflow.cs File with Second Exception Handler*

```csharp
using System;
using System.Workflow.ComponentModel;
using System.Workflow.Activities;

namespace SharedWorkflows
{
    /// <summary>
    /// Throw an exception and observe how it is handled
    /// </summary>
    public sealed partial class ExceptionWorkflow
        : SequentialWorkflowActivity
    {

...

        /// <summary>
        /// Handle a DivideByZeroException
        /// </summary>
        /// <param name="sender"></param>
        /// <param name="e"></param>
        private void codeHandleDivide_ExecuteCode(
            object sender, EventArgs e)
        {
            FaultHandlerActivity faultActivity
                = ((Activity)sender).Parent as FaultHandlerActivity;
            String message = String.Empty;
            if (faultActivity != null)
            {
                message = faultActivity.Fault.Message;
            }
            Console.WriteLine("Handle DivideByZeroException: {0}",
                message);
        }
    }
}
```

When you execute the ConsoleException application, the revised results look like this:

```
Executing ExceptionWorkflow Value 1
Handle DivideByZeroException: Error 1
Completed ExceptionWorkflow Value 1

Executing ExceptionWorkflow Value 2
Handle ArithmeticException: Error 2
Completed ExceptionWorkflow Value 2

Press any key to exit
```

This time the Console messages show that each type of exception is handled by a separate FaultHandlerActivity. In a real application, this allows you to declare a different set of activities to execute in order to handle each distinct type of exception. However, the second main line activity of the workflow (codeOtherActivity) still doesn't execute. The next example will remedy this situation.

Containing the Exception

In the previous examples, you were able to handle two different exception types using fault handlers that were declared globally for the entire workflow. This handled the exceptions and prevented them from being reported to the host application. However, when the exceptions were raised, the flow of control immediately went to the appropriate fault handler, bypassing any other main line activities of the workflow.

While this may be the desired result for some workflows, it may not be suitable in all situations. Instead, you may want to contain the damage from an exception, allowing other activities to execute even if an exception is raised in one part of the workflow. To accomplish this, you can move the fault handling activities closer to the point of failure.

In this example, you will modify the same ExceptionWorkflow developed in the previous examples. You will first move the CodeActivity that raises the exceptions into a SequenceActivity. Since the SequenceActivity is a composite, it supports the declaration of fault handling activities. You will then move the FaultHandlerActivity instances you previously declared for the workflow to the new SequenceActivity. This causes the exceptions to be caught within the SequenceActivity instead of the workflow, allowing the other main line CodeActivity to execute.

To make these modifications, open the ExceptionWorkflow in the workflow designer and add a SequenceActivity to the top of the workflow. Drag the codeCauseException activity into the new SequenceActivity. The workflow should now look like Figure 12-8.

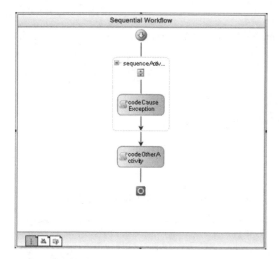

Figure 12-8. *Revised ExceptionWorkflow with SequenceActivity*

Now you need to move the existing FaultHandlerActivity instances from the workflow into the SequenceActivity. The easiest way to do this is with one simple cut-and-paste operation. First switch to the Fault Handlers view of the workflow and select both of the FaultHandlerActivity instances. You do this by clicking on the first one, then while holding down the Ctrl key, click on the second. You can cut both instances by right-clicking and selecting Cut from the context menu. Figure 12-9 shows this Cut operation.

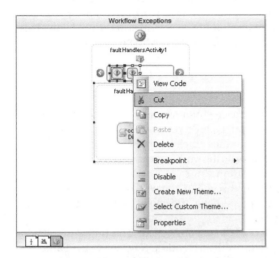

Figure 12-9. *Cutting the FaultHandlerActivity instances from the workflow*

You can now switch back to the SequentialWorkflow view, and then go into the Fault Handlers view of the SequenceActivity. Once there, paste the two activities into the FaultHandlersActivity. When you're done, the two FaultHandlerActivity instances (along with their children) should be declared within the SequenceActivity instead of the workflow.

■**Note** After pasting the two FaultHandlerActivity instances, the faultHandlerArithmetic may be listed first, which is the incorrect sequence. To correct this, you can drag the faultHandlerDivide activity to the left of the faultHandlerArithmetic.

Once these structural changes are made, you should be ready to run the ConsoleException application again without any code changes. This time, the results should look like this:

```
Executing ExceptionWorkflow Value 1
Handle DivideByZeroException: Error 1
Executing the other CodeActivity
Completed ExceptionWorkflow Value 1

Executing ExceptionWorkflow Value 2
Handle ArithmeticException: Error 2
Executing the other CodeActivity
Completed ExceptionWorkflow Value 2

Press any key to exit
```

As is the case in the last example, each exception is handled by its own FaultHandlerActivity. But now (finally), the second main line CodeActivity executes. When an exception is raised by the codeCauseException activity, it is now caught by the fault handlers declared within the

SequenceActivity. Once the exception is handled, any remaining activities within the workflow (the codeOtherActivity activity) are allowed to execute normally.

Where you place the fault handling activities is completely up to you. Depending on the requirements of the workflow, you may want to handle the faults at the workflow level. Or you may determine that it is best to handle them within one of the composite activities of the workflow. This latter approach contains the exception and allows other portions of the workflow to execute.

Rethrowing an Exception

One other useful pattern that you may use is to handle an exception within a workflow but then rethrow the exception. The benefit of this approach is that it allows you to declare cleanup activities within the workflow to handle the exception, but it also notifies other components in the application that an exception has occurred. The other components may be the workflow class itself, other composite activities farther up the activity stack, or the host application.

The ThrowActivity is used to declaratively throw a new exception. But when it is used as a child of a FaultHandlerActivity, you can bind the ThrowActivity properties to the parent FaultHandlerActivity, allowing the original Type of Exception to be rethrown.

To see this in action, you can modify the ExceptionWorkflow once again. This time you will add a ThrowActivity to the faultHandlerArithmetic to rethrow the exception. Navigate to the Fault Handlers view of the SequenceActivity and select the faultHandlerArithmetic activity. Add a ThrowActivity as the last child of the faultHandlerArithmetic. Switch to the Properties window of the new ThrowActivity and bind the properties to the parent faultHandlerArithmetic activity. Table 12-1 shows the property bindings that you need to make.

Table 12-1. *Property Bindings for throwActivity1*

Property	Binding
Fault	Activity=faultHandlerArithmetic, Path=Fault
FaultType	Activity=faultHandlerArithmetic, Path=FaultType

The revised faultHandlerArithmetic with the ThrowActivity is shown in Figure 12-10.

After saving your changes and rebuilding the SharedWorkflows project, you should be able to execute the ConsoleException application. Your results should now look like this:

```
Executing ExceptionWorkflow Value 1
Handle DivideByZeroException: Error 1
Executing the other CodeActivity
Completed ExceptionWorkflow Value 1

Executing ExceptionWorkflow Value 2
Handle ArithmeticException: Error 2
EXCEPTION: ArithmeticException: Error 2
Completed ExceptionWorkflow Value 2

Press any key to exit
```

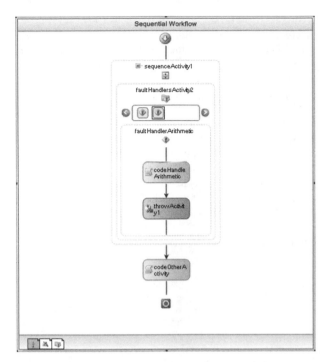

Figure 12-10. *The faultHandlerArithmetic with the ThrowActivity*

The DivideByZeroException is handled the same way as the previous example. But the ArithmeticException is handled by the CodeActivity (writing a message to the Console) and then rethrown by the ThrowActivity. This causes the second workflow instance to terminate before it has a chance to execute the other main line CodeActivity (codeOtherActivity).

Compensation and Exceptions

Exception handling and compensation are closely related but they address different problems. *Exception handling* provides a way to clean up any partially completed work. *Compensation* is the undoing of work that is completed but needs to be reversed due to an error elsewhere in the workflow.

■**Note** For more information on compensation, please refer to Chapter 10.

If you use a compensatable activity such as the CompensatableSequenceActivity, you can declare a set of activities to execute if compensation is necessary. If an unhandled exception is thrown in the workflow, the compensation logic that you declare is automatically executed. However, the key to the automatic compensation logic is that it is triggered by an unhandled exception. What happens if you also wish to handle the exception using fault handling? The answer is that the exception is no longer considered unhandled and the automatic compensation logic is not triggered.

However, you can have the best of both worlds using the CompensateActivity. The CompensateActivity allows you to manually execute the compensation logic for an activity. In the example that follows, you will develop a workflow that declares fault handling and compensation activities. When an exception is raised, it is caught by a FaultHandlerActivity, thus bypassing any automatic compensation logic. But within the FaultHandlerActivity, the CompensateActivity is used to manually trigger compensation. In a real application, the fault handling activities would be used to clean up any partially completed work. The compensation logic would be used to undo the work of the activity that previously completed.

Implementing the CompensateWorkflow

Add a new sequential workflow to the SharedWorkflows project and name it CompensateWorkflow. To define the main line of execution for the workflow, add a SequenceActivity to the empty workflow and name it sequenceMain. Next, add a CompensatableSequenceActivity as a child of sequenceMain. Now add a CodeActivity as a child of the CompensatableSequenceActivity and name it codeMainLine. Double-click the codeMainLine activity to add a handler for its ExecuteCode event.

Finally, add a ThrowActivity as a child of sequenceMain (not a child of the CompensatableSequenceActivity). Set the FaultType of the ThrowActivity to System. ApplicationException.

The main line view of the workflow should look like Figure 12-11.

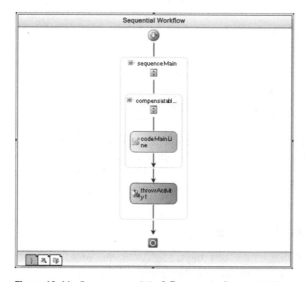

Figure 12-11. *CompensateWorkflow main line activities*

To define the compensation handler activities, right-click the CompensatableSequenceActivity and select View Compensation Handler. Add a single CodeActivity to the CompensationHandlerActivity and name it codeMainLineCompensation. Double-click the CodeActivity to add a handler for the ExecuteCode event. The compensation handler should look like Figure 12-12.

You can now return to the main view of the workflow by selecting View CompensatableSequence from the CompensatableSequenceActivity context menu.

The fault handling logic will be added to the sequenceMain activity. Right-click that activity and select View Fault Handlers. Drag and drop a FaultHandlerActivity onto the FaultHandlersActivity and name it faultHandlerAppException. Set the FaultType property of this activity to handle System. ApplicationException as the exception Type.

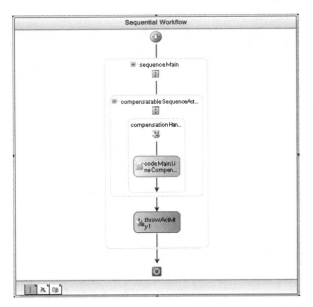

Figure 12-12. *Compensation handler for CompensateWorkflow*

You will now add two child activities to faultHandlerAppException to handle the exception. First add a CodeActivity, name it codeHandleAppException, and double-click it to add a code handler. Second, add a CompensateActivity. The CompensateActivity has a TargetActivityName that identifies the activity whose compensation logic you wish to execute. Choose sequenceMain for this property. The finished fault handler view should look like Figure 12-13.

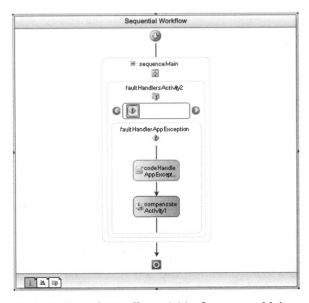

Figure 12-13. *Fault Handler activities for sequenceMain*

The workflow requires a small amount of code that should be added now. To keep this example as simple as possible, all of the code handlers write a message to the Console to let you know when they execute. Listing 12-5 is the completed code for the CompensateWorkflow.cs file.

Listing 12-5. *Complete CompensateWorkflow.cs File*

```csharp
using System;
using System.Workflow.Activities;

namespace SharedWorkflows
{
    /// <summary>
    /// Manually execute compensation code
    /// from a fault handler
    /// </summary>
    public sealed partial class CompensateWorkflow
        : SequentialWorkflowActivity
    {
        public CompensateWorkflow()
        {
            InitializeComponent();
        }

        private void codeMainLine_ExecuteCode(
            object sender, EventArgs e)
        {
            Console.WriteLine("Execute the main line CodeActivity");
        }

        private void codeMainLineCompensation_ExecuteCode(
            object sender, EventArgs e)
        {
            Console.WriteLine("Compensating the main line");
        }

        private void codeHandleAppException_ExecuteCode(
            object sender, EventArgs e)
        {
            Console.WriteLine("Handle the ApplicationException");
        }
    }
}
```

Test the Workflow

To execute this workflow, add a new Sequential Workflow Console Application to the solution and name it ConsoleCompensate. Delete Workflow1 that was added to this project, and add the usual set of project references (SharedWorkflows and Bukovics.Workflow.Hosting).

Add a new C# class to the project and name it CompensateTest. Listing 12-6 shows you the code you need to add to the CompensateTest.cs file.

Listing 12-6. *Complete CompensateTest.cs File*

```
using System;
using System.Workflow.Runtime;

using Bukovics.Workflow.Hosting;
using SharedWorkflows;

namespace ConsoleCompensate
{
    /// <summary>
    /// Test the CompensateWorkflow
    /// </summary>
    public class CompensateTest
    {
        public static void Run()
        {
            using (WorkflowRuntimeManager manager
                = new WorkflowRuntimeManager(new WorkflowRuntime()))
            {
                manager.WorkflowRuntime.StartRuntime();

                Console.WriteLine("Executing CompensateWorkflow");
                manager.StartWorkflow(
                    typeof(SharedWorkflows.CompensateWorkflow), null);
                manager.WaitAll(5000);
                Console.WriteLine("Completed CompensateWorkflow");
            }
        }
    }
}
```

You'll also need to add this code to the Program.cs file.

```
using System;

namespace ConsoleCompensate
{
    public class Program
    {
        static void Main(string[] args)
        {
            CompensateTest.Run();

            Console.WriteLine("Press any key to exit");
            Console.ReadLine();
        }
    }
}
```

When you execute the ConsoleCompensate application, you should see these results:

```
Executing CompensateWorkflow
Execute the main line CodeActivity
Handle the ApplicationException
Compensating the main line
Completed CompensateWorkflow
Press any key to exit
```

As you can see from these results, the main line CodeActivity that was a child of the CompensatableSequenceActivity completed. The exception in the main line of the workflow was then thrown and caught by the fault handler. Next, the CodeActivity that was declared in the fault handler executed (writing the message). Finally, the CompensateActivity executed, causing the compensation logic that was declared within the CompensatableSequenceActivity to execute.

In many situations, you will choose between fault handlers and compensation, not both. But in some situations, you may need to declare both types of recovery mechanisms within the same workflow. When you do, remember that the automatic compensation logic only works when an exception is unhandled. If you handle an exception with a fault handler, you will need to use the CompensateActivity to manually trigger compensation.

Using CancellationHandlerActivity

WF provides a declarative way to define activities to execute when composite activities are canceled. While this isn't directly related to exception and error handling, I've included it in this chapter since it is part of the same general theme of workflow and activity termination.

The ability to declare cancellation logic is useful in situations when you have more than one activity that is processing (in an active state) at the same time. A good example is when you are using a ParallelActivity. In a ParallelActivity there are two or more parallel branches of execution. Since all execution branches use the same workflow thread, they don't execute simultaneously but instead take turns executing their child activities. If the ParallelActivity is terminated for any reason (perhaps one of the branches raises an exception), all of the execution branches must be canceled. If cancellation handling activities have been declared for any of the branches, they will be executed in order to perform cleanup logic during cancellation.

Another example is a ListenActivity that contains multiple EventDrivenActivity instances. Each EventDrivenActivity is waiting to receive a different external event. Once one of the events has been received, the other EventDrivenActivity branches must be canceled.

Cancellation handler activities are declared as children of a CancellationHandlerActivity. One (and only one) CancellationHandlerActivity may be added to a composite activity.

Implementing the CancelHandlerWorkflow

In this example, you will implement a workflow that uses a ParallelActivity to illustrate the behavior of a CancellationHandlerActivity. The ParallelActivity will contain two execution branches, each one defined by a SequenceActivity. One of the SequenceActivity instances will include a WhileActivity that loops forever and also declares a CancellationHandlerActivity. The other SequenceActivity will throw an exception in order to terminate the entire ParallelActivity (and the workflow). As the first SequenceActivity is canceled, the cancellation handler activities that have been declared will execute.

Add a new sequential workflow to the `SharedWorkflows` project and name it `CancelHandlerWorkflow`. Drag and drop a `ParallelActivity` onto the empty workflow. The `ParallelActivity` automatically creates two `SequenceActivity` instances which are sufficient for this example. Add a `WhileActivity` to the `sequenceActivity1` and then add a `CodeActivity` to the `WhileActivity`. Name the `CodeActivity` `codeLeftBranch`, and then double-click it to add a handler for the `ExecuteCode` event.

The `WhileActivity` should execute forever, so you can add a condition to accomplish this. Select Code Condition for the Condition property, and then enter a name of `RunForever` as the code Condition name. You will add code for this condition later.

Turning your attention to `sequenceActivity2` (on the right side), add a `CodeActivity` and name it `codeRightBranch`. As usual, double-click the activity to add a code handler. Beneath the `CodeActivity`, add a `ThrowActivity` and set the `FaultType` to `System.ApplicationException`. This will throw the exception that causes the entire workflow to terminate.

The main line activities of the `CancelHandlerWorkflow` should look like Figure 12-14.

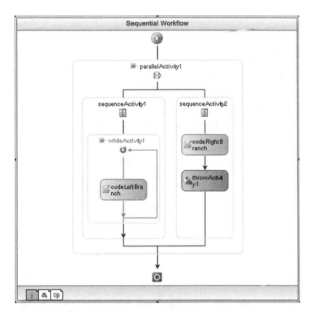

Figure 12-14. *CancelHandlerWorkflow main line activities*

To add cancellation handler activities, select `sequenceActivity1`, right-click and select View Cancel Handler. The designer view will change to an open `CancellationHandlerActivity`. Add a `CodeActivity` and name it `codeCancelHandler`. Double-click the new activity to add a code handler for the `ExecuteCode` event. The cancellation handler view should look like Figure 12-15.

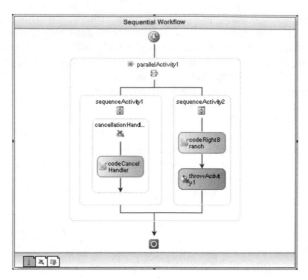

Figure 12-15. *Cancellation handler for CancelHandlerWorkflow*

This completes the visual design of the workflow. You can now add the necessary code to the CancelHandlerWorkflow.cs file. Listing 12-7 shows the completed code that you need.

Listing 12-7. *Complete CancelHandlerWorkflow.cs File*

```csharp
using System;
using System.Workflow.Activities;

namespace SharedWorkflows
{
    /// <summary>
    /// Use a CancellationHandler
    /// </summary>
    public sealed partial class CancelHandlerWorkflow
        : SequentialWorkflowActivity
    {
        public CancelHandlerWorkflow()
        {
            InitializeComponent();
        }

        private void codeLeftBranch_ExecuteCode(
            object sender, EventArgs e)
        {
            Console.WriteLine("Executing left branch CodeActivity");
        }

        private void codeRightBranch_ExecuteCode(
            object sender, EventArgs e)
        {
            Console.WriteLine("Executing right branch CodeActivity");
        }
```

```
        private void codeCancelHandler_ExecuteCode(
            object sender, EventArgs e)
        {
            Console.WriteLine(
                "Executing CancellationHandler CodeActivity");
        }

        private void RunForever(object sender, ConditionalEventArgs e)
        {
            e.Result = true;
        }
    }
}
```

The RunForever method always returns true in order to execute the WhileActivity forever. All of the CodeActivity handlers simply write a message to the Console to let you know when they execute.

Testing the Workflow

Just like the last workflow, this one doesn't require any input parameters. Therefore, you can test this workflow using the ConsoleCompensate application you used for the last example. The only necessary change is to replace all occurrences of CompensateWorkflow with CancelHandlerWorkflow in the CompensateTest.cs file.

After making the change and rebuilding the project, you should be able to execute it and see these results:

```
Executing CancelHandlerWorkflow
Executing right branch CodeActivity
Executing left branch CodeActivity
Executing left branch CodeActivity
Executing left branch CodeActivity
Executing left branch CodeActivity
Executing CancellationHandler CodeActivity
Completed CancelHandlerWorkflow
Press any key to exit
```

The results show that the left branch of the ParallelActivity executed until the exception was raised by the right branch. Your results may be slightly different since the WhileActivity may execute a different number of times depending on your processor speed. Once the exception is raised, the workflow began the process of terminating by canceling all active children. As the left branch was being canceled, the cancellation handler was executed, resulting in the message highlighted.

You won't need cancellation handlers for all of your workflows. But cancellation handler activities are a good place to declare logic if you need to perform cleanup work as an activity is canceled.

Summary

The focus of this chapter was exception and error handling. The chapter provided a brief overview of workflow exception handling and then launched into a discussion of the FaultHandlerActivity. A series of short examples were presented that demonstrated how to declaratively handle exceptions within the workflow model.

Another example showed you how to use fault handling and compensation within the same workflow and how the two mechanisms can work together.

In the final section of the chapter, the CancellationHandlerActivity was discussed and demonstrated using a short example. This activity enables you to declare logic to execute when an active composite activity is canceled.

In the next chapter, you will learn how to dynamically apply updates to executing workflow instances.

■ ■ ■

CHAPTER 13

Dynamic Workflow Updates

The focus of this chapter is dynamic workflow updates. WF provides the ability to make dynamic changes to the structure of a workflow instance. Structural changes might include adding or removing activities based on updated business requirements. When updates are applied to a workflow instance, they only affect that one instance. All other instances of the same workflow, current and future, use the original workflow definition.

This chapter begins with an overview of the dynamic update process. Following the overview, a series of examples are presented that demonstrate how to apply a set of changes to a workflow instance. The first two examples demonstrate external changes to a workflow instance, where the host application is applying the updates. The next example shows you how to dynamically update a workflow instance from within the workflow.

The rule definitions for a workflow are a likely candidate for dynamic updates. The last two examples in the chapter show you how to update a single rule condition from the host application, and how to completely replace the rule definitions for a workflow.

Understanding Dynamic Updates

You have already seen that all workflows have a structure that you declare at design time. You declare this structure using the workflow designer by dragging and dropping activities onto the workflow and then setting property values. The structure includes not only the placement of activities but also the relationships (bindings) between the activity and workflow properties. You count on the fact that the structure you defined won't change at runtime.

For instance, you may have designed and implemented a workflow that includes an `IfElseActivity` with two `IfElseBranchActivity` instances. You have confidence in the fact that when you execute an instance of that workflow, those two `IfElseBranchActivity` instances are still there. And the workflow doesn't spontaneously grow a third `IfElseBranchActivity` by itself. The workflow may include some activities that react to data and affect the flow of control within the workflow. Examples of such activities are the `WhileActivity`, the `ReplicatorActivity`, and the `ConditionedActivityGroup`. However, these activities still don't change the structure of the workflow. The structure of a live workflow instance matches the structure of the workflow that you defined. The structure doesn't change at runtime.

That is until now. WF also supports dynamic updates to workflow instances that permit you to make structural changes. The dynamic updates are applied to a single active instance of a workflow, not to a workflow definition. To change the definition, you still use the workflow designer to make changes in the normal fashion. The workflow definition acts as a template that is used to create new workflow instances. Therefore, new instances of the same workflow type are created with the original defined structure. They don't include any dynamic updates that you might have applied to another workflow instance.

What kind of updates can you apply? You can add new activities, or delete existing ones. You can replace an existing activity with a different one. You can modify property bindings, or even replace Declarative Rule Conditions. To accomplish most of these tasks, you will need to be proficient at navigating the tree of activities within a workflow. But if you can find the activity you wish to modify, you can modify it.

Why Use Dynamic Updates?

Why would you use dynamic updates? In most situations, you won't need to dynamically update active workflow instances. But business requirements do change and they may require changes to the workflow structure. If you have long-running workflow instances that are active, you may have no choice but to dynamically update them. The alternative to dynamic updates is to stop all running workflow instances and then restart them with the revised workflow definition. If they are state machine workflows, you would then have to bring them back into the state that they were in prior to the update. In this case, applying dynamic updates to active workflows may be the preferred approach.

In addition to changes in business requirements that necessitate workflow changes, you may also decide to incorporate the use of dynamic updates into your original design. For instance, you may develop a library containing dozens of custom activities, with each one performing a different business function. How would you declare the structure for a workflow that has to execute just one of these custom activities based on a runtime parameter? One option is to use a large number of `IfElseBranchActivity` instances. Each `IfElseBranchActivity` would have a condition that checks a runtime parameter and executes the appropriate custom activity if the condition is `true`. This workflow structure would work, but it is hardly simple or elegant. It requires you to prewire all of the possible conditions that execute each activity into the workflow. It also becomes difficult to add new functionality when new custom activities are added to the library.

On the other hand, the use of dynamic updates actually simplifies the design of this workflow. Instead of declaring all of the possible conditions and activities at design time, you can add code to the workflow that dynamically adds the appropriate activity at runtime. All that is needed is an association between the runtime parameter that determines which activity to execute and the `Type` of the activity. An instance of the activity can be created using reflection and then added to the appropriate location within the workflow structure. This design (using dynamic updates) is much simpler and more extensible than one that declares all possible conditions at design time.

Applying Dynamic Updates

Dynamic updates can be applied internally by the workflow instance itself, or externally by the host application. Internal updates are accomplished by code in the workflow class, perhaps in the code handler for a `CodeActivity`, or by a custom activity that you've developed to update other parts of the workflow instance. Each workflow instance executes on a single thread, executing a single activity at any one time. Because of this design, it is safe for code within the workflow (or an activity within the workflow) to apply a dynamic update at any time. The code that is applying the dynamic update is assured that no other workflow code is executing simultaneously.

When applying dynamic updates from the host application, the rules are more restrictive. A host application can only update a workflow instance if it is not actively executing. This makes sense since workflow instances execute on a separate thread that is managed by the workflow runtime. Attempting to update part of a workflow instance that is currently executing would likely produce undesirable results and is prohibited. Therefore, workflow instances must be in a nonexecuting state before the host application can dynamically apply updates to them. The following states are possible update points:

- The workflow has been created but not yet started.

- The workflow has been suspended but not yet resumed.

- The workflow is currently idled.

The easiest way to determine when a workflow is in one of these states is to handle a subset of the WorkflowRuntime events. The WorkflowCreated event is raised when you call the CreateWorkflow method of WorkflowRuntime. At this point the workflow is created and you can safely apply updates to the instance. When you call the Start method on the WorkflowInstance that is returned from CreateWorkflow, the workflow begins execution and it is no longer safe to apply updates until the workflow is suspended or idled. Calling the Start method raises the WorkflowStarted event.

The WorkflowSuspended event is raised when a workflow instance is suspended. A workflow can be suspended by the SuspendActivity declared within the workflow. If you know in advance that you want to support dynamic updates for a workflow, you might include this activity at predetermined points in the workflow to provide an opportunity for the host application to apply updates. When a workflow is suspended, it remains in this nonexecuting state until you call the Resume method on the WorkflowInstance.

Finally, the WorkflowIdled event notifies you when a workflow instance is idle. During this idled state, dynamic updates are permitted. A workflow enters the idled state when it is waiting for an event-driven activity such as a DelayActivity or a HandleExternalEventActivity. Idled workflows do not require any direct intervention from you to resume execution. They will automatically resume execution when the delay expires or the external event is received.

Changes to a workflow are made with the WorkflowChanges class (located in the System. Workflow.ComponentModel namespace). You start by creating an instance of this class that represents the proposed changes to the workflow. The constructor for this class requires the root activity of the workflow being changed. If you are applying changes internally within a workflow, you pass the C# this keyword to represent the root of the current workflow.

If you are applying changes externally from the host application, you must call the GetWorkflowDefinition method of the WorkflowInstance object to obtain the root activity and pass it to the WorkflowChanges constructor. As the name implies, GetWorkflowDefinition returns the definition of the workflow instance, not the instance itself. WF doesn't actually permit you to have external access to the live instance of a workflow, only its definition. The activity returned by GetWorkflowDefinition doesn't contain any runtime property values, so don't attempt to reference them using this definition.

Once a WorkflowChanges instance is created, you make proposed changes to the TransientWorkflow property of the WorkflowChanges object. The TransientWorkflow property is a cloned version of the workflow structure that accepts changes and is later applied to the real workflow instance. Your proposed changes generally take the form of adding or removing activities. To add an activity, you need to first locate the existing activity that will be the parent of the new activity. You can locate the parent by traversing the entire activity tree yourself (referencing the Activities property of the CompositeActivity object available from the TransientWorkflow property), or using the GetActivityByName method of the TransientWorkflow property (a CompositeActivity instance) to directly find the parent by name. Once the parent activity is found, you use the Add method to add the new activity to the existing parent. If you need to position the new activity between two existing activities, you use the Insert method.

Removing an existing activity works in a similar way. You first locate the existing activity that you wish to remove. Once located, you remove it from its parent activity (using the Remove method of the Parent.Activities property of the CompositeActivity).

After you have made your proposed changes to the WorkflowChanges object, you validate and then apply them to the workflow instance. The Validate method of WorkflowChanges checks your proposed changes against the existing workflow structure. If there are any errors, they are returned as a collection of ValidationError objects. If errors are returned, they indicate some type of structural problem with your changes. For instance, you might have added the same activity to two different parents. That's not allowed. Or you might have added a property binding to an activity (using an ActivityBind object) using an incorrect path that points to a nonexistent workflow property.

If there are no validation errors, you can apply the proposed changes to the workflow instance. If you are updating the workflow externally from the host application, you call the ApplyWorkflowChanges method of the WorkflowInstance object. If you are applying changes internally from within the workflow, you call the protected ApplyWorkflowChanges method of the workflow class (supported by both the sequential and state machine workflow classes). In either case, you pass the WorkflowChanges object containing the proposed changes to the method.

Remember that your changes only affect a single workflow instance. Subsequent instances of the same workflow that are created and started will have the original structure without your changes.

Preventing Dynamic Updates

WF provides a way to control when dynamic updates are allowed for a workflow instance. The sequence and state machine workflow classes provide a property named DynamicUpdateCondition. This is an optional rule or code condition that you can define to control when updates are allowed.

If you don't define a condition, updates to the workflow are always permitted (as long as the workflow is not actively executing as discussed previously). If you do define a condition, it is evaluated when you call the ApplyWorkflowChanges method. If the condition evaluates to true, the updates are permitted. If the condition evaluates to false, the updates are not allowed and an InvalidOperationException is raised.

In the remainder of this chapter, several examples are presented that demonstrate how to apply updates externally from the host application as well as internally from within a workflow.

Applying Updates from the Host Application

In this first example, you will develop a simple workflow that you will then update from the host application. A new activity will be added to one instance of the workflow and one of the existing activities removed from another.

To begin this example, create a new project using the Empty Workflow Project template and name the project SharedWorkflows. When creating a new project, you will also be prompted to save the solution file. You can use the same solution for all of the projects in this chapter. Add a sequential workflow to the project and name it DynamicWorkflow.

Implementing the DynamicWorkflow

The first activity that this workflow requires is a SuspendActivity. When this activity is executed, the workflow will be suspended and the host application will have an opportunity to apply updates.

Note Instead of suspending the workflow, you can also apply updates after the workflow is created but before it is started. This approach is used in another example later in this chapter.

Add two CodeActivity instances following the SuspendActivity. Name the first one codeFirstPart and the second one codeLastPart. After naming the activities, double-click each of them to add a handler for the ExecuteCode event.

Add a SequenceActivity between the two CodeActivity instances and name it sequencePlaceholder. At design time, you will leave this composite activity empty. At runtime, the host application will look for this activity to use it as a container for the new activity. This approach isn't strictly necessary, since the host application could instead insert a new activity between the two CodeActivity instances. However, providing this activity as a placeholder does simplify the code slightly and is especially handy if you want to add multiple activities. It's easier to add a set of child activities to this one composite activity instead of inserting them in the correct position between existing activities. Obviously, you would only include an empty activity such as this if you were planning in advance to support updates to the workflow.

The final workflow should look like Figure 13-1.

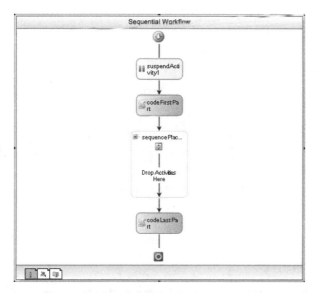

Figure 13-1. *Complete DynamicWorkflow*

The code for the DynamicWorkflow is straightforward. A single Int32 property named TestNumber is defined and referenced by the code handlers for the two CodeActivity instances. The real purpose of the property is to demonstrate how dynamically added activities can have their properties bound to workflow properties. The handlers for the two CodeActivity instances write a message to the Console so that you can see when they execute. The complete code that you need for the DynamicWorkflow.cs file is shown in Listing 13-1.

Listing 13-1. *Complete DynamicWorkflow.cs File*

```
using System;
using System.Workflow.Activities;

namespace SharedWorkflows
{
    /// <summary>
    /// Workflow that will be dynamically updated
    /// by the host application
    /// </summary>
    public sealed partial class DynamicWorkflow
        : SequentialWorkflowActivity
    {
        private Int32 _testNumber;
```

```
        public Int32 TestNumber
        {
            get { return _testNumber; }
            set { _testNumber = value; }
        }

        public DynamicWorkflow()
        {
            InitializeComponent();
        }

        private void codeFirstPart_ExecuteCode(
            object sender, EventArgs e)
        {
            Console.WriteLine(
                "Executing the First Part for TestNumber {0}", TestNumber);
        }

        private void codeLastPart_ExecuteCode(
            object sender, EventArgs e)
        {
            Console.WriteLine(
                "Executing the Last Part for TestNumber {0}", TestNumber);
        }
    }
}
```

Implementing a Custom Activity

In order to add a new activity to the workflow, you need to implement a self-contained custom activity to add. A custom activity is a natural choice for dynamically adding activities since the business logic is all encapsulated within the activity. You can dynamically add standard activities to a workflow, but you can only control their behavior using their public properties. Since you are dynamically adding the activity at runtime, you don't have an opportunity to add code to event handlers the way you can at design time.

Add a new custom activity class to the SharedWorkflows project and name it NewFunctionActivity. You can change the base class for this activity from SequenceActivity to Activity since you don't need a composite for this example.

This activity defines the same TestNumber property as the workflow. However, this time a dependency property is used instead of a normal C# property. As you will see in the host application code, the plan is to add a binding to this activity that binds this property to the same property of the workflow. You can only bind activity properties to a workflow if they are implemented as a dependency property.

The Execute method of the activity writes a message to the Console, referencing the value of the TestNumber property. When you see this message, you'll know that the activity was successfully added to the workflow at runtime, and that the activity binding for the TestNumber property correctly obtained the property value from the workflow.

The complete code that you'll need for the NewFunctionActivity.cs file is shown in Listing 13-2.

Listing 13-2. *Complete NewFunctionActivity.cs File*

```
using System;
using System.ComponentModel;
```

```csharp
using System.Workflow.ComponentModel;
using System.Workflow.Activities;

namespace SharedWorkflows
{
    /// <summary>
    /// A custom activity that is dynamically added
    /// to a workflow instance
    /// </summary>
    public partial class NewFunctionActivity : Activity
    {
        public static DependencyProperty TestNumberProperty
            = System.Workflow.ComponentModel.DependencyProperty.Register(
                "TestNumber", typeof(Int32), typeof(NewFunctionActivity));

        [Description("A simple number used for testing")]
        [Category("ProWF")]
        [Browsable(true)]
        [DesignerSerializationVisibility(
            DesignerSerializationVisibility.Visible)]
        public Int32 TestNumber
        {
            get
            {
                return ((Int32)(base.GetValue(
                    NewFunctionActivity.TestNumberProperty)));
            }
            set
            {
                base.SetValue(
                    NewFunctionActivity.TestNumberProperty, value);
            }
        }

        public NewFunctionActivity()
        {
            InitializeComponent();
        }

        /// <summary>
        /// Display a message to prove that we executed
        /// </summary>
        /// <param name="executionContext"></param>
        /// <returns></returns>
        protected override ActivityExecutionStatus Execute(
            ActivityExecutionContext executionContext)
        {
            Console.WriteLine(
                "Executing the New Functionality for {0}", TestNumber);

            return base.Execute(executionContext);
        }
    }
}
```

Implementing the Host Application

The host application for this example is a `Console` application. You can add a new Sequential Workflow Console Application to the solution and name it `ConsoleDynamicUpdate`. Delete `Workflow1` that was added to this project by the template, since it will not be used. Add project references for `SharedWorkflows` and `Bukovics.Workflow.Hosting`. `Bukovics.Workflow.Hosting` was developed in Chapter 4.

Next, add a new C# class named `DynamicUpdateTest` to the `ConsoleDynamicUpdate` project. This class will contain all of the code necessary to host the workflow runtime, start multiple instances of the `DynamicWorkflow`, and apply updates to the workflow instances.

The complete code for the `DynamicUpdateTest.cs` file is shown and discussed in Listing 13-3.

Listing 13-3. *Complete DynamicUpdateTest.cs File*

```
using System;
using System.Collections.Generic;
using System.Workflow.Runtime;
using System.Workflow.ComponentModel;
using System.Workflow.ComponentModel.Compiler;

using Bukovics.Workflow.Hosting;
using SharedWorkflows;

namespace ConsoleDynamicUpdate
{
    /// <summary>
    /// Test the DynamicWorkflow
    /// </summary>
    public class DynamicUpdateTest
    {
        private static Int32 _testNumber = 0;

        public static void Run()
        {
            using (WorkflowRuntimeManager manager
                = new WorkflowRuntimeManager(new WorkflowRuntime()))
            {
                manager.WorkflowRuntime.StartRuntime();

                //handle the WorkflowSuspended event
                manager.WorkflowRuntime.WorkflowSuspended
                    += new EventHandler<WorkflowSuspendedEventArgs>(
                        WorkflowRuntime_WorkflowSuspended);
```

After starting an instance of the workflow runtime, the code adds a handler for the `WorkflowSuspended` event. This event is raised as each workflow instance executes the `SuspendActivity` and is our opportunity to modify the workflow instance.

```
                //
                //add a new activity to this workflow
                //
```

```
Console.WriteLine("Executing DynamicWorkflow for 1001");
Dictionary<String, Object> wfArguments
    = new Dictionary<string, object>();
_testNumber = 1001;
wfArguments.Add("TestNumber", _testNumber);
manager.StartWorkflow(
    typeof(SharedWorkflows.DynamicWorkflow), wfArguments);
manager.WaitAll(5000);
Console.WriteLine("Completed DynamicWorkflow for 1001\n\r");

//
//let this activity execute normally without changes
//
Console.WriteLine("Executing DynamicWorkflow for 2002");
wfArguments.Clear();
_testNumber = 2002;
wfArguments.Add("TestNumber", _testNumber);
manager.StartWorkflow(
    typeof(SharedWorkflows.DynamicWorkflow), wfArguments);
manager.WaitAll(5000);
Console.WriteLine("Completed DynamicWorkflow for 2002\n\r");

//
//remove the first activity from this worfklow
//
Console.WriteLine("Executing DynamicWorkflow for 3003");
wfArguments.Clear();
_testNumber = 3003;
wfArguments.Add("TestNumber", _testNumber);
manager.StartWorkflow(
    typeof(SharedWorkflows.DynamicWorkflow), wfArguments);
manager.WaitAll(5000);
Console.WriteLine("Completed DynamicWorkflow for 3003\n\r");
    }
}
```

Three separate instances of the DynamicWorkflow are started. Based on the value of the TestNumber parameter, the workflow instance will run normally, have an instance of the NewFunctionActivity added, or have an existing activity deleted.

```
/// <summary>
/// A workflow instance has been suspended
/// </summary>
/// <param name="sender"></param>
/// <param name="e"></param>
private static void WorkflowRuntime_WorkflowSuspended(
    object sender, WorkflowSuspendedEventArgs e)
{
    //should we update the structure of the workflow?
    switch (_testNumber)
    {
```

```
                case 1001:
                    AddNewActivity(e.WorkflowInstance);
                    break;
                case 3003:
                    DeleteActivity(e.WorkflowInstance);
                    break;
                default:
                    break;
            }

            //resume execution of the workflow instance
            e.WorkflowInstance.Resume();
        }
```

Within the WorkflowSuspended event handler, the code determines what type of modification to make to each workflow instance. One of the three instances is left untouched as a control, allowing you to see the results of an unmodified workflow.

After applying any changes, the Resume method is called on the workflow instance to resume execution.

```
        /// <summary>
        /// Add a new custom activity to the workflow instance
        /// </summary>
        /// <param name="instance"></param>
        private static void AddNewActivity(WorkflowInstance instance)
        {
            //create a workflow changes object
            WorkflowChanges wfChanges = new WorkflowChanges(
                instance.GetWorkflowDefinition());

            //find the SequenceActivity that is a placeholder
            //for new activities
            CompositeActivity placeholder
                = wfChanges.TransientWorkflow.GetActivityByName(
                    "sequencePlaceholder") as CompositeActivity;
            if (placeholder != null)
            {
                //create an instance of the new activity
                NewFunctionActivity newActivity
                    = new NewFunctionActivity();

                //bind the TestNumber property of the activity
                //to the TestNumber property of the workflow
                newActivity.SetBinding(
                    NewFunctionActivity.TestNumberProperty,
                    new ActivityBind("DynamicWorkflow", "TestNumber"));
                //add the new custom activity to the workflow
                placeholder.Activities.Add(newActivity);
                //apply the changes
                ValidateAndApplyChanges(instance, wfChanges);
            }
        }
```

To add a new activity to an instance, a WorkflowChanges instance is created using the workflow definition returned by the GetWorkflowDefinition method. The placeholder SequenceActivity named sequencePlaceholder is then located. This is the composite activity that will be the parent for the new activity. The TransientWorkflow property of the WorkflowChanges object is used whenever you need to navigate the existing tree of activities.

An instance of the NewFunctionActivity is then created and an ActivityBind object added to bind the TestNumber property of the activity with the same named property of the workflow. After adding the new activity to the sequencePlaceholder activity, the private ValidateAndApplyChanges method is executed. The code for this method is shown later in the listing.

```
/// <summary>
/// Delete an activity from the workflow instance
/// </summary>
/// <param name="instance"></param>
private static void DeleteActivity(WorkflowInstance instance)
{
    //create a workflow changes object
    WorkflowChanges wfChanges = new WorkflowChanges(
        instance.GetWorkflowDefinition());

    //find the activity we want to remove
    Activity activity =
        wfChanges.TransientWorkflow.GetActivityByName(
            "codeFirstPart");
    if (activity != null)
    {
        //remove the activity from its parent
        activity.Parent.Activities.Remove(activity);
        //apply the changes
        ValidateAndApplyChanges(instance, wfChanges);
    }
}
```

To delete an existing activity, a WorkflowChanges object is created in the same way as the previous method. The existing codeFirstPart activity is then located and deleted from its parent activity. The parent in this case is actually the workflow class.

```
/// <summary>
/// Apply the changes
/// </summary>
/// <param name="instance"></param>
/// <param name="wfChanges"></param>
private static void ValidateAndApplyChanges(
    WorkflowInstance instance, WorkflowChanges wfChanges)
{
    //validate the structural changes before applying them
    ValidationErrorCollection errors = wfChanges.Validate();
    if (errors.Count == 0)
    {
        try
        {
            //apply the changes to the workflow instance
            instance.ApplyWorkflowChanges(wfChanges);
        }
```

```
                        catch (Exception e)
                        {
                            Console.WriteLine("Exception applying changes: {0}",
                                e.Message);
                        }
                    }
                    else
                    {
                        //the proposed changes are not valid
                        foreach (ValidationError error in errors)
                        {
                            Console.WriteLine(error.ToString());
                        }
                    }
                }
```

This final method validates the changes and then applies them to the workflow instance. If any validation errors are encountered, they are written to the Console.

```
            }
        }
```

To execute this test code, you also need a small amount of code in the Program.cs file. Here is the code that you need:

```
using System;

namespace ConsoleDynamicUpdate
{
    public class Program
    {
        static void Main(string[] args)
        {
            DynamicUpdateTest.Run();

            Console.WriteLine("Press any key to exit");
            Console.ReadLine();
        }
    }
}
```

Testing the Workflow

After building the solution, you should be ready to execute the ConsoleDynamicUpdate application. Your results should look like this:

```
Executing DynamicWorkflow for 1001
Executing the First Part for TestNumber 1001
Executing the New Functionality for 1001
Executing the Last Part for TestNumber 1001
Completed DynamicWorkflow for 1001
```

```
Executing DynamicWorkflow for 2002
Executing the First Part for TestNumber 2002
Executing the Last Part for TestNumber 2002
Completed DynamicWorkflow for 2002

Executing DynamicWorkflow for 3003
Executing the Last Part for TestNumber 3003
Completed DynamicWorkflow for 3003

Press any key to exit
```

The first workflow execution (1001) was the one that received a new activity. The results show that the new activity executed in the proper sequence (between the two CodeActivity instances) and that it received the correct value of 1001 for its TestNumber property.

The second instance (2002) executed without any changes. However, it does demonstrate that the previous changes to the 1001 instance were not permanent. The second instance did not include the additional activity and instead executed using the default workflow definition.

For the third instance (3003), the code removed the first CodeActivity instance. The highlighted results show that the only activity that remained in the workflow was the final CodeActivity.

Restricting Dynamic Updates

This example builds upon the previous one to demonstrate the use of the workflow DynamicUpdateCondition. If this rule or code condition is set, the condition is evaluated each time you call the ApplyWorkflowChanges method to update the workflow. If the condition evaluates to true, the changes are allowed. If the condition is false, an InvalidOperationException is thrown and the changes are prohibited.

Open the DynamicWorkflow in the workflow designer and switch to the Properties window for the workflow. Set the DynamicUpdateCondition property to Code Condition and then expand the property and enter IsUpdateAllowed as the code handler name. You could also use a Declarative Rule Condition if you prefer.

Add this code to the condition handler in the DynamicWorkflow.cs file:

```
/// <summary>
/// Determine if dynamic updates are allowed
/// </summary>
/// <param name="sender"></param>
/// <param name="e"></param>
private void IsUpdateAllowed(object sender, ConditionalEventArgs e)
{
    e.Result = (TestNumber != 3003);
}
```

The condition returns true (allowing updates) for all workflows except those that have a TestNumber value of 3003. If you execute the same ConsoleDynamic application used in the previous example, you should see these results:

```
Executing DynamicWorkflow for 1001
Executing the First Part for TestNumber 1001
Executing the New Functionality for 1001
Executing the Last Part for TestNumber 1001
Completed DynamicWorkflow for 1001
```

```
Executing DynamicWorkflow for 2002
Executing the First Part for TestNumber 2002
Executing the Last Part for TestNumber 2002
Completed DynamicWorkflow for 2002

Executing DynamicWorkflow for 3003
Exception applying changes: Workflow changes can not be applied to instance
'3708be69-437b-4236-a788-4539e312ebf9' at this time. The WorkflowChanges
Condition property on the root activity has evaluated to false.
Executing the First Part for TestNumber 3003
Executing the Last Part for TestNumber 3003
Completed DynamicWorkflow for 3003

Press any key to exit
```

The results for the first two workflow instances are the same as the previous example. However, the last instance prohibited the dynamic update since it had a TestNumber value of 3003 (the magic forbidden value). The message from the InvalidOperationException is shown in the results.

■**Note** The workflow instance ID shown in the exception message will be different when you run this test on your machine. It is, after all, a Guid, and in Microsoft parlance, it should be globally unique.

It is interesting to note that the DynamicUpdateCondition is not checked when you call the Validate method of the WorkflowChanges object. The Validate method only checks for structural integrity of the workflow changes and doesn't have access to the runtime values needed to evaluate the DynamicUpdateCondition. The condition isn't checked until you call ApplyWorkflowChanges. For this reason, you should always wrap the call to this method in a try/catch block in order to catch any possible exceptions.

Applying Updates from Within a Workflow

In the previous examples, you modified a workflow externally from the host application. In this example, you will develop a workflow that is capable of modifying itself. The workflow will be passed a property that identifies the Type of the activity to add along with another property that identifies the dependency property of the activity to use for binding. Using these properties, the workflow will create an instance of the new activity and add it to the workflow instance.

Implementing the SelfUpdatingWorkflow

Begin by adding a new sequential workflow to the SharedWorkflows project, naming it SelfUpdatingWorkflow. The visual design of this workflow is similar to the DynamicWorkflow that you implemented for the previous examples. It contains two CodeActivity instances (named codeFirstPart and codeLastPart) with a SequenceActivity (named sequencePlaceholder) between the two activities. Remember to double-click each CodeActivity to add a handler for the ExecuteCode event. Since this workflow will update itself, it does not require a SuspendActivity. The purpose of that activity in the previous workflow is to provide the host application with an opportunity to update the workflow.

Figure 13-2 shows the complete visual design of SelfUpdatingWorkflow.

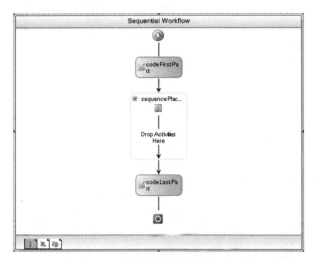

Figure 13-2. *Complete SelfUpdatingWorkflow*

The workflow needs to add the new activity when it is first created but before it begins execution. A good way to accomplish this is to add a handler to the Initialized event of the workflow. From the Properties window for the workflow, specify a name of WorkflowInitialized for the Initialized event. This adds a handler for this event to the workflow code file.

You can now switch to the code view for the SelfUpdatingWorkflow.cs file. Listing 13-4 is the complete listing of code that you'll need for this file.

Listing 13-4. *Complete SelfUpdatingWorkflow.cs File*

```
using System;
using System.Reflection;
using System.Workflow.ComponentModel;
using System.Workflow.ComponentModel.Compiler;
using System.Workflow.Activities;

namespace SharedWorkflows
{
    /// <summary>
    /// Workflow that will be dynamically updated
    /// internally
    /// </summary>
    public sealed partial class SelfUpdatingWorkflow
        : SequentialWorkflowActivity
    {
        private Int32 _testNumber;
        private Type _newActivityType;
        private DependencyProperty _numberProperty;

        public Int32 TestNumber
        {
            get { return _testNumber; }
            set { _testNumber = value; }
        }
    }
```

```
public Type NewActivityType
{
    get { return _newActivityType; }
    set { _newActivityType = value; }
}

public DependencyProperty NumberProperty
{
    get { return _numberProperty; }
    set { _numberProperty = value; }
}
```

In addition to the TestNumber used in the previous example, this workflow requires two additional properties. NewActivityType identifies the Type of activity that will be created and added to the workflow. NumberProperty identifies the DependencyProperty of the new activity that should be bound to the TestNumber workflow property. By passing these values as properties, the workflow has the flexibility to add any activity that is specified by the host application. For this example, the assumption has been made that the new activity defines an Int32 property that requires binding to a workflow property.

```
public SelfUpdatingWorkflow()
{
    InitializeComponent();
}

private void codeFirstPart_ExecuteCode(
    object sender, EventArgs e)
{
    Console.WriteLine(
        "Executing the First Part for TestNumber {0}", TestNumber);
}

private void codeLastPart_ExecuteCode(
    object sender, EventArgs e)
{
    Console.WriteLine(
        "Executing the Last Part for TestNumber {0}", TestNumber);
}
```

The same CodeActivity handlers that you used in the previous workflow are included here. Each one writes a message to the Console to let you know when they execute.

```
/// <summary>
/// Initialize a new workflow instance
/// </summary>
/// <param name="sender"></param>
/// <param name="e"></param>
private void WorkflowInitialized(object sender, EventArgs e)
{
    //should we update the structure of the workflow?
    if (NewActivityType != null)
    {
        AddNewActivity();
    }
}
```

The handler for the Initialized event checks the NewActivityType property. If the value is non-null, it executes the private AddNewActivity method to create and add the new activity.

```csharp
/// <summary>
/// Add a new custom activity to this workflow instance
/// </summary>
/// <param name="instance"></param>
private void AddNewActivity()
{
    //create an instance of the specified new activity
    if (NewActivityType != null && NumberProperty != null)
    {
        //create a workflow changes object
        WorkflowChanges wfChanges = new WorkflowChanges(this);

        //find the SequenceActivity that is a placeholder
        //for new activities
        CompositeActivity placeholder
            = wfChanges.TransientWorkflow.GetActivityByName(
                "sequencePlaceholder") as CompositeActivity;
        if (placeholder == null)
        {
            return;
        }

        //construct an instance of the activity
        //using reflection
        ConstructorInfo ctor
            = NewActivityType.GetConstructor(Type.EmptyTypes);
        Activity newActivity = ctor.Invoke(null) as Activity;

        //bind the TestNumber property of the activity
        //to the TestNumber property of the workflow
        newActivity.SetBinding(NumberProperty,
            new ActivityBind(this.Name, "TestNumber"));

        //add the new custom activity to the workflow
        placeholder.Activities.Add(newActivity);

        //validate the structural changes before applying them
        ValidationErrorCollection errors = wfChanges.Validate();
        if (errors.Count == 0)
        {
            //apply the changes to the workflow instance
            this.ApplyWorkflowChanges(wfChanges);
        }
        else
        {
            //the proposed changes are not valid
            foreach (ValidationError error in errors)
            {
                Console.WriteLine(error.ToString());
            }
        }
    }
}
```

To add the new activity to the workflow, a WorkflowChanges instance is first created. This time, the root activity of the current instance is passed to the constructor. The sequencePlaceholder activity is located by name since it will be used as the parent of the new activity. Reflection is then used to create an instance of the activity based on the Type passed in the NewActivityType property. Once it is created, an ActivityBind is added to the activity to bind the TestNumber property of the workflow to the unnamed activity property identified by NumberProperty. After adding the new activity as a child of sequencePlaceholder activity, the changes are validated and applied.

```
    }
}
```

Implementing the Host Application

To test this new workflow, you can add a new Sequential Workflow Console Application to the solution and name it ConsoleSelfUpdating. Delete Workflow1 that was automatically added to this project, and add the usual project references for SharedWorkflows and Bukovics.Workflow.Hosting.

Add a C# class named SelfUpdatingTest to the project. Listing 13-5 is the complete code for the SelfUpdatingTest.cs file.

Listing 13-5. *Complete SelfUpdatingTest.cs File*

```
using System;
using System.Collections.Generic;
using System.Workflow.Runtime;

using Bukovics.Workflow.Hosting;
using SharedWorkflows;

namespace ConsoleSelfUpdating
{
    /// <summary>
    /// Test the SelfUpdatingWorkflow
    /// </summary>
    public class SelfUpdatingTest
    {
        public static void Run()
        {
            using (WorkflowRuntimeManager manager
                = new WorkflowRuntimeManager(new WorkflowRuntime()))
            {
                manager.WorkflowRuntime.StartRuntime();

                //
                //add a new activity to this workflow
                //
                Console.WriteLine("Executing SelfUpdatingWorkflow for 1001");
                Dictionary<String, Object> wfArguments
                    = new Dictionary<string, object>();
                wfArguments.Add("TestNumber", 1001);
                //pass the Type of new activity to add along with the
                //dependency property to bind
```

```
wfArguments.Add("NewActivityType",
    typeof(NewFunctionActivity));
wfArguments.Add("NumberProperty",
    NewFunctionActivity.TestNumberProperty);
manager.StartWorkflow(
    typeof(SharedWorkflows.SelfUpdatingWorkflow), wfArguments);
manager.WaitAll(5000);
Console.WriteLine("Completed SelfUpdatingWorkflow for 1001\n\r");
```

The host passes the two additional properties for the first workflow instance. The first property identifies the NewFunctionActivity (developed in the first example of this chapter) as the activity to add. The second property identifies TestNumberProperty as the dependency property of the activity that should be bound to the workflow TestNumber property. This should result in the additional activity being added to the first workflow instance and executed. The second workflow instance (shown next) does not set these properties. This second instance should execute normally without any changes.

```
            //
            //let this activity execute normally without changes
            //
            Console.WriteLine("Executing SelfUpdatingWorkflow for 2002");
            wfArguments.Clear();
            wfArguments.Add("TestNumber", 2002);
            manager.StartWorkflow(
                typeof(SharedWorkflows.SelfUpdatingWorkflow), wfArguments);
            manager.WaitAll(5000);
            Console.WriteLine("Completed SelfUpdatingWorkflow for 2002\n\r");
        }
    }
}
```

You will also need to add this code to the Program.cs file.

```
using System;

namespace ConsoleSelfUpdating
{
    public class Program
    {
        static void Main(string[] args)
        {
            SelfUpdatingTest.Run();

            Console.WriteLine("Press any key to exit");
            Console.ReadLine();
        }
    }
}
```

Testing the Workflow

After building the solution, you can execute the ConsoleSelfUpdating application and should see these results:

```
Executing SelfUpdatingWorkflow for 1001
Executing the First Part for TestNumber 1001
Executing the New Functionality for 1001
Executing the Last Part for TestNumber 1001
Completed SelfUpdatingWorkflow for 1001

Executing SelfUpdatingWorkflow for 2002
Executing the First Part for TestNumber 2002
Executing the Last Part for TestNumber 2002
Completed SelfUpdatingWorkflow for 2002

Press any key to exit
```

The results show that, as expected, the first workflow instance added the additional activity and executed it. The correct value (1001) was also passed to the new activity due to the activity binding that was added by the workflow. The second instance executed without the additional activity.

Updating a Rule Condition

One of the benefits of rule conditions is that they are easier to modify at runtime compared to code conditions. Code conditions are expressed as code that is compiled into the workflow. To modify a code condition, you have to rebuild the workflow. On the other hand, rule conditions are expressions that are serialized to a separate `.rules` file. The `.rules` file is built into the workflow project as an embedded resource and deserialized at runtime. Since rule conditions are expressed in this separate resource and not in code, you can dynamically update them at runtime as this example will demonstrate.

In this example, you will develop a simple workflow that includes a set of `IfElseBranchActivity` instances. The `IfElseBranchActivity` instances use rule conditions to declare the condition for each branch. Using dynamic updates, the host application will update one of the rule conditions, changing the default workflow behavior.

Implementing the DynamicConditionWorkflow

Add a new sequential workflow to the `SharedWorkflows` project and name it `DynamicConditionWorkflow`. Add an `IfElseActivity` to the workflow. By default, an `IfElseActivity` adds two `IfElseBranchActivity` instances when it is created. This example requires three instances, so add another one to the `IfElseActivity` now.

Before you complete the visual design of the workflow, you'll need to add a public property named `TestNumber` to the workflow class. This is an `Int32` and is defined in the same way as the previous workflow examples earlier in this chapter. You need to add this property first in order to enter a rule expression that references this property.

The first two `IfElseBranchActivity` instances will each define a Declarative Rule Condition. The last `IfElseBranchActivity` doesn't require a condition. Name the condition for the first branch (on the left side) `conditionOne` and enter this expression:

```
this.TestNumber > 100
```

The second `IfElseBranchActivity` condition should be named `conditionTwo` and contain this expression:

```
this.TestNumber > 50
```

Add a CodeActivity to each of the IfElseBranchActivity instances, and double-click each one to add a code handler. This completes the visual design of the workflow. The final workflow should look like Figure 13-3.

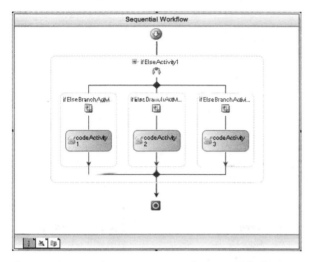

Figure 13-3. *Complete DynamicConditionWorkflow*

Listing 13-6 is the completed code that you'll need to add to the DynamicConditionWorkflow.cs file.

Listing 13-6. *Complete DynamicConditionWorkflow.cs File*

```
using System;
using System.Workflow.Activities;

namespace SharedWorkflows
{
    /// <summary>
    /// Workflow with Rule Conditions that
    /// are updated externally
    /// </summary>
    public sealed partial class DynamicConditionWorkflow
        : SequentialWorkflowActivity
    {
        private Int32 _testNumber;

        public Int32 TestNumber
        {
            get { return _testNumber; }
            set { _testNumber = value; }
        }

        public DynamicConditionWorkflow()
        {
            InitializeComponent();
        }
```

```
        private void codeActivity1_ExecuteCode(
            object sender, EventArgs e)
        {
            Console.WriteLine("Condition One is true");
        }

        private void codeActivity2_ExecuteCode(
            object sender, EventArgs e)
        {
            Console.WriteLine("Condition Two is true");
        }

        private void codeActivity3_ExecuteCode(
            object sender, EventArgs e)
        {
            Console.WriteLine("Neither condition is true");
        }
    }
}
```

In addition to the TestNumber property, the only other code that you need is for the individual CodeActivity handlers. Each handler writes a message to the Console so that you will know when each activity executes and which condition evaluates to true.

Implementing the Host Application

As usual, the host application for this example is a Console application. Add a new Sequential Workflow Console Application to the solution and name it ConsoleDynamicCondition. Delete Workflow1 that was added to this project and add the usual project references for SharedWorkflows and Bukovics.Workflow.Hosting. Add a new C# class to the project and name it DynamicConditionTest. Listing 13-7 is the complete listing of code for the DynamicConditionTest.cs file.

Listing 13-7. *Complete DynamicConditionTest.cs File*

```
using System;
using System.Collections.Generic;
using System.Workflow.Runtime;
using System.Workflow.ComponentModel;
using System.Workflow.ComponentModel.Compiler;
using System.Workflow.Activities.Rules;

using System.CodeDom;

using Bukovics.Workflow.Hosting;
using SharedWorkflows;

namespace ConsoleDynamicCondition
{
    /// <summary>
    /// Test the DynamicConditionWorkflow
    /// </summary>
    public class DynamicConditionTest
    {
        private static Boolean _firstWorkflow = true;
```

```
public static void Run()
{
    using (WorkflowRuntimeManager manager
        = new WorkflowRuntimeManager(new WorkflowRuntime()))
    {
        manager.WorkflowRuntime.StartRuntime();

        //handle the WorkflowCreated event
        manager.WorkflowRuntime.WorkflowCreated
            += new EventHandler<WorkflowEventArgs>(
                WorkflowRuntime_WorkflowCreated);
```

The workflow that this host application executes does not include a SuspendActivity like the first example in this chapter. Instead, this host application will make its workflow modifications immediately after the workflow instance is created but before it is started. To accomplish this, the code handles the WorkflowCreated event. Within the handler for this event, the code determines whether it should update the rule condition.

```
        //
        //modify the rule for this workflow
        //
        Console.WriteLine("Executing DynamicConditionWorkflow - 1st");
        Dictionary<String, Object> wfArguments
            = new Dictionary<string, object>();
        wfArguments.Add("TestNumber", 200);
        manager.StartWorkflow(
            typeof(SharedWorkflows.DynamicConditionWorkflow), wfArguments);
        manager.WaitAll(5000);
        Console.WriteLine("Completed DynamicConditionWorkflow - 1st\n\r");

        //
        //let this activity execute normally without changes
        //
        Console.WriteLine("Executing DynamicConditionWorkflow - 2nd");
        wfArguments.Clear();
        wfArguments.Add("TestNumber", 200);
        manager.StartWorkflow(
            typeof(SharedWorkflows.DynamicConditionWorkflow), wfArguments);
        manager.WaitAll(5000);
        Console.WriteLine("Completed DynamicConditionWorkflow - 2nd\n\r");
    }
}
```

Two instances of the DynamicConditionWorkflow are started. The rule condition for the first instance should be modified while the second instance should execute unchanged. Both instances of the workflow are passed the same value of 200 for the TestNumber parameter.

```
/// <summary>
/// A workflow was created but not yet started
/// </summary>
/// <param name="sender"></param>
/// <param name="e"></param>
private static void WorkflowRuntime_WorkflowCreated(
    object sender, WorkflowEventArgs e)
{
    //should we update the workflow?
```

```
        if (_firstWorkflow)
        {
            ModifyRuleCondition(e.WorkflowInstance);
            _firstWorkflow = false;
        }
    }
```

The WorkflowCreated event is raised by the WorkflowRuntime each time the CreateWorkflow method is called. This example uses the WorkflowRuntimeManager class that was developed in Chapter 4 to call the CreateWorkflow method. If this is the first workflow instance, the private ModifyRuleCondition method is executed to dynamically update one of the conditions for the instance.

```
    /// <summary>
    /// Modify a single rule condition
    /// </summary>
    /// <param name="instance"></param>
    private static void ModifyRuleCondition(WorkflowInstance instance)
    {
        //create a workflow changes object
        WorkflowChanges wfChanges = new WorkflowChanges(
            instance.GetWorkflowDefinition());

        //retrieve the RuleDefinitions for the workflow
        RuleDefinitions ruleDefinitions
            = (RuleDefinitions)wfChanges.TransientWorkflow.GetValue(
                RuleDefinitions.RuleDefinitionsProperty);

        if (ruleDefinitions != null)
        {
            if (ruleDefinitions.Conditions.Contains("conditionOne"))
            {
                //retrieve the rule that we want to change
                RuleExpressionCondition condition
                    = ruleDefinitions.Conditions["conditionOne"]
                        as RuleExpressionCondition;

                //change the rule by setting the right side of the
                //operation to 300 instead of the original value of 100.
                //was:  this.TestNumber > 100
                //now:  this.TestNumber > 300
                CodeBinaryOperatorExpression codeExpression =
                    condition.Expression as CodeBinaryOperatorExpression;
                codeExpression.Right = new CodePrimitiveExpression(300);

                ValidateAndApplyChanges(instance, wfChanges);
            }
        }
    }
```

Just like the previous examples, a WorkflowChanges instance is created using the workflow definition. Using the TransientWorkflow property, the current rule definitions are retrieved. The definitions take the form of a single RuleDefinitions object that is retrieved from the workflow definition using the GetValue method. The rule definitions are identified by their static dependency property (RuleDefinitions.RuleDefinitionsProperty). The RuleDefinitions object provides a Conditions property that is a collection of all defined conditions.

Once the code has retrieved the rule definitions, the condition that is used for the first IfElseBranchActivity (conditionOne) is retrieved as a RuleExpressionCondition object. The Expression property of this object represents the expression that is evaluated at runtime. It is actually a CodeBinaryOperationExpression (a CodeDom object). The right side of this expression is modified, changing the value from 100 to 300. Once this modification is made, the expression will compare the TestNumber property to a literal value of 300 instead of the original value of 100.

```
/// <summary>
/// Apply the changes
/// </summary>
/// <param name="instance"></param>
/// <param name="wfChanges"></param>
private static void ValidateAndApplyChanges(
    WorkflowInstance instance, WorkflowChanges wfChanges)
{
    //validate the structural changes before applying them
    ValidationErrorCollection errors = wfChanges.Validate();
    if (errors.Count == 0)
    {
        try
        {
            //apply the changes to the workflow instance
            instance.ApplyWorkflowChanges(wfChanges);
        }
        catch (Exception e)
        {
            Console.WriteLine("Exception applying changes: {0}",
                e.Message);
        }
    }
    else
    {
        //the proposed changes are not valid
        foreach (ValidationError error in errors)
        {
            Console.WriteLine(error.ToString());
        }
    }
}
```

The proposed changes to the workflow are first validated and then applied to the workflow instance using this private ValidateAndApplyChanges method.

```
}
```

You also need to add this code to the Program.cs file in order to execute the workflow testing code.

```
using System;

namespace ConsoleDynamicCondition
{
    public class Program
    {
        static void Main(string[] args)
```

```
        {
            DynamicConditionTest.Run();

            Console.WriteLine("Press any key to exit");
            Console.ReadLine();
        }
    }
}
```

Testing the Workflow

After building the solution, you should be ready to execute the ConsoleDynamicCondition application. Your results should look like this:

```
Executing DynamicConditionWorkflow - 1st
Condition Two is true
Completed DynamicConditionWorkflow - 1st

Executing DynamicConditionWorkflow - 2nd
Condition One is true
Completed DynamicConditionWorkflow - 2nd

Press any key to exit
```

The first workflow instance was the one that was modified and the second was unmodified. Both workflow instances were passed a TestNumber value of 200. Under normal circumstances, conditionOne (TestNumber > 100) should have been true for both instances. This is the case for the second workflow instance that was left untouched.

But for the first workflow instance, this expression was modified to be TestNumber > 300 instead of TestNumber > 100. Therefore the first condition was false, which caused the second condition (TestNumber > 50) to be evaluated.

Replacing a Rule Definition

In the previous example, you updated a single rule condition by directly updating the CodeDom objects of a rule condition. An alternative to updating a single rule condition is to replace the entire RuleDefinitions object that the workflow uses. The RuleDefinitions object is the deserialized version of the .rules file that is an embedded resource of the workflow project.

One approach to managing rules outside of the compiled workflow project is to load and deserialize a version of the .rules file at runtime. The serialized version of the rules can be persisted as a file or even stored in a database. The persistence mechanism is really up to you and depends on your application requirements. At runtime, you deserialize the rule definitions from their persisted state and perform a dynamic update on the workflow to replace the original rule definitions with the version stored externally.

In this example, you will modify the ConsoleDynamicCondition host application from the previous example. At runtime, you will load a new set of rule definitions from a file and dynamically update the workflow to use the new rules.

Modifying the RuleDefinitions

First, you need to save and then modify the original `.rules` file from the `DynamicConditionWorkflow`. To do this, make a copy of the `DynamicConditionWorkflow.rules` file and name the copy `ModifiedRule.rules`. This new file will be read directly by the host application at runtime and should not be added to any project. However, you do need to make sure that this file is copied into the directory that you will use when starting the application.

The `ModifiedRule.rules` file is a serialized version of the `RuleDefinitions` class. It contains workflow elements (such as the root `RuleDefinitions` element) and also `CodeDom` elements (e.g., `CodeBinaryOperatorExpression`). For this example, you will modify the condition named `conditionOne` so that the `CodeBinaryOperatorExpression.Right` element is set to 300 instead of the original value of 100. This is the same change that was made by the host application code in the previous example. Listing 13-8 shows the entire `ModifiedRule.rules` file after this one modification has been made. In the actual file, some of the lines extend beyond the maximum line length for this book. For this reason, I've reformatted some single lines into multiple lines.

Listing 13-8. *ModifiedRule.rules File*

```xml
<RuleDefinitions xmlns="http://schemas.microsoft.com/winfx/2006/xaml/workflow">
  <RuleDefinitions.Conditions>
    <RuleExpressionCondition Name="conditionOne">
      <RuleExpressionCondition.Expression>
        <ns0:CodeBinaryOperatorExpression Operator="GreaterThan"
          xmlns:ns0="clr-namespace:System.CodeDom;Assembly=System,
          Version=2.0.0.0, Culture=neutral, PublicKeyToken=b77a5c561934e089">
          <ns0:CodeBinaryOperatorExpression.Left>
            <ns0:CodePropertyReferenceExpression PropertyName="TestNumber">
              <ns0:CodePropertyReferenceExpression.TargetObject>
                <ns0:CodeThisReferenceExpression />
              </ns0:CodePropertyReferenceExpression.TargetObject>
            </ns0:CodePropertyReferenceExpression>
          </ns0:CodeBinaryOperatorExpression.Left>
          <ns0:CodeBinaryOperatorExpression.Right>
            <ns0:CodePrimitiveExpression>
              <ns0:CodePrimitiveExpression.Value>
                <ns1:Int32 xmlns:ns1="clr-namespace:System;Assembly=mscorlib,
                  Version=2.0.0.0, Culture=neutral,
                  PublicKeyToken=b77a5c561934e089">300</ns1:Int32>
              </ns0:CodePrimitiveExpression.Value>
            </ns0:CodePrimitiveExpression>
          </ns0:CodeBinaryOperatorExpression.Right>
        </ns0:CodeBinaryOperatorExpression>
      </RuleExpressionCondition.Expression>
    </RuleExpressionCondition>
    <RuleExpressionCondition Name="conditionTwo">
      <RuleExpressionCondition.Expression>
        <ns0:CodeBinaryOperatorExpression Operator="GreaterThan"
          xmlns:ns0="clr-namespace:System.CodeDom;Assembly=System,
          Version=2.0.0.0, Culture=neutral, PublicKeyToken=b77a5c561934e089">
          <ns0:CodeBinaryOperatorExpression.Left>
            <ns0:CodePropertyReferenceExpression PropertyName="TestNumber">
              <ns0:CodePropertyReferenceExpression.TargetObject>
                <ns0:CodeThisReferenceExpression />
              </ns0:CodePropertyReferenceExpression.TargetObject>
```

```
            </ns0:CodePropertyReferenceExpression>
          </ns0:CodeBinaryOperatorExpression.Left>
          <ns0:CodeBinaryOperatorExpression.Right>
            <ns0:CodePrimitiveExpression>
              <ns0:CodePrimitiveExpression.Value>
                <ns1:Int32 xmlns:ns1="clr-namespace:System;Assembly=mscorlib,
                  Version=2.0.0.0, Culture=neutral,
                  PublicKeyToken=b77a5c561934e089">50</ns1:Int32>
              </ns0:CodePrimitiveExpression.Value>
            </ns0:CodePrimitiveExpression>
          </ns0:CodeBinaryOperatorExpression.Right>
        </ns0:CodeBinaryOperatorExpression>
      </RuleExpressionCondition.Expression>
    </RuleExpressionCondition>
  </RuleDefinitions.Conditions>
</RuleDefinitions>
```

In Listing 13-8, I highlighted the one small change that you need to make to this file. The original value for this expression is 100 (the right side of the `TestNumber > 100` expression). As shown in this listing, I've changed this value to 300.

Note For this example, you are manually modifying the serialized version of the rule definitions. This is obviously not the optimal way to manage rule changes. WF provides the classes necessary to host the workflow designer and rule editors within your own application. Using these classes, you can develop your own external rule editor that enables you to more easily update serialized rules such as those shown here. Chapter 17 discusses hosting the WF designers.

Modifying the Host Application

To apply this serialized version of the rule definitions, you need to make a few modifications to the `ConsoleDynamicCondition` application that you developed in the previous example. Listing 13-9 shows just the sections of the `DynamicConditionTest.cs` file that require modification.

Listing 13-9. *Revised DynamicConditionTest.cs File*

```
using System;
using System.Collections.Generic;
using System.Workflow.Runtime;
using System.Workflow.ComponentModel;
using System.Workflow.ComponentModel.Compiler;
using System.Workflow.Activities.Rules;

using System.IO;
using System.Xml;
using System.Workflow.ComponentModel.Serialization;
//remove using statement for System.CodeDom - no longer needed

using Bukovics.Workflow.Hosting;
using SharedWorkflows;
```

```
namespace ConsoleDynamicCondition
{
    /// <summary>
    /// Test the DynamicConditionWorkflow
    /// </summary>
    public class DynamicConditionTest
    {

...


        /// <summary>
        /// A workflow was created but not yet started
        /// </summary>
        /// <param name="sender"></param>
        /// <param name="e"></param>
        private static void WorkflowRuntime_WorkflowCreated(
            object sender, WorkflowEventArgs e)
        {
            //should we update the workflow?
            if (_firstWorkflow)
            {
                ReplaceRuleDefinition(e.WorkflowInstance);
                _firstWorkflow = false;
            }
        }
    }
```

In the handler for the WorkflowCreated event, you can remove the call to ModifyRuleCondition since it is now replaced with a new ReplaceRuleDefinition method. The entire body of the ModifyRuleCondition method can be deleted from this class.

```
        /// <summary>
        /// Replace the entire rule definition for a workflow
        /// </summary>
        /// <param name="instance"></param>
        private static void ReplaceRuleDefinition(WorkflowInstance instance)
        {
            //create a workflow changes object
            WorkflowChanges wfChanges = new WorkflowChanges(
                instance.GetWorkflowDefinition());

            //get a stream from an externally saved .rules file
            Stream stream
                = new FileStream(@"ModifiedRule.rules",
                    FileMode.Open, FileAccess.Read, FileShare.Read);
            //read the .rules file using an XmlReader
            using (XmlReader xmlReader = XmlReader.Create(
                new StreamReader(stream)))
            {
                WorkflowMarkupSerializer markupSerializer
                    = new WorkflowMarkupSerializer();
                //deserialize the rule definitions
                RuleDefinitions ruleDefinitions
                    = markupSerializer.Deserialize(xmlReader)
                        as RuleDefinitions;
```

```
            if (ruleDefinitions != null)
            {
                //replace the embedded rules definition
                //with the new one that was deserialzed from a file
                wfChanges.TransientWorkflow.SetValue(
                    RuleDefinitions.RuleDefinitionsProperty,
                    ruleDefinitions);

                ValidateAndApplyChanges(instance, wfChanges);
            }
        }
    }
```

In the new `ReplaceRuleDefinition` method, the `ModifiedRule.rules` file is read and deserialized using the `WorkflowMarkupSerializer` class (found in the `System.Workflow.ComponentModel.Serialization` namespace). The result of deserializing this file is a `RuleDefinitions` object. Using the `TransientWorkflow` property of the `WorkflowChanges` object, the entire set of rule definitions for the workflow instance is replaced with this new object.

```
...
    }
}
```

Testing the Revised Application

After building the solution, you can execute this revised version of the `ConsoleDynamicCondition` application. The results should be exactly the same as the previous example and are shown here:

```
Executing DynamicConditionWorkflow - 1st
Condition Two is true
Completed DynamicConditionWorkflow - 1st

Executing DynamicConditionWorkflow - 2nd
Condition One is true
Completed DynamicConditionWorkflow - 2nd

Press any key to exit
```

Summary

The focus of this chapter was dynamic workflow updates. WF provides the ability to dynamically change the structure of a workflow instance. The chapter began with an overview of the dynamic update mechanism along with some reasons why you might want to use dynamic updates. Dynamic updates are yet another tool that enables you to quickly respond and adapt to changes in your workflow design.

Examples in this chapter showed you how to apply updates to a workflow instance from the host application or from within the workflow itself. One example demonstrated the use of the `DynamicUpdateCondition` to restrict when dynamic updates are allowed for a workflow instance. Other examples demonstrated ways to update rule conditions for a workflow.

In the next chapter, you will learn about the WF support for workflow tracking, which enables you to instrument your workflows to monitor their status.

CHAPTER 14

■ ■ ■

Workflow Tracking

The focus of this chapter is workflow tracking. *Tracking* is a built-in mechanism that automatically instruments your workflows. By simply adding a tracking service to the workflow runtime, you are able to track and record status and event data related to each workflow and each activity within a workflow.

The chapter begins with a general discussion and overview of the tracking mechanism provided by WF. The first example in this chapter introduces the SqlTrackingService, which is a ready-to-use service that records tracking data to a SQL Server database. A follow-up example demonstrates how to enhance the default tracking to create user tracking points within your workflow or activity code. Additional examples show you how to view tracking data for each rule that is evaluated and how to extract values from individual fields in a workflow. The use of custom tracking profiles is also demonstrated.

The database used by the SqlTrackingService does require some routine maintenance. This is discussed in a section that follows the SQL tracking examples.

The chapter concludes with an example implementation of a custom tracking service. This service writes the tracking data directly to the Console instead of persisting it.

Understanding Workflow Tracking

Visibility is one of the key benefits to using WF. So far, you've seen evidence of this visibility at design time. Using the workflow designer, you visually declare what steps a workflow should execute, the sequence of each step, and the conditions that must be true for each step to execute. You can later view the workflow model that you designed and quickly discern the relationships between activities. This design time visibility eases the initial development and, more importantly, future maintenance of the workflow.

Visibility at runtime is also an important key benefit of using WF. Since workflows execute within the confines of the workflow runtime engine, they truly operate in a black box. This boundary between the host application and the runtime environment increases the need for some way to monitor the progress of individual workflows. Without a built-in mechanism to monitor their execution, you would have to instrument each workflow using your own code.

But imagine a built-in mechanism that can monitor each workflow throughout its entire life cycle, tracking important events along the way. Imagine if this same mechanism extended to individual activities within the workflow and tracked the status of each activity as it executes. Such a mechanism would be able to record the results from individual rules within a RuleSet, or even extract individual field or property values from an activity or workflow. And best of all, all of this would take place automatically under the covers, without any changes to your workflows.

This accurately describes the workflow tracking mechanism that is provided with WF. Aspects of the workflow tracking are discussed in the sections that follow.

Tracking Services

Workflow tracking in WF is enabled by adding a pluggable tracking service to the workflow runtime. WF includes a standard tracking service (SqlTrackingService in the System.Workflow.Runtime. Tracking namespace) that saves tracking data to a SQL Server database. You can use this tracking service out of the box, or you can develop your own if you prefer to send tracking data to a different destination (e.g., the Console, a file, the Windows event log, or your own application database).

Unlike other core workflow services, you are not limited to a single tracking service at any one time. You can add multiple tracking services to the runtime at startup and each service will have the opportunity to work with and record the same tracking data.

Tracking Event Types

Once a tracking service is added to the runtime, tracking data is (by default) automatically passed to the service for all workflows. In the case of the SqlTrackingService, the data is saved to a SQL Server database. The available tracking data is categorized into three different types of events:

- Workflow events
- Activity events
- User events

Workflow events correspond to changes in the workflow status. Each time the workflow status changes, a workflow tracking event is raised and passed to any loaded tracking services by the workflow runtime. The possible workflow events are defined in the TrackingWorkflowEvent enumeration and are listed in Table 14-1.

Table 14-1. *TrackingWorkflowEvent Values*

Value	Description
Aborted	A workflow instance has aborted
Changed	A dynamic change has been made to a workflow instance
Completed	An instance has completed
Created	A new workflow instance has been created
Exception	An unhandled exception has been raised
Idle	An instance has become idle
Loaded	An instance has been loaded into memory
Persisted	An instance has been persisted
Resumed	An instance that was suspended has now been resumed
Started	An instance has started execution
Suspended	An instance has been suspended
Terminated	An instance has been terminated
Unloaded	An instance has been unloaded from memory

Activity events correspond to changes in execution status for an individual activity. The possible activity status values are defined in the `ActivityExecutionStatus` enumeration and are listed in Table 14-2.

Table 14-2. *ActivityExecutionStatus Values*

Value	Description
Canceling	An activity is being canceled
Closed	An activity is closed
Compensating	An activity is currently being compensated
Executing	An activity is executing
Faulting	An activity is currently in the faulting state
Initialized	An activity is in the process of being initialized

User tracking events can be generated at any point in the life cycle of a workflow. Their definition is totally under your control. The easiest way to create user tracking events is to explicitly instrument workflow or custom activity code by calling the `TrackData` method. This method is provided by the base `Activity` class (and also supported by the `ActivityExecutionContext` class). When you call this method within your workflow or activity code, you pass any type of data that you like, along with a string key name to identify the data.

You can use these events to track the progress of your workflows at any arbitrary point within your code, even if that point doesn't correspond to one of the standard activity or workflow status changes already discussed. And since you can pass any type of data with each event, this is another alternative mechanism to pass data to the host application (the other primary mechanism being the use of local services).

In addition to explicitly calling the `TrackData` method from within your code, you can also generate user tracking events by adding a `UserTrackPoint` to a tracking profile. Using the `UserTrackPoint` class along with the `UserTrackingLocation` class, you can define an activity, an argument type, and a set of conditions to match. Once the user track point is established, a user tracking event will be generated when an activity matches the conditions that have been defined. Tracking profiles are discussed next.

Custom Tracking Profiles

By default, all of the possible workflow and activity events are generated for all workflow and activity types. Of course, you do need to first enable workflow tracking by adding a tracking service to the workflow runtime. However, you are not limited to this default behavior. The tracking infrastructure allows you to define separate tracking profiles for each workflow `Type`.

The freedom to define multiple tracking profiles provides you with a great deal of flexibility. For instance, you might decide that you are not concerned with all of the activity events for a particular workflow. To remove the tracking of those unnecessary events, you can build a tracking profile for that workflow `Type` that includes only the events that you want. Or perhaps you want to monitor all possible events for a workflow, but only for one or two selected activities. To accomplish that, you can build a tracking profile that defines tracking locations for only the selected `Type` of activity.

Some advanced features of workflow tracking require you to create custom tracking profiles. For instance, WF workflow tracking provides the ability to extract and record field or property values from a running workflow. Extracting instance data such as this is not the default behavior and requires the use of a custom tracking profile that has specific knowledge of the fields and properties of the workflow.

If you are using the SqlTrackingService provided with WF, the database schema provides for the persistence of custom tracking profiles. If a custom profile is not defined for a given workflow Type, a default tracking profile is used. The default profile is also persisted in the database, allowing you to customize it to meet your needs.

If you develop your own custom tracking service, you decide how to persist tracking profiles, or even if you want to support them. Depending on your requirements, you may decide to forgo handling of custom tracking profiles and only use a default profile. Tracking profiles are serialized to XML and are easily saved to a file or to a table in your own database.

Using the Tracking Data

Once you have captured tracking data, how do you access and use it? If you are using the standard SqlTrackingService provided with WF, you can access the data by directly querying the tracking database. The standard database schema that is required by the SqlTrackingService includes a number of views and stored procedures that you can use to query the data.

However, WF also provides the SqlTrackingQuery class that provides easy access to the data. Under the covers, this class queries the tracking database for you, but then provides access to the tracking data via properties of the class. Each event category (workflow, activity, and user) has its own property that provides a collection of event records.

SqlTrackingQuery provides the ability to retrieve the tracking information for a single workflow instance (identified by the instance ID Guid). Or you can query for a collection of workflows based on selection criteria that you provide. For example, you can retrieve tracking data for just those work-flows that have been suspended, or for all workflows of a particular Type.

If you are using your own custom tracking service, you will need to provide your own mecha-nism to retrieve and use the tracking data. Of course, depending on what your tracking service initially does with the data, a retrieval mechanism might not be necessary. For instance, if your tracking service is directly writing tracking data to the Console or logging it to the Windows event log, there is no need to have a separate retrieval mechanism. On the other hand, if you are persisting the tracking data to your own database or to a set of log files, you will likely want to develop a way to access the data.

Benefiting from Workflow Tracking

Using the WF workflow tracking facilities provides a number of benefits to your workflow-driven applications. Some of these benefits are summarized here:

- Tracking is accomplished without application code. Enabling basic tracking of workflow and activity events doesn't require any additional code to your activities or workflows.

- Tracking is accomplished in a consistent way. All workflow applications can take advantage of workflow tracking in the same manner. You don't need to reinvent a new instrumentation mechanism for each new workflow application.

- Tracking services are flexible. You can use the SqlTrackingService that is provided with WF or develop your own custom tracking services that meet the specific requirements of each appli-cation. Regardless of which tracking services are used, the workflow runtime, workflows, and individual activities interact with them in the same consistent way.

- Tracking profiles are flexible. You can use a default tracking profile or define profiles that are different for each workflow Type. Tracking profiles can be programmatically updated and persisted.

- Tracking data is flexible. You can track workflow and activity events, custom user track points, and rule evaluation results, and extract workflow or activity field and property values.

- Tracking provides a central repository of data. All workflows, regardless of their type and purpose, can produce tracking data that is captured and persisted in a central repository. The data in this repository can be viewed and analyzed to track workflow progress, provide alerts when exceptional conditions occur, assist with tuning of workflow performance, and feed external applications.

- Tracking is efficient, seamless, and reliable. When using WF tracking, you don't need to task workflow developers with the job of adding instrumentation code to each workflow and activity. They can focus their time and energy on developing business solutions instead of building a tracking infrastructure.

- Tracking provides visibility. Workflows no longer have to operate in a black box. With workflow tracking enabled, you can monitor the progress of each individual activity and workflow. You can examine the raw data from past workflow instances to predict future behavior and tune workflow performance.

In the sections that follow, I walk through a series of examples that demonstrate how to use the built-in workflow tracking support in WF.

Using the SqlTrackingService

In this first example, you will develop a host application that uses the standard SqlTrackingService to capture workflow tracking data. A simple workflow will be developed to exercise the tracking service. After the workflow completes, the SqlTrackingQuery class will be used to retrieve the tracking data and then write it to the Console.

Preparing the Tracking SQL Database

The SqlTrackingService is an out-of-box tracking service that is designed to persist tracking data to a SQL Server database. Just as with the built-in persistence support included with WF, a set of scripts is included that defines the schema and associated database objects that the SqlTrackingService requires. Prior to using the SqlTrackingService, you need to create a tracking database and execute the setup scripts. If you haven't already set up the required tracking database, follow the steps in the "Preparing the SQL Tracking Database" sidebar now.

PREPARING THE SQL TRACKING DATABASE

You can follow these steps to create a SQL database that is suitable for use with the SqlTrackingService:

1. If you haven't already done so, install either the full or the Express version of SQL Server 2005. If you have already executed the examples from previous chapters that require a database for workflow persistence, you already have SQL Server installed. The example code in this chapter assumes that you are using the Express version. You'll need to adjust the database connection strings if you are using the full version of SQL Server. The steps outlined here use the sqlcmd command-line utility that is distributed with SQL Server. If you have optionally installed SQL Server Management Studio Express, you can use it instead of sqlcmd to execute the SQL commands and scripts.

2. Create a local database to use for workflow tracking. Open a Windows command prompt and enter the following command (don't forget to replace localhost\SQLEXPRESS with your own server name if necessary):

```
sqlcmd -S localhost\SQLEXPRESS -E -Q "create database WorkflowTracking"
```

This creates a local database named WorkflowTracking using the default settings for a new database.

3. Now that you have a database, you need to populate it with the tables and stored procedures that the SqlTrackingService expects. The SQL scripts to create these objects are distributed with the WF runtime and are located in this directory: [WindowsFolder]\Microsoft.Net\Framework\v3.0\Windows Workflow Foundation\SQL\[Language]. [WindowsFolder] is the actual folder where Windows is installed and [Language] is the language based on the regional settings of your machine. For my machine, it's EN for *English*. Within this folder, you'll see a number of SQL scripts, including the two that you need for workflow tracking: Tracking_Schema.sql and Tracking_Logic.sql.

4. Using your open command prompt, switch to the directory where the SQL scripts are located. Now using sqlcmd, execute the first script like this:

```
sqlcmd -S localhost\SQLEXPRESS -E -d WorkflowTracking -i Tracking_Schema.sql
```

5. Execute sqlcmd again to create the stored procedures:

```
sqlcmd -S localhost\SQLEXPRESS -E -d WorkflowTracking -i Tracking_Logic.sql
```

If all of these steps succeed, a local database named WorkflowTracking should now be populated with the tables and stored procedures that are required for workflow tracking.

Developing a Test Workflow

To demonstrate the tracking service, you need a simple workflow to execute. Like previous chapters, this one uses a single project to contain all of the test workflows. Create a new project with the Empty Workflow Project template and name it SharedWorkflows. Save the solution file when prompted, since you'll be adding other projects to the solution.

Add a new sequential workflow to the project and name it TrackingExampleWorkflow. The workflow requires just three activities: two CodeActivity instances with a DelayActivity in between them. Name the first CodeActivity codeFirstActivity and the second codeLastActivity. After naming the CodeActivity instances, double-click each of them to assign a handler for the ExecuteCode event. Set the TimeoutDuration of the DelayActivity to one second (00:00:01). The purpose of the short delay is just to collect a slightly more interesting variety of tracking data.

The completed visual design of the TrackingExampleWorkflow should look like Figure 14-1.

To complete this workflow, add code to the CodeActivity handlers to write a message to the Console. These messages let you know when each activity executes and don't serve any other purpose. This workflow doesn't require any properties at all since that's not the focus of this demonstration. The completed code for the TrackingExampleWorkflow.cs file is shown in Listing 14-1.

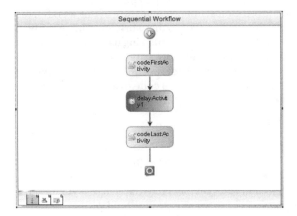

Figure 14-1. *Complete TrackingExampleWorkflow*

Listing 14-1. *Complete TrackingExampleWorkflow.cs File*

```
using System;
using System.Workflow.Activities;

namespace SharedWorkflows
{
    /// <summary>
    /// A simple workflow used to demonstrate tracking
    /// </summary>
    public sealed partial class TrackingExampleWorkflow
        : SequentialWorkflowActivity
    {
        public TrackingExampleWorkflow()
        {
            InitializeComponent();
        }

        private void codeFirstActivity_ExecuteCode(
            object sender, EventArgs e)
        {
            Console.WriteLine("Executing first activity");
        }

        private void codeLastActivity_ExecuteCode(
            object sender, EventArgs e)
        {
            Console.WriteLine("Executing second activity");
        }
    }
}
```

From Listing 14-1, you should be able to identify the most important feature of this workflow as it relates to tracking. That feature? There is no tracking-related code in this workflow. Out of the box, the workflow tracking service provided with WF will be able to produce tracking data without a single line of additional code being added to the workflow. The workflow isn't aware that every activity will be tracked throughout its lifetime. All instrumentation of the workflow occurs within the workflow runtime and doesn't rely on the workflow developer to add any special code to each workflow.

Developing the Host Application

The host application for this example is yet another Console application. Add a Sequential Workflow Console Application to the solution and name it ConsoleTracking. You can remove the Workflow1 that is autogenerated by the project template since it won't be used. You'll need to add the usual project references to this project (SharedWorkflows and Bukovics.Workflow.Hosting). If you haven't already added the Bukovics.Workflow.Hosting project to the solution, you should do that now.

Add a C# class named TrackingTest to the project. This class will contain all of the code needed to host the workflow runtime, add the SqlTrackingService to the workflow and execute the test workflow. Listing 14-2 is the completed code that you need to add to the TrackingTest.cs file.

Listing 14-2. *Complete TrackingTest.cs File*

```
using System;
using System.Collections.Generic;
using System.Workflow.ComponentModel;
using System.Workflow.Runtime;
using System.Workflow.Runtime.Tracking;

using Bukovics.Workflow.Hosting;
using SharedWorkflows;

namespace ConsoleTracking
{
    /// <summary>
    /// Test the TrackingExampleWorkflow
    /// </summary>
    public class TrackingTest
    {
        private static String _connStringTracking = String.Format(
            "Initial Catalog={0};Data Source={1};Integrated Security={2};",
                "WorkflowTracking", @"localhost\SQLEXPRESS", "SSPI");
```

This SQL connection string will be used later in the class when constructing an instance of the SqlTrackingService. Notice that this connection string assumes that you are using a SQL Server Express instance on your local development machine. If you are using the full version of SQL Server or if your server is located on a different machine, you'll need to modify this connection string.

```
        public static void Run()
        {
            using (WorkflowRuntimeManager manager
                = new WorkflowRuntimeManager(new WorkflowRuntime()))
            {
                //add services that we require
                AddServices(manager.WorkflowRuntime);
```

```
                //start the runtime
                manager.WorkflowRuntime.StartRuntime();

                Console.WriteLine("Executing TrackingExampleWorkflow");
                WorkflowInstanceWrapper instance =
                    manager.StartWorkflow(
                        typeof(SharedWorkflows.TrackingExampleWorkflow), null);
                manager.WaitAll(2000);
                Console.WriteLine("Completed TrackingExampleWorkflow\n\r");
            }
        }
```

An instance of the workflow runtime is created and then passed to the private `AddServices` method. This method (shown next) is used to add the `SqlTrackingService` to the runtime. The code then creates and starts an instance of the `TrackingExampleWorkflow` and then waits for it to complete.

```
        /// <summary>
        /// Add any services needed by the runtime engine
        /// </summary>
        /// <param name="instance"></param>
        private static void AddServices(WorkflowRuntime instance)
        {
            //use the standard SQL Server tracking service
            SqlTrackingService tracking
                = new SqlTrackingService(_connStringTracking);

            //add the service to the runtime
            instance.AddService(tracking);
        }
```

The `AddServices` method creates an instance of the `SqlTrackingService`, passing it the SQL connection string defined at the beginning of this class.

The `SqlTrackingService` also provides a `PartitionOnCompletion` property that optionally enables automatic partitioning. The `SqlTrackingService` has the capability of partitioning the tables that store tracking data on a daily, weekly, monthly, or yearly basis. The default is monthly, meaning that as you begin each new month, a new set of tracking tables are created within the database. The tables for the previous month will continue to exist until you explicitly drop them. For this example, the `PartitionOnCompletion` property is not set, which leaves this feature off.

Partitioning is not required, but it does make the job of managing the tracking database much easier. For instance, if you only care about the current month of tracking data, you can use a stored procedure provided with WF to drop all data for a previous month. More information on maintenance of the tracking database is provided in the "Maintaining the SQL Tracking Database" section of this chapter.

Finally, the code adds the `SqlTrackingService` instance just created to the workflow runtime.

```
    }
}
```

You will also need to add a small amount of code to the `Program.cs` file to execute the `Run` method of this class. The `Program.cs` code looks like this:

```
using System;

namespace ConsoleTracking
{
    public class Program
    {
        static void Main(string[] args)
        {
            TrackingTest.Run();

            Console.WriteLine("Press any key to exit");
            Console.ReadLine();
        }
    }
}
```

■**Caution** If you are using the SqlTrackingService and the SqlWorkflowPersistenceService at the same time, there are several guidelines that you should keep in mind in order to experience the best possible performance. You should use the same database and server for both of these services. If the two services use different databases or database servers, a distributed transaction must be obtained from the DTC (the Distributed Transaction Coordinator). A distributed transaction is more expensive in terms of performance and should be avoided.

If you do use the same database for both of these services, you should also load the SharedConnectionWorkflowCommitBatchService in place of the default commit batch service. This service uses a single shared connection between the tracking and persistence databases to avoid the use of distributed transactions.

Executing the Host Application

When you execute the ConsoleTracking application, your results should look like this:

```
Executing TrackingExampleWorkflow
Executing first activity
Executing second activity
Completed TrackingExampleWorkflow

Press any key to exit
```

This begs the question, where is the tracking data? The tracking data was saved to tables in the WorkflowTracking database that you created. This initial version of the host application doesn't include any code to retrieve and display the tracking data. In the next section, you will develop code that retrieves the tracking data for a workflow instance and writes it to the Console.

CONFIGURING SQLTRACKINGSERVICE WITH APP.CONFIG

You can also configure and load the `SqlTrackingService` with entries in the `App.config` file for the application. For example, here is an `App.config` file that configures `SqlTrackingService`:

```xml
<?xml version="1.0" encoding="utf-8" ?>
<configuration>
  <configSections>
    <section name="WorkflowRuntime"
      type="System.Workflow.Runtime.Configuration.WorkflowRuntimeSection,
        System.Workflow.Runtime, Version=3.0.00000.0, Culture=neutral,
        PublicKeyToken=31bf3856ad364e35" />
  </configSections>
  <WorkflowRuntime>
    <CommonParameters>
      <!--Add parameters common to all services-->
      <add name="ConnectionString"
          value="Initial Catalog=WorkflowTracking;
            Data Source=localhost\SQLEXPRESS;
            Integrated Security=SSPI;" />
    </CommonParameters>
    <Services>
      <!--Add core services here-->
      <add type="System.Workflow.Runtime.Tracking.SqlTrackingService,
        System.Workflow.Runtime, Version=3.0.00000.0, Culture=neutral,
        PublicKeyToken=31bf3856ad364e35"/>
    </Services>
  </WorkflowRuntime>
</configuration>
```

To load the service using this file instead of via code, you would specify the configuration section name (WorkflowRuntime) in the `WorkflowRuntime` constructor like this:

```csharp
//load the tracking service via the app.config.
//requires a reference to System.Configuration
using (WorkflowRuntimeManager manager
    = new WorkflowRuntimeManager(
        new WorkflowRuntime("WorkflowRuntime")))
{
...
}
```

As the code comments indicate, you need to add a reference to the `System.Configuration` assembly whenever you access an `App.config` section. In the `ConsoleTracking` example application, you would omit the call to the `AddServices` private method since the services are now loaded via the `App.config` entries.

Retrieving Tracking Data

To make the example `ConsoleTracking` application more interesting, you will now add code that queries and retrieves the tracking data for the current workflow instance after it completes. The code then writes that data to the `Console` for your viewing pleasure.

Implementing the TrackingConsoleWriter

The code to retrieve and write the tracking data is really common code that can be used by any number of applications. For this reason, the code is implemented as a new class in the Bukovics.Workflow.Hosting project instead of inline in the ConsoleTracking project. This is the first addition to this project since it was originally developed in Chapter 4.

Add a new C# class to the Bukovics.Workflow.Hosting project and name it TrackingConsoleWriter. Listing 14-3 is the completed code that you'll need for this class.

■**Note** The code in Listing 14-3 presents the completed TrackingConsoleWriter class. The class includes some code that isn't required for this current workflow but will be used for other examples later in this chapter. Rather than revisiting and enhancing this code with each example, I decided to present all of the code at this time.

Listing 14-3. *Complete TrackingConsoleWriter.cs File*

```
using System;
using System.Collections.Generic;
using System.Workflow.Runtime.Tracking;
using System.Workflow.Activities.Rules;

namespace Bukovics.Workflow.Hosting
{
    /// <summary>
    /// A utility class that retrieves tracking data from
    /// the SQL tracking database and writes it
    /// to the Console
    /// </summary>
    public class TrackingConsoleWriter
    {
        private String _connectionString = String.Empty;

        public TrackingConsoleWriter(String connString)
        {
            _connectionString = connString;
        }
```

This class is essentially a wrapper around the SqlTrackingQuery class, which queries the tracking database and provides access to tracking data via properties of the class. In order to query the database, you need a connection string, so this class accepts one as a parameter to the constructor and saves it in an instance variable.

```
        #region Single Instance Data

        /// <summary>
        /// Write tracking data for a single workflow instance
        /// to the Console
        /// </summary>
        /// <param name="instanceId"></param>
        public void DisplayTrackingData(Guid instanceId)
        {
            //retrieve the tracking data
            SortedList<Int32, TrackingRecord> records
                = QueryTrackingData(instanceId);
```

```
            //write the tracking data to the Console
            WriteSingleInstanceToConsole(instanceId, records);
    }
```

DisplayTrackingData is one of the public methods exposed by this class. You pass it a workflow instance ID and it will retrieve the tracking data and write it to the Console.

```
        /// <summary>
        /// Retrieve tracking data from the database for a
        /// workflow instance.
        /// </summary>
        /// <param name="instanceId"></param>
        /// <returns>
        /// Returns a sorted list of all available TrackingRecords
        /// </returns>
        private SortedList<Int32, TrackingRecord> QueryTrackingData(
            Guid instanceId)
        {
            //create a sorted list for all of the tracking records
            SortedList<Int32, TrackingRecord> records
                = new SortedList<int, TrackingRecord>();

            try
            {
                //create an object that queries the tracking database
                SqlTrackingQuery query
                    = new SqlTrackingQuery(_connectionString);

                //retrieve tracking data for a workflow instance
                SqlTrackingWorkflowInstance instance = null;
                query.TryGetWorkflow(instanceId, out instance);

                //build a sorted list of TrackingRecords
                BuildSortedList(records, instance);
            }
            catch (System.Data.SqlClient.SqlException e)
            {
                Console.WriteLine("SqlException in QueryTrackingData: {0}",
                    e.Message);
            }

            return records;
        }
```

The QueryTrackingData private method retrieves tracking data for a single workflow instance. It uses an instance of the SqlTrackingQuery class to perform the query and return the data in an organized way. The TryGetWorkflow method of SqlTrackingQuery is called to retrieve the data and return it as a SqlTrackingWorkflowInstance object. Once retrieved, the SqlTrackingWorkflowInstance is passed to the private BuildSortedList method.

As shown in this example, you should always wrap your calls within a try/catch block when using the SqlTrackingQuery class. Internally, SqlTrackingQuery executes SQL queries to access the tracking database and is capable of throwing a SqlException if a problem occurs.

```
/// <summary>
/// Build a sorted list of TrackingRecords for a single
/// workflow instance
/// </summary>
/// <param name="records"></param>
/// <param name="instance"></param>
private static void BuildSortedList(
    SortedList<Int32, TrackingRecord> records,
    SqlTrackingWorkflowInstance instance)
{
    if (instance != null)
    {
        //add workflow events to the sorted list
        foreach (TrackingRecord record in instance.WorkflowEvents)
        {
            records.Add(record.EventOrder, record);
        }

        //add activity events to the sorted list
        foreach (TrackingRecord record in instance.ActivityEvents)
        {
            records.Add(record.EventOrder, record);
        }

        //add user events to the sorted list
        foreach (TrackingRecord record in instance.UserEvents)
        {
            records.Add(record.EventOrder, record);
        }
    }
}
```

The private BuildSortedList method retrieves the three different types of tracking events (workflow, activity, and user) and consolidates them into a single sorted list. Each one of the events has its own record type, but they all derive from the base TrackingRecord class that is used here.

Although the event types are segregated into three different SqlTrackingWorkflowInstance properties, they form a contiguous series of individually numbered events. The EventOrder property of each TrackingRecord identifies the sequence of the event. In order to get the complete tracking picture for a workflow instance, you have to look at events of all three event types.

For instance, the workflow events usually contain a record with EventOrder of 1 that corresponds to when the workflow was created. This is followed by another record with an EventOrder of 2 that indicates when the workflow was started. After that, the next events (EventOrder of 3, 4, etc.) might be activity or user events.

The purpose of this method is to return one sorted list of event records that are in sequence based on their EventOrder property. Once a sorted list is produced, another method of this class can write the events to the Console knowing that they are already in the correct sequence regardless of their event type.

Of course, you are not required to handle the events in this way. This was a conscious design decision to display a consolidated list of all events in sequence. In your applications, you are free to use these tracking events in any way (and sequence) that you like.

```
/// <summary>
/// Write tracking data for a single instance to the Console
/// </summary>
/// <param name="instanceId"></param>
/// <param name="records"></param>
private void WriteSingleInstanceToConsole(
    Guid instanceId, SortedList<Int32, TrackingRecord> records)
{
    Console.WriteLine("Tracking data for workflow instance {0}",
        instanceId);

    foreach (TrackingRecord record in records.Values)
    {
        if (record is WorkflowTrackingRecord)
        {
            WorkflowTrackingRecord wfRecord
                = record as WorkflowTrackingRecord;
            Console.WriteLine("{0:HH:mm:ss.fff} Workflow {1}",
                wfRecord.EventDateTime,
                wfRecord.TrackingWorkflowEvent);
        }
        else if (record is ActivityTrackingRecord)
        {
            ActivityTrackingRecord actRecord
                = record as ActivityTrackingRecord;
            Console.WriteLine("{0:HH:mm:ss.fff} {1} {2}, Type={3}",
                actRecord.EventDateTime,
                actRecord.ExecutionStatus,
                actRecord.QualifiedName,
                actRecord.ActivityType.Name);
            WriteBodyToConsole(actRecord);
        }
        else if (record is UserTrackingRecord)
        {
            UserTrackingRecord userRecord
                = record as UserTrackingRecord;
            if (userRecord.UserData is RuleActionTrackingEvent)
            {
                WriteRuleData(userRecord);
            }
            else
            {
                Console.WriteLine(
                    "{0:HH:mm:ss.fff} UserData from {1} {2}:{3}",
                    userRecord.EventDateTime,
                    userRecord.QualifiedName,
                    userRecord.UserDataKey,
                    userRecord.UserData);
            }
        }
    }

    Console.WriteLine("End of tracking data for {0}\n\r",
        instanceId);
}
```

The WriteSingleInstanceToConsole method is passed the sorted list of events and writes all of them to the Console. The Type of each TrackingRecord is checked to determine the event type and then cast to the appropriate class in order to reference the type-specific members.

The WriteBodyToConsole method that is referenced for an ActivityTrackingRecord is used to display additional information for some tracking records. Likewise, the code that handles the UserTrackingRecord checks the UserData property to determine whether it contains rule-specific data. If so, the WriteRuleData method is invoked. Both of these methods handle special cases that are not used for this first tracking example. However, additional examples later in this chapter will produce tracking data that exercises this code.

```
/// <summary>
/// Write any annotations and body data to the Console
/// </summary>
/// <param name="record"></param>
private void WriteBodyToConsole(ActivityTrackingRecord record)
{
    //write annotations
    if (record.Annotations.Count > 0)
    {
        foreach (String annotation in record.Annotations)
        {
            Console.WriteLine("     {0}", annotation);
        }
    }

    //write extracted data
    if (record.Body.Count > 0)
    {
        foreach (TrackingDataItem data in record.Body)
        {
            Console.WriteLine("       {0}={1}",
                data.FieldName, data.Data);
        }
    }
}
```

The WriteBodyToConsole method is used to write additional data contained within an ActivityTrackingRecord if it exists. Each ActivityTrackingRecord can optionally contain annotations that describe the tracking data. The Body property of the tracking record contains optional data that has been extracted from an activity. The code in this method will be used by the extracting data example later in this chapter.

```
/// <summary>
/// Write rule data to the Console
/// </summary>
/// <param name="userRecord"></param>
private static void WriteRuleData(UserTrackingRecord userRecord)
{
    RuleActionTrackingEvent ruleAction
        = userRecord.UserData as RuleActionTrackingEvent;
```

```
        Console.WriteLine(
            "{0:HH:mm:ss.fff} RuleAction from {1} Rule:{2} Result:{3}",
            userRecord.EventDateTime,
            userRecord.QualifiedName,
            ruleAction.RuleName,
            ruleAction.ConditionResult);
    }
```

The WriteRuleData method writes rule tracking data if it exists. The rule tracking data is passed as a RuleActionTrackingEvent object in the UserData property of the UserTrackingRecord.

```
    #endregion

    #region Display All Workflow Instances

    /// <summary>
    /// Write tracking data to the Console for
    /// all workflow instances
    /// </summary>
    public void DisplayAllTrackingData(SqlTrackingQueryOptions options)
    {
        //retrieve all workflow instances
        IList<SqlTrackingWorkflowInstance> workflows
            = QueryWorkflowList(options);

        SortedList<Int32, TrackingRecord> records
            = new SortedList<int, TrackingRecord>();
        //process all workflow instances in the collection
        foreach (SqlTrackingWorkflowInstance wf in workflows)
        {
            //build a sorted list of TrackingRecords
            records.Clear();
            BuildSortedList(records, wf);
            //write the tracking data to the Console
            WriteSingleInstanceToConsole(wf.WorkflowInstanceId, records);
        }
    }
```

The DisplayAllTrackingData method is another public method that is exposed by this class. This method retrieves tracking data for all workflows that match the specified options. The options are passed as a SqlTrackingQueryOptions instance. Options might be as simple as the workflow status (e.g., return only completed workflows), or might include specific workflow Types or other conditions.

This method calls the private QueryWorkflowList method to retrieve the tracking data, then builds a sorted list and calls WriteSingleInstanceToConsole for each workflow instance that is retrieved. The result is that tracking data for all retrieved workflow instances is written to the Console.

This method is not used by any examples in this chapter but is included in this class for completeness. This method (along with the private methods that it calls) illustrates how to use the SqlTrackingQuery class to retrieve data for multiple workflows.

```
        /// <summary>
        /// Retrieve tracking data for all workflow instances
        /// matching the specified options
        /// </summary>
        /// <param name="options"></param>
        /// <returns></returns>
        private IList<SqlTrackingWorkflowInstance> QueryWorkflowList(
            SqlTrackingQueryOptions options)
        {
            IList<SqlTrackingWorkflowInstance> workflows
                = new List<SqlTrackingWorkflowInstance>();

            try
            {
                //create an object that queries the tracking database
                SqlTrackingQuery query
                    = new SqlTrackingQuery(_connectionString);

                //retrieve all workflows based on query options
                workflows = query.GetWorkflows(options);
            }
            catch (System.Data.SqlClient.SqlException e)
            {
                Console.WriteLine("SqlException in QueryWorkflowList: {0}",
                    e.Message);
            }

            return workflows;
        }
```

The QueryWorkflowList method retrieves a collection of SqlTrackingWorkflowInstance objects. Each instance represents the tracking data for one of the retrieved workflows. To retrieve this data, the SqlTrackingQuery class is used once again, this time calling the GetWorkflows method.

```
        #endregion
    }
}
```

Using the TrackingConsoleWriter

Now that you've implemented the TrackingConsoleWriter, you can use it from the ConsoleTracking application. Add code to the TrackingTest class of the ConsoleTracking project to create an instance of the TrackingConsoleWriter and then call the DisplayTrackingData method. The additional code should be added to the end of the static Run method as shown here:

```
public static void Run()
{

    …


    //query and display tracking data for this single instance
    TrackingConsoleWriter trackingWriter
        = new TrackingConsoleWriter(_connStringTracking);
    trackingWriter.DisplayTrackingData(instance.Id);
}
```

The TrackingConsoleWriter is passed the SQL connection string for the tracking database during construction. The DisplayTrackingData method is passed the instance ID for the workflow that just completed.

After building the solution, you can execute the ConsoleTracking application again. You should now see these results:

```
Executing TrackingExampleWorkflow
Executing first activity
Executing second activity
Completed TrackingExampleWorkflow

Tracking data for workflow instance 314a7b67-3281-45e3-b43d-0f2fe7d70bce
00:25:27.390 Workflow Created
00:25:27.390 Workflow Started
00:25:27.390 Executing TrackingExampleWorkflow, Type=TrackingExampleWorkflow
00:25:27.390 Executing codeFirstActivity, Type=CodeActivity
00:25:27.390 Closed codeFirstActivity, Type=CodeActivity
00:25:27.390 Executing delayActivity1, Type=DelayActivity
00:25:27.390 Workflow Idle
00:25:28.390 Closed delayActivity1, Type=DelayActivity
00:25:28.390 Executing codeLastActivity, Type=CodeActivity
00:25:28.390 Closed codeLastActivity, Type=CodeActivity
00:25:28.390 Closed TrackingExampleWorkflow, Type=TrackingExampleWorkflow
00:25:28.390 Workflow Completed
End of tracking data for 314a7b67-3281-45e3-b43d-0f2fe7d70bce

Press any key to exit
```

■ **Note** Since it is a Guid, the workflow instance ID that you see will be different when you execute this application.

Following the completion of the workflow, the tracking data for the instance is now displayed. The first two lines show workflow events, indicating that the workflow was created and then subsequently started. Following that, you will see activity events indicating that the workflow class itself is executing, followed by the first CodeActivity executing and then closing. In the middle of the execution for the DelayActivity, the workflow becomes idle, which is to be expected during a delay. Following the delay, the final CodeActivity executes and then the workflow is completed.

Each event is associated with a DateTime that indicates when the event occurred. For this listing, this property is formatted to show only the time portion.

With just a small amount of code during startup of the workflow runtime (to add the SqlTrackingService), you have a fairly large amount of tracking data. And no changes were required of the workflow to produce this data. This same level of detail is automatically captured for any type of workflow that you execute while the SqlTrackingService is loaded.

But this is really just the beginning of the workflow tracking story. The sections that follow expand on this example to demonstrate additional features of WF tracking.

Creating User Track Points

In the previous example, you saw how the standard set of workflow and activity events are tracked without adding any additional code to the workflow. This example builds upon the previous one to introduce user track points.

A *user track point* is simply a tracking point that you add to a workflow or custom activity in code. It is a user track point because it can occur at any point in the code that you like. When you call the TrackData method (implemented by the base Activity class), you are creating a user track point. When you call this method, you can pass any type of data that you like. This data, along with a string name to identify the data, is passed to any registered tracking services as a user tracking event.

This mechanism allows you to explicitly create your own tracking points based on your knowledge of the application. By creating a user track point, you are signifying that there is some significance to the data, or that this particular point in the activity or workflow code is important. When retrieving the tracking data for a workflow instance, the data you pass to the TrackData method is made available in a UserTrackingRecord.

Enhancing the TrackingExampleWorkflow

To add user track points to the TrackingExampleWorkflow, open it in the code editor and add calls to the TrackData method as shown in Listing 14-4.

Listing 14-4. *Revised TrackingExampleWorkflow.cs with User Track Points*

```
using System;
using System.Workflow.Activities;

namespace SharedWorkflows
{

    ...

        private void codeFirstActivity_ExecuteCode(
            object sender, EventArgs e)
        {
            Console.WriteLine("Executing first activity");
            TrackData("accountKey", 123456);
        }

        private void codeLastActivity_ExecuteCode(
            object sender, EventArgs e)
        {
            Console.WriteLine("Executing second activity");
            TrackData("approvalMessage", "approved");
        }
    }
}
```

This revised code includes two user track points, one for each of the CodeActivity handlers. The data passed to the TrackData method is a simple integer and String, but you can also pass complex objects of your own creation. The overloaded version of the TrackData method shown here also passes a userDataKey parameter as the first argument. This identifies the data in the tracking records. Any data passed to TrackData is serialized using binary serialization. If for some reason it can't be serialized, the ToString method is called on the object to extract the data for tracking.

Testing the Revised Workflow

There are no changes needed to the ConsoleTracking application to test the revised workflow. After rebuilding the SharedWorkflows project, you should be able to execute the ConsoleTracking application and see these results:

```
Executing TrackingExampleWorkflow
Executing first activity
Executing second activity
Completed TrackingExampleWorkflow

Tracking data for workflow instance 7604d971-2585-4b03-ac19-cf7947706303
01:00:31.860 Workflow Created
01:00:31.877 Workflow Started
01:00:31.877 Executing TrackingExampleWorkflow, Type= TrackingExampleWorkflow
01:00:31.890 Executing codeFirstActivity, Type=CodeActivity
01:00:31.890 UserData from codeFirstActivity accountKey:123456
01:00:31.907 Closed codeFirstActivity, Type=CodeActivity
01:00:31.907 Executing delayActivity1, Type=DelayActivity
01:00:31.907 Workflow Idle
01:00:32.907 Closed delayActivity1, Type=DelayActivity
01:00:32.907 Executing codeLastActivity, Type=CodeActivity
01:00:32.907 UserData from codeLastActivity approvalMessage:approved
01:00:32.907 Closed codeLastActivity, Type=CodeActivity
01:00:32.907 Closed TrackingExampleWorkflow, Type= TrackingExampleWorkflow
01:00:32.907 Workflow Completed
End of tracking data for 7604d971-2585-4b03-ac19-cf7947706303

Press any key to exit
```

The highlighted lines show that the two calls to the TrackData method successfully captured the data. Notice also that the user data is shown in the correct sequence between the start and end of each CodeActivity.

Tracking Rules Evaluation

Workflow tracking is also capable of recording each Rule in a RuleSet as it is evaluated. The rule name along with the result of the rule evaluation (true or false) is tracked. To demonstrate this, you need a simple workflow that executes a RuleSet.

Implementing the TrackingRulesWorkflow

Add a new sequential workflow to the SharedWorkflows project and name it TrackingRulesWorkflow. Before defining any rules, you need to add a few instance variables to the workflow. The variables have no special purpose other than to provide fields for the rules to evaluate and update. Listing 14-5 is the complete code that you'll need for the TrackingRulesWorkflow.cs file.

Listing 14-5. *Complete TrackingRulesWorkflow.cs File*

```
using System;
using System.Workflow.Activities;

namespace SharedWorkflows
{
    /// <summary>
    /// A workflow that demonstrates tracking of rules
    /// </summary>
    public sealed partial class TrackingRulesWorkflow
        : SequentialWorkflowActivity
    {
        private Int32 field1 = 20;
        private Int32 field2 = 0;
        private String field3 = String.Empty;

        public TrackingRulesWorkflow()
        {
            InitializeComponent();
        }
    }
}
```

Now add a PolicyActivity to the workflow, create a new RuleSet, and add the two rules defined in Table 14-3.

■**Note** If you need a reminder on how to define a RuleSet, please refer to Chapter 11.

Table 14-3. *Rules for the TrackingRulesWorkflow*

Rule	Condition	ThenAction	ElseAction
ruleOne	this.field1 >= 10	this.field2 = this.field1 * 100	this.field2 = this.field1
ruleTwo	this.field2 < 100	this.field3 = "not so big"	this.field3 = "big number"

The Rule Set Editor for the PolicyActivity is shown in Figure 14-2.

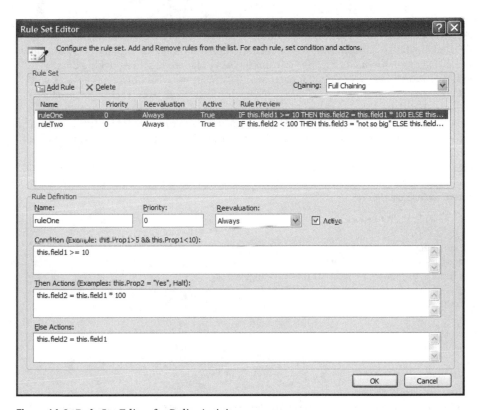

Figure 14-2. *Rule Set Editor for PolicyActivity*

Testing the Workflow

You can execute the TrackingRulesWorkflow with the ConsoleTracking application developed for the previous examples. The only required code changes are to the TrackingTest class. Replace all instances of the TrackingExampleWorkflow with the TrackingRulesWorkflow.

After rebuilding the solution, you are ready to execute the revised ConsoleTracking application. Here are the results that I receive when I run this application:

```
Executing TrackingRulesWorkflow
Completed TrackingRulesWorkflow

Tracking data for workflow instance 9723abbf-979f-4024-8458-b5ff09941a45
00:25:35.247 Workflow Created
00:25:35.337 Workflow Started
00:25:35.337 Executing TrackingRulesWorkflow, Type=TrackingRulesWorkflow
00:25:35.397 Executing policyActivity1, Type=PolicyActivity
00:25:35.487 RuleAction from policyActivity1 Rule:ruleOne Result:True
00:25:35.497 RuleAction from policyActivity1 Rule:ruleTwo Result:False
00:25:35.507 Closed policyActivity1, Type=PolicyActivity
00:25:35.507 Closed TrackingRulesWorkflow, Type=TrackingRulesWorkflow
00:25:35.507 Workflow Completed
End of tracking data for 9723abbf-979f-4024-8458-b5ff09941a45

Press any key to exit
```

The highlighted lines are the rule tracking data that was recorded during execution of the PolicyActivity. The results show that ruleOne evaluated to true while ruleTwo was false.

The rule tracking data is captured as a user tracking event, but it isn't immediately obvious how you retrieve the rule data. When you use the SqlTrackingQuery class to retrieve tracking data, a SqlTrackingWorkflowInstance is returned for each workflow instance. This object has a UserEvents property that contains a collection of UserTrackingRecord objects. Each UserTrackingRecord has a UserData property. If the UserTrackingRecord contains rule data, the UserData property will be an instance of a RuleActionTrackingEvent object. After casting UserData to a RuleActionTrackingEvent, you can reference the RuleName and ConditionResult properties that identify the rule and the result of the rule evaluation.

The TrackingConsoleWriter class that was developed earlier in this chapter contains a method named WriteSingleInstanceToConsole. This method has code to handle rule data that is similar to the abbreviated code shown here:

```
if (record is UserTrackingRecord)
{
    UserTrackingRecord userRecord
        = record as UserTrackingRecord;
    if (userRecord.UserData is RuleActionTrackingEvent)
    {
        WriteRuleData(userRecord);
    }
    else
    {
    …
    }
}
```

This example demonstrated that rule tracking data is easily accessible and doesn't require adding any additional code to each rules workflow. However, while the standard rule tracking data includes the result of each rule, it doesn't include the field values that were used during the rule evaluation. But retrieving the field values is also possible with workflow tracking.

Workflow tracking is capable of extracting field or property values during workflow execution, but that does require the use of a custom tracking profile. Developing a custom profile to extract workflow data is the subject of the next section.

Extracting Data with a Custom Tracking Profile

In addition to the built-in tracking functionality that you've already seen, WF tracking also enables you to extract data from an activity or workflow. This is accomplished by adding extract definitions to either an activity or user track point. Each extract definition identifies the field or property that you wish to extract, making the data available for retrieval in a tracking record.

In order to add extract definitions, you need to define a custom tracking profile. The fields that you wish to extract are most likely very specific to a particular Type of workflow and would not be suitable in the default tracking profile that is used by all workflow types.

In the example that follows, you will learn how to add entries to a custom tracking profile to extract field values from a workflow. The same workflow that was used in the last example (TrackingRulesWorkflow) will be used here without any changes. The profile will extract the fields at two tracking locations: before and after the RuleSet is evaluated. Once these values are extracted, you will be able to see the field values before the RuleSet evaluation, the result of how each rule is evaluated (as you saw in the last example), and the resulting field values after the RuleSet evaluation. You will finally have the complete tracking picture for rules evaluation.

The code needed to add the extract definitions is a relatively small portion of the overall code that you'll need. The bulk of the code is housekeeping logic used to retrieve, update, and delete custom tracking profiles.

Working with Tracking Profiles

Tracking profiles are simply a way for you to define the type of tracking data that you want to capture. They act as a filter, passing just the data that meets the selection criteria to a tracking service for processing and persistence. Tracking profiles are defined individually by workflow Type.

You haven't been bothered with a tracking profile up until this point since workflow tracking provides a default profile. This default profile is used for all workflow types unless you explicitly create one for a workflow Type. The default profile tracks all possible workflow, activity, and user events.

The database schema used by the SqlTrackingService provides a set of tables, views, and stored procedures for persistence and management of tracking profiles. The SqlTrackingService attempts to retrieve a tracking profile as tracking begins for a given workflow instance. If a custom profile is found, it is used; otherwise, the default profile is used. This means that in order to use a custom tracking profile, it is not enough to simply create the profile in memory. You must persist it to the SQL tracking database before it can be used.

All tracking profiles contain a version number. Each time you modify an existing profile, you must increment the version number. The profile with the highest version number for a workflow Type is the one that is used at runtime.

The tables and views associated with tracking profiles are listed in Table 14-4.

Table 14-4. *Tracking Profile Tables and Views*

Table	View	Description
Type	vw_Type	Identifies each workflow type by its full Type and Assembly name. Each workflow is assigned a unique ID number that is used to identify the tracking profiles associated with the workflow.
TrackingProfile	vw_TrackingProfile	Contains a row for each version of a tracking profile. Each row has a unique identifier along with a WorkflowTypeId that corresponds to a row in the Type table. The actual tracking profile is persisted in the TrackingProfileXml column as a serialized XML string. Multiple rows may exist for each workflow type since a unique Version number is assigned to each profile.

Some of the stored procedures that you can use to manage tracking profiles are summarized in Table 14-5.

You can work with tracking profiles in two forms. You can create and update a profile using the WF object model (the TrackingProfile and related classes), or you can serialize and deserialize a profile to XML. Once it is in XML form, you can parse and update the elements in the profile programmatically to modify the profile. Regardless of the mechanism you use to maintain tracking profiles, they are stored in their serialized XML format within the tracking database.

Each TrackingProfile object contains three properties (WorkflowTrackPoints, ActivityTrackPoints, UserTrackPoints) that correspond to the three types of tracking data. Each one of these properties is a collection of tracking point objects of a type that corresponds to each property (WorkflowTrackPoint, ActivityTrackPoint, UserTrackPoint).

Table 14-5. *Tracking Profile Stored Procedures*

Procedure Name	Description
GetTrackingProfile	Retrieves a tracking profile by workflow Type, Assembly, and Version.
UpdateTrackingProfile	Creates or updates a custom tracking profile for a workflow Type.
DeleteTrackingProfile	Deletes a tracking profile. Note: This procedure performs a logical delete on an existing profile by setting the version to –1. To physically remove a tracking profile, you need to delete the row from the TrackingProfile table.
GetCurrentDefaultTrackingProfile	Retrieves the current default profile.
GetDefaultTrackingProfile	Retrieves a particular version of the default profile. The version retrieved may not be the current one that is in effect.
UpdateDefaultTrackingProfile	Applies changes to the default tracking profile.

Each of these tracking point objects has a MatchingLocations property that you use to identify the tracking locations that qualify tracking data. Think of the MatchingLocations property as your primary filter. For instance, for a WorkflowTrackPoint, you can use the MatchingLocations property to identify the workflow events (e.g., Created, Started, etc.) that you wish to match. The ActivityTrackPoint and UserTrackPoint extend this concept by also providing an ExcludedLocations property. As the name implies, you use this property to specify conditions that will disqualify the tracking data.

The ActivityTrackPoint and UserTrackPoint both support an Extracts property. This is the property that you use to define the individual fields or properties to extract. Also included is an Annotations property that allows you to add descriptions of the extracted data.

Implementing the TrackingProfileHelper

Creating a custom tracking profile isn't difficult, but it is slightly tedious. In addition to the code that actually creates or modifies a profile, you need code that can retrieve a profile from the database or apply your changes as an update. To assist with these efforts, the code that follows is a tracking profile helper class. It contains a number of methods that take care of the database access when working with tracking profiles.

Since it is designed to be reused, I've placed this code in the Bukovics.Workflow.Hosting project. Add a new C# class to this project and name it TrackingProfileHelper. Listing 14-6 is the complete code for the TrackingProfileHelper.cs file with inline comments describing the code.

Listing 14-6. *Complete TrackingProfileHelper.cs File*

```
using System;
using System.IO;
using System.Data;
using System.Text;
using System.Data.SqlClient;
using System.Collections.Generic;
using System.Workflow.Runtime.Tracking;
```

```
namespace Bukovics.Workflow.Hosting
{
    /// <summary>
    /// Routines that assist with tracking profile management
    /// </summary>
    public class TrackingProfileHelper
    {
        private String _connectionString = String.Empty;

        public TrackingProfileHelper(String connString)
        {
            _connectionString = connString;
        }
```

Since you always need a connection string to reference the SQL tracking database, I decided to pass this in during construction.

```
        /// <summary>
        /// Retrieve the tracking profile for the workflow type
        /// </summary>
        /// <param name="workflowType"></param>
        /// <returns></returns>
        public TrackingProfile RetrieveProfile(Type workflowType)
        {
            TrackingProfile profile = null;
            try
            {
                String profileXml = null;
                using (SqlConnection conn
                    = new SqlConnection(_connectionString))
                {
                    SqlCommand command = new SqlCommand(
                        "GetTrackingProfile", conn);
                    command.CommandType = CommandType.StoredProcedure;
                    command.Parameters.Add(new SqlParameter(
                        "@TypeFullName", workflowType.FullName));
                    command.Parameters.Add(new SqlParameter(
                        "@AssemblyFullName", workflowType.Assembly.FullName));
                    command.Parameters.Add(new SqlParameter(
                        "@Version", null));
                    command.Parameters.Add(new SqlParameter(
                        "@CreateDefault", true));

                    command.Connection.Open();
                    using (SqlDataReader reader = command.ExecuteReader())
                    {
                        while (reader.Read())
                        {
                            profileXml = reader["TrackingProfile"] as String;
                        }
                        reader.Close();
                    }
                }
```

```
                if (profileXml != null)
                {
                    TrackingProfileSerializer serializer
                        = new TrackingProfileSerializer();
                    using (StringReader reader = new StringReader(profileXml))
                    {
                        profile = serializer.Deserialize(reader);
                    }
                }
            }
            catch (SqlException e)
            {
                Console.WriteLine(
                    "SqlException in RetrieveProfile: {0}", e.Message);
                throw;
            }

            return profile;
        }
```

The RetrieveProfile method is designed to retrieve the current profile for the specified work-flow Type. It returns a TrackingProfile object that can be manipulated by the calling code. The GetTrackingProfile stored procedure is used to retrieve the profile from the database. This stored procedure returns the current default profile if one doesn't exist for the specified workflow Type. The code passes true to the @CreateDefault parameter. This causes the stored procedure to insert a new profile for the workflow Type using the default profile as a template.

When the profile is retrieved from the database, the TrackingProfile column in the result set contains the serialized XML version of the profile. This is passed to an instance of the TrackingProfileSerializer class, which deserializes it into a TrackingProfile object.

```
        /// <summary>
        /// Update a tracking profile
        /// </summary>
        /// <param name="profile"></param>
        /// <param name="workflowType"></param>
        public void UpdateProfile(TrackingProfile profile, Type workflowType)
        {
            try
            {
                String profileXml = null;
                TrackingProfileSerializer serializer
                    = new TrackingProfileSerializer();
                using (StringWriter writer = new StringWriter(new StringBuilder()))
                {
                    serializer.Serialize(writer, profile);
                    profileXml = writer.ToString();
                }
```

```
        if (profileXml != null)
        {
            using (SqlConnection conn
                = new SqlConnection(_connectionString))
            {

                SqlCommand command = new SqlCommand(
                    "UpdateTrackingProfile", conn);
                command.CommandType = CommandType.StoredProcedure;
                command.Parameters.Add(new SqlParameter(
                    "@TypeFullName", workflowType.FullName));
                command.Parameters.Add(new SqlParameter(
                    "@AssemblyFullName", workflowType.Assembly.FullName));
                command.Parameters.Add(new SqlParameter(
                    "@Version", profile.Version.ToString()));
                command.Parameters.Add(new SqlParameter(
                    "@TrackingProfileXml", profileXml));

                command.Connection.Open();
                command.ExecuteNonQuery();
            }
        }
    }
    catch (SqlException e)
    {
        Console.WriteLine(
            "SqlException in UpdateProfile: {0}", e.Message);
        throw;
    }
}
```

The UpdateProfile method performs the work to persist a TrackingProfile object to the database for a specified workflow Type. It uses the UpdateTrackingProfile stored procedure to perform the database update. The TrackingProfileSerializer is again used to serialize the TrackingProfile object into an XML string prior to persistence.

```
/// <summary>
/// Delete a tracking profile for a workflow
/// </summary>
/// <param name="workflowType"></param>
public void DeleteProfile(Type workflowType)
{
    try
    {
        using (SqlConnection conn
            = new SqlConnection(_connectionString))
        {
            SqlCommand command = new SqlCommand(
                @"DELETE FROM TrackingProfile
                  WHERE WorkflowTypeId IN
                  (SELECT TypeId FROM Type
                   WHERE TypeFullName = @TypeFullName
                   AND  AssemblyFullName = @AssemblyFullName)",
                conn);
```

```
                    command.Parameters.Add(new SqlParameter(
                        "@TypeFullName", workflowType.FullName));
                    command.Parameters.Add(new SqlParameter(
                        "@AssemblyFullName", workflowType.Assembly.FullName));
                    command.Connection.Open();
                    command.ExecuteNonQuery();
                }
            }
            catch (SqlException e)
            {
                Console.WriteLine(
                    "SqlException in DeleteProfile: {0}", e.Message);
                throw;
            }
        }
    }
```

The DeleteProfile method removes all profiles for the specified workflow Type. This method executes a SQL delete directly rather than using a stored procedure. The DeleteTrackingProfile stored procedure provided by WF soft deletes a profile, marking it with a version number of –1. For purposes of this test, I want to make sure that I physically delete all traces of the tracking profile for a workflow. I use a subselect against the Type table to identify the WorkflowTypeId to delete in the TrackingProfile table.

```
    }
}
```

Creating the Tracking Profile

In this example, you will create the tracking profile directly in the ConsoleTracking host application. In a real application, you would likely develop a separate application that permits easy creation and maintenance of tracking profiles.

To create the tracking profile, modify the TrackingTest.cs file with the changes noted in Listing 14-7.

Listing 14-7. *Revised TrackingTest.cs File with Tracking Profile Creation*

```
using System;
using System.Collections.Generic;
using System.Workflow.ComponentModel;
using System.Workflow.Runtime;
using System.Workflow.Runtime.Tracking;

using Bukovics.Workflow.Hosting;
using SharedWorkflows;

namespace ConsoleTracking
{
    /// <summary>
    /// Test the TrackingExampleWorkflow
    /// </summary>
    public class TrackingTest
    {

        ...
```

```
public static void Run()
{
```

...

```
        //add a custom tracking profile for this workflow
        AddCustomTrackingProfile();

        //start the runtime
        manager.WorkflowRuntime.StartRuntime();
```

Add a call to a new AddCustomTrackingProfile method (implementation shown in the following code) immediately before the call to the StartRuntime method. This method will create the custom tracking profile for the workflow. The call to AddCustomTrackingProfile can be done any time prior to starting the workflow.

...

```
        //delete the tracking profile that we created
        DeleteCustomTrackingProfile();
```

At the very end of the static Run method, add a call to another new method named DeleteCustomTrackingProfile. This method will remove the custom profile from the tracking database.

```
    }
}

/// <summary>
/// Add a custom tracking profile for this workflow
/// </summary>
private static void AddCustomTrackingProfile()
{
    //get the default profile for the workflow
    TrackingProfileHelper helper
        = new TrackingProfileHelper(_connStringTracking);
    TrackingProfile profile = helper.RetrieveProfile(
        typeof(SharedWorkflows.TrackingRulesWorkflow));
```

To create a new profile for a workflow, you have two choices. One option is to build a profile completely from scratch using the profile object model. This option is demonstrated later in the chapter for a custom tracking service. The second option is to retrieve an existing profile and then modify it to meet your needs. The second option is demonstrated here.

The code uses the TrackingProfileHelper class (just discussed in the previous section) to retrieve an existing version of the profile for the TrackingRulesWorkflow type. Since a profile for this workflow doesn't already exist, the default profile is returned in the TrackingProfile object.

```
        if (profile != null)
        {
            //add an activity track point that captures workflow
            //field values prior to the RuleSet execution
            ActivityTrackingLocation location = new ActivityTrackingLocation();
            location.ActivityTypeName = "PolicyActivity";
            location.ExecutionStatusEvents.Add(
                ActivityExecutionStatus.Executing);
            ActivityTrackPoint point = new ActivityTrackPoint();
```

```
point.Extracts.Add(new WorkflowDataTrackingExtract("field1"));
point.Extracts.Add(new WorkflowDataTrackingExtract("field2"));
point.Extracts.Add(new WorkflowDataTrackingExtract("field3"));
point.Annotations.Add("Before RuleSet execution");
point.MatchingLocations.Add(location);
profile.ActivityTrackPoints.Add(point);
```

This code defines the tracking location for the first set of field extracts. The chosen location is the ActivityExecutionStatus.Executing status. This means that the fields identified by the WorkflowDataTrackingExtract objects (field1, field2, field3) will be extracted when the named activity type begins execution. In this case, the named activity type is a PolicyActivity. I've also included an annotation to indicate that these values are prior to the RuleSet execution.

```
//extract values for the same fields after RuleSet execution
location = new ActivityTrackingLocation();
location.ActivityTypeName = "PolicyActivity";
location.ExecutionStatusEvents.Add(
    ActivityExecutionStatus.Closed);
point = new ActivityTrackPoint();
point.Extracts.Add(new WorkflowDataTrackingExtract("field1"));
point.Extracts.Add(new WorkflowDataTrackingExtract("field2"));
point.Extracts.Add(new WorkflowDataTrackingExtract("field3"));
point.Annotations.Add("After RuleSet execution");
point.MatchingLocations.Add(location);
profile.ActivityTrackPoints.Add(point);
```

A similar set of code is used to define the second tracking location. In this case, ActivityExecutionStatus.Closed is specified as the location for these extracts. This causes these same fields to be extracted when the PolicyActivity closes, or completes. A different annotation is added in order to make it clear that these values are after the RuleSet execution.

```
//assign a new version that +1 greater than the last
profile.Version = new Version(
    profile.Version.Major, profile.Version.Minor + 1, 0);
//apply the update to the tracking profile
helper.UpdateProfile(
    profile, typeof(SharedWorkflows.TrackingRulesWorkflow));
```

The profile version number must be incremented, otherwise an exception will be thrown when these updates are applied to the database. The UpdateProfile method of the TrackingProfileHelper is invoked to apply the updated profile to the database.

```
    }
}

/// <summary>
/// Delete the tracking profile for this workflow
/// </summary>
private static void DeleteCustomTrackingProfile()
{
    //get the default profile
    TrackingProfileHelper helper
        = new TrackingProfileHelper(_connStringTracking);
    helper.DeleteProfile(
        typeof(SharedWorkflows.TrackingRulesWorkflow));
}
```

This method is called at the end of the test to delete the tracking profile that was added. In this particular example, the deletion of the tracking profile is important. The code in the AddCustomTrackingProfile method assumes that it can safely add the new track points to the profile. It doesn't check to see if they have already been added. If you don't delete the tracking profile each time, you will end up with multiple track points extracting the same data. This is an interesting effect, but hardly useful.

Once again, in a real application, it wouldn't make much sense to create and then delete a profile each time you execute a workflow. But for purposes of this demonstration, this works fine.

```
    }
}
```

Testing the Tracking Profile

After building the solution, you should be ready to execute the ConsoleTracking application. With this custom profile in place, you should see results that look like this:

```
Executing TrackingRulesWorkflow
Completed TrackingRulesWorkflow

Tracking data for workflow instance 67f3f17c-911a-4cec-b3cf-1fe1fcdbf6e1
01:57:16.780 Workflow Created
01:57:16.780 Workflow Started
01:57:16.780 Executing TrackingRulesWorkflow, Type=TrackingRulesWorkflow
01:57:16.780 Executing policyActivity1, Type=PolicyActivity
      Before RuleSet execution
         field1=20
         field2=0
         field3=
01:57:16.780 RuleAction from policyActivity1 Rule:ruleOne Result:True
01:57:16.780 RuleAction from policyActivity1 Rule:ruleTwo Result:False
01:57:16.780 Closed policyActivity1, Type=PolicyActivity
      After RuleSet execution
         field1=20
         field2=2000
         field3=big number
01:57:16.780 Closed TrackingRulesWorkflow, Type=TrackingRulesWorkflow
01:57:16.797 Workflow Completed
End of tracking data for 67f3f17c-911a-4cec-b3cf-1fe1fcdbf6e1

Press any key to exit
```

Now, in addition to the rule evaluation results, you also have the before and after values of the fields used by the RuleSet. When retrieving the tracking results, the extracted data is in a series of TrackingDataItem objects in the Body property of the ActivityTrackingRecord. In the TrackingConsoleWriter class developed earlier in this chapter, the WriteBodyToConsole method is responsible for writing this data, along with the annotations, to the Console.

Maintaining the SQL Tracking Database

As you've already seen, WF includes the SQL scripts necessary to set up a database for use with the SqlTrackingService. Most of the time, the database will record workflow tracking data automatically and won't require any manual intervention from you.

However, since it is a database, it does require some routine maintenance. In this section, I highlight some of the routine maintenance tasks that you might need to perform on the tracking database along with any stored procedures that WF provides to assist you.

Partitioning

Partitioning is one of the major areas that might require initial setup and routine maintenance. When you use partitioning, the tracking data for completed workflows is moved from the normal set of tracking tables to another set of tables that are segregated by some defined time period. That time period can be daily, weekly, monthly, or yearly.

For example, if you set the partitioning to daily, the tracking data for workflows that you execute today will end up in a set of tables that are reserved for today's data. A set of tracking tables will be created that contain today's date as part of the table name. When you execute additional workflows tomorrow, they will end up in their own set of daily tracking tables.

Why use partitioning? One good reason is that it makes maintenance of the database easier. When you are finished using the tracking data for a particular time period, you can remove those tables without the need for a complex query to identify the subset of rows to delete. WF provides a stored procedure that simplifies the job of removing a partition. Partitioning also makes the job of reporting and analysis much easier. Often when working with tracking data, you will want to limit your queries to a particular time period, perhaps analyzing past performance of selected workflows. By physically segregating the data by time period, your queries are easier to write and should perform better.

Setting the Partition Interval

The default partition interval is monthly. If you wish to change it to one of the other available intervals, you execute the SetPartitionInterval stored procedure. This procedure accepts a single parameter that determines the new partition interval. The possible values are d (daily), w (weekly), m (monthly), and y (yearly).

Automatic or Manual Partitioning

You can automatically partition the data for completed workflows, or you may choose to use manual partitioning. To automatically partition data, set the PartitionOnCompletion property of the SqlTrackingService class to true. When this property is true, tracking data for workflows will first be written to the standard set of tables. When the workflow completes, the tracking data will then automatically move from the standard tables to the partitioned tables. Be aware that automatic partitioning could potentially reduce performance, especially in an application that executes a large number of workflows.

■**Caution** In the current release of WF, there is a problem with the use of automatic partitioning. If you set the PartitionOnCompletion property to true, the SqlTrackingQuery class is unable to retrieve any user event data from partitioned tables. If PartitionOnCompletion is false (using manual partitioning), the SqlTrackingQuery class retrieves the user events correctly. Microsoft has acknowledged that this is a problem that will be corrected in a future release or service patch.

If you don't want to accept the possible performance hit associated with automatic partitioning, you can manually partition your tracking data. To do this, start by setting the PartitionOnCompletion property of the SqlTrackingService class to false (or don't set it at all since false is the default). With automatic partitioning off, all tracking data will be written to the standard set of tables and will not be moved when a workflow instance completes. Later, when you have a window of downtime for your application, you can manually partition the tracking data.

To manually partition data, you execute the PartitionCompletedWorkflowInstances stored procedure. This procedure moves any new data that has not been partitioned into the appropriate set of partitioned tables. Please keep in mind that this approach works best if your application has a window of time set aside for routine maintenance tasks such as this. You wouldn't want to execute this stored procedure during the busiest part of the day when everyone is using your application.

Both approaches have their pros and cons. Automatic partitioning doesn't require any intervention since it occurs in the background. But it does potentially reduce performance on a very busy system. Manual partitioning requires execution of a stored procedure, although this could easily be scheduled rather than manually executed. However, executing this stored procedure may adversely affect performance, since it is potentially moving a large amount of data between tables all at once. You would only want to execute it during a regularly scheduled maintenance window.

Accessing Partitioned Data

When you need to directly execute a query against all tracking data, you should use the views that are provided in the database. As new partitions are added to the database, the database views are updated to include each new set of partition tables.

When you select data from a view, you are actually selecting from a union of the primary tracking tables and all available partitions. This provides you with easy access to all tracking data, regardless of the partitioning scheme that you use. When you use the SqlTrackingQuery class to retrieve data, it also uses the consolidated view of the tracking data that includes all partitions.

Detaching or Dropping a Partition

When you no longer want to use a set of partitioned data, you have two options. You can detach the partition or you can drop it.

When you execute the DetachPartition stored procedure, you are logically removing the partition from the standard views. This stored procedure internally executes the RebuildPartitionViews procedure to update the views. When you detach a partition, the set of partitioned tables still exists. They are not deleted. You can still execute queries against those tables, but you will have to do so directly instead of using the standard views.

When you execute the DropPartition stored procedure, you are physically dropping the tables for a partition. Prior to dropping the tables, they are removed from the views.

Caution Never attempt to delete partitioned tables directly. Doing this can cause problems if the tables are still referenced by the standard views. Only detach or drop a partition with the stored procedures that are provided with the WF tracking database.

Both of these stored procedures accept a combination of partition name and partition ID. You can identify these values by querying the vw_TrackingPartitionSetName view.

Developing a Tracking Service

The SqlTrackingService that is included with WF is a good all-purpose tracking service that provides a rich set of functionality. Once you perform the initial setup of the database, using this service is easy. However, just as each application has its own set of business requirements, you may have special needs when it comes to workflow tracking.

For instance, your application may require a much smaller footprint, and the use of SQL Server might be prohibited. You might want to persist tracking data to a file, write it to the Console, log it to the Windows event system, send it as an e-mail, or do just about anything else with it.

To meet these special needs, you can develop your own tracking service. To accomplish this, you need to implement two classes. First, you need a tracking service that is derived from the abstract TrackingService class (found in the System.Workflow.Runtime.Tracking namespace). The tracking service class is the one that is loaded into the workflow runtime and is responsible for interacting with the runtime. It provides support for retrieval of tracking profiles and also hands the runtime a tracking channel when it asks for one.

A tracking channel is the second class that you need to implement. This class must be derived from the abstract TrackingChannel class (found in the same namespace). A tracking channel is the conduit between the workflow runtime and your host application. If a tracking record meets the selection criteria defined in the tracking profile, it is passed from the workflow runtime through the tracking channel. Within the tracking channel, you can handle the data any way you like.

In the example that follows, you will implement a relatively simple tracking service. To keep the service as simple as possible, it will write tracking data directly to the Console. This avoids the additional code that would be necessary to persist the data and keeps the focus on the actual requirements of a tracking service rather than a particular implementation.

Implementing a Tracking Channel

The tracking channel is responsible for handling the tracking data passed to it from the workflow runtime. In this example class, the tracking channel writes the tracking data directly to the Console. Much of this code is borrowed from the TrackingConsoleWriter class presented earlier in this chapter.

A custom tracking service is clearly a reusable piece of software, so I added this class (and the tracking service that follows) to the Bukovics.Workflow.Hosting project. Add a new C# class to this project and name it ConsoleTrackingChannel. Listing 14-8 is the complete code for the ConsoleTrackingChannel.cs file.

Listing 14-8. *Complete ConsoleTrackingChannel.cs File*

```
using System;
using System.Workflow.Runtime.Tracking;
using System.Workflow.Activities.Rules;

namespace Bukovics.Workflow.Hosting
{
    /// <summary>
    /// A tracking channel that writes tracking data
    /// directly to the Console
    /// </summary>
    public class ConsoleTrackingChannel : TrackingChannel
    {
        /// <summary>
        /// Invoked by the runtime to send tracking data
        /// to the service
```

```
    /// </summary>
    /// <param name="record"></param>
    protected override void Send(TrackingRecord record)
    {
        if (record is WorkflowTrackingRecord)
        {
            WorkflowTrackingRecord wfRecord
                = record as WorkflowTrackingRecord;
            Console.WriteLine("{0:HH:mm:ss.fff} Workflow {1}",
                wfRecord.EventDateTime,
                wfRecord.TrackingWorkflowEvent);
        }
        else if (record is ActivityTrackingRecord)
        {
            ActivityTrackingRecord actRecord
                = record as ActivityTrackingRecord;
            Console.WriteLine("{0:HH:mm:ss.fff} {1} {2}, Type={3}",
                actRecord.EventDateTime,
                actRecord.ExecutionStatus,
                actRecord.QualifiedName,
                actRecord.ActivityType.Name);
            WriteBodyToConsole(actRecord);
        }
        else if (record is UserTrackingRecord)
        {
            UserTrackingRecord userRecord
                = record as UserTrackingRecord;
            if (userRecord.UserData is RuleActionTrackingEvent)
            {
                RuleActionTrackingEvent ruleAction
                    = userRecord.UserData as RuleActionTrackingEvent;
                Console.WriteLine(
                    "{0:HH:mm:ss.fff} RuleAction from {1} Rule:{2} Result:{3}",
                    userRecord.EventDateTime,
                    userRecord.QualifiedName,
                    ruleAction.RuleName,
                    ruleAction.ConditionResult);
            }
            else
            {
                Console.WriteLine(
                    "{0:HH:mm:ss.fff} UserData from {1} {2}:{3}",
                    userRecord.EventDateTime,
                    userRecord.QualifiedName,
                    userRecord.UserDataKey,
                    userRecord.UserData);
            }
        }
    }
```

The Send method is one of the two abstract methods that you must implement. It is invoked by the workflow runtime each time it has tracking data to pass to a tracking service. Prior to invoking this method, the workflow runtime has already qualified the tracking data for the current workflow instance, verifying that it meets the conditions defined in the tracking profile for that workflow Type.

The Send method is passed a TrackingRecord instance. This could be any one of the three types of tracking records. The code shown here determines the type of record and writes an appropriate message to the Console to show that the data was received.

If you are implementing a tracking service that needs to persist the data, this is where that would occur.

```csharp
/// <summary>
/// Write any annotations and body data to the Console
/// </summary>
/// <param name="record"></param>
private void WriteBodyToConsole(ActivityTrackingRecord record)
{
    //write annotations
    if (record.Annotations.Count > 0)
    {
        foreach (String annotation in record.Annotations)
        {
            Console.WriteLine("     {0}", annotation);
        }
    }

    //write extracted data
    if (record.Body.Count > 0)
    {
        foreach (TrackingDataItem data in record.Body)
        {
            Console.WriteLine("       {0}={1}",
                data.FieldName, data.Data);
        }
    }
}
```

The WriteBodyToConsole private method is invoked by the Send method. It is used to write annotations and data items to the Console.

```csharp
/// <summary>
/// The workflow instance has completed or terminated
/// </summary>
protected override void InstanceCompletedOrTerminated()
{
    Console.WriteLine("Workflow instance completed or terminated");
}
```

The InstanceCompletedOrTerminated method is the other abstract method that you must implement. It is called whenever a workflow instance either completes normally or is terminated.

```csharp
    }
}
```

Implementing a Tracking Service

A custom tracking service has two primary tasks. First, it provides tracking profiles to the workflow runtime. Second, it returns an instance of the tracking channel to the runtime. Any tracking service that you implement must derive from the abstract TrackingService class.

To implement a custom tracking service, add a new C# class to the Bukovics.Workflow.Hosting project and name it ConsoleTrackingService. Listing 14-9 is the complete listing for this class.

Listing 14-9. *Complete ConsoleTrackingServices.cs File*

```
using System;
using System.Collections.Generic;
using System.Workflow.ComponentModel;
using System.Workflow.Runtime.Tracking;

namespace Bukovics.Workflow.Hosting
{
    /// <summary>
    /// A tracking service that uses the ConsoleTrackingChannel
    /// to write tracking data to the Console
    /// </summary>
    public class ConsoleTrackingService : TrackingService
    {
        private TrackingProfile _defaultProfile;

        public ConsoleTrackingService()
            : base()
        {
            //create and save a default profile
            _defaultProfile = BuildDefaultProfile();
        }
```

During construction, this class creates a single copy of a default profile. This same copy is returned to the workflow runtime by several of the methods of this class. One of the design decisions to keep this example simple was to always return a default profile. Custom profiles for individual workflow types are not supported. The private BuildDefaultProfile method is shown later in this listing.

```
        /// <summary>
        /// Retrieve the tracking channel
        /// </summary>
        /// <param name="parameters"></param>
        /// <returns></returns>
        protected override TrackingChannel GetTrackingChannel(
            TrackingParameters parameters)
        {
            //return an instance of the custom tracking channel
            return new ConsoleTrackingChannel();
        }
```

The GetTrackingChannel abstract method must be implemented by your class. It is called once by the workflow runtime during startup of the service to retrieve the tracking channel. In this example service, the code returns an instance of the ConsoleTrackingChannel implemented in the previous section.

```
        /// <summary>
        /// Retrieve a tracking profile for a workflow instance
        /// </summary>
        /// <param name="workflowInstanceId"></param>
        /// <returns></returns>
        protected override TrackingProfile GetProfile(
            Guid workflowInstanceId)
        {
            //always return the default profile
            return _defaultProfile;
        }
```

```
/// <summary>
/// Retrieve a tracking profile for a workflow type
/// </summary>
/// <param name="workflowType"></param>
/// <param name="profileVersionId"></param>
/// <returns></returns>
protected override TrackingProfile GetProfile(
    Type workflowType, Version profileVersionId)
{
    //always return the default profile
    return _defaultProfile;
}

/// <summary>
/// Called to retrieve a tracking profile
/// </summary>
/// <param name="workflowType"></param>
/// <param name="profile"></param>
/// <returns></returns>
protected override bool TryGetProfile(
    Type workflowType, out TrackingProfile profile)
{
    //always return the default profile
    profile = _defaultProfile;
    return true;
}
```

All three of these methods are variations on the same theme. The runtime calls them to retrieve a profile for a workflow Type, or a particular version of a profile for a workflow Type. In this implementation, all three of these methods return the default profile. If you need to support individual profiles by workflow Type, you would retrieve and return an appropriate TrackingProfile here.

```
/// <summary>
/// Called to reload a tracking profile that has changed
/// </summary>
/// <param name="workflowType"></param>
/// <param name="workflowInstanceId"></param>
/// <param name="profile"></param>
/// <returns></returns>
protected override bool TryReloadProfile(
    Type workflowType, Guid workflowInstanceId,
    out TrackingProfile profile)
{
    //always return false to indicate that the profile
    //has not changed
    profile = null;
    return false;
}
```

The TryReloadProfile method is called to determine if a tracking profile should be reloaded. If a profile has changed and should be reloaded, return true and pass an instance of the updated profile in the out parameter. Otherwise, return false and set the out parameter to null.

```
/// <summary>
/// Creates and saves a default tracking profile
/// </summary>
/// <returns></returns>
private TrackingProfile BuildDefaultProfile()
{
    //return a default profile that tracks all possible
    //workflow events and activity status values
    TrackingProfile profile = new TrackingProfile();

    //
    //create a workflow track point and location
    //
    WorkflowTrackPoint workflowPoint
        = new WorkflowTrackPoint();
    //add all possible workflow events
    List<TrackingWorkflowEvent> workflowEvents
        = new List<TrackingWorkflowEvent>();
    workflowEvents.AddRange(
        Enum.GetValues(typeof(TrackingWorkflowEvent))
            as IEnumerable<TrackingWorkflowEvent>);
    WorkflowTrackingLocation workflowLocation
        = new WorkflowTrackingLocation(workflowEvents);
    workflowPoint.MatchingLocation = workflowLocation;
    profile.WorkflowTrackPoints.Add(workflowPoint);
```

The BuildDefaultProfile method is a private method that is executed during construction of this class. It creates a single default profile that is returned whenever a profile is requested by one of the other public methods.

The profile created here includes all possible workflow, activity, and user events. In this first section of code, a WorkflowTrackPoint is created. It defines a WorkflowTrackingLocation that includes all possible workflow events.

```
    //
    //create an activity track point and location
    //
    ActivityTrackPoint activityPoint
        = new ActivityTrackPoint();
    //add all possible activity execution status values
    List<ActivityExecutionStatus> activityStatus
        = new List<ActivityExecutionStatus>();
    activityStatus.AddRange(
        Enum.GetValues(typeof(ActivityExecutionStatus))
            as IEnumerable<ActivityExecutionStatus>);
    ActivityTrackingLocation activityLocation
        = new ActivityTrackingLocation(
            typeof(Activity), true, activityStatus);
    activityPoint.MatchingLocations.Add(activityLocation);
    profile.ActivityTrackPoints.Add(activityPoint);
```

In a similar manner to the WorkflowTrackPoint, this section of code creates an ActivityTrackPoint. It uses an ActivityTrackingLocation that includes all possible activity execution status values.

```
//
//create a user track point and location
//
UserTrackPoint userPoint = new UserTrackPoint();
UserTrackingLocation userLocation
    = new UserTrackingLocation(
        typeof(Object), typeof(Activity));
userLocation.MatchDerivedActivityTypes = true;
userLocation.MatchDerivedArgumentTypes = true;
userPoint.MatchingLocations.Add(userLocation);
profile.UserTrackPoints.Add(userPoint);
```

A single UserTrackPoint is added to the profile with this code. The UserTrackingLocation specifies that this track point applies to the Activity class and to a user data type of Object. The MatchDerivedActivityTypes and MatchDerivedArgumentTypes properties of the UserTrackingLocation are both set to true. This is important since this indicates that this tracking location should match any types that derive from Activity and any data types that derive from type Object. This effectively means it should match everything.

```
//set the profile version
profile.Version = new Version(1, 0, 0);
return profile;
```

The final step is to assign a version number to the profile. This is important even though the profile is not persisted in this example.

```
        }
    }
}
```

Testing the Custom Tracking Service

You can test the custom tracking service with just a few changes to the ConsoleTracking application developed throughout this chapter.

Open the TrackingTest.cs file in the code editor and make the changes indicated in Listing 14-10. You may wish to first make a backup copy of this file prior to making any changes. Doing this will allow you to easily execute the previous version that used the SqlTrackingService.

Listing 14-10. *TrackingTest.cs Changes for a Custom Tracking Service*

```
using System;
using System.Collections.Generic;
using System.Workflow.ComponentModel;
using System.Workflow.Runtime;
using System.Workflow.Runtime.Tracking;

using Bukovics.Workflow.Hosting;
using SharedWorkflows;

namespace ConsoleTracking
{
    /// <summary>
    /// Test the TrackingExampleWorkflow
    /// </summary>
```

```
public class TrackingTest
{
    private static String _connStringTracking = String.Format(
        "Initial Catalog={0};Data Source={1};Integrated Security={2};",
            "WorkflowTracking", @"localhost\SQLEXPRESS", "SSPI");
```

You can remove this connection string since it is no longer needed.

```
    public static void Run()
    {
        using (WorkflowRuntimeManager manager
            = new WorkflowRuntimeManager(new WorkflowRuntime()))
        {

...


                //add a custom tracking profile for this workflow
                AddCustomTrackingProfile();
```

Remove this call to AddCustomTrackingProfile since it updates the SQL tracking database that isn't used with the custom tracking service. Notice also that the WorkflowRuntime is constructed using the default constructor. You may have previously modified the constructor to reference an App.config section. For this example, there is no need to use the constructor that retrieves entries from the App.config file.

...

```
                Console.WriteLine("Executing TrackingExampleWorkflow");
                WorkflowInstanceWrapper instance =
                    manager.StartWorkflow(
                        typeof(SharedWorkflows.TrackingExampleWorkflow), null);
                manager.WaitAll(2000);
                Console.WriteLine("Completed TrackingExampleWorkflow\n\r");
```

Change the Type of workflow to execute back to TrackingExampleWorkflow. This workflow contains user track points that will exercise that section of the code in the custom tracking channel.

...

```
                //query and display tracking data for this single instance
                TrackingConsoleWriter trackingWriter
                    = new TrackingConsoleWriter(_connStringTracking);
                trackingWriter.DisplayTrackingData(instance.Id);

                //delete the tracking profile that we created
                DeleteCustomTrackingProfile();
```

Delete this code that displays the tracking data as well as the call to the DeleteCustomTrackingProfile method. In this example, you don't need to display the tracking data since the tracking service writes it directly to the Console for you.

...

```
        /// <summary>
        /// Add any services needed by the runtime engine
        /// </summary>
        /// <param name="instance"></param>
```

```
    private static void AddServices(WorkflowRuntime instance)
    {
        //use the custom Console tracking service
        ConsoleTrackingService tracking
            = new ConsoleTrackingService();
        //add the service to the runtime
        instance.AddService(tracking);
    }
```

This is the revised AddServices method. To use the new custom tracking service, the code creates an instance of the class and adds it to the workflow runtime.

The private AddCustomTrackingProfile and DeleteCustomTrackingProfile methods that follow this section of code can also be removed.

...

```
    }
}
```

After making these changes, you should be able to build the solution and execute the ConsoleTracking application. When I execute the revised application, I see these results:

```
Executing TrackingExampleWorkflow
00:48:48.953 Workflow Created
00:48:49.000 Workflow Started
00:48:49.015 Executing TrackingExampleWorkflow, Type= TrackingExampleWorkflow
00:48:49.281 Executing codeFirstActivity, Type=CodeActivity
Executing first activity
00:48:49.281 UserData from codeFirstActivity accountKey:123456
00:48:49.281 Closed codeFirstActivity, Type=CodeActivity
00:48:49.281 Executing delayActivity1, Type=DelayActivity
00:48:49.281 Workflow Idle
00:48:50.281 Closed delayActivity1, Type=DelayActivity
00:48:50.281 Executing codeLastActivity, Type=CodeActivity
Executing second activity
00:48:50.281 UserData from codeLastActivity approvalMessage:approved
00:48:50.281 Closed codeLastActivity, Type=CodeActivity
00:48:50.281 Closed TrackingExampleWorkflow, Type= TrackingExampleWorkflow
00:48:50.281 Workflow Completed
Workflow instance completed or terminated
Completed TrackingExampleWorkflow

Press any key to exit
```

Since the code for the custom tracking channel was borrowed from the TrackingConsoleWriter class developed earlier in the chapter, the results are very similar to the prior examples. One difference is that the messages written directly by the workflow are interspersed with the tracking data. This is due to the fact that the tracking data is being written to the Console in real time as it is received rather than after the workflow completes.

With the pluggable service architecture provided with WF, you are able to develop specialized tracking services that meet your exact needs. You have the flexibility to use the standard SqlTrackingService or use one of your own designs.

Summary

The focus of this chapter was workflow tracking. In this chapter, you learned that WF provides a rich tracking mechanism that enables you to monitor the progress of each workflow and activity. You learned that you can extend the default event and status monitoring by adding your own user tracking points in code. You learned how to view the results of each rule as it is evaluated and how to extract field values from a running workflow using a custom profile.

This chapter also outlined some of the routine maintenance tasks that are necessary when working with the SQL Server database used by `SqlTrackingService`.

The chapter concluded by presenting an example implementation of a custom tracking service. This service wrote tracking data to the `Console` instead of capturing it in a database.

In the next chapter, you will learn how to use web services with WF workflows.

CHAPTER 15

Web Services and ASP.NET

The focus of this chapter is web services and the use of workflows from ASP.NET applications. WF provides support for web services in a number of ways. You can develop a workflow and expose it to clients as a web service. You can also invoke a web service declaratively from a workflow. WF also permits you to host the workflow runtime and invoke workflows from an ASP.NET client application.

The first example in this chapter demonstrates how to publish a workflow as a web service. A follow-up example enhances the example workflow to send web service fault information back to the calling client. In these first examples, the workflow instance completes when the response is sent back to the calling client. WF also supports stateful workflows where a web service client can make repeated calls to the same workflow instance. This is presented in another example.

Other examples included in this chapter show you how to invoke a web service from within a workflow and how to invoke a workflow from an ASP.NET Web Forms application.

Publishing a Workflow As a Web Service

WF provides the ability to publish a workflow as a web service. When you do this, you expose the service methods implemented by the workflow to a wide variety of clients. Any client that is capable of invoking a web service can be a consumer of the workflow logic. This includes traditional Windows applications using Windows Forms or Windows Presentation Foundation (WPF) as well as web-based applications using ASP.NET. Web services can also be invoked from non-Windows clients, provided they interoperate with the standard web service protocols supported by Microsoft.

Understanding the Web Service Activities

WF supplies a set of standard activities that must be used within a workflow to publish it as a web service. The WebServiceInputActivity receives any input from the invoking web service client and also marks the beginning of a web service call. Each WebServiceInputActivity is associated with a single web service method. The web service methods must first be defined in a C# interface that is referenced by the WebServiceInputActivity.

Each WebServiceInputActivity is followed by the set of activities that you wish to execute to service the web service request. That can include any standard or custom activities that are required by the application.

If the web service request requires a response, the WebServiceOutputActivity is added to the workflow. This activity sends a response back to the invoking client and is placed after any standard or custom activities that perform the real work of the request. Each WebServiceOutputActivity must be matched to a single WebServiceInputActivity. These two activities form the bookends of the web service request. The WebServiceOutputActivity must not execute prior to the WebServiceInputActivity. The web service request officially completes when the WebServiceOutputActivity executes.

If you encounter an error condition during execution of the workflow, you can send a web service fault to the client instead of a normal response. This is accomplished with the WebServiceFaultActivity. Like the WebServiceOutputActivity, the WebServiceFaultActivity is associated with an instance of the WebServiceInputActivity. You can either send a normal web service response (using WebServiceOutputActivity) or a web service fault (using WebServiceFaultActivity) but not both. To use the WebServiceFaultActivity, you assign a .NET Exception to the Fault property to identify the type of problem.

Figure 15-1 illustrates the relationship between these web service activities.

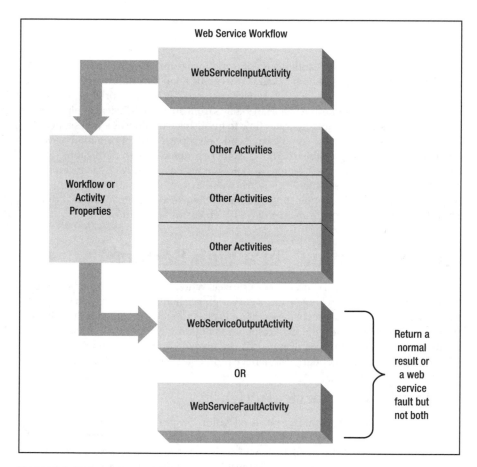

Figure 15-1. *Web service activities*

In Figure 15-1, the WebServiceInputActivity is shown updating workflow or activity properties. Any input parameters that are passed to the web service method are made available to the workflow via the WebServiceInputActivity. In a workflow that is exposed as a web service, this replaces the traditional approach of passing input values via a Dictionary of parameters.

Once you select the interface type and method name for the WebServiceInputActivity, a list of the defined parameters for the method is provided in the Properties window. You can then define the parameter bindings that will populate activity or workflow properties with the input values. Likewise, if the web service method returns a result value, the value is passed to the WebServiceOutputActivity via a parameter binding that you define.

As shown in Figure 15-1, you include the activities that perform the real work of the web service method between the `WebServiceInputActivity` and the `WebServiceOutputActivity`. When you need to return a web service fault, you use the `WebServiceFaultActivity`.

Publishing and Configuration

Once you have defined a web service workflow, you publish the project containing it to make it available to clients. Publishing a project is as easy as selecting the Publish as Web Service option from the Visual Studio Project menu. When you publish a project, a separate web service project is generated and added to the current solution. This new project contains the `.asmx` files that identify each workflow to publish as a web service. A sample `Web.config` file is also generated that includes the minimal set of entries needed to support the workflow runtime and access a workflow as a web service. After testing, you would ultimately deploy these entries to a production IIS web site to make them available to clients outside of your development environment.

There are a number of entries that you need to include in the `Web.config` file. Some of these are added for you since they represent the minimal set of entries needed to host a workflow as a web service. A complete `Web.config` file is shown later in this chapter, but a brief summary of the most important entries is provided here.

Loading the ManualWorkflowSchedulerService

The default scheduler used by the workflow runtime executes workflows asynchronously on its own threads. The `ManualWorkflowSchedulerService` (in the `System.Workflow.Runtime.Hosting` namespace) is an alternate scheduler service that executes a workflow synchronously on the caller's thread.

By loading this service in the `Web.config`, you instruct the workflow runtime to execute the workflow using the original thread that made the ASP.NET web service request. This helps to control the number of threads that are in use at any one time and also executes the workflow synchronously on the calling thread.

It is important to set the `UseActiveTimers` property of this service to `true` during construction. If you are loading this service via the `Web.config` file entries, you can also set this property to `true` there. If you don't set this property to `true`, any `DelayActivity` instances within your workflows will not behave as you might expect. When set to `false`, the workflow instance won't automatically begin again after the delay of a `DelayActivity` expires. By setting this property to `true`, the service will use a separate thread to detect the expiration of a delay and will automatically resume the workflow instance.

Loading the WorkflowWebHostingModule

The `WorkflowWebHostingModule` (in the `System.Workflow.Runtime.Hosting` namespace) is an ASP.NET HTTP module that is also included in the generated `Web.config` file. HTTP modules are part of the ASP.NET request pipeline and are called with each request and response.

The purpose of this particular module is to route a web service request to the correct workflow instance. To accomplish this, ASP.NET cookies are used. Each cookie contains the instance ID (`Guid`) that identifies the workflow instance in use by the client. When this default HTTP module is used, web service clients must support cookies.

Loading a Persistence Service

Although it isn't a strict requirement (and it isn't automatically added to the generated `Web.config` file), a persistence service should generally be loaded when hosting workflows in the ASP.NET environment. The `SqlWorkflowPersistenceService` can be used for out-of-the-box persistence to a SQL Server database, or you can develop your own service.

Persistence is especially important in the ASP.NET environment in order to reduce the number of workflows in memory at any one time. When a workflow becomes idle or is suspended, there is no need to keep it in memory. But you can't remove it from memory unless it is persisted. Therefore, a persistence service provides the mechanism that permits idled workflows to be removed from memory.

Developing a Web Service Workflow

In this first example, you will develop a workflow that divides two numbers and returns the result. The workflow itself is simple, yet it does demonstrate the minimal steps that are necessary to expose a workflow to web service clients.

Defining the Web Service Interface

To begin this example, create a new project named SharedWorkflows using the Empty Workflow Project template. When prompted, save the solution file. Add a normal C# interface to the project and name it IMathService. All web service workflows require an interface that defines the available web service methods. The purpose of the IMathService interface is to define the single DivideNumbers method that the example workflow will implement. Listing 15-1 is the complete code for the IMathService.cs file.

Listing 15-1. *Complete IMathService.cs File*

```
using System;

namespace SharedWorkflows
{
    public interface IMathService
    {
        /// <summary>
        /// Perform a division operation
        /// </summary>
        /// <param name="dividend"></param>
        /// <param name="divisor"></param>
        /// <returns></returns>
        Double DivideNumbers(Double dividend, Double divisor);
    }
}
```

Defining the MathServiceWorkflow

Next, you need to develop a workflow that implements the IMathService interface as a web service. To begin this task, add a new sequential workflow to the project and name it MathServiceWorkflow.

The workflow requires instance variables for each of the input parameters (the dividend and divisor) along with one for the result (the quotient). Listing 15-2 shows the code for the MathServiceWorkflow.cs file at this point.

Listing 15-2. *MathServiceWorkflow.cs File with Variables*

```
using System;
using System.Workflow.Activities;

namespace SharedWorkflows
{
    /// <summary>
    /// A workflow exposed as a web service
    /// </summary>
    public sealed partial class MathServiceWorkflow
        : SequentialWorkflowActivity
    {
        public Double dividend;
        public Double divisor;
        public Double quotient;

        public MathServiceWorkflow()
        {
            InitializeComponent();
        }
    }
}
```

The input parameters (dividend and divisor) will be bound to a WebServiceInputActivity. When the workflow is executed as a web service, the instance variables will be populated with the input values provided by the caller. The quotient variable will be bound to the ReturnValue parameter of a WebServiceOutputActivity. When the WebServiceOutputActivity executes, the value of the quotient variable is returned as a response to the caller.

After switching to the workflow designer view, add three activities to the workflow. The first activity is a WebServiceInputActivity (named divideNumbersInput), followed by a CodeActivity (named codeDoDivision), and finally a WebServiceOutputActivity (named divideNumbersOutput).

There are several properties that you need to set for the divideNumbersInput activity. First, select SharedWorkflows.IMathService as the InterfaceType, then select DivideNumbers as the MethodName. You have now identified the web service interface and method that this WebServiceInputActivity handles.

The IsActivating property defaults to false, but you need to set it to true. A value of true indicates that the receipt of the specified web service request is the one that should activate a new instance of the workflow. You can only set IsActivating to true for the first WebServiceInputActivity in a workflow.

The WebServiceInputActivity implements the IEventActivity and is one of the event-driven activities that wait for an event to trigger execution (another example being the HandleExternalEventActivity). When the event (the web service call) for the designated interface and method is received, the activity can stop waiting and begin execution of the activities that follow it.

When you select DivideNumbers as the MethodName, the Parameters section of the Properties window is populated with entries for the two input parameters (dividend and divisor). You should now bind these parameters to the workflow variables defined previously. The binding values to use are shown in Table 15-1.

Table 15-1. *Property Bindings for divideNumbersInput*

Property	Binding
dividend	Activity=MathServiceWorkflow, Path=dividend
divisor	Activity=MathServiceWorkflow, Path=divisor

The codeDoDivision activity requires a handler for the ExecuteCode event, so double-click it now to create one.

The divideNumbersOutput activity must be associated with a WebServiceInputActivity. The association is made with the InputActivityName property. Set this property to divideNumbersInput to link this output activity that ends this web service request to the input activity that started it. The ReturnValue parameter of the divideNumbersOutput must be bound to the quotient workflow variable in order to return the result of the division. Table 15-2 shows the binding values that you need to use for this parameter.

Table 15-2. *Property Binding for divideNumbersOutput*

Property	Binding
ReturnValue	Activity=MathServiceWorkflow, Path=quotient

Figure 15-2 is the completed visual design of the MathServiceWorkflow.

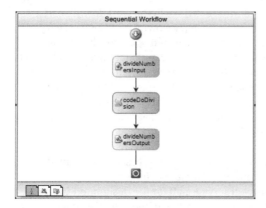

Figure 15-2. *Complete MathServiceWorkflow*

The final task before this workflow is finished is to add code to the codeDoDivision ExecuteCode handler to perform the division. Listing 15-3 shows the additional code that you need to add to the MathServiceWorkflow.cs file.

Listing 15-3. *Additions to the MathServiceWorkflow.cs File*

```
using System;
using System.Workflow.Activities;

namespace SharedWorkflows
{
    /// <summary>
    /// A workflow exposed as a web service
    /// </summary>
    public sealed partial class MathServiceWorkflow
        : SequentialWorkflowActivity
    {

...

        private void codeDoDivision_ExecuteCode(
            object sender, EventArgs e)
        {
            //do the division
            quotient = dividend / divisor;
        }
    }
}
```

Publishing the Workflow

After building the solution, you should be ready to publish the workflow as a web service. To do this, you select the SharedWorkflows project in the Solution Explorer and then select Publish as Web Service from the Project menu. You can also right-click the project and select the same item from the context menu.

The result of the Publish as Web Service option is a new project named SharedWorkflows_ WebService that is added to the solution. This new project contains a file named SharedWorkflows. MathServiceWorkflow_WebService.asmx and a Web.config file.

The contents of the generated .asmx file look like this:

```
<%@ WebService Class="SharedWorkflows.MathServiceWorkflow_WebService" %>
```

The WebService directive defines web service attributes that are used by ASP.NET. The Class attribute identifies the class that implements the web service. You didn't implement this class yourself, but it is present in the SharedWorkflows compiled assembly. It was generated for you and provides web service access to the real MathServiceWorkflow that you implemented. The generated class derives from the WorkflowWebService class (in the System.Workflow.Activities namespace). This class is the base class for all workflow web services.

The generated Web.config file contains the minimal set of entries that you need to test your workflow via a web service call. I made a few modifications to the generated Web.config. First, I added an entry to load the SqlWorkflowPersistenceService to provide workflow persistence. Workflow persistence isn't a requirement for this example workflow, since it doesn't contain any activities that would cause it to become idle after it begins. However, it is generally a good idea to use a persistence service when exposing a workflow as a web service.

I also removed the generated entry that added the `DefaultWorkflowCommitWorkBatchService`. This is the default commit work (transaction) service that is automatically loaded by the workflow runtime if no other commit work batch service is specified. It doesn't harm anything to leave the generated entry for this service, but it doesn't add any value. Finally, I added an entry that sets the `UseActiveTimers` property to `true` as previously discussed.

My revised `Web.config` file is shown in Listing 15-4. Some of the lines have been reformatted to fit the page size limitations of this book. I've highlighted the lines that load the workflow services and add the `WorkflowWebHostingModule` HTTP module.

Listing 15-4. *Web.config File*

```xml
<?xml version="1.0"?>
<configuration>
  <configSections>
    <section name="WorkflowRuntime"
      type="System.Workflow.Runtime.Configuration.WorkflowRuntimeSection,
        System.Workflow.Runtime, Version=3.0.00000.0, Culture=neutral,
        PublicKeyToken=31bf3856ad364e35" />
  </configSections>
  <WorkflowRuntime Name="WorkflowWebServices">
    <Services>
      <add type=
        "System.Workflow.Runtime.Hosting.ManualWorkflowSchedulerService,
        System.Workflow.Runtime, Version=3.0.0.0,
        Culture=neutral, PublicKeyToken=31bf3856ad364e35"
        UseActiveTimers="true"/>
      <add type=
        "System.Workflow.Runtime.Hosting.SqlWorkflowPersistenceService,
        System.Workflow.Runtime, Version=3.0.00000.0,
        Culture=neutral, PublicKeyToken=31bf3856ad364e35"
        UnloadOnIdle="true" LoadIntervalSeconds="5"
        ConnectionString="Initial Catalog=WorkflowPersistence;
          Data Source=localhost\SQLEXPRESS;Integrated Security=SSPI;" />
    </Services>
  </WorkflowRuntime>
  <appSettings/>
  <connectionStrings/>
  <system.web>
    <compilation debug="false">
      <assemblies>
        <add assembly="System.Design, Version=2.0.0.0,
          Culture=neutral, PublicKeyToken=B03F5F7F11D50A3A"/>
        <add assembly="System.Drawing.Design, Version=2.0.0.0,
          Culture=neutral, PublicKeyToken=B03F5F7F11D50A3A"/>
        <add assembly="System.Transactions, Version=2.0.0.0,
          Culture=neutral, PublicKeyToken=B77A5C561934E089"/>
        <add assembly="System.Workflow.Activities, Version=3.0.0.0,
          Culture=neutral, PublicKeyToken=31BF3856AD364E35"/>
        <add assembly="System.Workflow.ComponentModel, Version=3.0.0.0,
          Culture=neutral, PublicKeyToken=31BF3856AD364E35"/>
```

```
        <add assembly="System.Workflow.Runtime, Version=3.0.0.0,
          Culture=neutral, PublicKeyToken=31BF3856AD364E35"/>
        <add assembly="Microsoft.Build.Tasks, Version=2.0.0.0,
          Culture=neutral, PublicKeyToken=B03F5F7F11D50A3A"/>
        <add assembly="System.Messaging, Version=2.0.0.0,
          Culture=neutral, PublicKeyToken=B03F5F7F11D50A3A"/>
        <add assembly="System.Runtime.Remoting, Version=2.0.0.0,
          Culture=neutral, PublicKeyToken=B77A5C561934E089"/>
        <add assembly="System.DirectoryServices, Version=2.0.0.0,
          Culture=neutral, PublicKeyToken=B03F5F7F11D50A3A"/>
        <add assembly="System.Windows.Forms, Version=2.0.0.0,
          Culture=neutral, PublicKeyToken=B77A5C561934E089"/>
        <add assembly="Microsoft.Build.Utilities, Version=2.0.0.0,
          Culture=neutral, PublicKeyToken=B03F5F7F11D50A3A"/>
        <add assembly="Microsoft.Build.Framework, Version=2.0.0.0,
          Culture=neutral, PublicKeyToken=B03F5F7F11D50A3A"/>
      </assemblies>
    </compilation>
    <authentication mode="Windows"/>
    <httpModules>
      <add type="System.Workflow.Runtime.Hosting.WorkflowWebHostingModule,
        System.Workflow.Runtime, Version=3.0.0.0, Culture=neutral,
        PublicKeyToken=31bf3856ad364e35" name="WorkflowHost"/>
    </httpModules>
  </system.web>
</configuration>
```

Testing the Web Service

To test the web service workflow, you can develop a client application to invoke the web service. However, there is a much easier way to test this workflow. ASP.NET automatically generates a test web page for any .asmx-based web service. Using this test web page, you can enter input values, execute the web service, and then view the result.

Instead of deploying the web service to IIS, an easier way to test it is to use the ASP.NET Development Server (WebDev.WebServer.exe) that is included with Visual Studio. The Development Server will automatically start when you execute the web service project from within Visual Studio. To do this, set the SharedWorkflows_WebService project as the startup project in Visual Studio. Now select Start Without Debugging (CTRL+F5) from the Debug menu.

■**Note** If you select Start Debugging (F5) instead, you will receive a dialog box informing you that you can't debug the web service. The reason is that the Web.config sets compilation debug="false". If you want to debug the web service, you must first set this value to true.

After starting the project, you should see the ASP.NET Development Server Start and then add its icon to the taskbar notification area. An instance of your default browser should also launch and present a directory list of the files in the SharedWorkflows_WebService project folder. In my browser, I see this list:

```
Bin
SharedWorkflows.MathServiceWorkflow_WebService.asmx
Web.config
```

If you select the .asmx entry, you will be presented with a generated page with the operations supported by the MathServiceWorkflow_WebService. Figure 15-3 shows you a partial view of this page.

Address http://localhost:1269/SharedWorkflows_WebService/SharedWorkflows.MathServiceWorkflow_WebService.asmx

MathServiceWorkflow_WebService

The following operations are supported. For a formal definition, please review the **Service Description**.

- **DivideNumbers**
  DivideNumbers

Figure 15-3. *MathServiceWorkflow_WebService generated page*

If you now select the DivideNumbers link, another page that exercises this web service method will be generated and shown. Figure 15-4 shows a partial view of this page.

MathServiceWorkflow_WebService

Click here for a complete list of operations.

DivideNumbers

DivideNumbers

Test

To test the operation using the HTTP POST protocol, click the 'Invoke' button.

Parameter	Value
dividend:	
divisor:	
	Invoke

Figure 15-4. *DivideNumbers request page*

You can now enter values for the dividend and divisor and invoke the web service workflow. For example, I entered a dividend of **3333** and a divisor of **3**. After pressing the Invoke button, a new results page is presented with the correct result of 1111. Figure 15-5 shows the results page.

```
<?xml version="1.0" encoding="utf-8" ?>
<double xmlns="http://tempuri.org/">1111</double>
```

Figure 15-5. *Results page for DivideNumbers*

■Note You may have noticed that the published web service uses `http://tempuri.org/` as the default namespace. When developing your own web services, it is recommended that you change this default namespace to something that is more meaningful and that ensures that your web services are unique.

However, when a workflow is published as a web service, WF doesn't provide a way to change the default namespace. There are workarounds (hacks) for this problem that have been identified, but they are not something that I would recommend at this point. They require you to modify the registry in order to save the temporary generated files, locate the files in the temporary directory, manually modify them, and include them in your web service project.

The WF team is aware of this major deficiency and will hopefully come up with a better workaround by the time you are reading this.

If you happen to execute the web service again, you will notice that it produces an error message that looks something like this.

```
System.InvalidOperationException:
Workflow with id &quot;03ff8f3f-5925-4925-932f-ab016c268897&quot;
not found in state persistence store.
```

What's going on here? Remember that the `WorkflowWebHostingModule` HTTP module that is loaded communicates with web service clients using cookies. It passes back a temporary cookie that contains the workflow instance ID `Guid`. The cookie is named `WF_WorkflowInstanceId` and is set to expire at the end of the current session.

When you execute the web service again using this generated test page, the existing cookie is returned to the service and an attempt is made to reload the previous workflow instance. Since this workflow completed when it finished with the first divide operation, the requested instance doesn't exist in the persistence database. This results in the error.

A real web service client would determine what to do with this cookie. In this particular web service, the workflow ends as soon as the web service method returns, and there is no need to save the cookie. However, the client would use this cookie if a long-running workflow is being invoked. If multiple calls are being made to the same workflow instance, the cookie would be used to identify the existing workflow instance to use.

If you want to get around this problem without developing your own web service client, you need to close all of the browser windows to remove the session cookie. If you then start a new browser session, you will be able to execute the web service again without any problems.

When you are finished testing this workflow, you can shut down the ASP.NET Development Server by clicking the icon in the taskbar notification area and selecting Stop.

You have now seen that with a minimal amount of effort you are able to publish a workflow as a web service. In the next section, you will enhance this workflow to return a web service fault if an attempt is made to divide by zero.

Returning a Web Service Fault

If an exceptional condition occurs while executing a web service method, a web service fault should be returned to the client. If an unhandled exception is thrown within a web service workflow, the .NET exception is automatically returned as a fault. In addition to this automatic behavior, you can also explicitly send a fault by declaring it in your workflow model.

This is accomplished with the WebServiceFaultActivity, which must be associated with a WebServiceInputActivity. This activity includes a Fault property that identifies the .NET exception associated with the fault. You must model your workflow so that you execute either a WebServiceOutputActivity or a WebServiceFaultActivity. You can't execute both activities in a single workflow instance. If you do attempt to include both activities in the same line of execution, the workflow will not build due to this error.

For example, consider the MathServiceWorkflow that you implemented in the previous section. The initial version of this workflow doesn't perform any validation of the input parameters. If you enter a divisor of zero, it will attempt to perform the division. Since the dividend and divisor are both defined as a Double, the floating-point division by zero will return infinity. You may prefer to receive a web service fault that notifies you of the problem instead of receiving a result of infinity.

In the example that follows, you will modify the MathServiceWorkflow to perform some minimal validation on the input parameters. If the divisor is equal to zero, the workflow will return a web service fault using the WebServiceFaultActivity. Otherwise, the division will be performed and the result returned to the client.

Modifying the MathServiceWorkflow

Open the MathServiceWorkflow in the workflow designer and add an IfElseActivity immediately following the divideNumberInput activity. Rename the IfElseBranchActivity on the left side to ifDivisorZero, and the branch on the right to ifDivisorNotZero.

Select Code Condition for the Condition property of ifDivisorZero and enter a condition name of IsDivisorZero. You'll add code to this code condition when you have finished with the visual design of the workflow.

Add a WebServiceFaultActivity to the ifDivisorZero branch on the left. Select divideNumbersInput for the InputActivityName property. Setting this property associates this activity with the WebServiceInputActivity defined at the beginning of the workflow. For this example, you want to bind the Fault property to a workflow field that contains the exception to throw. The easiest way to do this is to open the binding dialog for the Fault property and select the Bind to a New Member tab. From here, you can enter a member name of **fault** and select Create Field as the type of member to create. When you select OK, a new field of type Exception is added to the workflow and the proper binding to this field is added to the Fault property.

Drag the original codeDoDivision and divideNumberOutput activities into the right-side branch (ifDivisorNotZero). Your completed workflow should look like Figure 15-6.

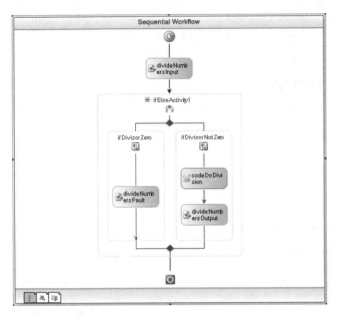

Figure 15-6. *Modified MathServiceWorkflow*

The additions that you need to make to the MathServiceWorkflow.cs code are shown in Listing 15-5.

Listing 15-5. *Additions to the MathServiceWorkflow.cs File*

```
using System;
using System.Workflow.Activities;

namespace SharedWorkflows
{
    /// <summary>
    /// A workflow exposed as a web service
    /// </summary>
    public sealed partial class MathServiceWorkflow
        : SequentialWorkflowActivity
    {

…

        private void IsDivisorZero(
            object sender, ConditionalEventArgs e)
        {
            e.Result = (divisor == 0);
        }

        public Exception fault =
            new DivideByZeroException("divisor must not be zero");
    }
}
```

The IsDivisorZero method is the code condition that checks whether the divisor is equal to zero. The fault field was originally added as a type of Exception. I changed this to a DivideByZeroException and constructed it with an appropriate error message.

Testing the Revised Web Service

After building the solution, you should be ready to test the revised MathServiceWorkflow. You don't have to republish the workflow as a web service since you didn't add or remove a workflow.

If you start the SharedWorkflow_WebService project without debugging (CTRL+F5), you can try a division by zero. This time, instead of returning infinity, a fault is returned. What you see depends on the browser that you are using. If you are using Internet Explorer, you receive this error:

```
HTTP 500 - Internal server error
```

If you use Mozilla Firefox (as I usually do), the actual fault message isn't hidden from you:

```
System.DivideByZeroException: divisor must not be zero
```

A real client application would be able to handle the web service fault much more gracefully than this generated test page.

Developing a Stateful Web Service

In the previous examples, the workflow ended as soon as it returned a web service response. While this may be fine for some of your applications, you will also likely need other workflows that maintain state and support multiple web service calls.

For instance, an order entry application might need to use web services to create a new workflow instance that represents an order. After creating that order workflow, it might call a different web service method that adds line items to the order. Finally, it could call another method that completes the order and ends the workflow. Obviously all of these web service calls must work with the same workflow instance since it must maintain state for the order. And that workflow instance must support more than one web service method.

Because of the way web services are implemented in WF, stateful web services such as this are supported. The WorkflowWebHostingModule provides cookie-based support that identifies the workflow instance ID. By passing this ID between the client and the workflow runtime, the client can invoke multiple web service methods against the same workflow instance. When you add persistence to the mix, you also have the ability to unload idle workflows from memory while they are waiting for the next web service call.

In the example that is presented next, you will develop a workflow that supports multiple web service calls. A division operation is supported, just like the previous examples. But this time the workflow will support new methods that explicitly start and end the workflow. I've also included a method that retrieves the current value of the quotient field, proving that the client is indeed working with the same workflow instance.

Defining the Web Service Interface

Although the design of this workflow is similar to the previous examples, it is different enough to warrant a new workflow. In the steps that follow, I present it as a new workflow, but you may find it quicker to copy some of the activities and code from the MathServiceWorkflow developed earlier in the chapter.

First, you need to define the new interface containing the web service methods. Add a new C# interface to the SharedWorkflows project and name it IMathServiceStateful. Listing 15-6 is the complete contents of the IMathServiceStateful.cs file.

Listing 15-6. *Complete IMathServiceStateful.cs File*

```
using System;

namespace SharedWorkflows
{
    public interface IMathServiceStateful
    {
        /// <summary>
        /// Activate the workflow
        /// </summary>
        void StartWorkflow();

        /// <summary>
        /// Perform a division operation
        /// </summary>
        /// <param name="dividend"></param>
        /// <param name="divisor"></param>
        /// <returns></returns>
        Double DivideNumbers(Double dividend, Double divisor);

        /// <summary>
        /// Retrieve the last divide result
        /// </summary>
        /// <returns></returns>
        Double GetLastQuotient();

        /// <summary>
        /// Allow the workflow to stop
        /// </summary>
        void StopWorkflow();
    }
}
```

In addition to the DivideNumbers method used in previous examples, I've added StartWorkflow, StopWorkflow, and GetLastQuotient methods.

Implementing the MathServiceStatefulWorkflow

Add a new sequential workflow to the SharedWorkflows project and name it MathServiceStatefulWorkflow. Before you start the visual design of this workflow, switch to code view and add the public fields that you will need. Adding these first allows you to easily bind activities to them when you are in the workflow designer. Listing 15-7 is the MathServiceStatefulWorkflow.cs file with the instance fields.

Listing 15-7. *MathServiceStatefulWorkflow.cs File with Instance Fields*

```
using System;
using System.Workflow.Activities;

namespace SharedWorkflows
{
    /// <summary>
    /// A stateful workflow exposed as a web service
    /// </summary>
    public sealed partial class MathServiceStatefulWorkflow
        : SequentialWorkflowActivity
    {
        public Double dividend;
        public Double divisor;
        public Double quotient;
        public Boolean isTimeToStop = false;

        public MathServiceStatefulWorkflow()
        {
            InitializeComponent();
        }
    }
}
```

The dividend, divisor, and quotient fields serve the same purpose as the previous examples. The isTimeToStop field will be used by a code condition to keep the workflow alive between web service calls.

Since this workflow requires a larger number of activities compared to the previous examples, I'll present a picture of the completed workflow first. You can use the completed workflow shown in Figure 15-7 as a guide when you add the activities.

At the top of the workflow is a WebServiceInputActivity named startWorkflowInput. Set the InterfaceType property to SharedWorkflows.IMathServiceStateful and select StartWorkflow as the method. This method doesn't require any input parameters, so there are no parameters to bind.

Set the IsActivating property to true if it isn't already set for you. This indicates that the StartWorkflow method is the one that will result in the creation of a new instance of this workflow. As you will see, only the first WebServiceInputActivity instance can be the one that activates a workflow. All of the other WebServiceInputActivity instances will set the IsActivating property to false.

Once the workflow is started, you want it to exist until you explicitly tell it to complete with the StopWorkflow method. To accomplish this, add a WhileActivity to the workflow. This activity will use a condition that keeps the workflow alive. Set the Condition property to Code Condition and enter a name of CheckIsTimeToStop.

Next, add a ListenActivity as a child of the WhileActivity. Remember that the WebServiceInputActivity implements the IEventActivity interface and is considered one of the event-driven activities. The ListenActivity is used here because you want the workflow to listen for any of the remaining web service methods (DivideNumbers, GetLastQuotient, StopWorkflow). As you can see in Figure 15-7, the ListenActivity has three distinct execution branches under it, each one corresponding to one of the web service methods.

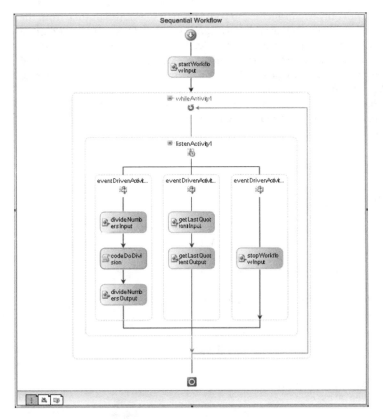

Figure 15-7. *Complete MathServiceStatefulWorkflow*

The leftmost branch corresponds to the DivideNumbers method. It requires a WebServiceInputActivity (divideNumbersInput), a CodeActivity (codeDoDivision), and a WebServiceOutputActivity (divideNumbersOutput). Set the InterfaceType and MethodName to use for the WebServiceInputActivity. Add parameter bindings to both of the web service activities that bind them to the appropriate workflow instance fields. Set the InputActivityName property of the divideNumbersOutput to divideNumbersInput. For this WebServiceInputActivity (and all others that you will add), the IsActivating property should be set to false. Before leaving this first branch, double-click the codeDoDivision activity to add a handler for its ExecuteCode event.

■**Note** To keep this example as simple as possible, I've left out the activities from the previous example that sent a web service fault. If you prefer, you can add these activities to the DivideNumbers branch, but they are not required.

The next branch corresponds to the GetLastQuotient method. It requires a WebServiceInputActivity (getLastQuotientInput) and a WebServiceOutputActivity (getLastQuotientOutput). Set the InterfaceType and MethodName for the input activity. Set the InputActivityName of the getLastQuotientOutput activity to getLastQuotientInput. The input activity doesn't require any parameter bindings, but the ReturnValue of the output activity should be bound to the quotient workflow field.

The `ListenActivity` starts with only two branches, so you'll need to select Add Branch from the context menu to add the third branch. The final branch corresponds to the `StopWorkflow` method. It requires a single `WebServiceInputActivity` (`stopWorkflowInput`). Set the `InterfaceType` and `MethodName` and then double-click the activity to add a handler for the `InputReceived` event. This event is raised when the activity first receives the web service call. In this example, you will use the code handler for this event to stop the `WhileActivity` from executing.

You should now be finished with the visual design of the workflow and can turn your attention back to the code. The additional code that you need to add to the `MathServiceStatefulWorkflow.cs` file is shown in Listing 15-8.

Listing 15-8. *Additional Code for the MathServiceStatefulWorkflow.cs File*

```
using System;
using System.Workflow.Activities;

namespace SharedWorkflows
{
    /// <summary>
    /// A stateful workflow exposed as a web service
    /// </summary>
    public sealed partial class MathServiceStatefulWorkflow
        : SequentialWorkflowActivity
    {

...

        private void codeDoDivision_ExecuteCode(
            object sender, EventArgs e)
        {
            //do the division
            quotient = dividend / divisor;
        }

        private void CheckIsTimeToStop(
            object sender, ConditionalEventArgs e)
        {
            e.Result = !(isTimeToStop);
        }

        private void stopWorkflowInput_InputReceived(
            object sender, EventArgs e)
        {
            //Stop the WhileActivity from executing
            isTimeToStop = true;
        }
    }
}
```

The `CheckIsTimeToStop` method is the code condition for the `WhileActivity`. Since the `isTimeToStop` field is initialized to `false`, this condition will return `true` until the value of the field is changed, keeping the workflow alive. The field is set to `true` by the `InputReceived` handler for the `stopWorkflowInput` activity when it receives the `StopWorkflow` call from a web service client.

Publishing the New Workflow

To publish this new workflow, you could select Publish as Web Service from the `SharedWorkflows` project menu. But that would generate a brand-new web service project, which you don't really need. The alternative is to add a new `.asmx` file to the existing `SharedWorkflows_WebService` project that corresponds to the new workflow.

The new `.asmx` file should be named `SharedWorkflows.MathServiceStatefulWorkflow_WebService.asmx` and contains the line shown here:

```
<%@ WebService Class="SharedWorkflows.MathServiceStatefulWorkflow_WebService" %>
```

Testing the Web Service

After building the solution, you can set the `SharedWorkflows_WebService` as the startup project and select Start Without Debugging (CTRL+F5). Your default browser should now present a list that includes both web services (the original one and this new one). Select the `SharedWorkflows.MathServiceStatefulWorkflow_WebService.asmx` service and you should now see a list of the four available operations.

To activate an instance of the workflow, you must begin with the `StartWorkflow` method. The `WebServiceInputActivity` associated with this method is the one with `IsActivating` set to true. Following the `StartWorkflow` method, you can invoke the `DivideNumbers` method as you did in the previous examples. Since you are invoking the same workflow instance with each call, you can call `DivideNumbers` multiple times without any problems. Previously, a second call to `DivideNumbers` resulted in an error because the workflow instance had already ended.

After performing some division, you can invoke the `GetLastQuotient` method. It should return the same result as the last `DivideNumbers` call. This proves that you are communicating with a stateful workflow instance that is maintaining the value of its instance variables between calls.

Finally, you can call the `StopWorkflow` method. This sets the `WhileActivity` condition so that the workflow completes. Additional calls to the workflow at this point will result in an error, since the instance no longer exists.

By keeping a workflow instance alive like this, you can interact with it across multiple web service calls. Using this technique, you can implement workflow-based applications, expose them to clients via web services, and still have the ability to maintain state.

Invoking a Web Service from a Workflow

Since WF enables you to expose a workflow as a web service, it makes sense that it also permits you to invoke a web service. The `InvokeWebServiceActivity` can be used when you need to invoke a web service from within a workflow.

To use the `InvokeWebServiceActivity` in a workflow, you add a web reference to the project containing the workflow. This generates a proxy class that enables you to make calls to the web service. The `ProxyClass` property of the `InvokeWebServiceActivity` is set to the name of this generated proxy class. The `MethodName` property identifies the web service method that you wish to invoke. Once the `MethodName` is selected, the input and result parameters are shown in the Parameters section of the Properties window. You can then bind each parameter to a workflow or activity member.

Implementing the InvokeWebServiceWorkflow

In this example, you will develop a workflow that uses the `InvokeWebServiceActivity` to call a web service method. The `DivideNumbers` method from the `MathServiceWorkflow` presented earlier in this chapter is the target web service method for this example.

Add a new Sequential Workflow Console Application to the solution and name it
ConsoleInvokeWebService. Unlike most other Console applications presented in this book, this one
doesn't need to reference the SharedWorkflows project. This project will define its workflow locally
within the project instead of referencing it in the SharedWorkflows project. This helps to emphasize
that you are referencing the MathServiceWorkflow as a web service instead of directly as a workflow.
However, you do need to add a project reference to the Bukovics.Workflow.Hosting project.

You can now turn your attention to the workflow design. Rename the workflow that was added
by the project template from Workflow1 to InvokeWebServiceWorkflow. Switch to code view for the
workflow and add several instance fields to the workflow as shown in Listing 15-9.

Listing 15-9. *InvokeWebServiceWorkflow.cs File with Instance Fields*

```
using System;
using System.Workflow.Activities;

namespace ConsoleInvokeWebService
{
    /// <summary>
    /// Invoke a web service from a workflow
    /// </summary>
    public sealed partial class InvokeWebServiceWorkflow
        : SequentialWorkflowActivity
    {
        public Double dividend = 100;
        public Double divisor = 4;
        public Double quotient;

        public InvokeWebServiceWorkflow()
        {
            InitializeComponent();
        }
    }
}
```

These fields will be bound to parameters of the InvokeWebServiceActivity that are used when
calling the web service method. I've given the dividend and divisor initial test values to eliminate
the need to pass them in as parameters.

After switching to the workflow designer, add a single InvokeWebServiceActivity to the workflow. When you add this activity, you are immediately prompted to add a web reference to the project
using the Add Web Reference dialog shown in Figure 15-8.

You have several options available to find the web service to reference. For this example, you
can select Web Services in This Solution. A list of web services in the current solution should be
presented, which includes the SharedWorkflow.MathServiceWorkflow_WebService. After selecting
this web service, a confirmation dialog shows you the list of operations available from the selected
web service. This is shown in Figure 15-9.

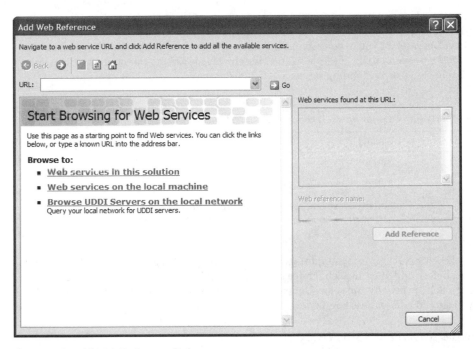

Figure 15-8. *Add Web Reference dialog*

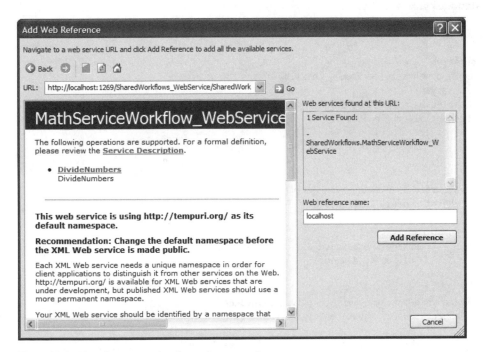

Figure 15-9. *List of supported web service operations*

You can now select Add Reference to add the web service reference to the project. If you review the Properties window for invokeWebServiceActivity1, you should see that the ProxyClass and URL properties have been set for you to correspond with the web reference you added. You now need to set the MethodName property to DivideNumbers and bind the DivideNumbers parameters to the workflow fields. Table 15-3 lists the binding values that you need.

Table 15-3. *Property Bindings for invokeWebServiceActivity1*

Property	Binding
(ReturnValue)	Activity=InvokeWebServiceWorkflow, Path=quotient
dividend	Activity=InvokeWebServiceWorkflow, Path=dividend
divisor	Activity=InvokeWebServiceWorkflow, Path=divisor

The InvokeWebServiceActivity supports two events named Invoking and Invoked. These events are raised just before and after the web service method is called. To add handlers for these events you can right-click the activity and select Generate Handlers. Listing 15-10 shows the additional code that you should add to these handlers.

Listing 15-10. *Revised InvokeWebServiceWorkflow.cs File*

```
using System;
using System.Workflow.Activities;

namespace ConsoleInvokeWebService
{
    /// <summary>
    /// Invoke a web service from a workflow
    /// </summary>
    public sealed partial class InvokeWebServiceWorkflow
        : SequentialWorkflowActivity
    {

...

        private void invokeWebServiceActivity1_Invoking(
            object sender, InvokeWebServiceEventArgs e)
        {
            Console.WriteLine(
                "Invoking web service dividend={0}, divisor={1}",
                    dividend, divisor);
        }

        private void invokeWebServiceActivity1_Invoked(
            object sender, InvokeWebServiceEventArgs e)
        {
            Console.WriteLine("Invoked web service result={0}",
                quotient);
        }
    }
}
```

When you add a web reference, an app.config file is also added to the project. This file contains entries that identify the URL to use when invoking the web service at runtime. By changing the values here, you can redirect this application to reference the web service at a different location. Listing 15-11 shows you the contents of this generated file.

Listing 15-11. *Generated app.config File*

```xml
<?xml version="1.0" encoding="utf-8" ?>
<configuration>
  <configSections>
    <sectionGroup name="applicationSettings"
      type="System.Configuration.ApplicationSettingsGroup, System,
      Version=2.0.0.0, Culture=neutral, PublicKeyToken=b77a5c561934e089" >
      <section name="ConsoleInvokeWebService.Properties.Settings"
      type="System.Configuration.ClientSettingsSection, System,
      Version=2.0.0.0, Culture=neutral, PublicKeyToken=b77a5c561934e089"
        requirePermission="false" />
    </sectionGroup>
  </configSections>
  <applicationSettings>
    <ConsoleInvokeWebService.Properties.Settings>
      <setting
        name="ConsoleInvokeWebService_localhost_MathServiceWorkflow_WebService"
          serializeAs="String">
            <value>http://localhost:1269/SharedWorkflows_WebService
                /SharedWorkflows.MathServiceWorkflow_WebService.asmx</value>
      </setting>
    </ConsoleInvokeWebService.Properties.Settings>
  </applicationSettings>
</configuration>
```

■**Note** The highlighted line that identifies the URL is actually a single line that has been split to fit the format of this book.

Testing the Workflow

You now need to add code to the project to host the workflow runtime and start the test workflow. Add a new C# class named InvokeWebServiceTest to the project. Listing 15-12 is the complete listing for this class.

Listing 15-12. *Complete InvokeWebServiceTest.cs File*

```csharp
using System;
using System.Workflow.Runtime;

using Bukovics.Workflow.Hosting;

namespace ConsoleInvokeWebService
{
    /// <summary>
    /// Test the InvokeWebServiceWorkflow
    /// </summary>
```

```
public class InvokeWebServiceTest
{
    public static void Run()
    {
        using (WorkflowRuntimeManager manager
            = new WorkflowRuntimeManager(new WorkflowRuntime()))
        {
            //start the runtime
            manager.WorkflowRuntime.StartRuntime();

            Console.WriteLine("Executing InvokeWebServiceWorkflow");
            WorkflowInstanceWrapper instance =
                manager.StartWorkflow(
                    typeof(InvokeWebServiceWorkflow), null);
            manager.WaitAll(10000);
            Console.WriteLine("Completed InvokeWebServiceWorkflow\n\r");
        }
    }
}
}
```

You also need a small amount of code in the `Program.cs` file as shown here:

```
using System;

namespace ConsoleInvokeWebService
{
    public class Program
    {
        static void Main(string[] args)
        {
            InvokeWebServiceTest.Run();

            Console.WriteLine("Press any key to exit");
            Console.ReadLine();
        }
    }
}
```

After building the solution and setting `ConsoleInvokeWebService` as the startup project, you should be ready for a test. When you execute the `ConsoleInvokeWebService` application, the ASP.NET Development Server will start (if it isn't already running) and the application will execute. Here are my results:

```
Executing InvokeWebServiceWorkflow
Invoking web service dividend=100, divisor=4
Invoked web service result=25
Completed InvokeWebServiceWorkflow

Press any key to exit
```

In this example, you executed the web service that was developed earlier in the chapter. That web service just happened to be implemented as a workflow, but that is certainly not a requirement.

You can use the InvokeWebServiceActivity to access any compatible web service regardless of how it was implemented.

Using Workflows from ASP.NET

You can also execute workflows directly from your ASP.NET Web Forms applications without using web services. To do this, you need to load the workflow runtime into the ASP.NET hosting environment and then reference it when you want to start a workflow. This is accomplished with a set of entries in the Web.config file and a small amount of code.

It is important to load the ManualWorkflowSchedulerService into the runtime when executing workflows from ASP.NET. As I already mentioned in the web service introduction earlier in this chapter, this service uses the host thread (an ASP.NET thread, in this case) to execute a workflow. When this service is loaded, each workflow executes synchronously on the current ASP.NET thread. If you don't load this service, workflows are executed asynchronously using threads managed by the workflow runtime.

In this example, you will learn how to execute a workflow from an ASP.NET Web Forms application. You will create another workflow that divides numbers and then develop a simple web site that executes the workflow. The single page web site will provide input fields that permit you to enter the parameters (dividend and divisor) needed to execute the workflow.

Implementing the DivideNumberWorkflow

You first need to implement a simple workflow that divides numbers. This workflow is similar to the ones presented earlier in this chapter with one major difference. This one isn't designed to be exposed as a web service.

Add a new sequential workflow to the SharedWorkflows project and name it DivideNumbersWorkflow. Add a single CodeActivity to the workflow and name it codeDoDivision. Double-click the activity to add a handler for the ExecuteCode event. The complete code for this workflow is shown in Listing 15-13.

Listing 15-13. *Complete DivideNumbersWorkflow.cs File*

```
using System;

using System.Workflow.Activities;

namespace SharedWorkflows
{
    /// <summary>
    /// Workflow that does division
    /// </summary>
    public sealed partial class DivideNumbersWorkflow
        : SequentialWorkflowActivity
    {
        private Double dividend;
        private Double divisor;
        private Double quotient;

        public Double Dividend
        {
            get { return dividend; }
            set { dividend = value; }
        }
```

```
        public Double Divisor
        {
            get { return divisor; }
            set { divisor = value; }
        }

        public Double Quotient
        {
            get { return quotient; }
            set { quotient = value; }
        }

        public DivideNumbersWorkflow()
        {
            InitializeComponent();
        }

        private void codeDoDivision_ExecuteCode(
            object sender, EventArgs e)
        {
            //do the division
            quotient = dividend / divisor;
        }
    }
}
```

The code for the workflow defines three fields (dividend, divisor, and quotient) and their associated properties. The code handler for the codeDoDivision activity performs the division using the field values.

Implementing the UseWorkflowWebsite

Begin development of the client application by adding a new web site to the current solution, naming it UseWorkflowWebsite. Select ASP.NET Web Site as the project template, File System as the Location, and Visual C# as the Language. The project template creates Default.aspx and Default. aspx.cs files that you will use as the page that accepts input parameters and executes the workflow. You will implement the web page after you configure the web site to load the workflow runtime.

Since the code in this web site will reference the DivideNumbersWorkflow directly, it requires a reference to the project containing this workflow. Go ahead and add a reference to the SharedWorkflows project at this time.

Modifying the Web.config

A Web.config file should have been added to the project for you as a byproduct of adding the reference to the SharedWorkflows project. You will need to add entries to this file to configure the services used by the workflow runtime. As a shortcut, you can copy the entries from the Web.config used earlier in this chapter (Listing 15-4). The Web.config used earlier can be used with one minor change. Since this example doesn't use web services (it invokes the workflow directly), you don't really need to load the WorkflowWebHostingModule. This is the HTTP module that passes a cookie to identify the workflow instance ID. The lines that you should remove from the copied Web.config are shown here:

```
<httpModules>
  <add type="System.Workflow.Runtime.Hosting.WorkflowWebHostingModule,
    System.Workflow.Runtime, Version=3.0.0.0, Culture=neutral,
    PublicKeyToken=31bf3856ad364e35" name="WorkflowHost"/>
</httpModules>
```

Loading the Workflow Runtime

When invoking workflows from an ASP.NET client application, you don't want the overhead of loading the workflow runtime with each request. Instead, you should load the workflow runtime once during application startup. To do this, you can add a Global.asax file to the project and add code to this file to load the workflow runtime during startup.

Select Add New Item for the project and select Global Application Class. Use the default name of Global.asax. The generated file contains placeholders for common application events. The only two that you care about are Application_Start and Application_End. You can remove the placeholders for the other events. Listing 15-14 shows the code that you need to add to these two event handlers.

Listing 15-14. *Global.asax Application Code File*

```
<%@ Application Language="C#" %>

<script RunAt="server">

    void Application_Start(object sender, EventArgs e)
    {
        //create an instance of the workflow runtime, loading
        //settings from the Web.Config
        System.Workflow.Runtime.WorkflowRuntime workflowRuntime =
            new System.Workflow.Runtime.WorkflowRuntime("WorkflowRuntime");

        //start the workflow runtime
        workflowRuntime.StartRuntime();

        //save the runtime for use by individual pages
        Application["WorkflowRuntime"] = workflowRuntime;
    }

    void Application_End(object sender, EventArgs e)
    {
        //shut down the workflow runtime
        System.Workflow.Runtime.WorkflowRuntime workflowRuntime =
            Application["WorkflowRuntime"]
                as System.Workflow.Runtime.WorkflowRuntime;
        workflowRuntime.StopRuntime();
    }
</script>
```

The Application_Start method is executed when the application is first initialized. Within this event handler, an instance of the WorkflowRuntime is created. Notice that the code uses the constructor that accepts a configuration section name. The name passed to the constructor corresponds to the section name within the Web.config file that identifies the services to load. After starting the workflow runtime, the code saves a reference to the workflow runtime as an attribute of the Application object.

Placing this reference in the Application object makes it available to any page-level code that requires the workflow runtime.

The Application_End method retrieves the WorkflowRuntime instance from the Application object and then performs an orderly shutdown of it by calling the StopRuntime method.

Implementing the Web Page

You can now turn your attention to the web page itself (the Default.aspx file in the project). Open this file, switch to the Design view, and add a series of controls that will allow entry of the workflow input parameters. You'll need to add three TextBox controls (one each for the dividend, divisor, and quotient) along with three Label controls to identify each TextBox. You also need one Button that will be used to invoke the workflow.

My web page is shown in Figure 15-10, but feel free to improve on my overly simplistic UI design.

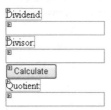

Figure 15-10. *Web page design.*

Provide a meaningful ID for each TextBox (I assigned IDs of dividend, divisor, and quotient). I also set the quotient TextBox to ReadOnly, since it isn't used as input. Assign an ID of btnCalculate to the Button control. You can double-click the button to add a handler for its Click event.

You need to add code to the Click event handler to parse the dividend and divisor input, invoke the workflow, and then display the result in the quotient control. Listing 15-15 shows the complete code that you need to add to the Default.aspx.cs file.

Listing 15-15. *Complete Default.aspx.cs File*

```
using System;
using System.Collections.Generic;
using System.Workflow.Runtime;
using System.Workflow.Runtime.Hosting;

using SharedWorkflows;

public partial class _Default : System.Web.UI.Page
{
    /// <summary>
    /// The calculate button was pressed
    /// </summary>
    /// <param name="sender"></param>
    /// <param name="e"></param>
```

```
protected void btnCalculate_Click(object sender, EventArgs e)
{
    //retrieve the workflow runtime
    WorkflowRuntime workflowRuntime
        = Application["WorkflowRuntime"] as WorkflowRuntime;
    //retrieve the scheduler that is used to execute workflows
    ManualWorkflowSchedulerService scheduler =
        workflowRuntime.GetService(
            typeof(ManualWorkflowSchedulerService))
                as ManualWorkflowSchedulerService;
```

The button click handler begins by retrieving a reference to the WorkflowRuntime that was saved in the Application object during startup. It then retrieves the ManualWorkflowSchedulerService from the runtime using the GetService method. This service was added to the WorkflowRuntime with Web.config entries instead of explicitly in code. The scheduler service will be used to execute the workflow on the current ASP.NET thread.

```
    //handle the WorkflowCompleted event in order to
    //retrieve the output parameters from the completed workflow
    workflowRuntime.WorkflowCompleted
        += new EventHandler<WorkflowCompletedEventArgs>(
            workflowRuntime_WorkflowCompleted);
```

A handler is added for the WorkflowCompleted event. Even though the workflow will execute synchronously on the current thread, you still need to handle this event to retrieve any output parameters from the workflow. In this example, you need to retrieve the value for the Quotient property.

```
    //get the input parameters
    Double dividendValue;
    Double divisorValue;
    Double.TryParse(dividend.Text, out dividendValue);
    Double.TryParse(divisor.Text, out divisorValue);

    //pass the input parameters to the workflow
    Dictionary<String, Object> wfArguments
        = new Dictionary<string, object>();
    wfArguments.Add("Dividend", dividendValue);
    wfArguments.Add("Divisor", divisorValue);
```

This code parses the dividend and divisor into Double values and adds them to a Dictionary of workflow input parameters.

```
    //create and start the workflow
    WorkflowInstance instance = workflowRuntime.CreateWorkflow(
        typeof(SharedWorkflows.DivideNumbersWorkflow), wfArguments);
    instance.Start();

    //execute the workflow synchronously on our thread
    scheduler.RunWorkflow(instance.InstanceId);
```

An instance of the DivideNumbersWorkflow is created using the CreateWorkflow method of the WorkflowRuntime. After calling the Start method on the WorkflowInstance, it is passed to the RunWorkflow method of the ManualWorkflowSchedulerService. This executes the workflow using the current ASP.NET thread.

```
    }

    /// <summary>
    /// The workflow has completed
    /// </summary>
    /// <param name="sender"></param>
    /// <param name="e"></param>
    void workflowRuntime_WorkflowCompleted(
        object sender, WorkflowCompletedEventArgs e)
    {
        //get the result from the workflow
        if (e.OutputParameters.ContainsKey("Quotient"))
        {
            Double quotientValue
                = (Double)e.OutputParameters["Quotient"];
            quotient.Text = quotientValue.ToString();
        }
    }
}
```

The WorkflowCompleted event handler retrieves the output from the Quotient property and displays it in the quotient TextBox.

```
}
```

Testing the Web Site

After building the solution, you should be ready to test the web site. Set UseWorkflowWebsite as the startup project and select Start Without Debugging (CTRL+F5). If all goes well, an instance of your default browser should start and you should see the web site, ready to handle your most difficult division problems. Figure 15-11 shows you an example of the working web site.

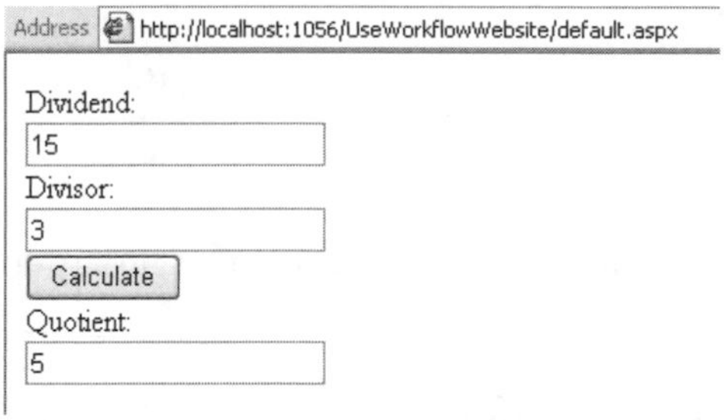

Figure 15-11. *Working invoking web site*

As you can see with this example, invoking a workflow from a web site is a straightforward matter. Once the workflow runtime is configured and loaded, it takes just a few lines of code to execute a workflow.

Summary

The focus of this chapter was the use of workflows with web services and ASP.NET applications. With a minimal amount of effort, you can develop and publish a workflow that clients can invoke using web services. This was demonstrated by several examples in this chapter.

This chapter also demonstrated how to invoke a web service from a workflow. As this chapter showed, ASP.NET applications are also able to use workflows. The final example in this chapter showed you how to implement a simple web site that hosts the workflow runtime and executes a workflow.

In the next chapter, you will learn about workflow serialization and markup. The techniques presented in the next chapter provide alternate ways to declare and manage workflow definitions.

CHAPTER 16

Workflow Serialization and Markup

The focus of this chapter is the use of workflow markup and serialization. WF provides several authoring modes that you can use when defining the workflow model. This chapter discusses those authoring modes, spending most of the time demonstrating the use of workflow markup. Workflow markup is a serialized representation of the workflow model that is saved as a `.xoml` file.

The chapter begins with an overview discussion of each authoring mode supported by WF. Following the overview, examples are presented that implement the same workflow using each authoring mode. The chapter includes examples using the code-only, code-separation, and no-code authoring modes. Several examples also demonstrate how rules are used with each authoring mode.

In addition to authoring modes and workflow markup, this chapter also discusses serialization and deserialization of the workflow model. The serialization techniques demonstrated in this chapter are useful if your application hosts the workflow designers or otherwise requires the ability to modify the workflow model. Several examples also show you how to compile workflow markup to a new assembly using the `WorkflowCompiler` class and the `wfc.exe` command-line workflow compiler.

Understanding Workflow Authoring Modes

One of the key benefits of developing workflow applications is the clear separation between the workflow model and your business logic. The business logic is generally implemented as code in the workflow class or in custom activities. You can also implement business logic as rules within a `RuleSet`.

The workflow model defines the sequence in which the business logic is to be executed. The sequence can be defined using simple `if/else` conditions, while loops, parallel activities, replicated activities, and so on. The workflow model is the glue that connects the business logic, orchestrating the discrete activities according to your design.

WF supports several authoring modes that you can use when defining the workflow model. What you have used throughout this book is known as the code-only authoring mode. As the name implies, the model is constructed completely in code using the WF object model. Also available are authoring modes that declare the workflow model in XML files. These modes are known as *no-code* and *code-separation*.

Your choice of authoring mode determines, in part, how you package and distribute your workflow-enabled application. It can also affect the way you create new workflow instances at runtime. In the next few sections, I provide a brief overview of each authoring mode. Later in the chapter, you will see examples that demonstrate how to use each authoring mode.

Code-Only Authoring Mode

The code-only authoring mode works by generating a separate code file that contains the workflow model. For example, if you create a new workflow named `Workflow1`, a file named `Workflow1.cs` is added to the project. This file is used by you when you add event-handling code and other business logic to the workflow class. A second source file named Workflow1.Designer.cs is also added to the project. This file contains the workflow model that is maintained by the workflow designer. Since the workflow designer adds or removes code to this file, it is off limits to you and should not be manually modified.

Both of these files define the workflow class using the partial C# keyword. This allows the definition of the workflow class to be split into multiple files. When the project is built, the contents of both files are combined to produce a single workflow .NET Type.

If the workflow uses rules or rule conditions, a separate Workflow1.rules file is created. This file contains a serialized version of the rule definitions for the workflow. When the project is built, the .rules file is stored as an embedded resource within the assembly.

At runtime, the compiled workflow Type is specified in the WorkflowRuntime.CreateWorkflow method to identify the type of workflow to create. The rule definitions (if they exist) are loaded by the workflow runtime from the embedded resource within the assembly.

The code-only authoring mode is illustrated in Figure 16-1.

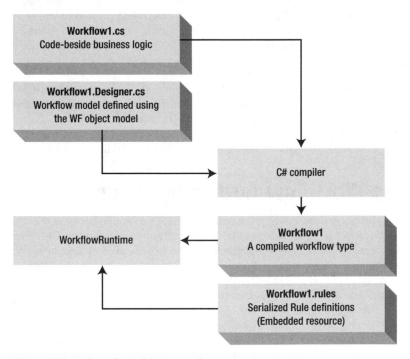

Figure 16-1. *Code-only authoring mode*

The advantages of the code-only authoring mode are that it is familiar, easy to use, and efficient. The Windows Forms designer support in Visual Studio uses the same approach of splitting the designer-maintained code and the code that you maintain into two separate files. So this is a familiar approach that is consistent with the way other designers work within Visual Studio.

It is relatively easy to use since the difficult work is done for you. You don't have to manually construct the workflow object model in code. The designer-generated code handles that for you.

And it is an efficient way to develop a workflow. All of the files that make up the workflow definition are contained within a single project and are compiled into binary form. At runtime, the compiled .NET workflow Type is used to create a workflow instance. There is no need to manage and maintain a set of files that are loaded separately at runtime.

The primary disadvantage to the code-only authoring mode is that it limits your ability to modify the workflow model. Since the model is compiled into a workflow Type along with the business logic, you can't easily modify just the model. You can use the dynamic workflow updates described in Chapter 13. But that's really the only way to modify the workflow model short of opening Visual Studio, modifying the model with the workflow designer, and then rebuilding the project.

Code-Separation Authoring Mode

WF also supports an authoring mode called *code-separation*. In this mode, the workflow model is maintained by the workflow designer in a separate source file with a .xoml extension. This is an XML file that declares the workflow model using the Extensible Application Markup Language (XAML, or just *markup*). XAML is a serialization format that specifies object instances as XML elements and properties of those objects as XML attributes.

A second source file is created that is used for any event-handling code and other business logic. This is referred to as the *code-beside file*. For example, if you create a new workflow named Workflow1 using code-separation, two files named Workflow1.xoml and Workflow1.xoml.cs are created and added to the project. If the workflow uses rules, they are maintained in a separate .rules file just as in the code-only authoring mode.

■Note It's easy to confuse the markup file extension (.xoml) with the format of the file's contents (XAML). You may wonder why a .xaml extension isn't used for the workflow markup files. One reason is that Windows Presentation Foundation (WPF) also makes extensive use of XAML. When you open a .xaml file, Visual Studio has to know whether to open the workflow designer or one that works with WPF XAML. A different file extension (.xoml) for the workflow markup files solves this problem. All files with a .xoml extension open the workflow designer as the default view.

To create a code-separation workflow, you select one of the available code-separation item templates from the Add New Item menu. For instance, instead of selecting the item template named Sequential Workflow (*code*), you select Sequential Workflow (*with code-separation*). Similarly named templates are available for adding state machine workflows. You can also add a code-separation custom activity to a project by selecting the Activity (with code-separation) template.

When you build the project, the workflow compiler generates a temporary C# source file from the .xoml markup file. The generated code is a partial C# class that is combined with the code-beside .xoml.cs file during compilation. The net result is a compiled workflow Type that can be used by the workflow runtime to create workflow instances.

The code-separation authoring mode is illustrated in Figure 16-2.

The code-separation authoring mode offers the same advantages as the code-only mode (familiar development experience, easy to use, and efficient). Defining the workflow model as markup (XAML) doesn't initially add any value. After all, the end result of the build process is the same .NET workflow Type you would have if you used code-only authoring.

The primary advantage of using code-separation is the potential that it offers. Declaring the workflow model as markup makes it more accessible to your own development and application tools. It keeps your options open.

For instance, you can develop your own tools that modify the workflow model by deserializing and serializing the markup file. After updates to the markup file are applied, you can recompile the markup into a complete workflow Type again (using the command-line workflow compiler or the WorkflowCompiler class). This capability is important if you wish to provide your end users with the ability to modify the workflow, perhaps by hosting the workflow designers within your application. You certainly can update the workflow model in code using the workflow object model. But it is easier to do so when it is described in markup instead of code.

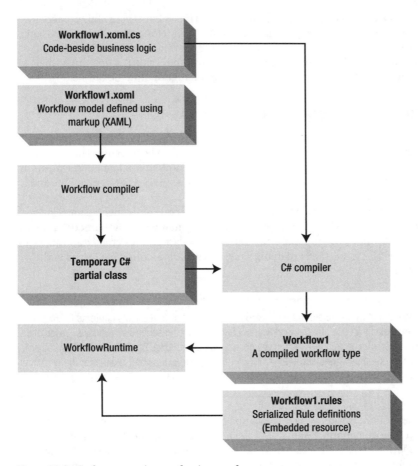

Figure 16-2. *Code-separation authoring mode*

No-Code Authoring Mode

The final authoring mode is called *no-code* (or sometimes *markup-only*). As you might guess from the name, the distinguishing characteristic of this authoring mode is that there is no code-beside file. The entire definition of the workflow model is done using markup (XAML).

Don't look for a New Item template within Visual Studio for this authoring mode. Visual Studio doesn't provide direct support for creating .xoml files without a code-beside file. The no-code authoring mode is primarily designed to facilitate the use of external workflow designers, not Visual Studio.

If you do wish to use Visual Studio to design a no-code workflow, you can start with a new code-separation workflow. After you add the new workflow, you can delete the code-beside file (e.g., Workflow1.xoml.cs). You can then drag and drop activities onto the workflow designer and set activity properties as you would normally.

However, you can't add any activities that require a code-beside file without crossing the line back into the code-separation authoring mode. For instance, you can add a CodeActivity to a no-code workflow. But if you double-click the activity, a code-beside file will be added automatically to the project in order to provide a home for the ExecuteCode event handler. When this happens, you're back in code-separation mode.

This highlights one of the features (or restrictions) of the no-code authoring mode. You can only use workflow types and members of those types that already exist. You can't directly create any new types or members when using no-code authoring. No-code authoring enforces a clear boundary between defining new workflow types and declaring instances of those types in the workflow model. The workflow markup can only create instances of types that have been defined, implemented, and compiled.

For example, using no-code authoring, you can't add a new event handler to the workflow class. But you can bind an event to an existing event handler in the workflow class. You can't add a new input or output property. But you can bind the dependency properties of an activity to existing properties of the workflow class (or of another activity).

Therefore, when using the no-code authoring mode, your work is separated into two distinct tasks. First, you design and implement workflow types. These are the building blocks that you will later assemble using markup. Included are custom activities and custom workflow classes. The custom activities are used to encapsulate task-specific business logic and expose public, bindable, dependency properties that provide access to input and output values. Custom workflow classes provide the input and output properties that are required by a particular workflow task. Defining properties in a custom workflow class is required if you want to pass input parameters to a no-code workflow during workflow creation. Custom workflow classes can also provide standard event handler code that can be bound to activity events. The deliverable from this first development task is a library of types that can be referenced by the markup.

The second task is to assemble the workflow using the library of custom and standard types. Instead of building upon one of the standard workflow classes, you can use a custom workflow class as the base Type of the workflow. By doing this, you provide access to the properties and other members that you define in the custom class. You can then define the workflow model by declaring instances of standard and custom activities. Properties of the activities can be set directly or bound to other activities or the workflow class.

The no-code authoring mode is illustrated in Figure 16-3.

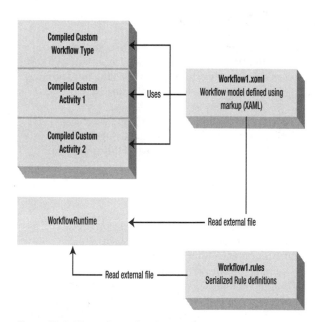

Figure 16-3. *No-code authoring mode*

As shown in Figure 16-3, the file containing the workflow markup references the library of custom workflow types that you developed. The references to the assemblies containing these types are established with namespace entries within the markup file. The markup file (.xoml) and the .rules file (if needed by the workflow) are accessed directly by the workflow runtime. This is a major difference from the other authoring modes, which create a workflow instance from a compiled Type.

■**Note** In addition to loading markup files directly at runtime, you can also compile them into a new assembly using the command-line workflow compiler (wfc.exe) or the WorkflowCompiler class. This option is discussed later in this chapter.

The no-code authoring mode provides flexibility as its primary advantage. Since the workflow model is defined in a separate markup file, it is easy to update the model without rebuilding the workflow types that are referenced by the model. If it is required, you can incorporate a workflow designer into your application that updates the markup files with a revised workflow model. In summary, no-code workflows are highly dynamic and easily modified.

However, no-code workflows require more up-front planning and discipline. Since you can't add new members or add new code to the workflow types that you reference, you must place the bulk of your business logic in custom activities or a base workflow class. Placing your business logic in custom activities is actually the recommended approach to workflow development, but it does require additional up-front planning.

If you are developing a high-performance application that will execute a large number of workflows, you may need to consider the trade-offs of flexibility vs. performance. Loading and parsing a workflow model from XAML is not as efficient as loading a compiled Type. If performance is an issue, you may want to precompile your markup files and then load them as a compiled Type.

Developing a Code-Only Workflow

Code-only workflows are what you have been using throughout this book, so this example doesn't present any groundbreaking information. But before you see examples that use workflow markup (XAML), I thought it would be beneficial to review a code-only example as a baseline implementation. Following this code-only example, workflows with the same functionality are implemented using each of the other authoring modes.

This example workflow uses a single IfElseActivity that contains two IfElseBranchActivity instances. Each execution branch contains a single CodeActivity that writes a message to the Console. Based on the value of an input parameter, one of the branches is executed and the appropriate message written.

Implementing the Workflow

To begin development of this example, create an Empty Workflow Project and name it SharedWorkflows. Next, add a new sequential workflow (code) to the project and name it CodeOnlyWorkflow.

Add an IfElseActivity to the workflow, which automatically includes two IfElseBranchActivity instances. Add a CodeActivity to each branch, naming the one on the left codeNumberIsPositive and the one on the right codeNumberNotPositive. Double-click each CodeActivity to add handlers for their ExecuteCode events. Set the Condition property of ifElseBranchActivity1 (on the left side) to Code Condition and provide a Condition name of IsNumberPositive. This creates a code condition event handler with this name in the workflow class.

Figure 16-4 shows the completed workflow in the designer.

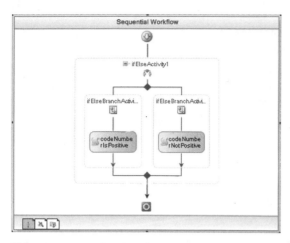

Figure 16-4. *Completed CodeOnlyWorkflow*

To complete the workflow, you need to define a single integer property named TheNumber that is set as an input parameter when the workflow is executed. You also need to add code for the two CodeActivity handlers and the IsNumberPositive code condition. The IsNumberPositive method returns true if the value of TheNumber is greater than zero. The complete code for the CodeOnlyWorkflow.cs file is shown in Listing 16-1.

Listing 16-1. *Complete CodeOnlyWorkflow.cs File*

```
using System;
using System.Workflow.Activities;

namespace SharedWorkflows
{
    /// <summary>
    /// A code only workflow
    /// </summary>
    public sealed partial class CodeOnlyWorkflow
        : SequentialWorkflowActivity
    {
        private Int32 _theNumber;

        public Int32 TheNumber
        {
            get { return _theNumber; }
            set { _theNumber = value; }
        }

        public CodeOnlyWorkflow()
        {
            InitializeComponent();
        }
```

```
        private void IsNumberPositive(
            object sender, ConditionalEventArgs e)
        {
            e.Result = (TheNumber > 0);
        }

        private void codeNumberIsPositive_ExecuteCode(
            object sender, EventArgs e)
        {
            Console.WriteLine("The number is positive");

        }

        private void codeNumberNotPositive_ExecuteCode(
            object sender, EventArgs e)
        {
            Console.WriteLine("The number is NOT positive");
        }
    }
}
```

I've highlighted the call to the InitializeComponent method in the constructor. This method is implemented in the other half of this partial class in the CodeOnlyWorkflow.Designer.cs file and is used to create the tree of workflow objects.

Testing the Workflow

To create a host application to execute the workflow, add a new Sequential Workflow Console project to the current solution and name it ConsoleCodeOnly. Delete the generated Workflow1 files and add references to the SharedWorkflows and Bukovics.Workflow.Hosting projects.

Add a C# class named CodeOnlyTest to the project. This class will host the workflow runtime and start an instance of the CodeOnlyWorkflow. Listing 16-2 is the complete code for the CodeOnlyTest.cs file.

Listing 16-2. *Complete CodeOnlyTest.cs File*

```csharp
using System;
using System.Collections.Generic;
using System.Workflow.Runtime;

using Bukovics.Workflow.Hosting;

namespace ConsoleCodeOnly
{
    /// <summary>
    /// Execute the CodeOnlyWorkflow
    /// </summary>
    public class CodeOnlyTest
    {
        public static void Run()
        {
            using (WorkflowRuntimeManager manager
                = new WorkflowRuntimeManager(new WorkflowRuntime()))
            {
```

```
        //start the runtime
        manager.WorkflowRuntime.StartRuntime();
        Console.WriteLine("Executing Workflow");
        //pass a number to test
        Dictionary<String, Object> wfArguments
            = new Dictionary<string, object>();
        wfArguments.Add("TheNumber", 1);

        //start the workflow
        WorkflowInstanceWrapper instance =
            manager.StartWorkflow(typeof(
                SharedWorkflows.CodeOnlyWorkflow), wfArguments);

        //wait for the workflow to complete
        manager.WaitAll(2000);
        Console.WriteLine("Completed Workflow\n\r");
    }
   }
  }
}
```

The code passes the number 1 as TheNumber parameter. This should result in execution of the first execution branch in the workflow since the number is positive. You also need this small bit of code in the Program.cs file:

```
using System;

namespace ConsoleCodeOnly
{
    public class Program
    {
        static void Main(string[] args)
        {
            CodeOnlyTest.Run();

            Console.WriteLine("Press any key to exit");
            Console.ReadLine();
        }
    }
}
```

After building the solution and setting ConsoleCodeOnly as the startup project, you can execute the application and should see these results:

```
Executing Workflow
The number is positive
Completed Workflow

Press any key to exit
```

The results may not be very exciting, but they are at least accurate.

Reviewing the Generated Code

Normally at this point I would move on to the next example. But in this case, the whole purpose of this example is to contrast a code-only workflow with the other authoring modes that will be presented next. So it makes sense to take a few minutes and review the code that is generated for you by the workflow designer.

If you expand the CodeOnlyWorkflow.cs file in the Solution Explorer, you will see another source file named CodeOnlyWorkflow.Designer.cs. This file contains the designer-generated code that constructs the workflow model. The generated code should look like Listing 16-3. You can open up this source file and look at it, but you should never modify it.

Listing 16-3. *Generated CodeOnlyWorkflow.Designer.cs File*

```
using System;
using System.ComponentModel;
using System.ComponentModel.Design;
using System.Collections;
using System.Drawing;
using System.Reflection;
using System.Workflow.ComponentModel.Compiler;
using System.Workflow.ComponentModel.Serialization;
using System.Workflow.ComponentModel;
using System.Workflow.ComponentModel.Design;
using System.Workflow.Runtime;
using System.Workflow.Activities;
using System.Workflow.Activities.Rules;

namespace SharedWorkflows
{
    partial class CodeOnlyWorkflow
    {
        #region Designer generated code

        /// <summary>
        /// Required method for Designer support - do not modify
        /// the contents of this method with the code editor.
        /// </summary>
        [System.Diagnostics.DebuggerNonUserCode]
        private void InitializeComponent()
        {
            this.CanModifyActivities = true;
            System.Workflow.Activities.CodeCondition codecondition1
                = new System.Workflow.Activities.CodeCondition();
            this.codeNumberNotPositive
                = new System.Workflow.Activities.CodeActivity();
            this.codeNumberIsPositive
                = new System.Workflow.Activities.CodeActivity();
            this.ifElseBranchActivity2
                = new System.Workflow.Activities.IfElseBranchActivity();
            this.ifElseBranchActivity1
                = new System.Workflow.Activities.IfElseBranchActivity();
            this.ifElseActivity1
                = new System.Workflow.Activities.IfElseActivity();
```

```
            //
            // codeNumberNotPositive
            //
            this.codeNumberNotPositive.Name = "codeNumberNotPositive";
            this.codeNumberNotPositive.ExecuteCode
                += new System.EventHandler(this.codeNumberNotPositive_ExecuteCode);
            //
            // codeNumberIsPositive
            //
            this.codeNumberIsPositive.Name = "codeNumberIsPositive";
            this.codeNumberIsPositive.ExecuteCode
                += new System.EventHandler(this.codeNumberIsPositive_ExecuteCode);
            //
            // ifElseBranchActivity2
            //
            this.ifElseBranchActivity2.Activities.Add(this.codeNumberNotPositive);
            this.ifElseBranchActivity2.Name = "ifElseBranchActivity2";
            //
            // ifElseBranchActivity1
            //
            this.ifElseBranchActivity1.Activities.Add(this.codeNumberIsPositive);
            codecondition1.Condition += new System.EventHandler<
                System.Workflow.Activities.ConditionalEventArgs>(
                    this.IsNumberPositive);
            this.ifElseBranchActivity1.Condition = codecondition1;
            this.ifElseBranchActivity1.Name = "ifElseBranchActivity1";
            //
            // ifElseActivity1
            //
            this.ifElseActivity1.Activities.Add(this.ifElseBranchActivity1);
            this.ifElseActivity1.Activities.Add(this.ifElseBranchActivity2);
            this.ifElseActivity1.Name = "ifElseActivity1";
            //
            // CodeOnlyWorkflow
            //
            this.Activities.Add(this.ifElseActivity1);
            this.Name = "CodeOnlyWorkflow";
            this.CanModifyActivities = false;

        }

        #endregion

        private CodeActivity codeNumberNotPositive;
        private CodeActivity codeNumberIsPositive;
        private IfElseBranchActivity ifElseBranchActivity2;
        private IfElseBranchActivity ifElseBranchActivity1;
        private IfElseActivity ifElseActivity1;
    }
}
```

As you can see from Listing 16-3, the designer-generated code is all contained in a single InitializeComponent method. You should note that this is the method that is executed from the class constructor shown in Listing 16-1. The code in this method is fairly straightforward. Instances of each activity are created, properties are set, event handlers are added, children are added to parents, and so on. There is nothing in this code that is difficult to understand and you could have easily written this code yourself by hand. But instead, the workflow designer handles that task for you.

Developing a Code-Separation Workflow

In this example, you will develop the same workflow presented in the last example (Figure 16-4) using the code-separation authoring mode instead of code-only. When you're done, the workflow should produce the same results as the previous example.

Implementing the Workflow

Add a new sequential workflow to the SharedWorkflows project, but this time make sure you select the Sequential Workflow (with Code-Separation) new item template. Name the new workflow CodeSeparationWorkflow.

Add the same set of activities that you added in the previous example (one IfElseActivity with one CodeActivity within each IfElseBranchActivity instance). Use the same names for the CodeActivity instances that you used in the previous example (codeNumberIsPositive and codeNumberNotPositive). Double-click each CodeActivity to add a handler for its ExecuteCode event. Select the same kind of Condition (Code Condition) and the same condition name (IsNumberPositive). The workflow should look exactly like the code-only workflow in Figure 16-4. From its visual appearance, you can't tell whether it is a code-only or a code-separation workflow.

Using Listing 16-1 as your guide, add the definition for the integer property (TheNumber), the code for the IsNumberPositive event handler, and the code for the two CodeActivity instances.

When you're done, your code should look exactly like Listing 16-1 with one notable difference. The CodeSeparationWorkflow.cs file doesn't have a constructor. The purpose of the constructor in Listing 16-1 is to call the InitializeComponent method that constructs the tree of workflow objects (the workflow model). That code isn't needed in a code-separation workflow since the workflow model is constructed from the markup (XAML).

Testing the Workflow

To test the code-separation version of this workflow, you can use the same ConsoleCodeOnly application that you developed for the last example. The only required modification is to change the CodeOnlyWorkflow reference to CodeSeparationWorkflow in the CodeOnlyTest.cs file.

After building the solution, you should be able to execute the ConsoleCodeOnly application and see the same results as the previous example ("The number is positive").

Reviewing the Markup

The default view associated with .xoml files is the workflow designer; so if you open the CodeSeparationWorkflow.xoml file, you will see the workflow markup rendered in the designer. However, the .xoml file contains XAML and you can also view it with the XML Editor provided with Visual Studio. To see the underlying XAML, first close the file in the workflow designer if it is open. You need to do this since you can't open a source file again if it is already opened by the workflow designer. Now right-click the CodeSeparationWorkflow.xoml file and select Open With. Select XML Editor and you should see the XAML shown in Listing 16-4.

Listing 16-4. *CodeSeparationWorkflow.xoml File Shown as XML*

```
<SequentialWorkflowActivity x:Class="SharedWorkflows.CodeSeparationWorkflow"
  x:Name="CodeSeparationWorkflow"
  xmlns:x="http://schemas.microsoft.com/winfx/2006/xaml"
  xmlns="http://schemas.microsoft.com/winfx/2006/xaml/workflow">
  <IfElseActivity x:Name="ifElseActivity1">
    <IfElseBranchActivity x:Name="ifElseBranchActivity1">
      <IfElseBranchActivity.Condition>
        <CodeCondition Condition="IsNumberPositive" />
      </IfElseBranchActivity.Condition>
      <CodeActivity x:Name="codeNumberIsPositive"
        ExecuteCode="codeNumberIsPositive_ExecuteCode" />
    </IfElseBranchActivity>
    <IfElseBranchActivity x:Name="ifElseBranchActivity2">
      <CodeActivity x:Name="codeNumberNotPositive"
        ExecuteCode="codeNumberNotPositive_ExecuteCode" />
    </IfElseBranchActivity>
  </IfElseActivity>
</SequentialWorkflowActivity>
```

If you compare this listing to the generated code shown in Listing 16-3, you will immediately notice the difference in size. Both of these listings are describing a workflow with exactly the same functionality and structure. Because the XAML is much more concise, it takes just 18 lines to fully describe the workflow model. The code-only version takes 90 lines. The reason for the dramatic difference in size is that the code and the XAML approach the problem of defining the workflow model in different ways. The code does so in a procedural way, while the XAML is completely declarative, just like the workflow model itself.

In addition to being concise, the workflow XAML follows a set of rules that make it very logical and easy to understand. XML elements are object instances, and XML attributes represent properties of those objects. For instance, consider this line:

```
<CodeCondition Condition="IsNumberPositive" />
```

The `CodeCondition` element creates an instance of the `CodeCondition` object. The `Condition` property is then set to a value of `IsNumberPositive`.

Elements that are nested as children of another element are child objects of the parent object. For instance, the `IfElseActivity` is the parent of the two `IfElseBranchActivity` instances. Each `IfElseBranchActivity` has a child `CodeActivity`.

The root element (`SequentialWorkflowActivity`) identifies the base class that you are extending to create this workflow. The `x:Class` entry is not always required but is in this case. It identifies the new class name that is assigned to this workflow. An `x:Class` entry is required when you are declaring a code-separation workflow that will be compiled into a new .NET Type. If you are not compiling the workflow into a new `Type`, the `x:Class` entry should be omitted. This would be the case if you are declaring a workflow in markup that you intend to load directly into the workflow runtime (a no-code workflow).

The `xmlns` entries on the root element are also important. They provide the references to the types that are represented by the XAML elements. This line

```
xmlns="http://schemas.microsoft.com/winfx/2006/xaml/workflow"
```

identifies the default namespace for the document and associates it with the XML schema for workflow XAML documents. It is this namespace entry that provides access to all of the standard workflow types.

This line

```
xmlns:x="http://schemas.microsoft.com/winfx/2006/xaml"
```

provides access to additional elements defined in the Microsoft XAML schema. In the next example, you will see how to add your own namespace entries to reference your own custom types within XAML.

Developing a No-Code Workflow

This example presents a workflow with the same behavior as the two previous examples (shown in Figure 16-4), but it uses the no-code authoring mode. However, using the no-code authoring mode presents a few challenges. First, the workflow requires a property definition in order to pass in a value for TheNumber as an input parameter. And the previous examples relied on a code condition and code handlers for the two CodeActivity instances. All of this code is added to the workflow class, which is something that you can't do with a no-code workflow.

The solution is to develop a new base workflow class (MarkupOnlyBaseWorkflow) that will be used instead of the standard SequentialWorkflowActivity. The base class will define TheNumber property and also the IsNumberPositive code condition handler. Instead of using instances of CodeActivity to write a Console message, a new custom activity (WriteMessageActivity) will be developed that writes a message to the Console. Instances of this custom activity will be created in the workflow markup instead of using CodeActivity.

One final challenge when using no-code authoring is that a different overloaded version of the WorkflowRuntime.CreateWorkflow method must be used when you create a workflow instance. This will require changes to the WorkflowRuntimeManager class that these examples use to create workflow instances.

Implementing the Base Workflow Class

To implement a custom workflow class, add a normal C# class to the SharedWorkflows project and name it MarkupOnlyBaseWorkflow. This class should derive from the standard SequentialWorkflowActivity and defines the property that you need (TheNumber) as well as the IsNumberPositive code condition handler. Listing 16-5 is the complete code that you need to add to the MarkupOnlyBaseWorkflow.cs file.

Listing 16-5. *Complete MarkupOnlyBaseWorkflow.cs File*

```
using System;
using System.Workflow.Activities;

namespace SharedWorkflows
{
    public class MarkupOnlyBaseWorkflow
        : SequentialWorkflowActivity
    {
        private Int32 _theNumber;

        public Int32 TheNumber
        {
            get { return _theNumber; }
            set { _theNumber = value; }
        }
```

```
        public void IsNumberPositive(
            object sender, ConditionalEventArgs e)
        {
            e.Result = (TheNumber > 0);
        }
    }
}
```

Implementing the Custom Activity

You now need to implement a custom activity that will write a message to the Console. This takes the place of the CodeActivity instances used in the previous examples. Add a new Activity to the SharedWorkflows project and name it WriteMessageActivity. Listing 16-6 is the complete code for the WriteMessageActivity.cs file.

Listing 16-6. *Complete WriteMessageActivity.cs File*

```
using System;
using System.ComponentModel;
using System.Workflow.ComponentModel;

namespace SharedWorkflows
{
    /// <summary>
    /// A custom activity that writes a message to the Console
    /// </summary>
    public partial class WriteMessageActivity : Activity
    {
        public static DependencyProperty MessageProperty
            = System.Workflow.ComponentModel.DependencyProperty.Register(
                "Message", typeof(String), typeof(WriteMessageActivity));

        [Description("A string message to write")]
        [Category("Pro Workflow")]
        [Browsable(true)]
        [DesignerSerializationVisibility(
            DesignerSerializationVisibility.Visible)]
        public String Message
        {
            get
            {
                return ((String)(base.GetValue(
                    WriteMessageActivity.MessageProperty)));
            }
            set
            {
                base.SetValue(
                    WriteMessageActivity.MessageProperty, value);
            }
        }
    }
```

```
        public WriteMessageActivity()
        {
            InitializeComponent();
        }

        protected override ActivityExecutionStatus Execute(
            ActivityExecutionContext executionContext)
        {
            if (Message != null)
            {
                Console.WriteLine(Message);
            }
            return base.Execute(executionContext);
        }
    }
}
```

Most of the code in this activity is used to define a dependency property named Message. This is the String message that will be written to the Console. It is important to define this as a DependencyProperty, otherwise you won't be able to bind values to this property in the workflow markup.

Defining the Workflow Markup

The markup file will be loaded directly by the workflow runtime as a file. It doesn't need to be added to a project as an embedded resource or compiled. However, prior to testing the workflow, the markup file should be copied into the same directory as the test application.

To create a markup file, you can use the XML Editor included with Visual Studio. Select File ➤ New ➤ File, then select XML File as the file type. Give the file a name of MarkupOnlyWorkflow.xoml. Listing 16-7 contains the workflow markup that you should add to this file.

Listing 16-7. *Complete MarkupOnlyWorkflow.xoml File*

```xml
<?xml version="1.0" encoding="utf-8" ?>
<proWF:MarkupOnlyBaseWorkflow
  x:Name="MarkupOnlyWorkflow"
  xmlns:x="http://schemas.microsoft.com/winfx/2006/xaml"
  xmlns="http://schemas.microsoft.com/winfx/2006/xaml/workflow"
  xmlns:proWF="clr-namespace:SharedWorkflows;Assembly=SharedWorkflows">
  <IfElseActivity x:Name="ifElseActivity1">
    <IfElseBranchActivity x:Name="ifElseBranchActivity1">
      <IfElseBranchActivity.Condition>
        <CodeCondition Condition=
          "{ActivityBind Name=MarkupOnlyWorkflow, Path=IsNumberPositive}"/>
      </IfElseBranchActivity.Condition>
      <proWF:WriteMessageActivity x:Name="writeMessagePositive"
        Message="The number is positive"/>
    </IfElseBranchActivity>
    <IfElseBranchActivity x:Name="ifElseBranchActivity2">
      <proWF:WriteMessageActivity x:Name="writeMessageNotPositive"
        Message="The number is NOT positive"/>
    </IfElseBranchActivity>
  </IfElseActivity>
</proWF:MarkupOnlyBaseWorkflow>
```

This markup is similar to the file that you saw previously in Listing 16-4, with a few important differences. First, the root element of the markup identifies the MarkupOnlyBaseWorkflow Type as the base class for this workflow instead of the standard SequentialWorkflowActivity. Notice that this root element (along with the other custom type) is prefixed with a namespace identifier of proWF. Any namespace identifier (e.g., ns0, ns1) could be used, but I prefer to use a meaningful name as an identifier. The most important line in the markup is this one:

```
xmlns:proWF="clr-namespace:SharedWorkflows;Assembly=SharedWorkflows">
```

This line provides a reference to the SharedWorkflows assembly and namespace where the custom types are located. It associates that reference with the proWF namespace identifier.

Notice that instances of the WriteMessageActivity are used where the previous version of this workflow used a CodeActivity. The Message property of the WriteMessageActivity is set here within the markup.

This workflow uses a CodeCondition just like the previous examples. To assign the code handler for this condition, an ActivityBind object is used. The ActivityBind identifies the object name (MarkupOnlyWorkflow) and the path within the object (IsNumberPositive) to use for the Condition property.

The name of the workflow instance (MarkupOnlyWorkflow) is assigned with the x:Name attribute. The x:Class attribute is not included in this markup since we are not defining a new .NET Type. The x:Name attribute provides a name for the workflow instance, while the x:Class attribute is used to provide a name for a new Type.

Enhancing the WorkflowRuntimeManager

The WorkflowRuntimeManager class was originally developed in Chapter 4 and is located in the Bukovics.Workflow.Hosting project. It is essentially a wrapper around the WorkflowRuntime, which assists with the hosting and workflow management duties.

For this example, you need to make a small enhancement to this class. When creating a workflow directly from markup, you need to call a different overloaded version of the WorkflowRuntime. CreateWorkflow method. Open the WorkflowRuntimeManager.cs file and add a new overloaded version of the StartWorkflow method shown in Listing 16-8.

Listing 16-8. *Additional StartWorkflow Method for the WorkflowRuntimeManager.cs File*

```
using System;
using System.Xml; //added for markup support
using System.Collections.Generic;
using System.Threading;
using System.Workflow.Runtime;

namespace Bukovics.Workflow.Hosting
{
    /// <summary>
    /// A wrapper class to manage workflow creation
    /// and workflow runtime engine events
    /// </summary>
    public class WorkflowRuntimeManager : IDisposable
    {
...
```

```csharp
/// <summary>
/// Create and start a workflow using markup (xoml)
/// </summary>
/// <param name="markupFileName"></param>
/// <param name="rulesMarkupFileName"></param>
/// <param name="parameters"></param>
/// <returns>A wrapped workflow instance</returns>
public WorkflowInstanceWrapper StartWorkflow(String markupFileName,
    String rulesMarkupFileName,
    Dictionary<String, Object> parameters)
{
    WorkflowInstance instance = null;
    WorkflowInstanceWrapper wrapper = null;
    XmlReader wfReader = null;
    XmlReader rulesReader = null;
    try
    {
        wfReader = XmlReader.Create(markupFileName);
        if (!String.IsNullOrEmpty(rulesMarkupFileName))
        {
            rulesReader = XmlReader.Create(rulesMarkupFileName);
            //create the workflow with workflow and rules
            instance = _workflowRuntime.CreateWorkflow(
                wfReader, rulesReader, parameters);
        }
        else
        {
            //create the workflow with workflow markup only
            instance = _workflowRuntime.CreateWorkflow(
                wfReader, null, parameters);
        }

        wrapper = AddWorkflowInstance(instance);
        instance.Start();
    }
    finally
    {
        if (wfReader != null)
        {
            wfReader.Close();
        }
        if (rulesReader != null)
        {
            rulesReader.Close();
        }
    }
    return wrapper;
}

...

    }
}
```

The new StartWorkflow method accepts two String file names and a Dictionary of workflow parameters. One file name identifies the workflow markup file (.xoml) and the other identifies the file containing the rules (.rules). The rules file is optional. The version of the WorkflowRuntime. CreateWorkflow method that accepts two XmlReader instances is used. One XmlReader is for the workflow markup and the other is for the rules. Since the XmlReader class is used, I also added a using statement for the System.Xml namespace where this class is located.

Testing the Workflow

To test the workflow, add a new Sequential Workflow Console project to the solution and name it ConsoleMarkupOnly. Delete the generated Workflow1 files since they are not needed. Add a reference to the Bukovics.Workflow.Hosting project. You don't need a project reference to the SharedWorkflows project since the references to the types in this assembly are made in the markup file and not directly in this project. However, the SharedWorkflows assembly (SharedWorkflows.dll) must be copied to the same local directory as the ConsoleMarkupOnly executable when you run this test. This is necessary to resolve the references to the base workflow and custom activity types.

Add a C# class named MarkupOnlyTest to the project and add the code shown in Listing 16-9.

Listing 16-9. *Complete MarkupOnlyTest.cs File*

```
using System;
using System.Reflection;
using System.Collections.Generic;
using System.Workflow.Runtime;
using System.Workflow.ComponentModel.Compiler;

using Bukovics.Workflow.Hosting;

namespace ConsoleMarkupOnly
{
    /// <summary>
    /// Execute the MarkupOnlyWorkflow
    /// </summary>
    public class MarkupOnlyTest
    {
        public static void Run()
        {
            using (WorkflowRuntimeManager manager
                = new WorkflowRuntimeManager(new WorkflowRuntime()))
            {
                //start the runtime
                manager.WorkflowRuntime.StartRuntime();

                Console.WriteLine("Executing Workflow");
                //pass a number to test
                Dictionary<String, Object> wfArguments
                    = new Dictionary<string, object>();
                wfArguments.Add("TheNumber", 1);
```

```
        try
        {
            //start the workflow
            WorkflowInstanceWrapper instance =
                manager.StartWorkflow(
                    "MarkupOnlyWorkflow.xoml", null, wfArguments);
        }
        catch (WorkflowValidationFailedException e)
        {
            foreach (ValidationError error in e.Errors)
            {
                Console.WriteLine(error.ErrorText);
            }
        }
        catch (Exception e)
        {
            Console.WriteLine(e.Message);
        }

        //wait for the workflow to complete
        manager.WaitAll(2000);
        Console.WriteLine("Completed Workflow\n\r");
    }
  }
 }
}
```

To create and start an instance of the workflow, the new overloaded version of the StartWorkflow method is used. The name of the markup file (MarkupOnlyWorkflow.xoml) is passed to the method as an argument along with the Dictionary containing the input parameter. For this test, a null is passed in place of the rules file name.

When creating markup files (especially if they are hand-coded), it is easy to make a mistake. If an error is detected, a WorkflowValidationFailedException is thrown by the WorkflowRuntime as the markup file is parsed and validated. You should always catch this exception when you work with markup files. The exception provides an Errors property that contains a collection of errors.

To round out this test application, you only need to add the usual bit of code to the Program.cs file that executes the test:

```
using System;

namespace ConsoleMarkupOnly
{
    public class Program
    {
        static void Main(string[] args)
        {
            MarkupOnlyTest.Run();

            Console.WriteLine("Press any key to exit");
            Console.ReadLine();
        }
    }
}
```

You are now ready to rebuild the solution and execute the ConsoleMarkupOnly application. The testing code assumes that the markup file is in the same directory as the host application, so make sure you copy the MarkupOnlyWorkflow.xoml file to the correct directory before you execute the application. Here are the results when I execute this test:

```
Executing Workflow
The number is positive
Completed Workflow

Press any key to exit
```

Using Rules with a No-Code Workflow

The no-code workflow that was just presented used a code condition to determine whether the value of TheNumber property is greater than zero. You can substitute a rule condition for the code condition and receive the same results. To see this in action, you can modify the code used in the last example.

■**Note** You may also want to take another look at Chapter 13. That chapter also provides a discussion of how to deserialize rules, but in the context of dynamic workflow updates. In that chapter, an example demonstrates how to deserialize and use rules from an external .rules file with a compiled workflow Type.

Defining the Rule Condition

First, create a file named MarkupOnlyWorkflow.rules using the XML Editor of Visual Studio. Listing 16-10 shows you the serialized definition of the rule condition that you need to add to this file.

Listing 16-10. *Complete MarkupOnlyWorkflow.rules File*

```
<RuleDefinitions xmlns="http://schemas.microsoft.com/winfx/2006/xaml/workflow">
  <RuleDefinitions.Conditions>
    <RuleExpressionCondition Name="IsNumberPositive">
      <RuleExpressionCondition.Expression>
        <ns0:CodeBinaryOperatorExpression Operator="GreaterThan"
          xmlns:ns0="clr-namespace:System.CodeDom;Assembly=System,
          Version=2.0.0.0, Culture=neutral, PublicKeyToken=b77a5c561934e089">
          <ns0:CodeBinaryOperatorExpression.Left>
            <ns0:CodePropertyReferenceExpression PropertyName="TheNumber">
              <ns0:CodePropertyReferenceExpression.TargetObject>
                <ns0:CodeCastExpression TargetType=
                  "SharedWorkflows.MarkupOnlyBaseWorkflow, SharedWorkflows,
                  Version=1.0.0.0, Culture=neutral, PublicKeyToken=null">
                  <ns0:CodeCastExpression.Expression>
                    <ns0:CodeMethodInvokeExpression>
                      <ns0:CodeMethodInvokeExpression.Parameters>
                        <ns0:CodePrimitiveExpression>
                          <ns0:CodePrimitiveExpression.Value>
                            <ns1:String xmlns:ns1=
                              "clr-namespace:System;Assembly=mscorlib,
                              Version=2.0.0.0, Culture=neutral,
```

```
                              PublicKeyToken=b77a5c561934e089"
                         >MarkupOnlyWorkflow</ns1:String>
                     </ns0:CodePrimitiveExpression.Value>
                   </ns0:CodePrimitiveExpression>
                 </ns0:CodeMethodInvokeExpression.Parameters>
                 <ns0:CodeMethodInvokeExpression.Method>
                   <ns0:CodeMethodReferenceExpression
                     MethodName="GetActivityByName">
                     <ns0:CodeMethodReferenceExpression.TargetObject>
                       <ns0:CodeThisReferenceExpression />
                     </ns0:CodeMethodReferenceExpression.TargetObject>
                   </ns0:CodeMethodReferenceExpression>
                 </ns0:CodeMethodInvokeExpression.Method>
               </ns0:CodeMethodInvokeExpression>
             </ns0:CodeCastExpression.Expression>
           </ns0:CodeCastExpression>
         </ns0:CodePropertyReferenceExpression.TargetObject>
       </ns0:CodePropertyReferenceExpression>
     </ns0:CodeBinaryOperatorExpression.Left>
     <ns0:CodeBinaryOperatorExpression.Right>
       <ns0:CodePrimitiveExpression>
         <ns0:CodePrimitiveExpression.Value>
           <ns1:Int32 xmlns:ns1="clr-namespace:System;Assembly=mscorlib,
             Version=2.0.0.0, Culture=neutral,
             PublicKeyToken=b77a5c561934e089">0</ns1:Int32>
         </ns0:CodePrimitiveExpression.Value>
       </ns0:CodePrimitiveExpression>
     </ns0:CodeBinaryOperatorExpression.Right>
   </ns0:CodeBinaryOperatorExpression>
 </RuleExpressionCondition.Expression>
</RuleExpressionCondition>
</RuleDefinitions.Conditions>
</RuleDefinitions>
```

Normally you wouldn't want to hand code a rule condition like this. If you frequently work with externally defined rules such as this, you will want to develop a stand-alone rule editor or build rule editing functionality into your application. In either case, WF provides the ability to host the workflow designers (including the rule editor) within your own application. Hosting the workflow designers is discussed in Chapter 17.

If you look closely at this rule, you will notice a reference to the GetActivityByName method. This is needed to properly reference activities when the workflow is loaded directly from markup and not compiled. If this were a code-only workflow, you would be able to define a rule such as this:

```
this.TheNumber > 0
```

But that syntax works because code-only workflows are compiled into a .NET Type. The reference to this and TheNumber are resolved from the compiled workflow class, which is derived from the base Type (SequentialWorkflowActivity). If you are using a rule along with workflow markup, you need to modify the rule so that it obtains a runtime reference to the correct activity instance and Type. For example, this is how the serialized rule shown in Listing 16-10 is defined in a more readable form:

```
((SharedWorkflows.MarkupOnlyBaseWorkflow)this.GetActivityByName(
    "MarkupOnlyWorkflow")).TheNumber > 0
```

This rule accomplishes the same thing as this.TheNumber > 0, but it does so in a way that will work for any authoring mode. In this case, the GetActivityByName method retrieves a reference to the root workflow activity, which is then cast to the correct type (MarkupOnlyBaseWorkflow). TheNumber property is then safely referenced. You can also use the GetActivityByName method to retrieve a reference to any child activity of the workflow.

If you are using workflow markup with rules, this is the syntax that you should use to get the correct results.

Modifying the Workflow Markup

Next, modify the MarkupOnlyWorkflow.xoml to use a RuleConditionReference instead of a CodeCondition. Listing 16-11 contains the revised version of this file.

Listing 16-11. *Revised MarkupOnlyWorkflow.xoml File with Rule Condition*

```xml
<?xml version="1.0" encoding="utf-8" ?>
<proWF:MarkupOnlyBaseWorkflow
  x:Name="MarkupOnlyWorkflow"
  xmlns:x="http://schemas.microsoft.com/winfx/2006/xaml"
  xmlns="http://schemas.microsoft.com/winfx/2006/xaml/workflow"
  xmlns:proWF="clr-namespace:SharedWorkflows;Assembly=SharedWorkflows">
  <IfElseActivity x:Name="ifElseActivity1">
    <IfElseBranchActivity x:Name="ifElseBranchActivity1">
      <IfElseBranchActivity.Condition>
        <RuleConditionReference ConditionName="IsNumberPositive" />
      </IfElseBranchActivity.Condition>
      <proWF:WriteMessageActivity x:Name="writeMessagePositive"
          Message="The number is positive"/>
    </IfElseBranchActivity>
    <IfElseBranchActivity x:Name="ifElseBranchActivity2">
      <proWF:WriteMessageActivity x:Name="writeMessageNotPositive"
          Message="The number is NOT positive"/>
    </IfElseBranchActivity>
  </IfElseActivity>
</proWF:MarkupOnlyBaseWorkflow>
```

The highlighted line is the only change that you need to make to this file. Remove the CodeCondition and replace it with a RuleConditionReference that references the IsNumberPositive rule condition.

Testing the Workflow

Finally, you need to make one minor change to the MarkupOnlyTest.cs file in the ConsoleMarkupOnly project. The required change is to pass the name of the .rules file in addition to the workflow markup file when calling the StartWorkflow method. Here is the modified code:

```
WorkflowInstanceWrapper instance =
    manager.StartWorkflow(
        "MarkupOnlyWorkflow.xoml",
        "MarkupOnlyWorkflow.rules",
        wfArguments);
```

When you build the solution and execute the ConsoleMarkupOnly project, you should see the same results as the previous example. Remember to copy both of the files (MarkupOnlyWorkflow.xoml and MarkupOnlyWorkflow.rules) into the executable directory in order for the code to find and load them.

Serializing to Markup

In the previous examples of this chapter, you have seen that you can construct the workflow model entirely in code (code-only authoring) and also using workflow markup (code-separation and no-code authoring). Since both of these mechanisms describe the same workflow model, it makes sense that WF would provide an easy way to convert between the two formats.

WF includes the WorkflowMarkupSerializer class (located in the System.Workflow. ComponentModel.Serialization namespace), which provides a way to convert from one format to the other. Using the Serialize method of this class, you can create a markup file from an in-memory workflow model. The Deserialize method reverses the process, reading a markup file and handing you an object containing the definition of a workflow model.

Also included are other serializer classes that derive from WorkflowMarkupSerializer. For instance, the ActivityMarkupSerializer class handles serialization of simple activities while the CompositeActivityMarkupSerializer class contains code that targets composite activities.

The ability to easily convert the workflow model between formats is important if you need to host the workflow designers in your application, or otherwise provide for customization of the workflow model within your application.

In the following example, you will manually construct a workflow model in code and then serialize it to a markup file. To verify that you have constructed a valid workflow model, the newly created markup will be used to create and execute a workflow instance.

To begin this example, add a new Sequential Workflow Console Application project to the solution and name it ConsoleSerializeWorkflow. Add a reference to the SharedWorkflows and Bukovics. Workflow.Hosting projects. Add a C# class named SerializeWorkflowTest to the project. Listing 16-12 is the complete code for the SerializeWorkflowTest.cs file. I've included a few comments that highlight selected portions of the code.

Listing 16-12. *Complete SerializeWorkflowTest.cs File*

```csharp
using System;
using System.IO;
using System.Xml;
using System.Collections.Generic;
using System.Workflow.Activities;
using System.Workflow.Runtime;
using System.Workflow.ComponentModel;
using System.Workflow.ComponentModel.Compiler;
using System.Workflow.ComponentModel.Serialization;

using Bukovics.Workflow.Hosting;
using SharedWorkflows;

namespace ConsoleSerializeWorkflow
{
    /// <summary>
    /// Create a workflow in code and serialize it to markup
    /// </summary>
    public class SerializeWorkflowTest
    {
        public static void Run()
        {
```

```
//create a workflow in code
Activity workflow = CreateWorkflowInCode();

//serialize the new workflow to a markup file
SerializeToMarkup(workflow, "SerializedCodedWorkflow.xoml");
```

The test code first calls the private CreateWorkflowInCode method (shown later in this listing) to create the workflow model in code. Once the model is created, it is passed to the SerializeToMarkup method that serializes it to a markup file. Following this, the newly created workflow model is used to create a workflow instance.

```
using (WorkflowRuntimeManager manager
    = new WorkflowRuntimeManager(new WorkflowRuntime()))
{
    //start the runtime
    manager.WorkflowRuntime.StartRuntime();

    Console.WriteLine("Executing Workflow");
    Dictionary<String, Object> wfArguments
        = new Dictionary<string, object>();
    wfArguments.Add("TheNumber", 1);

    try
    {
        //start the workflow
        WorkflowInstanceWrapper instance =
            manager.StartWorkflow(
                "SerializedCodedWorkflow.xoml",
                null, wfArguments);
    }
    catch (WorkflowValidationFailedException e)
    {
        foreach (ValidationError error in e.Errors)
        {
            Console.WriteLine(error.ErrorText);
        }
    }
    catch (Exception e)
    {
        Console.WriteLine(e.Message);
    }

    //wait for the workflow to complete
    manager.WaitAll(2000);
    Console.WriteLine("Completed Workflow\n\r");
}
```

An instance of the new workflow is created and started using the WorkflowRuntimeManager object. The StartWorkflow method is passed the name of the serialized markup file to load.

```csharp
/// <summary>
/// Create a workflow by hand
/// </summary>
/// <returns></returns>
private static Activity CreateWorkflowInCode()
{
    MarkupOnlyBaseWorkflow workflow = null;

    //create the root workflow object
    workflow = new MarkupOnlyBaseWorkflow();
    workflow.Name = "CodedWorkflow";

    //create an IfElseActivity
    IfElseActivity ifElse
        = new IfElseActivity("ifElseActivity1");

    //
    //Add the left side branch to the IfElseActivity
    //
    IfElseBranchActivity branch
        = new IfElseBranchActivity("ifElseBranchActivity1");
    //add a condition to the branch
    CodeCondition condition = new CodeCondition();
    //bind the ConditionEvent to the IsNumberPositive member
    ActivityBind bind = new ActivityBind(
        "CodedWorkflow", "IsNumberPositive");
    condition.SetBinding(CodeCondition.ConditionEvent, bind);
    branch.Condition = condition;
    //add a custom WriteMessageActivity to the branch
    WriteMessageActivity writeMessage = new WriteMessageActivity();
    writeMessage.Name = "writeMessagePositive";
    writeMessage.Message = "The number is positive";
    branch.Activities.Add(writeMessage);
    //add the branch to the IfElseActivity
    ifElse.Activities.Add(branch);

    //
    //add the right side branch to the IfElseActivity
    //
    branch = new IfElseBranchActivity("ifElseBranchActivity2");
    //add a custom WriteMessageActivity to the branch
    writeMessage = new WriteMessageActivity();
    writeMessage.Name = "writeMessageNotPositive";
    writeMessage.Message = "The number is NOT positive";
    branch.Activities.Add(writeMessage);
    //add the branch to the IfElseActivity
    ifElse.Activities.Add(branch);

    //add the IfElseActivity to the workflow
    workflow.Activities.Add(ifElse);

    return workflow;
}
```

The task of the CreateWorkflowInCode method is to create a workflow model entirely in code. To create the model, individual workflow activities are created, properties are set, and the relationships between objects are created by adding child objects to their parent. The MarkupOnlyBaseWorkflow class (developed earlier in this chapter) is used as the root workflow object for this workflow. Instances of the WriteMessageActivity custom activity are added to the model to write messages to the Console.

```
/// <summary>
/// Serialize a workflow to markup (xaml)
/// </summary>
/// <param name="workflow"></param>
/// <param name="fileName"></param>
private static void SerializeToMarkup(
    Activity workflow, String fileName)
{
    try
    {
        using (XmlWriter xmlWriter = XmlWriter.Create(fileName))
        {
            WorkflowMarkupSerializer markupSerializer
                = new WorkflowMarkupSerializer();
            markupSerializer.Serialize(xmlWriter, workflow);
        }
    }
    catch (Exception e)
    {
        Console.WriteLine("Exception during serialization: {0}",
            e.Message);
    }
}
```

The SerializeToMarkup method takes the workflow model that was constructed in code and writes it to a file as serialized markup. An XmlWriter is constructed for the output file and passed to the Serialize method of a WorkflowMarkupSerializer object. Since this method is working with file I-O, there are a number of things that could go wrong (unable to create file, invalid path, etc). This code takes a shortcut and only catches the base Exception class, but you might want to catch individual I-O-related exceptions and react to each one differently.

You also need this small bit of code added to the Program.cs file:

```
using System;

namespace ConsoleSerializeWorkflow
{
    public class Program
    {
        static void Main(string[] args)
        {
            SerializeWorkflowTest.Run();

            Console.WriteLine("Press any key to exit");
            Console.ReadLine();
        }
    }
}
```

After building the solution and setting `ConsoleSerializeWorkflow` as the startup project, you should be able to execute the test application and see these results:

```
Executing Workflow
The number is positive
Completed Workflow

Press any key to exit
```

Compiling a Workflow

One other option that is available is to compile the workflow markup (XAML) into an assembly. You might choose to use this option if you need the flexibility of defining the workflow model in markup but want better control and type safety.

When you load workflow markup directly into the `WorkflowRuntime`, it is first parsed and validated before a workflow instance is created. Any errors in the markup are discovered only then, as you are attempting to use it. On the other hand, precompiling your workflow markup into assemblies performs the parsing and validation steps much sooner in the process. Errors in the markup are discovered before you attempt to create an instance of the workflow. This is really the age-old argument of compiled vs. interpreted languages. Which mechanism you use depends on the requirements for your application.

By compiling workflow markup into assemblies, you also eliminate the slight performance hit associated with parsing and validating the markup at runtime. For some applications, the distribution of markup files also complicates the deployment of the application and is possibly even a security risk, since they are easily viewed by any text editor.

This example builds upon the code from the previous example (Listing 16-12). In addition to creating the workflow model in code and then serializing it to a markup file, you will also compile the markup, creating a new assembly. The code is also modified to create and start the workflow instance using the `Type` from the new assembly instead of directly from the markup file.

Listing 16-13 shows the modifications that you need to make to the `SerializeWorkflowTest.cs` file (originally presented in Listing 16-12).

Listing 16-13. *Revised SerializeWorkflowTest.cs File to Compile the Workflow*

```csharp
using System;
using System.IO;
using System.Xml;
using System.Collections.Generic;
using System.Workflow.Activities;
using System.Workflow.Runtime;
using System.Workflow.ComponentModel;
using System.Workflow.ComponentModel.Compiler;
using System.Workflow.ComponentModel.Serialization;

using Bukovics.Workflow.Hosting;
using SharedWorkflows;

namespace ConsoleSerializeWorkflow
{
```

```
/// <summary>
/// Create a workflow in code and serialize it to markup
/// </summary>
public class SerializeWorkflowTest
{
    public static void Run()
    {
        //create a workflow in code
        Activity workflow = CreateWorkflowInCode();

        //serialize the new workflow to a markup file
        SerializeToMarkup(workflow, "SerializedCodedWorkflow.xoml");

        //create a new assembly containing the workflow
        CompileWorkflow("SerializedCodedWorkflow.xoml",
            "MyNewAssembly.dll");
```

Add this call to a new private `CompileWorkflow` method. The purpose of this method (shown later in this listing) is to compile the workflow markup file into a new assembly. The new assembly name for this example is `MyNewAssembly.dll`.

```
        using (WorkflowRuntimeManager manager
            = new WorkflowRuntimeManager(new WorkflowRuntime()))
        {
            //start the runtime
            manager.WorkflowRuntime.StartRuntime();

            Console.WriteLine("Executing Workflow");
            Dictionary<String, Object> wfArguments
                = new Dictionary<string, object>();
            wfArguments.Add("TheNumber", 1);

            try
            {
                //get a Type object for the newly compiled workflow
                Type workflowType = Type.GetType(
                    "ProWF.MyNewWorkflowClass,MyNewAssembly");
                //start the workflow using the Type
                WorkflowInstanceWrapper instance =
                    manager.StartWorkflow(workflowType, wfArguments);
```

Change the code that creates and starts an instance of the workflow to use the compiled `Type` instead of directly reading the workflow markup. Prior to creating a workflow instance, you need to load the compiled workflow `Type` from the new assembly. You can also remove the `catch` statement for the `WorkflowValidationFailedException` since the validation is now done when the workflow is compiled instead of at runtime.

```
            }
            catch (Exception e)
            {
                Console.WriteLine(e.Message);
            }
```

```
            //wait for the workflow to complete
            manager.WaitAll(2000);
            Console.WriteLine("Completed Workflow\n\r");
        }
    }

    /// <summary>
    /// Create a workflow by hand
    /// </summary>
    /// <returns></returns>
    private static Activity CreateWorkflowInCode()
    {

...

            //add the IfElseActivity to the workflow
            workflow.Activities.Add(ifElse);

            //provide a class name for the new workflow
            workflow.SetValue(WorkflowMarkupSerializer.XClassProperty,
                "ProWF.MyNewWorkflowClass");
```

When you compile markup, you are creating a new .NET Type. Within the markup, the x:Class attribute is used to identify the new Type name (see Listing 16-4). Without this name, the workflow markup won't compile. To add this attribute to the markup, add the highlighted code immediately before the CreateWorkflowInCode method returns the constructed workflow. The code sets the new Type name using the SetValue method of the base Activity class. WorkflowMarkupSerializer. XClassProperty identifies the dependency property associated with the x:Class attribute.

```
            return workflow;
        }

    private static void CompileWorkflow(
        String fileName, String assemblyName)
    {
        WorkflowCompiler compiler = new WorkflowCompiler();
        WorkflowCompilerParameters parameters
            = new WorkflowCompilerParameters();
        parameters.OutputAssembly = assemblyName;
        parameters.ReferencedAssemblies.Add("SharedWorkflows.dll");
        WorkflowCompilerResults results
            = compiler.Compile(parameters, fileName);
        if (results.Errors.Count > 0)
        {
            foreach (System.CodeDom.Compiler.CompilerError error
                in results.Errors)
            {
                Console.WriteLine("Compiler error: Line{0}: {1}",
                    error.Line, error.ErrorText);
            }
        }
    }
```

The CompileWorkflow method is new and should be added in its entirety. To compile the markup into an assembly, an instance of the WorkflowCompiler class is created. The WorkflowCompilerParameters class provides a way to set a number of properties used during the compilation process. In this example, only a few of the properties are set, including the output assembly name. The ReferencedAssemblies property is used to identify other assemblies that are referenced by the workflow being compiled. Since the workflow references custom types from the SharedWorkflows assembly, that assembly is adding as a referenced assembly.

A WorkflowCompilerResults object is returned by the Compile method. If any errors are discovered during the compilation process, the Errors property of this object contains a collection of errors.

```
    }
}
```

If you build the solution and execute the ConsoleSerializeWorkflow project, you should see exactly the same results as you saw in the previous example. In addition to the expected results, if you look at the executable directory, you should see the new assembly that you created (MyNewAssembly.dll).

Compiling a Workflow with Rules

If the workflow markup that you wish to compile uses rules, the rules must be compiled as an embedded resource in the new assembly. To accomplish this, you need to identify the rules file in the EmbeddedResources property of the WorkflowCompilerParameters class.

To illustrate this, you can update the code from the previous example (Listing 16-13) to use a rule condition instead of a code condition. The compiled workflow will then include the rules file as an embedded resource.

First of all, you need a rules file to embed as a resource. Listing 16-14 is a rules declaration that you should save as a file named ProWF.MyNewWorkflowClass.rules in the executable folder. The file name contains the namespace and workflow class name. This naming format should be used since the workflow runtime will attempt to load the rules from this resource name.

Listing 16-14. *Complete ProWF.MyNewWorkflowClass.rules File*

```
<RuleDefinitions xmlns="http://schemas.microsoft.com/winfx/2006/xaml/workflow">
  <RuleDefinitions.Conditions>
    <RuleExpressionCondition Name="IsNumberPositive">
      <RuleExpressionCondition.Expression>
        <ns0:CodeBinaryOperatorExpression Operator="GreaterThan"
          xmlns:ns0="clr-namespace:System.CodeDom;Assembly=System, Version=2.0.0.0,
          Culture=neutral, PublicKeyToken=b77a5c561934e089">
          <ns0:CodeBinaryOperatorExpression.Left>
            <ns0:CodePropertyReferenceExpression PropertyName="TheNumber">
              <ns0:CodePropertyReferenceExpression.TargetObject>
                <ns0:CodeCastExpression TargetType=
                  "SharedWorkflows.MarkupOnlyBaseWorkflow,
                  SharedWorkflows, Version=1.0.0.0,
                  Culture=neutral, PublicKeyToken=null">
                  <ns0:CodeCastExpression.Expression>
                    <ns0:CodeMethodInvokeExpression>
                      <ns0:CodeMethodInvokeExpression.Parameters>
                        <ns0:CodePrimitiveExpression>
                          <ns0:CodePrimitiveExpression.Value>
                            <ns1:String xmlns:ns1=
```

```
                        "clr-namespace:System;Assembly=mscorlib,
                        Version=2.0.0.0, Culture=neutral,
                        PublicKeyToken=b77a5c561934e089"
                          >CodedWorkflow</ns1:String>
                      </ns0:CodePrimitiveExpression.Value>
                    </ns0:CodePrimitiveExpression>
                  </ns0:CodeMethodInvokeExpression.Parameters>
                  <ns0:CodeMethodInvokeExpression.Method>
                    <ns0:CodeMethodReferenceExpression
                      MethodName="GetActivityByName">
                      <ns0:CodeMethodReferenceExpression.TargetObject>
                        <ns0:CodeThisReferenceExpression />
                      </ns0:CodeMethodReferenceExpression.TargetObject>
                    </ns0:CodeMethodReferenceExpression>
                  </ns0:CodeMethodInvokeExpression.Method>
                </ns0:CodeMethodInvokeExpression>
              </ns0:CodeCastExpression.Expression>
            </ns0:CodeCastExpression>
          </ns0:CodePropertyReferenceExpression.TargetObject>
        </ns0:CodePropertyReferenceExpression>
      </ns0:CodeBinaryOperatorExpression.Left>
      <ns0:CodeBinaryOperatorExpression.Right>
        <ns0:CodePrimitiveExpression>
          <ns0:CodePrimitiveExpression.Value>
            <ns1:Int32 xmlns:ns1="clr-namespace:System;Assembly=mscorlib,
              Version=2.0.0.0, Culture=neutral,
              PublicKeyToken=b77a5c561934e089">0</ns1:Int32>
          </ns0:CodePrimitiveExpression.Value>
        </ns0:CodePrimitiveExpression>
      </ns0:CodeBinaryOperatorExpression.Right>
    </ns0:CodeBinaryOperatorExpression>
  </RuleExpressionCondition.Expression>
  </RuleExpressionCondition>
  </RuleDefinitions.Conditions>
</RuleDefinitions>
```

Next, modify the SerializeWorkflowTest.cs file to construct the workflow model with a rule condition instead of a code condition. Also add code to reference the ProWF.MyNewWorkflowClass.rules file as an embedded resource when compiling the workflow. Listing 16-15 highlights the changes that you need to make.

Listing 16-15. *Revised SerializeWorkflowTest.cs for Rules Compilation*

```
using System;
using System.IO;
using System.Xml;
using System.Collections.Generic;
using System.Workflow.Activities;
using System.Workflow.Runtime;
using System.Workflow.Activities.Rules; //added for rule condition reference
using System.Workflow.ComponentModel;
using System.Workflow.ComponentModel.Compiler;
using System.Workflow.ComponentModel.Serialization;
```

```csharp
using Bukovics.Workflow.Hosting;
using SharedWorkflows;

namespace ConsoleSerializeWorkflow
{
    /// <summary>
    /// Create a workflow in code and serialize it to markup
    /// </summary>
    public class SerializeWorkflowTest
    {

...


        /// <summary>
        /// Create a workflow by hand
        /// </summary>
        /// <returns></returns>
        private static Activity CreateWorkflowInCode()
        {

...


            //
            //Add the left side branch to the IfElseActivity
            //
            IfElseBranchActivity branch
                = new IfElseBranchActivity("ifElseBranchActivity1");
            //add a rule condition to the branch
            RuleConditionReference ruleCondition
                = new RuleConditionReference();
            ruleCondition.ConditionName = "IsNumberPositive";
            branch.Condition = ruleCondition;
            //add a custom WriteMessageActivity to the branch
            WriteMessageActivity writeMessage = new WriteMessageActivity();
            writeMessage.Name = "writeMessagePositive";
            writeMessage.Message = "The number is positive";
            branch.Activities.Add(writeMessage);
            //add the branch to the IfElseActivity
            ifElse.Activities.Add(branch);

...
```

Replace the CodeCondition with the highlighted code that creates a rule condition.

```csharp
        }

        private static void CompileWorkflow(
            String fileName, String assemblyName)
        {
            WorkflowCompiler compiler = new WorkflowCompiler();
            WorkflowCompilerParameters parameters
                = new WorkflowCompilerParameters();
            parameters.OutputAssembly = assemblyName;
            parameters.ReferencedAssemblies.Add("SharedWorkflows.dll");
            //add the .rules file for this workflow as a resource
            parameters.EmbeddedResources.Add("ProWF.MyNewWorkflowClass.rules");
```

Add this line to identify the .rules file as an embedded resource in the compiled assembly.

```
            WorkflowCompilerResults results
                = compiler.Compile(parameters, fileName);
            if (results.Errors.Count > 0)
            {
                foreach (System.CodeDom.Compiler.CompilerError error
                    in results.Errors)
                {
                    Console.WriteLine("Compiler error: Line{0}: {1}",
                        error.Line, error.ErrorText);
                }
            }
        }
    }
}
```

After building the solution, you can execute the ConsoleSerializeWorkflow and should see the same results. If you disassemble the new assembly that was created (MyNewAssembly.dll) using the ildasm.exe utility (included with Visual Studio and the Windows SDK), you will see in the assembly manifest that the .rules file is included as an embedded resource like this:

```
.mresource public ProWF.MyNewWorkflowClass.rules
{
  // Offset: 0x00000000 Length: 0x00000C5D
}
```

Compiling from the Command Line

The last two examples that compiled the workflow markup into an assembly used the WorkflowCompiler class provided with WF. Also provided with WF is a command-line workflow compiler (wfc.exe) that offers the same capabilities as the WorkflowCompiler class.

■**Note** The wfc.exe workflow compiler is packaged and distributed with the Windows SDK. To execute this utility, you need to set the environment variables required by the SDK utilities. The easiest way to do this is to open the Windows SDK command shell and execute wfc.exe from there. A shortcut to the command shell can be found off of the Start menu: Start ➤ All Programs ➤ Microsoft Windows SDK ➤ CMD Shell.

For example, here is a sample wfc.exe command that compiles the markup and .rules files used in the last example. Before trying this command, make sure you switch to the directory containing both of the input files and the SharedWorkflows.dll:

```
wfc.exe SerializedCodedWorkflow.xoml /target:assembly
    /debug:- /resource:ProWF.MyNewWorkflowClass.rules
    /reference:SharedWorkflows.dll /out:MyNewAssembly.dll
```

■**Note** The wfc.exe command is shown here as separate lines to fit the format of this book. It is actually entered as a single line.

The output of this command will be the same `MyNewAssembly.dll` created by the previous example that uses the `WorkflowCompiler` class.

The `wfc.exe` compiler supports a number of command-line options. Please consult MSDN for a complete list of options, or you can enter **wfc /?** for a short list of options. The Windows SDK documentation also has a topic named "How To: Compile Workflows" that provides additional information.

Deserializing Markup

The `WorkflowMarkupSerializer` class can also be used when you need to deserialize a workflow markup file into an object. The `Deserialize` method of this class accepts an `XmlReader` object and returns an object that represents the workflow model. You might need to deserialize a markup file if you want to modify the workflow model in code.

Deserializing a markup file is a straightforward task, but you do need to pay special attention to the process if the markup file contains references to custom types. The deserialization process must be able to resolve all `Type` references, otherwise it fails. If a markup file references a custom `Type`, you must provide the `WorkflowMarkupSerializer` with a reference to the assembly containing the `Type`. This is accomplished with a `DesignerSerializationManager` object that contains a `TypeProvider`. You add the assembly reference via methods of the `TypeProvider`. These steps are illustrated in the following example.

In this example, you will use the serialization methods of the `WorkflowMarkupSerializer` class to modify an existing markup file. First, you will call the `Deserialize` method of this class to create an object representing the workflow model from a markup file. After making a minor change to the model, you will then use the `Serialize` method to create a revised markup file. This example only modifies the workflow model, it doesn't execute the workflow.

To implement this example, add a new Sequential Workflow Console project to the solution and name it `ConsoleDeserializeWorkflow`. Add a project reference to the `SharedWorkflows` project. Delete the `Workflow1` that was automatically generated since it won't be needed.

Add a new C# class named `DeserializeWorkflowTest` to the project and add the code shown in Listing 16-16.

Listing 16-16. *Complete DeserializeWorkflowTest.cs File*

```csharp
using System;
using System.IO;
using System.Xml;
using System.ComponentModel.Design;
using System.ComponentModel.Design.Serialization;
using System.Workflow.ComponentModel;
using System.Workflow.ComponentModel.Compiler;
using System.Workflow.ComponentModel.Serialization;

using SharedWorkflows;

namespace ConsoleDeserializeWorkflow
{
    /// <summary>
    /// Workflow serialization and deserialization
    /// </summary>
```

```
public class DeserializeWorkflowTest
{
    public static void Run()
    {
        //deserialize the workflow from a markup file
        Activity workflow =
            DeserializeFromMarkup("SerializedCodedWorkflow.xoml");

        if (workflow != null)
        {
            //modify the workflow definition in code
            ModifyWorkflow(workflow);

            //serialize the new workflow to a markup file
            SerializeToMarkup(workflow,
                "SerializedCodedWorkflowRevised.xoml");
        }
        else
        {
            Console.WriteLine("Unable to deserialize workflow");
        }
    }
```

The static Run method contains the top-level code for this example. The workflow is first deserialized from markup by calling the DeserializeFromMarkup method. If the deserialization is successful, the ModifyWorkflow method is called to apply a minor update to the workflow model. Finally, the SerializeToMarkup method is called to write the revised version of the workflow model to a new markup file.

For this example, the markup file created and used by the previous examples (SerializedCodedWorkflow.xoml) is the input markup file.

```
/// <summary>
/// Deserialize a workflow from markup (xaml)
/// </summary>
/// <param name="fileName"></param>
/// <returns></returns>
private static Activity DeserializeFromMarkup(String fileName)
{
    Activity workflow = null;

    try
    {
        //add a TypeProvider to resolve SharedWorkflow references
        ServiceContainer container = new ServiceContainer();
        TypeProvider provider = new TypeProvider(container);
        provider.AddAssembly(
            typeof(SharedWorkflows.MarkupOnlyBaseWorkflow).Assembly);
        container.AddService(typeof(ITypeProvider), provider);

        //add the ServiceContainer with the TypeProvider to
        //a serialization manager
        DesignerSerializationManager dsm
            = new DesignerSerializationManager(container);
```

```
        using (dsm.CreateSession())
        {
            using (XmlReader xmlReader = XmlReader.Create(fileName))
            {
                //deserialize the workflow from the XmlReader
                WorkflowMarkupSerializer markupSerializer
                    = new WorkflowMarkupSerializer();
                workflow = markupSerializer.Deserialize(dsm, xmlReader)
                    as Activity;

                if (dsm.Errors.Count > 0)
                {
                    foreach (WorkflowMarkupSerializationException error
                        in dsm.Errors)
                    {
                        Console.WriteLine(
                            "Deserialization error: {0}", error);
                    }
                }
            }
        }
    }
    catch (Exception e)
    {
        Console.WriteLine("Exception during deserialization: {0}",
            e.Message);
    }

    return workflow;
}
```

The DeserializeFromMarkup method handles the deserialization from the markup file. The
example markup file contains references to custom types in the SharedWorkflows assembly. In order
for the WorkflowMarkupSerializer to resolve those references, the code adds the SharedWorkflows
assembly to a TypeProvider. The TypeProvider is first added to a ServiceContainer object, and the
ServiceContainer is then used during construction of the DesignerSerializationManager object.

This example uses the AddAssembly method of the TypeProvider to provide the assembly reference. You could also use the AddAssemblyReference method if you prefer. AddAssembly requires you
to pass an Assembly object, while AddAssemblyReference only requires the Assembly name.

The Deserialize method of WorkflowMarkupSerializer is passed the
DesignerSerializationManager instance along with an XmlReader that provides access to the markup
file. The result of the deserialization is an object derived from the base Activity class. If there are any
errors during deserialization, the Errors property of the DesignerSerializationManager provides
access to the collection of errors.

```
/// <summary>
/// Modify the workflow definition in code
/// </summary>
/// <param name="workflow"></param>
private static void ModifyWorkflow(Activity workflow)
{
```

```
            //locate the activity to change
            WriteMessageActivity wmActivity
                = workflow.GetActivityByName("writeMessagePositive")
                    as WriteMessageActivity;
            if (wmActivity != null)
            {
                //change the message
                wmActivity.Message = "This is a revised message";
            }
        }
```

In the ModifyWorkflow method, a simple change is made to the workflow model. The writeMessagePositive activity is retrieved by name and the value of the Message property is changed.

```
        /// <summary>
        /// Serialize a workflow to markup (xaml)
        /// </summary>
        /// <param name="workflow"></param>
        /// <param name="fileName"></param>
        private static void SerializeToMarkup(
            Activity workflow, String fileName)
        {
            try
            {
                using (XmlWriter xmlWriter = XmlWriter.Create(fileName))
                {
                    WorkflowMarkupSerializer markupSerializer
                        = new WorkflowMarkupSerializer();
                    markupSerializer.Serialize(xmlWriter, workflow);
                }
            }
            catch (Exception e)
            {
                Console.WriteLine("Exception during serialization: {0}",
                    e.Message);
            }
        }
```

The SerializeToMarkup method is similar to code that you have already seen. The serialize method of the WorkflowMarkupSerializer class is used to serialize the workflow model to a markup file using an XmlWriter.

```
    }
}
```

You also need this small amount of code in the Program.cs file:

```
using System;

namespace ConsoleDeserializeWorkflow
{
    public class Program
    {
        static void Main(string[] args)
        {
            DeserializeWorkflowTest.Run();
```

```
            Console.WriteLine("Press any key to exit");
            Console.ReadLine();
        }
    }
}
```

You can now build the solution and execute the `ConsoleDeserializeWorkflow` project. Before you execute this project, make sure that the `SerializedCodedWorkflow.xoml` file from the previous examples is in the executable directory. Also, make sure that the `SharedWorkflows.dll` assembly is in the directory.

When you execute this project, you should see a new markup file named `SerializedCodedWorkflowRevised.xoml` created in the executable directory. If you open this file in the XML Editor, you will see that the value for the `Message` property has been modified as shown here:

```
<ns0:WriteMessageActivity Message="This is a revised message"
    x:Name="writeMessagePositive" />
```

Summary

The focus of this chapter was workflow serialization and the use of markup to define the workflow model. WF provides several authoring modes that you can use to define the workflow model. Several of those authoring modes use workflow markup, which is a serialized representation of the workflow model that is saved to a `.xoml` file. The use of workflow markup is an important option since it provides you with additional flexibility to manage the workflow model separately from the compiled workflow types.

This chapter discussed the differences between each of the authoring modes and then launched into a series of examples that demonstrated each authoring mode. The code-only, code-separation, and no-code authoring modes were all demonstrated in this chapter. Examples were also presented that showed you how to use rules along with workflow markup.

The use of the `WorkflowMarkupSerializer` class was also demonstrated. This class provides methods that permit you to serialize a workflow model definition to a markup file and also deserialize it to reverse the process. You can also compile workflow markup to an assembly. This chapter showed you how to accomplish this using the `wfc.exe` command-line workflow compiler and in code using the `WorkflowCompiler` class.

In the next chapter, you will have an opportunity to use some of the techniques that you learned here when you host the workflow designers in your own application.

CHAPTER 17

Hosting the Workflow Designers

The focus of this chapter is hosting the workflow designers in your own application. You might need to do this if you want to provide someone other than a Visual Studio developer with the ability to modify workflow definitions. Hosting a customized version of the workflow designers goes hand in hand with no-code workflows. The main advantage of using no-code workflows is that they are distributed in a form that is easy to modify (.xoml markup files). A customized workflow designer provides a way to modify those markup files.

This chapter begins with an overview of the classes and interfaces that are used to build a designer application. Following this brief overview, the chapter presents the code for a working workflow designer application. This is not a general-purpose designer that takes the place of Visual Studio. Instead, it targets the narrow set of functionality needed to maintain no-code workflows. After reviewing the code for this working example, you should be able to apply the basic ideas and concepts presented here to your own designer application that is customized for your needs.

Understanding the Workflow Designers

As you learned in Chapter 16, WF supports a number of ways to declare your workflow model. In addition to the *code-only* mode that declares the workflow model entirely in code, you can use the *code-separation* and *no-code* modes. These modes declare the workflow model in .xoml files, which specify the model using XAML (Extensible Application Markup Language, or just *markup*). The primary advantage to using markup is that it is easy to modify without firing up Visual Studio and rebuilding your application. This is particularly true with no-code workflows where there is no code-beside file that requires compilation.

This chapter presents the second half of the markup and serialization story. Chapter 16 described how to use each workflow authoring mode within Visual Studio and also how to serialize and deserialize workflow definitions to and from markup. This chapter shows you how you can build an application that works with that markup outside of Visual Studio.

By now, you have discovered that WF includes a great set of workflow designers that are tightly integrated with Visual Studio. These designers provide a visually rich development environment that allows you to easily design and maintain workflow models, custom activities, and rules. These same designers are available for use within your own applications. In keeping with the other components in WF, the designers are not packaged as a complete application. Instead, they are provided as a set of classes that you can reference and use within your own application.

But be forewarned: you do have to write a considerable amount of code for any nontrivial designer application. This complexity is not unique to workflow designers. You potentially have the same level of complexity for any type of custom designer. Much of the complexity in developing an application with a workflow designer comes from the myriad interfaces and services that you must use or implement. Hosting the actual workflow designers is the easy part. You are also responsible for developing the peripheral components and services that actually make the design experience a pleasant one. Components such as context menus, the toolbox, and the properties window must be implemented by you.

Using the workflow designers is not a one-size-fits-all proposition. You have the freedom to implement just the designer functionality that you need. If you need a designer with very limited functionality—perhaps only permitting property changes to existing activities—you can implement that. If you need an application that permits adding and removing activities and generally working with the entire workflow model, you can implement that. Do you need a read-only workflow viewer that doesn't allow any changes? You can implement that as well. Do you want to support the generation of code-beside files and the ability to compile workflows into assemblies? That is also possible with enough code. Do you need an application that externally edits .rules files? That is most certainly possible. Just remember that the complexity of your designer application is directly proportional to the features that you wish to support. Start with just the features that you really need, and enhance your application later.

Designer Namespaces

Depending on the needs of your designer application, you will use classes in these namespaces:

- System.Workflow.ComponentModel.Design: This namespace contains the core workflow designer interfaces and classes.

- System.Workflow.ComponentModel.Compiler: This namespace contains the workflow interfaces and classes that are used if you need to generate code-beside files or compile workflows.

- System.ComponentModel.Design: This namespace contains a large set of standard .NET types that are used regardless of the kind of custom designer application that you build. The types in this namespace are not directly related to the workflow designers, but they do form the foundation and plumbing that is used by the workflow designers.

- System.Drawing.Design: This namespace contains types that are used to enhance a design time user interface.

Designer Classes

Regardless of the designer functionality that you wish to implement, you will need to work with these core designer classes:

- System.ComponentModel.Design.DesignSurface: This is a general-purpose design canvas.

- System.Workflow.ComponentModel.Design.WorkflowDesignerLoader: This class is responsible for serialization and deserialization of the workflow model as well as the creation and loading of services used by the designer.

- System.Workflow.ComponentModel.Design.WorkflowView: This class implements the visual representation of the workflow model (the designer that you see and interact with). It is an instance of this class that is added as a UserControl to your host application.

Of these classes, the most important one is the WorkflowDesignerLoader. This is an abstract class that you must fully implement in a derived class. It is responsible for loading the workflow model (and rules if necessary) from some persisted store (e.g., .xoml and .rules files or a database) and populating a tree of visual objects in the designer. Likewise, when it is time to save any changes to the model, this class must serialize and persist the data to a durable store.

The WorkflowDesignerLoader is also the place where a number of optional services are loaded. These services are described further in the next section.

The relationship between these classes is illustrated in Figure 17-1.

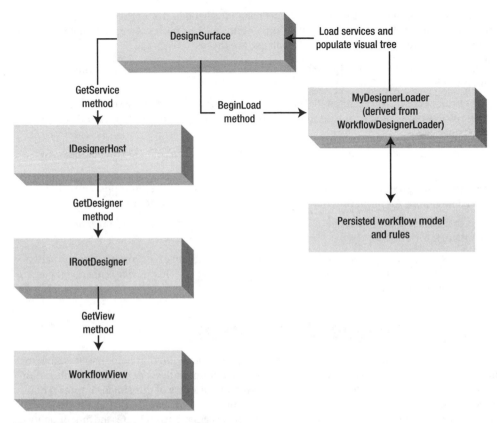

Figure 17-1. *Designer object relationships*

As shown in Figure 17-1, there exists a close relationship between the DesignSurface and the WorkflowDesignerLoader. The host application (or custom control if you are building your workflow designer as a reusable control) creates an instance of both of these classes. The BeginLoad method of the DesignSurface is then called, passing an instance of your loader class derived from WorkflowDesignerLoader to the DesignSurface. This allows the WorkflowDesignerLoader derived class to add the necessary services to the DesignSurface and to interact with the designer when necessary. For example, when a workflow is deserialized from markup, the WorkflowDesignerLoader-derived class adds the tree of individual activities to the designer.

Once a workflow is loaded, the WorkflowView is the control that contains the visual representation of the workflow model. Ultimately, the WorkflowView must be added to a Panel or some other control within the application in order to view it. But to obtain the WorkflowView takes a few steps. As illustrated in Figure 17-1, you first call the GetService method of the DesignSurface, requesting the IDesignerHost object. Using the IDesignerHost object, you call the GetDesigner method to obtain an IRootDesigner for the type of workflow that was just loaded. Different designers are possible. For instance, a sequential workflow uses a different designer than a state machine workflow. Once the IRootDesigner is retrieved, the GetView method is called to obtain the WorkflowView object.

Designer Services

If these services are needed, they should be loaded by the class that you derive from WorkflowDesignerLoader during initialization. Each service is identified by an interface and is designed to serve a particular purpose that has been standardized in the world of .NET designers. You are responsible for developing a class that implements each service `interface` that you wish to use. Some of the more likely services that you will use are these:

- `System.ComponentModel.Design.IMenuCommandService`: Provides support for context-sensitive menus within the designer.

- `System.Workflow.ComponentModel.Compiler.ITypeProvider`: Provides assembly references that resolve types used by the designer or when generating code-beside files and compiling workflows.

- `System.Drawing.Design.IToolboxService`: Provides methods to manage the toolbox used with a designer.

- `System.Drawing.Design.IPropertyValueUIService`: Provides images, tooltips, and other additional attributes for properties that are displayed in a properties window.

- `System.ComponentModel.Design.IEventBindingService`: Provides a way to register event handlers for events.

- `System.Workflow.ComponentModel.Design.IMemberCreationService`: Provides functionality that allows you to create, update, and remove code elements. This service is needed if you are generating or maintaining code-beside files.

Building a Designer Application

In the remainder of this chapter, I present a single designer application that demonstrates how to use the workflow designer classes. It would be difficult to demonstrate every possible combination of features that you could include in a workflow designer in the space of this single chapter. That might require an entire book instead of just this one chapter.

I made the conscious decision to avoid implementing a designer that duplicates the functionality in Visual Studio. Instead, I want to implement a designer that targets a narrow set of functionality, but fills a real gap. The gap that I've chosen to target is no-code workflows. Visual Studio isn't designed to handle no-code workflows, since it assumes that you can always add code to a code-beside file. It doesn't limit the scope of what you can do when maintaining a workflow. When maintaining a no-code workflow, you should be limited to only referencing the existing members of the workflow and activity types.

■Tip The designer application that I present in this chapter requires a lot of code. There's just no way to get around the fact that a workflow designer application such as this has a lot of moving parts that must be implemented and work together for the application to work correctly. In keeping with the other chapters in this book, I present and annotate all of the code that you will need to implement this application. However, since a lot of code is required, this would be a good time to download the source code for this book (if you haven't already done so). You can then load up the code in Visual Studio and follow along as I describe each code segment.

The designer that you will implement in this chapter supports this functionality:

- Serializing and deserializing workflows to and from `.xoml` files.

- Saving and loading rule definitions to and from `.rules` files.

- Changes to the structure of the workflow model (adding, moving, and deleting activities).

- Editing of rule condition, `Rule`, and `RuleSet` definitions.

- Workflow and activity property changes using a properties grid control.
- Adding references to custom assemblies to identify custom activity and workflow types.
- A toolbox populated with standard and custom activities from referenced assemblies.
- Maintenance of existing workflows, as well as the creation of new ones.
- New workflows created from the standard workflow types or from custom workflows in referenced assemblies.
- Binding of activity and workflow events to existing members.

The major features that this designer doesn't support are these:

- Generation of a code-beside file.
- Compilation of workflows.
- Changes to the workflow name or the base Type of the workflow.

Creating the Designer Project

To begin development of the designer application, create a new project using the Windows Application project template. Name the project WorkflowDesignerApp. You'll need to add these assembly references to the project:

- System.Workflow.Activities
- System.Workflow.ComponentModel
- System.Workflow.Runtime
- System.Design

This project requires the development of a number of classes. The details for each class are presented in the sections following this one, but Table 17-1 is a summary of the necessary classes.

Table 17-1. *Summary of Designer Classes*

Class Name	Base Class or Interface	Description
MainForm	Form	The main form of the application that contains the other controls
AssemblyReferenceForm	Form	A dialog that permits you to add references to other assemblies
NewWorkflowForm	Form	A dialog that permits you to select the base Type and workflow name when creating a new workflow
WorkflowDesigner	UserControl	A custom control that encapsulates much of the logic that hosts the workflow designer classes
WorkflowLoader	WorkflowDesignerLoader	A custom implementation of the workflow loader

Table 17-1. *Summary of Designer Classes (Continued)*

Class Name	Base Class or Interface	Description
WorkflowMenuService	MenuCommandService, IMenuCommandService	A service that provides for context-sensitive menus within the designer
WorkflowToolboxService	UserControl, IToolboxService	An implementation of a toolbox control and associated toolbox services
WorkflowPropertyValueService	IPropertyValueUIService	A service that provides tooltips, images, and other attributes for properties within a property grid
WorkflowEventBindingService	IEventBindingService	A service that provides for binding of workflow and activity events to existing workflow members
EventPropertyDescriptor	PropertyDescriptor	A property descriptor class that is used by the WorkflowEventBindingService

■**Tip** Because of the numerous dependencies between these classes, it is likely that code presented in one class will make references to other classes that have not yet been presented. For this reason, you can't incrementally build and test the application until most of the individual classes are in place.

Implementing WorkflowLoader

The WorkflowLoader class must derive from the abstract WorkflowDesignerLoader class (found in the System.Workflow.ComponentModel.Design namespace). It handles several important tasks:

- It loads all of the other services in the Initialize method.
- It deserializes the workflow from a markup file (.xoml) in the PerformLoad method.
- It serializes the workflow to a markup file in the PerformFlush method.

Add a new C# class (not a workflow class) to the WorkflowDesignerApp project and name it WorkflowLoader. Listing 17-1 is the complete listing of the WorkflowLoader.cs file with my annotations within the listing.

Listing 17-1. *Complete WorkflowLoader.cs File*

```
using System;
using System.IO;
using System.Xml;
using System.Reflection;
using System.Collections.Generic;
using System.Drawing.Design;
```

```
using System.ComponentModel.Design;
using System.ComponentModel.Design.Serialization;
using System.Workflow.ComponentModel;
using System.Workflow.ComponentModel.Design;
using System.Workflow.ComponentModel.Compiler;
using System.Workflow.ComponentModel.Serialization;
using System.Workflow.Activities.Rules;

namespace WorkflowDesignerApp
{
    /// <summary>
    /// A workflow designer loader for markup and .rules files
    /// </summary>
    public class WorkflowLoader : WorkflowDesignerLoader
    {
        private String _markupFileName = String.Empty;
        private Type _newWorkflowType;
        private IToolboxService _toolboxService;
        private TypeProvider _typeProvider;
        private String _newWorkflowName = String.Empty;

        public String MarkupFileName
        {
            get { return _markupFileName; }
            set { _markupFileName = value; }
        }

        public Type NewWorkflowType
        {
            get { return _newWorkflowType; }
            set { _newWorkflowType = value; }
        }

        public String NewWorkflowName
        {
            get { return _newWorkflowName; }
            set { _newWorkflowName = value; }
        }

        public TypeProvider TypeProvider
        {
            get { return _typeProvider; }
            set { _typeProvider = value; }
        }
```

The class begins with declarations of several instance variables and properties. The MarkupFileName property contains the name of the markup file that is currently loaded. The NewWorkflowType and NewWorkflowName properties are used during the creation of a new workflow. The TypeProvider object maintains a collection of assembly references. It is exposed here as a property in order to allow it to be created outside of this class and passed in. This permits multiple classes and components in this application to all work with the same TypeProvider instance.

```
        #region Required implementations for abstract members

        public override string FileName
        {
            get { return _markupFileName; }
        }

        public override System.IO.TextReader GetFileReader(
            string filePath)
        {
            return null;
        }

        public override System.IO.TextWriter GetFileWriter(
            string filePath)
        {
            return null;
        }

        #endregion
```

The abstract base class (WorkflowDesignerLoader) defines a few members that must be implemented. In this case, the FileName property simply returns the name of the markup file that is loaded. The GetFileReader and GetFileWriter members are not needed for this example application.

```
        #region Initialization

        /// <summary>
        /// Initialize the workflow designer loader
        /// </summary>
        protected override void Initialize()
        {
            base.Initialize();

            //add any necessary services
            IDesignerLoaderHost host = LoaderHost;
            if (host != null)
            {
                //add the custom MenuCommandService
                host.AddService(
                    typeof(IMenuCommandService),
                    new WorkflowMenuService(host));

                //add the TypeProvider
                host.AddService(
                    typeof(ITypeProvider), _typeProvider, true);

                //add the toolbox service
                _toolboxService = new WorkflowToolboxService(host);
                host.AddService(
                    typeof(IToolboxService), _toolboxService);

                //add the property value UI service
                host.AddService(
                    typeof(IPropertyValueUIService),
                    new WorkflowPropertyValueService());
```

```
            //add the event binding service
            host.AddService(
                typeof(IEventBindingService),
                new WorkflowEventBindingService(host));
        }
    }

    #endregion
```

The Initialize method is called just before the PerformLoad method and is your opportunity to add services to the designer host. The LoaderHost property of the base class contains an IDesignerLoaderHost object that is the recipient of the new services that are created in this method. With the exception of the TypeProvider, these are all custom services that you must implement. The implementations for these services are shown in the sections and code listings following this one. Note that each service is uniquely identified by an interface. All other components in the application that reference one of these services do so using the interface.

```
    #region Load the markup and add activities to the designer

    /// <summary>
    /// Load the markup file and add the workflow to the designer
    /// </summary>
    /// <param name="serializationManager"></param>
    protected override void PerformLoad(
        IDesignerSerializationManager serializationManager)
    {
        base.PerformLoad(serializationManager);
        Activity workflow = null;

        if (!String.IsNullOrEmpty(MarkupFileName))
        {
            //load a workflow from markup
            workflow = DeserializeFromMarkup(MarkupFileName);
        }
        else if (NewWorkflowType != null)
        {
            //create a new workflow
            workflow = CreateNewWorkflow(
                NewWorkflowType, NewWorkflowName);
        }

        if (workflow != null)
        {
            IDesignerHost designer
                = (IDesignerHost)GetService(typeof(IDesignerHost));
            //add the workfow definition to the designer
            AddWorkflowToDesigner(designer, workflow);
            //activate the designer
            designer.Activate();
        }
    }
```

The PerformLoad method is the top-level method that is responsible for loading a workflow definition. The code in this method is capable of either loading an existing workflow from markup or creating a new workflow based on the new workflow Type and name specified as properties. Once a workflow is loaded (either through deserialization or creation of a new workflow), it is passed to the private AddWorkflowToDesigner method that adds the individual workflow objects to the designer.

```
/// <summary>
/// Deserialize the markup file
/// </summary>
/// <param name="fileName"></param>
/// <returns></returns>
private Activity DeserializeFromMarkup(String fileName)
{
    Activity workflow = null;

    //construct a serialization manager.
    DesignerSerializationManager dsm
        = new DesignerSerializationManager();
    using (dsm.CreateSession())
    {
        using (XmlReader xmlReader
            = XmlReader.Create(fileName))
        {
            //deserialize the workflow from the XmlReader
            WorkflowMarkupSerializer markupSerializer
                = new WorkflowMarkupSerializer();
            workflow = markupSerializer.Deserialize(
                dsm, xmlReader) as Activity;

            if (dsm.Errors.Count > 0)
            {
                WorkflowMarkupSerializationException error
                    = dsm.Errors[0]
                        as WorkflowMarkupSerializationException;
                throw error;
            }
        }

        //deserialize a .rules file is one exists
        String rulesFileName = GetRulesFileName(fileName);
        if (File.Exists(rulesFileName))
        {
            //read the .rules file
            using (XmlReader xmlReader
                = XmlReader.Create(rulesFileName))
            {
                WorkflowMarkupSerializer markupSerializer
                    = new WorkflowMarkupSerializer();
                //deserialize the rule definitions
                RuleDefinitions ruleDefinitions
                    = markupSerializer.Deserialize(dsm, xmlReader)
                        as RuleDefinitions;
```

```
                    if (ruleDefinitions != null)
                    {
                        //add the rules definitions to the workflow
                        workflow.SetValue(
                            RuleDefinitions.RuleDefinitionsProperty,
                            ruleDefinitions);
                    }
                }
            }
        }

        return workflow;
    }
```

The DeserializeFromMarkup private method handles retrieval and deserialization of an existing workflow. It uses the WorkflowMarkupSerializer class to deserialize the workflow definition from a .xoml file. If a .rules file exists for the workflow, it is also deserialized and added to the workflow definition. For additional information on the use of the WorkflowMarkupSerializer class, refer to Chapter 16.

```
    /// <summary>
    /// Determine the name of the .rules file
    /// </summary>
    /// <param name="fileName"></param>
    /// <returns></returns>
    private static String GetRulesFileName(String fileName)
    {
        String rulesFileName = Path.Combine(
            Path.GetDirectoryName(fileName),
            Path.GetFileNameWithoutExtension(fileName) + ".rules");
        return rulesFileName;
    }


    /// <summary>
    /// Create a new workflow using the specified Type
    /// </summary>
    /// <param name="workflowType"></param>
    /// <returns></returns>
    private Activity CreateNewWorkflow(Type workflowType,
        String newWorkflowName)
    {
        Activity workflow = null;

        ConstructorInfo cstr
            = workflowType.GetConstructor(Type.EmptyTypes);
        if (cstr != null)
        {
            workflow = cstr.Invoke(new Object[] { }) as Activity;
            workflow.Name = newWorkflowName;
            //set a default file name
            _markupFileName = newWorkflowName + ".xoml";
        }
        return workflow;
    }
```

The CreateNewWorkflow method is invoked by the PerformLoad method to create a new workflow based on the specified workflow Type.

```
/// <summary>
/// Add the workflow definition to the designer
/// </summary>
/// <param name="designer"></param>
/// <param name="workflow"></param>
private static void AddWorkflowToDesigner(
    IDesignerHost designer, Activity workflow)
{
    //add the root activity to the designer
    designer.Container.Add(workflow, workflow.QualifiedName);

    //add any child activities
    if (workflow is CompositeActivity)
    {
        List<Activity> children = new List<Activity>();
        //get a collection of all child activities
        GetChildActivities(
            workflow as CompositeActivity, children);
        foreach (Activity child in children)
        {
            designer.Container.Add(child, child.QualifiedName);
        }
    }
}


/// <summary>
/// Recursively get a collection of all child activities
/// </summary>
/// <param name="composite"></param>
/// <param name="children"></param>
private static void GetChildActivities(
    CompositeActivity composite, List<Activity> children)
{
    foreach (Activity activity in composite.Activities)
    {
        children.Add(activity);
        if (activity is CompositeActivity)
        {
            //make recursive call
            GetChildActivities(
                activity as CompositeActivity, children);
        }
    }
}

#endregion
```

The AddWorkflowToDesigner method is invoked after a workflow has been loaded or created. It is used to add the individual activity objects of the workflow to the designer. It uses the GetChildActivities method to recursively retrieve a collection of child activities to add to the designer.

```
#region Cleanup methods

/// <summary>
/// Remove the workflow from the designer
/// </summary>
/// <param name="designer"></param>
/// <param name="workflow"></param>
public void RemoveFromDesigner(IDesignerHost designer,
    Activity workflow)
{
    if (workflow != null)
    {
        designer.DestroyComponent(workflow);
        if (workflow is CompositeActivity)
        {
            List<Activity> children = new List<Activity>();
            //remove all child activities
            GetChildActivities(
                workflow as CompositeActivity, children);
            foreach (Activity child in children)
            {
                designer.DestroyComponent(child);
            }
        }
    }
}

#endregion
```

The RemoveFromDesigner public method can be invoked to remove the current workflow (if there is one) from the designer. It is not directly used within this class but is invoked from the designer component (WorkflowDesigner) prior to loading a new workflow definition.

```
#region Save the workflow design to a markup file

/// <summary>
/// Flush the current workflow model to a xoml file
/// </summary>
public override void Flush()
{
    PerformFlush(null);
}

/// <summary>
/// Write the current workflow model to a xoml file
/// </summary>
/// <param name="serializationManager"></param>
protected override void PerformFlush(
    IDesignerSerializationManager serializationManager)
{
    base.PerformFlush(serializationManager);

    //get the designer
    IDesignerHost designer
        = (IDesignerHost)GetService(typeof(IDesignerHost));
```

```
        //get the root activity of the workflow
        Activity workflow = designer.RootComponent as Activity;

        //serialize to a markup file
        if (workflow != null)
        {
            SerializeToMarkup(workflow, _markupFileName);
        }
    }
}
```

The PerformFlush method is responsible for flushing (saving) the current workflow design to a markup file. The private SerializeToMarkup method is called to perform the actual serialization to markup.

```
/// <summary>
/// Serialize the workflow to a xoml file
/// </summary>
/// <param name="workflow"></param>
/// <param name="fileName"></param>
private void SerializeToMarkup(
    Activity workflow, String fileName)
{
    //clear the class name property since we are
    //never creating a new class type.
    workflow.SetValue(
        WorkflowMarkupSerializer.XClassProperty, null);

    using (XmlWriter xmlWriter = XmlWriter.Create(fileName))
    {
        WorkflowMarkupSerializer markupSerializer
            = new WorkflowMarkupSerializer();
        markupSerializer.Serialize(xmlWriter, workflow);
    }

    //Serialize rules if they exist
    RuleDefinitions ruleDefinitions = workflow.GetValue(
        RuleDefinitions.RuleDefinitionsProperty)
            as RuleDefinitions;
    if (ruleDefinitions != null)
    {
        if (ruleDefinitions.Conditions.Count > 0 ||
            ruleDefinitions.RuleSets.Count > 0)
        {
            String rulesFileName = GetRulesFileName(fileName);
            using (XmlWriter xmlWriter
                = XmlWriter.Create(rulesFileName))
            {
                WorkflowMarkupSerializer markupSerializer
                    = new WorkflowMarkupSerializer();
                markupSerializer.Serialize(
                    xmlWriter, ruleDefinitions);
            }
        }
    }
}
```

The SerializeToMarkup method uses the WorkflowMarkupSerializer class to serialize the workflow definition to a markup file (.xoml). It also serializes any rule definitions (if they exist) to a .rules file.

```
    #endregion
    }
}
```

Implementing WorkflowMenuService

The WorkflowMenuService is responsible for building context-sensitive menus that appear when you right-click a selected item in the designer. An instance of this class is created and loaded into the designer by the WorkflowLoader class (see Listing 17-1). This class is derived from the MenuCommandService class, which implements the IMenuCommandService interface.

Add a new C# class to the project and name it WorkflowMenuService. Listing 17-2 is the complete code you need for the WorkflowMenuService.cs file.

Listing 17-2. *Complete WorkflowMenuService.cs File*

```csharp
using System;
using System.Collections;
using System.Drawing;
using System.Windows.Forms;
using System.Collections.Generic;
using System.ComponentModel.Design;
using System.Workflow.ComponentModel.Design;
using System.Workflow.ComponentModel;

namespace WorkflowDesignerApp
{
    /// <summary>
    /// A workflow menu service that provides a
    /// context-menu for the selected component
    /// </summary>
    public class WorkflowMenuService : MenuCommandService
    {
        public WorkflowMenuService(IServiceProvider provider)
            : base(provider)
        {
        }

        /// <summary>
        /// The context menu is about to be shown. Build the
        /// available list of menu items based on the
        /// selected activity.
        /// </summary>
        /// <param name="menuID"></param>
        /// <param name="x"></param>
        /// <param name="y"></param>
```

```
public override void ShowContextMenu(
    CommandID menuID, int x, int y)
{
    base.ShowContextMenu(menuID, x, y);
    if (menuID == WorkflowMenuCommands.SelectionMenu)
    {
        ContextMenu contextMenu = new ContextMenu();
        //add a context menu item for each designer
        //verb that is available
        foreach (DesignerVerb verb in Verbs)
        {
            MenuItem menuItem = new MenuItem(verb.Text,
                new EventHandler(OnMenuClicked));
            menuItem.Tag = verb;
            contextMenu.MenuItems.Add(menuItem);
        }

        //add any context menu items based on the
        //selected object
        foreach (MenuItem menu in BuildItemsForSelection())
        {
            contextMenu.MenuItems.Add(menu);
        }

        //show the newly constructed context menu
        //on the workflow view
        WorkflowView workflowView =
            GetService(typeof(WorkflowView)) as WorkflowView;
        if (workflowView != null)
        {
            //show the context menu
            contextMenu.Show(workflowView,
                workflowView.PointToClient(new Point(x, y)));
        }
    }
}
```

The ShowContextMenu method is invoked when the user right-clicks somewhere within the workflow designer. The code in this method first creates a MenuItem object for each DesignerVerb that is defined in the Verbs property of the base class. The list of verbs is populated by the workflow designer; you don't need to explicitly define them. They include the standard workflow commands such as View Cancel Handlers, View Fault Handlers, Add Branch, and so on.

After adding the standard designer verbs, the code calls the BuildItemsForSelection private method and adds a MenuItem for each object returned from the method. The BuildItemsForSelection method (shown next) produces a list of other menu items based on the Type of the selected item.

Finally, the ShowContextMenu method shows the context menu that was just created.

```
/// <summary>
/// Build the menu items based on the selected context
/// </summary>
/// <returns></returns>
```

```csharp
private IList<MenuItem> BuildItemsForSelection()
{
    List<MenuItem> items = new List<MenuItem>();

    //determine if all selected items are valid for
    //our context menu
    Boolean isActivity = false;
    Boolean isComposite = false;
    ISelectionService selectionService
        = GetService(typeof(ISelectionService))
            as ISelectionService;
    if (selectionService != null)
    {
        ICollection selectedObjects
            = selectionService.GetSelectedComponents();
        if (selectedObjects.Count > 1)
        {
            //more than one object has been selected.
            //just make sure that all selected objects
            //derive from Activity
            isActivity = true;
            foreach (Object selection in selectedObjects)
            {
                if (!(selection is Activity))
                {
                    //not a valid selection
                    isActivity = false;
                    break;
                }
            }
        }
        else
        {
            //only a single item was selected, so we can
            //be more specific with the context menu
            foreach (Object selection in selectedObjects)
            {
                isComposite = (selection is CompositeActivity);
                isActivity = (selection is Activity);
            }
        }
    }

    if (isActivity)
    {
        //if the selection was valid, add menu items
        Dictionary<CommandID, String> commands
            = new Dictionary<CommandID, String>();
        commands.Add(WorkflowMenuCommands.Copy, "Copy");
        commands.Add(WorkflowMenuCommands.Cut, "Cut");
        commands.Add(WorkflowMenuCommands.Paste, "Paste");
        commands.Add(WorkflowMenuCommands.Delete, "Delete");
```

```
                if (isComposite)
                {
                    //add other menu items if a composite is selected
                    commands.Add(WorkflowMenuCommands.Collapse, "Collapse");
                    commands.Add(WorkflowMenuCommands.Expand, "Expand");
                }

                //add the divider
                items.Add(new MenuItem("-"));

                //add the menu items
                foreach (KeyValuePair<CommandID, String> pair in commands)
                {
                    //get the MenuCommand to execute for the menu item
                    MenuCommand command = FindCommand(pair.Key);
                    if (command != null)
                    {
                        MenuItem menuItem = new MenuItem(pair.Value,
                            new EventHandler(OnMenuClicked));
                        menuItem.Tag = command;
                        items.Add(menuItem);
                    }
                }
            }

        return items;
    }
```

The `BuildItemsForSelection` private method builds additional `MenuItem` objects depending on the `Type` of the selected object in the designer. The menu items that I have chosen to add are completely arbitrary and include common editing options such as Copy, Cut, Paste, and Delete. I have also chosen to add the Collapse and Expand options if the selected object is a `CompositeActivity`. Those are my selections, but you are free to modify this code to create just the menu items that you want to support in your designer application. You can also add a `MenuItem` for any custom commands that you wish to fully implement yourself.

The set of available workflow commands is defined in the `WorkflowMenuCommands` class. Each command corresponds to a command function that is supported by the workflow designer.

```
        /// <summary>
        /// Common handler for all context menu items
        /// </summary>
        /// <param name="sender"></param>
        /// <param name="e"></param>
        private void OnMenuClicked(Object sender, EventArgs e)
        {
            if (sender is MenuItem)
            {
                MenuItem menu = sender as MenuItem;
                if ((menu != null) && (menu.Tag is MenuCommand))
                {
                    ((MenuCommand)menu.Tag).Invoke();
                }
            }
        }
```

All of the MenuItem instances use this OnMenuClicked method to handle their OnClick event. The code in this method retrieves the MenuCommand that was saved in the Tag property of the MenuItem and invokes it. This executes one of the standard designer functions that is handled and implemented by the workflow designer.

```
        }
}
```

Implementing WorkflowEventBindingService

The WorkflowEventBindingService implements the IEventBindingService interface. In general designer usage, a service that implements this interface is responsible for assigning handlers for component events. In the case of the workflow designer application that you are building, this service (and its related classes) creates ActivityBind objects that bind activity or workflow events to members of the base workflow class.

Just like the other services, an instance of this class is created by the Initialize method of the WorkflowLoader. To implement this service, add a new C# class to the project and name it WorkflowEventBindingService. Listing 17-3 is the complete code listing for the WorkflowEventBindingService.cs file.

Listing 17-3. *Complete WorkflowEventBindingService.cs File*

```csharp
using System;
using System.Reflection;
using System.Collections;
using System.Collections.Generic;
using System.ComponentModel;
using System.ComponentModel.Design;

namespace WorkflowDesignerApp
{
    /// <summary>
    /// Workflow event binding service
    /// </summary>
    public class WorkflowEventBindingService : IEventBindingService
    {
        private IServiceProvider _serviceProvider;

        public WorkflowEventBindingService(
            IServiceProvider serviceProvider)
        {
            _serviceProvider = serviceProvider;
        }

        #region IEventBindingService Members

        public string CreateUniqueMethodName(
            IComponent component, EventDescriptor e)
        {
            return String.Empty;
        }
```

```csharp
/// <summary>
/// Get a list of any methods in the root component class
/// that are candidates as event handlers for the
/// specified EventDescriptor.
/// </summary>
/// <param name="e"></param>
/// <returns></returns>
public ICollection GetCompatibleMethods(EventDescriptor e)
{
    List<String> compatibleMethods = new List<String>();

    IDesignerHost designerHost =
        _serviceProvider.GetService(typeof(IDesignerHost))
            as IDesignerHost;
    if (designerHost == null || designerHost.RootComponent == null)
    {
        return compatibleMethods;
    }

    //get the event handler Type for the event
    EventInfo eventInfo
        = e.ComponentType.GetEvent(e.Name);
    ParameterInfo[] eventParameters = null;
    if (eventInfo != null)
    {
        //get the member info for the Invoke method
        MethodInfo invokeMethod =
            eventInfo.EventHandlerType.GetMethod("Invoke");
        if (invokeMethod != null)
        {
            //get the parameters associated with this method
            eventParameters = invokeMethod.GetParameters();
        }
    }

    if (eventParameters != null)
    {
        //get the methods in the root component
        Type rootType = designerHost.RootComponent.GetType();
        MethodInfo[] methods = rootType.GetMethods(
            BindingFlags.Public | BindingFlags.NonPublic |
            BindingFlags.Instance | BindingFlags.DeclaredOnly);

        //look for a method with a matching set of arguments
        foreach (MethodInfo method in methods)
        {
            ParameterInfo[] parameters
                = method.GetParameters();
            if (parameters.Length == eventParameters.Length)
            {
```

```
                    if (IsCandidateMethod(eventParameters, parameters))
                    {
                        compatibleMethods.Add(method.Name);
                    }
                }
            }

            //provide an entry that allows the selection
            //to be cleared
            compatibleMethods.Add("[Clear]");
        }

        return compatibleMethods;
    }
```

The GetCompatibleMethods method returns a string collection of members that are event handler candidates. This list is used to build the drop-down list of available event-handling members in the properties grid. For example, if you select a CodeActivity in the designer and open the drop-down list of members for the ExecuteCode event, this method would be responsible for producing the list of candidate workflow members.

This method is passed an EventDescriptor object that identifies the selected event. The code uses the event Type identified by the EventDescriptor to retrieve a list of arguments for the Invoke method of the event. It uses this list of arguments to match against the methods of the base workflow class. If the method arguments match, the workflow method is a possible candidate as an event handler for this event. This code only looks at methods in the workflow class and doesn't include those that are defined in base classes. You can modify this behavior by changing the set of BindingFlags passed to the GetMethods call.

```
/// <summary>
/// Do the method parameters match what the event expects?
/// </summary>
/// <param name="eventParameters"></param>
/// <param name="parameters"></param>
/// <returns></returns>
private static Boolean IsCandidateMethod(
    ParameterInfo[] eventParameters,
    ParameterInfo[] parameters)
{
    Boolean isCandidate = true;
    for (Int32 i = 0; i < eventParameters.Length; i++)
    {
        if (!eventParameters[i].ParameterType.IsAssignableFrom(
            parameters[i].ParameterType))
        {
            isCandidate = false;
            break;
        }
    }
    return isCandidate;
}
```

The private IsCandidateMethod is used to compare the set of event parameters to those of a workflow method. If the method has the same number and Type of arguments, true is returned from the method.

```
public EventDescriptor GetEvent(PropertyDescriptor property)
{
    if (property is EventPropertyDescriptor)
    {
        return ((EventPropertyDescriptor)
            property).EventDescriptor;
    }
    else
    {
        return null;
    }
}
```

GetEvent is one of the required methods defined by the IEventBindingService interface. It returns an EventDescriptor for a given PropertyDescriptor. The EventPropertyDescriptor class that is referred to in this method is shown and discussed in the next section of this chapter. It is derived from PropertyDescriptor and contains the logic that manages the ActivityBind objects for a workflow event.

```
/// <summary>
/// Convert a collection of event descriptors to
/// property descriptors
/// </summary>
/// <param name="events"></param>
/// <returns></returns>
public PropertyDescriptorCollection GetEventProperties(
    EventDescriptorCollection events)
{
    List<PropertyDescriptor> properties
        = new List<PropertyDescriptor>();
    foreach (EventDescriptor eventDesc in events)
    {
        properties.Add(new EventPropertyDescriptor(
            eventDesc, _serviceProvider));
    }
    PropertyDescriptorCollection propertiesCollection
        = new PropertyDescriptorCollection(
            properties.ToArray(), true);
    return propertiesCollection;
}

/// <summary>
/// Convert an EventDescriptor to a PropertyDescriptor
/// </summary>
/// <param name="e"></param>
/// <returns></returns>
public PropertyDescriptor GetEventProperty(EventDescriptor e)
{
    return new EventPropertyDescriptor(e, _serviceProvider);
}
```

These two methods (GetEventProperties and GetEventProperty) are required IEventBindingService members. They convert one or more EventDescriptor objects to their associated PropertyDescriptor. This is where an instance of the custom EventPropertyDescriptor class is created from the EventDescriptor.

```
/// <summary>
/// Display the code editor?
/// </summary>
/// <param name="component"></param>
/// <param name="e"></param>
/// <returns></returns>
public bool ShowCode(TComponent component, EventDescriptor e)
{
    return false;
}

public bool ShowCode(int lineNumber)
{
    return false;
}

public bool ShowCode()
{
    return false;
}
```

These ShowCode methods are called when the user switches from designer to code view. Since this application doesn't work with a code-beside file, there is nothing to do here, other than to return false to indicate that no code was shown.

```
    #endregion
}
}
```

Implementing EventPropertyDescriptor

The EventPropertyDescriptor class is used by the WorkflowEventBindingService discussed in the previous section. It is derived from the base PropertyDescriptor class and provides the code needed to add an ActivityBind object that binds the event to a workflow member.

Add a C# class named EventPropertyDescriptor to the project. Listing 17-4 is the complete code for this class.

Listing 17-4. *Complete EventPropertyDescriptor.cs File*

```
using System;
using System.Collections;
using System.ComponentModel;
using System.ComponentModel.Design;
using System.Reflection;
using System.Workflow.ComponentModel;

namespace WorkflowDesignerApp
{
    /// <summary>
    /// A PropertyDescriptor for workflow events that
    /// Adds or Removes ActivityBind objects
    /// </summary>
```

```
public class EventPropertyDescriptor : PropertyDescriptor
{
    private EventDescriptor _eventDescriptor;
    private IServiceProvider _serviceProvider;
    private DependencyProperty _eventProperty;

    public EventPropertyDescriptor(EventDescriptor eventDesc,
        IServiceProvider serviceProvider)
        : base(eventDesc)
    {
        _eventDescriptor = eventDesc;
        _serviceProvider = serviceProvider;

        //get the dependency property that defines the
        //component event from the ComponentType object.
        FieldInfo eventFieldInfo =
            _eventDescriptor.ComponentType.GetField(
                _eventDescriptor.Name + "Event");
        if (eventFieldInfo != null)
        {
            _eventProperty = eventFieldInfo.GetValue(
                _eventDescriptor.ComponentType)
                    as DependencyProperty;
        }
    }
}
```

The constructor for this class accepts an EventDescriptor and an IServiceProvider instance.
The code immediately retrieves the DependencyProperty from the component that corresponds to
the selected event. This DependencyProperty is used later in the code when an ActivityBind object is
created to handle the event.

```
public EventDescriptor EventDescriptor
{
    get { return _eventDescriptor; }
}

public override bool CanResetValue(object component)
{
    return false;
}

public override Type ComponentType
{
    get { return _eventDescriptor.ComponentType; }
}

public override object GetValue(object component)
{
    return null;
}

public override bool IsReadOnly
{
    get { return false; }
}
```

```csharp
public override Type PropertyType
{
    get { return _eventDescriptor.EventType; }
}

public override void ResetValue(object component)
{
    //reset by setting the property value to null
    SetValue(component, null);
}

/// <summary>
/// Set the new binding for an event
/// </summary>
/// <param name="component"></param>
/// <param name="value"></param>
public override void SetValue(object component, object value)
{
    DependencyObject dependencyObject
        = component as DependencyObject;
    String eventHandlerName = value as String;
    if (dependencyObject == null || _eventProperty == null)
    {
        return;
    }

    //is an event handler already defined for this event?
    String currentHandlerName = String.Empty;
    if (dependencyObject.IsBindingSet(_eventProperty))
    {
        currentHandlerName =
            dependencyObject.GetBinding(_eventProperty).Path;
    }

    //the handler name is the same so just get out now
    if (eventHandlerName == currentHandlerName)
    {
        return;
    }

    IDesignerHost designerHost
        = _serviceProvider.GetService(
            typeof(IDesignerHost)) as IDesignerHost;
    //use the IComponentChangeService to notify the
    //designer of the change
    IComponentChangeService changeService
        = _serviceProvider.GetService(
            typeof(IComponentChangeService))
                as IComponentChangeService;
    if (changeService != null)
    {
        //notify that the component is changing
        changeService.OnComponentChanging(
            component, _eventDescriptor);
    }
```

```
            //set or remove the binding
            String bindingName = String.Empty;
            if (eventHandlerName == null ||
                eventHandlerName == "[Clear]")
            {
                //remove the old binding
                dependencyObject.RemoveProperty(_eventProperty);
            }
            else
            {
                //Add a new ActivityBind object to the component
                ActivityBind bind = new ActivityBind(
                    ((Activity)designerHost.RootComponent).Name,
                        eventHandlerName);
                dependencyObject.SetBinding(_eventProperty, bind);
                //save the new binding name so we can notify others
                //of the change below
                bindingName = eventHandlerName;
            }

            if (changeService != null)
            {
                //notify that the component has changed
                changeService.OnComponentChanged(
                    component, _eventDescriptor,
                    currentHandlerName, bindingName);
            }
        }
    }
```

The SetValue method is where the most important work of this class takes place. This method is called when a candidate workflow method is selected by the user. If an ActivityBind object has already been set for this event, the path name of the existing ActivityBind is compared to the selected event name. The path name corresponds to the method name. If the method names are the same, there is no need for a change.

If the method names are different, the designer is notified of the change using an object that implements the IComponentChangeService interface. Depending on the value of the selected method, the existing ActivityBind object is removed, or a new one is created and added to the component.

```
        public override bool ShouldSerializeValue(object component)
        {
            //yes, persist the value of this property
            return true;
        }

        /// <summary>
        /// Provide a custom type converter to
        /// use for this event property
        /// </summary>
        public override TypeConverter Converter
        {
            get
            {
                return new WorkflowEventTypeConverter(
```

```
                    _eventDescriptor);
        }
    }
```

The Converter property of the base class is overridden so that the code can provide a custom TypeConverter. The custom WorkflowEventTypeConverter is shown next and is implemented as a private subclass.

```
#region Private WorkflowEventTypeConverter class

/// <summary>
/// Implement a TypeConverter for workflow event properties
/// </summary>
private class WorkflowEventTypeConverter : TypeConverter
{
    EventDescriptor _eventDescriptor;

    public WorkflowEventTypeConverter(
        EventDescriptor eventDesc)
    {
        //save the EventDescriptor that we convert
        _eventDescriptor = eventDesc;
    }

    /// <summary>
    /// Get a list of standard values that are supported for this
    /// event.  Use the GetCompatibleMethods method of the
    /// IEventBindingService to retrieve the list of valid values
    /// for the current event property
    /// </summary>
    /// <param name="context"></param>
    /// <returns></returns>
    public override TypeConverter.StandardValuesCollection
        GetStandardValues(ITypeDescriptorContext context)
    {
        ICollection compatibleMethods = new ArrayList();
        if (context != null)
        {
            IEventBindingService bindingService
                = (IEventBindingService)context.GetService(
                    typeof(IEventBindingService));
            if (bindingService != null)
            {
                //use the IEventBindingService to generate
                //a list of compatible methods
                compatibleMethods
                    = bindingService.GetCompatibleMethods(
                        _eventDescriptor);
            }
        }

        return new StandardValuesCollection(compatibleMethods);
    }
```

The GetStandardValues method of the TypeConverter is called whenever the drop-down list is selected for an event in the properties grid. The code in this method calls the GetCompatibleMethods method of the WorkflowEventBindingService (shown in Listing 17-3) to retrieve the list of candidate methods for the event.

```
        public override bool GetStandardValuesSupported(
            ITypeDescriptorContext context)
        {
            //Yes, a call to GetStandardValues should be made
            return true;
        }

        public override bool GetStandardValuesExclusive(
            ITypeDescriptorContext context)
        {
            // Only the values returned from GetStandardValues
            // are valid. You can't enter new string values.
            return true;
        }
    }
```

These two method overrides are small but important. The GetStandardValuesSupported method returns true to indicate that the GetStandardValues method should be called. If you don't return true, GetStandardValues will never be called.

The GetStandardValuesExclusive method also returns true. This indicates that only the values that are returned from the GetStandardValues method are allowed for an event. In other words, the user is not allowed to enter a name for a new event handler. This makes sense given the scope of this particular designer application (editing no-code workflows). If you are developing a designer that supports code-beside file generation and workflow compilation, you probably want to return false from this method.

```
        #endregion
    }
}
```

Implementing WorkflowPropertyValueService

The WorkflowPropertyValueService implements the IPropertyValueUIService interface and provides enhancements to the properties grid. This interface identifies the service that provides tooltips, additional images, and features for the properties grid. Add a new C# class named WorkflowPropertyValueService to the project. Listing 17-5 is the complete code listing for this class.

Listing 17-5. *Complete WorkflowPropertyValueService.cs File*

```
using System;
using System.Drawing.Design;
using System.Collections;
using System.ComponentModel;

namespace WorkflowDesignerApp
{
    /// <summary>
    /// A service that provides images and tooltips for
    /// property grid entries
    /// </summary>
    public class WorkflowPropertyValueService
```

```
    : IPropertyValueUIService
{
    private PropertyValueUIHandler _UIHandler;
    #region IPropertyValueUIService Members

    /// <summary>
    /// Add a handler
    /// </summary>
    /// <param name="newHandler"></param>
    public void AddPropertyValueUIHandler(
        PropertyValueUIHandler newHandler)
    {
        if (newHandler != null)
        {
            //combine the handler with the current delegates
            _UIHandler += newHandler;
        }
    }

    /// <summary>
    /// Remove a handler
    /// </summary>
    /// <param name="newHandler"></param>
    public void RemovePropertyValueUIHandler(
        PropertyValueUIHandler newHandler)
    {
        if (newHandler != null)
        {
            //remove a handler
            _UIHandler -= newHandler;
        }
    }
```

The AddPropertyValueUIHandler and RemovePropertyValueUIHandler methods are defined by the IPropertyValueUIService interface and are required. They are used by the designer framework to add or remove PropertyValueUIHandler delegates. This delegate is used by the GetPropertyUIValueItems method (shown next) to prepare an array of PropertyValueUIItem objects.

```
    /// <summary>
    /// Get a list of UI items for a property
    /// </summary>
    /// <param name="context"></param>
    /// <param name="propDesc"></param>
    /// <returns></returns>
    public PropertyValueUIItem[] GetPropertyUIValueItems(
        ITypeDescriptorContext context, PropertyDescriptor propDesc)
    {
        PropertyValueUIItem[] result = new PropertyValueUIItem[0];
        if (propDesc == null || _UIHandler == null)
        {
            return result;
        }

        //call any subscribed handlers allowing them
        //to provide a list of UI items. the UI items
```

```
                //provide images and tooltips for the properties
                //grid.
                ArrayList propertyItems = new ArrayList();
                _UIHandler(context, propDesc, propertyItems);
                if (propertyItems.Count > 0)
                {
                    result = new PropertyValueUIItem[propertyItems.Count];
                    propertyItems.CopyTo(result);
                }
                return result;
            }
        }
```

The GetPropertyUIValueItems method is invoked once for each property as it is shown in a properties grid. It invokes the delegate that was added by the AddPropertyValueUIHandler method, allowing the method represented by the delegate to populate an array of PropertyValueUIItem objects. This array is used by the properties grid to enhance the display for a given property.

You won't find any code in this application that adds a delegate to this service. The delegate is added internally by the workflow designer and is used to provide additional information that is shown for a property.

```
        /// <summary>
        /// Notify any subscribers that the list of
        /// PropertyValueUIItems has changed
        /// </summary>
        public void NotifyPropertyValueUIItemsChanged()
        {
            if (PropertyUIValueItemsChanged != null)
            {
                PropertyUIValueItemsChanged(this, new EventArgs());
            }
        }

        public event EventHandler PropertyUIValueItemsChanged;

        #endregion
    }
}
```

Implementing WorkflowToolboxService

The WorkflowToolboxService serves a dual purpose. It implements the IToolboxService interface, which provides methods that can be used by the designers. It is also derived from UserControl and is the control that visually represents the toolbox in the designer application. In this application, the toolbox displays a list of standard workflow activities as well as any custom activities that are found in referenced assemblies.

This service is created by the WorkflowLoader, but it is also added to the WorkflowDesigner control as a child control. The WorkflowDesigner control (described in the next section of this chapter) includes code to add the toolbox control to a panel of the designer control.

To create this class, add a C# class to the project and name it WorkflowToolboxService. Listing 17-6 is the complete code for this class.

Listing 17-6. *Complete WorkflowToolboxService.cs File*

```
using System;
using System.Reflection;
using System.Collections;
using System.Collections.Generic;
using System.ComponentModel;
using System.ComponentModel.Design;
using System.Drawing;
using System.Drawing.Design;
using System.Windows.Forms;
using System.Workflow.Activities;
using System.Workflow.ComponentModel;
using System.Workflow.ComponentModel.Design;
using System.Workflow.ComponentModel.Compiler;

namespace WorkflowDesignerApp
{
    /// <summary>
    /// A UserControl and service that provides a toolbox
    /// list of workflow activities
    /// </summary>
    public class WorkflowToolboxService : UserControl, IToolboxService
    {
        private ListBox _activitiesList;
        private List<Type> _standardActivities = new List<Type>();
        private IServiceProvider _serviceProvider;

        public WorkflowToolboxService(IServiceProvider provider)
        {
            _serviceProvider = provider;
            Dock = DockStyle.Fill;

            //create a ListBox to view the toolbox items
            _activitiesList = new ListBox();
            _activitiesList.Dock = DockStyle.Fill;
            _activitiesList.ItemHeight = 23;
            _activitiesList.DrawMode = DrawMode.OwnerDrawFixed;
            _activitiesList.DrawItem
                += new DrawItemEventHandler(ActivitiesList_DrawItem);
            _activitiesList.MouseMove
                += new MouseEventHandler(ActivitiesList_MouseMove);
            Controls.Add(_activitiesList);

            //create a list of standard activities that we support
            _standardActivities.Add(typeof(CallExternalMethodActivity));
            _standardActivities.Add(typeof(CancellationHandlerActivity));
            _standardActivities.Add(typeof(CodeActivity));
            _standardActivities.Add(typeof(CompensatableSequenceActivity));
```

```
        _standardActivities.Add(
            typeof(CompensatableTransactionScopeActivity));
        _standardActivities.Add(typeof(CompensateActivity));
        _standardActivities.Add(typeof(ConditionedActivityGroup));
        _standardActivities.Add(typeof(DelayActivity));
        _standardActivities.Add(typeof(EventDrivenActivity));
        _standardActivities.Add(typeof(EventHandlersActivity));
        _standardActivities.Add(typeof(EventHandlingScopeActivity));
        _standardActivities.Add(typeof(FaultHandlerActivity));
        _standardActivities.Add(typeof(FaultHandlersActivity));
        _standardActivities.Add(typeof(HandleExternalEventActivity));
        _standardActivities.Add(typeof(IfElseActivity));
        _standardActivities.Add(typeof(InvokeWebServiceActivity));
        _standardActivities.Add(typeof(InvokeWorkflowActivity));
        _standardActivities.Add(typeof(ListenActivity));
        _standardActivities.Add(typeof(ParallelActivity));
        _standardActivities.Add(typeof(PolicyActivity));
        _standardActivities.Add(typeof(ReplicatorActivity));
        _standardActivities.Add(typeof(SequenceActivity));
        _standardActivities.Add(typeof(SetStateActivity));
        _standardActivities.Add(typeof(StateActivity));
        _standardActivities.Add(typeof(StateFinalizationActivity));
        _standardActivities.Add(typeof(StateInitializationActivity));
        _standardActivities.Add(typeof(SuspendActivity));
        _standardActivities.Add(typeof(SynchronizationScopeActivity));
        _standardActivities.Add(typeof(TerminateActivity));
        _standardActivities.Add(typeof(ThrowActivity));
        _standardActivities.Add(typeof(TransactionScopeActivity));
        _standardActivities.Add(typeof(WebServiceFaultActivity));
        _standardActivities.Add(typeof(WebServiceInputActivity));
        _standardActivities.Add(typeof(WebServiceOutputActivity));
        _standardActivities.Add(typeof(WhileActivity));

        //add toolbox items for all activities in the list
        CreateToolboxItems(_activitiesList, _standardActivities);
    }
```

The constructor for this class creates a ListBox control and adds it as a child control. The ListBox is the control used to display the individual toolbox items. A List of standard activity types is then populated and passed to the private CreateToolboxItems method.

```
    #region IToolboxService Members

    /// <summary>
    /// Get a category name for the items in the toolbox
    /// </summary>
    public CategoryNameCollection CategoryNames
    {
        get
        {
            return new CategoryNameCollection(
                new String[] { "WindowsWorkflow" });
        }
    }
```

```csharp
/// <summary>
/// Get the category name of the currently selected
/// tool in the toolbox
/// </summary>
public string SelectedCategory
{
    get { return "WindowsWorkflow"; }
    set { }
}


/// <summary>
/// Get the ActivityToolboxItem from the serialized
/// toolbox item
/// </summary>
/// <param name="serializedObject"></param>
/// <param name="host"></param>
/// <returns></returns>
public ToolboxItem DeserializeToolboxItem(
    object serializedObject, IDesignerHost host)
{
    ToolboxItem result = null;
    if (serializedObject is IDataObject)
    {
        result = ((IDataObject)serializedObject).GetData(
            typeof(ToolboxItem)) as ToolboxItem;
    }
    return result;
}

public ToolboxItem DeserializeToolboxItem(
    object serializedObject)
{
    return DeserializeToolboxItem(serializedObject, null);
}


/// <summary>
/// Get a serialized object that represents the toolbox item
/// </summary>
/// <param name="toolboxItem"></param>
/// <returns></returns>
public object SerializeToolboxItem(ToolboxItem toolboxItem)
{
    //use a DataObject which is a general data transfer
    //mechanism used for clipboard and drag-drop operations.
    DataObject dataObject = new DataObject();
    dataObject.SetData(typeof(ToolboxItem), toolboxItem);
    return dataObject;
}
```

The DeserializeToolboxItem and SerializeToolboxItem methods work with the ToolboxItem that is passed around as a DataObject. The DataObject is a general-purpose class that implements IDataObject and is a suitable data transfer object for clipboard and drag-and-drop operations. Since the toolbox must support drag-and-drop operations to the workflow designer, this is a logical choice to use as a wrapper for each ToolboxItem. ToolboxItem is a class provided in the System.Drawing.Design namespace that represents a single item in a toolbox.

```
/// <summary>
/// Set cursor for the currently selected tool
/// </summary>
/// <returns></returns>
public bool SetCursor()
{
    return false; //just use standard cursor
}


/// <summary>
/// Does the designer host support this toolbox item?
/// </summary>
/// <param name="serializedObject"></param>
/// <param name="filterAttributes"></param>
/// <returns></returns>
public bool IsSupported(object serializedObject,
    ICollection filterAttributes)
{
    return true;
}


public bool IsSupported(object serializedObject,
    IDesignerHost host)
{
    return true;
}
```

In the large section of code that follows, the class declares members that are required by the IToolboxService but are not fully implemented in this class. Many of these methods are used to provide interactive updating of a toolbox, allowing a user to add or remove items from the toolbox as you would in Visual Studio. This example application doesn't require any of the functionality provided by these members, but you are free to implement them in your application.

```
#region IToolboxService Members Not Fully Implemented

public void AddCreator(ToolboxItemCreatorCallback creator,
    string format, IDesignerHost host)
{
    throw new NotImplementedException(
        "Method not implemented");
}

public void AddCreator(ToolboxItemCreatorCallback creator,
    string format)
{
    throw new NotImplementedException(
        "Method not implemented");
}
```

```csharp
public void AddLinkedToolboxItem(ToolboxItem toolboxItem,
    string category, IDesignerHost host)
{
    throw new NotImplementedException(
        "Method not implemented");
}

public void AddLinkedToolboxItem(ToolboxItem toolboxItem,
    IDesignerHost host)
{
    throw new NotImplementedException(
        "Method not implemented");
}

public void AddToolboxItem(ToolboxItem toolboxItem,
    string category)
{
    throw new NotImplementedException(
        "Method not implemented");
}

public void AddToolboxItem(ToolboxItem toolboxItem)
{
    throw new NotImplementedException(
        "Method not implemented");
}

public ToolboxItem GetSelectedToolboxItem(
    IDesignerHost host)
{
    throw new NotImplementedException(
        "Method not implemented");
}

public ToolboxItem GetSelectedToolboxItem()
{
    throw new NotImplementedException(
        "Method not implemented");
}

public ToolboxItemCollection GetToolboxItems(
    string category, IDesignerHost host)
{
    throw new NotImplementedException(
        "Method not implemented");
}

public ToolboxItemCollection GetToolboxItems(
    string category)
{
    throw new NotImplementedException(
        "Method not implemented");
}
```

```
public ToolboxItemCollection GetToolboxItems(
    IDesignerHost host)
{
    throw new NotImplementedException(
        "Method not implemented");
}

public ToolboxItemCollection GetToolboxItems()
{
    throw new NotImplementedException(
        "Method not implemented");
}

public bool IsToolboxItem(object serializedObject,
    IDesignerHost host)
{
    throw new NotImplementedException(
        "Method not implemented");
}

public bool IsToolboxItem(object serializedObject)
{
    throw new NotImplementedException(
        "Method not implemented");
}

public void RemoveCreator(
    string format, IDesignerHost host)
{
    throw new NotImplementedException(
        "Method not implemented");
}

public void RemoveCreator(string format)
{
    throw new NotImplementedException(
        "Method not implemented");
}

public void RemoveToolboxItem(
    ToolboxItem toolboxItem, string category)
{
    throw new NotImplementedException(
        "Method not implemented");
}

public void RemoveToolboxItem(ToolboxItem toolboxItem)
{
    throw new NotImplementedException(
        "Method not implemented");
}
```

```csharp
public void SelectedToolboxItemUsed()
{
    throw new NotImplementedException(
        "Method not implemented");
}

public void SetSelectedToolboxItem(ToolboxItem toolboxItem)
{
    throw new NotImplementedException(
        "Method not implemented");
}
#endregion

/// <summary>
/// Refresh the toolbox items for all activities in the list.
/// </summary>
/// <remarks>
/// new added to method so we don't
/// override the Refresh method
/// of the UserControl
/// </remarks>
public new void Refresh()
{
    CreateToolboxItems(_activitiesList, _standardActivities);
}

#endregion

#region Toolbox Item Construction

/// <summary>
/// Create all toolbox items
/// </summary>
/// <param name="lb"></param>
private void CreateToolboxItems(
    ListBox listbox, List<Type> activities)
{
    listbox.Items.Clear();

    //add Toolbox items for referenced assemblies
    LoadReferencedTypes(listbox);

    //add Toolbox items for standard activities
    foreach (Type activityType in activities)
    {
        ToolboxItem item =
            CreateItemForActivityType(activityType);
        if (item != null)
        {
            listbox.Items.Add(item);
        }
    }
}
```

The private CreateToolboxItems method is invoked by the constructor and also the Refresh method. After clearing all items in the ListBox, it adds ToolboxItem instances for each custom activity that is found in the referenced assemblies. It does this by invoking the private LoadReferencedTypes method. Following this, it adds ToolboxItem instances for each standard activity.

```
/// <summary>
///Add Toolbox items for any WF types found
///in referenced assemblies
/// </summary>
private void LoadReferencedTypes(ListBox listbox)
{
    ITypeProvider typeProvider =
        _serviceProvider.GetService(typeof(ITypeProvider))
            as ITypeProvider;
    if (typeProvider == null)
    {
        return;
    }
    foreach (Assembly assembly
        in typeProvider.ReferencedAssemblies)
    {
        Type[] types = assembly.GetTypes();
        foreach (Type type in types)
        {
            //if the Type is assignable to Activity, then
            //add it to the toolbox
            if (typeof(Activity).IsAssignableFrom(type))
            {
                ToolboxItem item =
                    CreateItemForActivityType(type);
                if (item != null)
                {
                    listbox.Items.Add(item);
                }
            }
        }
    }
}
```

The LoadReferencedTypes method examines all types found in any referenced assemblies. Throughout this application, the list of referenced assemblies is maintained in the TypeProvider object (referenced by the ITypeProvider interface). If a Type directly or indirectly derives from the base Activity class, it is added as a ToolboxItem. The CreateItemForActivityType (shown next) is used to create the ToolboxItem.

```
/// <summary>
/// Create a ToolboxItem for the specified activity type
/// </summary>
/// <param name="activityType"></param>
/// <returns></returns>
private ToolboxItem CreateItemForActivityType(Type activityType)
{
    ToolboxItem result = null;
```

```
            //does the activity type include the ToolboxItemAttribute
            ToolboxItemAttribute toolboxAttribute = null;
            foreach (Attribute attribute in
                activityType.GetCustomAttributes(
                    typeof(ToolboxItemAttribute), true))
            {
                if (attribute is ToolboxItemAttribute)
                {
                    toolboxAttribute = (ToolboxItemAttribute)attribute;
                    break;
                }
            }

            if (toolboxAttribute != null)
            {
                if (toolboxAttribute.ToolboxItemType != null)
                {
                    //construct the ToolboxItemType specified
                    //by the attribute.
                    ConstructorInfo constructor =
                        toolboxAttribute.ToolboxItemType.GetConstructor(
                            new Type[] { typeof(Type) });
                    if (constructor != null)
                    {
                        result = constructor.Invoke(
                            new Object[] { activityType })
                                as ToolboxItem;
                    }
                }
            }
            else
            {
                //no attribute found
                result = new ToolboxItem(activityType);
            }

            return result;
        }
```

The `CreateItemForActivityType` method creates a `ToolboxItem` for the specified `Activity` class. To accomplish this, the code looks for a `ToolboxItemAttribute` on the `Activity` class. This attribute contains a `ToolboxItemType` property that identifies the `Type` that should be used to represent the activity when it is shown in a toolbox. An instance of the `ToolboxItemType` is then created and returned as the `ToolboxItem`.

You might recall that the `ToolboxItemAttribute` was discussed way back in Chapter 3. As I illustrated toward the end of that chapter, using the correct `ToolboxItem` is important since it not only affects the visual representation of the activity in a toolbox but it also implements design time behavior. For example, when you drag and drop an `IfElseActivity` onto the designer, it is the specialized `IfElseToolboxItem` class that is associated with the `IfElseActivity` that creates the first two `IfElseBranchActivity` instances for you.

```csharp
/// <summary>
/// Perform owner drawing of the toolbox items
/// </summary>
/// <param name="sender"></param>
/// <param name="e"></param>
private void ActivitiesList_DrawItem(
    object sender, DrawItemEventArgs e)
{
    if (e.Index < 0)
    {
        return;
    }

    ActivityToolboxItem item
        = ((ListBox)sender).Items[e.Index] as ActivityToolboxItem;
    if (item != null)
    {
        Graphics graphics = e.Graphics;
        if ((e.State & DrawItemState.Selected)
            == DrawItemState.Selected)
        {
            //draw a border around the selected item
            graphics.FillRectangle(
                SystemBrushes.Window, e.Bounds);
            Rectangle rect = e.Bounds;
            rect.Width -= 2;
            rect.Height -= 2;
            graphics.DrawRectangle(SystemPens.ActiveBorder, rect);
        }
        else
        {
            //not the selected item, just fill the rect
            graphics.FillRectangle(SystemBrushes.Window, e.Bounds);
        }

        //draw the toolbox item image
        Int32 bitmapWidth = 0;
        if (item.Bitmap != null)
        {
            graphics.DrawImage(item.Bitmap,
                e.Bounds.X + 2, e.Bounds.Y + 2,
                item.Bitmap.Width, item.Bitmap.Height);
            bitmapWidth = item.Bitmap.Width;
        }

        //add the display name
        graphics.DrawString(item.DisplayName,
            e.Font, SystemBrushes.ControlText,
            e.Bounds.X + bitmapWidth + 2, e.Bounds.Y + 2);
    }
}
```

When the ListBox was created in the constructor of this class, the DrawMode property was set to DrawMode.OwnerDrawFixed. This means that this class is responsible for drawing each entry in the ListBox. The drawing is done here in the ActivitiesList_DrawItem method. The code uses an owner draw mode so that it can show the image associated with each activity.

```
    #endregion

    #region Drag / Drop operation

    /// <summary>
    /// Begin a drag / drop operation
    /// </summary>
    /// <param name="sender"></param>
    /// <param name="e"></param>
    private void ActivitiesList_MouseMove(
        object sender, MouseEventArgs e)
    {
        if (e.Button == MouseButtons.Left)
        {
            if (_activitiesList.SelectedItem is ActivityToolboxItem)
            {
                ActivityToolboxItem selectedItem =
                    _activitiesList.SelectedItem
                        as ActivityToolboxItem;
                IDataObject dataObject = SerializeToolboxItem(
                    selectedItem) as IDataObject;
                DoDragDrop(dataObject, DragDropEffects.All);
            }
        }
    }
```

The ActivitiesList_MouseMove method is used to initiate a drag-and-drop operation when you begin to drag an activity from the toolbox onto the workflow designer.

```
    #endregion
    }
}
```

Implementing WorkflowDesigner

The WorkflowDesigner is a custom control that encapsulates the workflow designers, the toolbox, and the properties grid. Once constructed, an instance of this control is placed on the MainForm.

You begin development of the designer by adding a new User Control to the project and naming it WorkflowDesigner. The finished visual design for this control is shown in Figure 17-2.

Drag and drop a SplitContainer onto the new WorkflowDesigner control. Leave the default name of splitContainer1, but set the Dock property to Fill for this control. The Orientation for this control should be set to the default value of Vertical. This control includes two Panel instances—one labeled Panel1 and the other Panel2. The control labeled Panel2 in Figure 17-2 is the right-side Panel and will be the home for the workflow designer canvas.

Drag and drop another SplitContainer onto the left-side Panel (Panel1). You can use the default name of splitContainer2, but change the Orientation for this control to Horizontal. This creates the top and bottom panels shown on the left side of Figure 17-2. You also need to set the Dock property of splitContainer2 to Fill.

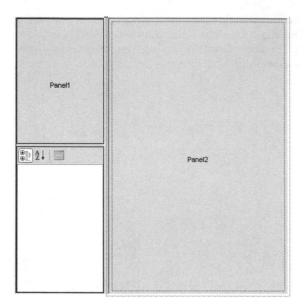

Figure 17-2. *WorkflowDesigner visual design*

The top Panel1 area shown in Figure 17-2 is where the toolbox will be placed. The bottom area will contain the properties grid that is used when editing properties. Drag and drop a PropertyGrid to this area now. The default name of propertyGrid1 is fine. This concludes the visual design of this control.

Listing 17-7 is the complete code that you need to add to the WorkflowDesigner.cs file.

Listing 17-7. *Complete WorkflowDesigner.cs File*

```
using System;
using System.Collections;
using System.Windows.Forms;
using System.Drawing.Design;
using System.ComponentModel.Design;
using System.Workflow.ComponentModel;
using System.Workflow.ComponentModel.Design;
using System.Workflow.ComponentModel.Compiler;

namespace WorkflowDesignerApp
{
    /// <summary>
    /// Implement a workflow designer control
    /// </summary>
    public partial class WorkflowDesigner : UserControl
    {
        private WorkflowLoader _wfLoader = new WorkflowLoader();
        private WorkflowView _workflowView;
        private Control _toolboxControl;

        private DesignSurface _designSurface;
        private TypeProvider _typeProvider;
```

```
public WorkflowDesigner()
{
    InitializeComponent();
}

public Control ToolboxControl
{
    get { return _toolboxControl; }
}

public TypeProvider TypeProvider
{
    get { return _typeProvider; }
    set
    {
        _typeProvider = value;
        //pass the TypeProvider to the loader
        _wfLoader.TypeProvider = _typeProvider;
    }
}
```

The TypeProvider is exposed as a public property, allowing this object to be created outside of this control and passed in. This is important since the TypeProvider maintains a list of assembly references and is used by several components of this application. When this property is set, it is also passed to the WorkflowLoader instance.

```
/// <summary>
/// Load a markup file into the designer
/// </summary>
/// <param name="markupFileName"></param>
/// <returns></returns>
public Boolean LoadWorkflow(String markupFileName)
{
    //remove the current workflow from the designer
    //if there is one
    ClearWorkflow();

    //create the design surface
    _designSurface = new DesignSurface();

    //pass the markup file name to the loader
    _wfLoader.MarkupFileName = markupFileName;
    _wfLoader.NewWorkflowType = null;

    //complete the loading
    return CommonWorkflowLoading();
}
```

The LoadWorkflow method is invoked from the MainForm to load an existing workflow definition into the designer. After clearing the existing workflow (if there is one) from the designer, a new DesignSurface is created. The markupFileName that is passed to this method is used to set the MarkupFileName property of the workflow loader. The NewWorkflowType property is set to null since this property is used only when creating a new workflow definition. Finally, the private CommonWorkflowLoading method is invoked.

```
/// <summary>
/// Create a new workflow using the specified Type
/// </summary>
/// <param name="workflowType"></param>
/// <returns></returns>
public Boolean CreateNewWorkflow(Type workflowType,
    String newWorkflowName)
{
    //remove the current workflow from the designer
    //if there is one
    ClearWorkflow();

    //create the design surface
    _designSurface = new DesignSurface();

    //pass the new workflow type to the loader
    _wfLoader.MarkupFileName = String.Empty;
    _wfLoader.NewWorkflowType = workflowType;
    _wfLoader.NewWorkflowName = newWorkflowName;

    //complete the creation of a new workflow
    return CommonWorkflowLoading();
}
```

The CreateNewWorkflow method is invoked from the MainForm to create a new workflow definition. It is passed the base workflow Type to use for the workflow along with the new workflow name. The code for this method is similar to the LoadWorkflow method just shown. The primary difference is that the MarkupFileName property of the loader must be set to String.Empty, and the NewWorkflowType and NewWorkflowName properties are set to real values. This signals to the code in the WorkflowLoader class that it should create a new workflow rather than load an existing one.

```
/// <summary>
/// Finish the process of loading an existing
/// or new workflow
/// </summary>
/// <returns></returns>
private Boolean CommonWorkflowLoading()
{
    Boolean result = false;

    //tell the designer to begin loading
    _designSurface.BeginLoad(_wfLoader);

    //retrieve the designer host
    IDesignerHost designer
        = _designSurface.GetService(typeof(IDesignerHost))
            as IDesignerHost;
    if (designer == null || designer.RootComponent == null)
    {
        return false;
    }
```

```
        IRootDesigner rootDesigner
            = designer.GetDesigner(designer.RootComponent)
                as IRootDesigner;
        if (rootDesigner != null)
        {
            SuspendLayout();
            //get the default workflow view from the designer
            _workflowView = rootDesigner.GetView(
                ViewTechnology.Default)
                    as WorkflowView;
            //add the workflow view to a panel for display
            splitContainer1.Panel2.Controls.Add(_workflowView);
            _workflowView.Dock = DockStyle.Fill;
            _workflowView.Focus();

            //link the propertyGrid with the designer
            propertyGrid1.Site = designer.RootComponent.Site;

            //setup the toolbar for the workflow using the one
            //constructed by the workflow loader
            IToolboxService toolboxService = designer.GetService(
                typeof(IToolboxService)) as IToolboxService;
            if (toolboxService != null)
            {
                if (toolboxService is Control)
                {
                    //add the toolbox control to a panel
                    _toolboxControl = (Control)toolboxService;
                    splitContainer2.Panel1.Controls.Add(
                        _toolboxControl);
                }
            }

            //get the ISelectionService from the workflow view
            //and add a handler for the SelectionChanged event
            ISelectionService selectionService
                = ((IServiceProvider)_workflowView).GetService(
                    typeof(ISelectionService)) as ISelectionService;
            if (selectionService != null)
            {
                selectionService.SelectionChanged += new EventHandler(
                    selectionService_SelectionChanged);
            }

            ResumeLayout();
            result = true;
        }
        return result;
    }
```

The CommonWorkflowLoading method is invoked when a new workflow is created or an existing one is loaded. It completes the work necessary to show the workflow designer and the toolbox.

The BeginLoad method of the DesignSurface is called first, passing in the WorkflowLoader instance. This results in the Initialize and PerformLoad methods of the WorkflowLoader being called. When the BeginLoad method returns, the new or existing workflow should be loaded and the workflow designer should be populated with the tree of activity objects that visually represent the workflow model.

Once the workflow is loaded, the WorkflowView is obtained and added to Panel2 of splitContainer1 (the right side of Figure 17-2). The Site property of the PropertyGrid control is set to the Site property of the RootComponent in the designer (IDesignerHost). This logically links the two so that the PropertyGrid is updated correctly as objects in the designer are selected.

The toolbox service is retrieved and added to Panel1 of splitContainer2. Remember that this is possible since the toolbox service uses UserControl as its base class. It is both a service and a visual control that displays the toolbox items.

```
/// <summary>
/// The selected object in the workflow view has changed,
/// so update the properties grid
/// </summary>
/// <param name="sender"></param>
/// <param name="e"></param>
private void selectionService_SelectionChanged(
    object sender, EventArgs e)
{
    ISelectionService selectionService
        = ((IServiceProvider)_workflowView).GetService(
            typeof(ISelectionService)) as ISelectionService;
    if (selectionService != null)
    {
        propertyGrid1.SelectedObjects = new ArrayList(
            selectionService.GetSelectedComponents()).ToArray();
    }
}
```

The selectionService_SelectionChanged method is the handler for the SelectionChanged event of the ISelectionService object. This service was obtained from the WorkflowView in the CommonWorkflowLoading just shown. This handler updates the PropertyGrid control with the list of properties retrieved from the ISelectionService object.

```
/// <summary>
/// Save the current workflow
/// </summary>
/// <param name="markupFileName"></param>
/// <returns></returns>
public Boolean SaveWorkflow(String markupFileName)
{
    _wfLoader.MarkupFileName = markupFileName;
    _designSurface.Flush();
    return true;
}
```

The SaveWorkflow method is called by the MainForm to save the current workflow definition to the designated markup file. The Flush method of the DesignSurface is called, which ultimately results in the PerformFlush method of the WorkflowLoader being invoked.

```csharp
/// <summary>
/// Remove the current workflow from the designer
/// </summary>
private void ClearWorkflow()
{
    if (_designSurface != null)
    {
        IDesignerHost designer = _designSurface.GetService(
            typeof(IDesignerHost)) as IDesignerHost;
        if (designer != null)
        {
            if (designer.Container.Components.Count > 0)
            {
                _wfLoader.RemoveFromDesigner(designer,
                    designer.RootComponent as Activity),
            }
        }
    }

    if (_designSurface != null)
    {
        _designSurface.Dispose();
        _designSurface = null;
    }

    if (_workflowView != null)
    {
        ISelectionService selectionService
            = ((IServiceProvider)_workflowView).GetService(
                typeof(ISelectionService)) as ISelectionService;
        if (selectionService != null)
        {
            selectionService.SelectionChanged -= new EventHandler(
                selectionService_SelectionChanged);
        }

        Controls.Remove(_workflowView);
        _workflowView.Dispose();
        _workflowView = null;
    }

    if (_toolboxControl != null)
    {
        Controls.Remove(_toolboxControl);
    }
}
```

Implementing MainForm

The MainForm is the primary form for the application that includes an instance of the WorkflowDesigner control and also a few menu definitions that allow you to interact with the designer.

To implement this form, rename Form1 that was automatically created with the project to MainForm. Next, drag and drop an instance of the WorkflowDesigner control onto the form. You may have to rebuild the project first in order for this control to appear in the Visual Studio toolbox. Change the name of the WorkflowDesigner instance to designer and set its Dock property to Fill, letting it use all of the real estate of the form. The finished visual design of the main form is shown in Figure 17-3.

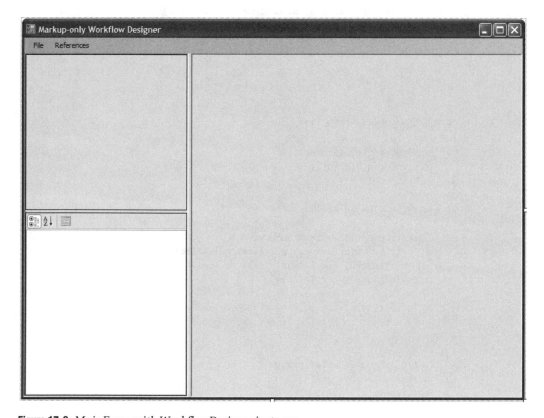

Figure 17-3. *MainForm with WorkflowDesigner instance*

As shown at the top of Figure 17-3, there are also a few menu items that you need to add to the form. Drag and drop a MenuStrip control to the top of the form for this purpose. The default name of menuStrip1 is fine. Table 17-2 shows the list of menu items that you should add to the MenuStrip.

Table 17-2. *MainForm Menu Items*

Menu Text	Control Name	Parent Menu Item
File	menuTopFile	None
Open Markup File...	menuOpenMarkup	menuTopFile
New Workflow...	menuNewWorkflow	menuTopFile
Save	menuSave	menuTopFile
Save As...	menuSaveAs	menuTopFile
References	menuTopReferences	None
Add Assembly References...	menuReferences	menuTopReferences

After setting all of the menu names, add a Click event handler for each item.

This completes the visual design of the main form. Listing 17-8 contains the code that you need to add to the MainForm.cs file.

Listing 17-8. *Complete MainForm.cs File*

```
using System;
using System.IO;
using System.Drawing.Design;
using System.Windows.Forms;
using System.ComponentModel.Design;
using System.Workflow.ComponentModel.Compiler;

namespace WorkflowDesignerApp
{
    /// <summary>
    /// The main form of the Markup-only workflow designer
    /// </summary>
    public partial class MainForm : Form
    {
        private String _loadedMarkupFileName = String.Empty;
        private TypeProvider _typeProvider;

        public MainForm()
        {
            InitializeComponent();
            _typeProvider = new TypeProvider(new ServiceContainer());
            designer.TypeProvider = _typeProvider;
        }
```

During construction, an instance of the TypeProvider is created. It is then passed to the WorkflowDesigner instance using the TypeProvider property.

```
#region Load and Save the Workflow

/// <summary>
/// Open an existing markup file
/// </summary>
/// <param name="sender"></param>
/// <param name="e"></param>
private void menuOpenMarkup_Click(object sender, EventArgs e)
{
    SetApplicationTitle(null);
    OpenFileDialog openFile = new OpenFileDialog();
    openFile.InitialDirectory = Environment.CurrentDirectory;
    openFile.Filter
        = "xoml files (*.xoml)|*.xoml|All files (*.*)|*.*";
    openFile.FilterIndex = 1;
    if (openFile.ShowDialog() == DialogResult.OK)
    {
        String fileName = openFile.FileName;
        try
        {
            //tell the designer to load the workflow markup
            if (designer.LoadWorkflow(fileName))
            {
                _loadedMarkupFileName = fileName;
                SetApplicationTitle(fileName);
            }
            else
            {
                MessageBox.Show("Unable to load markup file",
                  "Error loading markup",
                    MessageBoxButtons.OK, MessageBoxIcon.Error);
            }
        }
        catch (Exception exception)
        {
            MessageBox.Show(String.Format(
              "Exception loading workflow: {0}",
              exception.Message), "Exception in LoadWorkflow",
                MessageBoxButtons.OK, MessageBoxIcon.Error);
        }
    }
}
```

The Click event handler for the menuOpenMarkup menu item shows the standard open dialog and allows you to select an .xoml file to load. The selected file name is passed to the LoadWorkflow method of the WorkflowDesigner control to load the workflow definition.

```
/// <summary>
/// Save the workflow design to a markup file
/// </summary>
/// <param name="sender"></param>
/// <param name="e"></param>
```

```csharp
private void menuSave_Click(object sender, EventArgs e)
{
    if (!String.IsNullOrEmpty(_loadedMarkupFileName))
    {
        SaveWorkflowDefinition(_loadedMarkupFileName);
    }
}

/// <summary>
/// Save the workflow design to a new markup file
/// </summary>
/// <param name="sender"></param>
/// <param name="e"></param>
private void menuSaveAs_Click(object sender, EventArgs e)
{
    SaveFileDialog saveFile = new SaveFileDialog();
    saveFile.InitialDirectory = Environment.CurrentDirectory;
    saveFile.Filter
        = "xoml files (*.xoml)|*.xoml|All files (*.*)|*.*";
    saveFile.FilterIndex = 1;
    saveFile.FileName = _loadedMarkupFileName;
    if (saveFile.ShowDialog() == DialogResult.OK)
    {
        if (SaveWorkflowDefinition(saveFile.FileName))
        {
            SetApplicationTitle(saveFile.FileName);
        }
        else
        {
            SetApplicationTitle(null);
        }
    }
}
```

The Click event handler for the menuSaveAs menu item first prompts for a file name to use when saving the workflow definition to markup. The private SaveWorkflowDefinition is then invoked to handle saving of the workflow.

```csharp
/// <summary>
/// Save to markup
/// </summary>
/// <param name="fileName"></param>
/// <returns></returns>
private Boolean SaveWorkflowDefinition(String fileName)
{
    Boolean result = false;
    try
    {
        //let the designer handle the save operation
        if (designer.SaveWorkflow(fileName))
        {
            _loadedMarkupFileName = fileName;
            result = true;
        }
```

```
            else
            {
                MessageBox.Show("Unable to save markup file",
                  "Error saving markup",
                  MessageBoxButtons.OK, MessageBoxIcon.Error);
            }
        }
        catch (Exception exception)
        {
            MessageBox.Show(String.Format(
              "Exception saving workflow: {0}",
              exception.Message),
              "Exception in SaveWorkflowDefinition",
               MessageBoxButtons.OK, MessageBoxIcon.Error);
        }
        return result;
    }
```

The SaveWorkflowDefinition method calls the SaveWorkflow method of the WorkflowDesigner, passing it the name of the file to use when saving the definition.

```
    #endregion

    #region Update UI Elements

    private void SetApplicationTitle(String fileName)
    {
        if (String.IsNullOrEmpty(fileName))
        {
            this.Text = "Custom Workflow Designer";
        }
        else
        {
            this.Text = String.Format(
                "Custom Workflow Designer: {0}",
                Path.GetFileName(fileName));
        }
    }

    #endregion

    #region Assembly References

    /// <summary>
    /// Show the Add References dialog
    /// </summary>
    /// <param name="sender"></param>
    /// <param name="e"></param>
    private void menuReferences_Click(object sender, EventArgs e)
    {
        AssemblyReferenceForm form
            = new AssemblyReferenceForm(_typeProvider);
        form.ShowDialog();
```

```
        //rebuild the toolbox with referenced assemblies
        if (designer.ToolboxControl != null)
        {
            ((IToolboxService)designer.ToolboxControl).Refresh();
        }
    }
```

The Click event handler for the menuReferences menu item modally shows the
AssemblyReferenceForm. This form is described in the next section of this chapter and is used to add
assembly references. The references are used to find custom activity and workflow types. Notice that
the TypeProvider instance is passed to the constructor of this form.

```
    #endregion

    #region New Workflow

    /// <summary>
    /// Create a new workflow
    /// </summary>
    /// <param name="sender"></param>
    /// <param name="e"></param>
    private void menuNewWorkflow_Click(object sender, EventArgs e)
    {
        NewWorkflowForm form
            = new NewWorkflowForm(_typeProvider);
        if (form.ShowDialog() == DialogResult.OK)
        {
            try
            {
                //let the designer create a new workflow
                //base on the selected workflow Type
                if (designer.CreateNewWorkflow(
                    form.SelectedWorkflowType, form.NewWorkflowName))
                {
                    _loadedMarkupFileName
                        = form.NewWorkflowName + ".xoml";
                    SetApplicationTitle(_loadedMarkupFileName);

                    //immediately prompt to save the workflow
                    menuSaveAs_Click(this, new EventArgs());
                }
                else
                {
                    MessageBox.Show("Unable to create new workflow",
                        "Error creating workflow",
                        MessageBoxButtons.OK, MessageBoxIcon.Error);
                }
            }
```

```
            catch (Exception exception)
            {
                MessageBox.Show(String.Format(
                  "Exception creating workflow: {0}",
                    exception.Message),
                  "Exception in CreateNewWorkflow",
                   MessageBoxButtons.OK, MessageBoxIcon.Error);
            }
        }
    }
}
```

The Click event handler for the menuNewWorkflow menu item modally shows the NewWorkflowForm. This form prompts the user to select a new workflow Type and to also provide a name for the new workflow. When the form is closed, the CreateNewWorkflow method of the WorkflowDesigner is called to create the new workflow.

```
        #endregion
    }
}
```

Implementing AssemblyReferenceForm

The AssemblyReferenceForm is a simple form that is used to display the list of currently referenced assemblies and to add new ones. It is modally shown by the menuReferences_Click method of the MainForm. Figure 17-4 shows the completed visual design of this form.

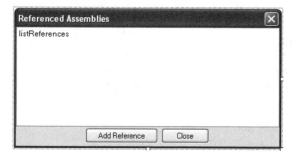

Figure 17-4. *AssemblyReferenceForm*

The form includes these three controls:

- A ListBox, which I have named listReferences. This control is used to display the names of any referenced assemblies. I set the Dock property of this control to Top so that it aligns itself nicely to the top of the form.

- A Button named btnAdd, which is used to add a new assembly reference.

- A Button named btnClose, which closes the form.

Both of the Button controls need handlers for their Click events.
Listing 17-9 is the complete code for the AssemblyReferenceForm.cs file.

Listing 17-9. *Complete AssemblyReferenceForm.cs File*

```csharp
using System;
using System.Reflection;
using System.Windows.Forms;
using System.Workflow.ComponentModel.Compiler;

namespace WorkflowDesignerApp
{
    /// <summary>
    /// A form used to add assembly references
    /// </summary>
    public partial class AssemblyReferenceForm : Form
    {
        private TypeProvider _typeProvider;

        public AssemblyReferenceForm(TypeProvider provider)
        {
            InitializeComponent();

            //build the list of referenced assemblies
            _typeProvider = provider;
            if (_typeProvider != null)
            {
                PopulateListWithReferences();
            }
        }
```

A TypeProvider instance is passed to the constructor of this form. Using this TypeProvider, the ListBox is populated with a list of any assemblies that are already referenced. This is done in the PopulateListWithReferences private method.

```csharp
        /// <summary>
        /// Build the list of referenced assemblies
        /// </summary>
        private void PopulateListWithReferences()
        {
            listReferences.Items.Clear();
            foreach (Assembly assembly in
                _typeProvider.ReferencedAssemblies)
            {
                listReferences.Items.Add(assembly);
            }
        }

        /// <summary>
        /// Add a new assembly to the list
        /// </summary>
        /// <param name="sender"></param>
        /// <param name="e"></param>
        private void btnAdd_Click(object sender, EventArgs e)
        {
            OpenFileDialog openFile = new OpenFileDialog();
            openFile.InitialDirectory = Environment.CurrentDirectory;
            openFile.Filter
```

```
            = "Dll files (*.Dll)|*.Dll|All files (*.*)|*.*";
        openFile.FilterIndex = 1;
        openFile.Multiselect = true;
        if (openFile.ShowDialog() == DialogResult.OK)
        {
            foreach (String filename in openFile.FileNames)
            {
                //add the referenced assemblies to the TypeProvider
                _typeProvider.AddAssemblyReference(filename);
            }
            PopulateListWithReferences();
        }
    }
}
```

The Click event handler for btnAdd uses the standard OpenFileDialog to prompt the user to select one or more assemblies to reference. Any assemblies that are selected are added to the TypeProvider using the AddAssemblyReference method.

```
        private void btnClose_Click(object sender, EventArgs e)
        {
            this.Close();
        }
    }
}
```

Implementing NewWorkflowForm

The NewWorkflowForm is used when the user wishes to create a new workflow definition instead of opening an existing one. It prompts the user to select the base Type and provide a name for the new workflow. Figure 17-5 is the completed visual design of this form.

Figure 17-5. *NewWorkflowForm*

The form requires these controls:

- A ListBox named listWorkflowTypes that is used to list the available workflow types. Set the Dock property to Top and add an event handler for the SelectedIndexChanged event.

- A TextBox named txtNewWorkflowName that is used for entry of the new workflow name.

- A Button named btnCreate.

- A Button named btnCancel.

Both of the Button controls require handlers for their Click events.

Listing 17-10 shows you the complete code for the NewWorkflowForm.cs file.

Listing 17-10. *Complete NewWorkflowForm.cs File*

```
using System;
using System.Windows.Forms;
using System.Reflection;
using System.Workflow.ComponentModel;
using System.Workflow.Activities;
using System.Workflow.ComponentModel.Compiler;

namespace WorkflowDesignerApp
{
    /// <summary>
    /// A form used to select the new workflow Type
    /// </summary>
    public partial class NewWorkflowForm : Form
    {
        private TypeProvider _typeProvider;
        private Type _selectedWorkflowType;
        private String _newWorkflowName = String.Empty;

        public NewWorkflowForm(TypeProvider provider)
        {
            InitializeComponent();
            _typeProvider = provider;
            if (_typeProvider != null)
            {
                PopulateWorkflowList();
            }

            btnCreate.Enabled = false;
        }
```

During construction, the ListBox is populated with the list of standard and referenced workflow types.

```
        public Type SelectedWorkflowType
        {
            get { return _selectedWorkflowType; }
        }

        public String NewWorkflowName
        {
            get { return _newWorkflowName; }
        }
```

The SelectedWorkflowType and NewWorkflowName properties expose the user's selections to the MainForm after this form closes.

```
        private void PopulateWorkflowList()
        {
            listWorkflowTypes.Items.Clear();
```

```
        //add standard workflow types
        listWorkflowTypes.Items.Add(
            typeof(SequentialWorkflowActivity));
        listWorkflowTypes.Items.Add(
            typeof(StateMachineWorkflowActivity));

        //add any workflow types found in referenced assemblies
        foreach (Assembly assembly in
            _typeProvider.ReferencedAssemblies)
        {
            Type[] types = assembly.GetTypes();
            foreach (Type type in types)
            {
                if (typeof(SequentialWorkflowActivity).
                        IsAssignableFrom(type) ||
                    typeof(StateMachineWorkflowActivity).
                        IsAssignableFrom(type))
                {
                    listWorkflowTypes.Items.Add(type);
                }
            }
        }
    }
```

The PopulateWorkflowList method populates the ListBox with the standard workflow classes and also any workflow types found in the referenced assemblies. Only types that descend from the standard workflow classes are included in the list.

```
    private void btnCreate_Click(object sender, EventArgs e)
    {
        if (txtNewWorkflowName.Text.Trim().Length > 0)
        {
            _newWorkflowName = txtNewWorkflowName.Text.Trim();
            this.DialogResult = DialogResult.OK;
        }
        else
        {
            MessageBox.Show("Please enter a new workflow name",
                "Name Required",
                MessageBoxButtons.OK, MessageBoxIcon.Exclamation);
        }
    }

    private void btnCancel_Click(object sender, EventArgs e)
    {
        _selectedWorkflowType = null;
        this.DialogResult = DialogResult.Cancel;
        this.Close();
    }
```

```
        private void listWorkflowTypes_SelectedIndexChanged(
            object sender, EventArgs e)
        {
            //save the selected workflow type
            if (listWorkflowTypes.SelectedIndex >= 0)
            {
                _selectedWorkflowType
                    = listWorkflowTypes.SelectedItem as Type;
                btnCreate.Enabled = true;
            }
        }
    }
}
```

Using the Designer

If you have stayed with me through all of that code, you will now be rewarded with a working work-flow designer application. Since this application targets the maintenance of no-code workflows, you can use the examples from Chapter 16 to test the designer. Chapter 16 provides a no-code markup file and rules, the SharedWorkflows.dll assembly containing custom base workflow and activity types, and a Console application (ConsoleMarkupOnly) that you can use to execute the workflow after you modify it.

Copy these files that you used in Chapter 16 into the bin\debug folder under the WorkflowDesignerApp project:

- MarkupOnlyWorkflow.xoml
- MarkupOnlyWorkflow.rules
- SharedWorkflows.dll
- Bukovics.Workflow.Hosting.dll
- ConsoleMarkupOnly.exe

You can now start the WorkflowDesignerApp (F5 from within Visual Studio). Once started, open the MarkupOnlyWorkflow.xoml file from the bin\debug folder using the File ➤ Open Markup File menu option. Once the workflow is loaded, the designer application should look like Figure 17-6.

■**Note** This workflow references types found in the SharedWorkflows assembly from Chapter 16. The designer assumes that any referenced assembles are in the same directory as the designer itself. That's the reason you copied the files from Chapter 16 into the bin\debug folder of the designer project.

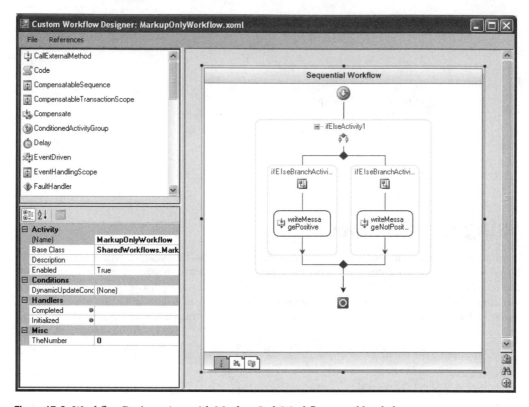

Figure 17-6. *WorkflowDesignerApp with MarkupOnlyWorkflow.xoml loaded*

Here are a few things that you can try or observe:

- Select different objects in the designer and notice how the properties grid is updated as each object is selected.

- Right-click an object in the designer to see the context menu that was constructed. Try some of the supported operations, such as Copy, Cut, and Paste to see how they work.

- Drag and drop new activities onto the designer.

- Expand the Condition property for the IfElseBranchActivity on the left side. Notice that the IsNumberPositive rule condition is there and that you can edit it in the Rule Condition Editor dialog.

- Change the Declarative Rule Condition to a Code Condition and notice that the drop-down list for the Condition property lists the IsNumberPositive method of the base class as a candidate method. This workflow is based on the MarkupOnlyBaseWorkflow class in the SharedWorkflows assembly that defines this method.

Now that you've done some initial exploration with the designer, reload a clean copy of the MarkupOnlyWorkflow.xoml file. The goal this time is to make a few changes to the workflow, save it back to the original file, and then execute the ConsoleMarkupOnly application (that you copied from Chapter 16) to execute the workflow. If you recall, the original results when you executed this application in Chapter 16 looked like this:

```
Executing Workflow
The number is positive
Completed Workflow

Press any key to exit
```

After loading the workflow in the designer, navigate to the writeMessagePositive activity on the left side of the workflow and change the value of the Message property to something different like this:

```
I just changed this message
```

Now use the File ➤ Save menu option to save the modified workflow definition back to the original file. When you execute the ConsoleMarkupOnly application again to run the workflow, you should see these different results:

```
Executing Workflow
I just changed this message
Completed Workflow

Press any key to exit
```

After switching back to the designer again, use the References ➤ Add Assembly References menu item that opens the Referenced Assemblies dialog. Initially, this dialog is empty since you haven't explicitly added any assembly references.

Note Even though this workflow already contains references to the SharedWorkflows assembly, the designer, as it is currently implemented, doesn't populate the list of references unless you use this dialog.

Click the Add References button and navigate to the SharedWorkflows.dll in the bin\debug folder. After selecting the assembly, the dialog should look like Figure 17-7.

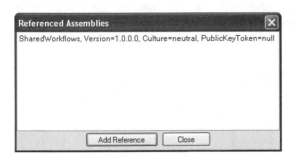

Figure 17-7. *Referenced Assemblies dialog*

After closing the dialog with the Close button, you should notice that the toolbox has been updated to include the WriteMessageActivity that it found in the SharedWorkflows assembly. This custom activity can be seen at the top of Figure 17-8.

Figure 17-8. *Toolbox with custom activity*

To make this workflow more interesting, drag and drop a new instance of the WriteMessageActivity from the toolbox to the top of the workflow. Enter some text for the Message property such as this:

```
I am starting
```

And to provide a balanced workflow, add another WriteMessageActivity instance to the bottom of the workflow with this Message:

```
I am ending
```

When you save the workflow and execute the ConsoleMarkupOnly application again, you should see these results:

```
Executing Workflow
I am starting
I just changed this message
I am ending
Completed Workflow

Press any key to exit
```

Clearly, the designer is updating and saving the workflow definition as expected.

You can also create a new workflow definition with this designer. To try this, select File ➤ New Workflow from the menu. You will be presented with the Select New Workflow Type dialog that looks like Figure 17-9.

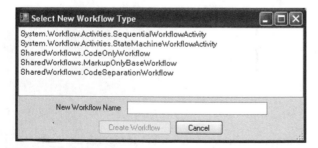

Figure 17-9. *Select New Workflow Type dialog*

The list of available workflow types includes the standard ones provided with WF along with any workflows found in the referenced `SharedWorkflows` assembly. You can choose one of the standard types or use the `MarkupOnlyBaseWorkflow` that the `MarkupOnlyWorkflow` uses. You also need to provide a New Workflow Name for the workflow. After clicking the Create Workflow button, the dialog will close and you will be prompted to save the workflow.

■Note If you are creating a new workflow, you will also need to create your own application to execute and test it. You can still use the `ConsoleMarkupOnly` application to execute the workflow, but the workflow must be named `MarkupOnlyWorkflow` and saved to a file named `MarkupOnlyWorkflow.xoml`, since that's what the `ConsoleMarkupOnly` application expects. Remember that the `ConsoleMarkupOnly` application from Chapter 16 also assumes that the workflow uses a rules file named `MarkupOnlyWorkflow.rules`.

The designer should now look like Figure 17-10. I've chosen to overwrite the existing `MarkupOnlyWorkflow.xoml` file with the new workflow definition so that I could execute it with the `ConsoleMarkupOnly` application.

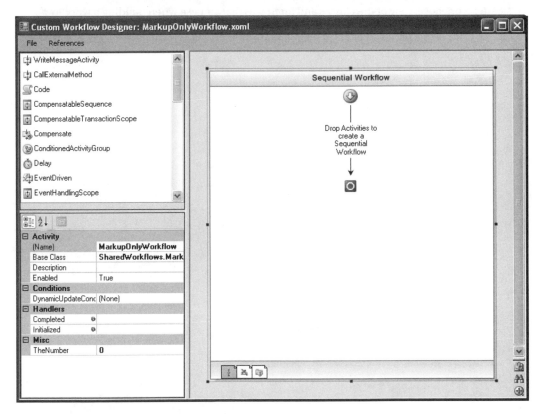

Figure 17-10. *Creating a new workflow definition*

You can now design a completely new workflow. Remember that this designer only supports no-code workflows. This means you can't create any new members (properties, fields, or members). You can only reference members that already exist in the base workflow Type that you selected.

This designer only hints at the capabilities that you can include in your own custom workflow designer.

Summary

The focus of this chapter was hosting the workflow designers in your own application. Hosting the WF workflow designers provides you with the ability to maintain workflow definitions with your own stand-alone designer application, or to embed some designer functionality in your core workflow application.

Visual Studio provides a great development environment for workflow definition. But it is a general-purpose development environment and is not suitable for nondevelopers who may need to only modify a workflow definition. When you host the workflow designers yourself, you can build an application that provides just the functionality that you require, restricting the user to just the limited set of capabilities that you wish to expose.

After a brief overview of the classes and interfaces that you use when building a workflow designer application, the bulk of this chapter presented a working designer application. The application presented here targeted the task of maintaining no-code workflows.

Index

Find it faster at http://superindex.apress.com

X

You Need the Companion eBook

Your purchase of this book entitles you to buy the companion PDF-version eBook for only $10. Take the weightless companion with you anywhere.

We believe this Apress title will prove so indispensable that you'll want to carry it with you everywhere, which is why we are offering the companion eBook (in PDF format) for $10 to customers who purchase this book now. Convenient and fully searchable, the PDF version of any content-rich, page-heavy Apress book makes a valuable addition to your programming library. You can easily find and copy code—or perform examples by quickly toggling between instructions and the application. Even simultaneously tackling a donut, diet soda, and complex code becomes simplified with hands-free eBooks!

Once you purchase your book, getting the $10 companion eBook is simple:

1. Visit **www.apress.com/promo/tendollars/**.

2. Complete a basic registration form to receive a randomly generated question about this title.

3. Answer the question correctly in 60 seconds, and you will receive a promotional code to redeem for the $10.00 eBook.

2560 Ninth Street • Suite 219 • Berkeley, CA 94710

eBookshop

THE EXPERT'S VOICE™

Offer valid through 8/19/07.